DATE DUE

HUMAN RIGHTS IN
ARAB THOUGHT

Human Rights in
Arab Thought
A Reader

Edited by
Salma K. Jayyusi

I.B. TAURIS
LONDON · NEW YORK

Reprinted in 2011 by I.B.Tauris & Co Ltd

6 Salem Road, London W2 4BU
175 Fifth Avenue, New York NY 10010
www.ibtauris.com

In the United States of America and Canada distributed by
Palgrave Macmillan a division of St. Martin's Press
175 Fifth Avenue, New York NY 10010

First published in 2009 by I.B.Tauris & Co Ltd

Library of Modern Middle East Studies, Vol. 44

ISBN 978 1 85043 707 9

A full CIP record for this book is available from the British Library
A full CIP record is available from the Library of Congress

Library of Congress Catalog Card Number: available

Typeset by Swales & Willis Ltd, Exeter, Devon
Printed and bound in Great Britain by
CPI Antony Rowe, Chippenham, Wiltshire

To the Arab prisoners of conscience
and to the Arab writers of conscience
I dedicate this book
for they have dared . . .

Contents

Acknowledgements   x
Preface   xiii
Note on translators   xvi

Introduction   1
Salma Khadra Jayyusi

PART 1
THE EARLY CONCEPT OF HUMAN RIGHTS IN ISLAM

1   The concepts of rights and justice in Arab-Islamic texts   17
    Muhammad 'Abid al-Jabiri

2   The concept of person in Islamic Tradition   62
    Mohammed Arkoun

3   Obedience and disagreement in the context of human
    rights in Islam   84
    Fahmi Jad'an

4   Human rights in the *hadith* – The model individual and the
    model community in Islam   103
    Husni Mahmoud

5   'Man' and 'the Rights of Woman' in Islamic discourse – between
    the idealism of texts and the crisis of reality   131
    Nasr Hamid Abu Zayd

6   The body: its images and rights in Islam   158
    Munsif al-Wahaybi

7   Concepts of human rights in Islamic doctrines (Sunnis, Shi'ites,
    Isma'ilis, Qarmatians, Mu'tazilis, Sufis, Wahhabis)   183
    Shamsuddin al-Kaylani

8   The Medina Charter   229
     Walid Nuwayhid

PART 2

HUMAN RIGHTS IN CONTEMPORARY
ARAB-ISLAMIC THOUGHT

9   The question of human rights in contemporary Islamic thought   253
     Ridwan al-Sayyid

10   The problematic of freedom and human rights in
     Arab-Islamic thought   274
     Yousef Salama

11   The issue of government in modern Islamic thought   303
     Ahmad Barqawi

12   The Islamic intellectual Mahmoud Muhammad Taha on
     the impasse of human rights in Islamic legislation   324
     Al-Nour Hamad

PART 3

THE CONCEPT OF HUMAN RIGHTS IN MODERN
SOCIAL AND POLITICAL ARABIC THOUGHT

13   Human rights in contemporary Arabic thought   343
     Burhan Ghalyoun

14   Human rights and social problematic in the Arab world   374
     Fahmiyya Sharafuddin

15   The rights of Palestinian refugees   391
     Salman Abu Sitta

16   Human rights in the heritage of the Yemeni National Movement   407
     Ahmad Qayid al-Sa'idi

PART 4

HUMAN RIGHTS IN MODERN ARABIC THOUGHT:
SPECIALIZED STUDIES

17   Human rights in the historical texts of the modern Arab world   435
     Bayan Nuwayhid al-Hout

18   Patriarchy and human rights   473
     'Abd al-Razzaq 'Eid

19   Civil and political rights in Arab constitutions   489
     Fateh Samih 'Azzam

20   Arab political parties and human rights   510
     Muhammad al-Sayyid Sa'id

21   Labour laws and human rights   536
     Asma Khader

22   Child rights in Arabic culture   562
     Violette Dagher

     Notes   573
     Index   655

Acknowledgements

This book is the legitimate child of an early sensibility, inculcated in me since childhood and directed towards right and justice. We grew up dangerously in Palestine, facing what is proving now to be one of the longest sustained onslaughts on the rights of people to life, property, continuity and identity. In my exuberant childhood I saw a great amount of grief afflicting many people, and some extremely painful scenes have remained with me to this day. They were all the result of a shrewd aggression directed against the rights of ordinary human beings to a normal life. My concept of human rights was born out of this arduous experience of watching grave injustice imposed on the Palestinians by a Zionism nurtured and protected by British colonialism. This sensibility could not, however, have been brought into consciousness, and given meaning in feelings and words, without the wisdom, compassion and humanitarian outlook of my parents, Subhi al-Khadra and Anisa Sleem, and it is to them, first and foremost, that I owe the basic attitudes against racism, and towards right and justice, which have at once accompanied, beautified and afflicted my life since I became conscious of the world, and which have eventually borne fruit – indirectly in many of my writings, but culminating now directly in this book.

In 1994–5 I was a fellow at the Wissenschaftskolleg zu Berlin (Institute of Higher Study in Berlin), and it was there that the idea of editing a comprehensive book on human rights in the modern Arab world began to take strong hold of me. Modern Arab governments had, by then, become notorious for infringing the human rights of the individual and the community, and I was deeply troubled by the fact that what was happening in the Arab world vis-à-vis this issue stood in direct contrast to the initial concept and practice of the early Arabs and of the first Muslims. I wanted this to be made known to the world. I had also been happily alert to the constant, unabated discussion in support of human rights that was proceeding, on an intellectual level, in the modern Arab world, despite the dangerous, unyielding watchfulness of the autocrats and their vindictive punishment of genuine dissidence. This, too, I wanted to be made known to the world.

However, I was at a loss. I needed more information about this issue in philosophical and legal terms, and a deeper, more structured knowledge, before I could approach such a vast topic armed with my anger, belief and rudimentary observations. And here was where my propitious encounter with the Polish human rights scholar Wiktor Osiatynsky, another fellow at the Wissenshaftskolleg, created the practical possibilities for me and for this book. With the patience, enthusiasm and expertise for which he is well known, Wiktor discussed with me at length the various issues which I attempted later on to implement in this book, and he laid down many of the questions to which I have tried to find answers through other specialists on human rights in the Arab world. I thank him most heartily for his vital help, and for his warm and enduring friendship.

When, later on, I spent time in Jordan as a Fulbright Fellow, I was able to find out more about the practice and violations of human rights, particularly in their social context, through my friend, the lawyer Asma Khader (former Minister of State in Jordan and formal official spokesperson). She had gathered, through her practice as a human rights lawyer, a rich repertoire of dramatic incidents and harrowing stories of violations and infringements which she was always happy to relay to me, and I owe her profound thanks.

Then, when the actual work on this book began, I needed, on account of my expatriate status in America, more detailed information about the state of human rights scholarship in the Arab world, and this I received from the Palestinian scholar and critic Dr Faisal Darraj. I owe him many thanks for this indispensable help. I am also truly sorry that unforeseen circumstances prevented him from participating in the actual writing of this book.

This English version owes a great deal to our style editor, Christopher Tingley. As none of the papers was written initially in English, he had to work on material translated by others. Beside the usual acumen and eagle-eyed vigilance he applies to every piece of work he undertakes, he has taken a special interest in the subject matter of this book and given it his finest editorial skills. I thank him warmly for a job excellently performed.

Among the other members of my family, I owe heartfelt thanks to my cousin Sawsan Nuweihed, a deeply pious and cultivated Muslim, who discussed with me many accounts of Islamic history which provide a truly proud heirloom for humanity in the field of human rights, and I thank her very much for the many hours of spiritual pleasure we spent together. I also owe a great deal to my daughters, Lena and May Jayyusi, with whom I have had a constant intellectual and spiritual exchange of ideas and concepts, and whose attitudes to the major issues that confront not just Palestinian but also contemporary human life in general were mature, learned and up-to-date. I am for this a happier mother and an even happier colleague.

Salma Khadra Jayyusi

Preface

This book has been produced with a view to examining the issue of human rights in the Arab world from a variety of standpoints, and from both a historical and a contemporary perspective.

In my Introduction I have tried to note the concern with human rights that has effectively marked Arab history in the earliest times, and have also attempted to identify problem areas regarding human rights (whether from external or internal causes) in the modern Arab world. In so doing I have tried to encapsulate some of the major themes present in the work as a whole, with the hope, however, of offering a new angle to the perception of human rights in the modern Arab world and the human rights problematic which I see existing among modern day Arabs.

Thereafter, the work, written by some of the most prominent thinkers of the modern Arab world, is divided into four principal sections:

Part One, entitled 'The early concept of human rights in Islam', deals with the historical background to the contemporary debate, demonstrating specifically, that a concern with human rights is not a modern feature of Arab-Islamic discourse but rather has its roots in the earliest period of Islam. Six contributors deal with this subject from various viewpoints. First comes a substantial essay by Muhammad 'Abid al-Jabiri, dealing with the rights and duties of man as viewed historically by Islam, and including a detailed enumeration of the various rights of man in Islam, both 'general' and 'special'. Mohammed Arkoun brings a multi-disciplinary insight to bear on the concept of 'the person' within Islamic tradition, noting the complex relationship between Quranic fact, subsequent Islamic discourse and modern identity. Fahmi Ja'dan examines the concepts of obedience and disagreement, noting the circumstances in which these are regarded as respectively obligatory and permissible. Husni Mahmoud, examines human rights issues in original Islamic texts, noting how the Prophet dealt with various human rights issues in a wide range of quoted *hadiths.* Next, Nasr Hamid Abu Zayd writes on 'man' and the 'rights of woman', noting the strong tension between the idealism implicit in texts and what he terms the 'crisis of reality'. Munsif al-Wahaybi treats an original subject: the rights of the body in Islamic culture, and Shams al-Din al-Kaylani speaks with painstaking care about the differences in the outlook on human rights of the various sects in Islam. Walid Nuwayhid writes on the Medina Charter, the contract concluded between the Prophet and the people of Medina, with a major emphasis on Medina's Jewish population, quoting the Charter in its entirety, providing explanation and commentary on one of the earliest declarations I know of regarding tolerance and the human rights of minorities within Islamic culture, and considering historical questions and the underlying rationale.

Part Two: With this essential perspective established, the work moves on to Part Two, which deals with 'Human rights in contemporary Arab-Islamic thought'. Ridwan al-Sayyid sets modern Western or universalist approaches alongside Islamic approaches, as reflected in parallel Islamic documents like the Cairo Declaration of Human Rights in Islam. Yousef Salama explores the problematic of freedom and human rights in Arabic thought on the individual and communal levels, with reference to the work both of older Arab intellectuals and of modern Islamist thinkers. Ahmad al-Barqawi tackles, with knowledge and honesty, a very crucial and sensitive subject dealing with the issue of government in modern Islamic thought, a subject that is always approached with care and courage because of the repercussions it might inflict. Al-Nour Hamad explores the impasse of human rights in Islamic legislation by specific reference to the life of the Sudanese Islamic intellectual Mahmoud Muhammad Taha.

Part Three: This part is concerned with 'The concept of human rights in modern social and political Arabic thought'. This part is itself divided into two sections dealing, respectively, with general and regional studies.

The first section begins with an essay in which Burhan Ghalyoun considers the modern Arab world in the context of the contemporary, explicitly expressed concern with human rights, dealing with the efforts of the Arab League, the project of national regeneration and 'emanation discourse' linking human rights specifically to Islamic ideas. Fahmiyya Sharafuddin explores the complex relationship between human rights and social problematic, noting such factors as the colonial heritage, relations with the 'Other' and the structure of authority within the Arab world.

The second section comprises two essays dealing with two different regions within the Arab world. Salman Abu Sitta considers the history of the Palestinian refugee question from 1948, reference to political developments and relevant writings being supplemented by personal experience and demographic research. Ahmad Qayid al-Sa'idi charts the progress of the Yemeni

National Movement, from the struggle against human rights abuses under the Imamate to the promulgation of the Yemeni National Charter.

Part Four: This part deals with 'Human rights in modern Arabic thought: specialized studies'. It comprises a series of six articles in miscellaneous areas relevant to human rights in the present-day Arab world. Bayan Nuwayhid al-Hout examines the issue of human rights in modern historical texts of the modern Arab world, referring to more than a dozen historians from various Arab countries. 'Abd al-Razzaq 'Eid considers patterns of patriarchy in the Arab world regarding women, the household and wider society, and the implications of these for human rights. Fateh 'Azzam considers civil and political rights as reflected in Arab constitutions, with citation of elements relevant to these issues in the documents of various Arab countries. Muhammad al-Sayyid Sa'id examines the state of human rights vis-à-vis Arab political parties, considered under the general categories of technocratic, pan-national, Islamist, Marxist and liberal. Asma Khader provides wide-ranging information on various aspects of labour law in the Arab world, with citation of the provisions made in this field by various Arab countries. Finally, Violette Dagher deals with children's rights, from the viewpoint both of historical Islamic thought and of present-day human rights initiatives.

Salma Khadra Jayyusi

Note on translators

Essays translated from Arabic

Muhammad 'Abid al-Jabiri, The concepts of rights and justice in Arab-Islamic texts (translated by Dr Abd al-Wahid Lulua)

Fahmi Jada'n, Obedience and disagreement in the context of human rights in Islam (translated by Dr Fuad Shaban)

Husni Mahmoud, Human rights in the *hadith* (translated by Dr Abd al-Wahid Lulua)

Nasr Hamid Abu Zayd, 'Man' and 'The Rights of Woman' in Islamic discourse (translated by Dr Abd al-Wahid Lulua)

Munsif al-Wahaybi, The body: its images and rights in Islam (translated by Dr Abd al-Wahid Lulua)

Shamsuddin al-Kaylani, Concepts of human rights in various Islamic doctrines (translated by Dr Fuad Shaban)

Walid Nuwayhid, The Medina Charter (translated by Dr Abd al-Wahid Lulua)

Ridwan al-Sayyid, The question of human rights in contemporary Islamic thought (translated by Dr Abd al-Wahid Lulua)

Yousef Salama, The problematic of freedom and human rights in Arab-Islamic thought (translated by Dr Fayiz Suyyagh)

Ahmad Barqawi, The issue of government in modern Islamic thought (translated by Dr Abd al-Wahid Lulua)

Al-Nour Hamad, The Islamic intellectual Mahmoud Muhammad Taha on the impasse of human rights in Islamic legislation (translated by Dr Abd al-Wahid Lulua)

Burhan Ghalyoun, Human rights in contemporary Arabic thought (translated by Dr Fayiz Suyyagh)

Fahmiyya Sharafuddin, Human rights and social problematic in the Arab world (translated by Dr Fayiz Suyyagh)

Salman Abu Sitta, The rights of Palestinian refugees (translated by Dr. Fayiz Suyyagh)

Ahmad Qayid al-Sa'idi, Human rights in the heritage of the Yemeni National Movement (translated by Dr Fayiz Suyyagh)

Bayan Nuwayhid al-Hout, Human rights in the historical texts of the modern Arab world (translated by Dr Abd al-Wahid Lulua)

Abd al-Razzaq 'Eid, Patriarchy and human rights (translated by Dr Fayiz Suyyagh)

Muhammad al-Sayyid Sa'id, Arab political parties and human rights (translated by Dr Fayiz Suyyagh)

Asma Khader, Labour laws and human rights (translated by Dr Fayiz Suyyagh)

Violette Dagher, Child rights in Arabic culture (translated by Dr Fayiz Suyyagh)

Originally translated from French

Mohammed Arkoun, The concept of person in Islamic tradition (translated by Christopher Tingley)

Originally submitted in English

Fateh Samih 'Azzam, Civil and political rights in Arab constitutions

Introduction

Salma Khadra Jayyusi

I.

This book forms an integral part of a project designed to explore the fundamental elements of human rights in Arabic thought, not only with regard to the present – in which concepts of human rights have become embedded in the world at large and ingrained as a stable component and regular preoccupation in contemporary Arabic thought – but also going beyond this present era, exploring remote periods before the issue of rights was ever a subject of discussion and theorization, or the outcome of a conscious intellectual debate, or a problematic lending itself to deliberation and elaboration, but had rather arisen from lived experience. This experience had shaped early the human factor in Arabia, and richly reinforced man's instinctive insight and natural, spontaneous sensibility with respect to justice and right.

This book demonstrates clearly how the concept of right and dignity was already entrenched among some of the early Arabs, not as something structured or moulded by pure theory but as a natural state of mind. In pre-Islamic Mecca, the 'Fudhoul Pact', whereby Meccan notables pledged to protect visitors and strangers within their city against any injustice inflicted on them, was not the outcome of an established civil law. It rather reflected a deep-rooted, conscious foresight regarding the principles of human transaction and exchange. The notions of the times were effectively embodied in the sonorous words of the sixth-century poet 'Amr bin Kulthoum:

> When the king degrades and oppresses,
> We will not accept humiliation.

In Islam, early in the seventh century, the Prophet accorded protection to the Jews of Yathrib (later called Medina), and laid down civil rights for them, in the 'Medina Charter', which is the subject of a full essay in this book. He also instituted a tolerant stance towards the followers of other monotheistic faiths. This outlook stemmed (so early in human history) from a deep-seated humane vision of justice, and of right to freedom of faith. Similarly, the 'Covenant of 'Umar', granted by the second Orthodox caliph 'Umar ibn al-Khattab on his arrival in Jerusalem (then called Aelia, Iliya' in Arabic) following the Arab conquest of the city, assured the Christians there of security and the freedom to live in peace. This was a further manifestation of the tolerance of Islam. The Covenant reads, in part, as follows:

> This is the assurance of safety that the servant of Allah, 'Umar, Commander of the Faithful, has granted to the people of Iliya' [Jerusalem].
>
> He has given them assurance of safety for their lives and property, for their churches and their crosses, for their sick and their healthy, and for all the rituals of their religion.
>
> Their churches shall not be used as dwellings, nor shall they be demolished, and nothing shall be diminished – neither their churches nor the estates thereof, nor their crosses nor any part of their property.
>
> They shall not be coerced in matters pertaining to their religion and none of them shall be harmed.[1]

'Umar gave them the option either to remain in Aelia or to leave with the Byzantines, with a guarantee of safe conduct, for their lives, property, churches and crosses, till they reached their destination.

By this and many similar actions, the new Muslims of the seventh century AD established religious pluralism in the part of the world newly come under their rule – and it was this tradition that was so abruptly undermined, indeed utterly negated, at the end of the fifteenth century, by the triumphant Spanish conquistadores. These last brought the inquisition courts to the world, nine centuries after Muhammad and 'Umar, and when they themselves had witnessed eight centuries of enlightened, tolerant Arab-Islamic civilization in Muslim Spain.

To this day, after centuries of a rule whose autocratic nature has ravaged the resources of citizens and citizenship, Arabs still invoke the call of 'Umar ibn al-Khattab 'How can you enslave people when their mothers bore them free?' Still they recall people's objection to the first Umayyad caliph Mu'awiya (d. 60/680), who wished his son Yazid to succeed him: 'You seek, in the tradition of a Khosrow [an ancient king of Persia whose name the Arabs took as a symbol of autocratic Persian rule] . . . an unyielding hereditary reign.'

This intellectual and cultural heritage, apparent in the early days of Islam, was undoubtedly the product of a mature, humanistic frame of mind that had grown in the Arabian Peninsula, out of a spiritual maturity cultivated and nurtured over centuries. This spontaneously enlightened tendency, in a culture existing before the mid-seventh century AD, must stand as a witness to the humane advancement of the nation that produced it. It also signifies an early measure of intellectual and spiritual evolution that had both defied and transcended the rough geographical elements and harsh primitive environment of Arabia at the time. This has not happened often in history.

A number of essays in this book cast a clear light on the early Arab drive towards the establishment of human rights and the securing of human dignity; and, given the constant present-day attacks on Arabs because they live wholly or partly deprived of civil rights, it is only just that we should, in this book, strive to show the range of liberal thought offered by so many inspired Arab thinkers, both classical and modern; to acknowledge the contribution of those who have championed the greatest cause to have exercised humanity through its long history. The Arabs of early classical times manifest enlightened thought in many of its forms. And, in modern times, the generations who received and absorbed these ideas were by no means unaware of, or detached from, an early Arab heritage that stands out as one of the most advanced in human history. Comparing the substance of this great legacy with its aftermath – as elucidated in this volume and elsewhere – it becomes clear enough how utterly paradoxical and ironic the whole situation has become. The splendid heritage has found issue in a bleakly contrasting state of affairs, with the Arab individual of modern times reduced to compliant acquiescence in the face of unrelenting coercion and challenge.

II.

This book suggests, often indirectly, the presence of a stubborn problematic; of a major discrepancy between theoretical conceptualization and concrete practice in the field of human rights in modern times. Drawing on various references, including many Arab studies, the essays show how individuals in the Arab world have clearly and consciously identified the underlying problem areas regarding human rights. Intellectuals, in fact, are all fully aware of the game as it has evolved in modern times, and of its fearful dimensions. Yet they have usually tended, even so, to veer away from the challenges involved, feel compelled to turn a blind eye to them. It is true that many of the rights in question, mostly of a social nature, were achieved over the course of the twentieth century. Our emphasis here, though, is on those political and civil rights (or lack of them) that involve participation in decision-making, freedom of expression and criticism, and the official practice of condemning those who oppose state policy and subjecting them to persecution. This last factor explains citizens' fear of expressing differing views, and the way they resort to a corresponding dissimulation in public. The coexistence of aware individuals and an unnatural situation of this kind, at a time rife with resounding calls in celebration of freedom and rights, implies a profound condemnation of the larger society within which they live. Over many centuries now, Arabs have settled for a type of civil life in which they can lend no voice, take part in none of the decisions that shape their destiny.

That is not to deny the presence of a struggle, throughout modern times, to change the way most Arabs are ruled, and to redirect the focus of those in power towards providing a broadly better and more just life for the citizen. Such a struggle has existed even in those Arab countries that have provided education, work and medicine for their citizens. There have, indeed, been many movements standing out against official practices and challenging the arbitrary violation of rights. We know well enough that the Arab world has witnessed many political parties, of various orientations: a diversity of nationalist ideologies, Islamist tendencies of various types, the full range almost of Marxist/communist affiliations and secular socialist parties. And we are aware, too, of the way Arab governments have, ruthlessly and with varying degrees of violence, combated these movements in an attempt to suppress all opposition to their policies. We are also aware of how the prisons of the Arab world are crammed with prisoners of conscience. Many of these have been detained over long periods, and some have been subjected to torture and some have even faced eventual liquidation. Nevertheless, the opposition shown by a committed individual member of a party or organization forms, in essence, part of a collective action. For, when an individual joins the political struggle, whether publicly or clandestinely, he embraces, often with all his heart and mind, an ideology he finds appropriate and applicable to the world around him, sharing this with many other members – whether in the Arab world, in the wider Islamic world, or in the world as a whole – who subscribe to his ideological standpoint. Such an individual, then, has the sense of a collective fraternal shield that provides further support for his position and equips him with the strength to confront and resist.

In contrast, the individual who stands alone against the world, without the support of a group, has been forced to keep a low profile when faced by the machinery of repression set up to punish any who oppose the status quo; all the more so when he has seen, with his own eyes, the dire penalties inflicted on those who have dared to criticize and protest. At their least devastating, such penalties might entail depriving the individual of his resources and means of livelihood, and labelling him *persona non grata*, after which he and his family will face grave consequences – at the very least he, and often his family and relatives as well, will be denied access to centres of power and sources of profit. This has happened all too often in the Arab world since the mid-twentieth century; since, that is, numbers of Arab countries have won their independence from foreign rule and come to be governed by their own nationals.

So it is that individuals backed by no party or organization, yet holding radical, opposing views, find no way out of their desperate plight but to emigrate from the country they love, the country they long to see playing its part in the movement of the modern, progressive world around them. This predicament is in part responsible for the brain-drain phenomenon in the modern Arab world. In other cases, where the individual is less bold in expressing criticism, or perhaps less sensitive to his vulnerable position in a world unable to preserve his rights, he will live in political isolation, keeping silent despite his discontent. In other cases still, a self-centred, self-interested individual, ambitious to grasp whatever spoils he can from the existing regime, may take a willing and conscious part in a grand game to reinforce the utter egocentricity of the ruling elite, and so enhance its insatiable love of power and ruthless drive to dominate others.

And so despotic rule, intolerant of all criticism, enters a vicious circle. We have seen a number of *coups d'état* designed to change the political landscape of this or that Arab country, but succeeding only in changing the ruler's face. The regime of this new ruler will, in most cases, provide merely another form of ceaseless domestic terror, another steady degradation of the initiative available to citizens, freezing any ability to establish their rights. Domestic terror has been powerfully depicted in the works of poets and other writers of various affiliations. Muhammad al-Maghout's work, for instance, has lucidly and vividly portrayed Arab citizens' sense of dread vis-à-vis the authoritarian powers that govern them and control their destiny. Such writing finds receptive ears and open hearts among large, sympathetic audiences throughout the Arab world; it supplies a clear enough message, and makes its mark, to a greater or lesser extent, on those who read it.

Yet for all that, consciousness of human rights, and awareness of their significance, has remained on the theoretical level only; and that chiefly among the intellectual elite. Barring a few exceptional cases, such feelings have not been linked, among non-committed citizens, to any will to challenge and to posit an ultimate rejection. In other words, the concept of human rights has not

permeated the core of society, or transformed itself into an essential component of public culture and of the day-to-day practice of this culture within the
community. A barrier has fallen, decisively, between the Arab's early awakening under the guidance of genuine Islam and the political practices of later
stages. This situation has marked the life of the Arabs, sealed it with acceptance
of a dominance whereby a single non-elected class looks, first and foremost, to
its own interest, seeking no concurrence with the majority but rather manipulating people as it pleases. The concept of individual rights can only become
second nature, ensuring a firm stand when those rights are violated, if such a
perception finds its place in day-to-day public culture, becomes an integral,
intrinsic element in day-to-day practice and natural conduct. The viewpoints
projected in Arabic creative writings about individuals denouncing and rejecting others' despotism are partly (if not quite entirely) inspired by theoretical
ideals and abstract theories. For, in truth, the stance of the Arab individual in
general is at best abundantly characterized by passive silence and compliance;
at its worst, it is marked by the crime of connivance and conspiracy against individual rights themselves. There are countless examples of each of these types –
in some cases (let it be said) from within various literary circles.

The situation has been aggravated over the years to a point where it has
become all but ingrained. The fact that many individuals have assumed positions of power and authority in this emasculated world, have betrayed their
responsibilities yet not been held accountable for what they have failed to do,
points to a deep-seated flaw within the very psyche of the Arab nation. The
truth is that Arab society has adopted, nurtured and exalted various specimens
of humanity who have plagued the official, economic, cultural and literary ech-
elons – characters who should have been cast out of the public sphere at the
very outset. They have dragged society down into a bottomless abyss, and the
full consequences of this have still to be seen.

Observers cannot but feel frustrated by a state of affairs that has sunk so
low, yet forms part and parcel of life in the Arab world. The problem of human
rights now seems, in the short term, insoluble. No matter how high idealistic
awareness soars, it soon collapses in the face of any attempt at actual implementation.

III.

The fundamental conflict outlined above – between theoretical awareness of
the sanctity of human rights and the static nature of a consciousness repressed

by constant violation of these rights – is what prompted me to edit this book. Why has the concept of the individual about human rights failed to find emotional support, failed to issue in an iridescent enthusiasm able to motivate the will for confrontation and open rejection? How can this constant, insidious invasion of individuals, and the flagrant violation of their dignity, be justified?

We have seen how any assault on the freedom of the national community has met with invariable public rejection, on both the spiritual and physical levels. Arabs have bravely defended the nation's right to free itself from colonial domination. Thousands of martyrs, from Morocco to Yemen, have fallen on the road to freedom. Against this kind of external aggression, the Arabs' sense of right and wrong has always been aroused and indeed ignited; they have always shown a steadfast readiness to make sacrifices, however costly, in order to denounce foreign invasion and be rid of its consequences. The emotional reaction to the colonial problematic in the Arab world has exerted tremendous influence on hearts and minds, nor has there ever been any need for clarification, urging or persuasion. I still recall my own reaction when, as a small girl at the elementary school in Acre, Palestine, I saw the first demonstration of my life, with its ringing denunciation of the prevailing political malaise and its rejection of the Balfour Declaration. I had heard much of this Declaration – it had by now become part of our daily bread – but it had not settled deep in my heart and consciousness as it finally did that day, when I heard the resounding voices of the high school students chanting: 'Britain! Don't make too much of your spoils. Don't ever think you can enjoy your conquest!' This cry, in fact, I later incorporated into one of my poems. This was the first collective experience to overwhelm my inner being, stirring a rejection of the forcible violation of our rights. We were all one bloc, the school pupil and the newspaper seller alike, in our emotional and mental outrage against the aggression and injustice that had stricken our country.

In such a fashion, awareness of collective rights became ingrained deep in the community. There is a peculiar magic to great collective experiences, an irresistible attraction, unleashing a powerful capacity to act, rebel and reject. By virtue of their communal muscle, they give the individual support and courage, even when he or she stands alone in the face of violence and the hangman's noose. The sense of fellow feeling and affinity in struggle grips the consciousness, equipping the individual with rigour and resolution.

Individual rights are a very different story. No sooner had an Arab national community, by its own courage and with enormous sacrifice of life and resources, rid itself of external (or sometimes internally-based) aggression, than it fell prey to the tyranny of 'pseudo-revolutionary' characters who used their newly-found positions of power to take total control; to assault and pillage the freedom and dignity of the individual. In such cases, personal and private interests surface, and the new masters rule as they please. Compliance and acquiescence in the head's dominance over the rest of the body becomes the recognized norm within the nation. The poet Ibn Hani' al-Andalusi (d. 362/973) encapsulated this propensity long ago in one of his most famous poems, addressed to the Fatimid caliph al-Mu'izz li Din al-Lah:

> What you decide, not what fate decides.
> Rule then, you are the one and the vanquisher.

Subsequently – in what Arab literary history describes as the 'Age of Decadence' (roughly from the end of the thirteenth to the beginning of the nineteenth centuries) – hypocrisy in poetry became the norm. Rulers were often placed side by side with God. And even now, a glance at daily newspapers in the Arab world will reveal a scarcely less submissive and obsequious attitude. Such flatterers have moulded language into an instrument for two-faced duplicity. Indeed, they have devised and exploited an adulatory vocabulary unknown even to the old classical masters of the Arab poetic eulogy.

The above discussion has shown how the group, be it a party or some other political organization, has always felt psychologically capable of challenging injustice and repression, particularly external aggression. Yet, as we have also seen, the infringement of individuals' rights, and the blocking of individuals from playing any part in deciding their own destiny, seems to evoke no sustained collective or popular response. Does this anomaly occur because Arabic culture, in its political and civil characteristics, is effectively grounded in concern for the rights, honour and dignity of the community rather than those of the individual?

Islamic culture undoubtedly provides a suitable environment for promoting collective attitudes. In the words of the Prophet: 'In its relations built on mutual affection, the community of believers is akin to a human body; when one limb is afflicted, the rest of the body falls sick.' As such, Islamic culture has brought Muslims together; has promoted among them a collective spirit that abhors isolationism, apathy and any withdrawal from the community: 'Align your ranks, for God does not look at the crooked line.' Such a position has often patterned and typified life, vision and response, stressing the importance of the community and communal experience, lessening the value of the 'different' individual within society.[2]

Over centuries Arab men became so accustomed to dissembling and evasion that they were not shocked by the tyrannical rule, in modern times, of Arab leaders who seized all privileges for themselves. So it was that, at the individual level, the ensuing debate did not glow with a proportionate measure of inner anger and bold rebellion against the usurpation of rights; the rejection of injustice lacked an emotional tinge. Latter-day Arabs did not (to evoke a verse by the Abbasid poet Bashshar ibn Burd) 'hasten with their swords to reprove and discipline a ruler turned tyrant'. Many of them, indeed, became mere cringing hypocrites vis-à-vis a ruler who had looted the treasury, begging him to pay them their own legitimate due.

IV.

One of the salient themes of this book is the issue of women's rights – some of the most important individual rights to have been usurped, consistently and ruthlessly, by a society rooted deep in an oppressive male culture. The voice of women has long been subdued and compliant – their mothers, after all, had been through the same enslavement and violation. For a lengthy period their case appeared closed and sealed.

Experience with educated women has, however, shown up the relative fragility of this situation, against a backdrop of heightened consciousness, worldwide, of women's natural qualifications and of their ability to face the challenges of life with learning and resolve. Moreover, the need for additional monthly income, to provide the household with extra material comfort, gave women a further reason for entering the workplace.

A process of cultural and intellectual awareness was at work among those Arab women possessing a measure of education. With schools and other educational institutions now open wide, women aspired to invest their personal and mental resources and satisfy their aspiration towards self-fulfilment. That is not to say there has been any universal attempt by women to secure society's acknowledgement of them as complete persons having no need of the men who are their greatest aggressors. Nevertheless, avant-garde working women, in the heart of a male chauvinistic society, are now marching (if unconsciously in some cases) towards this goal.

An essential component in any enlightened concept of human rights is treatment of the woman as a complete person. She must, that is to say, be treated on a par with man in terms of right to education, specialization, work, choice of future and of conducting her own personal affairs. Neither dependent on nor hostage to any other person, she is to be an individual in her own right. How often we have seen brilliant women subjugated, without hope of salvation, to worthless men. But how often, too, we have seen particular women assuming the role of true guardianship, working to support the family even as men vaunt their superior positions, still believing themselves to be guardians and masters.

This whole matter has, inevitably, become subject to certain social and economic variables. These factors, ingrained though they are within Arab society at large – within human society as a whole, indeed – are mostly, in my view, more amenable to change than the wider issue of civil and political rights filched from the individual by the authorities in most of the Arab world. Great hopes may be attached to Arab women's involvement in the workforce and to their participation in public life. The target goes, indeed, beyond dissipating and superseding a history of female enslavement by males, and proclaiming an authentic achievement and material independence which is in fact well grounded in Islam. This target involves a further proclamation, innocent yet ingenious, regarding a modernized vision of public life hostile to all forms of subjugation in society. The Arab woman – whether worker, educator, academic, lawyer, parliamentarian or writer – enters public life today as an untainted individual with a memory clear of connivance and injustice over others. She is free, in other words, of long centuries of indoctrination in hypocritical, submissive practices vis-à-vis those possessing the power to control individual lives. The human craving for independence, achievement and self-fulfilment has captured the hearts of a large sector of women throughout the Arab world. Nor does this apply only to those who have thrown away their veils, but to veiled women who, for all their compliance with tradition and acquiescence in a life of unobtrusive isolation, have surmounted many of the old-fashioned, dehumanizing, suppressive inhibitions – notably the old, total reliance on male support and approval.

V.

There are, perhaps, two main barriers to a proper understanding of the issue of rights in the Arab world: one having its origin outside Arabic culture, the other inside. The first is the pernicious example provided by Western democratic countries in their attitude to human rights outside their own borders – in the Third World generally and in the Arab and Islamic regions in particular. The second involves the power of inherited norms of individual behaviour, put forward under the guise of religion.

Regarding the first, some Western countries have a matchless capacity for (selectively) trumpeting human rights violations on the part of other peoples, especially, as said above, those in the Arab world. Of relevance here is the quite

naked official bias of countries like the United States and Britain, which sanction the most atrocious forms of premeditated aggression and obliteration on
the part of 'democratic' Israel, against people's dignity, and against people's
right to life, property and security in Palestine and other neighbouring Arab
countries. This bias is a matter of the utmost shame and disgrace, and will
undoubtedly be a source of embarrassment to future generations in the
Western countries in question. No situation lasts forever, and the West's
bedazzlement by Israel is bound to fade one day. Part of the infatuation rests
on biblical connotations that are actually fragile, and are beginning to be rigorously discredited by numbers of Western scholars. A second element prompting such an affiliation is the present strategic alliance with Israel against the
Arab world. A third aspect lies in the West's awareness of its persecution of
Jews through the ages; it is now striving to atone for this historical behaviour,
and so clear its conscience, through a show of repentance and recompense.
And yet this last stance, on the part of the West, has merely led on to a new cycle
of injustice, persecution and bloodletting against another people. This, in its
turn, will one day call for a further phase of atonement and conscience-clear-
ing. One wonders just how enlightened, conscientious persons in Britain, or in
other countries of the new colonial West, now look back on the infamous
Balfour Declaration and the cynical duplicity of the Sykes-Picot Agreement,
which led the Arabs to the protracted agony they now suffer.

Some western countries have gone to excessive lengths in contravening the
first principles of human rights, disregarding the essential right to life, medicine, education, housing and security. These are the rights of which the children of Iraq were deprived for more than a decade after the end of the first Gulf
War, years of siege, hunger, sickness and malnutrition. Such situations do not
simply stand in stark contradiction to the essential principles of human rights,
and to any appreciation of human life and dignity, but also show an astounding
lack of vision, prudence and acumen, an immense indifference to the life and
future of generations of Arab children still unborn; in other words, a quite
enormous apathy and lack of concern for the future of the world. The world we
live in cannot possibly enjoy a secure, prosperous future so long as injustice,
aggression, usurpation and carnage find support from superpowers that exercise hegemony by virtue of sheer technological prowess. It is inconceivable
that advocates of democracy and human rights can capture the hearts and
minds of a vast Arab society that feels betrayed and deeply wounded by those
same states that, to this day, use double standards and fail to practise what they
preach. The world will need to change, become fully aware of the problematic
situation and rise against it, before all hope and awareness is lost. The

extraordinary thing is that the onslaught against present-day men and women, through the sophisticated technology and economic hegemony of certain centres of power in the world, is taking place in an enlightened era; one that is heir to outstanding cultural and philosophical traditions, and to a treasure of splendid poetry, literature, art and sciences. In time this major human legacy, in the intellectual, spiritual and aesthetic fields, will inevitably be marshalled and rallied everywhere, from the United States to China and Japan, in the face of this hybrid state of affairs, self-contradictory and self-defeating. New generations of humanists and intellectuals – some as yet unborn – will pinpoint the problematic of a chasm that divides ideas from actions, and separates high ideals from a philosophy of authoritarian monopoly that has become the landmark of our age.

To put it briefly, the call for indigenizing human rights and eradicating domestic repression will, until that time, be engulfed in contradictions. Citizens in those societies where civil rights are not properly observed will have no authentic, consistent and honest role model to help them in their fight to resolve the overall problem. In this regard, the difficulties of setting up the 1948 Universal Declaration of Human Rights as a way forward to modernity, and to involvement in an ever-developing world, are surely obvious enough. 'Modernity', in the present world situation, appears to many as a superficial cover, beneath which lie inhuman aggression, injustice, repression and brute deprivation for the disadvantage of the world.

In the United States – the most vocal advocate of human rights as laid down in the Universal Declaration – most Arabs see only an exponent of a policy loaded against the rights of Arabs. And indeed any detached observer, viewing the human rights situation in an Arab context, will point out the damage being inflicted on the Arabs by the clearly biased policy of some of the Western powers; a policy which has hampered the efforts of those many Arab intellectuals, individuals and groups who are leading the struggle for the institution of human rights, especially regarding political activities and women, in an Arab society perplexed by contradictory criteria and standards. The aggression and notorious inattention to Arab sensibilities on the part of the outside world has weakened, significantly, the capacity of Arab intellectuals to carry out their necessary work. It must, too, have impeded the work of those institutions set up to advocate and promote the full application of human rights in the Arab world.

It should be pointed out here that America is not in fact a single face or a single voice. It is a country that permits diversity, plurality and difference by virtue of the individual freedom that citizens enjoy. It contains numerous men and women with a genuine interest in reaching out to the 'other' and in understanding this other's experiences and hardships. Tragically, this humanistic stance has receded considerably since the events of 11 September 2001.

Let us now consider the second barrier to a proper understanding of the issue of rights, namely, a number of obsolescent inherited norms now embedded in the Arab world under the guise of religion. The most cursory study of Islam's early history will show that such traditions have, in fact, no relevance to authentic Islam or its spirit.

The employment of religion as a pretext is both potent and immune from criticism, and the resulting traditions exert an immensely powerful impact on people's minds. The only way out of this quandary is to have Islam enter actively into the climate of modernization and modernity. It is indeed fully equipped to absorb developments and direct them beneficially; no truly pious Muslim could claim that Islam is incapable of assimilating human advancement and redirecting life into channels that are sound and secure. We are now looking at a modern era far distant from the first century of Islam, from the radiant joy that was open to the world, embodying a liberal call to promote people's happiness and good. The early Islamic discourse presented Islam as the 'seal' of religions – a message that needs urgently to be recalled by religious leaders who tend to block Islam away from development and close its conduits to the outside world. The Islam of al-Afghani and Muhammad 'Abduh, at the end of the nineteenth century, was actually far more flexible and liberal than what we see now, at the turn of the third millennium.

Islam must once more become open to interpretations, harmonizing it with a modernity of which it is fully capable. Genuine intellectual Muslims should have the right to do what their predecessors did so many centuries ago.

The most serious encumbrance in the life of modern Arabs is the inability to articulate their desire for modernization in all its various aspects. They cannot afford to wait endlessly for freedom of thought and expression, nor can they afford, in the current climate of human development, to wait very much longer before recognizing, clearly and with conviction, that they have sacred, inalienable rights, violated for centuries and under brutal assault from the two adversaries – one foreign, the other home-grown. These rights must be restored and reinstated.

The present Arab world is loaded with shortcomings which have become entrenched in the Arabs' whole way of life, accompanied by a destructive propensity to regionalism and a pathetic political illiteracy with all the consequences that entails. But of all the disasters that have befallen Arab society, the most tragic is the sustained suppression of thought and the constant desecration of human rights. Those lacking legitimate freedom and capacity for expression, whose political rights are not protected and respected, are in no position even to recognize, let alone resist, the vicious aggression against their existence, their culture, their identity and their future achievements.

Salma Khadra Jayyusi

PART 1

The early concept of human rights in Islam

Chapter 1: The concepts of rights and justice in Arab-Islamic texts

Muhammad 'Abid al-Jabiri

Introduction: The need to scrutinize the concepts

It would be quite erroneous to deal with Islamic texts – or with any other text from cultures prior to modern and contemporary European civilization – using the same approach and perspective that informs our contemporary discourse: a discourse governed, in one way or another, by the spirit of modern and contemporary European civilization itself, and by its concepts and perspectives. The connotations we link today with many words referring to the life of man, both material and moral, and especially in its economic, social, political and intellectual aspects, are the outcome of a vast development achieved over ages and centuries. To keep these same connotations in mind when dealing with traditional texts would be to commit a methodological blunder, and hence, an epistemological and historical one. We would be like someone who takes the word *rocket* (in Arabic *sarukh*) to mean 'shrieker', which is the basic Arabic lexical meaning. It is true that the Arabic equivalent has always denoted 'shrieking', but there is a huge difference between the connotation of the Arabic word today and its connotation before the present century.

This may be taken to apply to many words and terms informing our present-day discourse, such as 'right', 'individual', 'person', 'justice' and other concepts which will be discussed below. It is therefore necessary to begin by scrutinizing these concepts and carrying out the necessary groundwork. By so doing we can identify points of conjunction and disjunction, which should be recognized among the connotations of these concepts in our, contemporary discourse, and in those of our Arab-Islamic tradition.

Take, for instance, the term *human rights*, which has become current in our contemporary speech and which is the theme of this essay. The first thing to note concerning this term is that it was not known in Arab-Islamic texts before about the middle of the last century. (Nor in fact was it known in European texts going back about two centuries before that.) The closest equivalent term we find in Islamic texts, especially in jurisprudence (*fiqh*) is 'the rights of God and the rights of worshippers'. The difference between the terms shows the difference between the 'object thought of' in the Middle Ages and the 'object thought of' in the present age. The question is linked to two different types of relation controlling the status of man in this world. In the Middle Ages the concern was with the relation between man and God. In modern and contemporary ages the concern is more with the relation between man and the human community in which he lives, viewed from two different but complementary perspectives: one social, the other political. In the first perspective, the status of man is seen through the dichotomy of 'individual – society'; in the second, through the dichotomy of 'citizen – state'. Hence, the concept of 'human rights' in contemporary discourse refers to the rights of the individual in society on the one hand, and to his rights in the state on the other. The term 'the rights of God and the rights of worshippers' refers to quite another situation, that is, one not controlled by society or the state. Both terms have differed in their past and present meanings.

Nevertheless, the absence of a term, or the difference in the type of relations involved between one age and another, does not necessarily mean there is an unbridgeable gulf, or that what was not a subject of thought once, can never be a subject of thought. The concerns of man are, in essence, the same in all ages. The difference is usually in the form and the way of expression. In other words, what is different in the basic concerns of man, between one age and another, lies in the degree of awareness of those issues, not in the essence of the issues themselves. Our intention in this essay is, on the one hand, to approach the relevant Islamic texts in a manner that retains their historical significance, and, on the other, to heighten our awareness of their implications – and so widen the scope of our thought – in the light of our current preoccupations.

I. Right and duty

In Arabic, the concept of 'right' is alternatively and constantly connected with that of 'duty'. It is the preposition following the word that makes the difference in meaning. A 'right to him' means, exactly, a 'duty to him'; and a 'right on him' means a 'duty on him' or 'determined on him'. Most instances of the use of 'right' in the Quran come as a transitive verb with the preposition 'on', to mean a confirmation of the object or the assertion and necessity of it. 'When We decide to destroy a village We command the self-indulgent therein, so they transgress, and the judgment is proven right on them, then We destroy it utterly.' (17, *Al-Isra'*, 16) Also: 'We did indeed send, before you, messengers to their [respective] people, and they came to them with clear signs: then to those who transgressed, We meted out retribution: and it was right on Us to support the believers.' (30, *Al-Rum*, 47) In his comment on this verse, al-Zamakhshari says: 'He made [the believers] have a "right on" God to support them, and have a "duty on" Him to support and lead them to victory.' To support this interpretation, he quotes a *hadith* of the Prophet: 'A Muslim defending the honour of his brother Muslim would entail a "right on Allah" to protect him against hell fire on the Day of Resurrection.' In another *hadith,* the Prophet asked Mu'adh: 'Do you know the right of Allah on His worshippers and the right of worshippers on Allah?' He said: 'Allah and His Messenger know better.' The Prophet said: 'The right of Allah on worshippers is to worship Him and not to take any associates with Him. The right of worshippers on Allah is that He shall not torment any who does not take any associates with Him.' It is clear, then, how this type of constancy and alternation between 'right' and 'duty' denotes that what is a duty on one party is a right to the other party. What is a duty of God is a right of man, and what is a duty of man is a right of God.

II. The rights of God and the rights of men

The jurists (*faqih*s) distinguish between the rights of God and the rights of men in the following manner:

The rights of God cover belief, *salat,* fasting and all the others duties and *sunan* (religious laws) which have a purely devotional aspect, or which are accompanied by other duties or measures like the *zakat* of *fitr* (the Ramadan Feast), punishments for adultery and theft, or other expiatory acts.

The rights of men cover the rights of the relatives of a murdered person to retribution (killing the murderer, blood-money), the right to punishment for wounds (hand for hand, tooth for tooth, etc.), the right of a man whose honour has been impeached, the right of the wife over her husband, the husband over his wife, the rights of inheritors, etc. All these are rights due to certain individuals. The 'rights of God' are 'not for certain people, but for the benefit of all Muslims or a section therefrom'.[1]

When jurists define the 'rights of men' in such criminal and quasi-criminal areas, it does not mean that human rights in Islamic jurisprudence are limited to these areas and no other. The jurists themselves have enlarged Shariah rulings on the general basis that the intent of Shariah is to ensure 'the interests of worshippers in this world and in the hereafter', and they have classified these intents or general interests into three categories: necessities, needs and desirables. The necessities are 'indispensable for a righteous spiritual and worldly life which, when lost, the affairs of worldly life will not be on the right path. In the hereafter, such loss will lead to the loss of salvation and bliss, and descent into utter perdition'. Jurists specify five such necessities: the protection of life, reason, faith, progeny and property. This means that Shariah was laid down to protect five corresponding goals, namely man's right to life, thought, faith, procreation and acquisition of property. These are rights, essential for the physical and social well-being of man. In addition there are other quasi-necessary rights, which are the needs. These cover 'what is needed to provide ease and alleviate hardship which will in most cases lead to stressful situations as a result of missing what is required'; these include such things as the dispensation from fasting in Ramadan granted to travellers and the sick. Then there are the desirables, namely 'the adoption of proper and good habits and avoidance of bad ones shunned by decent minds. These can be termed as the loftiest of morals and manners.'[2]

III. The basis of 'right' on the human level in the 'duty of justice' on the divine level

This is how jurists view the rights of man. However, kalamologists, and the Mu'tazilis in particular, have based their view of the subject on their famous principle of 'good and better'. For them, God, in accordance with their principle of 'divine justice', never does what is 'bad'. When 'justice' is used 'to describe an action', says the *qadi* 'Abd al-Jabbar, 'it denotes any good action performed by a person to benefit one or harm another'. To help a man in need is justice; and the same applies to harming a sinner or a wrong-doer by imprisoning or fining him. In this sense, then, justice means 'to provide the right of one, and demand the right from another'. When 'justice' is used as an attribute of a person, it denotes that his actions are good. A just person is one who avoids major sins and endeavours to avoid minor ones. Hence the concept of 'adjustment and challenge' in criticizing the reporting of *hadith*. When the word is used as an attribute of God, it means, to the Mu'tazili, something different. According to the *qadi* 'Abd al-Jabbar: 'When we attribute justice and wisdom to the Everlasting, it means that He never does or chooses what is bad, nor fails to perform His duty; and that all His deeds are good.'

'Abd al-Jabbar's argument brings us closer to the Socratic theory that links virtue with knowledge. He says: 'God knows the badness of the bad, has no need of it, and knows that He has no need of it. One in such a state does not choose what is bad in any way.' The proof of this is that 'we know in our worldly life that if a person knows the badness of the bad, and has no need of it, he does not choose what is bad at all.' If 'one of us were given a choice between telling the truth and lying, and the benefit from one was equal to that of the other, and he was told, "if you tell a lie we will give you a *dirham*, if you tell the truth we will give you a *dirham*," and he knew the badness of lying and had no need of it, he would never choose lying over telling the truth, because he knows the badness of lying and that he has no need of it. The same situation holds in the case of the Everlasting; therefore He would never choose to do what is bad.' He cites significant evidence to support this Mu'tazili theory. 'God,' he says, 'emphasizes His disavowal of any injustice attributed to Him, or connected with His actions: "Your Lord is never unjust to His worshippers" (41, *Fussilat*, 46); "Allah is never unjust in the least degree' (4, *Al-Nisa'*, 40); "And your Lord will not treat anyone with injustice" (18, *Al-Kahf*, 49).'[3]

It follows from this that evil issues not from God but from men. Hence man's responsibility for his actions. Since responsibility is the basis of right and duty, it is therefore the basis of justice. It also entails freedom of will. For the Mu'tazili, therefore, to say that 'God would do the good or the better' implies man's ability to exercise the right of justice and the right of freedom, and to admit the necessity of responsibility.

The evils occurring in this world, such as pain, death and disaster, issue not from man but from a cause. 'That cause is not among our rights; but on the part of God it implies a lesson and a warning. In return, God provides ample compensations, that if one of us is given the choice between pain, along with those compensations, and health, he would choose pain to achieve those compensations.'[4] This is the Mu'tazili theory of 'compensation', or the right to compensation: God compensates man in the hereafter for the harm he suffers if that harm cannot be ascribed to men like him, since such harm, like natural disaster, is beyond their will and power.

This may lead to the following conclusion: The 'rights of man' in Mu'tazili texts are implied in their famous dictum: 'It is the duty of God to do what is good' (some say 'the better'). In other words, what establishes 'right' on the human level is 'the duty of justice' on the divine level.

IV. The right of the ruler and the right of the ruled: justice and obedience

IV.1 Justice: command or advice?

In addition to jurists and kalamologists concerned with 'right' and 'justice' in the relation between God and man, there were authors dealing with the 'principles of rule' and advice to sovereigns (producing 'mirrors for magistrates' in the European expression). Most of these were also in fact jurists or kalamologists, but they were mainly interested in 'rights' on the political level, that is, in the relation between ruler and ruled. They based this relation on 'justice' and 'obedience' as two interconnected 'rights', with the one calling for the other: the right of the prince over the subjects to obey him and the right of the subjects over the prince to be just. The ruler should mete out justice to the ruled in return for their obedience. These authors gleaned their material from texts and sayings ascribed to kings of Persia, Greek philosophers and Muslim scholars, in addition to the Holy Quran and the exalted *hadith*.

The noteworthy point about the treatment of justice in these 'political' works, whether in what is ascribed to the Prophet, to Companions of the Prophet or to wise men of other nations, is that it is less powerful than what is found in the Quran. In such works, exhortation to justice falls within the limits of advice, not legislation. In the Quran, the enjoinment of justice is comprehensive and absolute, as we see in many verses: 'Allah commands you to render back the trusts to whom they are due; and when you judge among men that you judge with justice' (4, *Al-Nisa'*, 58); 'Allah commands justice and the doing of good' (16, *Al-Nahl*, 90). The Quran insists there should be no discrimination between people, poor and rich, close or far relative, and enjoins justice to all. 'O you who believe! Stand out firmly for justice, as witnesses to Allah, even as against yourselves, or your parents, or your kin, or whether it be [against] rich or poor; for Allah can best protect both. Do not follow the whims lest you swerve, and if you distort or decline to do justice. Allah is well acquainted with all that you do.' (4, *Al-Nisa'*, 135) Also: 'O you who believe! Stand out firmly for Allah, as witnesses to fair dealing, and let not the hatred of others to you make you swerve to wrong and depart from justice. Be just: that is next to piety.' (5, *Al-Ma'ida*, 8) Justice is required even toward rivals and enemies. There are several reported *hadith*s of the Prophet that celebrate justice and encourage abiding by it. One such *hadith* is reported by al-Tirmidhi: 'The one most favoured by Allah on the day of Resurrection, and the nearest to Him, is the just ruler. The one most hateful to him, and the farthest from him, is the unjust ruler.'

Again: 'The greatest *jihad* [holy war] is a word of justice spoken before an unjust ruler.' Moreover: 'The just are gloriously seated to the right of the Compassionate: those who are just in their judgement of their kindred and others.' (Reported by al-Nassa'i and Muslim.)

When set alongside the Quran and *hadith,* the texts of authors on the principles of rule appear, as noted above, less powerful, since these authors hardly go beyond 'advice', although all consider justice a basis of government – indeed the main basis. Ibn al-Azraq, who attempted to collect and edit most of the relevant sayings ascribed to the wise men of Persia and other nations, wrote as follows:

> The sixth basis [of government] is the upholding of justice. It is the foundation of all the previous five principles. It has been said that no development is possible without justice, and so it became the basis of everything else. The circle of connections devised by Aristotle is the best proof of what we say. He believed as follows: 'The world is an orchard and the state is its fence; the state is a power kept alive by the law; the law is a policy managed by a sovereign; sovereignty is a system supported by the military; the military is an aid secured by money; money is wealth collected by the subjects, the subjects are followers administered by justice; justice is the acknowledged pillar of the world; and the world is an orchard with the state for a fence . . . each is connected to each.'[5]

'When this is established,' Ibn al-Azraq continues, 'the principle divides into two branches: the first is justice, which has two sub-divisions: the first of which is its religious benefits.' (He goes on to recount *hadith*s celebrating justice and the status of the just on the Day of Judgment, all of them similar to the ones cited above.) The second sub-division is worldly benefits, which include 'the assertion of sound reason through the exercise of justice. Some wise men were asked: "Who among the kings is more sound in reason and more perfect in conduct and worth?" The answer was: "He who throughout his life befriended justice and did his utmost to avoid injustice; he who met people with courtesy and dealt with them gently; he who never deviated from the policy of leniency in his rule and from firmness in upholding the right, so that the venturesome was not beyond his reach, nor the innocent fearful of his sway."' Among the worldly benefits realized by justice, Ibn al-Azraq mentions 'lasting grace through the exercise of justice.' He continues:

> They said: when you see rulers compete in justice and hold back from corruption and waywardness, then this is a lasting grace. But it is a transitory grace when you see injustice dominate and justice forgotten and ignored. Another benefit is the

steady progress of sovereignty in the practice of justice. One wise saying denotes that the most deserving person of constant sovereignty is the one adhering most to justice in his dealings with his subjects, and the one least perturbed by its practice. They say: whoever makes justice his means, the duration of his sovereignty will increase. A further benefit is that he will dominate the hearts of his subjects with his justice. It is reported of Plato that he said: the sovereign who exercises justice and righteousness will win the innermost feelings of his subjects; but he who exercises injustice and oppression will control nothing but their bodies and will see nothing but affectation, while the hearts harbour different intentions; the innermost feelings can be secured only through good and kind treatment. Furthermore, justice in the land is equal to life-giving rain, or still more beneficial. It is said that a just prince is better than a life-giving shower. Also, the justice of the sovereign is better than fertile seasons. And finally, no land becomes arid when the justice of the sovereign flows in it, and no land lies waste when shaded by a just sovereign.

Next in his discussion of justice, Ibn al-Azraq moves on to the second branch, that of injustice, exposing its dangers and relating what has been said in dispraise of it and warning against it, according to reported *hadith*s and sayings of wise men. He writes in the same manner he followed in praising justice.[6]

The writers on 'morals', in dealing with the issue of justice, follow a different approach from that of Ibn al-Azraq: they use the opinions of both Plato and Aristotle (mostly their genuine opinions, not those ascribed to them, as was the case in works on the principles of rule). One famous writer on morals was Ibn Miskawayh, whose best known book was the *Refinement of Morals* (Tahdhib al-akhlaq). However, since he based it almost entirely on Aristotle's *Ethics*, there is no need to discuss it here.

More profitable is an examination of the work of al-Raghib al-Asfahani, a major linguist and religious scholar who attempted to join the Greek and Islamic traditions. In the fifth chapter of his *The Way to the Dignities of Shariah*, under the title 'On Justice and Injustice; Love and Hatred', we read as follows:

Justice is a word based on equality, and it is used only in a genitive construction. As an abstract concept, it is a trait in man that requires equality. When applied, it is justice based on equality. When God is described as just, what is meant is that all His actions are perfect. When man follows the course of justice he is perfect in virtue, provided his actions are not self-centred. A just act may be undertaken by a person without his earning praise for it, as when he is hypocritically just, or seeking a worldly gain or fearing the punishment of the sovereign.

The author describes justice as the 'scale of God, which is flawless, and through which the affairs of the world are regulated'.[7] He quotes: 'It is Allah Who has sent down the Book in truth and the Balance' (42, *Al-Shura*, 17); 'And the Firmament He has raised high and has set up the Balance (of justice)' (55, *Al-Rahman*, 7). He explains 'balance' as 'justice', referring to a *hadith* of the Prophet which says: 'By justice heaven and earth were established.' Briefly discussing the 'virtue' of justice, the author details the 'types of justice', which he takes to be two in number. The first is absolute justice, which the mind approves, and which is not diminished at any time or described with its opposite in any manner. This is like doing a good turn to someone who did a good turn to you, or warding off harm from someone who warded off harm from you. The second type is limited justice, which is recognized as justice only through Shariah; this may at times be diminished or cancelled. This is like confronting evil with evil, as through enforcing punishment for certain crimes, sowing dissension or confiscating the property of the apostate. Such action may, at times, be metaphorically described as injustice. Thus, we read in the Holy Quran: 'The recompense for an injury is an injury equal thereto.' (42, *Al-Shura*, 40) The recompense for the injury is called injury, because, had it not been related to the former injury, it would have been an injury in itself. Commenting on the first type, some kalamologists have said that 'justice and injustice are known by reason before they are known by Shariah'. As for the second type (limited justice): 'Some have said it can be recognized only through Shariah. Generally speaking, Shariah is the consensus of justice, in which its attributes are recognized. If we could imagine Shariah to be non-existent, then justice would be non-existent, partially in some actions and wholly in many others. Commendable justice is that which is sought not hypocritically, in pursuit of fame, or by whim, or out of fear. It is rather that which is truly concerned with righteousness.'

Al-Asfahani then continues as follows:

> Man should exercise justice in five situations: the first between himself and the Almighty, by knowing His commands. The second is to be just with his own urges, by subjecting his whims to his reason. It is said that the most just man is the one who saves his reason from his whims. The third is between himself and his forefathers, which comes by practising what they advised and by praying for them. The fourth is between himself and the one with whom he is dealing: fulfilling what is right and being fair in transactions of all types. The fifth type of justice is extending advice to people, to the rulers and their followers.

Next al-Asfahani talks about injustice, describing it as 'deviation from justice'. Because of this:

It has been defined as placing a thing where it does not belong. We have said that justice is like the centre of a circle. Excessive deviation from it leads to aggression and tyranny. This is denoted by the holy verse, 'have really strayed far away from the path'. (4, *Al-Nisa'*, 167) Partial deviation from it is inequity, and injustice is the most common name. Since injustice is ignoring the right which is the centre of the circle, justice is therefore either far from or near to that centre. He who is too far from justice will find it more difficult to return to it . . .

Those by whom injustice is exercised are the same five mentioned above, the fifth being the ruler. Some wise men have said: 'The worst among people is the one who is unjust to himself, then to his relatives, then to all people. The best is he who is just to all people, then to his relatives, then to himself.' This is too general an opinion, since the unjust is not unjust to others until he is unjust to himself. Whoever intends injustice begins with himself, so he is ever unjust. And whoever metes out justice to people has been just to himself before being just to others.[8]

IV.2 Obligatory obedience

Alongside this profusion of texts celebrating justice and encouraging its exercise, as representing the essence of the right of subjects over the ruler, we find an equal number of texts encouraging obedience as this represents the right of the ruler over his subjects. What is notable here is the repetition of calls in the Quran to establish justice on the level of personal relations as well as on the level of government. These seem concerned with the issue of obedience only in respect of obedience to God and His Messenger, along with related matters. The exception is one single verse making additional mention of obedience to 'those charged with authority'. We shall see below the disagreement among exegetes and jurists about the meaning of 'those charged with authority'. On the other hand, we find a profusion of *hadith*s enjoining obedience to rulers, most of them directly linked to the political conflicts of the first Islamic century.

There is another observation worthy of note in this connection. While statements enjoining obedience to rulers abound in the texts, ascribed to the kings and wise men of Persia, we find hardly any corresponding statements ascribed to the Greeks. This is completely the contrary of what we have concerning the issue of justice, where the main reference of authority is to Plato and Aristotle. This may be explained by the characteristic preoccupations of people in Persia and Greece respectively. The need for obedience and justice together had its justification in the governmental system of the Persian Empire. In fact, the idea of connecting 'obedience' – as representing 'the right of the ruler over the subjects' – with 'justice' – as representing 'the right of the subjects over the ruler' – is of Persian origin, often linked to the name of Xerxes Anusherwan (the just king). In Greece the need for obedience was not mandatory in equal form and degree. The Greek city-state was in need of 'justice', which the Greeks took to mean balance among the classes of society and the assigning of people to the places where they belonged (in correspondence with the cosmic system). As for 'obedience', which meant 'the obedience of the subjects to the ruler', it had no place in their political thought. The ruler did not occupy the position of prince or emperor; he was elected by those enjoying the right of election, who were 'citizens' rather than 'subjects'. The Persian system of government was that of 'ruler and subjects'. That of Greece was one of 'citizens and slaves'. The first system needed to secure the obedience of the subjects to the ruler. The second required secure, continued stability of citizens' affairs (and the subjection of the slaves, who were mere tools).

Having made these observations, we may now return to the texts, beginning with that sole verse referring to 'those charged with authority'. We read: 'O you who believe! Obey Allah, and obey the Messenger, and those charged with authority among you. If you differ in anything among yourselves, refer it to Allah and His Messenger, if you do believe in Allah and the Last Day: that is best, and most suitable for final determination.' (4, *Al-Nisa'*, 59) Al-Zamakhshari takes 'those charged with authority among you' to mean just rulers; since Allah and His Messenger have no dealings with unjust rulers, then these cannot be coupled, in grammatical conjunction, with Allah and His Messenger in the enjoinment of obedience. The coupling is between Allah and His Messenger and rulers who prefer justice and choose what is right, who enjoin these two things and prohibit their opposite, like the Rashidin caliphs and those who followed in their footsteps. The Rashidi caliph would say: 'Obey me so long as I am just in my dealings with you; when I deviate, then I have no claim on your obedience.' Abu Hazim reports how Maslama ibn 'Abd al-Malik asked him: 'Were you not ordered to obey us [i.e. the Umayyads], in His saying, "those charged with authority among you?"' Abu Hazim answered: 'Has it [obedience] not been denied you when you deviate from the right way in His saying, "If you differ in anything among yourselves, refer it to Allah and His Messenger?"' Al-Zamakhshari further explains 'those charged with authority among you' to mean 'the chieftains of brigades'. A *hadith* is recorded to the following effect: 'He who obeys me has obeyed Allah; he who disobeys me has disobeyed Allah; he who obeys my prince has obeyed me; and he who disobeys my prince has disobeyed me.' It has also been said that the phrase denotes 'religious scholars who teach people their religion, enjoin what is right and prohibit what is wrong'. 'If you differ in anything among yourselves' has been explained as: 'if you disagree with those in charge among you about a religious question, then you should refer to Allah and His Messenger: that is, refer to the Book and the *sunna*.' Al-Zamakhshari comments further:

> How can it be mandatory to obey unjust rulers, when God has enjoined, in such clear terms, obedience on those in charge, commanding them to return the trust to where it is due, to be just in their ruling, and, finally, to refer to the Book and the *sunna* in questionable cases? Unjust rulers do not return the trust, do not rule justly, and do not refer to the Book or the *sunna*. They rather follow their own whims; therefore they do not enjoy the qualities of those who are regarded as 'charged with authority' by God and His Messenger. It would be more fitting to call them 'marauding thieves'.[9]

This is how the majority of the exegetes and jurists understand 'those charged with authority among you'. Such people are, they say, generally taken to be princes and rulers, or sometimes religious scholars. The oldest records, however, call them 'chieftains of brigades' appointed by the Messenger over army formations. Al-Shafi'i, in his *Treatise*, writes as follows:

> Some men of learning have said that 'those charged with authority' are the chieftains of the brigades appointed by the Messenger. This is how it has come down to us, and God knows the truth. This is plausible, since the Arabs around Mecca knew of no princedom, holding back from paying one another the fealty and obedience of submission to a prince. But when the leadership came into the hands of the Messenger of Allah, they could not see this leadership as being suited to other hands. Therefore, they were enjoined to obey those who are in charge, since these were appointed by the Messenger of Allah. It was not an absolute obedience, but limited by their rights and duties. 'If you differ in anything among yourselves, refer it to Allah.' This is concerning 'those charged with authority' whom they were commanded to obey. 'Refer to Allah and His Messenger' means refer to what Allah said, and to what the Messenger said, if you know it, or consult the Messenger on it if you are able to reach him, or ask those who can.'[10]

This is supported by something reported by al-Bukhari, quoting Ibn 'Abbas – the latter referring to the verse in question as being revealed in connection with 'Abd Allah ibn Hudhafa ibn Qays ibn 'Adiyy, who was commissioned by the Prophet to take charge of a brigade.

The opinion adopted by al-Zamakhshari is clearly based on the spirit of religion: he couples obedience with justice, government with righteousness, etc. Al-Shafi'i, relying on 'history', interprets the verse with reference to the historical situation prevailing at the time of the verse's revelation. Both opinions are worthy of consideration. Though this verse is the only reference in the Quran concerning obedience to 'those charged with authority', it is amazing how many *hadiths* are ascribed to the Prophet about the necessity of obeying princes, even when these are not just or righteous in their rulings. Here are some of the reported *hadiths* on the subject of obedience:

Ibn 'Umar reports how the Prophet said: 'Listening and obedience are a duty, unless a sinful deed is ordered. If it is, then there should be neither listening nor obedience.' (Source: al-Bukhari) Anas ibn Malik records how the Prophet said: 'Listen and obey, even if an Abyssinian with an uncomely head should be appointed chieftain over you.' (Source: al-Bukhari) Nafi' reports 'Abd Allah, who reports the Prophet as having said: 'Listening and obedience are a duty on the Muslim with respect to what he likes or dislikes, unless he is ordered to perform a sinful action. If he is so ordered, then there should be neither listening nor obedience.' (Source: al-Bukhari) 'Alqamah ibn Wa'il al-Hadrami, reports how his father said: 'Salama ibn Yazid al-Jufi asked the Messenger: 'O Prophet of Allah, if we were to be ruled by princes who demand their right and deny ours, what do you order us to do?' The Prophet ignored the question twice. At the third repetition of the question, al-Ash'ath ibn Qays restrained Salama . . . The Messenger of Allah said: 'Listen and obey. They have to do what they are charged with, and you have to do what you are charged with.' (Source: Muslim) Abu Salam tells how Hudhayfa ibn al-Yaman reported: 'I asked the Messenger: "We were in evil situations and Allah sent us good times. Will there be evil after this good?" He said: "Yes." I asked: "In what way?" He said: "After me there will come leaders who do not follow my guidance or my *sunna*. There will arise men with the hearts of devils in human bodies." I said: "What am I to do if I should witness that situation?" He said: "You should listen and obey the prince, even if he were to lash your back and seize your money. Listen and obey."' (Source: Muslim) Abu Hurayra records how the Prophet said: 'Whoever deviates from obedience and deserts the group dies a *jahili* (non-Muslim). Whoever fights under a misguided banner, supporting a faction or instigating one, and is then killed, his death is a *jahili* one. Whoever deviates from my followers, fighting right and left, not saving the believers and fulfilling no covenant, is no kin to me, and I am no kin to him.' (Source: Muslim) 'Abd Allah ibn 'Umar said: 'I heard the Messenger of Allah say: "Any who deviates from obedience will meet Allah on the Day of Resurrection void of any justification; and any who dies having made no Oath of Allegiance dies a *jahili*."' (Source: Muslim) 'Awf ibn Malik reports the Messenger as having said: 'The best among your leaders are those whom you like and who like you, those who bless you and whom you bless. The worst among your leaders are those whom you hate and who hate you, whom you curse and who curse you.' The Messenger was asked: 'Shall we not fight them with our swords?' He said: 'No, not so long as they lead you in the *salat*. If you find your leaders doing something you dislike, then avoid doing it, but do not deviate from obedience.' (Source: Muslim) Al-Arbad ibn Sariya reports: 'The Messenger led us in the *salat* one day, then gave a very eloquent sermon which brought tears to the eyes and caused hearts to sink. One of us said: "This sounds like a farewell sermon, O Messenger of Allah. What do you advise us to do?' He answered: "I advise you to be pious, to listen and obey even if addressed by an Abyssinian ruler. Those who survive me will witness a great difference. So you must abide by my *sunna* and by that of the Rashidin caliphs. Hold fast to it, and beware of novelty, as every novelty is a heresy, and every heresy is a deviation from the right.' (Source: Dawud)

Undoubtedly many of these *hadith*s are of somewhat dubious authenticity. What is noteworthy about them, however, is that the 'theme', especially in those that insist on non-violation of obedience toward the leader, reflect a general feeling of the necessity of authority in the state and the danger of its absence, and the need to avoid the rebellion and insurgence that plagued later Muslims while bringing no improvement in their situation. Hence the preference for security under an unjust ruler rather than having no ruler. This is illustrated in the following texts.

In the introduction to *The Crown*, a book ascribed to al-Jahiz, the author details the factors that led him on to write his book.

> A number of reasons led us to write this book of ours, among which is that, when the Almighty favoured kings with His grace, and endowed them with His sovereignty, and supported them in the lands and afforded them sway over the people, He imposed on the learned the duty of dignifying and revering them, supporting and praising them. He also imposed the duty of obeying, fearing them and submitting to them . . . Another reason is that the felicity of the commons lies in their revering and obeying their kings. Ardashir ibn Babek said: 'The felicity of subjects lies in their obedience to their kings . . . The kings are the foundation, the subjects the structure . . . What has no foundation will fall.'[11]

Such speeches are strewn throughout books dealing with 'mirrors for magistrates', 'annals' or 'anecdotes'. In later works such as *Selections from Every Fine Art* (Al-Mustatraf fi kulli fannin mustazraf), their treatment attains a kind of organization. Following the quotation of the sacred verse noted above, and some of the relevant *hadith*s, we read the following on the subject of obedience to 'those charged with authority':

> Among the principles of the exalted Shariah and the august creed is obedience to leaders, which is a duty for all subjects; since obedience to the sovereign unites the affairs of the faith and organizes the concerns of Muslims. Disobedience to the sovereign destroys the foundations of religious community. The highest degree of happiness is obedience to the sovereign. His obedience is a safeguard against all hardship. Through obeying the sovereign, laws are upheld, duties performed, bloodshed avoided, interests protected. How well it was expressed by the sages, that obedience to the sovereign is a guiding light, a violation of obedience a breach of faith. Obedience to the sovereign is allegiance to the divine religion. To deviate is to abandon the felicity of obedience for the wilderness of mutiny. Whoever betrays the sovereign has gone astray. Whoever offers him his sincere affection and advice attains the highest positions in religious and worldly life.[12]

These texts clearly indicate a tendency growing steadily in Islamic writings throughout the centuries: one which gives priority to 'the right of the ruler over the ruled', which entails "obedience" at the expense of justice, which entails "the right of the ruled over the ruler". This may be explained by two factors:

The first is the numerous revolts and seditions suffered throughout Islamic history, starting with the 'Great Sedition' which broke out following the assassination of 'Uthman ibn 'Affan, the third Rashidi caliph, and the ensuing power conflicts that led to the Siffin war, causing the death of many Companions and thousands of Muslims. A number of revolts followed (those of the Kharijis, Shi'ites, etc.), threatening the very Islamic state, even Islam itself. A number of *hadith* scholars and jurists set out to condemn sedition and 'deviation', calling for the necessity of 'obeying the ruler' even when he was a usurper of power, uncommitted to Shariah rule, etc. Obsession with the security of the 'state' was overwhelming; the predominant feeling was that, without a 'strong sovereign', no kind of community or religion could be upheld. Undoubtedly there were those who spoke on behalf of rulers and propagated the ideology of obedience in their service.

The second factor, more generally historical and embracing the Islamic civilizational experience along with other experiences, is linked to the nature of the 'state' and 'society' in ancient history and in the Middle Ages. The political structure of the times entailed ruler and subjects. Primacy belonged to the former, since he was the one who turned individuals, tribes and sects into "subjects". Hence 'obedience' to the ruler came before his own 'justice': subjects had to obey before the ruler could be just. The obedience of subjects comes before the justice of the prince, since this is the principle that makes him a prince. After that, he may or may not be just.

V. Ruler and subject: the purely Islamic perspective

If we move beyond such 'historical' justifications to a critical examination of advisory writings for sovereigns and a perusal of jurisprudential literature binding obedience to justice, we shall find that any reference to the justice of the prince is actually geared toward establishing the 'right of the prince to the obedience of his subjects'. The justice of the prince, in the minds of these authors, was intended for the 'elite'. In their usage, justice meant 'placing people where they belong'. In that age, those within Arab-Islamic society 'belonged' in one of three 'places': that of the prince, or caliph; that of the elite; or that of the commoners. Placing people where they belonged demanded recognition of a difference between these strata and the establishment of justice by assigning each stratum its function. The function of the prince was to rule, whereas that of the subjects, or commoners, was to obey. The function of the elite was to secure for the prince the silence and acquiescence of the commoners, that is, obedience given to him 'of their own accord'. This is the type of obedience inspired in the hearts of the commoners by 'those charged with authority'. It is the authority of the tribe, of 'knowledge', and consequently of religion itself. To assist the elite in performing this function, the prince has to recognize their 'place' as wielding an active moral authority over the commoners. Therefore, he has to treat this elite as possessing material rights to 'provisions and sustenance'.

What is significant in this connection is that the word *ra'i* (literally 'shepherd', hence 'ruler') is not used with reference to God in the religion of Islam. It is not one of the 99 attributes of God. The words *ra'i* and *ra'iyya* ('ruler' and 'subjects') never occur in the Quran. There is, however, an oft-quoted *hadith* which runs as follows: 'Each one of you is a *ra'i*, and each is responsible for his *ra'iyya*. The leader of the people is a *ra'i* and is responsible for his *ra'iyya*. So is the man responsible for his family. So is the woman responsible for the household of her husband. So is the slave responsible for his master's property. Each one of you is a *ra'i*, and each is responsible for his *ra'iyya*.' This *hadith* is at complete variance with the concept of 'ruler and subjects' as known in ancient oriental thought, whether Pharaonic, Babylonian, Hebraic or, later on, Persian. It gives a new sense to the function of *ra'i*, one that denotes keeping trust and recognizing responsibility, and emphasizes that such responsibility is assigned to every member of society, each according to his position. The expression 'each one of you is a *ra'i*' has a special significance, as it does not admit the existence of one *ra'i* alone; 'each one of you is a *ra'i*' in his own sphere. The 'leader of the people', or prince, has no special distinction, and he cannot in any way be compared to God. The only comparison allowed in the text is the comparison of the prince to the man in his home, the woman in her husband's homestead and the slave with respect to his master's property. All these share one thing only: responsibility. Each is responsible for the thing with which he was entrusted.

In conclusion it can be said that the concept of '*ra'i/ra'iyya*' as 'ruler/subjects' is foreign to Islam. In this field the concept nearest to the spirit of Islam is that of 'citizen'. The concept of the 'Muslim' in his relation to the *umma*, or Muslim nation, in Islamic discourse is, as will be shown later, the closest possible to the concept of 'citizen' in his relation to the state in modern political discourse.

As for the bases of government in Islamic political discourse, the first thing to be underlined is that the Prophet Muhammad refused on many occasions to let himself be called king or chief, emphasizing his identity as prophet and messenger only. What is significant in this connection is that his followers did not regard themselves as presided over or ruled; nor did the Quraysh or other opponents think of them as such. They called themselves, and the Arabs also called them, by a name devoid of any sense of kingship or presidency. They were simply the 'followers' of Muhammad, or his 'companions'.

From this perspective, the early kalamologists, who initiated political opposition discourse against the Umayyads, discussed the issue of government using religious concepts rather than political concepts lacking in the language of the time. Foremost among these, as will be shown in the next section, were such concepts as faith, predestination and justice.

VI. Justice on the divine and human levels

VI.1 *The divine level: tolerance and the question of faith*

The ideas propagated and defended by this first generation of 'cultured' Muslims – commonly divided into 'deferents' and 'determinists' – who carried out the kalamological' opposition to the Umayyads, might be said to focus on two basic points: on the one hand tolerance, and on the other the freedom of man, defining his responsibility. Argument on this question arose, as is well known, in the wake of the war between Mu'awiya and 'Ali ibn Abi Talib. After this war people were divided into two camps. One comprised the 'dissenters', who opposed Ali and accused him of 'unbelief' because he accepted 'arbitration' in an issue on which God's judgment was clear: namely the 'necessity' of fighting Mu'awiya as a 'transgressor' who challenged the leader and wanted the rule for himself. The other group was that of the 'deferents', who took no part in sedition and had no wish to be involved in struggle over government.

'Isolation' from sedition did not necessarily imply support for Mu'awiya, or any 'halting' in thinking about the problem. It rather meant raising the issue above the level of Umayyad political exploitation and 'external' extremism to the level of neutral objective thinking. Those who distanced and isolated themselves from the sedition were sure Mu'awiya was not an 'unbeliever'. Nor did 'Ali ibn Abi Talib think for one moment that, by fighting Mu'awiya, he was placing himself in the position of 'unbeliever'. Each believed himself to be fighting because he was right and his rival was wrong. But the war killed great numbers of Muslims, and killing is a major sin proscribed by God. (He has proscribed killing, adultery, stealing, wine, and abandoning *salat* and the Ramadan fast. As such, the issue of 'belief and unbelief' was associated with 'major sin'.) The question came to be formulated as follows: 'Is the perpetrator of a major sin a believer or an unbeliever?'

This issue assumed a further dimension when whole nations embraced Islam as a result of the *futuhat* (Islamic conquests). These nations did not know Arabic, or what was prescribed or proscribed. Nor did they know which religious duties to perform, or which proscriptions to avoid, and so major sins were committed. This led, inevitably, to the question of whether the faith of these nations was undermined on that account. The definition of 'faith' and 'belief' required an attitude of tolerance and leniency, and the avoidance of extremism and exaggeration. This was necessary not only to confront 'external' extremism, which used religion as a weapon in political conflicts, but also to deal with certain situations which emerged with the spread of Islam through the wars of conquest.

This led to the appearance of definitions of 'belief' that distinguished 'believing', in the strict linguistic sense, from 'practice', which entails the performance of religious duties and the avoidance of what is proscribed and prohibited. While most late historians of Islamic sects deny that Imam Abu Hanifa was a 'deferent' in their sense of the term – that is, one not abiding by religious duties or at least being lenient about them (which is actually a highly unfair interpretation) – Sunni sources could not absolve Abu Hanifa of a vision of belief based on leniency and the avoidance of exaggeration when defining the 'believer'. Abu 'l-Hasan al-Ash'ari does not hesitate to list Abu Hanifa and his followers among the 'deferent' groups. 'The ninth group of deferents,' he says, 'Abu Hanifa and his followers, claim that belief is knowing God, recognizing him, knowing the Messenger and recognizing what has come from God generally and without explanation.' Then he adds: 'Abu Hanifa does not consider belief to be what is deduced from religion; claiming that belief cannot be departmentalized, increased or decreased; and that people do not differ in their belief.'[13] This means that a Muslim may not be branded an unbeliever as a result of a deed committed or a duty omitted. Belief is one thing; practice (performing duties and forgoing proscribed activities) is quite another. Hence, belief is not increased by performing religious duties or decreased by neglecting them, since belief is in fact solely a belief in God, His Books and His Messengers. There are no degrees of belief: a person believes or does not believe. Moreover, belief is not bound by declaration of it, since its place is 'the heart'. It is a direct relation between the believer and God. Expression of belief by word of mouth is neither a condition nor a part of belief.

This, according to al-Ash'ari, is how Abu Hanifa understands 'belief'. In his *Greater Jurisprudence* (Al-Fiqh al-akbar), Abu Hanifa says: 'We do not regard a person who has sinned as an unbeliever, nor do we exclude anyone from belief.' Al-Ash'ari recounts the following incident:

> Abu Hanifa met 'Umar ibn Abi 'Uthman al-Shamzi in Mecca. 'Umar asked: 'Tell me what you think of a person who states that God proscribed the eating of pork but does not know whether pork is this particular meat.' Abu Hanifa said: 'He is a believer.' 'Umar asked again: 'And suppose this man were to state that God ordained pilgrimage to the Kaaba, but he is not sure whether it is not another Kaaba, in a different place?' Abu Hanifa answered: 'He is a believer.' Next: 'And if he were to say, I know that God has sent Muhammad, and that he is the Messenger of God, but I am not sure whether he might not be that Abyssinian there.' The answer was: 'He is a believer.'[14]

Although this is all based on strange and fabricated suggestions, the answers given by Abu Hanifa, who was quite aware of their strangeness, are compatible with his understanding of belief as 'the knowledge and recognition of God, the knowledge and recognition of the Messenger and all that has come from God, in its entirety, without any explanation'. It is clear these suggestions do not fall under 'knowledge and recognition' of God and His Messenger. They are related to the ignorance of the person who is supposed to be asking, because he 'does not know' certain matters, the knowledge of which is irrelevant to the sincerity of belief, or to the increase of it when known. This does not mean man is not required to know these matters. He is, in fact, required to know the duties and proscriptions and to obey the divine ordinance. But his being required to know this does not affect the meaning of belief. We can appreciate Abu Hanifa's point of view, and its profound implications, if we suppose he had given a different answer and considered the person in question an 'unbeliever'. The result would have been a death sentence for that person. But is it possible or conceivable to execute a person who has declared his belief that there is no god but God and that Muhammad is the Messenger of God, simply because he claimed that 'the pork proscribed by God may not be this particular meat'?

From this perspective, then, the first generation of 'men of culture' in Arab-Islamic civilization began their defence of a concept of 'belief' based on moderation and tolerance, a 'liberal' concept, if it might be so called, a concept informed by the principle that 'belief is not harmed by disobedience, nor is unbelief helped by obedience'. Just as the unbeliever remains in this state even if he has practised, say, *salat* and fasting, so the believer remains in this state even if he has not practised them, provided he does not deny the prescription of *salat* and fasting. The obvious aim of this principle is to annul the Khariji claim that whoever commits a sin is an unbeliever, and, as a further consequence, to annul their claim that it is necessary to dissent and to fight 'Ali and Mu'awiya, along with all those coming after them. The principle was, in fact, undoubtedly the best way to stop sedition through the power of reason. Moreover, followers of the principle attempted to take the question of 'unbelief' out of the domain of personal opinion and party ideology, to make it the concern of the nation as a whole. According to al-Ash'ari:

> They did not consider any interpreter an unbeliever, nor did they consider anyone as such unless he were branded an unbeliever by the consensus of the whole nation. They say: 'We are in a homeland of belief, and the people herein are believers, except for those who show what is contrary to belief.' Some say: 'Any act of disobedience, major or minor, which is not regarded by the whole Muslim nation as unbelief is not to brand its doer as a sinner, he is rather said to have sinned and disobeyed.'

In other words, there is no third value between belief and unbelief. Sin is not an absolute value, like belief or unbelief. It is merely a partial state: the person is a sinner because he sinned in performing a certain act; he is not an absolute sinner.

It was natural that this tolerant intellectual attitude toward 'belief' should lead on to other things, such as the question of promise and warning. Here again we find these 'men of culture' following a line of reasoning based on the principle that God is generous and merciful, and that man is a weak being. 'It is possible,' they say, 'that the Wise and Almighty may inform of His intention (such as saying He will torment whoever commits a certain disobedience), then make exceptions; His is the will to do or not to do, and He is truthful in either case.' They quote, in support, the verse: 'Allah does not forgive [the sin of] joining other gods with Him; but He forgives whom He pleases other sins than that' (4, *Al-Nisa'*, 48, 116) So much for warning. As for promise (like promising Paradise to the pious), there is, they say, no exception, since He said: 'The promise of Allah, never does Allah depart from His promise.' (30, *Al-Rum*, 6) Most of these 'men of culture' say: 'When God pardons any disobedient person on the Day of Judgment, He will pardon any disobedient believer in a similar situation; if He takes one out of the fire, He will take out another in the same situation'. Some of them went so far as to say: 'There is no warning to those who perform *salat*, the warning is for those who take other gods with Allah.' And: 'No one who faces the *qibla* [i.e., toward Mecca] enters hell.'[15]

It was inevitable that this argument, which was primarily intended to counter the 'Khariji' ideological notion of the 'charge of unbelief', should lead on inadvertently to an acceptance and justification of 'Umayyad predestination'; the first party to benefit from the argument would be the Umayyads themselves. 'No one who faces the *qibla* enters hell.' Undoubtedly, Wasil ibn 'Ata' had this in mind when he said: 'the perpetrator of a major sin [the Umayyads were meant at the time] is neither wholly a believer nor wholly an unbeliever: he is "betwixt and between".' Al-Shahrastani, commenting on Wasil's opinion, says:

> Belief is the sum total of good qualities, which, when found in a person, cause him to be called a believer by way of praise. The sinner is the one who does not possess these good qualities and so does not deserve to be praised as a believer. But he is not wholly an unbeliever, since he recognizes God and good deeds characterize him undeniably. But if he dies having committed a major sin without repentance, then he is a dweller in hell for ever, since there are only two groups in the hereafter: one in Paradise, the other in Hell. But his torment is lighter, and he is set in a circle above that of the unbelievers.[16]

Hence, the Umayyad rulers lie under conviction until they repent. Repentance requires forgoing the previous policy.

VI.2 Divine justice and liberty on the human level

In fact, the idea of 'betwixt and between' advanced by Wasil ibn 'Ata', while coming under the heading of 'belief', implies a new political stance. His insistence that the perpetrator of a major sin – that is, the one who is in this position of 'betwixt and between' and who dies without repentance – will definitely dwell in hell forever links the opinion directly to the question of 'free will' [Arabic *qadar*, which has the basic meaning 'power']. The meaning of the term as used here is different from the meaning of mere 'predestination' (which *qadar* can also denote). On the contrary, the word in this context means the 'free will' of man to perform his actions freely and by choice; hence he becomes responsible for his actions. This notion of 'free will' was primarily an attack on the Umayyads, who claimed that what they did was within the previous knowledge of God, and by His will and predestination. Being, as such, predestined in their actions, they were not responsible for what they did and so would not ultimately be dwellers in hell.

The question of 'free will' goes back to the time of the Prophet and his companions; there are Quranic verses emphasizing the freedom of man and his responsibility for his actions, and similar references in the *hadith*. Moreover, we are told by Ibn 'Umar that 'there is no predestination; the matter is one of choice'. Historians of the Muslim sects find evidence for the 'predestination' meaning in a conversation from the circle of al-Hasan al-Basri. According to Ibn Qutayba, Ma'bad al-Jahni and 'Ala' ibn Yasar came to al-Hasan al-Basri and said: 'O Abu Sa'id, these kings are shedding the blood of Muslims and seizing their property, saying that what they are doing is predestined by God.' Al-Hasan answered: 'The enemies of God have lied.'[17]

Al-Hasan al-Basri was the foremost religious authority of the time, and it was natural that his dictum concerning man's freedom in performing his actions, and his emphasis on man's responsibility for such actions, should arouse the displeasure and fear of the Umayyads. We find 'Abd al-Malik ibn Marwan writing to al-Hasan in reproachful tones, inquiring about the evidence for his dictum about 'predestination'.

> It has come to the attention of the Commander of the Faithful [the Caliph] how you have viewed predestination as freedom of the will. No one before you has seen what you have seen, nor are we aware of any such opinion expressed by any of the Companions known to us . . . We have not heard of any argument similar to yours. You are therefore instructed to explain and clarify your opinion to the Commander of the Faithful.

Al-Hasan al-Basri wrote an answering letter to the Caliph. If, he said, the Companions did not discuss 'free will/predestination', it was because 'they were agreed on a single thing and did not command anything that was wrong'. Among wrong deeds is 'when people ascribe to God things of which they are ignorant'. He was alluding to the Umayyad claim that God commands men to perform their deeds, which is contrary to the Quranic verse: 'To any of you that chooses to press forward, or to follow behind – Every soul will be in pledge for its deeds' (74, *Al-Muddaththir*, 37–38) He quotes several more verses to the effect that: 'God has not enforced anything on men; He has rather said: "If you do this, I will do that to you …" They are recompensed in accordance with their deeds.'

Among the early activists known for advocating the concept of 'free will' in opposition to the Umayyads was Ghaylan al-Dimashqi, who eventually paid with his life. Although historians of Islamic sects mention scores of treatises and texts by Ghaylan, just a few brief and scattered statements remain extant. The only text we have is his epistle to Caliph 'Umar ibn 'Abd al-'Aziz, in which he offers counsel and stresses man's freedom of choice and responsibility for his actions. It should be pointed out here that Ghaylan and his followers disseminated their enlightening ideas within the Umayyad court itself, and among tribes antagonistic to the Umayyads, so contriving to bring them together in accepting the 'free will' concept and its political implications. Thus appeared a class of 'educated activists' pushing for change toward the end of the Umayyad period. As may be gathered from the writings of historians of Islamic sects, who refer to them as 'determinists', they were not satisfied with discussions about 'free will'. They tried, further, to propagate an integrated ideology of enlightenment, adopting a rational and liberal view on all the issues current in their days.

According to these same historical works on Islamic sects, Ghaylan and his followers supplemented the concept of 'belief' by saying: 'May God do what is rationally unacceptable?' By this they mean that an evil deed is not a work of God, because it is not rational that God should oblige people to do something then punish them for it. Therefore, evil comes from human beings themselves and they carry it out by their own will and choice. But 'May God fail to do what is rationally acceptable?', as in the case of not leaving a disobedient person to dwell in hell for ever, is not considered part of 'belief' by these activists. Even so, they refer this to divine justice, saying: 'If God pardons a disobedient person on the Day of Resurrection, He may pardon any disobedient believer in a similar position. If He takes someone out of hell fire, He may take out another who is in a similar situation'. This 'equality' among people with regard to pardon and punishment on the Day of Resurrection implies a clear political context. 'Justice' and 'equality' in the hereafter entail justice and equality among people in this world. The principle assumes its direct political context in the following declaration by Ghaylan al-Dimashqi:

> Leadership is possible outside the Qurayshi dynasty. Anyone upholding the Book and the *sunna* may lay claim to it, and it is confirmed only by the consensus of the whole Muslim nation.

VII. The individual and forms of affiliation: the *umma*

There is no doubt that these enlightenment ideas run contrary to the ideology of obedience binding 'the justice of the prince' to 'the obedience of the sub-jects'. Yet they remain the product of their age and cannot, in consequence, be taken as a basis for the concept of 'human rights' in the contemporary sense. They are indeed addressing 'the rights of men', or, more precisely, 'the rights of worshippers', but they do not bring us to the contemporary discourse of 'human rights' for the simple reason that the concept of 'man' is absent, as are the notions of 'individual' vis-à-vis 'society' and 'citizen' vis-à-vis 'state', as defined in contemporary sociological and political discourse.

We shall once more find it necessary to refer to European culture, since the word 'individual', as used in contemporary Arabic discourse, is laden with con-notations not found in our Arabic culture. It is a direct translation from the European word, which, in contemporary European psychological, social and political discourse means 'the human being as distinguished from other beings, considered, primarily, vis-à-vis society and the state'. Thus the term 'individual' in European discourse – and consequently in contemporary Arabic discourse – is a term standing over against the terms 'society' and 'state'. Hence the phrase 'individual and society' in sociological discourse, which becomes 'citi-zen and state' in political discourse.

These meanings and connotations were completely absent from Arab-Islamic culture, and consequently absent from Arabic lexicons, which do not gloss 'individual' except in terms of numerical entity devoid of any social or political connotation. Thus we read in Ibn Manzur's *The Tongue of the Arabs* (Lisan al-'Arab), the largest lexicon in Arabic, the following explanation of 'individual' (*fard*). '*Al-Fard* [the individual] is God; it is the one who is distinc-tive; it is half of the couple; it is the wild bull; it is the camel which keeps apart in pasture and at the water; it is whatever stands alone.' There is absolutely no reference to 'society' as the party defining the individual, since 'society' in lexical Arabic does not embody modern sociological and political meanings. In the old Arabic usage 'society' denotes the time or the place of 'meeting'; it does not denote the human community called 'society' in modern Arabic, of which the individual is part, and where this community, as a group of organized traditional forces, exercises an influence on the individual. This latter usage is a reflection of European languages, where reference to the 'individual' deals, inevitably, with this individual's relation to society, a relation of mutual influence, of both affiliation and rejection.

The fact that Arabic does not use the term 'individual' to define a relation with the term 'society' does not mean Arabian civilization did not have individuals. On the contrary, the people who built up that civilization were individual human beings. The difference between the status of the 'individual' in modern society today and that in Arab-Islamic and similar ancient civilizations is that the 'other' party defining the individual in the latter was not 'society' or the 'state' but another entity altogether. In other words, the network of analysis helping us to identify the 'individual' in Arab-Islamic civilization is not the same as in European civilization (which includes city, university, society, party, labour union, the state, and so on). There are other networks pertaining to Arab society, which will be dealt with below.

In a book I published some years ago, I analyzed what I termed 'the structural elements of the Arabian political mind'.[18] These were three in number: the tribe, booty and creed. These are, in fact, the elements forming the fundamental structure of Arab-Islamic society in the Middle Ages; the structure that not only controls political thought and practice within that society but also informs the outer structure of society, the field of cultural, social, economic and political activities. In this outer structure, I singled out three hierarchical factors or levels: the caliph, the elite and the commoners. These two structures, the outer and the fundamental, characterize Arab society in the Middle Ages. By their interaction they delineate the social frameworks of affiliation which are, at the same time, the network by means of which all relations within the structure of the Arab society, including the relation between 'individual' and 'society', must be analyzed.

By referring to the elements of the two structures combined (tribe, booty, creed, caliph, elite, commons), and by viewing them as corresponding pairs, that is, networks for analysis, it becomes clear that the 'individual' in Arab-Islamic society was defined through the following five networks/pairs: ruler/subjects; elite/commons; donation/taxation (booty); creed/tribe; bedouins/town dwellers. That is to say, the status of the human being in Arab society was defined as: 1. ruler or one of the subjects; 2. member of the elite or the commons; 3. recipient of donations or taxpayer; 4. protected by the tribe or by the creed; 5. bedouin or town dweller. In other words, the 'individual' in Arab-Islamic civilization did not enter into a relationship with 'society' as one overall entity, since the latter did not transcend its five components; each component represented society according to the situation, and exerted a mutual impact on the individual.[19]

There are two other words with multiple meanings, some of them pertaining to the human individual. These are *shakhs* (= 'person') and *mar'* (= 'man'). But, like 'individual', they are not defined in Arabic by reference to 'society', the 'state' or any other human group. The word *shakhs* in Arabic denotes appearance and emergence. The lexicon *Lisan al-'Arab* defines *shakhs* as: 'man or any other object; anything whose body, when seen, is *shakhs;* it is any body which has a height and appearance, it confirms the self, so the word person is borrowed.' Needless to say, these meanings do not bring us any closer to the European word 'person', which is translated into Arabic as *shakhs*. Contrary to the Arabic word, which denotes a man or an object, the European 'person' is used of man alone: 'as a self-conscious being, in control of himself, and consequently responsible for his actions. It is the individual seen through his specific qualities as a human being.' Moreover: 'in psychology and ethics, the word "person" is used vis-à-vis the word "individual" to denote the human being as a being open to others like himself, integrated into a group of persons, and looking up to an ideal.'[20]

Yet Arabic has a word used for man alone: *mar'*, close to the meaning of 'person' and similarly not defined by 'society' or some other group. It indicates 'man', and the feminine is *mar'a* (= 'woman'). It is mostly used in praise and appreciation. It gave us the word *muru'a*, which means 'perfect manhood' or 'humanity'.

If these words are not defined by their relation to the word 'society', as in modern and contemporary European discourse, how, then, is the relation to be defined between 'the Arab man' and the authentically Islamic concept of *umma*?

Lisan al-'Arab glosses several meanings for the word *umma*, the relevant ones among which are: intention, creed, religion. 'We found our forefathers following a certain religion [*umma*].' (43, *Al-Zukhruf*, 22) 'You were the best of peoples evolved.' (3, *Al-'Imran*, 110) This means 'the best religion'. The verb from *umma* means 'to lead'. *Imama* and *imam* mean the leadership of the people. The 'imams' of the unbelievers are their chieftains. The *umma* is a human century. It is the 'nation' to whom a prophet was sent. The *umma* of Muhammad is the nation to whom he was sent, whether they believed in him or not. Every generation of people is a separate *umma*, so is every species of animals. It is the generation or the species of every living being. 'There is not an animal [that lives] on the earth, nor a being that flies on its wings, but [forms part of] communities [*umam*, plural of *umma*] like you.' (6, *Al-An'am*, 38) Whoever follows the right religion, contrary to all other religions, is *umma* in himself. The word also denotes the man who is distinctive. 'Abraham was indeed an *umma* by himself.' (16, *Al-Nahl*, 120) *Umma* in religion means a group of people with the same intention. When used of a man it means he is distinctive, as his intention is different from that of everyone else. Describing a man as *umma* means he is a model of good deeds. His *umma* is his people. It also indicates a community. An *umma* of believers is a group of these. The *umma* of God is His creation.

Obviously, none of these meanings corresponds to that of *umma* as used today in contemporary Arabic discourse, as a translation of the European 'nation', which, in its political context, means 'a group of people forming a political community, inhabiting a limited piece or pieces of land, represented by an independent authority'. Neither in Arabic nor in the European languages is there anything in the concept of *umma*/nation which makes it the other party defining the 'individual'. The concept of 'individual' is not competitive or incorporative with regard to the concept of 'nation'. The individual is a member of a nation, who considers himself a son of that nation, is proud of belonging to that nation, and is ready to make sacrifices for it. Consequently, his rights are not in contradiction with the rights of the nation. The ties that make a group of individuals a nation are moral and spiritual, and have no connection with 'rights', while the network of relations in 'society' is one of interests, hence of rights. We may say that the relations that join individuals together in society, like those connecting them to the ruler, are relations of power. But the essence of the individual's relation with the nation to which he belongs lies in relations of affiliation, of belonging, of pride and sacrifice.

'Human rights' in Arab-Islamic texts are not defined by the concept of nation. The concept of 'society', as we have shown above, is a barren concept, one rarely used, indeed, in these texts. What, then, defines the 'rights of man' in Arab-Islamic culture?

VIII. Honouring man

It should be emphasized from the outset that the concept of 'man' in our religious and traditional texts does not carry the same connotations given to it in our contemporary discourse, connotations that take their strength from the age of the Renaissance, and especially from visions of so-called humanism (six-teenth and seventeenth centuries). The concept of man in the European tradition was initiated and considered with a view to restoring recognition of the human individual, by liberating him from his feeling of guilt on account of 'original sin' (that of Adam, who, against the orders of his Lord, ate from the fruit of the tree of knowledge in Paradise and was punished by expulsion into the world, where, according to the Christian conception, he and his posterity were to suffer for ever), and then by restoring his unity as a human being made up of body and soul in an indivisible union. The second intention was to liberate man (or his spiritual life) from the authority of the church; and to liberate his body (or his material life) from the authority of the 'prince'. These two aspects – Adam's sin and the spiritual–temporal dichotomy – are not, as we shall see, present in Islamic thought. Consequently, these two aspects have no significance in defining the concept of 'man' in Islam. Yet it is quite possible to build up a concept of 'man', with the same implications given to him in contemporary thought, by reference to Islamic religious texts and without the need for superfluous interpretation. Here are some examples:

The most eminent text that comes to mind as a basis for the concept of man in Islam is the Quranic verse: 'We have honoured the sons of Adam; provided them with transport on land and sea; given them for sustenance things good and pure; and conferred on them special favours, above a great part of Our creation.' (17, *Al-Isra'*, 70) In his interpretation of this verse, al-Zamakhshari says: 'It has been said that God, in honouring the sons of Adam, honoured him with mind, with the faculty of speech and the power of discernment, with comely shape and upright stature, with the management of his worldly affairs and those of the hereafter . . . It has also been said, by control of earthly resources and their subjugation to men . . .'[21]

A dispute broke out between the Mu'tazilis and the Ash'aris about who is better before God: man or the angels? The Mu'tazilis clung to the literal meaning of 'great part' in 'We preferred them above a great part of Our Creation'. There are, they said, other creatures, such as the angels, not included in the 'great part' of the creatures above whom God preferred man. The Sunnis and Ash'aris referred to other verses that could be taken to suggest God preferred Adam to the angels. The meaning of the verse, they argued, in the light of these others, is that God created the children of Adam and 'many' other creatures, preferring Adam to that 'great part' of creation. In fact, a close examination of Quranic texts dealing with the honouring of man by God will provide evidence to support the Ash'ari point of view. One such text is: 'Behold! Your Lord said to the angels, "I will create a vicegerent on earth". They said: "Will You place

therein one who will make mischief therein and shed blood? – while we celebrate Your praises and glorify Your holy [name]?" He said, "I know what you
do not know". And He taught Adam the names of all things, then He placed
them before the angels, and said, "Tell me the names of these if you are right".
They said, "Glory to You: of knowledge we have none, save what You
have taught us: in truth it is You Who are perfect in knowledge and wisdom.'"
(2, *Al-Baqara*, 30–32)

The Sunnis support their view by reference to reported *hadith*s of the
Prophet, some related by Abu Hurayra. He recounts how the Prophet said:
'The believer is more honoured by God than His angels'; and again: "'Nothing
is more honourable before God on the Day of Resurrection than the children
of Adam." They asked: "Not even the angels?" He answered: "Not even the
angels. The angels are under direction, like the sun and the moon."' In another
hadith, the Prophet said: 'The angels said: "O Lord! You have given the children
of Adam the entire world where they eat, drink and clothe themselves. We sing
Your praise, but do not eat, drink or play. As You have given them the world,
give us the hereafter." He said: "I do not make the posterity of the one I created
with My own hands like the ones I ordered to be and they were."'

In addition to this honour and preference informing the concept of man in
the Quran, there are other verses giving him a further dimension as a vicegerent
for God on earth, as in the verse quoted above: 'Behold! Your Lord said to the
angels, "I will create a vicegerent on earth . . ."' Also: 'It is He Who has produced you from the earth and settled you therein.' (11, *Hud*, 61) Also: 'Then We
made you heirs in the land . . .' (10, *Yunus*, 14) The development of land means
the establishment of civilization in it, which requires knowledge of what is in
the land. This is the meaning of 'He taught Adam the names of all things'.

IX. Sin – and the body

Next comes the question of 'sin'. We read in the Quran how Adam and his wife
repented of their eating from the tree God had commanded them to avoid.
They asked for forgiveness, and God pardoned them. 'And their Lord called
unto them, "Did I not forbid you that tree and tell you that Satan was an
avowed enemy of you?" They said, "Our Lord! We have wronged our own
souls: If You do not forgive us and bestow on us Your mercy, we shall certainly
be lost."' (7, *Al-A'raf*, 22–3) Also: 'And His lord pardoned him. He is the Oft-
Pardoning, Most Merciful.' (2, *Al-Baqara*, 37) Thus Adam's sin was erased by
his repentance, and he and his posterity were freed from it. What is left is his

deeds on earth, to which he was commanded to descend and which he was command to develop, along with his posterity, who will all be judged by their deeds in it with reward or punishment.

What gives rise to reflection in the light of these Quranic quotations is that the Quran nowhere makes reference to the duality of soul and body, which so long preoccupied European religious and philosophical thought. Man, in the Quranic perspective, is a body and a soul. The Quran never belittles the body; on the contrary, the body is mentioned in terms of superiority and excellence. With reference to Talut (Saul), we read: 'Allah has chosen him above you and has gifted him abundantly with knowledge and bodily powers.' (2, *Al-Baqara*, 247) Also: 'We have created man in the best of moulds.' (95, *Al-Tin*, 4) Then: '[Allah] has given you shape, and made your shapes comely, and provided you with sustenance.' (40, *Ghafir*, 64) The human body and the comely shape, possessed by no other creature, are, we are told by al-Zamakhshari, one aspect of the honouring of man by God. Therefore the body, as well as the soul, has a right over man. One *hadith* tells us how the Prophet said to 'Abd Allah ibn 'Amr ibn al-'As: "'O 'Abd Allah! Have I not been told you fast the whole day and keep vigil at prayer all night?" He said: "Yes, O Messenger of Allah!" The Prophet said: "Do not do so! Fast and break your fast; keep vigil and sleep. Your body has a right over you. Your eyes have a right over you. Your wife has a right over you. Your palate has a right over you.' (Source: al-Bukhari).

We may conclude from this that 'man', in the Quran and in *hadith*, is an individual, integrated entity, liberated and honoured.

Three dimensions, then, inform the concept of 'man' in Islam: sound mind and the power of discernment; vicegerency based on developing the land and building civilization; and a complete and integrated individuality. These dimensions do not recognize the 'tribe' that held supremacy in Arab society before Islam; indeed, they abolish the role of the tribe altogether. This is a most important step in developing a sense of man's independence, without which his rights cannot be implanted, first in his consciousness and second in the social system. These dimensions branch into rights due to man alone, above all other creatures. The rights in question are of two types: generally comprehensive and international rights compatible with the modern concept of these rights; and rights of some special kind which must be explained to show their viability with reference to the situations of their formulation. I have detailed these rights in my book *Democracy and the Rights of Man* (Al-Dimuqratiyya wa huquq al-insan),[22] from which I shall quote here together with some additions.

X. The rights of man in Islam

X.1 General rights

1. The right to life: Life, in the Islamic perspective, is a gift from God to man. It is his right, and he has a duty to protect his life physically and spiritually; nor has anyone the right to interfere with this life either physically or spiritually. God has proscribed suicide for any reason whatever. 'Do not kill yourselves, for Allah has been to you most merciful. If any do that in rancour and injustice, soon shall We cast them into the fire, and easy is this for Allah.' (4, *Al-Nisa'*, 29–30) God has also proscribed the killing of human beings except for a just reason, the killing of captives and mutilating the bodies of the dead. Some Arabs, before Islam, would kill their children because they lacked the means of keeping them. This the Quran proscribed. 'Do not kill your children for fear of want: We shall provide sustenance for them as well as for you.' (17, *Al-Isra'*, 31) Islam also proscribed the burying of baby girls alive, as some Arabs would do before Islam for fear of shame. 'When the female [infant] buried alive is questioned – for what crime she was killed . . .' (81, *Al-Takwir*, 8–9.) Islam proscribes abortion too. As a general rule: 'If anyone slew a person – unless it be for murder or for spreading mischief in the land – it would be as if he slew the whole people: and if anyone saved a life, it would be as if he saved the life of the whole people.' (5, *Al-Ma'ida*, 32.) As for punishment of the sinner by death, Islam has provided every possible scope for alleviation by holding back execution where there is any room for doubt. One *hadith* says: 'Avoid punishment by the benefit of doubt.'

2. The right to enjoyment of life: The right to life in Islam is coupled with and supported by the right to enjoy it. 'O you who believe! Give of the good things which you have [honourably] earned, and of the fruits of the earth which We have produced.' (2, *Al-Baqara*, 267) Also: 'Say, "Who has forbidden the beautiful [gifts] of Allah which He has produced for his worshippers, and things clean and pure, [which He has provided] for sustenance?" Say, "They are, in the life of the world, for those who believe, [and] purely for them on the Day of Resurrection."' (7, *Al-A'raf*, 32) Moreover: 'Seek, with the [wealth] which Allah has bestowed on you, the Home of the Hereafter, and do not forget your portion in this world.' (28, *Al-Qasas*, 77) Similarly in the *hadith*: 'Do for your hereafter as if you were to die tomorrow; and do in this world as if you were to live for ever.' Also: 'If Allah gave you wealth, let the sign of His favour be visible on you.'

3. The right to freedom of belief: The Quran specifies freedom of belief and considers it an inalienable right of man. God created man and endowed him

with reason and discernment, showed him the right path and gave him freedom of choice. 'We have created man from a drop of mingled sperm in order
to try him: so We gave him [the gifts] of hearing and sight. We showed him the
way: whether he be grateful or ungrateful [rests on his will].' (76, *Al-Insan*, 2–3)
This meaning is emphasized by: 'Let there be no compulsion in religion. Truth
stands out clear from error.' (2, *Al-Baqara*, 256) Then: 'If it had been your
Lord's will, all who are on earth would have believed! Will you then compel
mankind, against their will, to believe!' (10, *Yunus*, 99) That is to say, God could
have forced mankind to believe, but He did not; they were given the choice.

    One of the questions raised in connection with freedom of belief in Islam is
that of apostasy. The issue is a debatable one, since an apostate may fall into
one of two categories:

1. One whose apostasy is confined to himself without any impact on society or
the state. There is no Quranic text demanding the execution of such an apostate.
He is only threatened with severe punishment in the hereafter. 'And if any of you
turn back from their faith and die in unbelief, their works will bear no fruit in this
life and in the Hereafter.' (2, *Al-Baqara*, 217) Also: 'Anyone who, after accepting
faith in Allah, utters unbelief – except under compulsion, his heart remaining
firm in faith – but such as open their breast to unbelief – on them is Wrath from
Allah, and theirs will be a dreadful penalty.' (16, *Al-Nahl*, 106) In these and similar verses we find that the rule for the apostate is a curse from God, His wrath,
and hell fire – but not execution. Moreover, the gate to repentance is open
before him.

2. The apostate who, in addition to renouncing Islam, sets out to fight against
Muslims and allies himself with the enemies of the faith comes under a different
ruling. This is a case akin to what is nowadays called 'treason' against country,
society and state. Abu Bakr fought the apostates, after the death of the Prophet,
because they were of this type; they began to attack the Islamic state and disobey
its orders. Those who refused to pay *zakat* after the death of the Prophet were a
debatable case among the Companions. Abu Bakr, in disagreement with 'Umar
ibn al-Khattab, considered them apostates, even though they declared their
continued allegiance to Islam as a religion and a faith. Abu Bakr fought them
because he considered them 'militants', dissenting from the state and failing to
recognize it. This explains why jurists issued their ruling against the apostate in
the same way as against the militant who rebelled against the state and resorted
to force of arms. Hence, the legal status of the apostate is not defined in Islam by
reference to 'freedom of belief' but to 'treason against the Islamic nation'.
Freedom of belief is one thing, apostasy quite another. To the best of our
belief, no one today defends 'treason against the nation' on the grounds
of freedom.

4. The right to knowledge: the Quran often couples the creation of man with the ascription of knowledge to him, as though knowledge were the first right of man. From the first stage of creation, 'He taught Adam the names of all things.' (2, *Al-Baqara*, 31) Also: 'Read! In the name of your Lord Who created – Created man out of a [mere] clot of congealed blood. Read! And your Lord is Most Bountiful – He Who taught [the use of] the pen – Taught man that which he did not know.' (96, *Al-'Alaq*, 1–5) As is well known, this *sura* was the first of the Quran to be revealed. In a well known *hadith*, we read: 'The quest for knowledge is the duty of every Muslim man and woman.' Also: 'Seek knowledge from the cradle to the grave.'

5. The right to disagreement: The Quran recognizes difference as an existential fact and an element of human nature. The difference among people in colour, language and nationality, and their division into nations and peoples and tribes, is all decreed by God's will, just as He willed the difference in the elements and the phenomena of the universe as a sign of His existence. 'And among His Signs is that He created for you mates from among yourselves . . . And among His Signs is the creation of the heavens and the earth, and the variations in your languages and your colours: in that are really signs for those who know.' (30, *Al-Rum*, 21–22) So much for the natural level. As for the level of creed and belief, the Quran recognizes variety and difference of religion in many verses. 'If your Lord had so willed, He could have made mankind one people, but they will not cease to dispute, except those on whom your Lord has bestowed His Mercy: and for this did He create them.' (11, *Hud*, 118–9) Also: 'To each among you have We prescribed a Law and a Way. If Allah had so willed, He would have made you a single nation.' (5, *Al-Ma'ida*, 48) Islam specifies, through the Quranic text, that the belief in all prophets and messengers is part of Islam itself. The monotheistic religions at the time of the Prophet were three: Judaism, Christianity and Sabaeanism. The Quran twice emphasizes their recognition, in almost identical wording. 'Those who believe [in the Quran] and those who follow the Jewish [scriptures] and the Christians and the Sabaeans, any who believe in Allah and the Last Day, and work righteousness, shall have their reward with their Lord: in them shall be no fear, nor shall they grieve.' (2, *Al-Baqara*, 62)

6. The right to consultation: The Quranic Text and Circumstantial Interpretations: The right to consultation is linked with the right to disagree, as specified by the Quran and the *hadith*, and also by the conduct of the Prophet and his Companions. The Quran is explicit in making consultation a basic quality defining the concept of the 'believer', placing it on a par with refraining from major disobedience and the performance of religious duties. 'Whatever

you are given [here] is [but] a convenience of this life: but that which is with
Allah is better and more lasting: [It is] for those who believe and put their trust
in their Lord: those who refrain from greater sins and shameful deeds, and
when they are angry, even then forgive: those who hearken to their Lord, and
establish regular prayers: who [conduct] their affairs by mutual consultation:
who spend out of what We bestowed on them for sustenance: and those who,
when an oppressive wrong is inflicted on them [are not cowed, but] help and
defend themselves.' (42, *Al-Shura*, 36–39) Exegetes say these verses were
revealed with reference to the Ansar 'who, before Islam, and before the arrival
of the Prophet to them, would come together and consult one another about
their affairs, for which the Prophet praised them, as they would not take a decision until they had reached an agreement' (al-Zamakhshari). Although the
phrase 'who [conduct] their affairs by mutual consultation' comes as a statement, it implies a command, as there are several examples in the Quran similar
to this. But the command to consult was openly expressed on other occasions,
when it was addressed to the Prophet himself. 'It is part of the mercy of Allah
that you were lenient with them. Were you severe or harsh-hearted, they would
have broken away from about you: so pass over [their faults], and ask for
[Allah's] forgiveness for them, and consult them in the affairs [of moment].
Then when you have taken a decision, put your trust in Allah, for Allah loves
those who put their trust [in Him]. (3, *Al-'Imran*, 159) It is reported of al-Hasan
ibn 'Ali ibn Abu Talib that he made the following comment on this verse:
'Allah knew that he [the Prophet] had no need of them, but He wished this to
be a rule after him [the Prophet]'. That is, He wished Muslims to follow in the
Prophet's footsteps.

   More might be quoted to this effect, making it clear that consultation in
Islam is a duty of the ruler and a right of the ruled. Indeed it is a right of the ruled
first, because the caliph at the time of the Rashidin was not installed before
consultation had been conducted. There was a dispute among jurists and
exegetes about whether consultation was compulsory or merely advisory,
whether the ruler had to abide by the decision from the consultation or merely
take it under advisement, being free thereafter to follow the opinion of the consultants or ignore it. The argument reflects the relation of jurists to rulers. If the
jurist were of independent mind, abiding by Islamic morality, he would say that
consultation was compulsory. If he were a spokesman for the rulers and could
justify their actions, or if he preferred certain considerations over others, he
would say consultation was merely advisory. Those who claimed consultation
was merely advisory looked on it as a desirable quality in the ruler, and did
not think of it as a right of the *umma* (Islamic nation). If, however, we view

consultation as a right of the *umma*, it will certainly become obligatory for the ruler. There is no authoritative text to bar consideration of it in this way, that is, as a right of the *umma* and not merely a quality in the ruler.

7. The right to equality: The Quran specifies equality among people in a decisive verse. 'O mankind. We created you from a single [pair] of a male and a female, and made you into nations and tribes, that you may know each other [not that you may despise each other]. Truly, the most honoured among you in the sight of Allah is [he who is] the most righteous. Allah has full knowledge and is fully acquainted [with all things].' (49, *Al-Hujurat*, 130) Exegetes understand equality, in this verse, as a negation of difference or preference due to lineage, emphasizing specific words – 'male' and 'female', 'nations' and 'tribes' – and concluding that the verse specifies preference on account of piety exclusively, not lineage. Such an interpretation was obviously appropriate to those times, when preference on account of lineage, and vaunting on the subject, was quite common. Nevertheless, to limit the meaning of this verse to the obvious construction – in this case the tribal aspect – is unfair, if only because there are other *hadith*s reported by the exegetes which extend disapproval of vaunting to cover other matters too, such as colour, wealth, prestige and anything else that might lead to self-praise. One such *hadith* is a speech made by the Prophet on the day of the conquest of Mecca: 'Praise be to Allah Who rescued you from the burdens and arrogance of *jahiliyya*. O you people! A man is one of two types: a pious believer honoured by Allah, and a wretched wanton disdained in the sight of Allah.' Then he recited the above-quoted verse. A decisive *hadith* in this connection is: 'No Arab is favoured over a non-Arab, nor a white man over a black, except in piety.' Also: 'People are equal like the teeth of a comb.'

These, then, are the rights of man in general – the basic rights as specified by the Holy Quran and the exalted *hadith*. Such are the rights of all human beings without exception or discrimination: the right to life, the right to enjoyment of life, freedom of belief, the right to knowledge, the right to disagree, the right to consultation, and the right to equality. Without enjoyment of these rights the human being falls short of the basis of his existence and the means of his prosperity and development.

In addition to these general rules, there are special rules pertaining to certain groups of people, such as the rights of parents, children, etc. Among such groups allotted special rights by the Quran is that of the 'weak and oppressed', who are given rights to the wealth of the rich. There is also the right nowadays called 'social security'. Let us see here how these rights can be authenticated to secure social justice.

X.2 Special rights

1. The rights of the weak and oppressed: righteousness, tribute and 'surplus':

The term 'weak and oppressed' occurs several times in the Quran to denote weak people as contrasted with 'the arrogant' who vaunt of their financial, political or military power, or about what they have in terms of material and moral power, with the suggestion that they are superior to others and worthier than others. The 'arrogant' person, therefore, is anyone who denies that he is equal to other persons and claims a kind of superiority for himself. The 'weak and oppressed', on the other hand, are those lacking the wealth, prestige or other powers which the 'arrogant' employ against them in their exercise of haughtiness and exploitation of others. In other words, the 'weak and oppressed' are those whose rights are forfeited in a society not based on equality and justice.

The Quran specifies a number of such weak and oppressed persons: they are the weak and the invalid among family members (elderly parents and other relatives), the poor, the needy, orphans, the wayfarer, those who ask for help, slaves and prisoners of war. The Quran stresses the rights of these people repeatedly, enjoining special attention for them and threatening anyone who violates their rights. One of the verses summing up these rights of the weak is: 'It is not righteousness that you turn your faces towards east or west; but it is righteousness to believe in Allah and the Last Day, and the angels and the Book and the Messengers; to spend of your substance out of love for Him, for your kin, for the orphans, for the needy, for the wayfarer, for those who ask, and for the ransom of slaves; to be steadfast in prayer, and practise regular charity, to fulfil the contracts which you have made; and to be firm and patient in suffering and adversity, and throughout all periods of panic. Such are the people of truth, the pious.' (2, *Al-Baqara*, 177)

Four points should be highlighted with respect to this verse:

The first point is 'righteousness', which means all good deeds and not merely the act of worship. The address in 'It is not righteousness that you turn your faces towards east or west' is directed to the People of the Book, because Jews pray facing Jerusalem, which lies to the west of Hijaz, while Christians pray facing the east. The meaning of the verse is that righteousness and good deeds in general are not limited to prayer, but cover other matters, mainly fulfilment of the rights of the weak and oppressed.

The second point is that this verse places belief in God and the Last Day on a par with the payment of money due to the oppressed specified in the verse.

This puts the rights of the weak and oppressed on the same level with the rights of God, namely worship.

The third point is that the verse regards money paid to the categories mentioned as being exclusive of *zakat*. In other words, the rights of the oppressed to God's wealth – which is in the hands of the rich – is not limited to *zakat*.

The fourth point is that the verse, by associating payment of money due to the poor and oppressed with the principles of Islam, such as testifying to the Oneness of God, *salat*, *zakat*, etc., raises the fulfilment of the rights of the weak and oppressed to the force of duty. The Quran further underlines this meaning by: 'And in their wealth and possession is the right of him who asked and him who is deprived' (51, *Al-Dariyat*, 19); and, in the *hadith*: 'In wealth there is right other than *zakat*.'

This shows that 'the rights of the weak and the oppressed' are of two types: one is their right to *zakat*, the other to 'righteousness'. The difference is that *zakat* is one of the pillars of Islam, along with attesting to the Oneness of God, *salat*, fasting and pilgrimage. As such, any Muslim wishing to join Islamic society must observe the payment of *zakat*, which is a kind of 'tax' signifying the allegiance of the individual to the state. The right to 'righteousness' specifies the rights of the individual over the state, especially, as will be shown below, the right to 'social security'.

It should be pointed out, first, that the 'tribute' imposed by Islam on non-Muslims within a Muslim society is a 'tax' in place of *zakat*. It is a duty binding the citizen to the state by a bond of allegiance and interest; a symbol of political allegiance and a contribution to the expenditure of the state in areas of public interest, such as security and development, which benefit citizens of all religions. Tribute differs from *zakat* because non-Muslim 'People of the Book', while under the protection of the state like other citizens, are not required to partake in *jihad* to propagate or defend Islam, either in person or through financial contributions. However, with regard to righteousness, justice and other rights, Muslims and non-Muslim are alike. This is clearly expressed in the following verse: 'Allah does not forbid you, with regard to those who did not fight you for [your] faith, nor drive you out of your homes, from dealing kindly and justly with them: for Allah loves those who are just. Allah only forbids you, with regard to those who fought you for [your] faith and drove you out of your homes, and supported [others] in driving you out, from turning to them [for friendship and protection]. It is such as turn to them [in these circumstances] that do wrong.' (60, *Al-Mumtahana*, 8–9)

But the rights of the weak and oppressed are not covered by the verse on 'righteousness' alone. The Quran stresses the fulfilment of these rights on several occasions. 'Give them something out of the means which Allah has given to you.' (24, *Al-Nur*, 33) Then: 'And those in whose wealth is a recognized right for the needy and deprived.' (70, *Al-Ma'arij*, 24–5) Also: 'They ask you how much they are to spend? Say: What is beyond your need.' (2, *Al-Baqara*, 219) The word 'beyond' [in the original Arabic] means 'surplus to', that is, what is more than is needed. Al-Nasafi explains the verse to mean: 'spend what is more than what you need.' Then he adds: 'Paying charity out of what was in excess of need was a duty in the early days of Islam. When a man had a farm, he would keep what he needed for a full year and give the surplus as alms. If he were a daily worker, he kept what he needed for his daily food and expended the surplus as alms. The verse of *zakat* was revealed to abrogate the verse of surplus.' In other words, when the Muslim community had limited resources, each member had to return to that community (by paying for the poor and the needy) whatever was in excess of his need, in order to keep a balance in living needs. But when the resources of the Muslim community began to flourish through gains from conquest, trade, etc., the tax of *zakat* replaced 'surplus'. As such, recourse to resources other than *zakat* was quite legitimate when the latter was insufficient to cover the needs of the poor and provide the minimum of balance in living needs.

Ibn Hazm explains the matter from the perspective of what we nowadays call 'social security'. God, he says,

> has imposed on the rich of every country the duty to provide for the poor. The sovereign obliges them to do so if the resources of *zakat* cannot meet the need . . . [The poor] are to be provided with the necessary food, with winter and summer clothing, and with abode to protect them from rain, sunshine and the eyes of onlookers.[23]

It is interesting, in this connection, to note the contract made by Khalid ibn al-Walid with the Christians of Hira in Iraq:

> I have provided that any elderly person among them who has become too weak to work, or is affected by a malady, or has been rich and has become so poor that those of his own religion have begun to help him with charity – that all these should be exempt from the *jizya* tax, and that all such, along with their dependents, should be supported by the Muslim treasury.[24]

As is well known, such contracts are considered a source of legislation in Islam. This contract was concluded at the time of Abu Bakr, who endorsed it, and it met with no objection from any of the Companions, so that the contract had the power of consensus. Khalid's commitment to the Christians of Hira corresponds, of course, to the right accorded to Muslims who come under the category of 'weak and oppressed'. As such, social security, in the present-day sense, is one of the rights of man in Islam, as specified in the Quran, in *hadith*, and in the conduct of the Companions.

2. The rights of women: To reach a full and thorough understanding of the rights of women in Islam, we have to consider three basic areas:

a the comprehensive rulings of Islamic Shariah;
b the partial rulings of Islamic Shariah;
c the reasonableness of these rulings as shown by the intents of Shariah and the occasions of revelation.

On the basis of these, it may be said that Islam, fundamentally and as a general and absolute rule, specifies equality between men and women. 'O mankind! We created you from a single [pair] of a male and a female, and made you into nations and tribes, that you may know each other [not that you may despise each other]. Truly the most honoured of you in the sight of Allah is [he who is] the most righteous of you.' (49, *Al-Hujurat*, 13) Also: 'And their Lord accepted [their prayers] and answered them: "Never will I suffer the work of any one of you, male or female, to be lost; you are members, one of the other.' (3, *Al-'Imran*, 195) Further: 'The believers, men and women, are protectors, one of another.' (9, *Al-Tawba*, 71) There are several *hadith*s that dignify the status of women, such as: 'Paradise is at the feet of mothers.' Other *hadith*s place men and women on the same level. For example: 'Women are fully equal with men.' As is well known, Islam imposes the same religious duties on men and women alike, regarding them as equal in responsibility.

There are indeed verses specifying the preference of some people over others; but such preference springs from reasons covered by the verse: 'The most honoured of you in the sight of Allah is [he who is] the most righteous of you.' Whoever is more righteous is preferred in honour. It is with this in mind that we must view the verse: 'Men are the protectors and maintainers of women, because Allah has given the one more [strength] than the other, and because they support them from their means.' (4, *Al-Nisa'*, 34) This verse was revealed in a specific context, namely the prohibition of illegal gain, as through robbery, treachery, looting, gambling and usury. By contrast, there is permission for trading carried out by agreement between seller and buyer. In this field of trade and profit, men have always been more concerned than women, hence making more profit. Women have been mostly concerned with work in the home; and, as such, men have been 'protectors and maintainers of women', that is, they have provided for their necessary expenditure, for food and clothing, etc. Also, men are not all alike in wealth and expenditure; there are differences among them. God has preferred active men over the lazy. In general, there is nothing in the Quran or the *hadith* to violate the principle of equality between man and woman, which is based on 'the most honoured of you in the sight of Allah are the most righteous'. Men and women are equal in the measure of righteousness. Women who are more righteous are more honoured in the sight of God than men who are less righteous.

The general tendency in Islamic legislation, therefore, is one of equality of men and women in rights and duties. Partial rulings that might appear to contradict this tendency must be investigated as to their *raison d'être* in the light of the intents of Shariah and the occasions of revelation. These will be discussed below:

1 The question of bearing witness

For testifying as a witness, the Quran, as is well known, specifies that at least two men, or else one man and two women, should be provided. 'And get two witnesses out of your own men. And if there are not two men, then a man and two women, such as you choose for witnesses, so that if one of them errs, the other can remind her.' (2, *Al-Baqara*, 282) It is clear from this verse that the sole rationale for Shariah, in asking for two women instead of one man, is the possibility that one of the two women may make an error or may forget. It is not that error and forgetfulness are specifically in the nature of women; the situation simply reflects the social and educational status of women at that time. But the question may be raised here: How will Islam rule on this issue when the social and educational status of women has been raised to the level of men's? Will there be application of the principle: 'When impediments are removed, matters return to their origin?' The 'origin' here is, as we have seen, equality between man and woman. Or is it necessary to abide by the literal text? This is not my field, and I have no intention of issuing a specialized legal ruling on the subject. However, I believe the matter is open to independent opinion. 'Umar ibn al-Khattab, for example, sanctioned this kind of independent opinion in a clear text when he refused to divide the land of Iraq among the Muslim fighters, preferring to leave it in the possession of its owners in return for payment of tax. Such a measure was, he considered, in the public interest at that time and for the future.

2 The question of inheritance

The Quran specifies that the girl should receive half the share of the boy in inheritance. 'Allah directs you as regards your children's [inheritance]: to the male a portion equal to that of two females.' (4, *Al-Nisa'*, 11) Since the Quran does not clarify the reasons for this differentiation, we have to refer to the intents of Shariah and the occasions of revelation. Arab society before Islam and in the time of the Prophet was a tribal and pastoral one, and relations between pastoral tribes were marked by conflict over pasture. In such a society marriage could lead to problems over inheritance when the father died and his daughter was married outside her own tribe. If the married girl took a share of her father's inheritance, whether livestock or merely the right to share grazing land, that portion would go to her husband's tribe at the expense of her father's, and this might result in conflict and war. To avoid such a situation, some tribes before Islam chose to deprive the female of any inheritance, while others allowed her a third or less. When we consider, in addition, the limited amount of property exchanged in tribal society, we realize how female inheritance might lead to economic disturbance among tribes, especially within a system where polygamy was widespread. Islam was undoubtedly aware of this situation and conscious of an interest in avoiding conflict. Accordingly, a kind of happy medium was fixed on to suit the new phase inaugurated by the Muhammadan state in Medina. The share of the female was fixed at one half that of the male, while the expenditure of the female, whether wife or mother, was to be the responsibility of the man.

3 Divorce and polygamy

There is, in my view, no justification for raising these two questions in connection with the rights of women in Islam. Far from enforcing or recommending either divorce or polygamy, Islam actually adopts quite the contrary standpoint. These two phenomena were quite popular among Arabs before Islam, and Islam attempted to keep them within bounds by laying down conditions not so very far removed from prohibition. Islam stipulates 'justice' in the case of polygamy, adding: 'But if you fear that you shall not be able to deal justly (with them), then only one.' (4, *Al-Nisa'*, 3) Then: 'You can never be just between women, even if it were your ardent desire.' (4, *Al-Nisa'*, 129) This indicates a clear tendency toward prohibition of the practice. Divorce is described in the *hadith* in the following terms: 'The most hateful permissible action in the sight of Allah is divorce.' It cannot be said, in view of this, that Islam undermines the right of women by permitting divorce or polygamy; neither is permissible 'absolutely' but only as a 'limited unforbidden action'. A state of justice is difficult to provide for in the case of polygamy; and divorce, as 'the most hateful permissible action in the sight of Allah', is not basically different from a prohibited action.

4 Women and sovereignty

The question of sovereignty (on which some jurists hold a strict opinion denying this right to women, referring to a *hadith* reported by Abu Bakra and by no one else) requires thorough investigation. Al-Bukhari quotes Abu Bakra as having said: 'Allah has favoured me with a word I heard from the Messenger at the time of the Battle of the Camel, as I was about to join and fight on his side in that battle. I remembered that when the Messenger heard how the Persians chose the daughter of Xerxes as their sovereign, he said: "no people will prosper if they choose a woman as their sovereign."' Quite apart from any adjustment or criticism to which Abu Bakra's report might be subject, reservation on the question is justifiable.

On the one hand, the *hadith* refers to the Battle of the Camel, which took place between 'Ali ibn Abi Talib on one side and, on the other, the Umayyad clan, Talha, al-Zubayr, and 'A'isha, the wife of the Prophet (who rode a camel, hence the name of the battle). Abu Bakra says he held back from joining the revolt out of respect for the *hadith* about the daughter of Xerxes. The presence of a woman in each case is clearly the only aspect common to the two situations. As such, the context noted by Abu Bakra reflects justification for a personal stance, and the *hadith* may hence be seen as recommending a high moral stand against participation in revolt, rather than being of a jurisprudential nature.

The wording of the *hadith* may be viewed as denoting a specific and not a general situation; hence it might be intended either as a prophecy as to what the Persians would come to or as a prayer against them.

What supports these reservations is that there is not the slightest reference in the Quran belittling the status of women as being inadequate to rule. On the contrary, the Quran very clearly specifies, as we have already seen, the equality between men and women. Support for this view may be found in the Quranic story of the Queen of Sheba, and of her rationality and good management. The Quran praises her as a 'queen' who, on receiving the epistle of the prophet Sulaiman (Solomon), abandoned the worship of the sun and responded to the call of 'monotheism'. 'She said, O chiefs! Here is delivered to me a worthy epistle * It is from Sulaiman, and is [as follows]: "In the name of Allah, the Most

Merciful, the Most Compassionate * Be not arrogant against me, but come to me in submission [to the true religion].' (27, *Al-Naml*, 29–31) The story ends with the Queen responding to the call to monotheism: 'She said, "O my Lord! I have indeed wronged my soul: I do [now] submit [in Islam] with Sulaiman, to the Lord of the worlds."' (Ibid., 44.) Thus it is that the Quran praises this woman who is a sovereign queen. Her status did not prevent her from following the course of prosperity and guidance: joining the religion of Sulaiman and submitting to God, the Lord of the worlds.

The *hadith* reported by Muslim, quoting 'Abd Allah ibn 'Umar and describing women as 'wanting in reason and religion', lacks any legislative power. It rather describes a specific situation. The text of the *hadith* is as follows: "Umar ibn 'Abd Allah tells how the Messenger of Allah said: "O you women! Give alms and ask more for forgiveness, as I see that you form a majority among the dwellers in hell fire." A prudent woman put in: "Messenger of Allah! Why should we be a majority among the dwellers in hell fire?" He said: "You curse a great deal and undermine friendship. I have not seen this more than in you [women] who are wanting in reason and religion [compared to men]." The woman asked: "O Messenger of Allah! What is the want of reason and religion?" He said: "The want of reason is because the testimony of two women is equal to that of one man. This is want of reason. The want of religion is when you stay nights on end without performing *salat*, and when you do not keep fasting in Ramadan."'

It is clear here that the 'want' is not a 'defect' but a dispensation afforded to women by Shariah. Women are given dispensation from certain religious duties, such as fasting in Ramadan when they are in their monthly period or confined after childbirth, in consideration of their physical condition and the physiological changes they undergo in these situations. The 'want in religion' in this case is not a moral or a behavioural matter, but a reality effected by a dispensation afforded to women by Shariah. This may be seen as an application of the principle of equality between men and women. If women were charged with *salat* and fasting in the cases mentioned above, while men were not subject to similar physical hindrance, it would be an injustice to the woman.

The 'want of reason' may be similarly interpreted. If the 'want of religion' is a kind of dispensation springing from a physiological cause, why can it not be possible to view 'want of reason' in the same manner: to say that the Shariah stipulation of testimony by two women to equal that of one man springs from psychological causes linked, ultimately, to social and cultural conditions? The Quran's reason for requiring that two women testify is stated quite clearly: 'If one of them errs, the other can remind her.' (2, *Al-Baqara*, 282)

Plato and Ibn Rushd on women

The Cordoban philosopher and incomparable Islamic jurist Ibn Rushd (Averroes) may have had the above interpretations in mind when commenting on Plato's opinion about the possibility of a woman assuming rule of a state. Ibn Rushd gave a social interpretation to the jurists' attitude to women's rule, an interpretation close to the one I have advanced. Here is what the eminent Cordoban judge and philosopher had to say on the issue:

> Plato wondered in his *Republic* whether it is possible to assign certain positions to women in his 'ideal city', meaning the positions which are usually assumed by men and not by women. He says: 'Women naturally participate in all occupations, and so do men; but in all women are weaker than men.' Then he adds: 'But we shall say, I fancy, that one woman is by nature fit for medicine, and another not; one musical, and another unmusical? . . . And is not one woman a lover of gymnastic and of war, and another unwarlike and no lover of gymnastic? . . . And one a lover and another a hater of wisdom; one spirited, another spiritless? . . . Then one woman will be capable of being a guardian and another not . . . Then for the purposes of guarding the city the nature of men and women is the same, except that women are naturally weaker, men naturally stronger?'

Such is Plato's position on the issue.[25] Ibn Rushd summarizes Plato's position as follows:

> The point at issue is this: is women's nature similar to or different from that of other citizens, especially the guardians of the state? If we find it similar, then women are necessarily on a par with men in the civil duties undertaken by every class of person. Among them we shall find soldiers, philosophers, rulers, etc. If we find it different, then they will be equipped only to perform duties most men are not equipped to perform, such as childbearing, raising children, and the like.

Ibn Rushd makes the following comments:

> I have said that, since women are of the same race as men (that is, the human race) concerning the sublime human aim [i.e., the primary aim of human existence], they are necessarily participants in this aim in one way or another; and, while men are more capable than women in most human activities, it is not impossible that women, in some activities, may be more capable than men. This is seen in musical performance (which was different from musicology, this being considered a mathematical science). On this account, it was said that music would be more perfect if it were composed by men and performed by women. This being the case, and since the nature of men and women is of the same kind,

and since the nature of the same kind turns into an activity of one kind in the city, then it is natural that women in the Republic might assume the same activities that men assume, except those which they cannot perform. It is necessary, then, that they should be assigned the easiest kind of work. This becomes clear upon investigation. We find women playing their part in crafts with the exception of those that are beyond their powers. And we find women more capable than men in certain crafts such as weaving, sewing and the like. As for women's participation in war and related activities, we find clear evidence for this among the inhabitants of the desert and the port.

He adds:

Moreover, since some women grow up endowed with a high degree of intelligence and excellence, it is not improbable to think of finding philosophers and rulers among them. But since people commonly suppose this type to be rare among women, we find that some legislation does not accept women in leadership with respect to the greater leadership [i.e., the caliphate], while other legislation remains silent on the point, since the existence of women of this type is not impossible in such a case.[26]

Such is the stance of Ibn Rushd on women, as reflected in his comments on Plato. I leave it to the reader to make his own evaluation of the philosopher's position.

Chapter 2: The concept of person in Islamic Tradition

Mohammed Arkoun

*In recent anthropological discussion, the moral (and aesthetic) aspects of a given culture, the eval-
uative elements, have commonly been summed up in the term 'ethos', while the cognitive, existential aspects have been designated by the term 'world view'. A people's ethos is the tone,
character and quality of life, its moral and aesthetic style and mood; it is the underlying attitude
towards themselves and their world that life reflects. Their world view . . . contains their most
comprehensive ideas of order.*

C. Geertz

I. Theoretical frameworks

It might be claimed that any social group or community identified as such constructs for itself a vision of what is called, in modern conceptualization, 'person'. This vision may be expressed implicitly, through beliefs, collective rituals
and customary codes, or explicitly, through precepts, proverbs, foundation
narratives, religious corpora and learned literature. For societies without writing, P. Bourdieu has developed the concept of 'practical sense', which permits
emphasis on the experiential character and the practical, empirical, unwritten
and speculative scope of the 'values', norms and 'symbolic capital' which
underlie and regulate the status of each member of the group and the mechanical solidarities that bind all the members together. 'Practical sense', so defined,
forestalls the emergence of a person or autonomous individual who might conceivably be critical, or indeed dissident, vis-à-vis the group or religious community.

It is important to keep such data in mind if we are properly to apply the difficult question of person within Islamic Tradition. The historical, geopolitical
and anthropological field worked upon by the 'Islamic fact' is so vast and varied as to be complex for the analyst. Even today it encompasses a number
of peoples or groups without writing, bound more to oral than to written

tradition, tied to behaviour, institutions and solidarities appropriate to the stage of 'practical sense' rather than that of the modern nation state. Where then, we must ask ourselves, are we to identify the historical emergences, the juridical, political and cultural manifestations, of the person? What status has the human person been accorded, finally, after 15 centuries of political experiments, juridical practices and doctrinal schemes within what I shall call Islamic Tradition?

Why, it may be asked, should we speak of Islamic 'Tradition', with a capital 'T', and not simply of Islam? And how is this Tradition to encompass, in practice, all the different historical and sociological manifestations involved, given the theological definitions which set in place an 'orthodox' tradition recognized by each community (*ahl al-sunna wa 'l-jama'a* for the Sunnis, *ahl al-isma wa 'l-'adala* for the Imami Shi'ites) against all the others which are pronounced heretical, errant or apocryphal? Islam is a generic name applied to all the theological, juridical and exegetical schools, and to all the peoples who have accepted and applied one school or another. In this sense there are as many 'Islams' as there are sociocultural and linguistic milieux sharing a long historical memory – one can speak of Indonesian Islam, Indian Islam, Turkish, Uzbeki, Senegalese, Iranian Islam, and so on. The affirmation, promotion, protection or oppression of the person will need to be evaluated for each local tradition, while, at the same time, taking into account the impact of Islamic Tradition.

The Islamic Tradition common to all Muslims, whatever their linguistic, cultural or historical reference, entails three great and binding foundational sources (*usul al-din* and *usul al-fiqh*): the Quran; the Prophetic traditions, or *hadith* (to which are added the teachings of the twelve or seven Imams in the case of the Twelver Shi'ites and Isma'ilis respectively); and the religious Law, or Shariah, accepted as the juridical codification of God's commandments by virtue of the technical work, known as *ijtihad*, undertaken by jurist theologians. These three foundational sources were theoretically defined, in the hierarchical order set out above, during the period (c. 661–950) in which Islamic thought was formed; in other words, all the texts, and teachings, and doctrinal formations laid down within this scripture-based Tradition belong to a period of the general history of thought which is styled medieval. We shall return to the problems raised by the periodization of the general history of civilizations, as this has been imposed by the European historiographical tradition since the sixteenth century. For the moment let us bear in mind that Tradition, so defined, can be written with a capital 'T' because it has always and everywhere sought to impose its supremacy, disregarding and where possible eradicating all previous local traditions, because these belong to the period styled by the Quran *jahiliyya*; that is, the state of ignorance of the true religion as defined by God, for the last time, in the Revelation transmitted through the Prophet (Muhammad). This theological definition of Tradition, which is bound to do away with all others, naturally disregards the concepts of tradition and custom as these have been developed by ethnography and cultural anthropology since the nineteenth century. The old tension between the scripture-based Tradition of the jurist-theologians and local traditions is today complicated by all the questioning which critical history, along with the various social sciences, has introduced into the study of every religious tradition – beginning with the traditions of Judaism and Christianity, which have been a direct focus of the ceaselessly renewed challenges of modernity. The capital 'T' also reflects the ways present-day Muslim thought resists the most indisputable teachings of modernity, in the name of a 'true religion' which no longer allows itself to be questioned even in terms of the educative tensions of its own past, when doctrinal pluralism was tolerated.

Neither 'noble' Tradition, having a universal force in the eyes of believers, nor local traditions – reduced to a residual state by the combined action of 'orthodox' religion and an *uncultivated* modernity – have as yet benefited from the explanations and opened vistas provided by *critical intellectual modernity* (which I contrast with the uncultivated modernity of the post-colonial states, upheld as these states are by technostructures lacking political focus and merchant classes lacking economic focus – each of these two being, usually, isolated elements within societies doomed to semantic disorder and in thrall to ungovernable forces of globalization). Thus the status of the human person, as defined in the Quran, in the Prophetic traditions and in juridical codes accepted and applied as Divine Law, has barely begun to open itself to the revisions and discussions inaugurated in Christian Europe, with the emergence, in the sixteenth century, of a humanist reason open to the pagan cultures of Graeco-Roman Antiquity and increasingly concerned to carve out its philosophical autonomy in the face of the dogmatic sovereignty of theological reason. This evolution continued with the reason of the Enlightenment, the philosophy of human rights and the establishment of a democratic de jure state bound, by renewable contract, with a civil society from which political sovereignty derives. Thus emerges the citizen individual, protected both in his relations with other citizens and in the free juridical construction of his private person, as a human being. The juridical freedoms guaranteed by the de jure state do not, naturally, do away with the sociological, economic and linguistic constraints that condition the construction and path of any human being.

Contemporary Islamic discourse proceeds through a formal annexation of modern values and positions, with the aid of an arbitrary selection of verses from the Quran and *hadith* wrenched from their historical and cultural contexts so as better to serve their apologetic purpose. For this reason I find myself unable, personally, to follow the lead of so many others in the operation of 'proving' that every modern development in the juridical, political and philosophical status of the person in Europe is already clearly stated and prescribed in the three corpora of Islamic Tradition. The fact is that present-day social frameworks of knowledge within societies called Muslim reflect the imaginary representations of 'true religion', and of the overall Muslim community for which salvation is promised, rather than giving encouragement to any scientific critique of all the alienating apologetic and ideological brands of discourse. We know, in this connection, the place and role of the nationalist discourse of liberation, begun in the 1950s and, since the 1980s, replaced and expanded by fundamentalist discourse in terms of a phantasmatical representation of self. We should note, nevertheless, that Muslims are not the only ones to practise this ideological cobbling in order to safeguard the validity of the living religious Tradition in the face of the concurrent model provided by modernity, which constructs the destiny of a human person without God; we witness, rather, a situation where each religious community strives to outbid the other in imposing its chronological precedence, and its priority generally, in affirming and implementing such modern concepts as freedom of conscience, tolerance in matters of religious freedom, freedom of expression, freedom of association and the vocation of the human person to exercise full autonomy, more particularly, in the realization of his spiritual destiny. This was a very old debate between the three monotheistic religions and philosophical reason in its Greek version, Islam experiencing this during the period corresponding to the High Middle Ages in Europe. What marks the difference, however, with Christianity and, in a lesser degree, Judaism is that in Islamic contexts philosophical reason was eliminated after the thirteenth century, while in Europe it was developed more and more influentially and productively thanks to its constant alliance with the scientific reason and political reason of the de jure state.

This alliance has sometimes led to excesses. A comparative critical history of modern religions and ideologies is beginning to show how annexations in reverse have also taken place in connection with the status of the human person. The ideas of fraternity and equality, the moral and spiritual presentation of man as a free spirit, who, as such, bears responsibility irrespective of frontiers, mechanical solidarities and illegitimate allegiances – these are put forward, in terms of an appeal to the discernment of the believer, in teachings of what (with a view to encompassing the Jewish, Christian and Islamic traditions) I call 'prophetic discourse'. These aspects of the history of the person have been better studied, relatively speaking, for Judaeo-Christianity than for Islam, to which the interrogations and new curiosities of the social sciences have always been tardily applied. We need, then, to remedy the conceptual displacements, the various misunderstandings, nourished by two mutually perceiving ideological cultures, between two imaginary entities called 'Islam' and 'the West'.

Let us try and establish the critical course which will, today, lead to the crucial question of the person being taken up globally, from the viewpoint of a humanism which will go beyond (without rejecting or seeking to invalidate) all those traditions of thought prior to the new cognitive scheme which must accompany globalization. It will obviously be necessary to examine the various contemporary Islamic contexts in order to determine how far they hold back or favourize the emergence of an autonomous person, free in his choices, in his commitments to lead his own existence in solidarity with his society and the evolution of the present-day world. This will show that the person's course of life and contexts of socialization, the interactive relations between the person and the group (patriarchal family, clan, village, quarter, community of orthodox believers), the status finally accorded the person in Islamic Tradition – all these have been irreversibly upset since the end of the Second World War and the beginning of the struggles for national liberation. There is thus a *before* and an *after* – institutional, semantic, sociological and anthropological – for the history of the person in Islamic contexts. The study of the *before* places us within the perspective of the long period that begins with the appearance of the 'Quranic fact', and continues, with perceptible differentiations but a profoundly marked structural and epistemic continuity, up to around 1940. The *after* constrains us to work within the short period in which brutal revolutions, violent upheavals, rapid disintegrations of every traditional code – whether customary, juridical, semantic, semiotic or anthropological – have followed one another without preparation or transition, within a highly compressed time frame in which a number of heterogeneous temporalities are clashing together. We shall refrain, therefore, from any static presentation of a 'paradigmatic Islam', unchanged and unchangeable; inasmuch as all the orthodox traditions set it up for reflection rather than living, and inasmuch as an Islamological approach respectful of these traditions continues to transpose it into European languages with a sometimes arrogant pretension to scientific qualities.

Let us begin from the Quran, not with a view to seeking out any statements prefiguring our modern conceptions of the person, but in order to distinguish

the cognitive status of 'prophetic discourse' from the normative devices introduced subsequently by theologico-juridical doctrines and by intellectual and
cultural evolution in urban milieux. The emergence and rapid expansion of a
self-declared Islamic state (the Umayyad Caliphate, followed by the Abbasid
Caliphate) favourizes the construction of what I shall call the 'Islamic fact', to
mark its distinctive characteristics as against the 'Quranic fact'. This terminology aims to problematize the whole inherited conceptualization of classical
and scholastic Islamic thought, transposed as this has been, without any critical deconstruction, by Islamological erudition. It is a question of dealing with
the central problem of the status of the person in Islamic contexts; and the first
task to this end is to rethink, or think over for the first time, all those questions
relative to the person which have been thrust into the unthinkable and kept in
the unthought by Islamic thought. Paradoxically, it is in the course of what I
have called the 'after', when the challenges of modernity, and now of globalization, are becoming more pressing, that the field of the unthinkable has
become most broadened due to the generalization of doctrinal terrorism as a
means of producing history in Islamic contexts.

II. The Quranic fact

The term Quran is too charged with theological content to serve as an opera-
tional concept for a critical revaluation and prospective redefinition of Islamic
Tradition as a whole. By speaking of 'Quranic fact', in the sense that we talk of
biological fact or historical fact, I wish to set at a critical distance all the doctrinal constructions, all the definitions – theologico-juridical, literary, rhetorical,
exegetical, and so on – which have been commonly regarded as indisputable
since an 'open Quranic corpus' was turned into a 'Closed Official Corpus'. Just
when this change occurred is difficult to say exactly. We can only indicate some
chronological points of reference, such as the history and *Tafsir* of al-Tabari
(d. 310/923), the *Risala* of al-Shafi'i (d. 204/820) and the collections of *hadith*
made by al-Bukhari (d. 256/870), Muslim (d. 261/875), al-Kulayni (d.
329/940), Ibn Babawayh (d. 381/991) and Abu Ja'far al-Tusi (d. 460/1068).
The works left behind by all these authors are decisive landmarks in the slow
historical process whereby concurrent Islamic orthodoxies were constructed,
theologically and politically. The collections of *hadith* swiftly became, in their
turn, closed official corpora, assuming the second rank in the hierarchy of
foundational sources (*usul*) defined as such by al-Shafi'i for an exegetically
trustworthy development of the Law which would henceforth be styled divine

(Shariah). As collective creations the Prophetic and Imami traditions reflect the slow linguistic, cultural and psycho-sociological processes leading to the establishment of a 'Muslim ethos' in the anthropological sense, as defined by C. Geertz (see the quotation at the head of this essay). They are informative too on the interactions between the teachings of a Quranic corpus on the way to closure and the ethno-cultural data proper to the different milieux in which the 'Quranic fact' has been introduced. The 'Muslim ethos' in process of formation does not have an equal impact for every group within a vast whole comprising, for instance, ancient Iran, the Berber regions, the Iberian Peninsula and the huge Turkish lands; even after the establishment of closed official corpora and their diffusion in written and oral form, the penetration of the 'Muslim ethos' was never to be either generalized in extent and depth for all the groups, nor irreversible in time, nor totally in conformity with the ideal orthodox definition perpetuated in spiritual, ethical and narrative literature.

The ideal orthodox definition of the person in 'Islam' takes no account either of the historical and sociological approach or of the anthropological problematization that I have set out above. Actually the Quran read by generations of the faithful as a closed official corpus does not function – linguistically, culturally or semiotically – either as it did at its stage of open oral statement up to the death of the Prophet, or as it did at the second stage, of a corpus in process of collection and written conveyance in a *mus-haf* which was subsequently declared closed. Such were the numerous steps involved in the formation of the 'Muslim ethos'. When we take into account all these methodological rules, any attempt to define the concept of person according to the Quran must inevitably take the form of a more or less coherent lexicological construction that respects the rules neither of a synchronic nor of a diachronic reading. It is precisely this in fact which has been made, and continues to be made, by the reading of believers, which obeys only the declarations of orthodox faith – accepts, in other words, the need for the insertion of self within a framework of identity determined by the contents of this faith. But if the reading of believers finds in this its sociological and psychological priority, we must not disregard the intellectual and social-historical costs involved, to the extent that such a reading perpetuates both the alienation of the person and the conditions within which a scholastic culture, giving rise to an institutionalized ignorance, can expand. This is just what has occurred in a number of Islamic contexts from the fifteenth and sixteenth centuries on. I insist, in this connection, on the reversibility of the conditions whereby the person is promoted in Islamic contexts. The humanist figure of the *adib*, open to diverse cultural currents between the ninth and eleventh centuries (c. 800–1030), disappeared along with the social, political and cultural conditions which made him possible.[1] A similar process can be seen with the figure of the mystic, who, at the same period, combined a rich personal experience of the divine with a considerable mastery of poetic and intellectual language whereby this experience was recorded in major works – I am thinking, for example, of al-Muhasibi (d. 243/857), whose name refers to his critical self-examination (*muhasabat al-nafs*). This kind of mystic figure was transformed, from the thirteenth to the nineteenth centuries on, into a petty scholar who was to islamize social groups maintaining an oral tradition, gather around himself disciples called brothers (*ikhwan*) and finally establish marabout dynasties governing quite powerful brotherhoods. We shall see later whether we ought to speak of regression or of a crisis of mutation with respect to the status of the person in the phase of national struggles for liberation and of Islamist opposition geared to seizing power.

Let us now briefly consider the means and mental tools provided by Quranic discourse for the construction of a new man clearly opposed to the old man of the *jahiliyya*, a polemic concept which, in the Quranic pairing *jahiliyya/'ilm-islam*, evokes the anthropological concept of 'uncultivated thought' as opposed to 'domesticated thought'. Quranic discourse utilizes the terms *nafs, ruh, ins, insan* and a rich vocabulary of perception and discursive activity[2] to construct, according to its appropriate perspectives, what it calls 'man'. We shall see that the spiritual vocation and ethico-political definition of man at the Quranic stage mask contents which are homologous to, if not identical with, those found in the Biblical and evangelic corpora. It is for this reason that I have introduced the concept of 'prophetic discourse', which, at its initial oral stage, utilizes the same linguistic mechanisms for the articulation of sense. The following are some samples of verses often selected, by advocates of an apologetic reading, for the way they lend themselves so comprehensively to an annexation of modern values by placing them under the authority of the Word of God:

We did indeed offer the Trust to the Heavens and the Earth and the Mountains; but they refused to undertake it, being afraid thereof: but man undertook it – he was indeed unjust and foolish. (33, *Al-Ahzab*, 72)

Behold, thy Lord said to the angels: 'I will create a vicegerent on earth.' They said: 'Wilt Thou place therein one who will make mischief therein and shed blood? – whilst we do celebrate Thy praises and glorify Thy holy (name)?' (2, *Al-Baqara*, 30)

And did not Allah check one set of people by means of another, the earth would indeed be full of mischief. (2, *Al-Baqara*, 251)

Say ye: 'We believe in Allah, and the revelation given to us, and to Abraham, Ishmael, Isaac, Jacob, and the Tribes, and that given to Moses and Jesus, and that given to (all) Prophets from their Lord: we make no difference between one and another of them: and we bow to Allah (in Islam).' (2, *Al-Baqara*, 136)

Verily, Man is in loss,

Except such as have Faith, and do righteous deeds, and (join together) in the mutual teaching of Truth, and of Patience and Constancy. (103, *Al-Asr*, 2–3)

But when the forbidden months are past, then fight and slay the Pagans wherever ye find them, and seize them, beleaguer them, and lie in wait for them in every stratagem (of war). But if they repent, and establish regular prayers and practise regular charity, then open the way for them: for Allah is Oft-forgiving, Most Merciful. (9, *Al-Tawba*, 5)

One could multiply indefinitely statements where the dialogue between God and man, man and God, develops within every register of discourse and within every sphere of knowledge and action. Indefatigably, in the most diverse contexts, the Ten Commandments are taught, set out to snatch man from the grip of blindness, violence, the 'uncultivated' life (*jahiliyya*) and the constraints of the group, including parents who refuse to enter into the new Alliance (*mithaq*): 'These are among the (precepts of) wisdom, which thy Lord has revealed to thee.' (17, *Al-Isra'*, 39) The verses quoted as a sample cannot, as has been said, reveal their true meanings, in the sense demanded by the historian, unless we duly consider the actual circumstances in which they were originally articulated at Mecca or Medina. This rule incumbent on the historian is, of course, systematically disregarded by believers concerned only with norms immediately applicable to their behaviour. According to the particular contingency faced, to the development of a conversation or the necessities of a line of argument, they will invoke, with equal conviction, verse 9, *Al-Tawba*, 5 to legitimize *jihad* or other verses more peaceful and more geared toward the promotion of the positive aspects of the person. The Quran as experienced has always had priority over the Quran as analyzed, expounded and known; yet the latter must retain primacy over the former if we are to limit the drift of the social and religious 'imaginary', to reject manipulations made with ideological ends in mind. This fight between priority and primacy lies at the heart of the history of all the foundational texts, and, consequently, of the sense and the effects of sense always conditioning the construction and action of the person. Apart from the reading of jurists, who are concerned to derive juridical norms which form an Islamic Law (Shariah) applicable to all, learned commentaries have had hardly any influence on common belief and individual reception of the Quran, which is more bound up with emotional ties, subjective expectations and group constraints on the expression of personal identity than with any learned exegetical explanations. Memorized verses are at the disposal of all and are invoked spontaneously, without any concern for the original context, to utter a prayer, to give thanks, to meditate on the inner equivalence between a situation as experienced and its beautiful, concise, eternally true expression in the Word of the Most High. The person, as a human being faced with the vicissitudes of existence, constructs himself, blossoms out or else founders in alienation, according to his degree of nearness to Quranic discourse in general (millions of Muslims do not know Arabic and, even among Arabic speakers, most do not have access to the archaic form of the Quranic language), and according to the use he makes of scattered texts, knitted into the here and now of daily existence.

We may note once more the relevance of the concept of 'prophetic discourse', which allows these analyses to be applied to all persons formed within the framework of identity associated with the long tradition of the teaching of the prophets from Abraham to Muhammad, a tradition expressed linguistically in the same discourse of mythic structure, and exploiting the same religious symbolic, the same metaphorical organization, to bring about 'the man of the Alliance' with a Living, Speaking God, One Who acts within earthly history so as to enrich and broaden, in terms of a benevolent pedagogy, the reciprocity of the perspectives man–God and God–man. Thanks to the revelational richness of 'prophetic discourse', man raises himself to the dignity of person through interiorizing God as an inner protagonist, with the help of prayer, thanksgiving and a meditative deciphering of all the signs (*ayat*) of creation and of that mark of Benevolent Care whereby man is singled out among all creatures to receive the heavy responsibility of directing a just order as 'God's deputy on earth'. All this leads to the emergence of a 'consciousness of self' in relation to the Absolute of a God Who is the ultimate Criterion and inevitable Referent for all the various activities of the 'person-creature'. The change to be wrought by modernity to this mode of the awakening and realization of consciousness of self will lie in a moving on from the 'person-creature' of God, bound to Him by a debt of sense and a loving acceptance of His commandments, to the 'person-individual-citizen', bound to the state by a social and juridical contract.

III. From the Quranic fact to the Islamic fact and 'modern identity'

There is no chronological succession between these three historical and cultural facts, especially when we bear in mind that modernity is less a matter of periodizing the history of thought than a problem of the *posture* of reason before the question: how can I gain adequate knowledge of the real, and, if I arrive at this knowledge, how can I communicate it without alienating the consciousness of self in any recipient? There is no room here to consider the analyses and historical restatements demanded by this definition of modernity (I have treated these at greater length in the second edition of my *Critique de la Raison Islamique*). The 'Quranic fact', the 'Islamic fact' and the emergence of a modern 'posture' of reason coexist at every stage of the history of thought, with interactions, educative tensions and frontal oppositions that are more or less fruitful or negative according to the particular contexts or ages involved. To set out these complex and evolving connections clearly would require a comparative history of these three poles of meaning and action, which engage the destiny of the person differently within Islamic, Christian, Jewish, Buddhist, Hindu or secularized modern contexts. We are a long way from this – so much does the European viewpoint on modern thought impose its periodization, its categorizations, its subject matter and its segmentation of the real, which is thereby transformed into unassailable paradigms of knowledge.

For the case of 'Islam' the dialectic of the 'Quranic fact' and the 'Islamic fact' remains to be defined. It supposes, indeed, the redefinition of the 'Quranic fact' *this side* of all the theological, juridical, mystical, literary and historiographical expansions essentially arising from the 'Islamic fact', which is itself indissociable from appropriations from a Quran recited, read and experienced as a closed official corpus in response to the double demand of the state-styled Islamic and the interpreting community which links its earthly destiny and eternal salvation to what it calls, indifferently, the Word of God, Revelation or the Quran.

At the stage of the 'Quranic fact', God presents Himself to man in a discourse articulated in the Arabic language; He sets Himself to perceive, to receive, to listen as the Person *par excellence*, possessing a fullness of fundamental attributes whose acquisition is only effectively possible for man through what mystics and philosophers have long called *ta'alluh*, 'the imitation of God'. Man must strive to attain the level of perfection embodied by this God Who reveals Himself in order to guide man in the realization of this essential Desire – the celebrated *'ishq*, that powerful motive for the moral, spiritual and intellectual search for the status of person (or, as it was known, Perfect Man, *al-Insan al-kamil*). 'Prophetic discourse' was the inexhaustible spring wherein the saints, the friends of God, the servants of God, the great witnesses to the spiritual found the living metaphors, the fruitful symbols, the organizing myths of their experience of the divine. It crosses the history of societies and cultures; it holds aloof from all partisan political commitments not based on 'true religion' (the problems posed by this concept were to be taken up by philosophic modernity but not definitively resolved), and leans, above all, on the trusting search, the search devotedly concerned with the greatest possible nearness to the Altogether Other and with the spiritual witness perpetuated, for men, by virtue of this search's unshakeable value.

The 'Islamic fact' retains and exploits this dimension of the 'Quranic fact' as a space of sacralization, of spiritualization, of transcendentalization, of ontologization, of mythologization, of ideologization of all the doctrinal schemes, all the juridical, ethical and cultural codes, all the systems of legitimation set in place by the social actors. The 'Islamic fact', like the Christian, Jewish, Buddhist fact, or any other, cannot be dissociated from the exercise of political power, in that the state, in all its historical forms, attempts to direct for its own benefit the spiritual dimension joined to the 'Quranic fact', while the latter's modes of presence in the 'Islamic fact' (notably ethical and juridical codes) resist any total, irreversible annexation. It is the high moments and most pertinent areas of this ongoing tension that witness the affirmations, the protests, the resistance by those most conscious of the recurrent factors of a confrontation complicated by the claims of 'modern identity' as defined by Charles Taylor in his *Sources of the Self: The Making of Modern Identity* (H.U.P., 1996).

It is to the 'Islamic fact' that we must link the development and historical action of what is called Muslim law, especially on that side of it applied as positive law (*fiqh*); in practice the role of 'Quranic fact' boils down to operations of sacralization, indeed of divinization, of corpora of norms that have become religious Law (Shariah). We are more aware, now, that the formation of the juridical schools (*madhahib*) continued up to the tenth century; and it was from the ninth century that the work of sacralization came to be seen as a religious necessity, to restrict the infiltration of local customs and practices. The inroads 'prophetic discourse' attempted to make with regard to the juridical emancipation of the person have been only partially successful, either in time or space, since parental solidarities continue to this day to weigh on the modern construction of the social bond and on the emergence of a civil society, a de jure state and the personal-individual-citizen as interactive actors in the historical march toward intellectual, spiritual and political modernity, all linked indissolubly together. I have given a particularly enlightening example of the manipulations of Quranic discourse itself, by jurists anxious to circumvent provisions considered too subversive for the customary order that preserved the force of patriarchal and clan solidarities in those key ethno-cultural areas where the power of the new Islamic state, first Umayyad then Abbasid, was exercised.[3]

After the triumph of what I have called the 'closed official corpus', Islamic Tradition ratified all the *faits accomplis* of exegesis and of the *corpora juris* accepted as orthodox. For this reason one cannot, today, either return to an open Quranic corpus or easily liberate the person from the kinds of status defined in that part of private law called personal status, *al-ahwal al-shakhsiyya*. The *fait accompli* of the closed official corpus is indeed historically irreversible – unless we can discover *mus-hafs* contemporary to the first official *mus-haf* – and the *corpora juris* declared orthodox continue to be perceived and experienced by the community of believers as juridical categorizations (*ahkam*) correctly derived from Quranic verses.

In the light of these explanations, we may better appreciate the need to rediscover what I venture to call 'spiritual responsibility', as a means of resistance, on the part of the human spirit, against the operations of reason itself as the latter works with the 'unthinkables' and 'unthoughts' of each sociocultural milieu and each historical period. I know that the concept of spirituality is difficult to apply credibly within a scientific thought which stresses the alienating functions of religion and a positivist explanation of man. It is because I recognize the need for a revaluation – historical, sociological, anthropological and philosophical – of the spiritual dimension of the human person that I propose the notion of 'spiritual responsibility' as a licensed field of research with a view to rehabilitating and reactualizing a concern lost as much in Islamic thought as in modern thought: the ethic of the person. I shall proceed with this heuristic definition in mind: *for the human spirit, to assume a spiritual responsibility means to provide itself with all the means, and to place itself at all times in the necessary conditions, so as to resist all operations (once these latter have been duly identified) which aim to alienate it, enslave it, mutilate it or mislead one or several of its faculties in an attempt to achieve an end contrary to what makes it the seat, the agent and the irreducible sign of the eminent dignity of the human person.*

An application of this definition to the concept of person as sanctioned by the law of the *fuqaha'* will allow us to detect the limits of status as found in the whole medieval mental space up to the sudden emergence of juridical modernity; a juridical modernity made possible by progress in scientific and philosophical thought on the human being. In Muslim law, the full-blown status of person is reserved for the orthodox Muslim who is male, free (as opposed to being a slave) and juridically fitted to respect the rights of God and human rights (*mukallaf*). Children, slaves and non-Muslims are potentially fitted to gain access to this status (the child when it reaches the age of responsibility, the slave when freed, the non-Muslim when converted); woman, however, while raised to a spiritual dignity equal to that of man, is kept to an inferior ritual and juridical status, since the Quran itself did not succeed in lifting all the taboos and restrictions weighing on the female condition in what it called the *jahiliyya*. It is a historical fact that all religions have perpetuated not only unthinkables and unthoughts with respect to the spiritual and juridical status of the human person, but also sacralized forms of religious status which continue, even now, to feed exclusions, schisms, inquisitions, persecutions, 'sacred' violence, claims, conquests in the name of a God Whom living traditions have, in fact, linked arbitrarily to mechanical solidarities, to strategies of power, to all the constraints of the 'imaginary production' of societies. Modernity may have abolished slavery, may have opened a space of citizenship in which distinctions between faiths are disregarded; but it has not yet finished the slow work of emancipation of the female condition and of the protection of the rights of the child.

It should be added that the theologies of 'true religion' (i.e., *din al-haqq* – this is a Quranic concept but Biblical too, taken up and developed by the three monotheistic religions up to Hegel, who attempted to give it a philosophical status) continue to disseminate their teachings and to bear down on the frontiers of the thinkable and unthinkable with regard to the status of the person. For its part, philosophical and scientific thought is less concerned to integrate the postures of theological thought and religious beliefs into its field of critical enquiry, in order to evaluate their precise scope and present functions, than to legitimize its own options and make them prevail. Even in the most secularized societies, the competition remains open between a humanism centred on God, on Whom man's salvation depends in this world and the next, and a humanism centred exclusively on man. We may note that the first borrows more from the second, than the second from the first; but we should add that the second is increasingly distancing itself from the classic notion of humanism, as the 'teletechno-scientific reason' (J. Derrida) driving on the processes of globalization asserts its hegemony over the theological and philosophical stages of reason. The status of the person thus finds itself fought over from several points of reference, ancient, traditional or new, while current debates or social scientific research fail to provide all the necessary enlightenment.

In contemporary Islamic contexts, the crisis for the status of the person is still more difficult to deal with. The rules of fraternity, solidarity and respect for the life and goods of persons, already so persistently harped on in the Quran, then in the whole living Tradition (*turath*), are 'applied' with tragic rigour in the generalized context of national and international terrorism. I prefer to abstain from any comment on a phenomenon which throws into crisis every form and every system of legitimation, old and new; we are dealing with terrorism

everywhere presented as the only path left for a human group to attain or re-
attain 'identities' wrested by other hegemonic groups or powers. The various
persecutions imposed by the inquisitions at the time of theological certainty
have been taken up today, with the same sense of conscious justification, by the
terrorist phenomenon. In both cases it will be noted that the conflict of interpretations rests on the same, still surviving contradiction: innocent persons are
physically done down so that the self-proclaimed rights of other persons can be
vindicated. We are not really concerned here with the political movements, the
ideological shifts, the clans and factions and ideals and causes, which lead to
such a radical negation of the human person; before a phenomenon so constant
throughout history, any political stance not preceded by a precise commitment,
religious or philosophical, aimed at the protection of the human person in so far
as this is tied in with the destiny of the human condition itself, will imply indefinite acceptance of the principle of war, as the sole means of installing the legitimacy which will subsequently ensure the emancipation of the person!

These trajectories, and frameworks of realization, of the human person continue to impose themselves in Islamic contexts, in that the application of the
'Quranic fact' to the functioning of the state has become radicalized over the
past 20 years; radicalized in the names of Islam and Islamic Law, according to
the terminology of militants, fundamentalism, integrationism, Islamism, political Islam – to the terminology of 'politologues'. Not only is the distinction
between Quranic fact and Islamic fact, outlined above, unthinkable, but the
terms 'Islam' and 'Islamic Law' come to denote, indistinctly, a populist brand
of theological axiology, ritualizations of collective behaviour, principles of
political commitment, militant practices observed with the same ritual punctil-
iousness as religious obligations in the proper sense. We have, in this way, a
complete system, sociologically and psychologically most efficient, for the formation of a new human being who views himself as radically and authentically
Muslim, bearer of the one true message of salvation for all mankind, responsible for the historical action necessary to block the devilish forces of modernization and secularization. Here are the lines of force of what I called, just
above, a populist brand of theological axiology. This terminology is dictated
neither by a theological reason, more intellectually trustworthy, to which future
reference would need to be made, nor by a philosophical or scientific reason
laying claim to a role of absolute normative authority. It is merely a matter of
broaching a typology of the social actors, of the kinds of discourse they produce, of regimes embodying truth, which they seek to make firm through political, juridical and economic institutions. I indicated earlier that populist culture,
along with the theological axiology it conveys, has already led to political

successes that make a mockery, in any substantial sociological or psychological sense, of what is called learned culture, of the postures of philosophical and scientific reason. This inversion of 'values' – spiritual, moral and intellectual on the one hand, political, economic and technological on the other – has been an incontrovertible datum of the history of thought, and therefore of the conditions within which the human being is formed and develops, since 'material civilization' in the historical Braudelian sense of the term first imposed its hegemony on the world.

We should consider in more detail the lapidary content and cognitive status of this populist brand of theological axiology. In this way we shall better measure the sociological extension of the concept of populist culture as I am trying to treat it here.

I shall start from a remarkable series broadcast by the Qatari al-Jazira television network under the general title *Al-Shariah wa 'l-hayat*. The guest on the evening of 28 December 1997, was Professor 'Adnan Zarzur, the author of a number of learned works on Islamic thought. He gave a concise, perfectly orthodox definition, one accepted by all contemporary Muslims, of the theological status of the Quran and of the procedures whereby all its verses are interpreted so as not only to ground (*ta'sil*) the thoughts and behaviour of believers in the divine Word but to ensure the cognitive validity of all the divine statements vis-à-vis all forms of knowledge, present and future, up to the final Day of Judgement. As the ultimate manifestation of Revelation, the Quran has divided the history of salvation, which embodies our chronological history on earth, into a before and an after; after 632 the theologico-juridical status of every human act is defined according to the limits (*hudud*) fixed by God Himself in the legislative verses; the far more numerous verses speaking of the creation of worlds and beings are signs provided for the spiritual meditation and the reflection of believers so as to integrate, within their individual consciousness, the nature of the Being of God, the meanings of the actions He has undertaken and the everlasting scope of His teaching. Within this theological perspective, the term *turath*, used to denote the classical cultural patrimony bequeathed by what historians call the civilization of classical Islam, denotes more especially what Christian theology calls 'living Tradition': the sum of the sacred texts – Quran and *hadith* – authenticated by the old doctors, together with all the authorized interpretations of these texts, form the Divine Body of Authority (*al-marji'iyya*) to which every product of human activity on earth must be referred, so as to determine its theologico-juridical status according to the five categorizations (obligatory, forbidden, recommendable, reprehensible, permitted) of the Law. This referral of the whole of human history on earth to a Tribunal decreed divine – though those seated there have been men elevated to the rank of imams (for the Shi'ites) or doctors duly qualified after the event (*a'imma mujtahidin*) (for the Sunnis) – is to be continuously applicable till the Day earthly history is replaced by the History of Salvation.

There is, in this formulation, an undeniable inner coherence which satisfies a kind of reason indivisible from what anthropologists call the social imaginary. The reason invoked in the course of theological enquiry is indifferent to all the reasonings of the human and social sciences; on the other hand, it is highly attentive and stringent regarding all the discursive operations made necessary by the collection and authentification of the official corpora it will pronounce closed. Once the process of dogmatic closure has been achieved, this same reason will, for the protection and everlasting preservation of the 'faith', use the ready-prepared arsenal of axiological postures, methodological practices, argumentative proceedings, rhetorical forms, and strategies of selection, insertion, rejection and total destruction of facts prior to and following on from the time of closure. Thenceforth, what the human and social sciences will call 'representations', or images each individual or collective subject possesses of itself, will dwell within the sphere of the unthinkable. It can be seen how the unthinkable and the unthought trace here a line of psychological cleavage between two mental configurations structured by two cognitive practices which, once systematized, permit the reproduction of two differentiated frameworks of the formation and development of the person.

I do not know how far Professor Zarzur would share these analyses, which, it will be seen, endeavour to problematize the two concurrent cognitive practices, and try never to affirm, even implicitly in the handling of concepts, the primacy of one or the other. I am speaking, alternately, the language of the social sciences and that of dogmatic theological reason, so as to transfer both alike to a cognitive practice whose legitimacy and productiveness will appear as this confrontation develops. The dogmatic posture makes no corresponding concession to concurrent kinds of discourse. Thus, in his presentation of theological axiology through a powerful media outlet, even someone like Professor Zarzur consigned to silence all discussions set up between the multiple schools before the closure of the official corpora and the construction of an orthodox *turath* – on the strength of which he gives a warning at once theological and 'scientific' to the regime of religious truth as such a regime functions for millions of Muslims throughout the world (a good many listeners to the series take part in the discussion from Europe). This is a measure of the sociological dimension, political weight and historical scope of what I have called the populist brand of theological axiology.

What turn might the programme – or rather the very numerous pro-grammes in the same style – have taken if Professor Zarzur, or any other teacher and scholar of his caliber, had had opposite him an advocate of the (still largely utopian) project of a *critique of Islamic reason* such as I have been working on in all my writings since the 1970s? The problem would be posed of *commu-nicability* between the two mental configurations and the cognitive systems they generate and reproduce; and, if communication proved possible to the fullest extent, then the unthinkables and the unthoughts accumulated on the two sides would be integrated, examined within a necessarily new space of the thinkable; reason, imagination, the imaginary, memory would receive other statuses, would enter another psychological configuration, and so give birth to new regimes embodying what continues, globally, to be called truth. I stress, with sadness, that neither the Western media nor those of Muslim countries, nor the universities, nor the research institutions, think to organize, encourage and multiply activities which would hasten the emergence of a new human being.

While awaiting a time when this utopia should be accorded an initial con-crete realization, we must explain why the dominant Islamic discourse has taken on such broad proportions and mobilizes so many fervent militants. I shall simply, here, enumerate the most decisive factors. Among the internal factors we may note: the demographic growth which has considerably broad-ened, over a short period, the sociological bases of a social imaginary fed at once by a nationalist discourse of anti-colonial fight and an Islamist discourse regarding the 'refounding' of an 'identity' betrayed by secularized 'elites'; the use of the media and public education for the purposes of ideological condi-tioning by one party states that are voluntarist, militarist and without demo-cratic culture; the recourse to a policy of 'traditionalization' aggravating the split between the modern and the 'religious' construction of the human being; the uprooting of peasant or nomad populations, who flock to the cities where traditional customary and cultural codes disintegrate, giving birth, instead, to a *populist* social imaginary, cut off, at one and the same time, from the urban elites and from those witnesses (increasingly rare and marginalized) to an Islamic tra-dition concerned to obey the sole authority (*hukm*) of God and, as such, to be independent vis-à-vis every type of power. I make a distinction here between, on the one hand, *'ulama'* familiarized with the media, who lend their assistance to the policy of traditionalization and add their weight substantially to the 'pop-ulist' imaginary, and, on the other, intellectuals, teachers, scholars, essayists, writers and artists who strive in their respective spheres to introduce a modern culture of perception, interpretation and creative interaction between a reconsidered Islamic tradition and a self-critical modernity. Unfortunately this latter current of thought and action exists only precariously, since its proponents are dispersed through the world, far from the sociological terrains now virtually abandoned to the mechanical forces of the factors enumerated above.

The external factors comprise, basically, the continuous pressures of economic and technological modernity on all those societies which have never taken part, at any stage, in the production and direction of this modernity. All the political 'elites' who have assumed control in these societies since the 1950s have taken immediate steps to ensure the acquisition of *power* in the practical sense of the term (through military disciplines, police networks for the control of the whole national territory, heavy industry and technological tools) over the development of the means of search for *sense*. The imbalance created by this policy has been aggravated all the more rapidly in that modernity has accelerated the rhythms of change in all fields of the historical production of societies. Thus it is that historical research on the past of each society is the most urgent kind of research, to restrict and correct the excesses of ideological manipulation – and also the most neglected. The perverse effects of material modernity continue to feed global rejections of modernity as a project of liberation for the human condition, while the legitimate needs of a vast population demand, everywhere, a recourse to modern means of production and exchange. The internal and external factors do not act separately; rather, the historical dialectic of the forces of modernity has a multiplicatory effect on the increasingly ungovernable play of all the factors.

I have, I hope, sufficiently shown how the 'Quranic fact', the 'Islamic fact' and 'modern identity' face one another, challenge one another and exclude one another, how they condition one another in their expressions and in their struggles for survival or hegemony. I have, I hope, sufficiently pointed out the gaping chasm that separates the respective protagonists advocating open competition between the model called Islamic and the Western model in producing the history of mankind for the third millennium. It remains to set down the resources and present orientations whereby 'modern identity' seeks to open the road to a solidary history of mankind, to put an end to the cultural and intellectual systems of reciprocal exclusion which continue to legitimize civil wars, structural violence, systems of inequality and hegemonic conquests, under the pretext of historical necessities of globalization.

'Modern identity' is a historical datum as massive, and as broadly encompassing in its definitions and applications, as 'religious identity' in its various realizations. And this is why they contend for the privilege of leading man toward his 'true' salvation. It should be clear by now that my position in the face of this age-old rivalry, marked by wars and costly revolutions, can be summed up in three verbs: *infringe, displace, transcend*. I have described at length the methodological and epistemological scope of these three cognitive operations as applied to the writing of the history of societies fashioned by the 'Islamic fact'; I refer the reader to the relevant study in *ARABICA* (1, 1996). I note that Christian theology is witnessing significant moves toward the displacement and transcendence of questions and solutions bequeathed by a two-millennium-old practice of living Tradition whose frontiers are now infringed. I am thinking especially of Father J. Dupuy's recent work *Vers une théologie chrétienne du pluralisme religieux* (Editions Cerf, 1997). The interest of this orientation of religious thought in the face of the fruitful or arrogant challenges posed by 'modern identity' lies in its demonstration of the possibility and promise of a systematic problematization of the two identities by one another. We should not forget that the reason of the Enlightenment has liberated us from what Voltaire called a 'wild beast' (dogmatic theological reason utilized by a Church-institution having power over souls and bodies). But this reason has, by the same token, ratified recourse to the violence of war to impose a new political legitimacy — a historical fact which is not without bearing on the barbarous instances of violence in the nineteenth and twentieth centuries and on what I have said about 'modern' terrorism. The establishment of the revolutionary violence of the modern political symbolic, in place of the religious symbolic now declared obsolete, has driven back into the 'darkness of the Middle Ages', that is, into ignorance, the unthought, and indeed the unthinkable, about numerous questions of an anthropological and philosophical nature. The return of God, following the vaunted declaration of His death, must mean not a return to mythologized 'values' and phantasmatical visions of the 'perfect man', but the opening of new spaces of scientific intelligibility and surer paths for the emancipation of the human condition.

I shall conclude this critical investigation by bringing to attention one of those new paths that neither religious thought nor modern thought has explored in any exhaustive and pertinent way: I mean the fundamental and permanent bonds between the three underlying productive forces of all human existence: *violence, sacredness* and *truth*. I am well aware that countless meditations, sermons, exhortations, analyses and inquiries have been devoted to these three themes in every tradition of thought; nor am I ignorant of the contributions made by contemporary anthropology and psycho-analysis; and R. Girard has, I know, reflected on the link between violence, sacredness and the response proposed by Christianity. But there still remains much to be done in this direction. In an earlier study[4] I broached the problem of what St. Augustine calls the 'just war' and the Quran *jihad* – a notion taken up once more by the Western countries allied against Iraq during the Gulf War. Throughout the history of humanity people have invoked the just war, the sacred struggle to protect the superior interests of a 'Truth' assailed by 'enemies' external to it: the defence or expansion of Christian territory, of the *Dar al-Islam*, of the modern capitalist nation states, of colonized regions, of the geopolitical spheres of the great powers. I have analyzed at length a text by Muhammad 'Abd al-Salam Faraj entitled 'The Absent Canonical Obligation' (*Al-Farida 'l-gha'iba*), showing how the author's efforts to reactivate the obligation of *jihad* within a majority Muslim society – Sadat's Egypt – and more generally within the *umma* as a whole, so as to vindicate exclusively the warring and terrorist face of *jihad*, runs counter to all the teachings of the Islamic Tradition on the dignity of the human person. This study, like so many others that have nevertheless been translated into Arabic, has found no significant echo either among intellectuals or within enlightened Muslim opinion. As for the Western public, it naturally prefers to reinforce its own imaginary about an Islam championing holy war against the infidels. So long as it is a question of confrontation, about a truth of self which each protagonist opposes to that of the other, without either side being prepared to reflect in depth on what such a truth of self actually implies, then the question of the human person is not on the agenda. The logic of war is rooted in the founding logic of truth of self. The culture in which these two logics can be brought out – logics which refer to the same processes for the construction of the human being – is not yet available even in those places most penetrated by 'modern identity'.

I realize the need to delve further and more deeply in the exploration of an Islamic consciousness not yet worked upon by the positive contributions of modernity. For this reason I have, for some years now, been working on an ambitious subject: *violence, sacredness and Truth according to sura 9, Al-Tawba*. Indeed, we cannot continue to invoke formal kinds of humanism taught by the great religious and philosophical texts while treating violence as a manifestation which is exceptional, which simply happens to occur within archaic societies, or imperfectly integrated sections of civilized societies, or wayward individuals who are immediately condemned or brushed aside in the name of a dominant morality and an effective law. Violence is an inherent aspect of the human being; there are always, within each person, quite strong and recurrent tensions between impulses to violence and aspirations toward the Good, the Beautiful, the True. Verse 2, *Al-Baqara*, 251, quoted earlier, provides a very simple reminder of this double face of man. In his attempts to check the ravages of violence, man has long had recourse to what is still called the 'sacred', referring things to a substantial reality endowed with effective powers, when it is really rather a matter of rituals and procedures of sacralization aimed at shielding beings, places and temporal sequences from profanation and sacrilege through violence. Sacrifices are instituted to turn the effects of violence toward a category of human being, toward a part of the human body, toward animals or natural elements. Thus functional and notional bonds are woven between *violence, sacredness and Truth* – just as clearly stated in verse 9, *Al-Tawba*, 5 quoted earlier. Only an anthropological reading of these three forces will lay bare the hidden mechanisms which are still at work on the consciousness of the group, the community and the nation, still demanding the integration of each member. This objectivication of interactions between realities still being posed and experienced as powers external to man simultaneously shows the person moving on to a new stage of knowledge and realization of self.

The struggles for respect for the rights of man, woman and child are joined within every country and every regime where Islam, Islamic Tradition and Shariah remain points of reference impossible to bypass. The spiritual, moral and cultural fullness of the person can be ensured only by way of a democratic regime, a de jure state, monarchical or republican according to the history of each country, and a civil society recognized as a partner from whom the sovereignty of the state derives. It has been conclusively shown, since the 1950s, that movement toward these institutions is more conditioned by the acquisition and diffusion of a *culture of democracy* than by material prosperity, which nevertheless remains a trump card when managed with the democratic participation of all the social actors. I have shown the decisive role played by the philosophical postulates which, implicitly or explicitly, govern all religious, juridical, moral and political thought. For this reason I would maintain that there is no viable democracy without debates among open, free, fruitful, critical societies; and these debates cannot attain the humanist aims of democracy unless they integrate philosophical interrogation at some level. We know the extent to which the dogmatic religious attitude excludes philosophical concern; and we are familiar too with the weakness, or often total absence, of the teaching of philosophy in the educative systems set in place by post-colonial regimes. If we add to this the total absence, everywhere, of a teaching of theology founded on a critique of theological reason, we shall clearly appreciate the kind of educative programme that should be set up as a matter of urgency, to create the modern intellectual and cultural conditions for the emergence and optimum development of the person in Islamic contexts.

Chapter 3: Obedience and disagreement in the context of human rights in Islam

Fahmi Jad'an

Introduction

The concepts of obedience (*ta'a*) and disagreement (*ikhtilaf*) lie at the heart of the Islamic theoretical and practical system. Indeed, our view of this system cannot be balanced and complete unless we recognize the significance of these two concepts, which need to be re-examined in the light of Islam itself and of ideological developments worldwide.

Obedience and disagreement move between two principal poles, with right (*haq*) at one end and duty (*wajib*) at the other. In the overall Islamic system, they are linked both to abstract doctrinal issues and to political philosophy.

Obedience is not a right of man as a member of the community. It is rather a right of three parties: God, the Prophet, and those charged with authority. The last-named, for practical purposes, comprise the state; specifically, the political authorities as represented by the imam or equivalent ruler. Yet, if obedience is a right belonging to these parties, it is a duty on members of the community – as human beings answerable to God and subject to His laws – which cannot simply be shrugged off.

Disagreement, on the other hand, is a right of man, in his capacity as a member of the community holding a certain belief that will normally dictate a certain kind of behaviour. Affirmation of the two principles of obedience and disagreement is not, nevertheless, an unconditional and absolute matter. Everything happens in conjunction with conditions, limitations and checks.

I.

Human society in Islam stems from the basic axiom that authoritative deterrents are an imperative condition for this society. The axiom was summed up by al-Ghazali in his statement, first, that 'authority is a prerequisite for the system of religion, and that the secular order is also a prerequisite for the system of religion,' and, second, that 'the system of religion cannot be accomplished without the secular order, and the latter cannot be accomplished without an imam who commands obedience'.[1] Ibn Khaldoun also supported this principle,[2] which had been represented in Islamic orthodox and juristic tradition by the idea that it was necessary to install an 'obeyed imam'. Faith is, undoubtedly, a necessary precondition for this Islamic social life, but it is not sufficient in itself. What guarantees the success and integrity of this socio-political enterprise, which is grounded in faith, is a strong political authority. This goal cannot, however, be attained without the just policy stipulated, according to writers on the rules of political government and on legal policy, by the relevant Quranic verses:

> God doth command you to render back your Trusts to those to whom they are due; and when ye judge between man and man, that ye judge with justice: verily how excellent is the teaching which He giveth you! For God is He Who heareth and seeth all things. O ye who believe! Obey God, and obey the Apostle, and those charged with authority among you. If ye differ in anything among yourselves, refer it to God and His Apostle, if ye do believe in God and the Last Day: That is best, and most suitable for final determination. (4, *Al-Nisa'*, 58–9)

This text brings together a cluster of basic concepts, in the forefront of which is the concept of obedience. The text raises no problems regarding obedience to God and the Prophet; what is intended here, clearly, is obedience to God's commands and prohibitions as stated in the Quran, and observance of the Prophet's proven tradition. Many questions, nevertheless, have been raised regarding obedience to 'those charged with authority'.

Foremost among the questions is this: Is such obedience imperative in all circumstances and under all conditions? In other words, does the Muslim have the 'right' to dissent from this obedience and disobey the authorities, so breaking the cycle of absolute compliance and endangering the unity and survival of the community? Further, if renunciation of obedience is admissible, in what sense is it so?

The Prophet, as quoted by Anas ibn Malik, told Muslims: 'Listen and obey, even if you are ruled by a black Abyssinian slave.' And Abu Hurayra quoted this saying of the Prophet: 'Whoever obeys me obeys God, and whoever disobeys me disobeys God; whoever obeys the ruler obeys me, and whoever disobeys the ruler disobeys me.'[3]

Third in importance – after the Quranic text and the Prophet's sayings – comes a statement made by the second caliph, 'Umar ibn al-Khattab: 'There is no Islam with no community [of believers], and there is no community with no ruler, and there is no ruler with no obedience.' The Companion of the Prophet 'Ubada ibn al-Samit is related as having said: 'We pledged obedience to the Prophet in good times and bad, in approved and forbidden matters, and not to dispute with those in authority, and to witness to the truth in any circumstances, not fearing admonition in obedience to God.'[4] Finally, the Companion 'Abd Allah ibn 'Umar wrote to 'Abd al-Malik ibn Marwan, in acknowledging him as Caliph: 'I pledge obedience to you according to the commands of God and the tradition of the Prophet, as far as it is in my power to do so.'[5]

Obedience, then, is a right of those in authority, and it is a duty enjoined on subjects. Al-Mawardi said of this: 'If the imam acts in accordance with the nation's rights that I have mentioned, he will have fulfilled God's rights in what they owe and in what they are entitled to; the ruler is then entitled to two kinds of right, obedience and support, unless his condition alters.'[6] Caliphs and other rulers held fast to their right to obedience, invoking the text, the concept of the 'unified nation' and avoidance of discord and division. In this they were supported by the 'ideologues' who subscribed to Prophetic tradition and enlisted themselves among the followers of the 'righteous ancestors' (al-salaf al-salih) or the followers of the sunna and community (ahl al-sunna wa 'l-jama'a).

The consensus was that obedience to those in authority was a duty. Some, indeed, pushed the matter to the limits, invoking a hadith quoted by Ibn 'Abbas: 'Whoever disapproves of a ruler's behaviour, let him bear it patiently; for whoever breaks ranks with the community, even by a handspan, will die like an unbeliever.'[7]

Although the Sunni system places considerable emphasis on the principle of justice as enjoined on the ruler, it nevertheless waives this principle in a limited number of situations. A good example of this is the saying ascribed to 'Amr ibn al-As, governor of Egypt during the caliphates of 'Uthman and Mu'awiya: 'An oppressive imam is better than a long-lasting discord.'[8] He justified this principle by citing the exigencies of security, stability and the unity of the nation. The viewpoint became part of Sunni belief and a main principle of their theory of the state. This can be seen in the works of al-Tartoushi, al-Mawardi, al-Ghazali, Ibn Jama'a, Ibn Taymiyya and others, where we read such statements as the following: 'The injustice of a ruler for forty years is better than a nation neglected for an hour'; 'an eternity of injustice is better than an hour of upheaval'; or 'an unjust ruler for sixty years is better than one night with no ruler.' Here again, of course, the justification is fear of discord and its evils, and the maintenance of the nation's unity and survival.

Nonetheless, such obedience which is the ruler's right and the subjects' duty has been questioned, or at least restricted, by some people; this is in fact an old viewpoint, based by some on the very Quranic verse (4, *Al-Nisa'*, 59) that calls for obedience. Such people noted that the verse clearly waives obedience to the ruler in case of dispute, when the matter is referred to God and His Prophet, that is, to the religious text. In justification of this stance, they cite the incident when the Umayyad rulers asked one of the Companions: 'Did God not command you to obey us through the expression "and those charged with authority"?' The Companion replied: 'Is obedience not waived if you refuse justice, in the text: "If ye differ in anything among yourselves, refer it to God and His Apostle, if ye do believe in God and the Last Day"?'[9]

Al-Hasan al-Basri indicated that 'the orders of the Commander of the Faithful are to be judged by God's Book; if they are found to be in agreement with it, they are to be followed; otherwise, they are to be discarded'. He further believed that obedience is due first to God, and that 'no obedience is due to anyone in disobedience to God'. Ibn Hanbal, for his part, stated as a matter of faith that 'jihad [is incumbent] under every caliph, whether he is beneficent or unjust; and perseverance [is incumbent] under the ruler's banner, be he just or oppressive. We should not rise in arms against the rulers even if they are oppressive.'[10] Hanbal ibn Ishaq affirmed, according to Ahmad, that 'it is not in the *sunna* doctrine to rise in arms against your imam'; and that 'whoever breaks ranks with the community, even by a handspan, he will die like an unbeliever'.[11] Similarly, Abu Ahmad al-Tahawi believed people had a duty to pray behind the devout and the iniquitous alike, and did not believe in raising a sword against any followers of the Prophet Muhammad, except when sanctioned by religious precepts. He did not, moreover, support 'dissent against our imams and those in authority, even when they practise injustice. Nor should we invoke [from God] evil against them, or disobey them; we should consider obedience to them part of obedience to God and a duty enjoined on us, unless they order us to disobey God's commands. We should pray to God that they be reformed and that they be healed'. Al-Tahawi further advised people 'to walk with the *sunna* and the community and avoid dissension, disagreement and discord'. Unity, he said, 'is just and right, and dissension is unjust and leads to suffering'.[12] As for cases subject to dispute, these 'ideologues' refer to the rest of the Quranic verse: 'If ye differ in anything among yourselves, refer it to God and His Apostle.' In this, there is a limitation on the authority of rulers and on the legitimacy of their commands.

In fact, the drawing of such limits occurs not only in disputes among believers, but also in some situations where there is a link between obedience and the ability to obey. However, the most serious case where it becomes a duty to suspend obedience to those in authority, stripping them of this right and absolving subjects from it as a matter of duty, is when the ruler 'orders [them] to commit wrongdoing'. Obedience to those in authority is a binding duty 'unless they order a wrongdoing, which annuls obedience'. The *hadith* anthologists Muslim and al-Bukhari both included, in their collections of 'authentic *hadith*s', a section on 'the incumbency of obedience to rulers except in cases of wrongdoing'.

For all that, the prevalent tendency in the past, among Sunnis and advocates of the *sunna* and community, was to call on people to give sound counsel to rulers rather than rising in arms against them and so causing discord. This stands in contrast to the violent confrontational approach adopted by the Dissenters, the Mu'tazilis and the religious leaders of the Zaydis and Shi'ites – as long as the Imam remained absent – in accordance with the principle of commanding what is righteous and preventing wrongdoing.[13] It accords, on the other hand, with the definitive principle formulated by Abu 'l-Hasan al-Ash'ari, who said that 'the sword is wrong, even if people are killed and the offspring are abducted; and the imam may be just or unjust, but we cannot remove him even if he is corrupt. They [the Sunni jurists] rejected rebellion against the ruler.'[14] This view finds contemporary expression in the views of the prominent Sunni scholar Muhammad Sa'id Ramadan al-Bouti, who comments as follows:

> The imam is the guardian of matters regarding all believers; he is therefore the guardian of every person who has no guardian. Thus his actions respecting their affairs are dependent on the common good. That is, his actions cannot be considered valid unless they serve people's well-being. God has commanded people to obey the ruler because of this guardianship which he holds, and which is based on the common good and the effort to attain this wherever possible. Their obedience to the ruler is not, in other words, because he holds sovereignty over them; obedience is simply their means of enabling him to accomplish the public interest and of facilitating his efforts to coordinate, with them, the interests of the individuals concerned. They are, therefore, not bound to obey a ruler who burdens them with excesses and requires of them duties from which they derive no benefit. But the legislator takes into account the discords and great harm that might result from their refusal to obey him in every matter not sanctioned by God or in any affairs in which they have no interest. These discords and evils, which might spring from their disobedience, are undoubtedly far more harmful and dangerous to them – in general – than the harm that would come to them from obeying his orders.[15]

The viewpoint of those calling for obedience, whether ancient or modern, can be summed up in the principle that obedience and avoidance of armed dissension are the natural behaviour of the Muslim as a member of an Islamic community governed by an administration based on Islam and its laws. This Muslim's right to dispute the state's authority is an undesirable one, even when we take into account the text commanding disobedience in the case of wrong-doing ordered by the imam, ruler, guardian or the state. This does not, even so, imply absolute consent and acceptance. 'Annulment of the sword' does not in fact mean annulment of other forms of protest or 'passive' rejection. History reveals many and various examples of such passive rejection, which have come very close to a form of civil disobedience. One of these was 'silence' in the face of the ruler's wrongdoing. Another kind of civil resistance was seen in those who abstained from 'working with the ruler' or 'visiting royal persons'. And then there were those who resigned themselves to 'exercise patience under the ruler's reign' and 'retired from discord' or declared themselves in 'disagree-ment' till the Day of Judgement.

Such standpoints and situations are comparable to the situation of those al-Ghazali called 'the relentless in religion', who represented, in the history of the Islamic state, 'a parallel or combatant force' proclaiming overt struggle against the 'royal state'. Such groups strove to rise in arms or act through revolutionary secret organizations, for their own reasons or for reasons described by al-Hasan al-Basri:

> The best of my nation's martyrs is a man who confronted an oppressive ruler, ordered him to do good, enjoined him against wrongdoing, and was killed for this reason. He is indeed a true martyr, and his place in Heaven is between Hamza and Ja'far [uncles of the Prophet who were killed in the cause of religion].[16]

Such forces of protest, known to us from history books, have not disappeared with the passing of the classical ages. They have reappeared in modern times, especially in recent decades, in the guise of radical or fundamentalist Islamic groups or movements, which have pushed the principle of 'righting wrongs' to the extreme. They have not limited their protest to the heart and tongue, but have reached for the ultimate measure according to the Prophet's saying: 'Whosoever of you sees an evil action, let him change it with his hand; and if he is not able to do so, then with his tongue; and if he is not able to do so, then with his heart – and this is the weakest of faith.'[17] Movements of this kind have not been satisfied with a standpoint of obedience under coercion, or with passive resistance, the eschewal of discord or retirement. Instead, they have resorted to revolt and rising in arms.

From an examination of these various aspects of the question of obedience, we may conclude that obedience is in principle an undisputed duty to God, His

Prophet and those in authority. This principle represents the coercive, forceful aspect of the authority of the text on the one hand and of the state on the other. Yet the subject – the human being governed by the authorities – does have rights, some of them natural, others legal. Natural human right is linked to ability: obedience to God, the Prophet and the authorities is expected insofar as man is capable of offering it. Such an ability is dependent, naturally, on a group of principles which themselves rely on other aspects of the Islamic system of thought, such as the issue of justice, the principle of not assigning duties beyond people's ability, the compliance of the state, ruler or authorities with God, His Prophet and Shariah, and various other principles. Where these conditions are not met, renunciation of obedience, and mutiny and dissent, become legitimate standpoints and rights which man may practise. In other words, non-compliance by the ruler, the state or the authorities with God's rights and the rights of citizens – as detailed in works on rules of governance and on proper regulation[18] – leads directly to a human right, legally binding, which is the right to difference or disagreement.

II.

If obedience is a duty, then its opposite, disagreement, is a right. This does not, however, apply to any disagreement. It is rather specific to acts that lead to the public good, and does not, as such, fall under atheism or dissent. It should be noted, in this regard, that 'division' or 'desertion' (*iftiraq*) – a term used in classical Islam – is not a right; it is, on the contrary, a loathsome course of action to be avoided. 'Division' is associated with breaking away from the one true doctrine, and from the imam and the community. Such action is condemned in Prophetic *hadith*, which compares it to the divisions of Jews and Christians into many sects: 'My nation will be divided into over seventy factions, only one of which will be saved.' If we survey the 72 or 73 factions noted by historians of Islamic division, as reflected in this saying, we find the division to be based not only on ideology but on practical political issues too. As such, division is the thing likely to break the community's back, leading to disintegration and eventual failure.

This concept of 'division' can, however, be indicated by another term, 'disagreement' (*ikhtilaf*), which does not necessarily imply dissent from the parameters of Islam. Abu 'l-Hasan al-Ash'ari's *Islamic Discourses* contain a further part that he calls *Disagreement Among Worshippers*, which begins: 'After the Prophet, people disagreed over many matters, some misleading others, and they were divided into many different factions; yet, Islam brings them all together.'[19] Moreover, while the *hadith* of the 'one faction which will be saved' seems to imply that the others will not be saved, this *hadith* – as al-Ghazali, for one, pointed out – does not in fact mean 'they all end in hell eternally', but that 'they will be there for periods according to the degree of disobedience'.[20] As such, 'disagreement among worshippers' indicates variations in their adherence to the precepts of Islam.

While factional differences may give occasion for warning and condemnation, there is another kind of difference which all religious scholars have regarded as a 'mercy' for the nation. This is confirmed even by some Prophetic sayings, such as: 'Disagreement among my nation is [a source of] mercy.' This refers specifically to jurisprudential disagreement, which indicates differences in rulings and is linked to one of the sources of jurisprudence; in other words to *ijtihad*: independent legal reasoning, or, more specifically, interpretative opinion. Clearly, such activity is the starting point for the various legal doctrines in Islam. These differences and kinds of pluralism have been considered means of providing comfort and latitude for believers in their day-to-day worldly affairs. It is only to be expected, of course, that juridical interpreters will be sometimes right and sometimes wrong. Yet error, here, is not to be regarded as deviation from the right path, nor does it entail condemnation and penalty. On the contrary, the one who makes such a mistake is rewarded for his effort, though not to the same extent as the one who makes sound judgements. This, perhaps, is why jurisprudential differences, like jurisprudential schools, have been innumerable. Such a kind of disagreement might be termed 'merciful disagreement', and it is certainly the right of any Muslim who has the basic qualifications for interpretative judgement.

There is, however, a third kind of difference, whereby the concept of 'truth' becomes intricate and problematic, and which gives rise to doubt, misunderstanding and complexity. This is ideological disagreement, which, in Islam, has been linked to the believer's relationship with the two acts of 'faith' (*iman*) and 'Islam'; for, despite the distinctions made by dialecticians and jurists between the act of 'faith' and the act of 'Islam', each has clear reference to the other and can only be understood in the context of the other. The real difference, perhaps, is that the former reflects the 'depth' of things, whereas the latter demonstrates the 'appearances'. Generally speaking, however, all names and epithets used for 'worshippers' or those 'of differing ideas' refer to what is in essence one. What defines the name given to the person who 'does not believe' or 'does not believe and does not act' is the absence of 'believing' or 'believing and action by tongue and limbs'. As such, he is an unbeliever, atheist, apostate, polytheist, sinner, hypocrite, etc. These names all stand in opposition to faith and to Islam as a specific religion. And, for all the endless differences between the followers of doctrines, groups and factions in defining the essence of the unbeliever, atheist, heresiarch, or whatever, all exhibit the same tendencies vis-à-vis judgement on the punishments to be imposed on this or that offender, whether execution, payment of tribute, everlasting hell, or censure.

In fact, traditional Islam denies those who hold profoundly different opinions – that is, followers of non-Islamic doctrines who openly proclaim atheism – the right to declare their atheism openly at all. The Quranic *sura* (109, *Al-Kafirun*) which might give the impression that atheists have their own religion, just as the Prophet and his followers have theirs – 'To you be your way, and to me mine' – was not in fact understood to indicate 'equality of freedom', that is, freedom of belief for Muslims and atheists alike. Most Quranic explicators did not take the verse to imply equality.[21] Religious scholars and dialecticians have dealt extensively with the rules governing atheism and heresy. As a representative of the *sunna* and community of believers, Abu Mansour al-Baghdadi made a division into two groups: 'atheists from whom tribute is not accepted' and 'those from whom tribute is accepted.' Regarding the former, the judgement is that they should be killed if they do not embrace Islam, enjoying no 'security'. Such people are subdivided into 15 categories: Sophists; Dahriyyas (materialists); Simniyyas (those who believe in materialist free will, equal values of evidences and deduction); adherents of the prime matter theory; naturalists; materialist philosophers; pagan soothsayers and astrologers; worshippers of human beings; those who privately worship a particular leader of their religion; worshippers of angels; believers in incarnation; believers in reincarnation or the transmigration of souls; Kharmadinians (followers of Mazdak); Batinis (adherents of esoteric sects adopting certain Magian and dualist doctrines); and Brahmins. Al-Baghdadi notes:

> These are the categories of atheists from whom tribute is not accepted, whose slaughtered meat is not to be eaten, and whose women cannot be married [by Muslims]. If they live in Muslim lands, they are invited to recant, and, if they do not do so, they are to be killed. If they live in non-Muslim lands, they are to be treated as people at war, not as free non-Muslims. The same applies to dualists who believe in primal forces of light and darkness, such as the Manicheans, Dissanians and Marconians. Also the worshippers of carved or crafted idols. No blood money, punishment or expiation is to be exacted against the person who kills one of these.[22]

As for those who pay tribute, that is, Sabians, Jews, Christians and Magians, these present a problem. Scholars have differed on the issue of blood money in respect of these. According to Abu Hanifa, blood money in such cases is equal to that of a Muslim, and a Muslim may be killed in reprisal for their death. Al-Shafi'i and Malik agree that no Muslim may on any account be killed in reprisal, though they differ in the matter of blood money for one of the tribute people. Malik sets the blood money for a Jew or a Christian at half that for a Muslim, whereas al-Shafi'i sets it at a third. The latter also sets the blood money for a Magian at a fifth of that for a Jew or a Christian, that is a fifth of a third of that for a Muslim.[23]

In reality, although Muslims in practice recognized ideological or religious differences with the extreme group – those not belonging to the tribute categories – they did not recognize the right of this group to disagree within the legal context of Islam.[24] Such a right was recognized only for Jews and Christians, and for those given equivalent consideration, such as the Sabians and the Magians of Hijr and Yemen.

The classical Arab and Islamic approach to the issue of freedom of belief is obviously different from that of the modern era, which has been exposed to Western principles of civilization, modernism and liberalism. Given the prevalence and pressure of these values, Renaissance and contemporary Muslim scholars have found themselves faced with conditions, both local and worldwide, which do not allow for the traditional methods and viewpoints characteristic of Islamic schools and jurists; and, as such, they have sought some modernist interpretative viewpoint capable of adapting the traditional view of 'those who differ' in doctrinal matters. Early in the modern period, an attempt was made to define the status of non-Muslims in a Muslim society, with regard to doctrinal matters, treatment and rights. At first, these issues were mostly treated according to traditional provisions regulating the affairs of 'free non-Muslims' (ahl al-Dhimma). Later – under pressure from modern values, post-modernism and advancing globalization – attention was focused on the issue of absolute freedom of belief. This meant going beyond the specific 'rights of free non-Muslims' to a consideration of all those who differed, including 'atheists', 'apostates', 'secularists' and those regarded by Muslim leaders and movements as enemies and deniers of Islam.

Contemporary literature on this issue is very extensive. Specially relevant, however, are the views advanced by Abdul-Aziz Jawish, *Shaykh* Mahmoud Shaltout and Rashid al-Ghanoushi, chiefly on account of the change these represent in the ruling on apostates, compared to the views of previous religious scholars and jurists who had ruled that apostates be killed. For Jawish:

No verse in the Quran states that those who apostatize from Islam to another religion should be killed . . . As for the Prophetic *hadith*s cited by al-Bukhari to support the summary killing of apostates, there is, in my view, nothing in these that either imposes judgement of death, clarifies the conditions of apostasy, or defines this.

He continues:

The rules governing the early Islamic period were not intended to be applied to other periods. They came about because, when the Prophet was spreading the call concerning the Oneness of God, apostates reverted to their former Jewish, Christian or idolatrous faith, which enabled them to plot against Muslims from within their ranks and expose their weaknesses. In those days, therefore, apostasy was not simply dissension from Islam; it was always accompanied by apostates' support for their peoples ... Some of these persons proclaimed their faith in Islam during the daytime and reverted to atheism at night. In the early years, apostates were generally those who entered Islam out of hypocrisy and left it to stir discord and compromise its plans.

In the third place, says Jawish:

The apostasy mentioned in the *Surat al-Baqara* [the second *sura* of the Quran] and elsewhere signified retreat from a position of supporting Muslims in their battle against their enemies for fear the latter might win the day; such people wished to put themselves in favour with these enemies in order to save their own lives.

Finally, we should, according to Jawish, take benefit from the example of the Prophet's judgement, knowledge and conduct, which teach us 'how to react to particular conditions and be guided by the requirements of the time'.[25]

As for *Shaykh* Mahmoud Shaltout, he comments as follows:

To commit offence against religion by apostasy is to deny what one has learned by virtue of religion, or to commit such an act as to take religion lightly or declare it a lie. In the Quran God says of this: 'And if any of you turn back from their faith and die in unbelief, their words will bear no fruit in this life and in the Hereafter; they will be companions of the Fire and will abide therein.' (2, *Al-Baqara*, 217) This verse, it will be noted, simply stipulates failure in this life and punishment by eternal hellfire in the afterlife. As for punishment by death in this life, it is indicated by jurists on the evidence of a Prophetic saying ascribed to Ibn 'Abbas, who said: 'The Prophet of God said: "If anyone changes his religion, you shall kill him."' Scholars have expressed various views on this saying ... The matter is seen in a new light when we consider how numerous scholars hold that punishment cannot be indicated on the basis of *hadith*s from a single source, and that atheism does not by itself call for death. What calls for death is waging war against Muslims, committing aggression against them and attempting to seduce them from their religion. The Quran, in many verses, rejects coercion in religion.

God said: 'Let there be no compulsion in religion: Truth stands out clear from Error.' (2, *Al-Baqara*, 256). God also says: 'Wilt thou then compel mankind against their will, to believe!' (10, *Yunus*, 99)[26]

As for that intellectual Islamic herald Rashid al-Ghanoushi, he advances a striking instance of *ijtihad*, taking pains to link the issue to modern-day concepts of human rights. His view is based on the 'commonweal' theory derived from al-Shatibi, author of *Agreements* (Al-Mwafaqat). Al-Shatibi arranges the universals and objectives of jurisprudence on three levels: necessary interest, needs, and ameliorative interests. Naturally, these levels are subject to an order of priorities, seeking to guarantee individual rights and the common good, and giving priority to the rights of the community where these conflict with individual rights. The theory of freedom in Islam is based, accordingly, on 'granting the individual freedom in everything, except when this freedom conflicts with justice or with the commonweal. For, if it transgresses these limits, it becomes aggression and should be arrested and limited. In light of this view, the Quranic verse "Let there be no compulsion in religion" (2, *Al-Baqara*, 256) becomes the major rule supporting freedom of belief.' For Islam, according to al-Ghanoushi, 'does not permit coercion of people to adopt it, nor does it permit anyone to force Muslims to abandon it. In order to guarantee the absence of compulsion, Islam has made it the duty of Muslims to acquire the power to resist those who attempt to turn them against their religion, and has at the same time commanded them to adopt, in their calling of people to Islam, the method of good judgement and kind counsel to clarify truth from error.'

The verse, 'Say, "The Truth is from your Lord: Let him who will believe, and let him who will reject (it)"' (18, *Al-Kahf*, 29), likewise supports this viewpoint. Freedom is the foundation of faith, and it tops the list of human rights.[27] As for freedom to express one's faith – whether to defend it, propagate it or criticize other faiths – al-Ghanoushi concurs with Isma'il al-Farouqi in the view that 'the free non-Muslim – that is, the non-Muslim citizen in a Muslim state – has the right to proclaim the values of his identity within his own community, or to the public, provided he does not violate the common feelings of Muslims . . . And if it is the right – the duty, indeed – of a Muslim to offer his faith to his fellow non-Muslim citizen, the latter has the same right.'[28]

Al-Ghanoushi supports this view by citing the viewpoint of Abu 'l-A'la al-Mawdoudi:

In the Islamic state, non-Muslims will enjoy exactly the same freedoms of speech, writing, opinion, thought and holding meetings as those enjoyed by Muslims . . . They will have the right to criticize Islam just as Muslims have the right to criticize their faiths and creeds, and they will have complete freedom to praise their own creeds. If a Muslim apostasizes, he, and not the non-Muslim, will bear the consequences. In the Islamic state, non-Muslims will not be coerced into adopting a creed or performing an action against their conscience. Furthermore, they will be entitled to behave exactly according to their convictions, provided this does not conflict with the laws of the state.[29]

With regard to 'apostasy' – conscious and voluntary atheism after becoming Muslim – the more likely opinion is that it is 'a crime not related to freedom of belief . . . but a political issue intended to protect Muslims and the systems of the Islamic state against its enemies. Furthermore, what has been ascribed to the Prophet regarding apostasy occurred in the context of his political guardianship over Muslims. Thus, punishment of the apostate should be deterrent, but not death; it is a political crime to be dealt with through laws regulating the crime of violent dissent from the state system and any attempt to unsettle it. It should be dealt with according to its extent and the danger it poses.'[30] This is not the majority opinion, but a modern interpretative one.

Islamic thought has thus been broadened to include the concept of the right to differ, and, indeed, to acknowledge the right to differ, not only with respect to Jews and Christians – there is nothing new about this – but with respect to all non-Muslims, including the followers of creeds, faiths, religions and philosophies that adopt suspicious, critical or dismissive stands vis-à-vis Islam. Yet what has not been acknowledged in the context of legitimate disagreement, here and elsewhere, is that disagreement should take on a 'practical' character; that is, that it should become a 'political crime' assuming the form of physically violent 'dissent', 'tyranny' or 'apostasy' against the state system.

This brings us back, naturally, to the extreme form of 'disagreement': that which refuses obedience to the state or the ruler and dissents from the community, thereby threatening to destroy its unity. This issue was the subject of extensive studies in former eras and is still fiercely debated in our own times.

The case of 'practical disagreement' is totally different from that of jurisprudential, religious or doctrinal disagreement. This is because the former has direct material consequences affecting the individual, the community and the state. The main issue here is that disagreement is linked to the general principle of evident wrongdoing in the actions of the ruler, the 'guardian', the community or the state. This occurs when the one governing does not implement the provisions of the religious laws; when he 'does not govern according to God's commands', when he does not dispense justice to the population, and when he commands disobedience to God. When this happens, the subjects have the right not to listen and not to obey.

The doctrinal basis of the requirement to amend wrongdoing and deny obedience is found in the Quranic verse: 'Let there arise out of you a band of people inviting to all that is good, enjoining what is right, and forbidding what is wrong: They are the ones to attain felicity.' (3, *Al-'Imran*, 104) The Prophetic *hadith* also embodying this principle states: 'Whosoever of you sees an evil action, let him change it with his hand; and if he is not able to do so, then with his tongue; and if he is not able to do so, then with his heart – and this is the weakest of faith.' There are in fact numerous Quranic verses and *hadith*s dealing with this matter.[31]

The early and modern Sunnis did not, as we have noted, go so far as to dissent and refuse obedience, and to require that wrongdoing be amended by the first tool – by the 'hand', that is, by physical force. Their purpose in this was to preserve the nation's unity. Others, however, like the Dissenters (Khawarij), Mu'tazilis and Zaydis in earlier periods, and contemporary radical Islamicist groups now, have accepted the principle of refusing obedience by means of belligerent dissent. The history of Islam has, of course, witnessed many 'revolutionary' movements, whether this involves justifying 'mutiny', 'rising in opposition' and promoting 'discord' by reference to the text, or whether it springs from the requirements of social justice, or the need to combat hypocritical tendencies or open heresy. We might consider, among those who have risen against the authorities and the nation for reasons other than religion or belief, the 'Apostasy Group' (ahl al-ridda), the 'Community of War' (ahl al-harb) and highwaymen. These latter groups are not among those demanding the 'amendment of wrongdoing' on the authority of the revealed text.

There are also those called by al-Mawardi and al-Farra' 'transgressors', on the basis of the Quranic verse: 'If two parties among the Believers fall into a quarrel, make ye peace between them: but if one of them transgresses beyond bounds against the other, then fight ye (all) against the one that transgresses until it complies with the command of God; but if it complies, then make peace between them with justice, and be fair; for God loves those who are fair.' (49, *Al-Hujurat*, 9) These 'transgressors' were a party of 'believers' characterized by a principle of their own contrivance, which involved withdrawing from the 'people of justice', differing with the majority or rising against the ruler on grounds of the revealed text. The Dissenters, who justified their revolt by 'God's command', and on the grounds of fighting an unjust or atheist ruler, could be placed in this category according to the views of traditional *sunna*. In fact, they come among the parties demanding 'amendment of wrongdoing', viewing disagreement in beliefs and actions as a legitimate right required by the religious texts themselves.

There are, undoubtedly, differences in the precise means used by those believing in the right to amend wrongdoing, be they Dissenters, Mu'tazilis, Zaydis or modern-day politico-religious groups. The Dissenters, for example, believed in the general principle of doing battle against the ruler and the community, and would accept no middle ground between peace and war. The Zaydis, on the other hand, associated revolt with their 'call' and with the appearance of the Zaydi Imam. The Mu'tazilis, while marked out by the basic doctrinal principle of commanding what is righteous and prohibiting wrongdoing, nonetheless regarded doing battle as a last resort, at the end of progressive steps beginning with 'conciliation'.[32] Only one Mu'tazili group is known to have risen up, under the leadership of Bashir al-Rahhal and Matar al-Warraq, and in concert with the Zaydi Imam Ibrahim ibn 'Abd Allah ibn al-Hasan ibn al-Hasan ibn 'Ali ibn Abi Talib, during the caliphate of Abi Ja'far al-Mansour in 145/762.[33] This is an exceptional case of a revolutionary amendment of wrongdoing, to be compared only with that entered into by Ahmad ibn Nasr al-Khuza'i, who comes close to the principles of believers in the Prophetic Traditions.[34] The more general Mu'tazili tendency was to employ advice, criticism, exhortation and condemnation; all the features of a strict reformist tendency.

As for modern hardline Islamic groups, they have taken as their motto the statement of Ibn Taymiyya: 'Whoever deviates from the Book should be set straight with force; this is why reformation of religion is done with the Quran and the sword.'[35] This reflects their belief that all religious worship should be directed by God, and that God's word should reign supreme. Yet Ibn Taymiyya himself believed that 'one of the basic principles of the *sunna* and the community of believers is adherence to the majority, forsaking battle against the ruler and foreswearing fighting in discord'.[36] In fact the reformist fundamentalism (*salafiyya*) of these groups differs from that of Ibn Taymiyya in interpreting the principles of reform to mean the necessity of dissent, revolt or rising against the ruler and the community, through *jihad*, confrontation, fighting and direct action. This is because 'the tyrants of this world cannot be removed except by force'; and because restoring 'the caliphate to the path of the Prophet' cannot be achieved without 'fighting the tyrants and declaring holy war against them; this is because they will never be deposed without a fight'. These modern movements further justify their violent actions by saying that 'today's rulers have no title to public authority because they have deviated from Islam by discarding God's Book, replacing legislation . . . Therefore, replacing them, rising against them and fighting them has become a duty, and confrontation has become inevitable, since the land has become a seat of atheism.'[37]

III.

It should be reiterated, then, that the two concepts of obedience and disagreement move between the two principles of right and duty. Obedience is the right of the Legislator (God) on the one hand and of the state on the other. As such, it is the duty of the Muslim, as long as the state recognizes the 'rights of God' and 'the rights of the subjects', or people, dispenses justice, grants rights to those entitled to them, and does not do anything in disobedience to God – that is, against Shariah law. In point of fact, this is hardly different from the case of the state and the citizen in modern political systems, where the state obliges citizens to act according to law and to obey the state, and where the state, too, is under an obligation to enforce the laws and not to deviate from them. If it does so deviate, then the representative systems – parliaments, national assemblies, or whatever – call it to account. In individual cases, meanwhile, citizens have recourse to the judicial authorities to obtain their rights. The modern political system in democratic regimes is, of course, founded on the principle of rotation of power; in other words, democracy implies legitimate disagreement in all circumstances except those of armed rebellion. In the latter case, the political authority has the right to put down the rebellion and bring the 'rebels' before the courts to receive the punishment they have brought on themselves by virtue of the law. This does not mean, even so, that the historical system of the caliphate is exactly equivalent, or even similar, to the modern democratic system. The differences are, indeed, obvious.

It is nonetheless important to realize that the principle of obedience – especially to rulers, that is, to the state – took on an absolute character in traditional Islamic political theory. It emerged as sacred and inviolable; anyone, indeed, who rebelled, and who died in that condition, died as an atheist. A system granting rulers this kind of extreme authority could only, finally, lead to a despotic system of absolute rule. Political jurists recognized this, and, in an attempt to mitigate its effect, were always at pains to praise the principle of justice, tirelessly exhorting caliphs, princes and sultans to follow such a policy. They presented their exhortations in an attractive guise, instilling in rulers' minds the idea that 'justice is the foundation of governance'. Works containing 'mirrors of kings' and 'advice to kings', in which writers on political ethics like al-Ghazali, al-Mawardi and al-Tartoushi excelled, were nothing if not tools of courteous instruction to despotic rulers. But these jurists rejected the principle of rebellion and armed dissent, concerned as they were to ensure the survival of the nation, and of its legal system and structural unity.

Disagreement, in various forms, was nevertheless inescapable; human beings always in practice behave in this way. While rulers may not welcome disagreement, especially practical disagreement, and while 'their' jurists may support them in this, religious texts permit disagreement in various forms and in varying degrees. Still, jurists are most careful to limit the extent of difference and disagreement – they are in fact comfortable with only one form, namely the jurisprudential disagreement which they consider a kind of mercy. Other forms they find abominable and abhorrent; and in this context they emphatically turn the principle of 'amending wrongdoing' against the dissidents themselves. Those who dissent, in creed and behaviour, find themselves faced with a powerful, cohesive 'regulating' establishment, designed to call the governed to account, control their actions and quell their wrongdoings, and not to be used against the rulers themselves. The latter are, indeed, treated with the utmost consideration: no one may question them or their wrongdoings, whatever theories might exist regarding the duties of the imam and the reasons for deposing him.

Yet, despite the survival of the old view on disagreement among a large contingent of modern Islamic thinkers and contemporary Islamic movements, real development has taken place in the interpretative opinions of particular Muslim scholars and particular Islamic revivalist movements, which have made serious efforts, in action or appearance, to manifest enlightened views on the subject. As a result, disagreement in all its forms has become the legitimate right of the individual Muslim. This applies equally to factional, partisan, interpretational, ideological and hardline practical disagreement. Only the last has become controversial over the past few decades.

Doctrinal disagreement is perhaps the form most closely linked to the human rights demanded by the modern world. The tendency of traditional jurisprudential theory was to deny such a right. Its judgement regarding apostates was death, and the same applied to all theists who openly proclaimed their unbelief. This stance has, however, been modified at the hands of a group of contemporary Muslim intellectuals, who, starting out from the premise 'let there be no compulsion in religion', believe each human being has the right to adopt any creed he wishes, religious or non-religious, Islamic or non-Islamic. In the modern world this naturally includes individuals and intellectuals avowing materialism, atheism, Marxism, secularism, liberalism, or whatever.

In contrast, confrontational disagreement – expressed, that is to say, through armed violence – has become the preserve of radical Islamic groups who base their claim to this right on their own particular understanding of certain Islamic texts, supplemented by the opinions of particular Islamic jurists like Ibn Taymiyya. The state, however, disputes this right, as does Islamic public opinion and the international community generally. In any case, no one who supports the right to disagree, within the modern ideology of human rights, sees this right as entailing a further right – in the event of disagreement over opinion or belief with the majority in the state – to resort to armed rebellion and to withhold obedience to the state and community. The only exceptions involve certain very specific situations, which are considered on a case-by-case basis and judged according to their particular circumstances, simple or complex.

Man is free in his choice of belief, and disagreement is his legitimate right. Such is the interpretative conclusion reached by numerous contemporary Muslim intellectuals, who attach themselves to Islamic missionary thought, or who are linked to certain political Islamic movements and parties, or to progressive religious trends in general. Until their ideas are put to the test of actual practice, one must provisionally accept their stated beliefs, though some have conspicuously departed from this trend in cases of disagreement over the past few decades.

The fact is that the conditions surrounding Islam at present, and those awaiting it in the course of the twenty-first century, simply will not permit any leaning towards confrontational fundamentalist formulas in the area of obedience and disagreement. Obedience is an indispensable requirement within civil communities, under the binding laws of civil states. Such laws are the state's inalienable right, and the public good absolutely demands them, with proper law and order taken as a matter of course. Disagreement has likewise become an integral part of modern society in the modern state, where public life is based on the principles of democracy, representative will and freedom. These principles tolerate disagreement in a variety of forms, excepting only that which issues in uprising against the state, the community and the law. There is, indeed, a certain aversion to the democratic system among some contemporary Islamic thinkers and active Islamic groups, because they sense this system gives authority to the people rather than to religious law. Over against this, however, is an enlightened current growing ever stronger in contemporary Islamic societies: one that attempts to set life, within these societies, on a course towards democracy, public liberties and cultural and doctrinal pluralism. Those espousing this trend believe the Islamic socio-political system to be quite capable of absorbing such values and of accepting interpretative doctrinal differences; and they further believe that the system has an inbuilt capacity to enforce these values within a framework of *shura* (consultation), acting in consort with the nation's representative majority.

Some forms of doctrinal freedom will, of course, fail to find acceptance with even the most progressive Islamicists, especially where such freedom results in defamation, insult or slander, or in stinging moral outrage touching Muslims and Islam's beliefs and prominent representatives. Some other forms of freedom, too – notably sexual freedom – will be neither accepted nor ignored. This will not, though, provide sufficient reason for these enlightened Islamic thinkers publicly to reject values whose acceptance has become imperative.

All this does not, needless to say, mean that Islam as a whole will take this free, enlightened direction in the foreseeable future. We are also witnessing a growing inflexibility within some contemporary Islamic politico-religious movements and regimes. This can only lend support to the view that the future will bring differences of opinions on these issues, that disagreement will be inevitable.

The main test, however, will be whether or not those holding different opinions can practise the right to disagree, or whether one party will rather try to enforce its interpretative opinion on the other; whether or not, in sum, these matters are decided by the interpretation or opinion of the representative majority.

Chapter 4: Human rights in the *hadith* – the model individual and the model community in Islam

Husni Mahmoud

I.

I.1.

Man represents a veritable model of the wondrous divine creation at work throughout the universe; and Islam's understanding of man, and the essence of his creation and psychology, represents one aspect of the divine truth, together with the prophetic knowledge embodied in the *sunna*, which is a clarification and detailed explanation of the Holy Quran. There is no wonder in this, for Muhammad the man was a pattern for the possibilities of a historical situation ripe for the call of Islam and divine revelation. Quite apart from the unique qualities that characterized Muhammad the prophet and man, it seems that life around him was vibrant with currents of vital wisdom, embodied in a large number of men and women who supported his message and formed a group known as the Companions – people whose deeds and mature knowledge of life are abundantly recorded in books of tradition and history. There is no doubt this mature knowledge, at this particular time, contributed to their acceptance of the new call and facilitated their allegiance to the faith.

The greatness of man's creation, and his separation from all the other creatures of God, Who made him in the best mould and endowed him with knowledge, caused him to be appointed vicegerent on earth, assigned to develop and prepare a flourishing life. 'Your Lord said to the angels, "I will create a vicegerent on earth."' (2, *Al-Baqara*, 30) This responsibility with which God charged man is a duty requiring the fulfilment of his human essence, the flourishing of his skills and abilities; and Islam, the religion of *fitra*, or nature, which fulfils the nature of this creation and responsibility, has accordingly guaranteed man certain rights necessary to carry out his task and realize the responsibility.

The source books of Islamic legislation provide abundant details of these rights, and of the rulings and encouragement enabling the individual and society to realize and abide by them, acting under their guidance. It might be more practical to trace all this in a range of reference books, so as to have a full picture of the position of Islam on these rights – a formidable task, however, and one requiring much time and energy. Since this is beyond my scope here, I have chosen to clarify the picture with regard to one significant source of Islamic jurisdiction: namely, the *Authenticated Hadith*s of al-Bukhari. This is a major source of the *sunna* and a pre-eminent compendium of the *hadith*s of the Prophet Muhammad, and its use will, I hope, suffice to realize my objective.

I.2.

Was it possible for the prophets and messengers, who were sent to their own peoples or to humanity at large, to be other than human beings? I am not attempting, in posing this question, to create a problem of interpretation, even if the Meccan unbelievers found it easy to make such a request/hypothesis, in order to avoid believing in heavenly messages and so justify their negative attitude toward them. Those who endorsed such a request/hypothesis might thereby have found a miracle capable of leading them to belief – or so they claimed. In fact each of the heavenly religions centred on the belief in one God has been marked by one or more miracles, but such miracles have not been sufficient to convince those who disbelieved, opposed or remained unsatisfied. God replied to such people in the Holy Quran, and on a number of occasions. 'If We had made it an angel, We should have sent him as a man, and We should certainly have caused them confusion in a matter which they have already covered with confusion.' (6, *Al-An'am*, 9) 'And they say, "What sort of a messenger is this, who eats food, and walks through the markets? Why has not an angel been sent down to him to give admonition with him?"' (25, *Al-Furqan*, 7) 'Say, "If there were settled, on earth, angels walking about, in peace and quiet, We should certainly have sent them down from the heavens an angel for a messenger."' (17, *Al-Isra'*, 95) 'The chiefs of the unbelievers among his people said, "He is no more than a man like yourselves: his wish is to assert his superiority over you: if Allah had wished [to send messengers] He could have sent down angels. Never did we hear such a thing among our ancestors of old."' (23, *Al-Mu'minun*, 24) 'Those who do not hope to meet with Us [on the Day of Judgment] say, "Why are not the angels sent down to us, or [why] do we not see our Lord? Indeed they have an arrogant conceit of themselves, and mighty is the insolence of their impiety!"' (25, *Al-Furqan*, 21)

   Prophets and messengers are, then, human beings; and the essence of human creation, as embodied in the prophet who communicates with his people and other men, is more conducive to understanding and conveys a greater intellectual and psychological conviction, although the communication of revelation to the Prophet was, in various ways, through the angel Gabriel. No element of the message is more convincing than the fact that the Prophet Muhammad should be a man leading a normal human life, in its material, worldly aspect, among his people and as one of them. Had this not been so, he would not have been able to reply to someone who boasted of spending the whole night in prayer, fasting continually and abstaining from contact with women. The Prophet told his people: 'By Allah, I am the most fearful of Him among you and the most pious, but I fast and break my fast, I pray and sleep, and I marry women. He who does not like my ways is not of my company . . . Oh young men! He who finds himself capable, let him marry; he who does not, let him fast, as this will protect him.'[1] This address can be taken as realistic and credible only if it comes from a man who addresses men in their own language, in accordance with their powers of perception and the reality of their lives. What can come closer to an understanding of human nature than the address – approaching, in its profound wisdom, the depths of the human soul in its most delicate feelings – where he says: 'No adulterer commits adultery while he is a true believer; no one drinks wine while he is a true believer; no true believer steals or commits robbery while people turn their eyes toward him in amazement, and hopes to remains a believer.'[2]

This subtle observation, based on a thorough knowledge of the human soul and its profound inner struggle, far surpasses the achievements of analytical psychology or modern literary criticism with regard to conscious and unconscious ideas, psychological struggle and dramatic movement. This Islamic insight is reflected in the Shariah, which specifies the nature of the punishment for committing a sin, an offence or a crime.

This understanding of the human soul is represented, in its epitome, in one *hadith*: 'A dead man is followed by three: two of whom leave him, and one stays with him. He is followed by his family, property and deeds. His family and property return, and his deeds remain with him.'[3] Such an understanding of man's nature and role in life entails basic rights, which Islam considers duties placed on man, to help equip him to perform the role with which he was entrusted by the Divine Legislator.

II.

For all the achievements of science and technology, and the things man has learned about himself, all humanity acknowledges its insufficient knowledge of man, of his body and his soul or psyche. Hence we have come to appreciate, in considering man, Socrates' motto, 'Know Yourself', a saying imbued with a philosophical spirit and indicative of the deficient nature of knowledge. God, Who created human beings, endowed His Prophet with a knowledge that elevated him to the level of comprehensive discernment and enabled him to grasp some of the implications necessary for legislation. Since Islam is not only a religion of worship, it was necessary to outline certain rules of conduct to inform the life of the Muslim and to guide Muslim society. Therefore, in addition to the Holy Quran, the Prophet represents, through his *sunna*, a source of legislation in the life of man and Muslim society. This legislation is based on the understanding and veneration of this divine creation, and deals with man's social relations in general and with his role and responsibility in human life. Islam has, therefore, specified certain basic rights, by which Muslims must abide and which they cannot surrender, enabling them to fulfil their humanity and celebrate their divine creation. Muslims are legally obliged to hold on to these rights, to the extent that, through social relations, they have become duties man must carry out for the good of the individual and society.

These rights/duties are best seen in the light of man's right to his life, with which he has been endowed by God, and of his duty to protect this life/trust, which he cannot surrender or abolish. This underlies the sublime image of responsibility indicated in the following *hadith*s: 'Let no one among you desire death when in adversity. If he must desire something, let him say: "Oh Allah! Keep me alive if life is good for me, and take my life if death is better for me."'[4] And: 'Let no one among you desire death; for if he has done well, he may do better; and if he has done ill, he may reform.'[5] Therefore, violation of this life, by a person alive or otherwise, is considered a crime punishable by Shariah, which places a suicide outside the witness of Islam and counts him among the unbelievers. The Messenger said of one man in his company, who claimed to be a Muslim: 'This man is one of the dwellers in Hell.' When this man was fighting against the pagans and the battle was raging, he fought most fiercely till he was covered with wounds and men had begun to doubt the Prophet's insight. When the man felt his severe pain, he picked up one of his arrows and killed himself with it. This caused some other Muslim fighters to come to the Messenger and say: 'Oh Messenger of Allah, you were right in what you said. The man has killed himself.' The Prophet then said to one of his followers: 'Rise and announce that none but a believer will enter Paradise, though God may support his religion even through a wrong-doer.'[6]

In addition, a human being should not expose this life, which he holds 'in trust', to any harm. The Shariah specifies that 'a sound body comes before a sound faith', because the sound body of the Muslim is basic as a means of carrying out duties and the exercise of religious rites. Hence, 'religious prohibitions give way to human necessities'. A sick person, or a traveller, under certain conditions, is excused from fasting. The Prophet said to a man who was shading himself from the hot sun: 'It is not a form of piety to fast when travelling.'[7] A traveller is permitted to combine the prayer (*salat*) times under certain conditions. The *salat* of a hungry or frightened person is, by juridical consensus, not acceptable. And it is a fact that *salat* and fasting are two basic elements of Islam. The legislator sanctifies human life, appreciates human limitations and sanctions a way out of certain difficulties. It is well known that ablution from 'ritual impurity' is made by water. The Prophet said: 'If a person under ritual impurity fears sickness, death or thirst, he may perform ablution by clean sand.'[8]

The Prophet prohibited any form of self-harm. It is reported that he sent a battalion under the command of a man from the Ansar (Medinan supporters), ordering the men to obey him. In a fit of anger, the man asked them: "'Has not the Prophet ordered you to obey me?'" They said: "He has." He ordered them to collect wood and build a fire, which they did. Then he commanded: "Go into that fire!" The men hesitated and clung to one another, saying: "We have taken refuge with the Prophet to avoid fire!" When the fire died down, the commander's anger cooled too. The Prophet, when he learned of the incident, said: "Had they entered it, they would not have gone out of it until the Day of Judgement. Obedience is due only to just orders.'"[9] And again: 'Deference and obedience are a duty, unless someone is ordered to perform an act of disobedience. If the order is such, then no listening or obedience is due.'[10]

It becomes obvious that a sound religion depends on a sound state of affairs within life. A sound religion is not achieved without the enjoyment of rights and duties specified by Islam. The imam al-Ghazali says: 'A sound system of religion is not possible without a sound system of life. A sound religion, by knowledge and worship, cannot be achieved without a sound mind, the continuation of life, adequate clothing, shelter, food and security . . . Sound religion depends on the presence of these basic needs . . . Otherwise, if a person is involved the whole time in protecting himself against the unjust, and gaining his living by contending with the stronger, when will he have time for work and learning, his only means to happiness in the hereafter? Therefore, a sound system of life, that is the fulfilment of needs, is a precondition for a sound system of religion.'[11]

In upholding this human right, which is also a necessity, Islam elevates the standing and value of the human being. Indeed, Islam, in expecting man to live his life in its sublime sense, vests him with human dignity, personal independence and the ability to cooperate and exchange interests within society. The Prophet encourages work that provides personal independence and dignity. 'No man has ever eaten food better than what he prepares with his own hands. The prophet David would eat of what his hands prepared.'[12] Abu Hurayra reports how the Messenger said: 'For someone to collect firewood in a bundle on his back is better than asking another who may give or refuse him.'[13] This *hadith* is reported in another version: 'If someone should take his rope and go [to the mountains?] and collect wood to sell it, then eat and give charity, this is better than asking people [for help].'[14]

These are the traits of character Islam has wished to build in the Muslim, and in the human being generally: to be strong, honoured and dignified in private and public life. Islam honours man even after his death. This is seen in walking behind the funeral and performing *salat* for the dead, and in refraining from abusing the dead. The Prophet said: 'Whoever walks behind the funeral of a Muslim, out of faith and hoping for reward, and remains after *salat* and burial, he will return with two measures of reward, each measure being as large as Mount Uhud. If he only performs *salat* and returns before burial, he returns with one measure of reward.'[15] In another *hadith* he says: 'Do not abuse the dead, for they have gone to meet their deeds.'[16] The Prophet performed *salat* for a pious Ethiopian, and also at the graveside of a humble man who had been buried the night before without the Prophet's knowledge, and at the graveside of a man who was looked down upon by others.[17]

The Prophet gives the highest example of honouring the human soul in this respect. He used to rise whenever a funeral was carried before him. Once he was told: 'But this is the funeral of a Jew!' His answer was: 'Isn't that a soul?'[18] Jabir ibn 'Abd Allah said: 'A funeral passed before us, and the Prophet rose up, so we followed suit and rose from our seats. We said: "Oh Messenger of Allah! This is the funeral of a Jew!" He said: "If you see a funeral, rise."'[19] The Muslims followed the example of their Prophet by rising for the funeral of a non-Muslim in Qadisiyya (in Iraq), saying that the Prophet had risen for the funeral of a Jew.[20]

Thus we see how human rights turn into duties binding sometimes the individual and sometimes society as represented by certain of its members. This is a sign of respect for the human soul, and an appreciation of its human right in life and in death, since it is a divine creation, granted to man by favour and grace. As such it is a duty to acknowledge this favour at all times, by revering the divine creation and showing gratitude and reverence for the gift and the grace. Is this duty, that right, not enough to drive man to sympathize with his brother in humanity and respect his human rights, since both of them are equally exposed to the problems of life, and equally subject to death, when each has to return the trust of life to its Creator and Giver? The Prophet, with his vision, was clearly aware of such feelings when he specified these rights for man and charged him with these duties and responsibilities.

III.

Besides valuing man as an individual, honouring him in life and death and specifying rights and duties designed to guarantee his well-being, Islam has considered the life of man in society and the vital relations between individuals and communities. It has therefore directed the life of the Muslim in society according to certain Muslim educational principles, which, when applied, cause the life of individual and society to flourish by means of the just balance achieved through mutual social rights and duties. Each member of society has rights that may be seen as duties when looked at from a different perspective. An individual may be a son, a father, a mother, a wife, or a citizen with various relations, all these states entailing rights merging with duties to produce a balanced individual when the Islamic theory of education is applied; for, just as man was created in the best mould, so Islam organizes the education of man in the best manner. In the *hadith*s 'The Muslim is the one from whose harmful tongue and hand Muslims are safe'[21] and 'No one of you will become a true believer until he wishes for his brother what he wishes for himself',[22] we find an intertwining of rights and duties. This takes the form of a process of grace involving the whole of society, with the human psyche raised to a state of harmony in relation to society, where every individual performs his duties while being aware of his rights. The two *hadith*s define the general framework for the believing Muslim in his relations with others, in every respect, including his way of thinking which will be liable to inform his speech and behaviour. The Prophet insisted on this ideal orientation in education, which should inform relations within society, on the basis of balanced and mutual rights and duties. The Prophet said: 'Do not hate, envy or avoid each other. Worshippers of Allah, be brothers. A Muslim is not permitted to abandon his brother for more than three days.'[23] In another *hadith* the Prophet says: 'Man is not permitted to abandon his brother beyond three nights, causing them to meet again coldly; but the better of the two is the one who begins the greeting.'[24]

The welfare of any society depends on the education of the individual and the preparation of the good citizen to take initiatives in life with full awareness and conviction, whether undertaken negatively or positively. When the Prophet said: 'Support your brother, whether oppressor or oppressed,' he was asked: 'When oppressed we support him, but how shall we support the oppressor?' He said: 'By holding his hands back from oppression.'[25] The role of the active individual, who understands the right he owes to his Muslim brother and recognizes the duties entailed by this right – to improve society and relations among its members through a sense of mutual cooperation – will come to the aid of the wronged person and restrain the wrongdoer. The Prophet said: 'No man accuses another of wickedness or disbelief but will have the charge rebound on him if the other man is free of the accusation.'[26] Again: 'If a man says to his brother, Oh unbeliever, one of them has admitted [to disbelief].'[27]

We may conclude this section on the education of the individual and society with a *hadith* addressed to 'A'isha, the Prophet's wife: 'The worst person before God on the Day of Resurrection is the one who [in life] has been abandoned by people to avoid his evil.'[28] This is a declared stance and ruling on the life of man based on man's conduct in society. Abu Hurayra reports how the Prophet was asked which action was best if a man could not do a good deed? The answer was: 'To avoid doing evil to others. This will be an act of charity toward yourself.'[29]

IV.

Within this framework, the Prophet indicated the role of the Muslim on various levels of relations and duties to others, starting with the parents and next of kin, then down to the other members of society, as informed by the general system assigned by Islam. The coordination of these levels stems from a truly humane Islamic education, which makes the Muslim a model in his role and relations with others, just as it makes Muslim society a model of good human society by virtue of the cooperation of its members and their sense of responsibility on every level.

The Prophet defines the rights of parents by linking them to the most fundamental pillar of Islam, that of belief in the Oneness of God. He considers unfilial behaviour the gravest of sins. He once asked his companions: 'Shall I tell you of the greatest enormity?' They said: 'Yes, Messenger of Allah.' He said: 'Assigning partners to Allah and displaying ingratitude to parents.'[30] He also placed these rights closest to God by associating them at one time with *salat* and at another time with *jihad*. Once the Prophet was asked: 'Which deed is the most desirable with Allah?' He said: 'Performing *salat* at the due time.' 'What next?' they asked. 'Next filial piety,' he answered. 'What next?' they asked. 'Next *jihad*, fighting for the cause of Allah,' he answered.[31] On yet another occasion, a man asked the Prophet: 'Shall I go to *jihad*?' He asked the man: 'Do you have parents?' The man said that he had. The Prophet commented: 'With them [doing what is their due] is your *jihad*.'[32]

In another insight rich with human significance, the Prophet once said: 'One of the worst iniquities is insulting one's own parents.' When asked how a man might insult his parents, he answered: 'A man may insult another man's father, causing the latter to insult this first man's father and mother.'[33] In another *hadith*, the mother's rights are placed high in rank, and ingratitude by her children is to be proscribed. 'Allah proscribed ingratitude toward mothers and forbade a newborn girl to be buried alive ...'[34] Honouring the mother's position is mandatory, even when she is not a Muslim. Asma bint Abu Bakr said: 'My mother came to me, wishing to join the covenant of the Prophet. So I asked the Prophet whether I should welcome her, and he said: "Yes."' Ibn 'Ayniyya said that God revealed, on this occasion, the Quranic verse: 'Allah does not forbid you from dealing kindly and justly with regard to those who did not fight you for [your] faith ...' (60, *Al-Mumtahana*, 8)[35] Concerning the rights of the parents, and the mother in particular, a man came to ask the Prophet: 'Oh Messenger of Allah! Who deserves my good company best?' The Prophet answered: 'Your mother.' The man asked: 'Who next?' The answer was: 'Your mother.' The man asked further: 'And who next?' The Prophet said: 'Then your father.'[36] A more popular *hadith* elevating the high standing of the mother says: 'Paradise is beneath the feet of mothers.'

In taking this humane attitude, the Prophet proceeds from the teachings of the Quran, where the rights of parents on their children are related to the worship of God and the belief in His Oneness: 'Your Lord decreed that you worship none but Him, and that you be kind to parents. Whether one or both of them attained old age in your life, do not say to them a word [showing your annoyance] nor repel them, but address them in terms of honour. And out of kindness, lower to them the wing of humility and say: "My Lord! Bestow on them Your mercy, even as they cherished me in childhood."' (17, *Al-Isra'*, 23–4) The relation between the duties of children and the rights of parents is thus bound fast by noble human feeling, which is the ornament of life. As the parents are the source of family life thus honoured by the Quran, so Islam, in similar fashion, is concerned about the issue from that source. The Prophet encouraged the Muslim to work for this world as though he would live for ever, and for the hereafter as though he were to die the next day. He also enjoined filial gratitude on the issue and inheritors, to provide a decent and happy life for their parents through the enjoyment of their God-given rights. In addition to untiring exhortation to Muslims to do good, help others and give charity, the Prophet called on the faithful to care for posterity and inheritors, specifying the rights of these and stipulating the duty of those possessing the means not to leave them in need or be obliged to ask others for help. 'Amir ibn Sa'd ibn Malik reported how his father said: 'In the year of the Farewell Pilgrimage, the Prophet visited me when I was sick and in the throes of death. I said: "Oh Messenger of Allah, you see how sick I am, and you know I am a rich man, and my daughter is my only inheritor. Shall I give two-thirds of my money in charity?" He said: "No." I said: "Shall I give half of it in charity?" He said: "No; give away one third, which is already a great deal. If you leave your posterity rich, this is better than leaving them in need, asking for help."'[37]

The Prophet prohibited the wasting of money on pretext of charity. Ka'b ibn Malik reports: 'I said to the Messenger of Allah: "Shall I give away all my wealth in charity as atonement?" He said, "Retain some of your wealth, as this is good for you. I retain the share I had in Khaybar [the Jewish area]."'[38] He also said: 'The best charity is what comes out of wealth; and it begin with your dependents.'[39]

Within the framework of relationship between rights and duties imposed on the Muslim, we find the Prophet emphasizing the rights of kinship to enhance social relations and mutual valuation among relatives. The Prophet said: 'Whoever wishes his livelihood to be enlarged, and his life prolonged, let him care for his kinsfolk.'[40] The Prophet was heard to say: 'The one who severs kin relation never enters Paradise.'[41] 'A'isha reported how the Prophet once said: 'Kinship is a branch; whoever joins it will be joined by it, whoever cuts it will be cut by it.'[42] He went so far as to join belief in God and the Day of Judgment with keeping good relations with kin. 'Whoever believes in Allah and the Day of Judgment, let him honour his guest; whoever believes in Allah and the Day of Judgment, let him keep good relation with his kinfolk; whoever believes in Allah and the Day of Judgment, let him speak well or keep silence.'[43]

All these duties imposed on the Muslim lead to a very active life within society, blessed by cooperation and mutual kindness, which act as a safeguard against any form of social corrosion and aid the growth and flourishing of human relations.

V.

V.1.

Islam does not stop at the rights and duties detailed above, but is concerned with society as a whole, under various circumstances. The judgements of the

Prophet, and their cognizance of developments in society, are remarkable for their flexibility. 'A'isha said: 'The Messenger was never given a choice between two matters without choosing the easier, except when it was a sin, from which he was the farthest of men.'[44] This means that Islam is capable of embracing life in its entirety, as long as there are people in authority who, in their understanding of life, do not deviate from the sources of legislation or obstruct the development of life as informed by faith.

In this section, we deal with the rights of neighbours, both general and specific, which were particularly emphasized by the Prophet. One might imagine a situation where a person is living far from his next of kin, yet has better relations with a neighbour whom he had never known before. The Prophet links the rights of the neighbour to the belief in God and the Day of Judgment: 'He who believes in Allah and the Day of Judgment shall not annoy his neighbour.'[45] The Prophet emphasized the rights of the neighbour in several *hadith*s. '[The Angel] Gabriel kept asking me to take good care of the neighbour until I thought he would give the neighbour a share of one's inheritance.'[46] He advised the Muslim women not to offend: 'Oh Muslim women! Let no one despise her neighbour in any manner whatever.'[47]

This makes the rights of neighbours akin to special human rights. The Prophet was particularly insightful on these rights. He once said: 'By Allah, he is not a believer'; and he repeated this three times. When asked who was meant, he answered: 'The one who does not trust his neighbour with his belongings.'[48] This shows what is demanded of such mutual neighbourly feeling. Once he was asked, 'Which is the greatest sin?' He said: 'To associate companions with Allah Who created you.' 'And what comes next?' he was asked. 'To kill your child for fear of its sharing your food,' he answered. 'And what is next to that?' he was asked. And he answered, 'To commit adultery with your neighbour's wife.'[49] This is an indication of the crucial nature of the rights of neighbours. It is no wonder, then, that these rights, in the view of Islam and of the Prophet, should attain the level of an inheritor, and of holiness.

V.2.

Islam takes a comprehensive view of the lives of human beings in this world and the next, and in their relations on every level. Hence the call for mutual social cooperation. Islam states that human beings are mere keepers and custodians of what they possess. 'Believe in Allah and His Messenger, and spend [in charity] out of the [possessions] whereof He has made you heirs. For those of you who believe and spend [in charity] – for them is a great reward.' (57,

Al-Hadid, 7) Islam also specifies that the poor and needy have a right to this wealth; hence mutual responsibility within Islam is designed to answer the needs of society and solve the problems of the poor and needy. The system of mutual responsibility depends partly on contributions from those who have the means. The *hadith*s depend, in this and all other respects, on the Holy Quran with respect to its call for the model human being and the ideal society. 'Alms are for the poor and the needy, and those employed to administer them [the funds]; for those whose hearts have been [recently] reconciled [to the Truth]; for those in bondage and in debt; in the cause of Allah, and for the wayfarer; Thus it is ordained by Allah, and Allah is full of knowledge and wisdom.' (9, *Al-Tawba*, 60) Then: 'Whatever you spend that is good is for parents and kindred, and orphans, and those in want, and for the wayfarers, and whatever you do that is good – Allah knows it well.' (2, *Al-Baqara*, 215) Moreover: 'The parable of those who spend their wealth in the way of Allah is that of a grain of corn: it grows seven ears, and each ear has a hundred grains. Allah gives manifold increase to whom He pleases, and Allah cares for all and He knows all things.' (2, *Al-Baqara*, 261) 'O you who believe! Give of the good things which you have [honourably] gained, and of the fruits of the earth which We have produced for you, and do not even aim at getting anything which is bad, in order to spend anything thereof.' (2, *Al-Baqara*, 267) Finally: 'Of their goods take alms, so you may purify and sanctify them; and pray on their behalf. Truly your prayers are a source of security for them, and Allah hears and knows.' (9, *Al-Tawba*, 103)

Since livelihood is ordained by God for human beings, and since it is inevitable that different classes should exist within society, certain duties must be imposed on people, each according to their means, to help others who are in need. The mere fact that individuals and people in authority, along with society at large, have been entrusted with such religious duty is a sublimation of the duty on the one hand, and, on the other, a recognition of the right of the less privileged members of society to a respectable human life. The various sources of financing the vital 'project', at the official level (the Treasury) and the popular level (alms, endowment, charity, etc.), are indicative of the Islamic legislator's concern about the human rights specified for all sectors of society needing help. This project of mutual social responsibility may be called a project of social security or of peaceful life. This explains the withholding of punishment from a thief when it is proved he committed theft out of a real need to live, when the 'project' could not for some reason satisfy that need.

This project of mutual social responsibility was not as easy to establish as it might seem, involving as it did various aspects of life within a steadily growing Muslim society – it entailed tending to the needs of the poor, the needy, wayfarers, widows, orphans, captives and slaves. This explains the concern of the Prophet, the first legislator after the Holy Quran, over educating Muslims in the sound principles of Islam, and directing them to perform such human and social duties through a sense of responsibility vis-à-vis the human rights of the other, and to take individual initiative for the benefit of the community and society at large. The Prophet says: 'Feed the hungry, visit the sick and liberate the captive.'[50] On one occasion he said: "I and the guarantor of the orphan are in Paradise so!" With that he pointed with his index and middle fingers, parting them a little.[51] He also said: 'The one who strives to help a widow, or a poor person, is like the one who fights for the cause of Allah, or the one who keeps vigilant prayers and day fasting.'[52] The Prophet's call to extend charity was governed by common sense and sensitivity. He did not demand that such help be beyond one's means. 'Avoid hellfire, even with half a date.'[53] As small a help as half a date for alms, a kind word, a good deed, removing an obstacle from the road, or refraining from evil, are all considered forms of help.[54]

In addition to the great emphasis he laid on charity, the Prophet specified the type and aim of charity, in order to organize the priorities and classes of recipients. No charity is acceptable from a man when he or his family is in need or if he is in debt, as debt ought to be paid before charity, gifts or liberating a captive. The Prophet said in this connection: 'He who takes people's money intending to waste it will be wasted by Allah, unless he was known for patience, and would prefer others to himself, even if he were in need.'[55] He also said: 'The best charity comes from the rich; and begin with your dependents.'[56] And: 'If a person spends on his family, anticipating Allah's reward, it is indeed a charity.'[57] To enforce this good character within the Muslim, the Prophet expressed admiration for the spirit of charitable giving even when exercised by a person before embracing Islam. 'Urwa ibn Hakam ibn Hizam reports: 'I said: "Oh Messenger of Allah! What do you say of acts of piety I would perform before Islam, such as alms-giving, liberating captives, supporting kindred? Is there a reward for that?" The Prophet said: "Your Islam is based on your previous good deeds."'[58]

V.3.

In addition to specifying human rights in the case of charity and alms-giving, the comprehensive view of Islam also specified human rights in the process of buying and selling, which is an important aspect of people's daily lives. Both buyer and seller have rights, which were specified by the Prophet in a number of *hadith*s. He established these rights on principles of equality and justice, and encouraged leniency and ease in transactions and in demanding repayment. He said: 'May Allah bless the liberal man in selling, buying or demanding repayment.'[59] With regard to the sound conduct of trade, the Prophet forbade thrusting an object on the buyer (*munabadha*) before he has a chance to look it over. He also forbade the *mulamasa*, or 'touching-sale', where the object is to be sold by merely touching it.[60] Moreover, he forbade selling livestock that has not been milked for days. 'Do not keep she-camels and ewes unmilked. Whoever buys them has the choice of milking or returning them with a measure of dates.'[61] He also forbade a townsman to sell a commodity brought for sale by a Bedouin. A man may not sell over his brother's sale, or bargain over his brother's bargain, until he obtains his permission.[62] He forbade cheating by inflating the price. He said: 'Three people God will not speak to, look at or purify; and they are severely punished: a man who has enough water on a trip, but refuses a drink to a wayfarer; a man who does not pledge allegiance to another except for worldly gain; and a man who bargains on a commodity in the late afternoon, then the seller swears by Allah that he was paid so much for it, so the buyer is obliged to take it.'[63]

Explaining some elements of the process of buying and selling, the Prophet said: 'The two parties to a sale remain in agreement until they separate. If they were truthful and open, their sale is blessed; if they kept secret intentions and were untruthful, their transaction will be condemned [by God].'[64] He was also considerate of the situation of the debtor, advising creditors to be lenient with him. He said: 'A man would lend money to people, and say to his servant: "If you find a man in a difficult situation, overlook the demand for repayment, in the hope Allah will overlook our trespasses."' The Prophet went on: 'When [that man] faced Allah, He overlooked his trespasses.'[65]

V.4.

Within his comprehensive view of life, the Prophet specified certain rights for the road and for houses on a thoroughfare. Concerning the roads, he advised: 'Beware of sitting in the roads!' The men who were addressed answered him: 'But we have no choice. This is where we sit together and talk!' He said: 'If you are forced to, then give the road its right.' They asked: 'And what is the right of the road?' He answered: 'To avert your glance, to remove obstacles, to enjoin what is right, to answer greetings, to forbid gently, and to prevent wrong-doing.'[66]

Concerning the inviolability of homes, he advised: 'If you enter a house, you may perform your *salat* wherever you wish, or wherever you are told to do so, and you should not eavesdrop.'[67] It is reported that a man peeped through a hole in the wall outside the Prophet's room, while the Prophet was scratching his head with a sharp object. When he became aware of it, he said to the man: 'Had I sensed you were peeping, I would have pierced your eye with this! Asking permission to enter a place was instituted to safeguard privacy.'[68] This severe answer underscores the right of people to privacy in their own homes. How does this compare, may we ask, with the violation of these rights through spying on private lives and exposing personal affairs, even by the official authorities in many cases? A serene human touch regarding respect for these rights may be sensed in the following *hadith*: 'If there should be three of you together, let not two of you whisper together, lest the third be vexed.'[69]

Another aspect of this sensitivity and consideration is the great regard he shows for these rights in the context of communal *salat*. The Prophet would draw attention to the health and bodily condition of people performing prayers, which calls on the imam leading the *salat* not to prolong it so as possibly to exhaust the weak and sick: 'If one of you should lead people in prayer, let him be brief, for there may be some who are weak or sick. If he should perform the *salat* for himself, then let him extend the *salat* as long as he wishes.'[70] A man came to the Prophet and said: 'Oh Messenger of Allah, I shall not attend the *salat* tomorrow, for such-and-such a person extends it too much.' He then said: 'I have never seen the Prophet more angry than in that day's sermon, as he said: "Oh people! Some of you are to be abhorred! If any of you should lead the *salat* in a group of people, let him be brief, since some may be old, or weak, or need to attend some business.'"[71] In another *hadith* he said: 'When I am leading a *salat*, intending to extend it, and hear a child crying, I curtail the *salat* for fear of putting the child's mother to trouble.'[72]

The Prophet was especially kind to children, underscoring their human rights to mercy and compassion. It is a known fact that he was patient with children even during his *salat*. It is related that he embraced the child al-Hasan ibn 'Ali in the presence of some companions, one of whom said: 'I have ten children, but I have never embraced any of them.' The Prophet looked at him and said: 'Whoever is not merciful does not deserve mercy.'[73] A Bedouin said to him one day: 'You embrace children, but we do not.' The answer was: 'What can I do when Allah has taken mercy out of your heart?'[74]

The protection of the rights of individuals was a major concern of the Prophet. He stated that 'a Muslim who intends to bequeath his property should have that intention registered swiftly, even before he has slept two nights.'[75] He was concerned not only with the human rights of the Muslim, but with those of *dhimmi*s, the covenanted non-Muslims, as well. He said: 'Whoever kills a *dhimmi* will not smell the breath of Paradise, a breath detected at a forty-year distance.'[76] A characteristic anecdote is related of a group of Muslims who came to a Jewish area, and said: 'Join Islam and live in peace. You should realize the earth belongs to Allah and His Messenger. We intend to evacuate you, so, if you have any property, you may sell it; otherwise, you should remember the earth belongs to Allah and His Messenger.'[77]

Within this context of deep regard for human rights and individual property, the Prophet once said in his address to the Muslims: 'There will come a time of great disruption and things not to your liking.' They asked: 'What do you command us to do, Oh Messenger of Allah?' He said: 'You should pay the dues which you owe, and demand from God the right which is due to you.'[78] Two anecdotes will suffice to show how the Prophet was extremely just in his rulings. He had assigned 4,000 [dirhams?] by way of subsidy for each of the early emigrants, and 3,500 for the son of 'Umar. When asked why 'Umar's son had received less when he was also an emigrant, he answered that he had emigrated with his parents, and this was not the same as someone who had emigrated alone. It was also related by 'A'isha that the Quraysh tribe was perturbed by a certain incident: a Makhzumi woman had stolen something, and the Prophet had refused the mediation of his close follower Usama ibn Zayd, who wished him to hold back from applying the punishment on her. The Prophet said in his address: 'Those before you have perished because, when a powerful person stole, they left him in peace, but when a weak person stole they applied the punishment on him. By Allah, if Fatima, the daughter of Muhammad, stole, I would have her hand cut off.'[79]

When such a humane Islamic education of the individual is effectively applied, a good individual will lead to a good society; the individual will represent the model, and society will represent the model sought in Islam, all working together as described by the following *hadith*: 'You see believers, in their mutual feelings of mercy, kindness and compassion, as one human body, in which, when one organ is affected, the entire body responds in sleeplessness and fever.'[80] In such a society, rights and duties will be fully respected, and everyone will enjoy security and peace.

VI.

In this section we shall attempt to present the image and rights of women, based on the *hadith*s included in the *Sahih al-Bukhari*. Since the woman, like the man, is a divine creation, with qualities of her own, her rights are specified in respect of those qualities, in addition to the rights she shares with the man.

Islam has honoured woman and raised her in dignity, after she had been as nothing before Islam. As 'Umar ibn al-Khattab said: 'When Islam came, and Allah mentioned them [in the Quran], we realized they have rights on us, without our having to include them in any of our affairs.'[81] Based on this valuation, the Prophet said: 'He who believes in Allah and the Day of Judgment, let him not annoy his neighbour. Be kind to women, since they were created from a rib [of Adam] . . . Be kind to women.'[82] The woman/female may be a mother, a wife, a daughter or a close kin. We noted above the incident of the man who asked the Prophet about the person most deserving of his care; and how the answer was 'your mother', repeated, then 'your father.'[83] This is not only because the mother has more burdens to bear than the father. It is also because the special nature of woman, with her maternal and other responsibilities, entails for her all the rights she has over her children, in excess of those enjoyed by the father. The daughter, as a responsible being, is honoured by the Prophet in being charged with the duty of performing the pilgrimage instead of a mother who cannot go, and in place of her old father. In this, there is a recognition by the Prophet of that duty and right, wherein the woman is considered equal to the man.[84] Of the same nature is the right of the mother to have charity paid in her name after her death. Ibn 'Abbas reports how Sa'd ibn 'Ubada's mother died in his absence. He asked the Prophet whether it was useful for him to pay charity for her, and was answered in the affirmative.[85]

The woman as wife has her own rights over her husband. There are several *hadith*s to this effect 'Your wife has a right on you.'[86] The Prophet exempted a man from joining in a campaign, since he was accompanying his wife on the pilgrimage. 'Go back and perform your pilgrimage with your wife.'[87] In a long *hadith*, the Prophet says to Sa'd ibn Abi 'Amir: 'Whatever you give is charity, even the morsel which you lift up to your wife's mouth.'[88] The degree of respect accorded to the woman/wife is expressed in the following *hadith*: 'No one should treat his wife as a slave, then sleep with her at night.'[89] The Prophet's view of the wife's position is manifest in the witness of 'A'isha, who said that the Prophet 'came to her when Allah ordered him to ask his consorts to have a choice [between continuing to lead a frugal life with the Prophet or to be released from the marriage bond]. He began with me, saying: "I am going to tell you something, but do not hasten to give an answer before you consult your parents," though he knew my parents would not order me to leave him. Then he recited the two verses: "Oh Prophet! Say to your consorts, If you desire the life of this world and its glitter – then come, I will provide for your enjoyment and set you free in a handsome manner. But if you seek Allah and His Messenger, and the Home of the Hereafter, truly Allah has for the well-doers amongst you a great reward." (33, *Al-Ahzab*, 28–9) So I asked: "In which of these two choices shall I consult my parents? I wish to seek Allah and His Messenger and the Home of the Hereafter." Then the other consorts of the Prophet did the same as I did."[90]

Islam has specified for woman certain human rights at every stage of her life, rights appropriate to that stage. In addition to her rights as mother or wife, Islam has specified for the woman basic rights when asked in marriage. These rights become duties binding on her father or guardian. The legislator has given her the right to accept or refuse the man who asks her hand. The Prophet said: 'A widow cannot be married without consultation; and a virgin cannot be married before she gives her consent.' They asked: 'And what is her consent?' He said: 'To keep silent.'[91] The legislation built on this rule was that if a man gives his daughter in marriage against her will, the marriage is repealed. It is reported that Khansa' bint Khidham of the Ansar was given in marriage by her father, after she had been divorced, but that she, being unwilling, appealed to the Prophet, and he annulled her marriage.[92]

One aspect of the control of betrothal and marriage is that a man cannot ask in marriage a girl or a woman already betrothed to another man. 'A man may not ask in marriage a woman already betrothed to a man, unless he breaks the betrothal.'[93] Ibn 'Umar reports that the Prophet forbade a man to ask a girl already betrothed until the first suitor left or gave permission.[94] In another *hadith* he adds: '. . . a woman should not ask for the divorce of another [woman] in order to take her place.'[95]

The above examples show the high regard with which women were treated in Islam, and the range of human rights guaranteed her at every stage of life. If, at any later period of history, these rights have been somewhat ignored or bypassed, the reason does not lie in the legislation or the principle, but with the people involved and their misunderstanding or misapplication of Shariah. In most cases, the passage of time over which that misapplication has occurred, and the blind submission to the attractions of modern Western life, have led to the neglect or violation of the Shariah principle and to the perpetuation of misconceptions and distortions concerning the attitude of Islam to women. A sound and objective understanding of this attitude, and a comprehensive view of the principles in question, will lead to a realistic appreciation of the attitude of Islam in this respect, even on controversial points, provided we fully understand the physiological and psychological nature of woman. Clearly such understanding and valuation informs the positive laws which exclude women, children and the elderly from certain requirements, despite the call for equality between men and women, and despite the violation of these laws on many occasions, especially in times of war but even in peaceful times. Such realistic understanding of woman's nature informs the call of the Prophet to consider the rights implied by this nature, and to proscribe the killing of women and children.[96] In one campaign, the Prophet was told a woman had been found killed. He condemned this and prohibited the killing of women and children. This policy was maintained by the caliphs and early Muslim military leaders, as is well documented in many books on war and traditions.

VII.

In this section we shall deal with a highly sensitive and complex question in the field of human rights: namely slaves and slavery.

At the time of Islam's rise, the phenomenon of slavery was deep-rooted and widespread in Arab and other societies east and west. The sources of this phenomenon ranged from the spread of wars and poverty to the practice of usury, to the extent that no system or exhortation succeeded in abolishing this phenomenon once and for all. An outright prohibition would have led to various and complex problems within the social fabric. The attitude of Islam was clear from the beginning, based on the Quranic text that specifies equality among Muslims: 'The most honoured among you is the most pious.' (49, *Al-Hujurat*, 13) This principle was embodied in the famous cry of 'Umar ibn al-Khattab: 'When did you enslave people while their mothers begot them free?' Islam has seen, in the freedom of the individual and the community, an embodiment of the true meaning of life, without which humanity cannot fulfil its potential. On this basis Islam prescribed the duty of the manumission of slaves as an atonement for many sins, and as an alternative to some punishments, considering this one way of seeking divine favour. Islam even legislated for the payment of ransom for captives in the Muslim wars. This was not effected by material payment only; the ransom sometimes took the form of a captive teaching Muslim children. This practice led many slaves to embrace Islam, which, in turn, led the converts to suffer various forms of oppression at the hands of slave-masters. Islam therefore legislated for the formation of a public treasury for alms and charity for the manumission of slaves. The Holy Quran specifies as follows: 'Alms are for the poor and the needy, and those employed to administer the [funds]; for those whose hearts have been [recently] reconciled [to the Truth]; for those in bondage and in debt; in the cause of Allah, and for the wayfarer; [Thus it is] ordained by Allah, and Allah is full of knowledge and wisdom.' (9, *Al-Tawba*, 60) Islam linked manumission to many principles and laws of religion. 'It is not righteousness that you turn your faces towards east and west; but it is righteousness to believe in Allah and the last day, and the angels, and the Book, and the Messengers; to spend your substance, out of love for Him, for your kin, for orphan, for the needy, for the wayfarer, for those who ask, and for the ransom of slaves; to be steadfast in prayer, and practise regular charity; to fulfil the contracts which you have made; and to be firm and patient in pain and adversity; and throughout all periods of panic. Such are the people of Truth, the God-fearing.' (2, *Al-Baqara*, 177)

The *hadith*s came to embody this religious objective. Since the institution of slavery could not be abolished at once, we find in the *hadith* three aspects of the good treatment of slaves. The Prophet enjoined the abolition of the word 'slave' or 'slave-girl'. He said: 'Do not say "my slave" or "my slave-girl", but say 'my young man" and "my young woman".'[97] Another *hadith* highlights the human feeling to be shown to slaves, and considers them equal to their masters. 'If one of you is handed his food by his servant, and did not ask the servant to sit near him, let him hand the servant one or two morsels, or one or two meals, as the master is responsible for the servant's need and welfare.'[98]

This exhortation to the good treatment of slaves is further confirmed by the account of al-Ma'rour ibn Suwayd, who said: 'I met Abu Dharr at Rabadha, wearing an elegant garment, and his young man was wearing the same. I asked him for an explanation, and he said: "I abused a man and slandered his mother. The Prophet said to me, "Abu Dharr, have you slandered his mother? You are a man with a streak of *jahiliyya* [pre-Islamic ignorance]. Your servants are your brothers, and Allah put them under your hands. Whoever has his brother under his hand, let him feed and clothe him as he does himself. Do not over-work them. If you do, give them a hand."'[99]

It was natural the Prophet should encourage slaves to embrace Islam, promising them salvation from the scourge of disbelief and the immunity offered by joining the faith. He said: 'If a slave has embraced Islam and behaved like a good Muslim, Allah will pardon him his previous sins. After that each good deed is requited ten to seven hundred times; every bad deed carries its equal punishment, except when Allah pardons that bad deed.'[100] Concerning the immunity guaranteed by the faith, he said: 'I was commanded to fight people until they say there is no god but Allah. If they say it, perform our *salat*, face our Kaaba, and sacrifice as we do, then their blood and property are inviolate, and God will be the judge of their acts.'[101] This immunity he further expresses from a legal point of view, though with similar sensitivity and discernment. Al-Miqdad ibn 'Amr al-Kindi, who took part in the battle of Badr, asked: 'Oh Messenger of Allah, if I were to meet an unbeliever and fight, and if he were to strike my hand and cut it with his sword, then take refuge at the top of a tree and say: "I submit to Allah in Islam," should I kill him after this?' The Prophet said: 'No, you should not kill him.' 'But, 'al-Miqdad objected, 'suppose he had cut off my hand before he said those words; should I kill him then?' The Prophet answered: 'You should not kill him; if you did, then he would be in your status [of belief] before you killed him, and you would be in his status [of disbelief] before he said what he said.'[102]

This mature judgement shows the Prophet's sharp realization of the subtle difference between disbelief and belief in Islam, despite the complex situation presented. It was the keen vision of the Prophet that led him to condemn the action of Khalid ibn al-Walid when he killed the captives from the tribe of Bani Judhayma, who failed to say clearly 'we submit to Islam' but lisped in pronouncing the phrase. He said: 'Oh my Lord Allah, I absolve myself twice from the misdeed of Khalid ibn al-Walid.'[103]

However, this immunity and state of grace is lost when a Muslim insists on doing what takes him outside the fold of Islam. In answer to a question, the Prophet said: 'When two Muslims cross swords with each other, the slayer and the slain go to Hell.' The Prophet's companions said: 'Oh Messenger of Allah, one is indeed a killer, but why should the one killed be punished also?' He answered: 'Because he too was bent on killing his adversary.'[104]

These are some aspects recommended by the Prophet in the treatment of slaves until they are manumitted, which he encouraged; and he specified a system whereby the slave regained his liberty and full rights while keeping allegiance to his old master.[105] The Prophet said: 'Whoever had a maid whom he taught and brought up well, then manumitted and married, will have two rewards.'[106] The Holy Quran has specified that setting a believer free from bondage is considered an atonement for some punishable acts and sin committed by a Muslim, such as premeditated murder and broken oaths or pledges. In one *hadith* we read: 'If a man manumits a Muslim [slave], Allah will save from the fire every one of his limbs for every limb of the freed man.'[107] It is natural to find in the *hadith*s details of Quranic legislation, with examples from the real lives of Muslims. The Prophet ruled the payment of blood money for the unborn baby whose mother had been killed inadvertently. When the guardian of the mother objected to the payment for someone 'who has not yet eaten or drunk or spoken', the Prophet commented: 'This is to talk like a brother of priests!'[108] A man confessed to the Prophet that he had slept with his wife during the fasting month of Ramadan. He said: 'Go and manumit a slave.'[109]

Concerning the manumission of a 'shared slave', the Prophet specified a full manumission. 'Whoever manumits a shared slave must do the job in full. If he has the means, he must pay the fair price and pay the partners their due before setting the slave free.'[110] The Prophet so appreciated the slave's status as a rational human being that he said: 'If the slave gave good advice to his master and was devoted in his worship of God, he will have two rewards.'[111] By the same token, he said: 'The leader in the communal *salat* should be the one best versed in the Quran; a slave is not barred from the task except for some other reason.' 'A'isha's slave Dhakwan led the *salat* for her. Among the early emigrants, Salim, a slave of Abu Hudhayfa, led the *salat* before the arrival of the Prophet, since he was best versed in the Quran.[112] The Prophet so valued the human status of the slave that he said: 'A virtuous bondsman has two rewards. By the One in Whose Hand is my soul, had it not been for striving in the cause of Allah, going on pilgrimage, and filial duty to my mother, I would have liked to die as a slave.'[113] Indeed, the Prophet's attitude to the manumission of slaves is in conformity with the Islamic view that considers the liberation of the human soul from bondage as equal to bringing it back to life. Islam considers bondage an image of death, since slavery is a remnant of disbelief, which is death itself. 'Can he who was dead, to whom We gave life ... be like him who is in the depths of darkness?' (6, *Al-An'am*, 122) Thus Islam was keen to realize for the manumitted slave the true meaning of life, and to place him within the human reality in which Allah created him, on the same footing with other free human beings.

VIII.

We may say that justice is the objective of the Islamic formation of the individual and society. Justice is the main objective of Islamic Shariah, since it is the basis of life, which is itself a constant struggle between justice and injustice. 'Injustice is darkness on the Day of Resurrection,' said the Prophet.[114] 'An act of injustice committed on earth will entangle the doer sevenfold its weight. Whoever takes a thing from earth without justice, this will plunge him sevenfold deep into the earth on the Day of Resurrection.'[115]

Justice is a duty on everyone, and its area of responsibility involves the relations of the individual with the family, the community and life in all its aspects. The Prophet said: 'Be just among your children in gifts ... Fear Allah and be just with your children.'[116] Al-Nu'man ibn Bashir relates how his father took him to the Prophet and said: 'I have offered this son of mine a servant.' The Prophet asked: 'Have you offered all your children the same?' His father said: 'No.' The Prophet said: 'Take back that servant.'[117]

In the words of the Prophet, when he sent Mu'adh ibn Jabal as an envoy to Yemen, we feel the enormous responsibility of justice and an aversion toward oppression. 'Beware the appeal of the wronged person, as there is no screen between it and Allah.'[118] Injustice may fall on a person's own self or on others; it may be issued by a judge against the plaintiff or the defendant, or by the ruler against subjects – all of which is proscribed. There are various Quranic verses that proscribe injustice: 'For Allah is never unjust to those who serve Him.' (3, *Al 'Imran*, 182) 'Allah is never unjust in the least degree.' (4, *Al-Nisa'*, 40) 'And not one will your Lord treat with injustice.' (18, *Al-Kahf*, 49)

The Prophet says: 'One Muslim is a brother of the other; he does not wrong him or renounce him.'[119] Also: 'He who has wronged another, let him right that wrong before the day when there will be no *dinar* or *dirham*. If he has good deeds, they will be decreased in proportion to the injustice he had done. If he has none, the bad deeds of the wronged person will be decreased in proportion to the injustice and added to those of the unjust.'[120]

In an attempt to avoid injustice, the Prophet advised a judge not to issue judgement when he is angry, lest the balance of justice be affected. 'Let none of you make a judgement on one of two people when he is angry.'[121] 'The best among you is the best in judgment.'[122] 'If Fatima, the daughter of Muhammad, stole, I would have her hand cut off.'[123] Such examples of fairness and human justice manifested by the Prophet are also seen in his attitude concerning al-Rubayyi', the paternal aunt of Hamid ibn Anas, when she broke one of her slave-girl's teeth. He insisted the ruling of the Holy Quran should decide the punishment. But the slave-girl pardoned her mistress. So he said: 'There are some among the worshippers of Allah who make an oath and keep it.'[124] A similar case was that of a Jew who pressed two stones against the head of a slave-girl who refused to forgive him; the Jew was punished in a like manner.[125]

The Prophet was very careful in making judgements, for fear of error and judging unjustly, specifically when one adversary was more eloquent than the other. He said: 'I am only a human being. One adversary might be more eloquent than the other, and I could believe him to be truthful, and judge in his favour. If I have made a judgment against a Muslim, the judgment is a brand of fire; let him take it or leave it.'[126]

He advised Muslims to listen to the ruler and obey him, unless he exhorts to wrongdoing, when he should not be obeyed. 'The Muslim has to listen and obey, in what he likes and dislikes, unless he is ordered to commit a transgression; then there should be no listening or obedience.'[127] 'Whoever obeys me has obeyed Allah; whoever disobeys me has disobeyed Allah. Whoever obeys the prince has obeyed me; whoever disobeys him has disobeyed me. The imam is a barricade, behind whom and by whom fighting is done. If he exhorts to the pious course and is just, he has his reward; if not, he has what he deserves from the ill incitement.'[128]

'Umar ibn al-Khattab was known for his justice. His Persian visitor, finding him asleep beneath a tree without a guard, in the manner of his people, was led to say: 'Because you were just, you felt safe and slept [peacefully].' It is also known that Abu Bakr and 'Umar refused to share the inheritance of the Prophet, giving his daughter Fatima and his two paternal cousins 'Ali and 'Abbas their share, according to what the Prophet himself had once said: 'We [prophets of God] are not inherited; what we leave behind should be distributed as charity.'[129]

This shows how Islamic traditions reject injustice; indeed, how they exhort to confrontation with injustice in order to uphold the balance of justice in the world. The absence of justice undermines the legitimacy of peace and security within a society, where peace is a mutual responsibility. Justice is a divine duty. Therefore: 'If any do help and defend themselves after a wrong [done] to them, against such there is no cause of blame. The blame is only against those who oppress men with wrong doing and insolently transgress beyond bounds through the land, defying right and justice: for such there will be a grievous penalty.' (42, *Al-Shura*, 41–2)

IX.

IX.1.

The building of the ideal Muslim society, through the observation of Muslims' rights and duties, depends on *shura*, or 'mutual consultation', which is the embodiment of the Muslim philosophy of government within state and society, informed by the Holy Quran and the *hadith*. Therefore, this philosophy of consultation is regarded with great veneration, a duty imposed by Shariah, to be followed in all transactions of the state. 'Those who hearken to their Lord, and establish regular prayer, who [conduct] their affairs by mutual consultation, who spend out of what We bestow on them for substance.' (42, *Al-Shura*, 38) And: "It is part of the Mercy of Allah that you deal gently with them. Were you severe or harsh-hearted, they would have broken away from about you. So pass over [their faults] and ask for [Allah's] forgiveness for them, and consult them in affairs [of moment]. Then, when you have taken a decision, put your trust in Allah, for Allah loves those who put their trust [in Him].' (3, *Al 'Imran*, 159)

Mutual consultation is compatible with the spirit of Islam, since it is assumed that the individual or ruler intends the public good for society. The Prophet was the model for Muslims in every situation. He would consult his Companions over the appointment of governors and commanders and other matters of state, and members of his family in family affairs. Abu Hurayra said: 'I have never seen anyone consult more than the Messenger of Allah.'[130] He would encourage leaders, governors and Muslims in general to consult with and advise each other. He said: 'If one of you asks his brother for advice, let him give it.'[131] And: 'If someone is asked for advice by a Muslim brother and gives unsound advice, he is a traitor to his brother.'[132] He also said: 'If one of you asks his brother for a piece of advice, let him be given that advice.'[133]

It is well known that the caliphal state was established by consultation when Abu Bakr was selected as caliph. The same applied in the selection of Umar. Both caliphs followed the *sunna* of the Prophet in managing affairs of state. Thus the principles of sound consultation provided human rights for everyone. The oppression and individual authority characterizing some periods of Muslim history was a violation of a basic principle of religion, and a disruption of a basic duty of the ruler.

IX.2.

In Islam knowledge and learning is regarded as, simultaneously, a right and a duty for every Muslim man and woman. It is well known that knowledge was one of the bases of Muslim civilization, which itself played an active role in human civilization as whole. We should keep firmly in mind the consensus of jurists and the schools of thought within Islam: that Muslim men of knowledge and learning should be the rulers and governors, and that authority should be in the hands of intellectuals and men of *ijtihad*. The Prophet said: 'Allah does not take away knowledge from His worshippers by force, but He takes away knowledge by taking away men of knowledge, so that when He leaves none of them, the people will choose ignorant heads, who are asked, but give opinion wanting in knowledge. So they become misled and misleading.'[134] 'Umar ibn 'Abd al-'Aziz used to say that 'knowledge does not perish until it becomes a secret'.[135]

IX.3.

There is another public human right which the Prophet recognized and through which he recommended a practice akin to the 'quarantine' measures of modern times. 'A'isha asked the Prophet about 'the plague'. He said: 'It was a punishment sent by Allah on whom He chose, then He turned it into a Mercy for believers. If a worshipper should be in a land where there is plague, but does not leave, abiding patiently, knowing that nothing will befall him except what Allah has ordained for him, he will have a reward equal to that of a martyr.'[136] He also said: 'If you hear of it in some land, do not go near it; and if it should break out in a land where you happen to be, do not leave and flee from it.'[137]

IX.4.

In addition to human rights, it may be significant to refer to the Prophet's concern for the rights of animals, which he regarded with great mercy and pity. Once he was asked: 'Do we have a reward concerning animals?' He answered: 'In every beating heart there is a reward.' He related that 'a man saw a parched dog eating the soft soil out of thirst. So the man took off his shoes and filled them with water for the dog to drink until it quenched its thirst. Allah appreciated the man's deed and admitted him to Paradise".[138] He also related the anecdote of a woman who imprisoned a cat until it died of hunger; and she was punished with hellfire. It is reported that he commented, addressing this woman: "You gave it nothing to eat and drink when you imprisoned it till it died of hunger, nor did you let it loose to go about looking for something to eat."[139]

This shows how Islam was far in advance of what we see nowadays in societies for animal welfare, even though animals in those days were closer to the wild state and not kept as pets inside houses.

X.

In conclusion, one may ask whether the image of human rights, as represented by the *hadith* of the Prophet culled from the *Sahih al-Bukhari*, is clear and composite as an image? How far can the Muslim or non-Muslim reader be convinced concerning the attitude of Islam toward the question of human rights?

It must be asserted that this image reflects a secure and sacrosanct attitude. It is true that a more comprehensive image might be obtained from a wider range of references than those of the *Sahih al-Bukhari*, but the present selection nonetheless represents the whole, as a blood sample represents the whole blood supply of a man's body. We may indeed gain further detail from a larger image, but these details will never contradict what we see in miniature. Islam harbours no contradictions; it is a composite but consistent creed harmonious, in its ideal and realistic aspects alike, in all matters concerning this world and the next.

It is hoped this essay has indicated the deep and comprehensive spirit of Islam vis-à-vis the issue of human rights; showing how the insight and practice of the Prophet demonstrates this, and, more importantly, how divine teachings are not liable to change or modification according to personal whim. Yet this implies no stiffness and callousness. The rights in question are sufficiently flexible to respond to attempts at adapting them to modern developments. These rights identify with duties within human life, and this gives them greater vitality to enhance the situation of man in this world and in the hereafter. Man was created by God in a certain form and for a certain purpose. Islam, accordingly, reveres this creation and endeavours to help man develop human life with dignity. Hence the guarantee of all these rights and duties, which are imposed individually and collectively with a view to better equipping man to realize his humanity. When the principles of Islam are applied in practice, the model man becomes possible, leading to the model society which, at a certain period of history, was able to create its own civilization in its own [Arabic] language – even though, as is well known, some of the followers of Islam had no knowledge of the language and early ambience of Islam. That this should be possible in such a short period of time indicates the humane nature of Islam and the genius of the language which transformed a heterogeneous community into a single human community guided by the light of Islam. Attempts by the enemies of Islam to undermine this human civilizational project spring from the merest fanaticism and rancor.

For all the prior existence and historical significance of the Code of Hammurabi, the modern world is more impressed with the French Revolution and its principles of Liberty, Equality and Fraternity, which emerged two centuries ago. The world also regards the UN Declaration of Human Rights as the first document in the history of humanity to recognize, with true clarity, the responsibility of the international community to recognize and protect human rights, and the first to aim to promulgate a comprehensive international order to protect these rights. This Declaration was issued late in 1948, after the bitter experience of two world wars had devastated humanity. The human rights of women were proclaimed in the International Conference on Human Rights, held in Vienna, under the auspices of the UN, in mid-1993.[140] And yet the world ignores the first comprehensive, organized constitutional precedent given to the world by Islam, in a body of legislation that has lived on for fifteen centuries and will remain active, dynamic and flexible in the lives of its adherents. No one can reasonably blame this order and its laws for misapplications during certain periods of history. Such misapplication has similarly plagued the principles of the French Revolution, the UN Charter and the Universal Declaration of Human Rights, through quite ridiculous double standards, in their application, that have aggravated the sense of injustice existing among many nations of the world. Since the real importance lies in the principle itself, it is sufficient credit to Islam, in addition to its precedent in honouring man and elevating his rights to the level of religious duties, that it was a religion stipulating, with a good measure of consensus, that authority and rule should be in the hands of men of learning, acting after mutual consultation. "Consult them in affairs [of moment]." (3, *Al 'Imran*, 159.) "Their affairs [of moment] are by mutual consultation." (42, *Al-Shura*, 38.) All this aims at the establishment of justice and the protection of human rights for all and everyone. The Prophet, in these legal rulings, was sent as a mercy for the whole of humanity, as is confirmed by the holy words: "We did not send you but as a Mercy for all humanity." (21, *Al-Anbiya'*, 107.)

Chapter 5: 'Man' and 'the Rights of Woman' in Islamic discourse – between the idealism of texts and the crisis of reality

Nasr Hamid Abu Zayd

Introduction

Muslims often stop to ponder this verse in the Holy Quran: 'We have honoured the sons of Adam; provided them with transport on land and sea; given them for sustenance things good and pure; and conferred on them special favours, above a great part of our creation.' (17, *Al-Isra'*, 70) This, Muslims agree, confirms that the Holy Quran and, consequently, Islam affirm and support human rights. Some might go so far, indeed, as to say that Islam anticipated twentieth-century civilization in specifying such rights. Undoubtedly Islam, like all religions, makes man the focus of interest, since it is in essence a discourse addressed to man by God. The discourse aims at establishing a relationship between the divine and the human, so that the latter may come into contact with the former and draw nearer to God's precincts through the act of 'obedience', or 'falling prostrate'. Thus, God commanded the Prophet not to obey those who prohibited him from performing the *salat*: "Fall prostrate, and come closer [to God]." (96, *Al-'Alaq*, 19.)

Be that as it may, we should not forget that the "man" honoured by religions, which guarantee him every right, is the man who adheres to a particular religion and follows the path of salvation it assigns to him. In contrast, the man who falls outside the sphere of a certain religion is, from the perspective of that religion, "irredeemable" and denied all rights, even if he enjoyed full rights from the perspective of the religion he follows. Deprivation of rights in one religion or the other is not limited to a threat of torment in the hereafter, since "degradation" in this world also serves to dehumanize man. Without this human quality, no kind of talk about rights is possible.

Muslims can very reasonably object to this generalized judgement, in that Islam recognizes all the religions that preceded Islam, the final revealed religion. Islam also respects the faithful followers of those preceding religions, and grants them all human rights as long as they themselves respect Islam and do not fight against its followers or ally themselves with its enemies. Indeed, the payment of *jizya*, demanded by Islam from non-Muslims and especially from "People of the Book", might possibly be justified to non-Muslims by saying that it was a "war tax" imposed in return for exemption from military service and fighting against the enemy, which were activities restricted to Muslims at the time.[1] Some may in fact interpret this extraction of tribute as part of a historical practice, recognized in olden times but not binding on Muslims today.[2]

If we are talking about 'Islam' with reference to its basic texts, the Quran and the authenticated *sunna* of the Prophet, we find endless evidence in the conduct of the Prophet, in his personal, social and political practices, to confirm the concept of respect for the rights of man as man, that is, irrespective of creed, colour or gender. The reason for the killing of some Jews in Yathrib (Medina) was their breach of the treaty of neutrality between the Muslims and the Meccan non-believers and their collusion with the unbelievers against Muhammad and his Companions.[3] This is similar, in modern terms, to the concept of 'national treason'. As such, an impartial scholar cannot use this incident as evidence of enmity toward Judaism as a religion.

Religious texts invariably convey idealistic principles concerning human nature. Yet the matter is left, in the end, to the activity of the human mind addressed, which, through the processes of 'explanation and interpretation', brings these principles down to reality in certain intellectual forms, informed by the nature of the epistemological 'frame of reference' of this interpreter or that; and it depends in equal measure on the general social and historical context of the age in which the process of understanding and explanation takes place. It is therefore possible to find various, even contradictory, versions within the corpus of Islamic thought, whether in its classical, traditional context, or in its modern phase from the beginning of the 'awakening' in the early nineteenth century up to the present. In the field of classical Islamic thought, we may trace these versions in a number of disciplines: namely, kalamology (principles of religion, or theology), and the principles of jurisprudence, philosophy and mysticism (*tasawwuf*).

There is a difference – indeed there are a number of differences – that can neither be ignored nor belittled between the level of abstract, intellectual formulation and that of social, historical and political practice in various Islamic societies. It is the difference between the 'ideal' and the 'real', whether the ideal in question is embodied in the divine discourse, as seen above, or in the theoretical formulation of human beings, in their interpretation of the divine discourse. This difference between the ideal and the real is found in all cultures and civilizations. The international document of human rights in the modern age – a formulation stemming from the long historical experience of man's struggle against all kinds of discrimination, segregation and oppression – has undoubtedly benefited from intellectual achievement in this field; the document guarantees man all rights, on the ideal level. But actual practice in advanced societies, where the human rights document was initiated, falls far below the standard of that ideal.

Partiality, based on culture, gender or race, represents a flagrant violation of human rights in each of these societies. Even worse are the policies pursued by the major developed countries against the small, undeveloped countries by way of degradation, impoverishment and exploitation. One might almost suspect that what is meant by 'man' in the Declaration of Human Rights is exclusively Western man. One might almost be led to believe, even, that Western European, and not Eastern European man is the 'man' in question. Thus the validity of the concept is diminished in political practice, as reflected in the relations of power, control and domination which make economic interest the ultimate aim and turn the ideals and principles into mere slogans.

This chasm between the ideal as posed by texts, be they religious or secular, and actual reality is the primary focus of this essay, which takes 'Islamic discourse' as its topic for analysis without any suggestion that it is a 'unique' discourse. Rather, it is offered as an example and a model expressive of the crisis of human existence from the dawn of history to the present: namely, the crisis of the gulf between the spiritual or intellectual 'ideal' and the 'actual' in its materiality and harshness. In its effort to analyse Islamic discourse, this study aims to deepen awareness of the crisis and so take one step forward toward a solution. This is offered as an alternative to the exchange of accusations, which can only worsen the crisis by numbing awareness.

The present analysis will focus mainly on Islamic discourse in its human dimension – that is, on the ways Muslims have understood divine discourse – in the hope of supplying a fair representation of the position on 'man' and the rights of woman as manifested in the four disciplines mentioned above: kalamology, jurisprudence, philosophy and mysticism. These disciplines are in fact the outcome of interaction between 'divine discourse' and historical social reality. They are the intellectual formulation of that constant 'tension' between the ideal and real.

I. Kalamology (scholastic Islamic theology)

Nowhere, perhaps, is the humanistic tendency more clearly manifested than in Mu'tazili thought, where the exaltation of 'reason' was more than the mere

result of coming into contact with other cultures generally and Greek philosophy in particular. It stemmed, in fact, from the whole socio-political attitude of
the early Mu'tazilis, an attitude primarily underlying their intellectual theses.
The Mu'tazili motto, that 'reason is the most equitable endowment of human
beings', was designed to counter the fanaticism that began to rear its head
immediately after the death of the Prophet, growing more ominously towards
the end of the Umayyad reign before reaching a peak of extremism in the
Abbasid age.[4] As Persians boasted to Arabs about their culture and traditions,
and Arabs boasted to Persians that they were the noblest among nations, since
the divine revelation had come to a Prophet from among themselves (and so
on), remonstration began to be made everywhere, especially in the writings of
al-Jahiz. Thus, it may be said that the Mu'tazili exaltation of reason and knowledge was an essential element of the movement's modernity, if we may use that
term. It was an attempt on their part to put an end to the bragging about ancestry, tribal allegiance and race, and to replace this with the values of 'reason and
knowledge' as a more objective criterion for assessing the social and spiritual
value of man. We must remember, in this connection, that the foremost theorists and leaders of the Mu'tazilis belonged socially to the *mawali*s,[5] a caste
deemed inferior to pure 'Arabs' – as may be gathered from the satire of the poet
Bashshar ibn Burd, levelled against the linguist and grammarian 'Abdullah ibn
Ishaq al-Hadrami (who could see nothing in Bashshar's poetry but grammatical errors):

> Had 'Abdullah been a *mawla*, I would have satirized him;
> But 'Abdullah is a *mawla* of *mawali*s.

This modernist, social attitude of the Mu'tazilis made them insist on the 'freedom' of the human will, not only because it provides evidence of divine 'justice'
– which is the bedrock of their intellectual system – but because it is impossible to prove the existence of God without such freedom. It is like a 'branch'
without which there is no 'origin'; since it is the branch that establishes the origin epistemologically, even though it is the 'origin' that establishes the 'branch'
existentially. This is how it is seen by the Qadi 'Abd al-Jabbar (d. 416/1025):

> [If one were to believe] that the Almighty was the creator and generator of men's
> actions, such belief [in man's inability to create his own action, or to have free-
> dom of choice] would mean that the Eternal [God] can be known as such,
> because the way to know Him is through His actions that indicate Him. If [such
> a believer] was unable to prove in [visible, tangible] reality the need of the created
> for a creator, he would be unable to refer [by analogy] the unseen to Him. So, he
> would be unable to see the need of created objects – which we cannot manage

on our own – for a creator. It follows that this would hinder knowledge of the Eternal, *per se*; so, how can it be said that He is the creator of [human] actions? And how can it be believed that a branch would abolish its [root] origin?[6]

It is only natural and logical that the concept of 'reason' should be the establishing concept of 'freedom' in all its manifestations, whether on the level of abstract knowledge or on that of action. On the epistemological level, reason, by its own unaided means, can attain to knowledge of the existence of God and to the knowledge of His qualities (oneness and justice), as well as to an awareness of its own duty of gratitude to God, Who created man and gave him the gift of life. Reason can also distinguish between the 'good' and 'bad' in objects and actions. The role of Shariah is to show the ways by which man can perform such intellectual duties, explaining the extent of acts of obedience – like *salat*, fasting, and almsgiving – and their times. These matters cannot be known by reason in detail, though reason can comprehend them in general. Indeed, 'reason' appears from this perspective as an absolute concept, liberated from the constraints of time/space, since it is a reason preoccupied with the universe and its creator on the one hand, and, on the other, liberated from the bonds of gender, race, culture and language in its capacity as human reason, indeed as the reason of the 'absolute man'. This cosmic, absolute man is able, through his cosmic, absolute reason, to penetrate the *terra incognita* of the cosmos, without guide from outside itself, because

> The knowledge of praise and blame and their applicability to actions . . . is a sign of sound reason, and it is not restricted to the fact that [such actions] have actually occurred. For [if one would] mix with people none of whom had committed an act of disobedience, there would be no place for blame; and if none had performed an act of obedience there would be no cause for praise. This will not affect what we mentioned earlier about the perfection of reason. Similar to that is saying, [if one] were created in a desert, he might be charged [with duties] when his mind came to perfection and when he could distinguish between praiseworthy and reproachable acts, even if he did not know the performer of such acts.[7]

But this exaltation of human reason epistemologically does not mean, for Mu'tazilis, the absolute exaltation of man on the scale of rational beings created by God. Men do not differ except in their ability to utilize that 'power' which is the 'essential reason' – that most equitable endowment of human beings – and to reach the stage of 'theoretical reason' which can attain to the knowledge of God, along with knowledge of His qualities of justice, and oneness, as well as the necessity of being grateful to Him. Since angels enjoy that knowledge as an endowment from God, they exist on a higher plane than man. But we have always to realize that the Mu'tazilis formulated their concepts according to notions of the 'social' man, not the absolute man in the metaphysical sense, even though, as noted above, they considered 'reason' an absolute power, liberated from the social conditions of place, time, culture and language. Another point of difference between angels and human beings led the Mu'tazilis to emphasize the concept of the 'supremacy' of the angels, in that they are naturally given to 'obedience': 'they do not disobey Allah in His commands, but perform what they are commanded.' (66, *Al-Tahrim,* 6) This confirms that the Mu'tazilis, in their judgment, had their eyes on the social being who can disobey and fail to heed the divine command, because he is the only being created free and not constrained. Perhaps he is the only being who dares defend his disobedience, claiming that he is 'constrained' and that the will of God directs his actions, as was maintained by the Umayyad rulers.[8]

By this means we can explain the difference between the Mu'tazili interpreters and their rivals, who called themselves 'the followers of *sunna* and majority' (*ahl al-sunna wa 'l-jama'a*), in interpreting the divine command to the angels to fall prostrate before Adam, as we read in the Holy Quran in a number of verses (2, *Al-Baqara,* 34; 38, *Sa'd,* 75; and others). Al-Tabari (d. 923), for instance, argues that God's command to the angels to fall prostrate before Adam was 'honouring' him, and that the angels' compliance was an act of obedience to God but that this does not suggest an act of 'worship'.[9] Another notable exegetist, al-Zamakhshari, does not disagree with al-Tabari here, but we find him striving, even so, to provide an intellectual justification for the divine command and the angels' obedience:

> What is inadmissible is falling prostrate to any other than God by way of worship. As an act of rendering honour, it is not rejected by reason except where God knows it to be evil and He prohibits the performance thereof.[10]

On this basis the divine command becomes 'an interest', the action of the angels 'an obedience', and the refusal of Satan 'a disobedience'. Satan's notion that he is better than Adam because he was created from fire, which is superior to the clay from which Adam was created, is vain in the view of al-Zamakhshari, because the command to fall prostrate is not connected with superiority. Satan, al-Zamakhshari argues, did not realize that

> when God commanded *His dearest worshippers and the nearest to Him* – the angels – who have a better right than others to refrain from humbling themselves to the meager human being, and to disdain the act of falling prostrate to him . . . they obeyed the command of God and were mindful of it, *paying no attention to the*

distinction between those falling prostrate and that to whom the act of prostration is performed, in glorification of the command of their Lord and His address.[11]

The Mu'tazili attitude, in the matter of preferring the angels to human beings, becomes much clearer when al-Zamakhshari uses an analogy to explain the significance of Satan's disobedience in Quranic discourse:

> It is similar to the king who orders his minister to visit some lowly servants; and the minister refrains from bringing himself low.[12]

The significance of the analogy, which makes 'some lowly servants' similar to Adam, provoked the spokesman of 'the followers of the *sunna* and majority', Ahmad ibn Muhammad al-Munir al-Iskandari al-Maliki, into an attack on al-Zamakhshari, describing him as 'utterly fanatical' in preferring the angels, not only over human beings but over prophets as well:

> He transgressed in his discourse on Adam by comparing his lower station to that of the angels, as he claims, with the order of a king to his minister to visit some lowly servants, making those lowly servants analogous to Adam, father to all prophets, peace be on them all.[13]

It is clear here that the question from the perspective of *ahl al-sunna* revolves around the preference between 'prophets' and 'angels', a comparison which must tend to prefer the prophets as they are 'infallible' and incapable of committing acts of disobedience. The Mu'tazilis are basically concerned with the social man who is liable to error, sin and wrongdoing, as a result of the 'freedom' of 'thought' and 'action' accorded him. On the other hand, not all prophets are infallible in the view of the Mu'tazilis, since Adam himself disobeyed the order of his Lord and ate from the forbidden tree. The prophets, however, are safeguarded against 'major' sins that might alienate people from their message and undermine their credibility. Thus we see that religious thought, as represented here in kalamology, or scholastic theology, chooses the texts that suit its point of view and support its way of thinking. What runs contrary to that thinking and perspective becomes a matter of texts open to interpretation and explanation. In this way the Mu'tazili emphasis on the 'epistemological' aspect of man, with a view to combating 'sectarianism' and 'fanaticism', has led to the placing of man on a level lower than that of the angels. This was to become a problem for Islamic philosophical thought, even one of its fundamental problems.

II. Philosophy

This epistemological aspect of man became the focus for philosophers, both for rational ones like al-Kindi and Ibn Rushd (Averroes) and for illuminists like al-Farabi and Ibn Sina (Avicenna). For all of them, knowledge is the only way to realize both types of happiness: of this world and of the hereafter. Knowledge is acquired by achieving an understanding of the 'essence' of existence through, on the one hand, meditation on physical objects, from the lowest to the highest, and, on the other, by understanding the essence of 'man' through introspection. Whether knowledge is 'acquired' – achieved, that is, by learning, inspection and deduction – or 'endowed' – that is, endowed in man by God through inspiration – the source of knowledge remains a great cosmic mind, which the philosophers call the 'active' or 'primordial' mind. It was called 'primordial' because it was the first of the emanations or creations that emerged into existence from God the Creator; and it was called 'active' because it is the 'active cause' of all that happens in the world. From the content of its knowledge each of the nine spherical minds (from the second to the tenth) derives the knowledge necessary to manage the affairs of its own sphere. In other words, these ten minds combine the two powers: the epistemological or 'scientific' on the one hand and the existential or 'practical' on the other.

We may note, in this connection, a *hadith* ascribed to the Prophet (though some scholars ascribe it to Plotinus), one so highly celebrated in Islamic quarters towards the end of the first/seventh and early second/eighth centuries that it became the subject of a number of interpretations and acquired meanings and types of significance not easy to count.[14]

> The first thing that God created was the mind. He said to it: Come along, so it did; then He said to it: Turn back, so it turned back. Then God said: By My Glory and Grandeur, I have not created anything nobler than you. With you I take, and with you I give; with you I reward, and with you I punish.

Whether by the deductive mental reflection of the rational philosophers, or through 'imagination', at the highest point of its serenity, according to illuminist philosophers, man communicates with the active mind to obtain full and complete knowledge.[15] If the first route, through reason and deduction, is 'rare and exclusive to great men', the second route, through imagination and inspiration, is restricted to prophets alone. 'All their inspiration and what they relay to us of revelation is an effect of imagination and one of its results.'[16] Both ways nevertheless lead to the same objective in practice. The Mu'tazilis effectively concluded as follows: There is nothing in the Quran except what is compatible with the manner of the mind. Had this been taken as evidence that it comes from God, it would have been easier to understand, since there is nothing in His evidence except what goes along safely with minds and is compatible with them.[17] Ibn Rushd had come to virtually the same conclusion, when he decided, based on the unity of the epistemological source, that 'Shariah' and 'evidence' are like two foster-sisters (note the precision and significance of the simile) who entertain no opposition or contradiction between themselves, because 'the right does not contradict the right, but agrees with it and is evidence for it'.[18]

Hence, it can be said that the 'man' the philosophers speak about, and place on a level near that of the prophet, is the philosophical man and not the normal social man. As such, the value of man is decided according to the level of his epistemological awareness, and this divides human beings into commoners and elite. The elite enjoy the two types of happiness: that of this world and that of the next. Commoners have to 'imitate' the elite to enjoy a degree of happiness. The elite enjoy a level of 'evidential' or 'inspirational' knowledge which is kept from the common people for fear of corrupting their faith. This division of human beings was attested by the most eminent rivals in the history of Arab-Islamic culture: Abu Hamid al-Ghazali, author of *The Destruction of the Philosophers* (Tahafut al-falasifa), and Abu 'l-Walid ibn Rushd, author of *The Destruction of Destruction* (Tahafut al-tahafut). In fact Islamic thought was beginning, gradually, to 'justify' the division of human beings within social reality, especially given the growing association between the intelligentsia and political authority, which has been a relationship of reliance and support for the first party, and one of manipulation for the second. Indeed, it may have been that the justification of intellectual, then epistemological, differences between human beings was a means by which a member of the educated elite tried to find – through the authority of knowledge – a place for himself within the social system, next to the authorities of financial and military power.[19]

III. Mysticism

The common man within society, unequipped with knowledge or learning, was destined to follow the way of 'imitation' or else perish on the way of perdition. This doomed creature is the 'animal man', so termed by the eminent Andalusi mystic Muhyi 'l-Din ibn 'Arabi, who formulated the notion of the 'perfect man'. It should be emphasized that this concept, as propounded by Ibn 'Arabi, is a composite of several intellectual elements and influences which cannot be reviewed here; in any case a number of studies, some noted below, have dealt with the matter. Nevertheless, the first and foremost of those elements, the Holy Quran, has not received sufficient attention from scholars for its formative and pivotal role in the establishment of the concept. Louis Massignon has reproached his fellow orientalists for confining themselves to the study of external influence on Islamic thought, rather than penetrating to the essence of Islam itself – a failure he attributes to their inability to use the Quran to come to an adequate understanding and analysis of thought. For the Muslim, this text represents an excellent and comprehensive dictionary. It is the compendium of the Muslim's knowledge and the key to his vision of the world.[20]

Indeed, the Holy Quran addresses the human being directly, informing him that God has subjected to him 'what is in heavens and on earth'. (31, *Luqman,* 20) 'He subjected to you the night and the day; the sun and the moon; and the stars are subjected by His command: truly in this are signs for men who are wise.* And the things on this earth which He has multiplied in varying colours [and qualities]: truly in this is a sign for men who celebrate the praises of Allah.* It is He Who has subjected the sea that you may eat thereof flesh that is fresh and tender, and that you may extract therefrom ornaments to wear; and you may see the ships therein that plough the waves, that you may seek of His bounty, and that you may be grateful.' (45, *Al-Jathiya,* 13) 'And marks, and by the stars [men] guide themselves.' (16, *Al-Nahl,* 12–16) These texts, and many more in the Holy Quran, affirm to the Muslim mind that the entire world is created and subjected to the service and interest of man; which means that man in the divine discourse is the centre of the universe and the end and aim of existence. This is the central idea that developed, in the mystical mind, into the theory of the 'perfect man'. Ibn 'Arabi notes:

> There is nothing in this world which is not subjected to this man as the fact of his image would show . . . Everything in the world is under man's subjugation. He who knows this is the perfect man; and whoever is ignorant of it is the animal man.[21]

But what is the 'fact of image' which made man deserving of this high status in the system of existence? It was the Quran, once more, which the Muslim mystics invoked to formulate their theory of man. The clay of which the body was created is formed of the four elements of nature: earth, air, water and fire.[22] This is in addition to God's honouring of Adam by creating him with His own hands. ('The one whom I have created with My hands.') (38, *Saad,* 75) Whether the reference to 'hands' is interpreted realistically or metaphorically, it was deemed an act of honour to Adam and a preference accorded to man over the rest of the creatures who did not achieve this honour, having been created by the command 'let there be'. The human image is perfected by the soul, which is of the 'divine breath'. ('We created man from sounding clay, from mud moulded into shape.') (15, *Al-Hijr*, 26) ('He fashioned him in due proportion, and breathed into him something of His spirit.') (32, *Al-Sajda*, 9) ('When I have fashioned him and breathed into him of My spirit.') (38, *Saad*, 72) Thus the human image combines the 'natural' and the 'divine', and man becomes the 'small collective universe', just as it may be said that the 'universe is a large-scale man', because in man are collected all the facts of the large universe.[23]

The Quran adds to all this the distinction of Adam over the angels, which became a justification for his being deserving of 'vicegerency'. This is because God 'taught Adam the names of all things; then He placed them before the angels and said, "tell Me the names of these if you are right".* They said, "Glory to You, of knowledge we have none, save what You have taught us: in truth it is You Who are perfect in knowledge and wisdom."* He said, "O Adam! Tell them their names". When he had told them, Allah said, "Did I not tell you that I know the secret of heavens and earth, and I know what you reveal and what you conceal?"' (2, *Al-Baqara*, 31–3) The mystics interpreted 'all the names' epistemologically as 'the divine names'; the 'teaching' they interpreted existentially, to mean the emergence of the divine names, which were 'inherent' in the 'divine self' before the creation of Adam, and their manifestation in the spirit of Adam. Just as intellectual circles in the early second/eighth century were alive with discussion about 'reason', as outlined above, so discussion about 'image' was found fascinating in epistemological circles in particular. The Prophet reportedly said: 'Allah created Adam in His own image.' The epistemologists understood 'His' to refer to God, which means, they argued, that Adam was created in the image of God. Others tried to deny the mystic significance of the possessive pronoun 'his', saying it rather referred to Adam. The meaning, they held, is that God created Adam in the image of Adam that he had. In other words, God gave Adam the image that he had. In fact this interpretation completely undermines the meaning of the *hadith*. There is no argument among Muslims about the fact that God created Adam. It is only logical that the act of 'creation' should imply giving the image. See, for instance: 'It is We Who created you and gave you shape.' (7, *Al-A'raf*, 11); 'It is Allah Who has given you shape.' (40, *Ghafir*, 64); 'He . . . has given you shape, and made your shapes beautiful.' (64, *Al-Taghabun*, 3) (The original Arabic for 'shape' in the Quran means 'image'.) In any case, this *hadith* is another version of what we read in *Genesis*, so there is no point in the last interpretation, which renders the *hadith* void of meaning.

Thus, we find that the mystical interpretation established the supremacy of Adam over the angels, but from a standpoint essentially different from that of the kalamologists. On the existential level, Adam represents the most complete and comprehensive manifestation of the natural and the divine, because the divine names and the cosmic facts appear in his image. Hence, he is the only being able to reach complete and comprehensive knowledge. According to Abu 'l-A'la 'Afifi, Ibn 'Arabi sees the whole of existence as

> a logical structure from top to bottom, where man has the central place by virtue of his distinguished character in which none of the other beings has a share. Ibn 'Arabi thinks that no one can realize the position of man in the universe or appreciate his work except one who is well-versed in the knowledge of God. And no one is capable of this knowledge of God except man; because through man God knew Himself, as man is the complete manifestation of divinity. Beings other than the perfect man know of God as much as they know of themselves; since beings are only His attributes; hence their knowledge is imperfect if we compare it with the knowledge of man in whom all the divine attributes are gathered together. Even angels have an imperfect knowledge, because all they know of the 'right' is 'infallibility', which is not connected to visible existence. Man alone knows both sides of the "right", because he himself is the right and the creation.[24]

Thus we find that the concept of 'man' in mystical discourse is generally concerned with the 'knowledgeable' man, the man who has achieved a full and complete knowledge of himself, existence and divinity. This man is the measure of truth, because he is perfection itself. He is the object of celebration, high in station, honoured in rank. But the 'unenlightened' man, the simple social man, has no place in this epistemological system. Hence it could be said that Islamic thought is, in this respect, no different from medieval thought in general, which assesses the value of man through this sharp division of human beings into 'elite' and 'common people'. It is always necessary, therefore, before launching into the traditional – often pointless – high praise of man, to investigate the significance of 'that man' in the intellectual discipline or discourse under study.

IV. Hayy ibn Yaqzan: the Allegory of Pure Mind

We need, first, to consider the significance of the title chosen by Abu Bakr ibn Tufayl (d. 581/1185) for his philosophical novel *Hayy ibn Yaqzan*. 'Hayy' represents 'life' (*hayat* in Arabic), which is manifested solely in the *yaqza* ('wake-fulness') of the mind. Whether in the 'deductive' system of the kalamologists or in the 'evidential' system of the philosophers, God has the attribute of 'life', because there is no 'knowledge' without life. All the attributes of the divine self, such as 'sempiternity', which distinguishes the creator from the created, and 'power', which is evidenced by the very act of creation, and 'wisdom', deduced from the perfection of creation and the lack of discrepancy among the parts of the world – all these lead, almost as a logical necessity, to the attribute of 'knowledge'. This coupling of the two attributes to a degree of concomitance, which makes each attribute imply the other, is found in Quranic discourse in more than one context. In the *surat Al-Baqara*, 255 ('Allah! There is no god but He – the Living, the Self-subsisting, the Eternal . . . He knows [what appears to His creatures] as before or after or behind them. Nor shall they compass aught of his knowledge except as He wills.'), we find the concomitance too obvious to need elaboration.[25] In another context, the attribute of 'life' is coupled with the revelation of the Book. ('Allah! There is no god but He – The Living, The Self-subsisting, Eternal. It is He Who sent the Book down to you in truth.') (3, *Al-'Imran*, 2–3.) Life is also coupled with creation ('And put your trust in Him Who lives and does not die . . . He Who has created the heavens and the earth and all that is between') (25, *Al-Furqan*, 58–9); and life is coupled, too, with the giving of life and the taking of it. ('He is the Living [One]: There is no god but He . . . It is He Who has created you . . . It is He Who gives life and death.') (40, *Ghafir*, 65–8) In the light of this concomitance, Ibn Tufayl chooses the name of his hero to denote the 'absolute' man, and to make an allegorical ref-erence to the potential of this 'living' and ever 'wakeful man' who is 'not taken by slumber or sleep'.

This absolute nature of the hero's character is confirmed when Ibn Tufayl presents two possibilities for his birth: the first, implicitly favoured by the author, is that he was born from nature, without father or mother. The detailed description of the process of natural 'birth' sounds like a parody of the story of the creation of Adam's body from the four elements of nature, with the body then given life by the divine breath. The clay from which 'Hayy' was born

> was fermented with the passage of years until the hot mingled with the cold, the humid with the dry, in equal and balanced proportions. That fermented clod of clay was very large. Parts of it were finer than other parts in temperate mood and readiness for the preparation of mixtures. The centre of the clod was most tem-perate and closest to the temper of man. That clod convulsed, and something like boiling happened to it, caused by its high viscosity. In its centre, a tiny viscid bubble appeared, and divided into two parts, with a thin diaphragm in between,

full of a fine airy body, of extreme temperate nature proper to it. To it then was attached the spirit, which is 'the affair of God'. It clung to it in a manner difficult to separate in sense and mind.[26]

Emphasis on the absolute nature of the hero, and indication of his status as the absolute man, grows steadily as the hero faces directly, for the first time, the problem of 'death' as represented in the death of the 'roe deer' who was like a mother to him. He is now seven years old, and is able to adjust to the life of the island with its various creatures by way of 'imitation' first; then he begins to devise solutions that deepen his awareness of his difference and independence from these creatures. In an attempt to discover the 'cause' which led to death, he dissects the body of the dead doe deer until he comes to the left cavity of the 'heart'. Finding it empty, he realizes this must be the site of the 'secret' of life, 'because [the secret] had left it and evacuated [its place]. Then the body suffered the incompetence [which it did] and lost perception and was bereft of movement . . . The body became base in his eyes, and of no value, in comparison with that thing which, he concluded, abides in the body for a while, then departs. Then he dwelt on thinking of that thing. What is it? How is it? What binds it to the body? What has become of it? From which exit did it leave the body? What was the cause of its annoyance, if it was forced to leave? What made it dislike the body so it left it, if it departed by choice?'[27]

Next 'Hayy' is guided to the process of 'burying' the body of the roe deer by imitation. He imitates the crow which has killed another crow and buried it. The scene in our novel is almost a representation of the Quranic scene with Cain and Abel, the two sons of Adam, except that the Quranic story specifies that it was God Who 'sent' the crow to the killer, 'to show him how to hide the shame of his brother.' (5, *Ma'ida,* 31) But this reference is not absent in our tale; for the feeling of 'Hayy' that he is more deserving than the crow to know of the burial process strongly suggests the Quranic original. Thus the text prepares the reader for the realization that the human mind, in its sincere and constant quest for knowledge and understanding, is accompanied by divine care and protection at all times.

This absolute cosmic hero, or pure mind, lives on a deserted island among other imaginary isles. It is an ideal island in its 'geographical' situation, and the climate is 'of the most temperate air on earth'. It has 'no excessive heat or cold'. Moreover, it is the best place to receive 'the high light shining on it'.[28] On this island there is no one but this person whom the reader cannot identify as a man or a woman, except through the masculine name 'Hayy', plus one single phrase in the entire text.[29] This man, however, needs no society or language, let alone learning or culture, for his perceptions to grow, his senses to open up, his mind to operate, or his consciousness to develop. He is very similar to the man described by the Mu'tazilis, but he goes beyond him in that his use of deductive knowledge does not stop at the question of the existence of God and the divine attributes of justice and oneness. Through deduction, he provides evidence for the 'creation' of the world, and deduces its need for a 'creator', one who is different from it in nature and qualities:

> Then whenever he beheld any being of beauty, magnificence, perfection, power, or with any other virtue in it, he reflected on it and realized that it flowed from the emanation of that Creator by choice – Praise His Majesty – and from His existence and action. He then realized that that Being is greater, more perfect, complete, beautiful, magnificent and enduring than those [creatures] and is in no way comparable to them. He kept on reviewing all the qualities of perfection and found that they all belong to Him, and emanate from Him, and that He is more worthy of them than all that is described by them other than Himself. He reviewed all qualities of imperfection, and found Him free from them. For can He not be free from them when imperfection can only mean sheer non-existence or what is implied therein? And how can non-existence[30] have a relation or connection with absolute existence, the self-existing, the Giver to every existing being of its existence? There is no existence but Him: He is the existence, the perfection, the completeness, the beauty, the magnificence, the ability, the knowledge, and He is Himself, and 'everything is perishing except His own Face'.[31] (28, *Al-Qasas*, 88)

This is the level reached by 'Hayy' at the age of 35: an intellectual knowledge based on contemplation of existential evidence. This knowledge moves his yearning to witness the beauty of the Being evidenced by his intellect. This is what distinguishes 'Hayy' from the Mu'tazili model, for 'Hayy' is the man of the philosophers, Aristotelians and Gnostics alike, as well as the man of the mystics. In short, he is the 'man of knowledge', the perfect and model man envisaged by the Islamic consciousness. Existential evidence is not enough for this man to achieve the happiness represented in embracing the absolute and uniting with it. The way to this is the elimination of needs, except what is necessary for the 'body', which is simply a miniature of the universe, in order to cleanse and purify the soul from other preoccupations, in preparation for reaching the state of readiness to join its primary source and origin. This is how our hero continues his efforts, moving from state to state, and from one station to another, until he perishes away from himself and all other selves:

> He did not see in existence except the One, the Living, the Eternal, and saw what cannot be described! Then he returned to observe the different beings, when he

awoke from his state, which was similar to intoxication. It occurred to his mind that he had no existence different from that of the Supreme Truth, and that the truth about his own existence was part of that transcendent Reality; what he had thought at first to be his existence, distinct from His existence, was not so in fact, for 'there is nothing except the Existence of the Right'. It was like the sunlight which falls on solid bodies, and you see it appearing therein. Although it is ascribed to the body wherein it appeared, it is in reality nothing but the light of the sun. When the body disappears, its light disappears with it and the sunlight remains as it is, neither diminished by the presence of that body, nor increased by its absence.[32]

The story comes to its climax and conclusion, and we, the readers, come to the quintessence and centre of significance. To the island comes 'Asal', an ascetic worshipper and hermit, seeking seclusion and privacy. His name (cognate with the Arabic sa'al: ask) indicates the 'questions' he is eager to ask, as

he was given to constant meditation, attachment to instructive lessons, and pro-found search for meanings' according to reports.[33] He subscribed to a revealed religion whose secrets he had penetrated, and he had delved deep into its spiri-tual meanings. He was not satisfied with the surface sense of words related 'in the description of the Almighty or the description of the resurrection, reward and punishment.

In all this he was at variance with a friend, who was a follower of the same reli-gion and his own compatriot; for this friend was 'more concerned with appar-ent [sense] and kept far away from interpretation, stopping short of flexibility of thought, meditation and free disposal'.[34] Hence this companion bears the name 'Salaman', which indicates a preference for 'safety' (Arabic salama), fol-lowing the group and holding fast to what its members say. Note how he is described by the narrator of the story, who speaks of

his cowardly nature in shying away from thought and disposal. His attachment to the group warded off his fears, removed interfering fancies, and saved from the intimations of Satan.[35]

'Hayy' and 'Asal' meet, and the latter begins to teach our hero the language, 'by pointing out to him the physical beings, pronouncing their names, repeating those names to him, and making "Hayy" pronounce them. "Hayy" began pro-nouncing those names accompanied by the gestures, until *he taught him all the names*, coaching him gradually until he began to speak in a short time'.[36] The surprise comes when 'Asal' hears 'Hayy' describing the facts of existence as he has seen and witnessed them. 'Asal' thereupon becomes certain that all that was related in his doctrine: the commands of God, His angels, Books and the Day of Judgement, His Heaven and Hell were all examples of what 'Hayy ibn Yaqzan' had seen. So [Asal's] vision was flung open, and the flame of his mind was sparked, the rational and the revealed corresponded, the ways of interpretation became more accessible to him, and there was no problem in the Shariah that did not become clear to him, no door was left unlocked and no obscurity unclarified. He became one of those who think and reason. Then he looked at 'Hayy ibn Yaqzan' with reverence and glorification, and was certain that he was one of the saints, on whom there is no fear, nor shall they grieve.[37]

'Asal', for his part, now begins to tell 'Hayy' about the island he has come from, and about the religion he believes in: its commands, prohibitions, forms of worship, transactions and the like. Here, 'Hayy' can see only complete agreement between what he has achieved in his isolation and retirement and what has been introduced by 'revelation' in general. He is, however, bewildered over certain details, unable to understand the wisdom contained in them. Such matters include the following: Why does revelation, in *matters related to the divine sphere and reward and punishment*, depend on similitude and parables rather than the presentation of facts in a clear language, without recourse to interpretation and difference? Is not the dependence on 'simile' in expressing these facts the cause which has 'led people to greatly magnify and believe things about the Essence of Reality of which He is free?' The other matter which bewilders 'Hayy' is the question of forms of worship and transactions: he sees an 'abridgement' in the revelation about forms of worship when compared with the 'details' and expansion in the transactions.[38]

The kalamologists had previously dealt with the problem of simile and metaphorical expressions in the Holy Quran in their discussion of the 'categorical and analogous' (*muhkam* and *mutashabih*) verses, a problem raised in Quranic discourse itself. ('In it are verses basic [categorical] ... others are analogous . . .') (3, *Al-'Imran, 7*) Their answers, irrespective of the various approaches and ideological tendencies, were briefly that the divine wisdom intended to stir the human mind towards *ijtihad* (interpretation), so that the *mujtahid*, or interpreter, might have more reward than the traditional follower.[39] But philosophical discourse in general – with its sharp division of human beings into elite and commons, or (to use Ibn Tufayl's expression) those 'of superior nature' and 'of defective nature' – made revelation a mere discourse to the commons, suitable to their defective nature – though it does also include 'indications and warnings' to the elite and the wise to enable them to interpret its metaphorical expressions and similes in a manner clarifying the real indications intended in the expressions in question. These fact-clarifying expressions were considered 'proscribed' to commoners and 'denied' to the non-elite, whether Aristotelian or Gnostic.[40]

'Hayy', with his companion 'Asal', now departs to the island from which the latter came, hoping the salvation of the islanders will be achieved at his hands as he expounds and clarifies the truth to them. But when he starts 'teaching them and spreading the secrets of wisdom before them', he finds them inattentive, disgusted and angered. As the narrator bluntly puts it, he had not known how stupid and defective they were, how poor in judgement and weak in resolution – that they were 'only like cattle – Nay, they are worse astray'. (25, *Al-Furqan*, 44)[41] 'Hayy' finally becomes convinced that common people are interested only in clinging to outward appearance, and are satisfied with similes and metaphors as literal facts. He realizes, accordingly, that 'all wisdom, guidance and prosperity in the words of the prophets and the texts of Shariah ah cannot be other than that, and can afford no more[42] Before leaving the island with 'Asal', to return to Hayy's own island, 'Hayy' goes to the islanders pretending repentance for the opinions he had previously expressed and advising them to remain in their present state, abiding by Shariah and outward actions. They should, he says, refrain from delving into what does not concern them, but rather continue to believe in the analogous verses and accept them, steering away from heresies and whims, following in the steps of the pious forefathers and shunning novelties and innovations.[43]

This is where the cosmic mind of the enlightened man anchors: isolation and aloofness, accepting the ignorance of the masses rather than striving to teach them, since there is no point in teaching people who are born with an unreceptive nature. Because they were born to an ignorant nature, formulated to it by an effective 'determinism', the enlightened man has no choice but to isolate himself and seek his personal salvation in the arms of the absolute, which may sometimes be analogous with the 'absolute' of political authority. Thus, the enlightened man alone deserves the title of 'man'. The common people are 'like cattle, nay they are worse astray'. In the second/eighth or third/ninth centuries, *'aql*, or 'reason' (hence the aptitude for learning and knowledge), was the most equitable distinguishing criterion among human beings. By the sixth/twelfth century 'reason' had come to be seen as a divine gift which God has assigned to a chosen minority of human beings. This represents a considerable retreat in the concept of man within Islamic discourse.

V. Fiqh (Jurisprudence)

In legal jurisprudence, man is generally the subject of what is a duty and what is prohibited, the two being aspects of a single aim: to prevent collision between individual wills and liberties. What should be legally permitted or prohibited is decided by a will higher than that of individuals, namely the will of society, according to what some philosophers call the 'social contract'. But we know from sociology that what is called a social contract is simply a matter of the terms imposed by the will of those social forces exercising control and domination, the powers that *possess* the means of control and domination, beginning with the possession of the 'tools of production' and going beyond the mere production of ideology – law being, in fact, one of the means by which these powers control and manage the affairs of society.

In the history of Islamic thought, *fiqh*, or jurisprudence, concerns the law or laws promulgated by society but based on the legislative texts contained in the Holy Quran, these latter making up a little more than one sixth of the Quran itself. Most of these texts deal with family matters, such as marriage, divorce and inheritance. Others deal with aspects of the commercial transactions of selling and buying, while still others deal with worship and morals.

Muslim jurists needed to formulate precise methods of deduction and interpretation to help them derive a complete legal structure from religious texts. They started by compiling the former laws, traditions and social practices which Islam did not prevent or proscribe, incorporating these into their jurisprudential system under such headings as 'the law of our predecessors', 'approval', 'public interests', etc., and 'intellectuals' like Abu Hanifa al-Nu'man formulated the concept of *qiyas*, or analogy, to apply those rulings actually specified by texts to similar cases. This was the principle approved by Imam al-Shafi'i, who specified its guidelines and conditions, making it a source of legislation after the Quran, the *sunna* and *ijma'* (consensus).[44]

Within this legal frame of reference, it is natural that emphasis with regard to the concept of man should fall on the dimension of *ta'a*, or obedience. The legislator is a holy and supreme authority that no worldly, earthly authority can reach – this ultimate authority being God, Who is the 'charger', while man is the 'charged', able to find no salvation except in obedience. Jurisprudential thought has distinguished three basic levels of action: *duty*, whereby man is punished for failure to perform an action; *the proscribed*, whereby man is punished for performing an action; and *the permitted*, into which other actions fall, whether mentioned in the text or not, these last therefore falling outside jurisprudential law and being a matter of individual or social 'liberties'. In the flourishing age of Islamic jurisprudence, permitted actions were further divided. Some were *commendable*, that is, those actions which bring man closer to 'good' deeds desired by the legislator; a man is rewarded for doing these but not punished for neglecting them. The other category was of *repugnant* actions, which draw man on to commit sin and acts of disobedience. These actions are undesirable to the legislator, and man is rewarded for avoiding them but not punished for performing them.

'Obligation' therefore falls on two of the five types of action. The other three fall under no obligation other than the moral, individual 'commitment' stemming from personal 'piety'. In all cases, the measure of value in jurisprudence is 'obedience', which alone assesses the value of man, indeed his very humanity within society as governed by this legal frame of reference. Although early jurisprudents distinguished between the 'right' of God over the individual and the community, and the rights and duties exchanged among individuals within the community, later jurisprudents tended to confuse the distinction between the 'social' and the 'religious', this leading to a 'distinction' among human beings on religious grounds. The result was those harsh judgments against non-Muslims which, fortunately, remained mere opinions ignored by Muslims in practice. The history of the Muslim conquests does not record a single case of mass killing or religious cleansing. Jurisprudential rulings were in fact mostly used to liquidate rivals following accusations of 'atheism', 'disbelief' or 'infidelity' to Islam.

VI. Man between 'thought' and 'reality'

From this review of the concept of 'man' in Islamic thought, it may be said that the man celebrated in many texts by the Quran and the *sunna* was subject to considerable limitations in the field of thought. He is the 'thinking' man of the Mu'tazilis, the 'enlightened' man of the philosophers and mystics, the 'charged' and obedient man of the jurisprudents. In most of these limitations there is no mention of man as a 'social being' who is neither enlightened nor obedient; and this it was that led to the exclusion of the non-Muslim, along with the Muslim who is not obedient. If the latter happens to be enlightened, he is classified as a *zindiq* (a heretic, wayward unbeliever) who deserves butchering or burning. Thus, when the text moves from its ideal and utopian position to the field of thought, intellectual bias and ideological fanaticism intervene to dictate exclusion and exile, for political and social reasons hiding behind religious and intellectual justifications.

In the social context, the controlling, domineering politician tends to exploit the intelligentsia for his own benefit, using all the means of attraction and intimidation – the policy of carrot and stick. This is ingeniously employed in dictatorial communities to tame the 'enlightened' and incorporate them into the power structure. Through the men of 'knowledge' it becomes easier to direct the common people to the path of obedience and submission. Obedient men of knowledge enjoy august favour, and are offered the titles of *imam*, *hujja* ('authority') and *thiqa* ('trustworthy'). If the man of 'knowledge' proves difficult to incorporate into the arena of obedience, he is branded a *zindiq*, an insurgent rebel against the faith. He is then oppressed, imprisoned, persecuted or killed, either by crucifixion, or by amputation, or, at very best, through the burning of his books. Among those to suffer, we may cite Ma'bad al-Jahni, al-Jud ibn Dirham, Ghaylan al-Dimashqi, Ibn al-Muqaffa', al-Hallaj, al-Suhrawardi, and Ibn Rushd (Averroes). Reference might also be made to the incessant attempts to tarnish and distort the thought of certain Islamic tendencies and sects that opposed official authority, such as the Khawarij, the Shi'ites and the Qarmatians.

Moving away from the field of the 'enlightened' and political 'opponent' to the ordinary 'man', we immediately find a figure ignored and neglected by historians, concerned as these have basically been with the history of 'messengers and kings'.[45] In the context of major events this ordinary man is a forgotten quantity, referred to as 'the commons', 'the rabble' or 'the riffraff'. This debasement of the common people is reflected in their treatment by rulers. An Egyptian Copt complained to 'Amr ibn al-'As, the governor of Egypt appointed by the second Rashidi Caliph, 'Umar ibn al-Khattab. When the Caliph received news of the man's grievance, he shouted in his governor's face: 'When did you enslave human beings who were born free?' This was not, though, repeated in the reign of his successor, 'Uthman ibn 'Affan. When people complained to him about the injustice of certain governors, he wrote to his governor in Egypt instructing him to chastise the commoners in question. Whether the letter was actually known to 'Uthman or sent without his knowledge is immaterial. In either case debasement of the commoners by political authority is current, starting from that period.

Under the Umayyads, rulers tried every means to employ the men of knowledge and the jurisprudents. While some accepted, others refused, paying the price for their refusal and independence by suffering imprisonment and persecution. 'Ideological deceit' was the Umayyad way of controlling the common people. The concept of *jabr*, or 'determinism', was a religious cover used to justify Umayyad injustice. The charge of 'hypocrisy' levelled against new converts to Islam (who were as such no longer technically bound to pay the *jizya*) was a pretext to continue the further levying of the tax, even though these people were now members of the Muslim community. The levy was necessary to ensure constant revenue, to guard against any drying up of the springs of wealth and pomp. 'God made us rulers, not tax-collectors' was the cry of Caliph 'Umar ibn 'Abd al-'Aziz. But it was heard no more after his death. The concept of *irja'* ('deferment') – leaving the judgment of man's belief to God alone on the Day of Reckoning – emerged as an ideological reaction to Umayyad cynicism about the motives and genuineness of new converts to Islam. But even this was soon to be absorbed into the state ideology. The 'deferred people' turned from 'rebelling' against the system to 'justifying' it. Deferment came to mean effective withdrawal from criticizing political injustice and corruption.[46] In the Abbasid age the situation was not much different. Al-Ma'mun sought to impose the doctrine of 'the creation *khalq* of the Quran' by force, thus putting an end to Mu'tazili thought and opening the door for the almost total domination of Hanbali orthodoxy.

Gradually, Islamic thought changed from a 'formulation' and guidance of reality to a mere 'justification' of it, by giving it ideological cover and religious legitimacy. The 'obedient enlightened' model virtually dominated the fields of thought, culture and literature in the fifth/eleventh century. Its role grew steadily, transforming Muslim thought to a veil preventing any awareness of the methods used by the authority to control, domineer, exploit and repress. Thus, Abu Hamid al-Ghazali fought his intellectual battles for the benefit of the Abbasid system, on several fronts. He gave the Ash'ari school of thought a philosophical foundation; he offered his version of a conciliatory sufism as an alternative to a vibrant and subversive movement; he justified the authority of the Abbasid Caliph against his Shi'ite enemies, indeed against the very foundation of Shi'ite thought; finally, he sought to undermine the intellectualism of philosophy and branded philosophers as heretics.[47] Consequently, *ijtihad* was frozen, and the tendency merely to explain and summarize came to dominate many fields of knowledge. The Ash'ari school of thought, mixed with mysticism, was no longer one among other tendencies. It became the 'doctrine' *par excellence*. Hanbali and Ash'ari views on the principles of religion were quoted in later works under the heading: 'That which must be believed and should not be ignored.' *Taqlid*, ('imitation') now dominated the Muslim mind, which became satisfied with reiterating and repeating the sayings of former authors. Philosophy and logic became proscribed, their learning and teaching prohibited. Subordination of the present to the past, and deference to the sayings of predecessors without inspection or discussion, became a form of 'submission', 'acceptance' and 'obedience' to any kind of authority wearing the robe of the past and seeking to protect 'tradition'. In this situation, 'obedience' became the sole criterion for man, leaving no sense of humanity beyond that even for the Muslim, let alone the non-Muslim.

VII. Man in political Islamic discourse

What distinguishes modern movements of political Islam from their traditional origins is their capacity for political mobilization and recruitment; they
are able to exploit the failure of all projects of modernization and development,
while simultaneously claiming to oppose subordination to foreign powers in
any economic, social, political or intellectual field. Their tangible success,
apparent in the spread of their slogans in popular and professional sectors
(even among some notable members of the elite), springs from their pragmatic
political interpretations of religious texts and doctrines, interpretations that
divert religion away from its basic functions – spiritual and moral – to perform
the role of an ideology of 'opposition' to current systems of government, in an
attempt to replace them in power. Yet this ideology of interpretation really
offers no credible alternative for tackling the country's crisis, or rescuing the
nation from its backwardness, since the ideology in question derives its basic
argument from the conventional thought of the ages of decadence.

It may be sufficient here to refer to the question of *hakimiyya* (authority),
which necessitates reference to Shariah, whether in the texts of the Quran and
the *sunna*, or in the interpretations of the jurisprudents, especially those of the
school of *ahl al-sunna* (the followers of *sunna*), in every detail of life, on either the
individual or the communal level. Such an approach obviously excludes, from
the field of organizing human life, any authority except that of jurisprudents
and preachers. These alone are to direct matters of economics, politics, culture,
thought, art, etc. The holding of political power is the only way for this 'authority' to assume its proper place, since 'God deters through the *sultan* (power)
what He does not deter through the Quran'. The Quran, in other words, is not
sufficient in itself, but must, inevitably, be joined with a state authority to
enforce on people the commitment to Quranic teachings and directions. Thus,
the notion of *hakimiyya* betrays the same elements of conventional thought that
marked the periods of decadence: namely, submission, acceptance and obedience. Politico-religious discourse tries, deviously, to reformulate these elements so as to imply both submission, acceptance and obedience to the highest
legitimacy – that of God – and rebellion and revolt against a political authority
not ruling according to divine revelation. The prevalence of general awareness,
as a result of the long absence of liberties and particularly of freedom of expression and thought, has helped this misleading interpretation to slip into minds
and settle there.

In the context of this political project, armed as it is with religious dicta
and terminology, where does the concept of 'man' lie? Any representative or

ideologue of this project could, of course, answer the question by invoking Quranic texts and the sayings and practices of the Prophet, that is to say, by invoking the ideal and the utopian.[48] But the actual practice of the project's representatives at the level of intellectual dispute and political argument – as carried out through *fatwas* (Islamic legal opinions) branding opponents as heretics and apostates, legitimizing their murder, plotting to separate a man from his wife, and so on – hints at a wide gulf between the 'texts' invoked and the *fatwas* and judgments themselves. This is borne out by numerous examples, one such being the testimony of the late *Shaykh* Muhammad al-Ghazali at the trial of the killers of Faraj Fuda, who was murdered by members of the Armed Flank in June 1992, following a statement by a 'Committee of Azhar Scholars' that he was a 'secular unbeliever'. According to al-Ghazali's statement, anyone not finding it necessary to apply Islamic Shariah was considered an 'apostate', subject to sentence of 'death' if he was asked to repent and did not do so. If those in authority did not apply this punishment on the apostate, any Muslim had the right to apply it without making himself liable to punishment by the divine law. A certain writer has tried, rightly or wrongly, to defend the dicta of this political project, seeking an outlet for the *Shaykh* from this 'predicament' that exposed the myth of so-called 'moderation'. In his weekly article, the writer in question attempted to distinguish between the value of *fatwa* and that of *shahada* ('testimony'), in a desperate effort to cover the shame of this fanatical and extremist discourse.

If this has been the attitude toward a believing Muslim who openly declares his Islam, the attitude towards non-Muslims is governed by downright arrogance, not to say a tendency to belittling and debasement. One cannot forget, in this context, the advice proffered by 'Umar 'Abd al-Kafi, a professor of Agricultural Science, who declared that Muslims should not make Copts welcome or show them any kindness, should refrain from joining in their festivals, even by the mere sending of congratulation cards. A certain person tried to devise an explanation of, even a justification for, such dangerous *fatwas*, which threaten the very texture of national unity, now and in years to come. Yet all his recognized skill in justification and reversing facts could go no further than a claim that the statements did not issue from his friend. His weekly article was entitled 'He reviled you, the one who informed you' – but denial was like the proverbial ostrich burying its head in the sand. 'Abd al-Kafi was soon to accompany the then minister of *awqaf* (religious endowments) to congratulate the 'Coptic Pope' in his church on Christmas Day. This was an apologetic visit in the form of an initiative, highly advertised by the official media, to free the state, as represented by its political system, from the charge of approving such irresponsible statements. But the secretary-general of the Muslim Brotherhood in Egypt – Mustafa Mashhur – surprised everyone and generally shocked the feelings of Muslims vis-à-vis the Copts, by reiterating the old jurisprudential attitude of excluding non-Muslims from 'the army' and military service in the 'Islamic state' which the Muslim Brothers had been trying to establish. His justification was the fear that non-Muslims (Egyptian Copts, for instance) might join the enemy if that enemy should be of their own religion. This undermined the national feeling of the Copts, since it would actually jus-tify their being made to pay *jizya*, for protection accorded them by the Muslim 'army'.

If we pass from these blatantly extremist attitudes to those usually described as moderate, or even 'enlightened', we find Yusuf al-Qardawi supporting those who describe people of a different religion as 'unbelievers', denying that this is 'extremism' or 'fanaticism'. The basis of religious belief, he noted, is that the believer thinks he is right and the other is wrong, and there should be no com-promise in this.[49]

These are just a few examples among many, all of which reflect a deep and wide gulf between the ideology of political Islam and the religious texts upon which this ideology claims to rely. As such, it can be said that the measures of exclusion and oppression directed at the person of a different religious belief, or at the Muslim who opposes the ideology of political Islam, are characteristic not so much of Islamic religion and doctrine as of this kind of thought *per se*; and that such measures form one of its most dangerous tools. To return to Islam in its basic texts is to be astonished at the ability of modern discourse to counterfeit and falsify religion for political and ideological ends, since there is in fact no worldly punishment for apostasy in Islam: the human being was given the freedom to choose between belief and disbelief. It would be a logical contradiction with Islam itself if the choice of belief or Islam were to be con-sidered the end of man's original right in freedom. What kind of freedom would this be, which limits man's freedom to one choice: the surrender of free-dom!

If the charge of 'secularism' in the statement of the Committee of Azhar Scholars justified the murder of Faraj Fuda, and the same charge, according to al-Ghazali's statement, acquitted the murderers, we find the former *Shaykh* of al-Azhar – the highest official religious authority not in Egypt alone but prob-ably in the entire Muslim world – declare in one of his speeches that 'there is no place for secularists in the land of Egypt'. This was a statement sometimes reit-erated by responsible officials of state and by leading figures in the governing party. This exclusion of secularism and secularists from the sphere of 'homeland' and 'patriotism' again depends on the tools of deceit, falsification and misleading statement, which equate 'secularism' with 'disbelief', finding in it nothing but enmity to religion. If we are all proud that Islam does not sanction priesthood, or give the man of religion authority over people, then what religion is closer to secularism than Islam? And what priesthood is more distant from Islam than the authority sought by the representatives of this discourse? Such discourse would undoubtedly result in the alienation of the Egyptian Copts, since they are 'secular' in their belief in separating the church from politics and the affairs of government and political authority. This is how the concept of 'man' diminishes in the political discourse of Islam, how it boils down to the model of the 'submissive Muslim', the acquiescing one, sheltering under the wing of unscrupulous political, utilitarian interpretations of religion and doctrine. This is how distances become wider, and differences deeper, between the 'idealism' of religious texts and the 'reality' of religious thought, whether official or in opposition.

This gulf between the 'ideal' and the 'real' in attitudes to man, or in dealings with him, is not so much an Islamic phenomenon as a human one. The violation of human rights everywhere in the world, despite the Declaration of Human Rights promulgated more than half a century ago, has led to the formation of human rights organizations to uncover the violations in question and draw attention to them. In the last decades of the twentieth century this violation grew ever worse and ever more fundamental, assuming, finally, the proportions of wars of extermination, together with blatant interference by international forces of domination and control bent on determining the destiny of nations and imposing governments on them under the pretext of human rights protection – a course as absurd as it was shameful. And since 'fundamentalism', in its religious, racial and cultural manifestations, has become a global trend, and one generally limiting the concept of 'man' to a racial dimension, it becomes mandatory on thinkers, intellectuals, writers and artists of all affiliations and ideologies to fight, each through their own means, this form of 'racism' which threatens to devour the entire world. They should also endeavour to crystallize a concept of man, as one who does not derive his humanity from membership of a certain race, gender or culture, or of a class in the economic, social or political sense. This is no easy task, given the cultural obstacles and language barriers involved. Politicians and economists buttress these obstacles and barriers by preventing some human communities from interacting with other 'lower' communities, by setting up 'iron curtains' under different names and pretexts. If the 'protected' communities had limited their aims to political coordination and economic cooperation, this would have been commendable. Instead they become, invariably, cultural impediments and intellectual barriers which hinder the possibilities of mutual understanding.

Perhaps the starting point is to understand oneself, and one's own culture and language, then move on to understand others and evaluate their culture, within the framework of their achievement in the relevant historical and social context, rather than imposing 'evaluation' criteria based on a different cultural system which considers itself better and higher. In other words, intellectuals and men of culture must emphasize their independence by rejecting the tools of enslavement and exclusion exercised by economists and politicians, and so create room for mutual understanding and cooperation, irrespective of national, racial, cultural or linguistic affiliations. This call for a combined effort among intellectuals and men of culture throughout the world, on the basis of mutual understanding, does not imply any attempt to abolish the special characteristics of any single culture. Rather, these characteristics, if not enhanced by mutual cooperation and understanding, will come to embody a form of 'sectarianism' leading on to enslavement and exclusion, with all the predictable consequences of these. Such cooperation and understanding should bring down the obstacles and barriers that confine the concept of man to a closed framework. When the concept opens up to include all human beings, without restriction or special consideration, it will be possible to bridge the gap between the 'ideal' and the 'real'.

Chapter 6: The body: its images and rights in Islam

Munsif al-Wahaybi

I. Why the body?

The body is a topic celebrated in contemporary humanistic culture, one addressed by individuals and groups of differing intellectual persuasions and studied through a variety of approaches: psychological, philosophical, sociological and anthropological. None of these scholars finds it necessary, any longer, to justify an investigation of the subject. According to the French philosopher Michel Bernard, life obliges man to look at his body day by day. By the body, and through the body, man feels, expresses himself, works, invents, dreams and imagines. From the body, man looks at the bodily realities of others, and joins himself to the affairs of the world. Gone are the times when the body was entrenched in myths and superstitions. Many old theories and images have begun to crumble: those that considered the body a hindrance, a prison, a grave, a shell sealed around the soul and preventing its light from shining, a mortal corpse divorced from worship and prayer, which has to be trained and famished – after which, as Shafiq al-Balkhi would say, the heart is enlivened and enabled to see with the divine light. In contemporary humanistic culture, the body has become 'a general symbol of the world' and the source of all current and potential human symbols. The body symbolizes everything, just as everything symbolizes the body. It has now, therefore, become impossible for criticism to avoid or ignore the body. The attitude toward the body, whatever its precise tendency, reflects an attitude toward society and the universe, defining the relation of man to himself and to others. Generally speaking, contemporary humanistic culture tends to celebrate the body as a source of enjoyment and creativity, a means of individual and communal liberation, listing it among the basic dimensions of existence, considering it the language of reality and imagination, making bodily dimensions the essence of humanity, celebrating nudism in painting, theatre, cinema and literature, finding in this a renewed reconciliation with nature and a discovery of bodily innocence.

This has not, it must be said, stopped modern societies from controlling the body and exploiting it through work and exercise, turning body culture, in many cases, into 'pornographic culture'. Contemporary Arab culture, on the other hand, has not given the subject the due its importance merits. Arabs have yet to write their history of sex and the body, despite a wealth of available material which might have been used as sources to clarify the suppressed and unconsidered aspects of this culture. Most studies touching on the subject focus merely on the emotional or sensual relation between the sexes, ignoring, apparently, the presence of a visible body, imagined, social, theological, political or mythical, which informs and controls such a relation, leaving the impact of its language and image on the human flesh. These studies addressing the relation between man and woman do not so much clarify the image of the body, the body of love or sex, as manifest an excited emotion or set up static aesthetic criteria. There is, it seems, no conception of the body in art or religion as an image informing a certain kind of discourse. The body is not excluded from this discourse which it informs and directs. It is the discourse which forms the shape and aspects of the body, as an activating and activated entity. It is the discourse which represents its drives and emotions, peels away the veils hiding it, and shows, through the body, the real human status in its two aspects: the living human aspect implying the potentials for action, love, imagination and invention, and the tragic aspect denoting the absence and exploitation of the body: its temporality and failure, its decay and inevitable destiny. The body is realized through speech and by speech. Therefore, any attempt to strip the body of its vibrant context, with a view to reducing it to static aesthetic criteria, or to force it into a ready-made ideological shell, will end only in disparate, abstract equations, not equations involving human emotions and attitudes.

The body is one. But it is also a number of bodies. It has various aspects: religious, moral, scientific, philosophical and literary. The fact that this essay addresses only the first (religious) aspect does not mean the others have been lost sight of. Islam is not merely a religion, but a culture and a civilization as well. To the Muslim, it is both a spiritual and a social need, a special view of the universe with all its components, formed by the collaboration of intricate factors which are not easy to probe within the limited scope of an essay. Nevertheless, they cannot, in connection with a multi-dimensional topic like 'the rights of the body in Islam', be neglected. Inevitably, therefore, we must refer to the religious text and the parallel text at one and the same time, while delving, also, into the linguistic material, the 'social fossil', as philologists would say. Each word implies not just an idea or a mental image, but also a mostly hidden image of an 'imagined' aspect of people, of their fancies and social thinking.

This 'imagined' aspect concerning the image of the body in Islam is found in the religious text, the language, and in Arabic culture before Islam. If Islam was able to fuse all these aspects into one entity, this is because Islam, being focused, like any religious discourse, on an absolute, has certain subjective qualities in the forms of its manifestation and contents. These qualities afford Islam the possibility of manipulating words and meaning, of profiting from the cultural repertory and communal memory and spreading all this across time and place, so allowing the words and meaning to take on their particular nuances and attractiveness, and exercise their influence on the communal conscience.

All this requires a kind of probing and lifting of the veils draped over the body and its rights in the civilization of Islam, a removal of the accumulated myths whereby reality is confused with imagination. To try and arrive at the facts uncontaminated by fancies is a formidable task, one hardly within the scope of this essay.

This essay will, in fact, concern itself with studying the linguistic items (body/rights) on one level, and, on a second level, the images of the body as manifested in Arabic culture before Islam. Once this is done, we can then proceed to address the issue of 'the rights of the body in Islam'.

II. The linguistic material: physique/body

The most significant meanings glossed by dictionaries for the item physique are: the body of man, *jinn*, angels; saffron; the calf of the children of Israel; dry blood. For the item body we have: the whole *body* and organs of men and all creatures of magnitude.

Under *right* are glossed the attributes of the Almighty. Right is: the Quran; the opposite of unjust; justice; Islam; property; the fixed being; truth; death; and resolve.

The word *physique*, though, occurs in an ambiguous context, being interchangeable with words like: soul, spirit, mind. This calls for some consideration of its various meanings.

Under *soul* the dictionaries gloss: spirit; blood; physique; essence; grandeur; dignity; resolution; pride; will; punishment. 'Allah warns you about His punishment' (3, *Al 'Imran*, 28, 30)

Soul covers: what has life; the Quran; revelation; Gabriel; Jesus the son of Maryam (Mary); breathing life into something; the order of prophethood; the words of the Almighty; His order; a man-faced angel; rest; mercy; the breath of religion; welfare; wind; power; compassion; support; state; fragrance.

Taking all these linguistic indications into consideration, we soon realize that the image of the physique must necessarily involve several dimensions and aspects, both in language and in religious terminology. Islam is probably no different from other religions in this respect. Judaism distinguishes spirit from soul. It views spirit as the source of life which runs in the blood; yet the soul indicates the spirit of God, which is the divine command. Judaism sees God in a 'human' image, giving Him physical qualities. The Old Testament portrays man as soul and body, the soul being connected to the divine self.

In Christianity, man is defined as body, soul and spirit. In St. Paul's First Epistle to the Thessalonians, we read: 'I pray God your whole spirit and soul and body be preserved blameless unto the coming of our Lord Jesus Christ. Faithful is he that calleth you, who also will do it.' (5, 23–4)

In Christianity, the religious connotation of 'spirit' is moral. Therefore, we find the spirit commanding man to fight his evil nature, his desires, instincts and vengeful tendencies, encouraging him to love, forgiveness and temperance.

Perhaps Islam is closer to Christianity in this respect, because it does not distinguish between the soul, the spirit and the body of man. The nature of the soul cannot be known in Islam. 'Say: the soul is a concern of my Lord; of knowledge you have been given but little.' (17, *Al-Isra'*, 85) It is a thing breathed into the body of man to begin life in him. Another verse reads: 'Behold! Your Lord said to the angels: "I am about to create man from sounding clay, from mud moulded into shape; * When I have fashioned him and breathed into him of my soul, fall prostrate before him."' (15, *Al-Hijr*, 28–9)

'Spirit' in Islam has obvious moral connotations. There is the evil commanding spirit, which is the seat of evil instincts and animal desires. 'Nor do I absolve my own self [of blame]: the [human] self is certainly prone to evil' (12, *Yusuf*, 53) Therefore, such self must be fought. There is also the self-reproaching spirit, which is the seat of conscience and deterrence, whereby it is prescribed to follow religious commands and abide by prohibitions.

The third type is the contented spirit, which is freed from the power of unruly desires and given to reason, contemplation and asceticism, so as to be worthy of reward. 'O you contented spirit, come back to your Lord, well pleased and well pleasing [to Him].' (89, *Al-Fajr*, 27–8)

Having shown that Islam does not distinguish between body, soul and spirit, we may now, in the context of such a unity, address the rights of the body imposed on the Muslim, whether in the spiritual-religious or the daily practical field. We shall separate these two fields only for methodological purposes, since Islam itself, being religion and practice at the same time, does not endorse such a division.

III. The right of purity

The body is charged with performing the greatest duty in Islam, which is *salat*, whether in its sense of worship, as in kneeling and falling prostrate, or in its sense of prayer for mercy and forgiveness. *Salat* as such is a bodily exercise, as is demonstrated by the linguistic root of the verb (*s-l-o*). The word *sala* means the middle of the back of man or of any four-legged creature. The call for *salat* in Islam is a call to the soul, the spirit or mind. It is also a call to the body, which must purify itself; that is, a call to wash off its impurity. The body must also be cleansed of sin (as the root for 'purity' denotes in language and terminology). This purification and cleansing will build and support the relationship with the 'holy'.

We are, therefore, dealing with a matter of individual behaviour, since the Muslim is religiously committed to purity of his body as much as to care for the purity of his behaviour and his spirit. 'By the soul and the proportion and order given to it; * and the enlightenment as to its wrong and its right.' (91, *Al-Shams*, 7–8) What characterizes the body of sin or piety characterizes the soul too, because the one is but a mirror of the other.

This demonstrates not only the strong bond between body and soul, but also the intimate quality of the individual in Islam. Yet it should not veil the communal image of Islamic societies, which are supposed, religiously, to fulfil the rights of the body as a whole. This may extend to a sense of horror at the impurity of the body, or at the impending punishment of the Muslim for failing to purify and care for the body.

We find these rights viewed with a degree of holiness both in spiritual and sublime matters, like *salat* and fasting, and in practical daily affairs, including intimate physical contact. The root *t-h-r* has given us the word *athar*, which refers to the 'pure' days of the woman, when she is not in her monthly period. This indicates the condition of purity that must be fulfilled before the body can exercise its right in pleasure.

IV. The right of pleasure (in sexual intercourse)

This item calls for patient consideration for a number of reasons, foremost among them the impression some people have gained about Islam – an impression based mainly on preconceived judgements and hearsay with regard, especially, to body, sex and the man–woman relationship. We have seen cases of general judgement lacking any foundation in truth, or else guided by exceptional cases lacking basis in a religious text. Some people believe Islam belittles the woman's body, undermining its rights or being inclined to slight its status. One example may suffice to show how an exceptional case, divorced from its far larger social context, may be construed by some as reflecting a constant, general phenomenon. For educated and ordinary Muslims alike, the circumcision of girls is ugly and repugnant, and we find it, as such, practised only in a restricted number of Islamic countries, notably in Africa. Some people may not realize that this is an 'imagined' and not a Muslim practice. The 'imagined' procedure has a logic different from that of religion, and an authority which may, in some cases, be stronger than that of the religious text itself. The circumcision of girls is linked to certain ancient concepts about the power of women, and the aim is not to deprive the body of its right to pleasure and enjoyment but rather to check its potential for enticement. These are notions linked with enchantment and magic in the Muslim imagination; in ancient societies they are aspects of power and authority. As such, the procedure may be viewed as akin to the punishment imposed on witches in medieval Europe, when they were bound and burned at the stake because they possessed, from the Christian perspective, an authority parallel to that of Church and state.

There are many instances, in the history of Muslims and others, when the body was tortured and persecuted because it was considered a source of allurement inspiring a kind of authority. These exceptions should not undermine the rights and inviolability of the body in Islam, or be used as a pretext to slander a culture of which some people know scarcely more than what is propagated by religious fundamentalists. Femininity in Islam is, like masculinity, a field open to various forms of practice, though Islamic communal fancy may brand it with its own mark and attach to it a profusion of its own reasonings and misconceptions. This topic is a very popular one in modern studies on the rights of Muslims in particular and human rights in general. We find it fitting, therefore, to approach the subject on three levels, which may give a clearer picture of the rights of the body in Islam. The first level is the image of the body in pre-Islamic culture, given that the culture of Islam was in some ways an extension of what came before it and in others a deviation from it. The second level is that of the body and its rights in traditional Sunni Islam. The third level addresses the body and its rights in Islam from a Sufi viewpoint. The following discussion will refer to various texts and examples which we regard as components of Islamic intellectual structure, or as the product of an Islamic civilization springing from an interaction among legislative, jurisprudential and cultural experiences accumulated through contact between Islam and other cultures. It should not be considered strange, therefore, to find in this essay, side by side,

religious texts from the Quran and *sunna*, others from jurisprudence or legislation, and still others from literary mythological texts. All these coalesce in
forming the image of the body and its rights in the civilization of Islam, within
a certain society of a historical period. All these aspects are generative in connecting various arts and disciplines in Islamic culture which identify, in one way
or another, the authority of the religious text in Islam, in its traditional Sunni
aspect.

V. Pre-Islamic culture

A number of annals confirm that the body in pre-Islamic Arab society was not
absent, ignored or considered a source of sin. This society endorsed, in addition to marriage, various types of sexual relations practised for pleasure, indicating a celebration of the female body as a source of enjoyment, a 'commodity'
that might be acquired, looted, rented or exchanged, or a 'property' that might
be transmitted by inheritance. These types of sexual revelation referred to by
annals and works of jurisprudence, some of which are mentioned in the Quran,
are ten in number, namely: *istibdaha'*, *mudamada*, *mukhadana*, prostitution, *dayzan*
(inherited marriage), *shaghar*, exchange of wives, marrying captive women,
adultery, and pleasure marriage.[1]

These sexual relations in pre-Islamic society may lead us to believe that sexual desire was uncontrolled by proscriptions and restrictions. They may even
lead us to feel pre-Islamic Arab society was one of sexual laxity and free
instincts. It would, however, be misleading to claim that pre-Islamic society
symbolized liberation of the body from every cultural or moral restriction, or
that the body among Bedouins was a source of individual and communal liberation. This 'sexual freedom' was limited to men as opposed to woman – an
indication of instinct satisfaction and of the man's tendency to possess the
female body. Hence, talk of 'sexual chaos' or 'absolute sexual freedom', in the
absence of laws or any taming of the instincts, finds no possible support or
basis either in pre-Islamic poetry or in the customs or traditions of the people.
Any attempt to prove such 'freedom' by reference to the poetry of al-A'sha or
Imru'u al-Qays raises many objections. The behaviour of each poet was an
individual phenomenon, an exception which should not be generalized to
apply to pre-Islamic society as a whole. In fact, that society did not endorse
such conduct. Imru'u al-Qays spent most of his life as an outcast, and one reason for this may have been that 'he was adulterous in his poetry'. The annals
record that his father expelled him twice: once on account of his ode *Qifaa*

nabki ('Let us halt and cry', his most famous poem) concerning Fatima, and a second time on account of his other famous poem *Ala-n'im sabahan ayyuha 'l-talalu 'l-bali* ('Good morrow, you, decayed ruin!').

This expulsion is proof that his poetry, especially his poetry on women and love, was an attempt to undermine the values and morals of pre-Islamic tribal life. Love and its practice was seen as a subversive act; destructive not only of the structure and unity of the family but also of the structure and unity of values. In addition to all this, the woman in the sexual relations and types of marriage referred to above was an object and not a person. She did not possess her body, nor could she use it according to her will.

If the woman was an 'object', a 'commodity' or a 'property', then the celebration of the parts of the body in the poem's erotic introduction may be seen as hiding a tendency to communicate with the female body as an object of pure sex, not as an entity capable of giving and receiving emotion. Hence, the celebration of love in pre-Islamic poetry is simply a celebration of the body; love of this nature is sensual and erotic, a mere biological love, in which the woman does not know the man and does not hope to integrate with the other or bypass him. In fact there was no one woman in particular, but a number of them.[2] The aim of the poet – although this image should not be generalized – was to penetrate the female body, to taste its delicacies, without penetrating to the humanity and entity of the woman. The portrayal of the parts of the body as a source of pure pleasure, or as a bundle of instincts, reaches its climax perhaps in these lines by Imru'u 'l-Qays:

> Many a pregnant and breastfeeding damsel like you I haunted,
> And kept her from an amulet-bearing, one-year-old babe.
> When it cried, behind her, she turned to it
> With part of her body, while beneath me her other part was always there.

In this obscene literary image, as with most of this poet's images, the body of the woman is split into two bodies, occupying the same time and place: the body of the mother and that of the lover. The two are joined in one person, and they are divided, at the same time, into two persons. Both are given over to satisfying instinct and securing pleasure. Such an obscene image, in the hands of Freudians, would undoubtedly yield much proof for their theses and hypotheses. The split female body is, in fact, simply a field of intricate symbols. Some of these symbols may refer to a guilt feeling, compensated for by giving the breast to the child, or to a mutual pleasure between the mother's body and that of the child, whose crying is a call for love. As the mother responds to this call, she satisfies her body and that of her lover simultaneously. Nevertheless, is the symbolism of the parts of the body limited to its being a source of pleasure and enjoyment alone? This reading may hold if restricted to the image in isolation, separate from the whole structure. However, since the image of the parts of the body is tied to that of the whole body, and since both are part of another body, which involves them as it involves other parts, that is, the body of the pre-Islamic poem, the 'metamorphoses of the body' can only be grasped in the context of the whole technical experience of the pre-Islamic poem.

V.1 Metamorphoses of the body in pre-Islamic tradition

The body eulogized by the poet is a 'generated' or 'invented' body, descending from the social body without being totally separated from its existence. It carries some traces of the original aspects and qualities. This magnified and partitioned body corresponds to the ideal image of the pre-Islamic body. It embodies the beautiful as an expression of the ideal in a tangible, artistic image, just as it embodies the majestic with all its connotations of greatness, grandeur, and transition from the visible to the imaginary and from the finite to the infinite. In this conjunction of the beautiful and the majestic lies the curiosity, the irony indeed, of the magnified/partitioned body. The beautiful is a harmony, a concord, a symmetry, a structure of coordinated factors which stimulate the poet to joy and freedom; as if he took some profound pleasure in discovering, in this magnified/partitioned body created by his imagination, not a means to satisfy a need only but a testimony to his creative act. Perhaps this pleasure, felt by pre-Islamic poet and audience alike, largely explains the secret of the exciting celebration of the body in pre-Islamic and Arabic poetry generally, of every type and form. The majestic expands 'the limits of harmony between the real and the ideal'.[3] The moment the pre-Islamic poet has supplied the finishing touches to the image of the female body in the erotic introductory lines of his poem, he moves to another scene. The majestic accelerates in power and magnitude, stopping at no limit or end, stressing, at the same time, the supremacy of the world over human power on the one hand, and, on the other, the insistence of man on emphasizing himself and his freedom. It is thus no wonder that the magnifying of the body in the pre-Islamic poem is coupled with magnifying of the self; the glorifying of the body with glorifying of heroism. Heroism was always coupled with glory, seen as a powerful will to renew life, an endeavour to achieve the ideal, and a challenge to the finite that finds its echo in the infinite. This makes physical love an accompaniment to chivalry. Through this love, the poet whets his power and inflames his desire for adventure, going beyond the female body to feats of heroism, as if 'nothing can quench his thirst, satisfy or stop him'.[4] Hence the character of the knight in pre-Islamic poetry is 'wandering and settled at the same time – at night he is enchanted by the day; in daytime he yearns for the female body'.[5] He is bewitched almost by the desire to have his life resemble the desert, 'absolute and relative, simple and complex, firm and falling apart like sand'.[6] Indeed, so it is in reality. Everything in the pre-Islamic poem takes the form of the boundless desert, from the body all the way up to the poet himself. There is no word more expressive of this state of affairs than the word *hamasa* (zeal, excitement) which the Arabs used in describing their poetry, before it was categorized into poetry of love, boasting, elegy or panegyric. *Hamasa* is a term lively, philosophical, comprehensive and profound, embodying the height of excitement about a state of living that extends the present into the past, the visible into the invisible or imagined. The zeal of love poetry is not limited to excitement about the female body, but branches into excitement about the heroic body, the body of love, which is itself then transformed to a celebration of the female essence, stretching out, finally, to what might be called a 'paganization of the body' or a 'myth of the body'. Through this excitement, the poet formulates the cosmic image of the body, an image where the body comes to resemble a form of grand metaphor, a body-ideal whose components the poet culls from common bodies and physiques of gods and totems which enjoyed sanctity in the old pre-Islamic times. The ancient Arabs represented the goddess al-'Uzza, for example, as a beautiful woman in the shape of a flower, and as one of the daughters of the arch god Hubal. This type of worship had its roots deep in history and the matriarchal system, when the woman held control. But while many nations knew such a system, where are the testimonies and documents to prove the Arabs knew it in their primordial days?

Might the spread of the matriarchal system among the ancient Arabs be attributed to the proliferation of communal marriage among them, whereby the child had no true father? Or does it relate to the absence of the father's authority, in the Freudian sense, in pre-Islamic tribal life? Or does it belong to the totemic stage, when the man found in the woman a source of magic, holding as she did the secret of fertility and the power to create life? Might the ancient Arabs' worship of the woman be proved by the popularity of religious or sacred prostitution in their pre-historic times? One might refer to the myth of Asaf and Na'ila to say that intercourse was not unknown in the pre-Islamic temple, and that the myth of metamorphosis was endorsed following the rejection and disappearance of this custom.[7] And could this be further indicated by the ancient annals concerning women attached to the service of the pre-Islamic temple, where they dedicated their bodies to the temple's priests, guardians and poets? This has perhaps

led some commentators to see the erotic introduction to the poem in this light –
saying, for example, that, 'if the various names, in the introductions bemoaning
the ruins in an image of horror and mysterious love, do not relate to goddesses
and saints, then they relate to these types of women with whom the poet found
favour as one of those who were in the service of the temple'.[8]

Such an interpretation, linking the celebration of the body in the preludes to
pre-Islamic Arabic poetry with reminiscences of the adulation of woman and
with ancient Arab legends, may be interesting, but it is not above controversy.
While the present writer may find a degree of satisfaction in such a construal, it
nevertheless raises questions to which ready answers are not easily found –
which are indeed bewildering, calling for careful consideration. Even if it were
possible to prove the authenticity of a good deal of pre-Islamic poetry, to
regard it as a historical source, what proof do we have for all the sources which
record pre-Islamic myths from the perspective of an Islamic mentality? In
order to authenticate a pre-Islamic myth, and use it with confidence to probe
the religious mentality of the ancient Arabs, is it not essential to conduct extensive research, compare various annals and have an extensive knowledge of the
mentality and imagination of the ancient Arabs? Such a type of research may
indeed be still in its early stages in Arabic culture, but we must question
whether it is a viable alternative to project modern mythological, anthropological or psychological concepts onto a historical stage about which the scholar
has but scant, partial and scattered data.

Some writers, in investigating the celebration of the body in ancient Arabic
poetry, may resort to recent findings about the body, so divorcing the phenomenon from its historical context. Does this not lead to a sort of identification with the other, and to excessive generalization? Psychology, for example,
stresses how the mother embeds one's erotic relationship with one's body and
one's perception of it, until the individual becomes the tender mother of his
own body; the individual then believes he should give his body the same love
his mother gave him in childhood. This could in fact be a universal human phenomenon, stemming from unconscious infantile residues, whereby the
mother's body might be associated with power and capacity as much as it is
associated with eroticism and the need for protection.

VI. The body in Islamic culture

Before Islam, the Arabs celebrated the body as a source of pleasure and a release
for tendencies, whims and instincts, linking all this with their set of

values, which reflected a power structure seen in such things as self-assertion, violence, assault, valour and pride. This led to the appearance of a type of 'obscene literature', marked by a disregard for many traditions and social norms. Muslim society, however, tended to regularize pleasure and tame the sexual instinct. The appreciation of the body in Islam was guided by the duality of pre-scription and proscription, or permission and deprivation. Within those limits we can discern the image of the body and its right to pleasure in sexual relations.

Like other revealed religions, Islam considers aspiration to perfection an indispensable trait for the believer. As such, Islam recognizes the right of the body to pleasure so long as this right is subject to proper control, in order to train the spirit and check desires. The incentive underlying the right to marriage is not simply control of desire but liberation from desire, which is considered an image of the devil and the spirit that spurs on to evil.

We are told by al-Ghazali that 'marriage is a help to faith, an insult to the dev-ils, a buttressed fort against the enemy of God, and a means to reproduction'. For all the restriction of this right, which is a form of religious duty in Islam, the body is not considered a hindrance or a source of sin. Islam has restricted the right through moral and social measures, honouring it by the institution of marriage, or the enjoyment of slave girls in early Islamic times. Hence, the right of copulation had its manners and ethics. This led to numerous works on the subject, especially by jurists. In fact, the extent to which the subject was taught in mosques and 'education circles' led some jurists to declare that 'by instruct-ing the youth in the conditions and ethics of copulation, one is hoping for divine reward'.[9] These rules and manners included cleanliness of the body, ejaculation only by the wife's permission, play, a gentle approach to the wife, caring and intimacy. We may note among these rules the duality of body/dress, which is more significant in our present times when nudity and physical inno-cence, under the influence of modernist and post–modernist culture, are rein-stated to respectable status.

VI.1 Body/garment

We often find ourselves quoting al-Ghazali, because the Islam circulated in various regions of the world is in the version he canonized. Among other aspects of proper sexual relations, he stresses that the man should cover him-self and his wife with a garment. He records a saying of the Prophet: 'If you approach your wife, the two of you should not strip off like donkeys.' He also records how the Prophet would cover his head and lower his voice when approaching his wife, and ask the woman to 'be tranquil'.

Such references are hard to understand outside their cultural context. Before Islam, Arabs would circumambulate the Kaaba naked, and one Arabian myth relates how Adam, the first man, circumambulated it 'naked, without a cover on his head'. A number of annals, too, record that men would perform this holy rite quite naked, and that some women would do the same, while others had a cloth around their body, with a vent either on the front or the back.

Al-Jahiz records how 'Diba'a al-Qurashiyya', a pre-Islamic woman famous for her beauty, would circumambulate the Kaaba naked. Once al-Muttalib ibn Abi Wada'a, seeing her, said: 'I saw her circumambulating the Kaaba naked. So I followed her from behind, then faced her direct as she approached. Never have I seen a more beautiful sight among God's creations.'

In the early days of Islam, a poem by Suhaym, a slave of the Hashas tribe, describes some women who would meet and celebrate love and beauty by tearing off their clothes and competing in showing off their beauty and charms. The poet did not hesitate to join them in the game of disrobing:

> Many a belted garment we have torn off,
> And many a veil, covering bewitching eyes!
> When one robe was torn, it was coupled by a veil,
> And so, till all remained with nothing on!

The garment is a profound social symbol, designed to cover whichever parts of the body must be covered and to show whichever may be shown. The women in Suhaym's poem, in their 'communal disrobing' celebration, were not merely tearing off woollen or leather fabric; they were, still more, tearing away the cultural masks and social restrictions preventing the liberation of the body, its breaking into a type of 'childish sexuality', whereby both men and women experience an undoubted pleasure in uncovering the body.

An image like this, viewed from a psychological viewpoint, may uncover the desire of the individual to see and be seen. There is a link between the image of the individual's body and that of others, stemming from this hidden desire to explore one's own body and to present it to others to explore.

What should be realized in this connection is that the Islamic cultural context is somewhat equivocal. A thing and its opposite may be found at one and the same time. This is to be attributed to the Islamic mentality and not to religion *per se*. When we are told how the Prophet advised covering the body during sexual relations, it is because religion as culture, in the anthropological sense, controls the body and 'exploits' it by various means, to turn it to its own language and the language of the society the religion hopes to construct.

In the Islamic view, a body uncovered by garments is not necessarily naked. It may be a hidden body. Nakedness is a speechless mask covering the real nature of the body. By the same token, a covered body is not necessarily a hidden one. A garment often leads to some degree of ambiguity, since it attracts the eye to hidden parts of the body, and 'sculptures' a body that is meant to be seen. Such a garment hides as much as it exposes. This explains the semantic ambiguity of the Arabic *libas*, which means 'garment' and, when used metaphorically, 'obscurity'. The ancient Arab would call the naked body *libas*, taking the flesh as a metaphor for dress. He would also call the woman and the man 'gown and robe'. Faith, bashfulness and covering the intimate parts of the body are all the 'garment of piety'. The ancient Arab would say 'I wore her as a garment' to denote his physical enjoyment of the woman. Al-Nabigha al-Ja'di writes:

> When her bed-partner turned her sides,
> She would wind and be his garment.

The Quran describes intimate relations between man and woman by using the body/garment metaphor. 'They are your garments and you are their garments.' (2, *Al-Baqara*, 187) This is because the naked body is not a single body; it is in a close sensual connection with another body. Each is a 'garment' for the other, as they meet in one 'dress', as al-Tabari would argue. The union of one with the other is akin to being dressed in the other's body, or finding serenity in the other.

All this leads us to say that the right or pleasure of sexual intercourse is controlled, in the Islamic perspective, by a religious vision that surrounds such relations with exciting holiness; the aim is not simply to check or satisfy the desire. Such a vision calls on Muslims to discharge sexual energy in order to insure the expansion of the religion itself. The 'power of copulation', according to al-Ghazali, is a 'means of reproduction through which the Prophet vies with other prophets'. Desire and procreation are 'destined and related. It is not acceptable to say that the aim is enjoyment. Procreation is the intention, as the aim of eating is not the food itself, but satisfying the need for it. Procreation is intended by nature and wisdom, and desire is the stimulus.'[10]

It is in this context that al-Ghazali explains the verse: 'Your wives as a tilth for you . . . ' (2, *Al-Baqara*, 223) Desire, he says, 'was created to be an agent entrusted with making the seeds grow, and making the female a help in the tillage, so that both will be enabled to procreate through copulation.' He focuses on desire as the divine inscription on the organs of the body, which no one can decipher unless favoured by a penetrating divine insight. 'Among the wonders of God is that He created a human being from water, making of him relative and kin, and imposed a desire upon the creation, forcing them to till and procreate . . . He created the couple; created the male and the two females (the testicles); created the sperm in the spine and provided it with veins and vessels in the testicles; created the womb a receptacle and store for the sperm; and made both male and female partake of that desire.' He goes on to affirm that copulation is a religious duty and not a mere right, and that abstention is an obstruction of a function of the body. 'To abstain from copulation is to abstain from tillage, to squander seed, to obstruct the tools created by God, to transgress over the intent of nature and the wisdom conceived from the aspects of creation ingrained on these organs by a divine hand, not by letters, figures or sounds, yet legible to everyone endowed with a penetrating divine insight, capable of grasping the subtleties of eternal wisdom.'

It is no wonder, then, that the right of copulation is viewed with such exciting holiness in Islam, since physical pleasure is a way to achieve the spiritual and fulfil divine wisdom. It is not an end in itself, since it is, as al-Ghazali would say, impaired by imperfection; such pleasure is rather a reminder of the promised pleasures of Paradise. 'One aspect of worldly desires is the desire for their continuation in Paradise . . . the lapsing imperfect desire begets a perfect enduring one.'

But the body in Islam has various images and different rights according to different schools of thought and discourses.[11] Islamic Sufism (mysticism) in all its aspects presents another image which cannot be grasped in its entirety. Nevertheless, it emphasizes that the body, as image and rights, is defined by social and cultural values, some of which are rooted in Islam, being manifested in the religious text, while other values are either imported or comprise certain items within Islamic civilization.[12]

VII. Images and rights of the body in Sufism

A student of the Sufi attitude toward the body is confronted by immature theories and fanciful judgements, entertained by some people without consideration of their validity. The Sufi, according to these people, is a homosexual pervert who does not satisfy his needs in a normal manner. Or the Sufi is a masochist who derives pleasure from pain, by training the body and torturing it through hunger and curtailing the desire for food and drink. Evidence to support these theories and judgements may be found in the lives and writings of some Sufis, but generalization on these grounds is liable to blur what might be considered a normal attitude to the body. We are dealing less with a moral issue than with a socio-cultural vision, formulated by intricate civilizational factors.

The attitude toward the body in Sufi literature is, in fact, multi-layered. According to Shafiq al-Balkhi, the first step toward Sufism lies in training the spirit by curtailing the desire for food and drink to the minimum necessary for life, and refraining from surfeit by night or day, since a full stomach 'detains the body from worship and *salat*'.[13]

Abu Bakr al-Razi adopts an ascetic Sufi approach in his philosophy. Lovers, he stresses, 'surpass beasts in failing to control themselves or check their whims, and in following their desires'. Pleasure, according to him, is merely a matter of returning a person to a pleasant state. He gives an example: of a man who leaves a cool, shady place for the heat of a desert, then returns to his former place, where the pleasure he finds causes his body to resume its former state. When this has happened, the pleasure disappears. Therefore, pleasure is a return to nature. But this step is not free from pain, since it cannot happen without pain preceding it, and it happens in proportion to the pain. Al-Razi concludes by saying that man's rational duty is to stop himself from falling in love, or to wean the self from love before it becomes too late; and he gives his attitude a philosophical interpretation by associating love with death, with a view to keeping man away from it. 'The separation from the beloved is a harm inevitable, either by death or some worldly accident which separates lovers.'

He rejects the argument that 'love enhances cleanliness, tact, looks or adornment.' For: 'What use is a comely body housing an ugly spirit? Is physical beauty sought by anyone except women and effeminate men?'[14] It is true that the other al-Razi, Fakhr al-Din, compares intellectual pleasures to sensual ones, but he considers the first higher in honour and perfection. He rejects the claim that the highest pleasure and the most perfect form of happiness lies in eating, copulation and possession. Fulfilment of desires is, he believes, merely answering a need. 'If fulfilling the desires of stomach and sex were a cause of man's perfection and happiness, then the more man is involved in these desires the more perfect his humanity would be.'[15]

Some Sufis may have become homosexual for cultural and psychological reasons that cannot be discussed here, or even for reasons linked to Sufism itself. Sufism is, finally, an intimate communal rite. Modern psychological research shows that sexual excitement is often found in public celebrations, which motivate sexual drives. This may lead to perversion in a single-gender group, or in a group which keeps the two sexes apart. None of this should eclipse the shining image of the body in many Sufi texts.

In Sufism the body, be it male or female, is generally regarded with praise and honour. Al-Ghazali records how someone was once criticizing the behaviour of the Sufis. A pious man asked: 'Where do you find them going astray?' 'They eat too much!' came the answer. 'If you were to feel the same hunger they do,' the pious man replied, 'you would eat as much as they do!' 'They copulate too much!' persisted the man. 'You too,' he was told, 'if you kept your sight away from sexual attraction, would copulate as much as they do!' He also records something said by al-Junayd: 'I feel the need for intercourse as much as I do for food.'

Al-Ghazali explains this inclination to celebrate the body, among some Sufis, by linking it to the context of Sufi experience itself. Copulation, he says, is not an obstacle to the worship of God. Hence the wife is to be considered a sustenance, an agent to purify the heart, to strengthen it in the course of its worship, to revive the spirit, to cheer it by good companionship and dalliance. 'Enjoying the company of women affords enough comfort to remove anguish and relieve the heart of its worries.' The Prophet, al-Ghazali says, sometimes received a revelation when he was in bed with his wife. He reports the Prophet to have said: 'O Um Salma, do not begrudge me my intimacy with 'A'isha. Believe me, the revelation never came to me when I was under the bedcover of any of you except her.'

The body, in this Sufi experience, is an 'instrument' which reminds of the promised pleasures of Paradise. Therefore, enjoying the body is not an end in itself. It is the fulfilment of a religious goal. However, the woman, in this experience, is not merely an intermediary between the human and the divine. The visible 'profane' is not only a way to the imagined 'holy'; it is also an image of it. If the woman is good-looking, of good character, has black eyes and hair, is fair-complexioned, intimately in love with her husband, and visibly so, turning her eyes to no one but him, desiring intercourse, then, according to al-Ghazali, she is the image of the houris, described in the Quran as 'fair [companions] good and beautiful' (55, *Al-Rahman*, 70), and 'beloved [by nature], equal in age'. (56, *Al-Waqi'a*, 37)[16]

These general descriptions delineate the ideal of the female body in the eyes of Sufis in particular and Muslims in general. It is obvious that this image is informed by the Quranic text and the Arabian environment, retaining many pre-Islamic criteria of beauty, with very few changes. The plump body remained an ideal of beauty for reasons connected with the Arabian life, enhanced by the Islamic conquests and the wealth they brought. The woman took to a life of comfort, and a chubby woman was seen as a mark of affluence. We have already referred to the image of the magnified and partitioned body in pre-Islamic tradition, regarded as a metaphor informed by ancient mythical and religious beliefs. While this interpretation fits the pre-Islamic vision, the recurrent image of the magnified body in the various aspects of the Islamic vision – sensual, 'Udhri (chaste) and Sufi – calls for a reading of this metaphor from other perspectives.

Why did this metaphor retain its glow, despite the change in circumstances, civilizational interactions and the collapse of ancient mythical and religious beliefs? It is true that, under the influence of the Quran and the intermingling of races, tastes began to favour the fair-skinned, chubby woman of long, flowing black hair and upright stature. It is also true that the flowering of civilization in the Abbasid era led people to favour the woman of slender body, not fat or flaccid. This is the ideal woman whose beauty was described by al-Jahiz.

> Most of the outstanding men of taste, who are experts on the rare qualities in women, prefer the delicately slender woman, who is neither fat nor slim. She must have a good stature, be comely built, have straight shoulders and a level back. She must not be bony, but somewhere between chubby and slim. That is why such a woman is described as hen tree-branch, a bamboo rod, or a rein-plait.[17]

The taste of the Abbasid age no longer favoured comparing the woman to the antelope, the deer, the sun or the moon, because, again according to al-Jahiz:

> [A beautiful maid] is better than an antelope, a deer or any other creature she has been likened to. The same holds true in the comparison with the sun. If the sun is considered beautiful, it is but one thing only. But in the face of a beautiful person are created various types of beauty of wondrous aspect and form. Who would ever deny that the human eye is better than that of the deer or the antelope, and that the difference between them is huge?[18]

Despite all this, the yearning for the magnified female body did not subside in the Islamic love poem, even in its Sufi aspect, even though it was combined with the image of the houris of paradise. It took on various forms and images, most prominent of which was the image of the cosmic life-giving female, intertwined with nature and its aspects.

VII.1 The cosmic life-giving female body: origins

The image of the life-giving female body in Sufi literature has roots in the pre-Islamic sensual love poem, and also in the 'Udhri Islamic love poem. What supports this idea is the image of the magnified body in both these genres and the chaste and pure diction of the Sufi poem.

The magnified body, previously referred to, stresses ample breasts and hips. There is hardly an old poem that does not celebrate this aspect of ideal female beauty. This cannot proceed from a void. It must have some roots in the communal unconscious and in mythical and religious beliefs. In many statues of goddesses, the chest and breasts are accentuated. The goddess Annat has large breasts from which water flows.[19]

Al-Hallaj uttered his enigmatic sentence which no one but a Sufi like himself could understand: 'My mother begat her father.' This is a reference to the mother who is his infinite, everlasting existence, latent in the divine existence.

The image of the cosmic life-giving female is not isolated from the tendency to unite with the divine being. This is the tendency called, by Ibn 'Arabi, the yearning that connects three parties: the divine being, the woman and the man. It is a mutual yearning: the man yearns to his Lord, as He is the origin; the Lord yearns to the man as he is the mirror in which He contemplates His image; the man yearns to the woman as the whole yearns to its part, as the woman is the mirror wherein his image is revealed. The woman yearns to the man as the part yearns to the whole. The three parties coalesce in one being, which is the beloved one, as this is the pivot of unity and supreme perfection. In such unity, the woman is accorded a distinguished status. She is, as al-Kashani would say, a part of the man, and each part indicates its origin. The woman indicates the man, and the indicator comes before the indicated. Ibn 'Arabi confirms this image when he says: 'Man (Adam) is placed between two females: the everlasting soul whence he issued, and Eve who issued from him. Adam does not create, as he is the prime reason, while Eve (the woman) is the collective soul which created the world.'[20] Commenting on this statement by Ibn 'Arabi, one writer noted how the language, in this context, denotes the metaphysical truth that the female is the origin of things. Every 'origin' is called 'mother' in Arabic.[21] It is obvious that this image of the cosmic female in the Sufi mind has extremely complex epistemological and philosophical roots. It is beyond the scope of this essay to explore these roots. We can only identify, in the Sufi context, their intricate aspects with regard to the visible and imagined body.

We should retain two interconnected elements of this image.

First: As an ideal of earthly beauty, the woman is a link between the human and the holy; and she is, at the same time, a mirror of the divine being in her real, tangible form. Some might suppose the symbolism of the cosmic female to be linked not to the physical functions of woman, but to the spiritual qualities which create love in the heart of man and move him toward a union with the holy beloved. But this view has little support in Sufi texts. We have seen how al-Ghazali excludes the power of copulation from Sufi asceticism. The poetry

of Ibn al-Farid and Ibn 'Arabi is not free of images saturated with manifestations of physical desire. Some jurists of Aleppo went so far as to say that Ibn
'Arabi's *Manifestation of Passions* (Tarjuman al-ashwaq) could not have been
inspired by divine mysteries. Certain extreme Sufi texts can be found which
argue the cancellation of religious duties, the permitting of what is proscribed
and freedom of interaction with women.

The Sufi love poem cannot stand except through a coupling of the spiritual
and physical. This is clearly shown by Corbin in his treatment of the creative
imagination of Ibn 'Arabi. 'As God cannot be seen except in a real form akin to
the aspect in which He is manifested, so is the holy form and the ideal image,
which can only be contemplated in a real form, whether tangible or imaginary.
This real form renders the ideal image visible without and within. If we catch
Ibn 'Arabi's reference to al-Nazzam,[22] whom he describes as a sign of a holy
sublime wisdom, we will realize how her ideal aspect, since the poet was overwhelmed by imagination, was transformed into a symbol resulting from the
light of manifestation, wherein one dimension of sublimity is disclosed.'
Corbin illustrates this in his comment on the image of the female manifested in
a poem by Ibn 'Arabi:

> Greetings to Salma, to whomever came of late;
> A piteous man, like me, has the right to greet.
> Why should she not answer with greetings
> To me? But one may not appeal to dolls!
> They journeyed as the night lowered down its veils,
> So I pleaded: 'A homeless, infatuated man in love!'
> A smile betrayed her teeth, a streak of light,
> I could not tell which one dispersed the night.
> She said: 'Suffice it not that in his heart
> I dwell, where he can see me at all times,
> suffice it not?'

It is pointless to wonder whether this image of the female is the personified
female or the divine truth. In the Sufi love poem it is not possible to see one
without the other. The female joins beauty to majesty, and manifest to invisible
divinity. This coupling of the visible and the imaginary is what led the Sufis to
resort, in their image of the cosmic female, to aspects of sensual love language
as well as to aspects of *'Udhri* love poem language. Many examples might be
taken to illustrate this point, but one will suffice here. The following is a poem
by Ibn 'Arabi, implying a reference to 'Umar ibn Abi Rabi'a, where the holy
(pilgrimage) and the profane are excitingly coupled together.

I sacrifice my soul to the fair, comely beauties,
Who captured my heart, while kissing the holy corner and the black stone.
When lost behind them, you cannot find your way
Except when guided by their fragrant trace.
No moonless night fell dark on me
But I remembered them, and then a moon would guide my way.
In courting, I wooed that one of them,
A beauty, no human was her like.
If she would show her face, a ray would shine
Like that of the sun, when free from dust.
The sun, her forehead; the night, her locks;
A sun and night; in wondrous unison.
At night, she is the light of day;
At noon, a night of black hair is our shade.

Second: The image of the cosmic female as a life-giving mother has developed, in Sufi gnosticism, into something akin to androgyny in mythology. The underlying reason for this is that the essence of Sufi love is a yearning to reclaim the lost human unity. Hence, it was inevitable femininity and masculinity should be sanctified at the same time, so that the beloved being would be an amalgamation of the two. Ibn 'Arabi addresses the analysis of this image by joining Adam to Maryam (Mary) and Eve to Jesus:

> The Almighty created Jesus through Maryam, so Maryam assumed the status of Adam, and Jesus assumed the status of Eve. As a female was begotten of a male, so a male was begotten of a female. Thus God concluded in a manner similar to that with which He began: Jesus and Eve as siblings and Adam and Maryam as their parents.[23]

This exciting image confirms once more, perhaps, the high status attained by the woman in Sufi gnosticism. It implies the principle of the agent and that of the recipient. 'The Sufi,' Corbin says, 'achieves the highest vision of revelation while meditating on the image of the female being, as the positive–negative duality leads to the expectation of some aspects of the androgyny myth. Moreover, the spirit of Muslim Sufism may lead, by virtue of its permanence, to the emergence of everlasting femininity as an image of the godhead, as the Sufi contemplates in the female the mystery of the compassionate God, whose creative act seems like a liberation of beings from their bondage.'[24]

In the gnostic tendency, which represents the more profound and complete image of Sufism, the world is divided into two parts: a higher world of light and a lower world of darkness. At the top of both worlds sits the God whom al-Suhrawardi calls 'the Light of Omnipotent Lights'. The first world is celestial and ethereal, the other terrestrial and involved. The first manages the world of celestial and human spirits.[25] It is the world of the 'Kingdom of God'. The other is the world of matter given over to Existence, or the 'tenebrous isthmuses' which are veils, or death, or absolute night.[26] Hence, the body in the illuminist philosophy of al-Suhrawardi is a barrier or a space dividing the human being from abstract thought or the truth of truths. This truth, the moving from the tangible to the ideal, cannot be achieved except through imagination. Through imagination the Sufi achieves the world of 'suspended ideals' whose aspects appear as an image in a mirror.

Al-Suhrawardi, therefore, cancels the visible body to replace it with an imaginary body, moving about in an imaginary world, which includes whatever is found of wealth and variety in the tangible world, but on an ethereal level. It is images and shadows that form the threshold to the Kingdom of God, where lie what might be called the dream cities of the Sufis. In the gnostic philosophy of al-Hallaj, the objective to which the Sufi aspires is an eternal union between man and the divine self. This union cannot be effected until three stages or obstacles have been passed. The first is the obstacle of veils (the level of the *murid*, or novice); the second is the obstacle of trial or resignation of the body (the level of the *murad*, or intention); the third is the obstacle to *ittihad*, or union. To pass through these stages the desirous spirit must be suppressed and subjugated to the articulate spirit. This is achieved through the practice of asceticism and spiritual exercise.

> He who trains his body in obedience, and occupies his heart with good deeds, and suffers patiently in parting with pleasures, and controls himself in avoidance of desires, will be elevated to the class of favoured ones. He will then ascend in the stages of purity until his nature is gleaned out of humanity. When there is nothing human left of him, he will be possessed by the divine soul of which was the soul of Jesus, the son of Maryam. Then he will be obeyed. All he desires is fulfilled through divine command. All his actions then will be acts of God . . .[27]

The obliteration of the body through asceticism, exercise and suppression of desires until it is purified and refined is, in the philosophy of al-Hallaj, a way to revive and create the body in a new guise. The novice, in this philosophy, is able to compress his body until it becomes an image or a mirror of the divine self:

> Praise be to Him, Who manifested His human form,
> The mystery of His piercing divine glory.
> Then He appeared manifest in His creation
> In the form of one who eats and drinks;
> Until His creatures had a sight of him,
> Like one eyebrow glimpsing another.[28]

If the Sufi could compress his body into this imaginary form, then he could, in the view of al-Hallaj, make an interpretation of the Quranic verse: 'He is the first and the last; the evident and the hidden.' (57, *Al-Hadid*, 3) The interpretation would take the following form: 'Here I am, the first and the last; the evident and the hidden; for I am the right and the whole, and my existence is in no need of proof since in everything I abide.'[29] This image led the Sufi to distinguish three types of love: divine, spiritual and natural. Divine love is the love of the creator for the created, and at the same time the love of the created for the creator, wherein the image of the Creator Himself is manifested. Spiritual love is that in which the created seeks the existence that is revealed to him, and strives to have that image identify with the image of the beloved. Natural love, on the other hand, is an overpowering and searching to satisfy the desires of the lover, irrespective of those of the beloved.[30] These three types of love meet in the Sufi when he achieves the stage of union or incarnation, where the spiritual and corporeal become two sides of the same reality. Al-Hallaj says:

> It's me I love, and who loves is me,
> Two souls are we, in one body incarnate.
> If you saw me, it's him you saw,
> If you saw him, you saw us both.[31]

In such an experience the body becomes absent while present, and present while absent. An interesting conflict arises between the visible and the imaginary, or between vision and insight. One may replace the other; so it can be said that the Sufi is haunted by a state that sounds like visual hallucination, which makes him see what cannot be seen. Perhaps it is this situation that led to the variety of manifestation images in Sufi literature. The Sufi-deified body cannot achieve the varied manifestation except through a kind of passion and intuition of imaginary sights. When such a state of the body is achieved, the Sufi becomes devoid of himself, because, as Imam al-Qushayri would say, the revelation of majesty necessitates obliteration and absence.[32] This is a status the Sufi can achieve only through progressively higher stages.

In this connection, al-Qushayri advances an interpretation of the following Quranic verse: 'And the moon We have assigned stages [to traverse] till it returns like an old [crooked] palm tree branch. Neither should the sun catch up with the moon, nor can the night outstrip the day: each swims along in [its own] orbit.' (36, *Yasin*, 39–40) He says: 'The novice, in his first stages of seeking union with the divine self and vanishing into it, is of feeble appearance and slender perception. Then he grows in insight and becomes like a full moon. Then he decreases in his guise as he approaches the sun. The nearer he comes, the more he slips into imperfection, until he vanishes.'[33] Thus is achieved the union between the celestial and the terrestrial, the eternal and the transient. In this union, the lover realizes, in Corbin's words, that the divine image is not outside him, but is inherent in his existence. 'At this vital point of the experience, the circle of love dialectic begins to close in on itself;'[34] for in the Sufi union an exciting duality emerges, which is the duality of the lover and the beloved, and love becomes a veil around the lover. To explain this duality, one may refer to the symbolism of Qays and Layla, which was very popular with the Sufis: they used it in explaining the divine manifestation, and the stage of obliteration and union. They made Qays utter their famous dictum – 'I am Layla' – following al-Hallaj's words 'I am the Truth.' This indicates that the mad Qays has vanished into Layla, and his love has become a veil enshrouding him and her at the same time, or that he is in love with his love for her, hence his love has kept him away from her.[35] Therefore, al-Shibli could say: 'O people! Here is the madman of Bani 'Amir who, when apart from Layla, would say, "I am Layla;" and he would be so overwhelmed with Layla that he would conceive of no sense or meaning except that of Layla, seeing everything through Layla.'[36] In view of this, Corbin says that the Sufi, in the early stages of his experience, would grope for the divine image in external natural phenomena, though they imply all his inherent existence. He searches around for this image in the visibles and the tangibles until he returns to the precincts of his soul to realize that the sought image is dormant in the depths of his existence:

> When my beloved appears to sight,
> With which eye do you see him?
> With his eye, but not with mine,
> For none but him can see him.[37]

VII.2 Significance of the deified body: The body as man's vista to his humanity

The image of the deified body in many texts of Sufi literature seems connected, from a certain ideological viewpoint, with the mythical mind, with its absolutism and timelessness, and its concepts that transcend man and history. It is based on the principle of absolute unity, and proceeds from the many to the one, considering it the centre and origin, mixing the absolute with the relative; and so the absolute loses its supremacy and the relative its specificity. Despite the significant truth of this comment, the image of the deified body implies, for some Sufis, a reconciliation with nature and a restoration of the lost unity of man, a vista for man to his humanity. Man, in this curious experience, is his own creator and lord. Of man as an absolute value, there is nothing more expressive than the testimony of the famous Sufi al-Jili: 'There is no I but I.' This sounds for all the world like Zoroaster confronting man with his destiny and self.

It is true that the image of the deified body assumes the Sufi dignity and its power to transform and convert objects. However, this dignity is no more than the language of metaphors and dreams, which can penetrate into the region of the 'inexpressible', obliterating whatever possibilities it can, as if in revenge for the usurpation and absence of the body in current socio-cultural relations and structures – and so magnifying the body and raising it to the status of divinity. It was because of this sublimation, perhaps, that Sufism was branded with introversion and detachment from society. Yet such criticism, levelled at Sufism or at modern literature with Sufi tendencies, fails to see how Sufism implies a refinement of the self, a recognition of individual personality that was suppressed in an Arab-Islamic civilization where the only authority was that of the group. It also finds, in the disbanding of social relations, a recognition of individual liberty and the authority of the ideal. One reasonable objection to the image of the deified body in Sufi literature may be addressed to the aspects of magnification, which often assume a magical expression, and to the concept of the conversion of objects rather than their growth and development.

Chapter 7: Concepts of human rights in Islamic doctrines (Sunnis, Shi'ites, Isma'ilis, Qarmatians, Mu'tazilis, Sufis, Wahhabis)

Shamsuddin al-Kaylani

I. The comparative approach: human rights in a variety of contexts

Numerous self-congratulatory Islamist writings insist on the precedence of Islam in the area of human rights legislation. Often, indeed, they conclude that Muslims do not need 'modern' human rights at all; the traditional rights provided for in the Holy Quran and Prophetic Tradition are, they believe, sufficient. There are also those who affect a blend of the two sources, placing Islamic concepts of human rights on a par with those springing from the modern European revolution.

By contrast, both the modernist elite and Islamist intellectuals, starting out from the same initial point, reach quite different conclusions: there is, they insist, a fundamental methodological gap regulating any comparison of human rights in Islam with those advanced in the context of modernity. In this regard, Bassam al-Tibi asserts that 'there is a conflict between a world view centred on man and another centred on God. The modern legal system, including the laws governing human rights, is an outcome of the modernist cultural agenda – that is, a product of the principle of human subjectivism, the vision which centres on man.'[1] The same argument is made by the Islamist Shaykh Rashid al-Ghanoushi. 'The Universal Declaration of Human Rights is,' he says, 'based on the precedence of man, who is himself the source of all rights and legislations; while the Islamist concept of human rights stems from the idea of transcendence. In this latter situation, the rights become sacred duties which God's vicegerent on earth cannot treat lightly. They do not belong to him; God is their sole proprietor.'[2]

The divergence between the two contexts becomes still clearer if we read the Islamic human rights document issued by UNESCO's Higher Islamic Council on 19 September 1981 alongside the preamble to the French Revolution's Declaration of the Rights of Man and Citizen (1789). The former presents human rights as religious duties, while the latter proceeds from the principle of the commonweal and aspires to create better human conditions on a universal scale. These latter, as Sami A. al-Sahiliyya observes, spring from motives of pragmatic expediency in conjunction with such ideal goals as liberty and dignity.[3]

The problem here lies not in any emphasis on different contexts; it lies, rather, in the reciprocal denial, by each party, of the value of the human rights advocated by the other. History and historical relativity are thus ignored. Denial by the modernists of the seeds of human rights in Islam is countered by the Islamists' denial of any value in the modern concepts of human rights.

The standpoint of Islamic religious scholars on human rights converges with that taken by their Christian counterparts; for the Catholic Church refused to sign the 1948 United Nations Universal Declaration of Human Rights on the grounds that it ignored God's rights. It was not until 1961, during the reign of Pope John XXIII, that the Church finally signed the Declaration.[4]

Despite all these difficulties, it is nevertheless imperative that we acknowledge the 'roots' of human rights present in Islam. This is also in fact the view reached by the Paris Academy of Political Ethics, which, following extensive debate, confirmed the use of the term 'origin' or 'origins' to describe the common ground existing between modern concepts of human rights and religious texts dealing with these rights.[5] In this connection, Mohammed Arkoun recognizes the presence in Islam of the 'petals' or 'seeds' of human rights – what he calls 'the "foundations" able to serve as a springboard to conduct a dialogue with the European intellect and interact with its historical experiment'.[6] These 'origins' can indeed be found in the major Islamic religious texts, and are able to supply the necessary basic features of human rights in many aspects of life.[7]

It will also be helpful, in making such a comparison, to take into account the period of time separating the advent of Islam (in the seventh century AD) from the modern era; for the concept of rights is one that takes shape gradually within cultures, giving expression to a particular social structure and its prevalent morals and values. On the other hand, there are quasi-natural abstract rights which form part of 'human nature' itself.[8] Ultimately, present-day concepts of human rights simply represent the crown of human culture as experienced over the centuries and forming the background for the historical achievements of modern culture.

The Quran and Prophetic Tradition mark the initial emergence of a proper position to be accorded to man as an individual created in the image of God and enjoined to emulate Him. When God appointed man as his vicegerent on

earth,[9] the mythological outlook on the world was discarded; the drama of periodic recreation was replaced by one giving greater relevance to human events
as the expression of God's will in history. Moreover, man's position in this history is all the more important because he is God's vicegerent. This experience
of historical awareness, based on the individual's faith and his accountability
before God, calls for a collective effort to respond to His exalted will.

Rights, as formulated in the modernist context, were not fundamentally
conceivable in the conditions of the seventh century. Yet, as Muhammad A. al-
Jabiri notes, 'we do come across texts and references to man, and to his universal and moral role, which provide genuine origins for modern concepts of
human rights.'[10]

Although the Quranic context of human rights differs from the modern
one, Islamic texts do give rise to the concept of the individual's spiritual and
moral character; and out of this came the notion of the moral being as bearer of
a spiritual message lodged in his consciousness. This development also emphasized the sublime values of the individual, whose relationship with God is not
dependent on any mediation. The Islamic texts reinforced the humanistic tendencies inherent in the two earlier monotheistic religions, Judaism and
Christianity, although the texts did not, it should be said, establish the legal and
institutional safeguards necessary to guarantee these rights, except through
divine justice.[11] And, while a distinction undeniably exists between the concept
of the 'moral person' and that of the 'citizen' (who enjoys legal independence
within a constitutional state), the task of the spiritual upliftment of the individual does equip the 'contractual' rights with stronger moral safeguards.

Islam advocated human equality and brotherhood, and it preached certain
commandments to humanity: 'Thou shalt not commit murder; thou shalt not
lie; and thou shalt not commit adultery.' It also commanded people to do what
was right and laid prohibitions against wrongdoing. These are all commandments making for an absolute guarantee of the protection of the contractual
rights brought about in the context of modern civilization. Religion, says Hans
Küng, 'provides man with the highest standard in matters of conscience, unrestricted by any conditions — a standard that is absolute and conclusive, yet
applicable in the most complex situations.'[12]

Having developed the concept of moral equality, man has added to it the
concept of legal equality — a course which, according to one authority, 'has
brought about a social and political revolution in Europe, resulting in the modern European Renaissance which ultimately adopted the concept of political
equality. This was the concept that provided the basis for a guaranteed equality
Islam had preached (and Christianity had advocated). Thus the individual won

the right to political participation, which in Islam had heretofore been the prerogative of those in authority.'[13]

II. The initial period: human rights and the eras of the Prophet and the first four caliphs

It is somewhat difficult to speak of 'human rights' vis-à-vis a particular Islamic doctrine without reference to the major sources of religion – the Quran, the Prophetic Tradition and the period of the first four (orthodox) caliphs – that underlie the visions of the various doctrinal sects in question.[14] One needs to return to the initial period before Islam became ideologically disjointed, even though, as Arkoun remarks, 'the segmentations and categorizations we know today were recorded two centuries after the rise of Islam'.[15]

Since the end of the Prophet's Medina period, and since the period of the orthodox (Rashidi) caliphs, who played an undeniable role in forming Islamic awareness, Muslims have dreamed ceaselessly of regaining the 'ideal state' – the Islamic Utopia – governed by the principles applied by the Prophet and the orthodox caliphs. 'With the passage of time,' Arkoun contends, 'this Islamic awareness became solid, coherent and irreversible.'[16]

It is possible to distinguish two historical periods with regard to Islamic awareness of human rights. First, there was the era of the Prophet, followed by that of the experiment of the four orthodox caliphs, which had at its core the discourse of a Quranic revelation open to interpretation. The second was the juridical period during which each doctrinal orientation operated independently in giving shape to the initial Islamic discourse. This discourse was also ideologically organized according to concepts which would, in time, constrict the receptivity of the Quranic text and set limits on the initial experiment itself. All these doctrines, nonetheless, existed within one principal ambit: whatever the specific doctrinal interpretations involved, common features remained in evidence – such as values and moral tendencies amenable to concepts of human rights.

As such, it is imperative to scrutinize these common concepts, which governed everyone's approach to human rights, even if each doctrine was clearly inclined to give precedence to one or the other of the values and tendencies in question.

A close study of the major initial texts (the Quran, the Tradition and the contributions of the orthodox period) will reveal these as being replete with a deep concern over man and over his rights, greatness and nobility. They show, beyond all doubt, an acute awareness of the values of justice, equality and human brotherhood regardless of colour or race, so constituting viable bases for modern human rights.

II.1   *The metaphysical covenant: honouring man*

The concept of 'obedience to God' is expressed in the Quran by the term 'covenant', which provides for a metaphysical agreement – to find its equivalent, in worldly terms, in Rousseau's 'social contract' – based on man's testimony to the Oneness of God and the promise to confer nobility on man if he abides by God's terms. The Quran states: 'When thy Lord drew forth from the Children of Adam – from their loins – their descendants, and made them testify concerning themselves: "Am I not your Lord?" they said: "Yea! We do testify."' (7, *Al-A'raf*, 172) This 'covenant of faith' is dependent upon uttering the 'testimony of faith': 'I testify that there is no God but God and that Muhammad is His Prophet.' This embodies man's free commitment to the testimony and to the irrevocable trust which he shoulders.[17]

By this covenant man will be blessed and exalted, for has God not created him 'in the best of moulds' (95, *Al-Tin*, 4)? And has God not addressed him in the singular[18] in the Quran: 'O man! What has seduced thee from thy Lord Most Beneficent? Him who created thee. Fashioned thee in due proportion?' (82, *Al-Infitar*, 6–7) And again: '. . . He began the creation of man with clay, and made his progeny from a quintessence of the nature of a fluid despised. But He fashioned him in due proportion, and breathed into him something of His spirit.' (32, *Al-Sajda*, 7–9) God honoured man still further by making him His vicegerent on earth: 'Behold, thy Lord said to the angels: "I will create a vicegerent on earth." They said: "Wilt thou place therein one who will make mischief therein and shed blood? Whilst we do celebrate Thy praises and glorify Thy holy (name)?" He said: "I know what ye know not."' (2, *Al-Baqara*, 30) Thus, God's action in making man His vicegerent raises him to the position of citizen in the Kingdom of God.[19] Khalid M. Khalid describes God's favour to man as an act of making him the centre and cause of existence, and the passage to things unseen and others known.[20]

God also 'taught Adam the nature [names] of all things' (2, *Al-Baqara*, 31), and ennobled him with His spirit, raising him in stature. God said: 'Behold! Thy Lord said to the angels: "I am about to create man, from sounding clay, from mud moulded into shape. When I have fashioned him [in due proportion] and breathed into him of My Spirit, fall ye down in obeisance unto him."' (15, *Al-Hijr*, 28–29) Furthermore, God liberated man from the sin that has dogged him in Christianity, and accepted his repentance: 'Then learnt Adam from his

Lord words of inspiration, and his Lord turned towards him; for He is oft-returning, Most Merciful.' (2, *Al-Baqara*, 37) Thus Adam has no need of any mediation to be saved; all he needs is to take the straight path.[21]

II.2   The right to life

This honouring of man in Islam is reflected in an emphasis on the protection of human life. We read in the Quran: '. . . if any one slew a person – unless it be for murder or for spreading mischief in the land – it would be as if he slew the whole people.' (5, *Al-Ma'ida*, 35) And the Prophet expresses the same idea: 'If a person commits murder in the East and another in the West condones the act, he would be a partner in it.'[22] In the same context, Islam prohibits suicide, duelling and the killing of the foetus.[23] Islam also prescribes severe deterrent punishments, appropriate to the period of Revelation, in order to protect life. In the Quran, God says: 'We ordained therein for them: "life for life, eye for eye, nose for nose, ear for ear, tooth for tooth, and wounds equal for equal."' (5, *Al-Ma'ida*, 48) The human body in Islam has its own sanctity, as witnessed in the Prophet's saying, as related by al-Bukhari: 'Your soul has its rights and your body has its rights.'[24]

II.3   Consultation and freedom of opinion

The Islamic metaphysical covenant is translated in earthly terms into a contract among people, in the form of 'consultation' (*shura*), which is described by M. 'Amara as 'a binding religious duty enjoined on every person, the governors and the governed in a state, and the family in a community, and in every aspect of human activity'.[25] God addresses the Prophet in these terms: '. . . Wert thou severe or harsh-hearted, they would have broken away from about thee: so pass over (their faults), and ask for (God's) forgiveness for them; and consult them in affairs (of moment).' (3, *Al 'Imran*, 159) The principle of consultation is strengthened by holding all family members responsible for the protection of justice. The Prophet says: 'Everyone of you is a guardian and is responsible for his wards.' The principle of consultation was not, however, institutional- ized, and some jurists have blamed this on the deviation of men such as 'Amr ibn al-'As and al-Mughira ibn Shu'ba.[26]

II.4   The right to opposition and freedom of opinion

'Enjoining people to do what is right and forbidding them from doing what is wrong' is one of the most crucial duties in Islam; and this can only be carried out in a climate guaranteeing freedom of opinion.[27] The Quran is very clear about this. In 3, *Al 'Imran*, 104, we read: 'Let there arise out of you a band of people inviting to all that is good, enjoining what is right, and forbidding what is wrong.' This is interpreted by Ibn Taymiyya as a means to 'reform the conditions of life for people in the context of obedience to God and His Prophet. This can be done only by enjoining what is right and forbidding what is wrong.'[28] The ultimate goal of this duty, as viewed by Muhammad Asad, is for the nation to establish itself on the principles of righteousness and justice.[29] In this respect, the first caliph, Abu Bakr, recalled how the Prophet of God had said: 'If people see something wrong but do nothing to change it, punishment would fall on all of them.'[30] The Prophet of Islam makes this matter very clear. He instructs Muslims in one of his sayings: 'Whosoever of you sees an evil action, let him change it with his hand; and if he is not able to do so, then with his tongue; and if he is not able to do so, then with his heart – and this is the weakest of faith.'[31] Al-'Ashmawi comments on this as follows:

> The individual Muslim was enjoined, personally and physically, to remedy faults in the Medina community, where no police force had been established. Every individual citizen of that community was himself a policeman, and all members of the community were expected to forbid wrongdoing.[32]

And when the second caliph, 'Umar, addressed people, saying, 'Whosoever of you sees in my actions a diversion from the right path, he should set me right', one of those in attendance replied: 'If we see wrongdoing in your actions, we shall straighten you with our swords.' 'I thank God,' 'Umar replied, 'that there are those among you who would straighten me with their swords.'[33]

II.5 *The right to equality and the unity of human destiny*

The Islamic belief in the Oneness of God – rejecting the idea of 'mediation' – laid the foundation for the mental-moral principle of the equality and brotherhood of all human beings. The new Quranic teachings rejected traditional pride based on ancestry, race, ethnicity and colour; 'the only criterion of pride left for Muslims became moral transcendence and good deeds.'[34] The Quran explicitly lays down this principle in 49, *Al-Hujurat*, 13: 'O Mankind! We created you from a single (pair) of a male and a female, and made you into nations and tribes, that ye may know each other (not that ye may despise each other). Verily the most honoured of you in the sight of God is (he who is) the most righteous of you.' Again, the Quran states that all people are descended from one being: 'It is He who hath produced you from a single person.' (6, *Al-An'am*,

98) This is also one of the principal themes of the Prophet's Speech of Valediction. 'O, people,' he said, 'your God is One; your father is one; you are all Adam's descendants, and Adam was created of dust. The best of you are the most pious. The only thing that distinguishes an Arab over a non-Arab is piety.'[35] Even Muhammad was considered equal to other human beings: 'Say thou: "I am but a man like you."' (41, *Fussilat*, 6) And on one occasion when one of Muhammad's Companions seemed intimidated in his presence, he reassured him, saying: 'Be comforted, for I am not an angel. I am but the son of a Qurayshi woman who eats dried meat.'[36]

II.6 Encouragement to free slaves

In keeping with its promotion of the principle of equality, Islam regards liberty as the natural state of man. This is the essence of 'Umar's angry response to the cruel treatment of helpless people: 'Wherefore do you enslave people who were born free?' Although Islam did not declare slavery unlawful – this would have been inconceivable in the historical context – the Quran nevertheless encouraged the practice of setting slaves free. This became, indeed, something ingrained; the practice came to be regarded as an act of worship and faith, cleansing man's sins. In 90, *Al-Balad*, 12–13, the Quran states: 'And what will explain to thee the path that is steep? (It is freeing the bondman.)'[37] Moreover, Islam limited the heretofore many sources of slavery to just one: war. This, at the time, was a common practice in international relations.[38] Other sources known at the time, such as default on debt, self-sale and kidnapping, were banned by Islam.[39] Additionally, Islam called for slaves to be treated as brothers. Such is the command given by the Prophet: 'They are but your brethren, so clothe, cover and feed them.'[40] In fact, as Karen Armstrong says, divine admonition comes close to sounding a warning note on the matter: 'And we wished to be gracious to those who were being depressed in the land, to make them leaders (in faith) and make them heirs.' (28, *Al-Qasas*, 5)

II.7 The rights of women

The Quran affirms the ontological union of women and men: 'O mankind! Reverence your Guardian-Lord who created you from a single person, created, of like nature, his mate.' (4, *Al-Nisa'*, 1) Islam has also honoured the descendants of Adam without any distinction among them. God promises in the Quran: 'Never will I suffer to be lost the work of any of you, be he male or female; ye are members, one of another.' (3, *Al 'Imran*, 195) Islam's attitude towards women was positive in the historical context of its beginning. The Quran prohibited the practice of burying girls alive, derided the Arab habit of mourning at the birth of a girl, and gave women the legal rights to inheritance and divorce. Most Western women did not obtain these rights until the nine-teenth century.[41] As for the wearing of veils, Roger Garaudi has argued that Islam made this prescribed only for the Prophet's wives, and that Muslims adopted the custom from Persia and Christian Byzantium.[42]

The practice of polygamy had been common before Islam; it was permitted with no limits by the Old Testament, which mentions the harem of David and the seven wives of Solomon, besides his concubines.[43] The Quran permits polygamy, but limits it to four wives, on the very firm condition of equity. The Quran clearly states: 'But if ye fear that ye shall not be able to deal justly (with them), then only one.' (4, *Al-Nisa'*, 3)

II.8 *The right to religious beliefs*

The Quran takes a central position among the monotheistic religions, with which it has a spiritual link vis-à-vis the history of mankind's salvation. The term 'Muslim' includes all those believing in monotheistic religions. This recognition of other believers, and the sharing of the basic revelation with them, leads naturally to religious tolerance. The Quran addresses all people: 'Say ye: "We believe in God, and the revelation given to us, and to Abraham, Ismail, Isaac, Jacob, and the Tribes, and that given to Moses and Jesus, and that given to (all) Prophets from their Lord: We make no difference between one and another of them; and we bow to God (in Islam)."' (2, *Al-Baqara*, 136)

Islam does not force 'peoples of the Book' to convert, and it advises its fol-lowers to conduct their dialogue with them with kindness: 'And dispute ye not with the People of the Book, except with means better (than mere disputa-tion).' (29, *Al-'Ankabut*, 46) And again, addressing the Prophet: 'Invite (all) to the way of thy Lord with wisdom and beautiful preaching; and argue with them in ways that are best and most gracious.' (16, *Al-Nahl*, 125)

Islam establishes for people of the Book certain recognized rights and priv-ileges, including the right to practise their religious worship and rites and to conduct their internal affairs, such as their personal status laws. This is a logical outcome of the spirit of toleration in Islam, a spirit confirmed in the Prophet's saying: 'Whosoever harms a Jew or a Christian, I will be his adversary on the Day of Judgement.'

These rights may seem incomplete by our modern standards of absolute equality, which is the foundation of the rights of citizenship. They shine, nevertheless, when compared with the state of denial, exile and annihilation of Muslims and Islam in Christian Europe. There is just no comparison between the final status of the Christian churches in Turkey, Iran and the Arab world and the fate of Muslims in Spain, Sicily and the Crimea.

The Islamic principle of justice is based on equity and the right to litigation on the one hand, and, on the other, on worship of one God and equality among people. The Quran instructs people: 'And when ye judge between man and man, that ye judge with justice.' (4, *Al-Nisa'*, 58) And again: 'God commands justice, the doing of good.' (16, *Al-Nahl*, 90) The Prophet includes in the admonition those who aid injustice: 'Whosoever aids an oppressor in doing injustice to suppress a just cause is outside the protection of God and His Prophet.'

Justice in the Islamic system is not limited to litigation; rather, it includes all relationships among people, including family relationships and those between the governors and the governed.[44]

Although these rights formally fall under the duty of obedience to God and are consecrated as divine obligations, nonetheless, on the level of moral values and of real-life relations between human beings, they jolted traditional tribal concepts, raised moral standards and – in varying degrees – galvanized people's values with the demands of the principles of daily life, like justice, equity, brotherhood and dignity. These Islamic rights have also practically expanded the limits of freedom of the individual and of society, by consecrating a system of jurisprudence and litigation far more just and progressive for this period.

III. The 'great discord' and opening up to disagreement; the religious schools

Muslims believe that the Prophet struck a balance between revelation and history, and that, by the time of his death, he left a complete religious belief and a unified Arabian Peninsula, thereby giving Arabs what has been described as a ticket to history.[45] Following the Prophet's death, the Arabs were able to reach a consensus on the succession of Abu Bakr, based on his spiritual closeness to the Prophet – his affinity with the Prophet's morality – and on a balance of power. Consequently, as al-Tabari noted, Abu Bakr assumed the succession to belong 'solely to this branch of the Quraysh'.[46] Abu Bakr was succeeded by 'Umar, who established a new system limiting the role of the tribe's nobility and leaning on persons of low birth but a noble Islamic record, such as 'Ammar ibn Yasir, 'Abdullah ibn Mas'ud and Abu Musa al-Ash'ari. 'Ammar, from a class of slaves who entered Islam, was appointed governor of Kufa. According to

Hisham Ju'ayt, 'Ammar and Ibn Mas'ud represented the Islamic elite at its purest.[47] 'Umar distinguished himself by personal involvement in the administration of justice and by controlling public moneys, and he was known for his frugal personal life. He also made sure to attend the meetings of the Prophet's Consultative Council of Companions.[48]

With 'Umar's death, an era of pure heroic Islamic history came to an end.[49] His successor, 'Uthman, followed a soft policy of nepotism, especially during the last years of his caliphate – a policy that broke with the recent but effective practice established by the Prophet, Abu Bakr and 'Umar. This 'deviation' (normal by today's standards) confronted a deep, strong Islamic sense of justice and equality, nurtured by the Quran and by the behavioural and ethical standards established by Abu Bakr and 'Umar.[50] In opposition to any form of nepotism and favouritism, the Companion Abu Dharr al-Ghufari would proclaim, in the face of 'Uthman and Mu'awiya, that 'this money belongs to the Muslim nation and must not be called God's money'.[51] When he told 'Uthman that 'wealthy people should not hoard more wealth', 'Uthman rejoined: 'I will not enforce asceticism on people.'[52] The same Islamic principles made 'Abdullah ibn Mas'oud reject his appointment by 'Uthman as 'our treasurer'. 'I am,' he said, 'keeper of the Muslims' treasury';[53] and he returned the key of the treasury to 'Uthman. Those who had assimilated the Quranic system of values were shocked by the clear difference between the requirements of Islamic ethics and the actions of the aging Caliph. The Quran 'reciters', who were in direct touch with the religious text and voluntarily devoted their lives to memorizing and teaching it, protested to 'Uthman: 'You have changed it and made replacements in it.' Six hundred of them marched to Medina to ask that he rescind these aberrations and begin dismissing his governors. Initially, it is reported, 'Uthman reached an agreement with them, guaranteed by some of the Prophet's Companions, to 'act according to the word of God and the Tradition of His Prophet; to give to the deprived; to allay the fear of the oppressed; and to permit the return of those exiled'.[54] Subsequently, however, he showed some reluctance, and was abandoned by the Immigrants and the Supporters (*al-Muhajirun* and *al-Ansar*). Later, 'Ali and al-Zubayr were to send their sons to defend 'Uthman, a standpoint subsequently regarded as defeatist.

At this point, we witness an astonishing and wonderful scene: the 'reciters', who upheld the Prophet's ideals, surrounded 'Uthman's house, demanding to see him and later demanding his removal. For 40 days they wavered over their decision to kill him. For his part, the Caliph, who was accused of deviating from the right path, and who held sway over a vast land, chose to stand alone, refusing to enlist the help of his police force or army. He would not even accept help from his many relatives and followers, but he also refused to abdicate, saying: 'I shall not take off a mantle in which God clothed me.'[55] He proceeded to read the Quran, eager to answer the Prophet's beckoning to him in his dream.

A fascinating scene! In the end they killed him, a dreadful act that was to jolt the nation's conscience and set a scar in the hearts of believers. It would also be the springboard for rifts and wars, and raise the spectre of ideological and social polarization.

After this 'incident' people rallied in terror around 'Ali ibn Abi Talib, hoping to save the nation's unity and heal its wounds. But 'Ali's legitimacy was not confirmed. Many Companions of the Prophet would not support him – not because he lacked the necessary qualifications, but because he had not taken a firm stand against 'Uthman's murderers (though he constantly denied any personal responsibility), and because, although most people condemned the killing, 'Ali did not visit any punishment on the killers.

Subsequently, 'A'isha, al-Zubayr and Talha rose demanding revenge, and Mu'awiya took a similar stand on his own account. Soon there was a confrontation between 'Ali on the one hand and, on the other, 'A'isha, al-Zubayr and al-Talha, in what was to become known as the 'War of the Camel'. This was followed by a confrontation between 'Ali and Mu'awiya in Siffin, averted in compliance with a call by Mu'awiya's followers to submit to the 'judgement of the Quran'. As a result, the Dissenters (*al-Khawarij*) deserted Ali, because he had accepted mediation. They then succeeded in killing him but failed in their attempt to assassinate Mu'awiya.

In the midst of these bloody events (known as the 'great discord'), in which ideals overlapped with the grey area of mundane interests, deep political differences took shape. These, in turn, led to the various Islamic groupings, which began as simple reflections of socio-political problems but ended as theological doctrines, with a corresponding transference from opinions on political matters to judgements on religious rules. Abu 'l-Fath al-Shahrastani aptly describes the situation: 'The fiercest argument within the nation was that over the Imamate [religious leadership], for there was no sword raised in Islam at any time that was worse than that over the Imamate.'[56]

Perhaps the best illustration of this point is in the names given to the Islamic doctrines themselves: 'Shi'a' is an Arabic word meaning 'those who pledged allegiance to the family of the Prophet'; 'Khawarij' is Arabic meaning 'those who dissented from Imam Ali; and 'Mu'tazila' signifies an early version of 'withdrawal from political life', in times of crisis.[57]

IV. Sunni doctrine

Followers of this doctrine have identified themselves as the orthodox group entrusted with the Prophet's Traditions and the heritage of the Prophet's successor caliphs and Companions. They give precedence, in their programme, to the concept of the community, or nation, which according to their doctrine becomes the custodian of Revelation and the party entitled to interpret religious law and to select the caliph. This, according to Dorothea Kravolski, distinguishes them from the She's, who have limited these privileges to the imam.[58]

The Sunnis took a conciliatory stand towards the opposing parties in the Great Discord: they recognized the legitimacy of 'Ali's claim; but they admitted the other Companions, who disputed with 'Ali, into Islamic brotherhood, that is, into the community of believers.

After 'Ali's death, when Mu'awiya held sway, the Sunnis supported him so as to maintain the unity of the nation and prevent internal discord. They nevertheless opposed the naming of his son Yazid as successor and his deviation from the principle of consultation (*shura*).[59]

During the Umayyad period, the Sunnis were known as 'the custodians of the Tradition'; and they were distinguished by their tendency to reach independent judgements rather than follow one single line of interpretation.[60] Imam Ahmad ibn Idris al-Shafi'i (d. 204/820) was later to provide this doctrine with its methodical formulation and to arrange its four main sources: the Book, Tradition, Consensus and Juristic Analogy.[61]

Al-Shafi'i especially emphasized the principle of 'consensus', which was to become the basis on which Sunnis constructed their political and jurisprudential theories. He also proposed the era of the first four (Rashidi) caliphs as a model to be emulated in the lives of community and state, and advocated the consensus model of the Companions and the principle of the common will, that is, the will of the majority.[62] From these principles the following Islamic concepts of human rights are derived:

IV.1 Rights of the individual and of communities

Concepts of human rights in Islamic doctrines have been governed by the ideas inherent in the major religious texts discussed at the beginning of this study. Each doctrinal group has, even so, emphasized one aspect which became the key to an order of priority for these rights. Subsequently, jurists undertook the task of classifying and arranging the rights in question.

Jurists took as their starting point the 'rights of God', making these the centre vis-à-vis all recognized rights of the individual. Since human beings are instructed to observe 'God's rights', they are bound to respect the social and political conditions that allow for recognition of these. Thus, the rights of man came, as Arkoun observes, to be considered a manifestation and precondition for respecting the rights of God.[63] Imam al-Ghazali (d. 505/1111) expresses a similar viewpoint:

> The system of religion, with its knowledge and observation, cannot be achieved except by maintaining physical health and security of life, and by obtaining the necessities such as clothing, habitation and food. But when a person is constantly preoccupied with guarding himself against injustice and seeking sustenance in hard times, how can he devote himself to learning and labour, which are the means to achieve happiness in the afterlife? I conclude, therefore, that the system of life, that is, obtaining necessities, is a condition for the system of religion.[64]

Al-Ghazali, then, regards 'human rights' as a means to the full practice of religion.

This is made clear in his definition of life. 'It is,' he says, 'a common term used to denote the seasons of life, including those of enjoyment, happiness, the fulfilling of needs, and obtaining necessities. It is also used to denote anything sought before death. One of these uses runs counter to religion, the other is a precondition for it.'[65]

Islamic jurists have placed the subjects of jurisprudence into two main categories: duties to God (i.e., God's rights) and duties of people to one another (people's rights). In some cases the latter also take the form of legal penalty, such as the rights of a murdered person's guardians to reprisal, the right of punishment for injuries (a hand for a hand and a tooth for a tooth), the right of a person to retribution for harm done to his honour or good reputation, the reciprocal rights of husband and wife, and the rights of heirs to inheritance.

These are the areas, within the discourse of Islamic jurisprudence, that are relevant to the field of human rights. They have been grouped according to their purpose and to the legislator's goals in laying them down, which is securing the interests of people in this life and in the hereafter.[66] Jurists have divided these goals, or common goods, into three categories. First, we have necessities without which people's lives would be wretched and corrupt. These are five: the maintenance of religion, the self, the mind, wealth and pedigree. Islamic jurisprudence has laid down laws to maintain each one of these necessities. The second category is that of man's needs, and it aims to alleviate hardships, as in the case of permitting a sick person to break his/her fast. The third category is that which seeks to improve life, and includes good manners and nobility of actions and character.[67]

Modern Islamic scholars have regarded these principles and objectives as the basis for the theory of personal and public rights and liberties in the Islamic context. It is necessary, nonetheless, to unravel their cultural intricacies and clarify their objectives, to examine them in light of their historical context, so as to cultivate the seeds that are in accordance with modern human rights.

Even without these juristic classifications, we may in fact discern that Sunni discourse is open to a complex of juristic, value and ethical principles which lead to a strengthening of the conscience and its freedom, to toleration, and to augmenting the position of the community of believers in matters of politics. All this is the outcome of the precedence accorded by Sunni discourse to the community of believers, and of its conciliatory stance in the face of disagreement.

These Sunni doctrinal principles are amenable to the following formula of human rights:

a   The right of personal conscience. This is based on the Sunni rejection of the concept of the Imam's infallibility, and its denial of the authority of any religious institution over what Muhammad 'Abduh calls 'people's faith and system of beliefs except for God and His Prophet'.[68] This rejection will, theoretically at least, open the door to religious freedom for the individual conscience.

b   The Sunni's conciliatory stance towards parties to the 'discord', and their clinging to the unity of believers, led to a forbearing attitude towards the parties in dispute. Ahmad ibn Hanbal (d. 241/855), along with other Sunni jurists like al-Bukhari (d. 256/870) and Abu Musa 'l-Ash'ari (d. 324/935), while recognizing the legitimacy of 'Ali's claim to the caliphate, over-looked the dispute among the Companions, and regarded the stand taken by Mu'awiya, Talha and al-Zubayr as a discretionary error not amounting to guilt. As such, they deserved to be spoken well of.[69]

On the basis of this principle, jurists were satisfied, when deciding on matters of faith, with 'opinion of conscience' and 'acceptance by the tongue'. This Abu Hanifa (d. 150/767) called 'acceptance and belief', and he never charged a believer with heresy as a result of guilt, even if this involved a cardinal error.[70] This was followed by the judgement of al-Baqillani.[71] Abu Musa al-Ash'ari described the situation in these terms: 'Faith is acceptance by conscience; statement by the tongue and the

practice of faith are only branches of it.'[72] Finally, al-Ghazali emphasized
that 'dispute over the Imamate is not ground for a charge of heresy'.[73]

c   Freedom to differ and freedom of opinion. Sunnis' rejection of a religious
institution and denial of the Imam's infallibility, and their emphasis on the
community of believers as a decisive factor in jurisprudence and the succession, open the door, in principle, to freedom of opinion. As Shaykh
Rashid Rida comments: 'For Sunnis, infallibility is not a trait of any human
being, except prophets.'[74] They even, indeed, go so far as to deny prophets
this trait, except in matters of cardinal error. Basing his study on this point,
Sir Hamilton Gibb decides that 'the humblest Muslim becomes – in matters of religion – equal to the Caliph',[75] and that theoretically no party has
the right to consider the others' vices a matter of heresy on which they
should be judged.[76] Gibb affirms that 'Sunni Islam enjoys an essential
characteristic, which is its toleration towards different viewpoints', citing
as proof the presence of the four doctrinal schools, which gives legitimacy
to modernization.[77]

   For these reasons, Sunnis denied that the Caliph should be the deciding
factor in matters of religion. Thus, Imam Anas ibn Malik (d. 179/975)
rejected Ja'far al-Mansour's request that he make his juristic work the
state's legal doctrine. 'The Prophet's Companions,' Anas replied, 'dis-
persed in the land, and [every one of them] made a personal judgement in
a province as he saw fit. The people of this city [Mecca] have an opinion,
those of Medina have another, and those of Iraq have another.'[78] Anas's
judgement was: 'that the oath is not binding on one who is subjected to
coercion (in the appointment of the Caliph); and no divorce can be
enforced by coercion.'[79] Abu Hanifa's views on freedom of opinion are
still more radical. 'The authorities,' he says, 'have no legal basis on which to
incarcerate or punish a person who objects to the legitimacy of the
caliphate and to its just legitimate government, and who insults the temporal Imam, or even calls openly for him to be killed, unless he intends to
start an armed revolt.'[80]

d   Freedom of worship. Basing their work on the principles of the 'initial
period' (discussed above), Islamic jurists set down laws governing the status of believers in other divinely inspired religions within the Muslim state.
These laws guaranteed freedom to carry on their worship and rituals, their
personal status affairs and their juristic traditions. In addition to Christians
and Jews, Manichaeans were treated as 'people of the Book'.[81]

   According to Philip Hitti and others: 'Muslims, generally speaking,
respected the status of non-Muslims in spite of their suffering religious

persecution during some periods. In cities, Christians and Jews held high government offices. This caused Muslim jealousy and covetousness.'[82]

e   Women's rights. Some Sunni jurists broadened the extent of women's rights, giving them the right to divorce based on a *hadith* quoted by al-Bukhari.[83] Abu Hanifa, according to Mustafa al-Shak'a, gave an adult woman the right to marry a man of her own choice, and to initiate the marriage contract. He also denied the father the right to force his daughter to marry against her wishes.[84] Abu Hanifa endorsed the appointment of women as judges in personal status courts; al-Tabari later endorsed their appointment in any judicial court. Hadi 'Alawi says that Abu Hanifa made a woman's blood money equal to that of a man, thus proclaiming equality in blood regardless of gender.[85]

f   The right to justice and equality. Sunnis were also in agreement with other Islamic doctrines on the principles of justice and equality.

g   The caliphate and the political rights of individuals and the community. For Sunnis governance comes close to being a civilian matter: decision-making is the right of the community (i.e., the nation) through consultation. According to al-Ash'ari: 'the Imamate is confirmed by agreement and selection, not by dictation and appointment.'[86] And al-Baqillani sums up the concept simply by saying: 'The Imamate [is by] selection.'[87]

The majority of Sunnis agree that 'the appointment of the Imam is a duty indicated in Islamic Law . . . and some believe that this duty is recognized by the intellect'.[88] The purpose of his appointment, they say, 'is the organization of communities, the enforcement of borders, the collection of alms and the reformation of the citizenry through the six universals: the maintenance of religion, the preservation of the self, the preservation of the mind, the preservation of pedigree, and of wealth, and of honour . . .'[89] They also, according to M. Abu Zahra, used in his appointment the consultation method followed during the period of the orthodox caliphs.[90]

Sunni scholars required certain personal qualities in the caliph, such as 'education, a sense of justice, high moral standards, piety, knowledge of religion, good breeding and military and political power'.[91] Yet, the chief weakness in Sunni political theory is the lack of any institution to regulate consultation and control its machinery.

Basing their treatment on this juridical notion of the caliphate, jurists distinguished between the Prophet's caliphs (the Successors), whose appointment came through selection, and the caliphate in later periods. The true Islamic caliphate, they said, came to an end, in al-Shak'a's words, 'with the murder of

'Ali',[92] turning then into coercive kingship. They regarded the current government with suspicion, considering its actions inconsistent with religious teachings; in consequence, 'they refused to grant it full recognition'.[93]

Ibn Khaldoun very succinctly traces the transformation of the caliphate into
kingship:

> You have observed how rule was transformed to kingship, retaining such
> notions of the caliphate as observing religion and its doctrines. The only notice-
> able change was in motives, which were first religious, then became tribalism
> and the sword. This was the case in the reigns of Mu'awiya, Marwan, his son
> 'Abd al-Malik, and the early Abbasid period up to al-Rashid and his sons.
> Subsequently, the caliphate remained only in name, and the system turned to one
> of pure monarchy. Ultimately, force ruled the day.[94]

While the central government system was strengthened, says Arkoun, the subject of legitimacy remained a matter of contention 'and never reached a consensus'.[95] This provided justification for the discussion of a rift between state
and society from the Umayyad period to the end of the Ottoman era, when,
according, to W. Kawtharani, the state 'was established through the power to
vanquish, never attaining legitimacy and never effecting integration with the
community'.[96] Al-Aroui describes the situation as follows:

> Islamic government at first took the form of the caliphate. Then it became a
> monarchy that regressed, generation by generation, into despotism, until it
> became impossible to retrieve the caliphate, short of a miracle similar to the first
> miracle.[97]

In this situation, jurists were torn between their utopian dream of retrieving the
institution of the caliphate and adjusting to the despotic current state that
coerced them into recognizing some kind of legitimacy through the pretexts of
protecting the nation from internal mutiny and external danger. Thus, jurists
avoided organizing themselves, within the current political system, with a
view to developing it into a legitimate state based on consultation. In consequence, the utopian dream became partnered by effective justification of the
status quo.

The outcome of these developments was a separation of legitimate political
action from realistic political action proportionate to the respective rights of
the community and the ruler, and to the distance separating the Quranic model
from the grey area of reality.

Subsequently, the Ottoman Sultanate was to set up a 'religious establishment' under its auspices, one which assimilated – from the reign of Suleyman I

('the Law-Giver') in the sixteenth century – most of the religious posts in society.[98] This sultanate state model fostered a distinction between the secular authority and the duties of the religious authorities, which were assigned to religious scholars and later to the Department of Religious Opinion (Dar al-Ifta'). The secular authority thus became dominant over the religious authority, which was in accordance with the principles of the modern political revolution. Islamic societies were not centred around a religious establishment which dominated the secular establishment (the state); rather they 'were marked by the presence of an absolute dominating authority, for which religion always played a deterrent refining role'.[99]

With the beginning of the nineteenth century, and confrontation with European superiority and recognition of its democratic institutions, a reformist vision was to take shape outside the sultanate religious establishment, one which would attempt to domesticate Western concepts of democracy and human rights. It was a process that recaptured the concepts of the initial Islamic period, reaffirmed by Muhammad 'Abduh and 'Abd al-Rahman al-Kawakibi in their belief that the political authority in Islam was a civil authority, and that Islam did not recognize a theocratic authority;[100] that Sunni Islam was in harmony with Protestant discourse.[101]

V. She's doctrine

The She's and Sunni doctrines were not formed at a single stroke. Rather, as Arkoun notes, 'they took shape gradually over the first few centuries of Islam'.[102] Proof of this is found in the controversy over the issue of succession. Arkoun sees how the two doctrines took shape materially and intellectually only after both sides had established their respective collections of Prophetic Traditions: those of al-Bukhari and Muslim on the Sunni side, those of al-Killini and Ibn Babawayh on the Shi'a side.[103] This was the culmination of a slow but continuous process of search and struggle over the first four Hijri centuries.

Once more according to Arkoun, initial Shi'a doctrine was not what it is today, 'for political partisanship on the side of 'Ali gradually and slowly developed into forceful religious partisanship'.[104] This transformation found expression in the periodic, unsuccessful Shi'ite revolts, and in their repeated tragedies. A strong emotional bond linked them to the family of the Prophet, and they came, as described by Julius Wellhausen, to look on the brief period of 'Ali's Imamate in Kufa as the ideal Utopia.[105]

'Ali's assassination, followed by the martyrdom of his son Hussein and the tragic end of Hujr ibn 'Adi, had a strong impact on the Islamic consciousness, and especially on the band that had rallied closely around 'Ali and his offspring.

The movement of the 'Penitents' (*al-Tawwaboun*) was formed as a result of self-reproach for the failure to help Husain, and, in 67/686, according to the historian al-Tabari, four thousand members marched and fought to the death,[106] driven more by a sense of guilt than by any urge to revenge.[107] Their death opened the door to an ongoing revolt[108] and consecrated the Imamate and the Imam's religious authority.[109] It also, according to Marshall Hodgson, constituted the major step towards 'making the political issue a religious cause'.[110] Subsequently, the movement led by al-Mukhtar ibn Abi 'Ubayd al-Thaqafi came to emphasize the religious character of the Imam's position, together with the notion of the Mahdi, or 'Rightly Guided One'. The movement also emphasized the Islamic principles of equality and justice, which were to be the introduction to Shi'ite discourse about human rights.[111] Later, Zayd ibn 'Ali (founder of the Zaydi doctrine) was to start his own revolt, raising the banner of justice and a return to God's Book, only to be killed in the process.[112] The precarious course of this doctrine was to witness the splintering of the Shi'ites into a number of denominations.

First, we have the Twelvers (*al-Ithna 'Ashariyya*). This movement, whose name long remained a term used to denote a political movement loyal to 'Ali and his offspring, was not transformed into a closed theological order until the time of the Sixth Imam Ja'far al-Sadiq (80/699–148/765) and Hisham ibn al-Hakam.[113] Since that time, says Hodgson, most Shi'ites have been inclined to this doctrine.[114] The Imamate theory, which separated Shi'a from Sunna, was formulated with the establishment of the Ja'fari religious doctrine. But, as Jan Richards says, the structure of this Imamate doctrine did not take clear shape till the end of the ninth century, with the death of the second Imam and the emergence of the theory of the 'great disappearance'. This was a reference to the doctrine of the disappearance of the Imam, described as the 'awaited guided one', and the 'governor of the time', whose return would fill the world with justice after it had been overwhelmed with injustice.[115]

Some of the beliefs of the Imamate doctrine have relevance to the principles of human rights:

V.1 General consideration

In contrast to the Sunni viewpoint, the Imamate doctrine did not see the position of the Imam as a matter for the community, or nation, to decide on. 'It is,' as Ibn Khaldoun explains, 'the pillar of religion and the foundation of Islam. Hence, no prophet should overlook [his appointment] and assign the task to the nation. Rather, he should appoint the Imam for the nation, one who should be infallible regarding major and minor sins. The Imamites believed that 'Ali (may God be pleased with him) was the one appointed by the Prophet, citing texts and interpreting them to suit their doctrine.'[116] They, in fact, were the ones who stipulated the need 'for his appointment and his infallibility and the need for textual proof'.[117] The Imam's appointment is seen by some as 'God's kindness to His creatures, and will steer them away from disobedience'.[118] Shi'ite authorities believe, moreover, that 'God in His omniscience chooses the Imam as He chooses the Prophet',[119] and that 'the jurist Muhammad ibn Makki al-Jizzini al-Amili (d. 786/1384), who wrote *Al-Lam'a al-Dimashqiyya* for the Khurasani Sultan 'Ali ibn al-Mu'ayyad, was the first to use the term 'Imam's deputy'.

'Ali and his eleventh child have a better claim than anyone else to the caliphate, and that, second to the Prophet, they are the best of creation'.[120] The Imamites thus 'raised this matter from the realm of politics, to make it one of the fundamentals of faith that the Imam's position is as divine as prophethood'.[121] The 'discipline of the caliphate/politics was transferred from anthropology to theology'.[122] Human beings 'are not entitled to appoint, nominate or elect him [the Imam],'[123] says one source; and al-Killini (d. 225/840), basing his statement on Imam al-Rida, stresses the close link between the disciplines of Prophethood and the Imamate, with the slight difference that 'the Prophet may hear the speech [of the Angel Gabriel] and may see him in person, whereas the Imam hears the speech but does not see the person'.[124] He also reports that Ja'far al-Sadiq said: 'Since that Spirit came down to the Prophet, he ascended to Heaven, [yet] he is among us.'[125] The Imam is thus 'a holy man', with a spiritual nature knowing what is concealed and what is revealed. It is impossible to interpret or 'recite the Quran' without him.[126]

From the era of Ja'far al-Sadiq and his interpreters, the lines of discussion became centred around the issues of 'guardianship' and the 'order of the concealed'; the end of prophethood is to merge with the beginning of guardianship, thereby completing the cycle of prophethood; for, as Henry Corbin observes, 'the guardianship is the concealed part of prophethood, and the concealed follows that which is revealed'.[127]

The Imam became 'the authority which leads man to God. Whoever forsakes him will perish, and whoever follows him will be saved.'[128] The Imamate doctrine extends to the ultimate belief that 'God does not leave the world without a manifestation to people, such as a prophet or guardian that is revealed and known, or absent and concealed'.[129] This theory was, it seems, introduced following the disappearance of the twelfth Imam in 328/940.

However, the death of the Twelfth Imam – or his absence, as Shi'ites believe – made it important to develop the theory of the Imamate; for the Shi'ites had constantly said that no period of time could pass without an Imam, who is God's manifestation and preserver of religion. This gave rise to the theory of the Great Disappearance and the awaited guided one who had entered the stage of concealment, but who is ever-present in the hearts of believers; he is sure to return to fill the world with justice.

V.2 Human rights in Imamate doctrine

a   Equality and Justice. The human rights observed by Shi'a doctrine are based on the same principles and values as those contained in the major initial religious texts – the Quran and Prophetic Tradition – with the addition of Ali's experience in Kufa and the lives of the imams. The Shi'ites, however, place more emphasis on the principles of justice, equality and treating the oppressed with justice. Husain Muruwwa notes, on this point, that 'the political stand of the Shi'ites was often that of the opposition, and had a social dimension, since they were an integral part of the social classes and groups that suffered from oppression'.[130]

The Shi'ites were heirs to the opposition against 'Uthman; and this opposition was characterized by a religious awareness formed during the Meccan period, taking definite shape among the ranks of the oppressed, who were, according to al-Jabiri, 'subjected to the cruellest torture by the Quraysh masses'.[131] At a later stage 'former slaves adopted Shi'ite beliefs, and the house of 'Ali became the representative of public opposition'.[132] These ex-slaves found blatant discrepancies between religious teachings about justice and actual Islamic governance.[133] In the course of Shi'ite movements, al-Mukhtar al-Thaqafi sounded the slogan: 'Whoever comes to us a slave will be a free man.'[134] According to al-Tabari, he attempted to placate former slaves, and he set slaves free.[135] His motto was: 'seeking to revenge the house of the Prophet and to defend the weak.'[136]

Becoming a Shi'ite was, for former slaves, 'a means of demanding justice'.[137] Ali's letter to his appointed governor of Egypt, Malik al-Ashtar, became the model for a Shi'ite Islamic constitution. In this letter, 'Ali wrote: 'Learn, O Malik, that I have assigned you to a province which has been subject to just as well as oppressive governments. People will observe your actions as you did the actions of former rulers. Let your most treasured thing be good deeds. Control your whims, and turn away from what is not rightfully yours. Fill your heart with mercy for your subjects and treat them with love and kindness; for they are to you one of two kinds: either a brother in religion or a fellow equal in creation. So grant them of your forgiveness and pardon as you would ask God to give you of His forgiveness and pardon.'[138]

b   Enjoining what is good and forbidding evil; freedom of opinion.

From their traditional stance in opposition, the Shi'ites underlined the Islamic principle 'to enjoin good and to forbid evil', considering this principle 'the best kind of worship and the noblest form of obedience. They saw it also as *jihad* and a call to the truth, promoting righteousness and resisting evil-doing and falsehood.'[139]

Nevertheless, while this principle was amenable to 'freedom of opinion' and the call to the true path while the Shi'ites were in opposition, it became supererogatory, in principle at least, under the rule of their Imam, who was inerrant.

c   For all the theocratic character of Imamate authority, the Shi'ites underlined certain principles which brought them closer to the Order of the Mu'tazilis. These principles, it seems, took shape during the Buwayhid period, which was contemporaneous with the 'Great Disappearance' that occurred as a result of Mu'tazili influence (334/945).[140] The Shi'ites stressed that beauty and ugliness are states of mind, 'and are judged by the mind before the law'.[141] They also said that God should not punish a person for an act he did not commit; for actions come from men, 'and if God forgives, it is His generosity; but if He punishes, it is man's guilt and his responsibility'.[142]

V.3 *Political rights of individuals and the community*

It is impossible to imagine legislated human rights in the context of a theory of theocratic state that considers the ruler 'infallible' and inerrant, uniting in his person both political and religious authority. The ruler does not speak 'of his own desire' (53, *Al-Najm*, 3); thus any opposition or differing opinion would be prejudged as heresy and deviation from the truth. Nevertheless, the way the Shi'ites dealt with authority, and their concepts of it, were to change following the 'disappearance' of the Imam. The Shi'ite political vision was transformed into an eschatological one, which contended that the Imam would not appear until the Day of Judgement, to save the world.[143] Thus it was possible for the Shi'ites to view politics as a worldly secular activity, and they proceeded to distinguish between the temporal/secular and religious guardianships. They went so far, indeed, as to contend that it was improper to establish a religious government, which meant the suspension of the Imam's project to set up an Islamic state, according to Imamate doctrine, during the Great Disappearance of the Imam (The Absent-Present), who was the only one entitled to the Imam's position.[144] This in turn meant indefinite suspension of the project to set up the Islamic state itself. As such, the Shi'ites had no religious objection to the establishment of a secular state, whereby politics were handled on a worldly secular basis. As Dorothea Kravolski notes, the Shi'ites did not 'require of any political authority anything more . . . than justice'.[145] And, since the Shi'ites did not recognize any authority other than that of the Imam, they became, after his disappearance, 'at liberty vis-à-vis the authority'.[146]

Two movements emerged among Shi'ite jurists. The first was that of the 'communicators', who ruled out the mediation of any religious establishment between the believer and God. These are compared by Richard to Lutherans in their emphasis on following the teachings of imams and in their 'view that all believers are emulators of imams; persons who give religious interpretations, they say, are equal to simple believers'.[147]

This 'communicator' tendency was confronted by a fundamentalist tendency prevalent in the Iranian cities of Qum and al-Rayy, led by Shaykh al-Mufid (d. 413/1021), al-Sharif al-Murtada (d. 436/1044), Shaykh al-Tousi (d. 459/1067) and al-Killini (d. 328/940), and followed by the She's jurists in Baghdad.[148] These jurists were the ones who came up with the religious interpreters' role and initiated the notion of a 'Shi'ite religious establishment'. The tendency was also encouraged and supported by the Buwayhid sultan in Baghdad.[149]

Ibn al-Muttahar al-Hilli (d. 726/1325) was the first scholar to speak of the religious interpreter (*mujtahid*) as a person who inferred a juristic ruling based on established jurisprudential evidence.[150] He also laid the foundation for jurists' monopoly over religious interpretation. Later, al-'Amili (d. 1011/1602) was to provide a final formulation for the conditions of interpretation.

While the fundamentalists offered to cooperate with the Alikhanis, Safavids and Qajaris, the Ikhbariyyoun (communicators) continued to dissociate themselves from politics.[151] The tendency of fundamentalist jurists to serve the Shi'ite 'vanquishing' state grew stronger, as did their willingness to infer the necessary rulings to adapt Shi'ism to the needs of this state. The nature of the jurist's guardianship was given procedural expression during the Buwayhid period; later, in an effort to define jurists' authority during the period of disappearance, the jurist Muhammad ibn Makki 'l-Jizzini 'l-'Amili (d. 786/ 1384), (who wrote *Al-Lam'a 'l-Dimashqiyya* for the Khurasani Sultan 'Ali ibn al-Mu'ayyad), was the first to use the term 'Imam's deputy'.[152]

The Shi'ite Safavid Sultanate (1501–1736), whose structure resembled that of the Ottoman state, made the Shi'ite religious establishment (*sadr al-sudour*) one of its main pillars, bringing together a large order of jurists.[153] Yet the formula of the 'reference of imitation', which had been given shape by the Buwayhid jurists, continued to provide a parallel form to that of the jurist enrolled in the official religious establishment. Moreover, the fundamentalist reference of imitation remained as a centre parallel to and independent of the state, distinct from the 'institution of ranks'.[154] However, the greater challenge and opposition to the authority of this institution was to come in the seventeenth century, from the communicator group headed by the jurist al-Astrabadi (d. 1614); these refused to become involved in politics, whether on the side of court or opposition,[155] so effecting a separation between politics and religion. The fundamentalists were nonetheless to regain the initiative through the efforts of Muhammad Baqir al-Bahbaha'i (d. 1793), with the support of the Qajari Sultanate, and so confirm the notion of the religious establishment and the role of religious clerics. This was to mark the final demise of the communicators. The theory of the jurist's guardianship, for which there was no precedence in She's jurisprudence, was voiced by Mulla Ahmad al-Turaqi (d. 1830). His argument, as described by the Isma'ili scholar Farhad Daftari, was that, in the absence of the inerrant Imam, the interpreter acts as a substitute for him.[156]

Later, too, as a result of several factors – global changes, contacts with the European constitutional way of life, a sense of danger, the influence of Ottoman reform, and Sunni reformist thought (Muhammad 'Abduh and al-Kawakibi) – a 'constitutional' movement would be launched in Iran within what came to be called 'religious circles'.

Scholars belonging to official religious establishments took the Shah's side against this constitutional movement (1905). In contrast, scholars in 'scientific circles' stood with it, those in question including al-Sayyid 'Abdullah al-Bahbaha'i and Muhammad al-Tabataba'i, with support from the Najaf authorities, Mulla Kazim Khurasani and 'Abdullah al-Mazandari. Al-Khurasani made the ruling that 'the laws of the constitutional council are revered sacred laws, and obedience to them is the duty of all believers'.[157] But the decisive step was to come when al-Mirza Muhammad Husain Na'ini (d. 1936) – who was the sole Shi'ite authority in 1920 – legislated 'the right of the nation's guardianship over itself during the period of disappearance'.[158] He also justified constitutional life from a juristic viewpoint, basing his opinion on the *shura* formula in force during the era of the Prophet and the orthodox caliphs. Na'ini, envisaging the possibility of Sunni-Shi'ite agreement over this issue,[159] insisted that blind obedience to Shi'ite clerics was the basis for 'the strengthening of slavery to the ruler'.[160]

Na'ini's argument could have led to a situation where politics would be regarded as a secular matter concerning the whole nation. This in turn would have left the door wide open for a constitutional life that confirmed the rights of individuals to expression and to running the affairs of their country democratically.

However, subsequent developments in Iran (and also in the Ottoman state) were not destined to follow this course. The First World War disrupted consti- tutional life, and the West backed the Shah's stand against the constitutional movement, and, later, against the Musaddeq movement. This strengthening of the imperial tendency, with American help, was to open the door to a strength- ening of the religious establishment and a revival of the guardianship of the jurist, first in theory and then in practice.

VI. The Isma'ilis and human rights

VI.1 Introductory considerations

The history of the Isma'ilis began with a dispute over the succession, following the death of Imam Ja'far al-Sadiq in 148/764. Ja'far had decreed his son Isma'il as successor, but Isma'il died, whereupon the Twelver Shi'ites claimed that Ja'far had subsequently also named his second son Musa to succeed him. According to the Isma'ili scholar Farhad Daftari, the other party – the Isma'ilis – held firm to Isma'il's imamate, which was to be followed by that of his son Muhammad.[161] This point, says Bernard Lewis, marked the beginning of 'Absence or Disappearance'.[162]

For Isma'ilis, Imam Muhammad was then succeeded by his son 'Abdullah (al-Radi), then by Ahmad (al-Wafi) (d. 212/827), who moved the centre of his movement to al-Sulaymiyya in Syria. This latter is credited, in collaboration with 'Abdullah al-Qaddah and others, with the authorship of *The Epistles of the Brethren of Purity*. Ahmad was succeeded by Muhammad al-Naqi (d. 279/892), then 'Abdullah, (d. 334/945), who moved to the Maghreb and established the Fatimid caliphate. Subsequently, his grandsons (d. 365/975) conquered Egypt, which remained under his successors until the arrival of Saladin.[163]

The Isma'ili movement went through five stages in its history:

1   Early Isma'iliyya, which adopted an eschatological vision based on the dis-
     appearance of Muhammad ibn Isma'il and his return. This is the idea
     retained by the Qarmatians.
2   Fatimid Isma'iliyya (296/909–487/1094), which later split into Nizariyya
     and Musta'liyya.
3   Musta'liyya came to an end with the fall of the Fatimid state (566/1171),
     and is now represented in India by Dawoudiyya and Shaykhaniyya.
4   Nizariyya Isma'iliyya during the Alamout period (483/1090) and up to the
     latter's destruction (654/1256).
5   Nizariyya Isma'iliyya of the post-Alamout period.[164]

VI.2 Isma'ili doctrine

The Isma'ilis took up the Shi'ite theocratic theory of the imamate and pushed
it to its limits, having first mixed it with a cosmic vision that borrowed a great
deal from Pythagoreanism, neo-Platonism and Zoroastrianism, out of which,
says Karen Armstrong, 'they devised a way to salvation. They also used a symbolism loosely associated with logic because, they think, it reveals a deeper
truth than that perceived by the senses.'[165]

   For the Isma'ilis, the imamate is an appointment made by God, a branch of
prophethood and a religious duty without which juristic theory would be
incomplete.[166] The imam, they say, may even have some attributes associated
with God; on the visible level, he is a human being created of clay, and he grows
sick and dies; but 'on the concealed level, he is the face of God, the hand of God,
and beloved of God; he is the right path; he is the Holy Quran'.[167] Furthermore,
the imam, who is of the offspring of Muhammad ibn Isma'il, exists till the end
of time, for his presence is necessary for all ages. The imams come in succes-
sions of seven, and the seventh (in this succession he is Muhammad ibn Isma'il)
is the 'universal intellect'. He is the mouthpiece of the miraculous powers, and
the six preceding imams are souls that pave the way for him.[168]

   The seventh imam, Muhammad ibn Isma'il, occupies a special position: he
is the author of a system of jurisprudence, the invalidator of one juristic system
and the originator of another. He combines pronouncement of a message with
the imamate. He is also, as the author of an authentic system, involved in interpretation. This imam also has a concealed nature, being the seventh imam who
records the system of the sixth (the Prophet Muhammad) by explaining its
meaning and revealing its concealed aspects.[169]

Perhaps the role accorded by Isma'ilis to the seventh imam is what prompted them to devise a metaphysical sevenfold structure for the world, for man and for the history of revelation. Al-Karamani, for example, divides his book *Peace of the Intellect* into seven 'secrets', to indicate the seven 'pronouncers', or prophets: Adam, Noah, Abraham, Moses, Jesus, Muhammad and the 'ever-present' (*qa'im al-zaman*). Around every pronouncer stand seven imams; there are seven heavens, seven stars, seven provinces; man has seven parts, he measures seven handspans, the same in width, he prostrates on seven limbs, and there are on his brow seven passages.[170]

The imam has been transformed to a deified man, who holds the visible and the concealed. So it is that the Isma'ilis developed 'imamate metaphysics'; and they effected a balance between these metaphysics and the world of divine creation. Thus the arrangement of the celestial orbits became the reflection of the world of religion, and to this end they established a complete theory of the archetype and the ideal; for the visible (the archetype) points to the concealed (the ideal). For Isma'ilis, the physical universe is an analogy of the spiritual universe (concealed), and the world of the imamate is an analogy of the world of celestial limits.

The first divine creation, the 'Primary Intellect' – the pre-existing, or the form/pen – is analogous to the Isma'ili concept of the 'pronouncer' – the Messenger. The second creation, the soul – Prime Matter, the text, the tablet – is analogous to their 'origin' – the first imam. The third creation – the Third Intellect – is analogous to the imam (that is, the rank of imams who succeed the imam/origin).

As for the seven succeeding creative intellects, they are represented by the Isma'ili ranks: the passageway; the inference; the proclamation; the absolute herald; the limited herald; the absolute authorized; the limited authorized and contender. This structure may be represented by the following table:

The Higher Limits	The Lower Limits
1 The First Creation (the image, Pen, the higher orbit)	is equivalent to the pronouncer (rank of the Messenger)
2 The Second Delegate (the tablet, Primary matter, second orbit)	is equivalent to the origin (rank of interpretation, the Imam)
3 The Third Intellect (Saturn)	is equivalent to the Imam (the rank of command)
4 The Fourth Intellect (Jupiter)	is equivalent to the passageway (the rank of sound judgement)

5 The Fifth Intellect (Mars)	is equivalent to the argument (the rank of judgement)
6 The Sixth Intellect (Sun)	is equivalent to the herald of the message (the rank of protest)
7 The Seventh Intellect (Venus)	is equivalent to the absolute herald (the rank of identifying the higher and concealed limits)
8 The Eighth Intellect (Mercury)	is equivalent to the limited herald (the rank of identifying the lower limits and worship)
9 The Ninth Intellect (Moon)	is equivalent to the absolute authorized (the rank of receiving the covenant)
10 The Tenth Intellect (sub-orbital manners)	is equivalent to the limited authorized (the rank of contender – enlister of supporters)[171]

VI.3 The Status of Man and his Rights in Isma'ili Cosmology

a   Elevating man:

Isma'ili doctrine has accorded man a distinguished position in the cosmos and used exalted language in his praise. Abu Hatim al-Razi, for example, indicates that human beings are the cream of the world, and that the whole world was created for their sake. And Abu Ya'qoub al-Sajistani says that man is the fruit of the 'luminous' noble world. For his sake prophets conveyed their warnings, so as to bear human beings from this 'house of death' to the 'eternal hereafter'.[172]

Sayyiduna 'Ali ibn Muhammad al-Walid places man at the highest point on the scale of creatures. Man, he says, is the choice and heart of creation, the beginning idea and the end of action, the goal of existence, where all ends. Man is the passage to the higher order of angels.[173] For the Brethren of Purity, man is the angel of the earthly heaven, the vicegerent of God in this world, as the sun is God's deputy in the heavens.[174] When man's soul rises to the higher world, 'it adorns that world'.[175] And although the Isma'ilis believed that the body decays when the soul leaves it, they showed their admiration for it, and their amazement at its symmetry and harmony. 'The body,' say the Brethren of Purity, 'has been built with the best proportions when it escapes the corruptions of the stars.'[176] They believe that God

created man 'in the best form', and attributed the impurities to which it is
subject to astronomical factors.[177]

The Isma'ilis applied the theory of correspondence to the balance
between man and the universe. God has summarized the universe in one
thing, man. Thus they called man a microcosm, and the universe a macro-
image of man.[178]

b   The unity of revelation, human and religious toleration, equality and the
     right to differ:
     On the basis of the unity of revelation indicated in the Quran, the
Isma'ilis were to offer an original concept of this unity, setting distinct roles
for every prophet's message within the total body of revelation. For them,
revelation begins with Adam and ends with the Absent Imam: 'Adam in the
religious context corresponds to progeny in the context of the foetus; similarly, Noah and the select of his people in the religious context correspond
to the sperm in the context of the foetus; Abraham corresponds to the
blood clot; Moses corresponds to the embryo; Jesus (peace be upon him)
and the elite of his followers correspond to the skeleton in the context of
the foetus; and Muhammad (peace be upon him) corresponds to the flesh
in the context of the foetus, which has attained its perfect form. No other
rank follows Muhammad until the rise of the "awaited" . . .'[179]

The Isma'ilis view religion like links in a chain. This is confirmed by
the Brethren of Purity's statement that 'the difference in the origins of religion is not an evil; some matters are favoured by one nation, but not by
others. In fact, differences may be beneficial, for they prompt the search
for arguments and proof, and reveal faults, so leading to reform of those
faults. It has been said: "disagreements among scholars are a source of
mercy."'[180]

Theoretically, this vision results in an attitude of tolerance towards religious differences and differences of opinion. Indeed, the Brethren of
Purity emphasize, in some of their writings, that differences are a condition for human perfection. They select attributes of a number of nations
and religions to form their concept of the 'perfect man'. These are: Arabs
for religion, Persians for pedigree, the Hanafis for doctrine, Iraqis for literature, Hebrews for investigation, Indians for insight, Greeks for sciences, Shamis (from the Levant) for toleration, royalists for morals, divine
believers for knowledge, and theologians for opinion.[181] This method of
thought leads to a strengthening of notions of equality, toleration and the
right to differ.

c   Freedom of worship and devotion:

Despite the theocratic nature of Isma'ili (i.e., Fatimid) government, and despite their merging of the religious and political authorities in the imam/ruler (who is inerrant), their rule was characterized by religious toleration and freedom of worship, barring some short intervals. It is reported, for example, that when the Fatimid military commander Jawhar al-Siqilli conquered Egypt in 358/969, he treated people kindly, announcing a general amnesty and assuring people through a distributed leaflet of 'guaranteeing safety of their lives and property ... and freedom of religious beliefs; only gradually did he introduce the Shi'ite form of prayers'.[182] In fact, the successes achieved by the Fatimids are partly to be attributed to their policy of religious toleration which, says Farhad Daftari, 'characterized the ruling family', and to their making use of individuals and communities 'regardless of race or religion'.[183] It has been said that 'the conditions of non-Muslims underwent great changes under the Fatimids, and they made many contributions in administrative, economic and political affairs, in an unprecedented manner'.[184] The Fatimid ruler al-'Aziz appointed many 'people of the Book', to various state positions: the Jew Ibn Kalas and the Christian 'Isa ibn Nastour (385/995–386/996) were ministers. This, according to Daftari, is in accordance with the religious toleration practised by the Fatimids.[185]

VII. The Qarmatians

VII.1 History and doctrine

The Qarmatians started as an Isma'ili movement, established by Hamdan ibn Ash'ath al-Qurmati, who was influenced by the religious leader Husain al-Ahwazi.[186] Hamdan's mission began in Wasit, between Kufa and Basra, which was 'home to a motley of Arabs and Black Africans, all poverty-stricken and disgruntled.'[187] From 261/874 to 278/891 he continued to organize his mission, and in 278/891 initiated a revolt and laid the foundations for a state over which he presided until 296/908.[188] Hamdan depended on the assistance of his brother-in-law 'Abdan, and he appointed, as missionary teachers, Zikrawayh ibn Mahrawayh to western Iraq and Sa'id al-Janabi to southern Persia. The latter was subsequently to move to al-Ihsa' and establish the Qarmati state in Bahrain in 286/899.[189] This last remained a powerful entity for at least 100 years, only to meet defeat, in 378/988, at the hand of the Abbassids. Thereafter it gradually declined.[190]

The Qarmatians retained their belief in early Isma'ili doctrine (up to the great reforms of 'Abdullah al-Mahdi in 286/899), along with the belief that 'Muhammad (peace be upon him) would be followed by seven imams; the last of these would be Muhammad ibn Isma'il, the guided rising Imam, the communicating prophet who has not died, but who is absent and concealed in the lands of the Romans. He is the awaited rising guided one [the Mahdi], who will bring forth a new religion to supersede Muhammad's message.'[191] They further maintained the consecration of the 'Saving Imam', along with cosmic notions associated with a strong eschatological vision and faith in the resurrection of this imam, who would bring justice to all. They also bound their salvation to the Imam's mediation, since, in al-Shahrastani's words, 'the truth is known by the teachings of the Imam who is knowledgeable in interpretation'.[192] A person cannot attain faith 'except by attaining interpretation, and this can be reached only by reading and practising the juristic writings of the covenanted one'.[193] The Qarmatians regarded their message as preparatory to the 'return' of Muhammad ibn Isma'il.[194]

The Qarmatians divided the religious history of man into ascending heptagonal cycles, each begun by a 'communicator' (prophet) followed by a spiritual revelation (that is, the foundation, the silent) which interprets religion. The seventh imam for every prophetic cycle becomes the communicator for the next cycle, abolishing one religion and beginning a new one. Thus, Muhammad ibn Isma'il, the seventh imam of the Muhammadan cycle, has entered the 'cave of concealment' to rise again, annul the religion of Islam and announce the final cycle of life. In this cycle there is no need for religion, since justice has prevailed, corruption has been wiped out, and time has come to an end.[195]

It was natural that there should, in 286/899, be a rift between Hamdan and 'Abdan on the one hand and the Isma'ilis on the other, after 'Abdullah al-Mahdi promoted himself and his ancestors from the rank of the 'sign' of the concealed Imam (Muhammad ibn Isma'il), by which he had previously been known, to the rank of the actual imams of the descendants of Muhammad ibn Isma'il. The result of this claim was to deny this last the title of 'the guided and resurrected one', something rejected by the Qarmatians.[196]

VII.2 Justice and equality: the Qarmatians' claim to human rights

The eschatological nature of Qarmatian doctrine, which includes a call for justice, together with its secret organization and its grass-root social basis, gave this movement a social character which, according to Daftari, posed a threat to the Abbasid system.[197] However, the social conditions of the time ruled out the

Qarmatians' utopian ideals, which emulated initial Islamic principles.[198] The new movement seems to have enlisted the help 'primarily of poverty-stricken farmers and bedouins, which deprived it of a civic presence. Thus, bedouin tribes in Bahrain and Syria formed the backbone of this movement . . . In Yemen it was supported by tribesmen, and in North Africa by the entire bedouin tribe of Katama.'[199]

To realize the extent of the Qarmatians' yearning for the ideals of justice and equality called for by the Quran, one has only to examine the qualities they bestowed on the Imam: he is expected, on his reappearance, to replace injustice by justice and inequality by equality. Only then would 'the bull and the lion drink from the same pond; the shepherd would entrust his sheep to the wolf; all innovations would be rejected; and justice would be dealt to those deserving of it.'[200]

During their revolt of 316/928, the Qarmatians wrote on their banners the Quranic verse: 'And we wished to be gracious to those who were being depressed in the land, to make them leaders (in faith) and make them heirs.'[201] Their social system adopted a trend of equality and collaboration. In 267/880, Hamdan came up with his programme of 'cooperation', according to which his followers surrendered their possessions to the community and become one family, where no person was distinguished from his brother by his wealth.[202] This partnership in wealth was, as de Goeji puts it, 'in total agreement with the hope of seeing the realization of the Kingdom of God on earth'.[203] Historians have seen the same aspirations on the part of the Qarmatians in Bahrain, in whom al-Janabi had planted the seed of 'total brotherhood among men, regardless of their religious, ethnic or geographic orientation'.[204]

Nasir Khosraw paints a lively picture of people's life in al-Ihsa', which he visited in 444/1052. He says, in *Safar Nama*:

> No tithe is levied from people, and should a person be in debt, he has to pay back only the capital. Every newcomer in the city is given enough money to start his business, of which he returns to the ruler whatever he wishes . . . Also there are in the city a number of mills owned by the Sultan which grind people's grain free of charge.[205]

VII.3 The system of government: opening up to consultation

Some scholars, such as de Goeji, hold that the Qarmatian system of government did not follow the kingship model. Abu Sa'id, they maintain, played the role of first among equal rulers, aided by a number of counsellors linked to him by family ties or by ideological orthodoxy. Those in the elite were called 'ideologues', to indicate their power of making decisions, and they made up a council to deal with important issues, chaired by Abu Saʿid.[206] It seems that this system was in operation when Nasir Khosraw visited al-Ihsaʾ, for he recorded the presence of six rulers sitting on a platform, 'issuing their orders in agreement and flanked by six ministers . . . discussing every case.'[207]

For all the idealistic nature of the justice and equality underlined by the Qarmatians, the social (bedouin) basis of the movement with its tribal tendency, together with the character of the age, severely damaged the legitimacy of their presentation of these concepts. Historians have pointed to the reliance of the Qarmatian state in al-Ihsaʾ on slaves in agriculture and the crafts.[208] Khosraw provides testimony to the 'presence of thirty thousand black and Abyssinian slaves working in agriculture and husbandry'.[209]

Moreover, the tribal character of the movement was to manifest itself in its harsh rough manner, and in its horrific cruelty to its enemies. Historians provide countless examples of their rigours and cruelty. Khosraw, for example, says that 'all bedouins to me are like the people of al-Ihsaʾ; they have no religion, and there are some whose hands have not touched water for a year . . . I could not drink the milk they offered me.'[210] And the Azhar scholar (d. 370/980) who was in their prison for two years said that the Qarmatians 'grew up in the desert, following water catchments in dry seasons; they tended their flocks, and survived on their milk, conversing in their bedouin manner to which they were used'.[211]

Historians have painted appalling pictures of their treatment of their enemies: a mixture of zeal and cruelty, entailing firm but unbending principles and an absolute rejection of differing opinions. Utopian justice thus became a curtain blinding them to the truth. The uncompromising rejection of their enemies' opinions flew in the face of the principle of justice itself.

The Qarmatian movement remained a product of its time and a fit expression of its social foundations. It was not dissimilar to the revolutionary movement within medieval Christianity; it too embodied a strong protest against an oppressive power, but nevertheless remained a prisoner of its historical circumstances. The Qarmatians were, on the level of ideology, 'a reproduction in a more petrified and closed form of the prevailing faith'.[212] Their utopian experiment with justice and equality is aptly described by de Goeji:

> They caused the cancellation of the weak influence made by Islam on the bedouins and the loss of this effective deterrent to old barbarism. Nonetheless, the Bahraini Qarmatians behaved with the conscience of one who served a just cause.[213]

VIII. The Mu'tazilis: a discourse of the mind and of freedom

The term 'withdrawal' (*i'tizal*) may first have been used to describe a group of Companions who took a neutral stand in the dispute between 'Ali and Mu'awiya. It represented a political idea with a religious colouring: 'If we cannot identify the aggressor, we will withdraw.'[214] The rise of Mu'tazili doctrine was, however, the result of a disagreement between Wasil ibn 'Ata' (d. 131/748) and his tutor Hasan al-Basri (d. 110/728) over the issue of 'the great sin; whether or not it amounts to atheism'. Wasil contended that it was 'between belief and atheism. This was more of a political opinion meant to define a stance toward the Umayyads. By this they took a middle position between the Dissenters and the Deferrers.'[215]

Yet the withdrawal movement was not strictly the product of this attitude; it was rather an expression of a wider intellectual movement whose political manifestation appeared during the time of the 'discord' and was subsequently nourished on constantly broadening and deepening views. The way for Mu'tazilis was paved by the Qadiriyya, or 'free-will school' (those who believed in man's power and ability to act independently); by men like Ma'bad al-Jahni, 'Amr Maqsous and Ghaylan al-Dimashqi. This latter wrote to the Umayyad caliph 'Umar ibn 'Abd al-'Aziz about man's freedom of choice:

> Is there, O Omar, a Wise One Who deprecates what He Himself has made, or makes what is disgraceful; punishes for what He Himself has ordained, or ordains what is punishable? Is there, O Omar, a Merciful One Who enjoins on people what is beyond their abilities, or punishes for obedience?[216]

Hasan al-Basri took the first step towards the abstract rationalism that was to be followed by the Mu'tazilis in their theoretical theses.[217] It was, however, in the works of Wasil ibn 'Ata' and 'Amr ibn 'Ubayd that the parameters of the Mu'tazili viewpoint or theory were to be defined.

VIII.1 *Reference to rational judgement*

The Mu'tazili movement embodied a rational theory of religion. The method was to refer the 'text' to rational interpretation and subject the interpretation to rational logic, referring any apparent difference between the text and reason – apart from the elements of faith – to the latter. What the Mu'tazilis did with respect to Islam seems fairly similar to what the early Greek philosophers did with Greek mythology.[218]

The Mu'tazili formula was not limited to treatment of the Oneness of God; it also dealt with the issues of faith and prophethood, morality and politics, and the relationship of God with the world and with man. The Mu'tazilis laid the groundwork for dialectics that adopted the principles of rational judgement vis-à-vis religion, as a means of confirming the doctrines of faith.[219] However, the deeper they went into philosophy, the more 'they referred to reason as the dispenser of the appearances of Quranic texts whenever they seemed to conflict with rational thinking.'[220] Al-Nazzam was even of the opinion that rational argument annulled the *hadith*s.[221]

The Mu'tazilis were very active in the cultural life, which reached their acme of variety and depth during the early period of the Abbasid state. They were able to respond to the attacks of the Manichaeans and to take apart their arguments, forcing them to refer to the judgement of reason. This meant, according to al-Jabiri, the immediate rejection of gnosticism. On the other hand, the Mu'tazilis, in their controversies with the Sunnis, were able to effect an important and fundamental development in Sunni thought, resulting in the doctrines of Mataruddiyya and Ash'ariyya.[222] It is, as such, fair to say that the Mu'tazilis were instrumental in bringing about 'a decisive change in the history of Arab thought. The Arab gained the confidence to subject the whole of existence, seen and concealed, to the criteria and rules of reason.'[223] The Mu'tazilis' rational logic was to be clear in all the subjects they treated.

VIII.2 Mu'tazila and human rights

In their treatment of human rights, the Mu'tazili began from the Islamic discourse of the initial period. But they differed from other Islamic doctrines in their arrangement of this discourse and in the precedence they gave to reason and the trust they placed in it. They also accorded greater value to the freedom of man and to his ability to make choices and to assume responsibility before himself, God and the community.

VIII.3 The foundations of Mu'tazili doctrine

Historians of Islamic movements are in agreement on defining the foundations of Mu'tazili doctrine, though they differ on the order of these. The Mu'tazili authority al-Khayyat arranges them as follows: 'belief in the Oneness of God, justice, the promise and the warning, the "rank between two ranks", and ordering what is good and forbidding wrongdoing.'[224] Al-Shahrastani calls the Mu'tazilis 'advocates of justice and the Oneness of God'.[225]

What concerns us here is their conclusions regarding the concepts of human rights and the moral and legal status they give to human beings.

VIII.3.1 The Oneness: denying the attributes; denying the 'Oldness' of the Quran

In all the subjects they dealt with, the Mu'tazilis used the strict logic of reason, in which they had limitless faith. Therefore, when they treated the concept of the Oneness of God, in which all Muslims believe, they subjected it to their own rational thinking. The *qadi* 'Abd al-Jabbar (d. 415/1024) regarded Oneness in the light of 'knowing what attributes distinguish the Oneness of God . . . such as that He is old and everything else is new, One and has no second'.[226] He is One 'and nothing is like Him'. They rejected the attribute of 'eternity' for God in order to exalt Him above multiplicity. As for God's attributes, they follow Abu Hudhayl al-'Allaf's statement that 'He is all-knowing, yet His knowledge is Himself; He is omnipotent, and His power is Himself'. They also follow al-Jiba'i in saying that 'God is all-knowing in Himself and omnipotent in Himself.[227] The Mu'tazilis then interpreted the *sura*s of the Quran in accordance with their concepts.

The Mu'tazilis then decided that the Quran is not 'old', that is, it is not an attribute equal to that of God; rather, it is an 'event', that is to say, created. Thus, to say that God is the Speaker means that He is Creator of the Quran; the Quran is command and proscription, message and inquiry, promise and warning: 'These are divergent facts and different attributes, whereas God, "the One", cannot be manifold with different attributes.'[228]

The Mu'tazilis agreed, according to al-Shahrastani, that the Quran 'is the word of God, "created in matter and space". It is, furthermore, letter and sound.'[229] The Quran is a group of letters and sounds inscribed on paper and transcribed on pages, that is, these occupy space; thus they are accidents and not essences. They perish as soon as they are spoken or written in space.

Such reasoning implies the involvement of culture and language in the act of acquisition of the revealed message. It also means recognition of the role and responsibility of reason in what Arkoun calls the act of ontological acquisition.[230] It means, further, 'a modernist attitude in the midst of the eighth century AD . . . initiating a novel approach capable of producing critical reasoning similar to the one the West witnessed at the beginning of the thirteenth century'.[231]

VIII.3.2 Justice; the freedom of the human individual; the mind's capacity
to recognize values

The Mu'tazilis apply the mind to the concept of divine justice in order to confirm the freedom of the human individual. The mind, they say, is capable of distinguishing between good and evil, and God 'admits no ugliness and chooses
only wisdom and truth'.[232] God is too exalted to partake of evil and injustice,
for, if He created injustice, He would be unjust, and, if He created justice, He
would be just. According to al-Shahrastani, 'the [Mu'tazilis] concluded that
God (be He exalted) does only what is righteous and good'.[233] Some of them go
so far as to believe that God must do what is good for human beings.[234] For, if
God's will were associated with all the good and evil in the world, both good
and evil would be God's purpose; thus good and evil, justice and injustice,
would be attributed to the willer, which is inapplicable to God.[235] Furthermore,
if man's actions were decided by God, reward and punishment would be nullified and meaningless; commands and prohibitions, prophets' messages, and
accounting and punishment would also be nullified. From these premises, the
Mu'tazilis emphasize that 'men's actions are their own doing, not created by
God'.[236] They add that 'God's power and will do not influence man's power
and will.[237] On this subject, Roger Garaudi concludes that man alone enjoys
this terrible distinction of the power to disobey.[238] Man can act according to his
rational judgement, thus choosing from among good and evil deeds – and
deservedly bears the responsibility for his acts.

    From their rational conception of justice, the Mu'tazilis reach a further con-
clusion: they rely on reason in determining good and evil in matters that concern human affairs, though some of them exclude the acts of worship. These
latter are determined by the 'text'.[239] Man, before the advent of religions, was
capable of distinguishing between good and evil, and beauty and ugliness, for
the attributes of beauty and ugliness are intrinsic in acts and things. Lying is
ugly and evil in itself, and truthfulness is beautiful and good in itself. Religions,
by commanding or prohibiting certain matters, simply take into account the
beauty and ugliness of things. Reason, therefore, is capable, before the revelation of religions, of discovering the evil and good nature of acts and things.
This was the case before religions; people referred to reason, and wise men dis-
approved of injustice and aggression and approved of aiding the oppressed and
rescuing the ruined.[240] Theoretically, this position leads to liberating men from
all kinds of blind imitation and to man's self-confidence and creative power of
distinction. It also leads to a daring involvement in taking part in the fate of
humanity before God. The Mu'tazilis push the rational boundaries of their

thought to the point where they claim that: 'God's orders and commandments are not enough for a definite distinction between good and evil, and truth and error; it is imperative that reason intervene – or rather, reason is entitled to intervene – with total independence of the postulates of revelation.'[241]

VIII.3.3 Promise and warning

Working from the fact that God will undoubtedly fulfil his promise of reward for the righteous and punishment for the rebellious, the Mu'tazilis reach the following conclusion: all meditation and intercession is meaningless. Every person reaps what he has sown, and seeking favour through saints becomes meaningless. They reject the supernatural power of saints, restrict the circle of miracles (al-Nazzam, in fact, limits them to the Quran) and insist that the power of magic is illusory.[242]

VIII.3.4 The caliphate by election

The majority of Mu'tazilis believed that the imamate, or caliphate, should be based on election by the nation. It can be verified only by election. Some of them, indeed, believed the consensus of the whole nation to be necessary.[243]

Mu'tazila as an intellectual movement developed at the heart of a flourishing civic and cultural civilization that had no fear of difference of opinion as long as this was not supported by arms. The beginning of the movement's decline dates from the eleventh century, which witnessed military control over the state, the rise of the military sector in the economy and the advance of imitation to the detriment of enlightenment. This trend was helped by the tendency of the Mu'tazilis themselves – in conjunction with the caliphs al-Ma'moun and al-Mu'tasim – to coerce people into adopting their doctrine. This facilitated elimination of the Mu'tazilis politically, socially and culturally following the Sunni coup during the reign of al-Mutawakkil. The result was a dissociation of philosophy, the religiously reasonable and the rational in its highest form, from 'withdrawal'. This, says al-Jabiri, paved the way for the 'irrational to gain new territory'.[244]

IX. Sufism: between the deification of man and the humanization of God

Sufism is not a discrete Islamic doctrine akin to Sunni and Shi'i doctrines. It is rather a trend or way of belief with which Sunnis and Shi'ites are alike associated. In a sense, indeed, it is not limited to Muslims; Sufism, considered simply as mysticism, is something practised by believers within many religions. Islamic Sufism has, nevertheless, its own distinctive character, stemming from its Islamic context and its association with the cultural and social concerns of the Arab-Islamic community.

According to Ibn Khaldoun:

> The method of these people has remained since the days of the Prophet's Companions and their successors: the method of righteousness and true faith. It is grounded in total dedication to the worship of God and abstention from the pleasures of life . . . When, in the second century and thereafter, people became immersed in the pleasures of life, those who devoted themselves to worship were called Sufis.[245]

Sufism grew out of the phenomenon of asceticism, which flourished in the middle of the first century and involved a renunciation of this world, over which Muslims were competing. Asceticism began as a negative movement of retreat, a moral stand against current conditions. Subsequently, during the second half of the first century, there developed the ascetics of Kufa, Basra and Egypt, who protested against current socio-political relations and against what Karen Armstrong describes as 'the excessive wealth of the Court and the decline of strict religious observance . . . Social justice remained a decisive factor in their faith.'[246] In consequence, they retreated into asceticism 'in protest against what they objected to in the system of government'.[247] The most prominent of these ascetics was Hasan al-Basri.[248]

The behavioural 'combatant' patterns subsequently adopted by Sufism were extensions of ascetic behaviour; and ascetic 'interpretations' were transformed to become the nucleus of the 'interpretative' Sufi method, which resembles those of esoteric systems.[249]

At the end of the second Hijri century, we witness the beginning of a Sufism in which Rabi'a al-'Adawiyya (d. 185/801) provides the notion of divine love and Ma'rouf al-Karkhi (d. 200/815) the notion of 'intuitive cognition' leading to God. With this, Sufism became a systematic spiritual life based on the rules and methods of mathematics, on self-denial and on self-knowledge.[250]

In the third Hijri century, philosophy merged with Sufism, and a number of Sufi schools were established, each with its own methodology. These did, however, share the goals of unity, annihilation or union with transcendence. The most important of these schools and their representatives were: the Baghdad School (Abu 'Abdullah al-Muhasibi, d. 243/857; Abu 'l-Qasim al-Junayd, d. 298/910; al-Sarraj, d. 286/899; al-Saqati, d. 253/867); the Nisabour School

(Hamdoun al-Qassar, d. 271/884); and the al-Shami and Egypt School (Dhu 'l-Noun al-Misri, d. 245/859).[251] Finally, with al-Hallaj (d. 309/922), al-Suhrawardi (d. 587/1191) and Ibn 'Arabi (d. 638/1240), the philosophy of Illuminism and Inspiration reached its zenith.

Sufism advocated certain notions relevant to the concept of human rights.

IX.1 The elevation of man

IX.1.1 Man's ennoblement through knowledge

The Sufis initiated a unique spiritual-existential experiment whereby they offered proof of man's supernatural ability to communicate directly with transcendence and to unveil the 'truth' hidden behind the veil of jurisprudence. Man, they believed, is able to go beyond the 'apparent' and grasp its deeper 'concealed' content. This ability is attained through inner knowledge, inspiration, vision, intuition, miracles or illumination (all synonyms for the same basic notion), which stand in total contradiction to the rational cognition advanced by dialecticians and to the demonstrative cognition advanced by jurists.

Islam advocates connection with God without mediation; but Sufism pushed this notion to its limits, prompted by the yearning for a most intimate contact with God. Sufis were looking for a knowledge of God of the kind that Muhammad experienced when he received the revelation.[252] The Sufi's vision and heart were riveted to three metaphysical moments of bonding between God and man, and he strove to recover these through introspection in his own life. The first was the moment of the 'covenant' when, as the Quran says: 'thy Lord drew forth from the children of Adam – from their loins – their descendants, and made them testify concerning themselves (saying): "Am I not your Lord (who cherishes and sustains you)?"' (7, Al-A'raf, 172) The second moment was when the Angel Jibril (Gabriel) dictated the word of God to the Prophet. The Sufis were confident of this to the point of dizziness, and, says Henry Corbin, 'concentrated their attention on the conditions which are necessary for this bonding'.[253] The third moment of vision, for the Sufis, was crystallized in the Prophet's midnight journey to the Seven Heavens (the Mi'raj) – his ascension and transcendence – through which Muhammad came to know the divine secrets. He thus became a model which the Sufis, each in his turn, strove to emulate.[254]

The Sufis used Plato's concept of the soul to describe the 'spiritual midnight journey'. The soul, they said, having descended to this world, constantly yearns to throw off its shackles and rejoin its original world. The Prophet's journey, in

Ibn Arabi's view, is symbolic of the life of the soul in this world, where God placed it in order to achieve perfection and ultimately reach its sublime goal of being in the presence of God.[255]

Sufis used the gnostic method to breach the wall that separates God from man. This, they believed, would elevate them to the level of guardianship equivalent to the Isma'ilis' Imam. The rank of guardianship, in its Sufi connotation, implies a level at which direct contact has been achieved between God and the gnostic (the guardian) and where no mediation is needed, not even the Prophet's according to some. Abu Yazid al-Bustami, for example, goes to the extraordinary lengths of asserting that 'my banner is greater than Muhammad's; my banner is illumined and stands over jinns and humans, all of whom are prophets'.[256]

Al-Suhrawardi explains the gnostic illuminism theory of 'light' through the well known Quranic verse: 'God is the Light of the heavens and the earth. The parable of His Light is as if there were a Niche and within it a Lamp: the Lamp enclosed in Glass: the Glass as it were a brilliant star . . .' (24, *Al-Nur*, 35)

Light, he says, emanates from the 'source of light' (that is, God), and descends one step at a time until it reaches the physical level of the body, where it dwindles into extinction. The movement of descending illumination is countered by a transcending movement by man, which is the 'act of cognition' or 'contemplation'. Both are existential gnostic movements leading to the meeting of man with God.[257]

IX.1.2 From yearning for divine meeting to the unity of existence

The Sufi experience, taken to its logical conclusions and based on its yearnings and spiritual tendency, leads from the level of a longing for divine meeting to the level of 'union'. This may lead to the deification of man and the humanization of God, or the converse. Man is no longer on the outside of the world, or of God; God is no longer one side of an equation facing man or outside him. He is 'the finite point in its growth and infinite blossoming. Thus the universe becomes an illumination of the Creator, and man becomes the likeness of God. The Divine is no longer outside this world. It is in it.'[258]

The Sufis describe this state as the 'oneness' where contact with God reaches a stage 'whereby duality between the lover and the beloved vanishes and they become one in essence and in reality. Allusions to the Sufi and to God are no more.'[259] This is what al-Bustami is referring to when he says: 'I am God; there is not deity but I, so worship me.' It is also the essence of God's 'dwelling' in man, as expressed in the following verses by al-Hallaj:

> Exalted be He Whose creation
> Shows the secret of His divine light;
> He then appeared to His creation
> Incarnate in the form of man.[260]

It is also Ibn 'Arabi's 'unity of existence', whereby the whole universe is perceived as one truth that accepts no duality or multiplicity. Truth (God) and men are thus two names and two faces of one reality, which, when viewed from the vantage point of its unity, we call the Truth (God); and when viewed from the vantage point of its multiplicity, we call creation (man). The world is a mirror which reflects the presence of God.[261]

IX.1.3 Man and his sublime role in the universe

The Sufis glorified man and exalted his image and role in the universe. They made man the source and origin of the world; thus the whole world is called the 'macrocosm' and man is called the 'microcosm'. Ibn 'Arabi exalted man (as the Brethren of Purity had also done) by regarding man as the individual king of the world's firmament, and the sun as the successor of God in the seven heavens and the earth.[262] Indeed, Ibn 'Arabi's system of thought made man the centre of the universe. He said:

> God, the Exalted, knew Himself, thus He knew the universe. God created man as a noble miniature in whom all the notions of the macrocosm are gathered, and made him a duplicate of the macrocosm and of the names of the Godhead. The Prophet (peace be upon him) said that God created Adam in His image . . . and because the perfect man is a perfection of this image, he is truly entitled to be the successor and deputy of God in the world.[263]

For Ibn 'Arabi, the first attribute of the perfect man is that he is an accurate, complete image of God, and for this reason he is God's successor on earth; the second is that man is capable of attaining the transcendent degrees of the prototypical perfect man, a rank which is realized in the Prophet.[264]

By contrast, al-Iji (d. 756/1355) considered man combines the nature of all beings: inanimates, plants, animals, devils and angels.[265] Before him, Husain ibn Mansour al-Hallaj had indicated that man is the image of God, and that this image has two natures: human and divine.[266] Ibn 'Arabi also advanced the notion 'that the world as created by God was a ghost without spirit; it was necessary to illuminate the mirror of the world, and Adam was the light or spirit of this reflection'.[267]

Man was for Ibn 'Arabi the source of all beings, the starting point of the world's relation to God and the image of God, for which he merited succession in the world. He was favoured by God over all other creatures, including the angels, and was the most beloved by God. On the basis of this exalted position occupied by man, God warns us against destroying this human creation, for that would be to destroy a perfect image and a challenge to God Himself. Ibn 'Arabi states in *Fusous al-hukm*: 'Know that pity for God's creation has precedence over jealousy for God.'[268]

IX.2 *Tolerance and the love of man*

The prominent Sufis took a highly tolerant attitude towards religion and doctrinal pluralism. In this, they pushed the Quranic notion of the unity of revelation to its limits, seeing in pluralism a variety of ways to discover the truth. Al-Hallaj, for example, began his career by calling on each man to search for God within himself. He avoided criticizing the nomenclatures distinguishing the various religious schools, for he wished people to return to the first source of high ideals and conceptions, preferring to view different rites as mediums through which we should pass to reach divine truth.[269]

According to Massignon, al-Hallaj, in the final stage of his intellectual development, showed 'a basic desire to unify the methods of worship for all human beings'.[270] And al-Suhrawardi formulated a highly complex system by which he attempted to bring together all the world's visions into one spiritual religion.[271]

Finally, Ibn 'Arabi developed a positive attitude to other religions; for had not God said: 'Wheresoever you turn, there is the face of God'? He thus called for religious toleration, opening his mind to the world with all its varieties of things, beings and religions. He said:

> My heart has come to embrace everything.
> A pasture for gazelles and a monastery for monks,
> A house of idols, a Kaaba for the pilgrim,
> Tablets of the Torah, and the book of the Quran.
> I believe in the religion of love wherever it takes me;
> Love is my religion and my faith.[272]

X. The Wahhabis: confirmation of the individual's relation with God

By the eighteenth century, more than two centuries had passed since the Arabs lost their role as intermediaries in East–West trade, and more than a century since the beginning of the disintegration and decline of the Ottoman Empire. Civic and cultural life, and the sciences, had become stale; imitation, narrow-mindedness and rigidity of opinion dominated the lives of Muslims. Communal and individual life alike had become strictly controlled by a network of rituals in which Sufi movements merged, having lost their spiritual vivacity and allowed the mythic symbolism in their discourse to gain ground.

Muslim life had fallen victim to apathy, rituals and imitation, and their relation with God was governed by all kinds of mediums: their Sufi *shaykh*s, various memories of the righteous people of old, tombs and relics of holy men. People flocked to these for mediation, with money and sacrificial gifts.

In the context of these heresies, which had extinguished the very flame of Islamic monotheism, the reformer Muhammad ibn 'Abd al-Wahhab (1713–1791) began his Wahhabi movement – in the selfsame Arabian Peninsula which had witnessed the entrance of the Arabs into history. He emphasized absolute monotheism, rejecting notions of incarnation and union and confirming man's responsibility. Supplication, he stressed, could be made only to God, and he called for opening the door to religious interpretative opinions.[273]

The Wahhabi reformer was influenced by Ibn Taymiyya, except that he parted ways with his mentor in his different interpretation of Islam: his teaching was not limited, in the current conditions, to a call to repentance. As Albert Hourani observes, he posed a challenge both to the Arab tribes and to the Ottoman Sultanate.[274] The Wahhabis were able to control Mecca and Medina, which damaged the prestige of the Ottoman Sultan. Furthermore, they set up the nucleus of a state of Arab character, so leading up to a confrontation with the Turkish race. The Wahhabis made the first attempt in modern times to breathe some life into Arab society through a return to early Islam.[275]

X.1 *Monotheism; the stress on individual conscience*

The central principles of Wahhabi discourse were Ibn 'Abd al-Wahhab's emphasis on monotheism and the Oneness of God, and an implied rejection of novel mediations between the individual and his God, rather confirming the pure personal relation of the believer with God. At the same time, Ibn 'Abd al-Wahhab defined his concepts of human rights in terms of the individual believer's responsibility before God, with no mediation involved.

'Everything,' says Ibn 'Abd al-Wahhab, 'that is worshipped other than God, nay, everything that distracts believers from God, is to be considered an idol.'[276] He insists that no medium must be used to reach God, 'except

knowledge, worship and noble deeds'.[277] He also considers 'seeking the protection of anyone other than God as idolatory',[278] quoting the Quran: 'Nor call
on any other than God; such will neither profit thee nor hurt thee.' (10, *Yunus*,
106) He even says that 'supplication to the Prophet is limited to asking for rain
only, and any other is not permitted'.[279]

He rejects the notion that 'mediation is imperative between the believer and
God just as it is with rulers; for a subject uses mediation to acquaint the ruler
with himself, whereas God is in no need of this.'[280] The Wahabis, in fact, equate
those who say they seek God's favour through the mediation of righteous persons with those who seek favour with their idols.[281]

The Wahhabis battled against 'innovations', excessive sanctification of persons and dependence on mediators, and – ultimately – they waged war against
those who opposed them, basing this on the principle of commanding what is
righteous and prohibiting what is wrong. Thus, whenever they conquered a village or city, they destroyed all its hallowed tombs. They levelled to the ground
the graves of the Prophet's Companions and only allowed their visit without
sanctification.[282] They destroyed many old domes, such as those of 'A'isha, at
the Prophet's birthplace, and those of Abu Bakr, 'Umar and 'Ali. When they
entered Medina, too, the Wahhabis levelled the tombs of the Companions and
came close to doing the same with the Prophet's tomb.[283] This behaviour led
Dozi to see some similarity between Muhammad ibn 'Abd al-Wahhab and
Martin Luther.[284] The Muslim reformer also aimed to redeem the purity of
early Islam and to cleanse it of all extraneous elements. He especially fought
against Sufism and condemned all notions of divine incarnation, including allegiance to saints and Sufi and Shi'ite imams.[285] In so doing, he left ample room
for the emergence of the 'moral character of the individual',[286] which remained,
nonetheless, deeply preoccupied with the endless stream of the Creator's
commands.

Chapter 8: The Medina Charter

Walid Nuwayhid

Introduction

The following is the text of the Medina Charter, the contract concluded by the Messenger in his place of immigration, with the people of Medina (originally called Yathrib) who embraced Islam, and with the Jewish residents there. It is the first contract in Islam to recognize the rights of man, whether immigrant or resident, Muslim or Jew.

1   In the name of Allah, the Merciful, the Compassionate. This is a contract between the Prophet Muhammad and the believers and Muslims of the Quraysh and of Yathrib, and those who followed and joined them and fought alongside them.
2   They are one nation, apart from other people.
3   Immigrants from the Quraysh are to retain their traditions concerning payment of blood money and the ransoming of captives, in fairness and justice among believers. The Banu 'Awf are to retain their traditions and pay their customary blood money. Each group shall continue ransoming its captives in fairness and justice among believers. The Banu Sa'ida are to retain their traditions concerning payment of customary blood money. Each group shall continue ransoming its captives in fairness and justice among believers. The Banu al-Harith are to retain their traditions concerning payment of customary blood money. Each group shall continue ransoming its captives in fairness and justice among believers. The Banu Jusham are to retain their traditions concerning payment of customary blood money. Each group shall continue ransoming its captives in fairness and justice among believers. The Banu al-Najjar are to retain their traditions concerning payment of customary blood money. Each group shall continue ransoming its captives in fairness and justice among believers. The Banu al-Nabit are to retain their traditions concerning payment of customary blood money. Each

group shall continue ransoming its captives in fairness and justice among believers. The Banu al-Aws are to retain their traditions concerning payment of customary blood money. Each group shall continue ransoming its captives in fairness and justice among believers.

4   Believers shall not leave one laden with debt among them without a charitable payment of ransom or blood money.

5   No believer shall ally himself with another believer's ally.

6   The pious believers shall oppose whoever among them acts unjustly, or seeks to profit from injustice, sin, aggression or evil caused to believers. They shall all rise against him, though he be the son of one of them.

7   No believer shall kill another believer in revenge for an unbeliever. No believer shall support an unbeliever against a believer.

8   The Covenant of Allah is one and the same. Even the lowest in status among the believers must be equally protected. Believers are each other's allies, apart from other people.

9   Jews who follow us shall enjoy support and equality. They shall not suffer injustice or hostile alliance.

10 Peace for believers is one and the same. No believers shall conclude peace alone, in any fight in the cause of Allah, except with fairness and justice among believers.

11 Groups that campaign with us shall take turns in action, one after the other.

12 Believers shall avenge their fellow believers for the lives they lost in the cause of Allah.

13 The pious believers shall follow the best guidance. No unbeliever shall protect Qurayshi men or trade, nor deny protection to a believer.

14 Whoever intentionally kills a believer, and is thus proven, is to be punished, except where the family of the murdered decide otherwise. All believers shall rise against the killer, and they may not do otherwise.

15 A believer who abides by this Charter, believes in Allah and the Day of Judgement, shall not protect or shelter a criminal. Whoever protects or shelters the same shall be subject to the curse and wrath of Allah on the Day of Resurrection. No objection or compensation may be entertained in such a case.

16 In case of disagreement on any point, the recourse is to the Almighty and to Muhammad.

17 The Jews are to share expenses when they take part in fighting wars.

18 The Jews of the Banu 'Awf are one nation with the believers. The Jews keep to their religion and the Muslims to theirs. This applies to themselves

and their allies, except for the unjust and the sinner, who hurts no one but himself and his family. What applies to the Jews of the Banu 'Awf applies to the Jews of the Banu al-Najjar. Similarly, what applies to the Jews of the Banu 'Awf applies to those of the Banu al-Harith. What applies to the Jews of the Banu 'Awf applies to those of the Banu Sa'ida. What applies to the Jews of the Banu 'Awf applies to those of the Banu Jusham. What applies to the Jews of the Banu 'Awf applies to those of the Banu al-Aws.

19 What applies to the Jews of the Banu 'Awf applies to those of the Banu Tha'laba, except for the unjust and the sinner, who hurts no one but himself and his family. The Jafna are a sub-tribe of the Tha'laba, and are like them. What applies to the Jews of the Banu 'Awf applies to the Banu al-Shutayba. Fidelity shall be a bar against sin. The allies of the Tha'laba are not different from that tribe, nor are the allies of the Jews different from the Jews themselves.

20 No one of the above shall establish an outside connection without permission from Muhammad.

21 A wound is not healed by revenge. Whoever kills has committed a crime against himself and his family, except for him who is wronged.

22 Jews shall bear their expenses; Muslims theirs. They shall support each other against aggression toward the signatories to this Charter. They shall exchange advice, and fidelity shall be a bar against sin.

23 No man is charged with the sin of his ally. The wronged person is to be supported.

24 Jews are to spend alongside believers so long as they are fighting.

25 The inner precincts of Yathrib are inviolable for the signatories to this Charter.

26 The neighbour is like oneself in matters of offence and sin.

27 No protection is to be offered in the inviolable state except by permission of the inhabitants.

28 Any misunderstanding or conflict that might lead to disruption among the signatories to this Charter shall be referred to the Almighty and to Muhammad, His Messenger. Allah is with the pious and faithful.

29 The Quraysh and their allies are not to be offered refuge or protection.

30 The signatories are to cooperate in defending Yathrib against any aggression.

31 If invited to conclude and uphold peace, they shall do so. If they invite others to do the same, believers shall respond, except to those who fight against religion. Each group shall have its share with the party that accepted it.

32   The Jews of al-Aws, themselves and their allies, enjoy what the signatories
      to this Charter enjoy, in addition to true fidelity on the part of the signato-
      ries to this Charter. Fidelity shall be a bar against sin. Whatever one gains is
      for himself alone. Allah is with the faithful and pious.

33   This Charter is no protection to the unjust and the sinner. Whoever leaves
      Yathrib is safe, and whoever stays is safe, except the unjust and the sinner.
      Allah is the refuge and protection to the faithful and pious. Muhammad is
      the Messenger of Allah.

I. Explanation and Commentary

The Charter comprises a number of items, the first being a preamble which, as
in the case of any political or social contract, defines the source of authority and
the parties to the contract. The Charter names 'believers' and 'Muslims', as if
distinguishing between them. Next it names the Quraysh (the emigrant
Meccans) and Yathrib (the tribes of Aws and Khazraj), then those who followed, joined them and fought on their side. Thus, we have the immigrant and
the resident (the Ansar). We also have the followers of non-Muslim believers:
the allies of the Quraysh, of the Aws and Khazraj, and the various groups in
Yathrib.

After the preamble come the articles detailing the principles and conditions
of the contract.

Article 2 specifies 'one nation, apart from other people'. This means that the
believers and Muslims of Mecca and Yathrib, and their followers, are 'one
nation [*umma*]'. This nation is distinct in creed and different in way of life from
the people of Yathrib. The distinction does not, nevertheless, imply a fundamental difference, since the paragraph equates the believers and Muslims of
both Mecca and Yathrib. 'Other people' means those who have not accepted
the call of Islam. After the emigration, Yathrib had two nations, one Muslim,
the other Jewish, but the state was common to all: one state for two religiously
different nations.

Article 3 specifies that Qurayshi emigrants are to retain their pre-Islamic system of relations, customs and style of conduct concerning payment of blood
money and the ransom of captives. After specifying the Qurayshi emigrants as
one group, the Charter mentions each tribe by name. In his *Sira* (biography of
the Prophet), Ibn Kathir says: 'Then he mentions each sub-tribe of the Ansar,
such as the Banu Sa'ida, Banu Jusham, Banu al-Najjar, Banu 'Amr ibn 'Awf,
and Banu al-Nabit.'[1]

But the Charter mentions more than this. It enumerates the following sub-tribes: the Banu 'Awf, Banu al-Harith, Banu Sa'ida, Banu Jusham and Banu al-Najjar – all subdivisions of the larger, more eminent tribe of Khazraj. Then the Charter enumerates the Banu 'Amr ibn 'Awf, Banu al-Nabit and Banu al-Aws (the allies of Islam). All these belong to the Aws tribe.

The Charter also mentions each tribe by name, to make eight, five of which are from the Khazraj, two from the Aws and one ally of the Aws. For each tribe of the Khazraj and Aws, the Charter assures respectful recognition of previous custom without modification, the retention of traditions predominant before emigration and the right of every tribe to internal independence. The Medinan *suras*, notably those concerned with social organization and laws, had not yet been revealed. In return for recognition of previous conditions, specificity and internal independence, the Charter demands acceptance of fairness and justice among believers; this is an Islamic principle of faith, joining old to new.

While the traditions of clans and tribes are retained, some aspects of them are redefined within a new context, emphasizing a social cooperation advanced by the new call for unity.

Article 4, as we are told by Ibn Hisham in his *Sira*,[2] is concerned with 'one laden with debt or family responsibilities' among believers. The Charter stresses the principle of social cooperation and solidarity with the poor and needy, especially when such a one falls captive or is in need of blood money. The Charter was drawn before *zakat* (alms tax) was imposed; hence the need for joint social responsibility and solidarity on the level of the Medinan state as a whole, and not on that of a particular tribe only. The fourth paragraph, then, is of a comprehensive nature, covering all of the eight tribes mentioned in paragraph three, in addition to all the believers of Yathrib.

Having called for the retention of tribal balance, traditions and customs, the Charter calls on the tribes to uphold civil peace in Yathrib by preventing new tribal alliances between the Ansar (Khazraj and Aws) and their followers, or between Jews and others. As such, article 5 cancels previous alliances and pre-cludes new ones, raising the old relations to the higher level of union in Medina (the new state). The unified solidarity (of believers and Muslims) replaces previous alliances and blocs. Protection becomes the responsibility of the state, not of the tribe.

Article 6 clearly specifies the responsibility of the state in securing internal peace and punishing wrongdoers. It stresses the unity of the group in imposing legal punishment on fomenters of unrest and in upholding this legal right. It further stresses the state's responsibility toward individuals and groups, and their joint duty with regard to defence, opposing injustice, preventing dissent and propagating peace. Here again the state replaces the tribe in bearing responsibility for punishing the wrongdoer, within legal limits. The state puts an end to revenge in order to prevent internal conflict and tribal disturbances based on acts of vengeance.

Article 7 defines individual responsibility under the new order. 'No believer shall kill another believer in revenge for an unbeliever.' It cancels previous alliances and establishes new relations. Muslims and non-Muslim believers are set apart from unbelievers. All conflicts are to be referred to the law, whether the problem is among believers, non-believers or between believers and non-believers. Law applies to all, not to one group against another. However, there is a difference between believers and non-believers, since the two are not equal when killed or protected. Though the law remains the same, a group of believers is not equal to one of unbelievers: an unbeliever's death may not be avenged by a believer's blood, because a believer has violated the code of his group if he kills another believer.

Article 8 specifies that 'the Covenant of Allah is one and the same'. The covenant here is an offer of security and protection, which is the responsibility of the state toward Muslims and believers (who are citizens of the state). The article establishes social equality between Muslims and believers. The poor are equal to the rich in all rights, in weal or woe, in offering protection and providing security. Security of the community and all people in Yathrib issues from God's Covenant, which is the contract concluded with the Messenger, providing security for His worshippers. Sovereignty rests here in the hands of the state, whose authority extends to all subjects and citizens. Individuals have a right over the state to defend them against foreign aggression and to provide for their internal security. In addition to security there is the support provided among believers only: the believer supports another, but not an unbeliever. Nevertheless, the believer has the right to protect the unbeliever if the latter requests it.

Article 9 defines the rights of non-Muslim believers. Jews are mentioned by name and are considered part of the state. They are citizens who have the right to support if involved in a conflict where they are in the right and are threatened with danger. Jews are not to be left exposed to any alliance against them. Among the terms of covenanted society, in such a case as Medina, is clarification of the terms of the Covenant even with respect to people of a different religious persuasion. The article provides, for Jews, rights parallel to those of Muslims.

Article 10 prohibits individual conclusion of peace. This is a step in which various tribes are to take part. It is mandatory on Muslims and believers to consolidate their efforts to defend Yathrib under the leadership of the state, not of the tribe.

Article 11 specifies that campaigning is a collective responsibility against the enemy. In the light of this, where one campaign is undertaken or led by one group of fighters, the next is to be led by another group so as to provide relief for the first.

Article 12 specifies that any believer or Muslim killed in battle shall be avenged by all believers. The collective responsibility of believers provides for the martyr and moves to take revenge on the unbelievers performing the killing. As such, responsibility is collective in defence and attack. Revenge, in the Islamic sense, means punishment according to the law.

Article 13 specifies as polytheists those people who have not accepted monotheism, even after the emigration. As such, unbelievers in the new monotheistic religion of Islam shall not be allowed to protect Qurayshi trade or men, or support the Quraysh against believers. Similarly, the polytheists of Yathrib are not to assist the Quraysh against the state, which includes Muslims and believers both among emigrants and among Ansar supporters, together with Jews. Any such financial assistance and protection extended to the Quraysh is to be considered treason against the various inhabitants of Yathrib. Whoever commits such a crime shall be punished according to the terms of the Charter as laid down for everybody. The article addresses all groups and warns them against undermining the unity and common destiny of Yathrib.

Article 14 is concerned with the intentional killing of a believer, which calls for punishment of the killer. The party to decide the punishment is the family of the victim. They may demand execution of the murderer, or accept blood money within legal limits, so as to preclude revenge. Fighting between the family of the victim and that of the killer is proscribed in Islam.

Article 15 calls on believers to cooperate in executing judgement on the killer or violator of the creed (belief in Allah, the Last Day and the Charter). As such, it is proscribed to protect the killer or fomenter of unrest. The guardian of the law is to execute legal judgement against such individuals. The right to object is withheld in order to prevent chaos and a return to tribal customs and traditions.

Article 16 specifies that the Messenger of Allah is the point of reference in legislation and the settlement of conflicts. This cancels the multiplicity of tribal differences by referring conflicts to a higher authority for settlement. The revealed Quran and *sunna* unify the group of Muslims and believers (emigrants and Ansar) in a joint destiny, in private and public affairs alike.

Article 17 marks the beginning of the second part of the Charter, on a tone of reconciliation with the Jews, having first delineated the general framework of relations between Muslims and believers, Meccan emigrants and Yathrib Ansar, and other tribes and unbelievers. The Charter recognizes all Yathrib inhabitants, emigrants, Ansar and others, defining their rights and duties as citizens, yet distinguishing between the Muslim, who is charged with the duty of fighting, and the non-Muslim, who may choose to take part in it or not. Even so, the non-Muslim, as a citizen, has a duty to contribute toward the expenses of war when he chooses not to fight. He also has a share in war booty if he takes part in raids and campaigns. The Charter was written before the imposition of the *jizya*, or poll tax, on non-Muslims. Therefore Jews had a share in the booty if they took part in the war alongside Muslims; and, correspondingly, they were bound to contribute to expenses, especially in the case of defence if Medina was attacked.

Article 18 begins to clarify the rights of each group by name, recognizing its religion and its right to be different and distinct. Each party has its religion. Each group has its commitments. As such, the Charter endeavours to regulate relations with each group within the limits of the law common to all. The Jews were a religious group, but they were not tribally united: each of their tribes had its own alliances with the Yathrib tribes (Aws and Khazraj) before the revelation of Islam and the arrival of Meccan emigrants in Medina. There were Jews, or Judaized tribes, of the Aws and Khazraj. Hence they were both Jews (believers) and groups basically belonging to Arab tribes. In view of this, the article approves their alliance with Muslims in both their religious and tribal aspect. It guarantees their religious freedom as a group and stipulates their responsibility as individuals when they commit any crime. The Jews form a nation as the Muslims form a nation. Yet they come under one state and one constitution, i.e., the Charter. Therefore, the Jews of the Banu 'Awf must support believers without renouncing their own religion, since they form 'one nation with the believers'. Their duty is to side with the Muslims, not to conspire against them; their right is to keep their independent religion as citizens. If any wish to join the nation of Islam, with no coercion involved, they may do so. The article does not stop with the Jews of the Banu 'Awf; all the other Jewish tribes are mentioned by name to prevent any misunderstanding. These Jewish tribes belong to either the Khazraj or the Aws.

Article 19 mentions the Jews of the Banu Tha'laba specifically, since they are a tribe related neither to the Arab tribes of Aws and Khazraj, nor to the tribes of Qurayza, Nadir, or Qaynuqa'. The Arab tribes migrated from Yemen into Yathrib, and are most probably related to the Arab Azd tribes. The Jewish tribes had probably emigrated to Yathrib from Syria after the fall of Jerusalem in Roman times (70 AD), finding refuge in the Arabian Peninsula. In addition to the broad tribal division of Arabs and Jews, there are smaller divisions of Arab Jewish or pagan tribes. These the Charter addresses clearly in one article, specifying commitments and conditions as in the case of the Banu 'Awf and other tribes linked to the Khazraj, though some of their members are of the Jewish faith. The Arabian tribe of Banu Tha'laba is divided into Jews and pagans. The article also mentions the tribe of Jafna as an ally of the Tha'laba, while the Banu Shutayba is yet another Jewish tribe mentioned. Also mentioned are the allies of the Tha'laba. These may have been polytheists who allied themselves with the Tha'laba. The 'allies of the Jews' may be certain groups having relations and common interests with the Jews of Yathrib before the emigration. They enjoy the same rights and have the same duties specified in the Charter. This article, like the previous one, is comprehensive; nevertheless it specifies every clan and tribe by name.

Article 20 is linked to the three previous ones in that it commits both parties to the contract. Each group has its own religion; each clan, tribe or sub-tribe its specificity and rights, provided it abides by the present Charter that covers all groups, irrespective of faith or ethnicity. The article categorically prohibits any connection outside the Medinan state without permission from the source of authority. The article also recognizes all conditions existing before the revelation and immigration to Medina, i.e., alliances, interest relations and friendships, provided these are reformulated within a common context and regrouped under the higher interests of the state. This is a precautionary measure to guard Medina internally, and prevent any infiltration by outside alliances liable to undermine its political structure.

Article 21 rules out the idea of revenge and forces every claimant to resort to the legal process for a judgement in his case. The article specifies the personal responsibility of the criminal and his crime. The judgement issued is to be individual not tribal, since the person himself and not his family is responsible for his actions, except when a person is unjustly charged.

Article 22 returns once more to specify the Jews by name and remind citizens of the necessity of fidelity and avoidance of treachery. The articles of the Charter are comprehensive, yet there are certain limitations of relation so as to avoid confusion between the rights and duties of the signatories to the Charter. Hence the distinction between the expenses to be borne by Jews and those by Muslims, except when Medina is attacked, or when the citizens go out to fight in defence of their city. In that case all Medinans have to bear their part in the expenses of the war, even those groups who are not obliged to fight. The safety of Medina involves the safety of all groups, which must bear their part of the expenditure even if they do not take part in fighting or defence. The

Charter was, as said, drawn up before the imposition of *jizya*; therefore Jews are given their share in the booty if they fight, provided they share in the expenses of war.

Article 23 reaffirms previous articles concerning individual punishment. The individual is responsible for his actions, not his family or tribe. Legal judgement is always in the interest of the wronged person against the aggressor.

Article 24 once more affirms the responsibility of Jews to share in the expenses of war and to support believers in their war against polytheists.

Article 25 specifies the inviolability of Medina. This is a reminder of the Medinans' sovereignty over their town. The article proscribes civil conflict and prohibits outsiders (the Quraysh and polytheists hostile to the call of Islam) from entering Yathrib. Sovereignty means the right of signatories to the Charter to prevent any outsider from interfering in the affairs of Medina.

Article 26 gives the same rights to the neighbour and the ally within the context of mutual guarantees and integration as defined by the Charter to the Medinans.

Article 27 provides that the granting of political asylum in Medina is a prerogative of the Medinans themselves, and of the source of authority in the state (the Prophet). This article embodies a development of a previous system whereby asylum was granted by one clan or tribe to another upon permission by the chieftain. The format is now different, since the signatories to the Medina Charter hold the right to decide on matters concerning asylum and protection. The article abrogates tribal authority, regulating matters of asylum within a common legal framework.

Article 28 confirms the reference to a single authority for the settlement of internal conflicts, be they political, social, economic or of a security nature. Any misunderstanding or conflict liable to lead to disruption or sedition must be referred to the Messenger for a fair and just settlement. This article provides for centralized control of the settlement of any conflict that might arise among the Medinans or signatories to the Charter.

Article 29 excludes the Quraysh and their allies from the system of asylum and protection, or even from the establishment of interest relations and friendship. The Charter imposes comprehensive sanctions on the Quraysh, and a boycott in every aspect of life: social, economic or political. This will deter any party from attempting to make contact with the Quraysh or establish alliances with them, the aim being to weaken their previous power and influence over Medinans.

Article 30 emphasizes cooperation in defending Medina against external aggression. Previous articles have emphasized internal security through a unified law and a defined source of the process of law. This one emphasizes the joint responsibility for defending Medina against danger from outside.

Article 31 emphasizes acceptance of peace from wherever the proposal may come, except from the party 'that fights religion'. This means that a call for peace is open to everybody inside or outside Medina. It is not confined to one group of people exclusively. 'Each group shall have its share with the party that accepted it', provided the decision to conclude peace be in the hands of the Medinans and their supreme authority.

Article 32 is concerned with the Jews of al-Aws and their allies. In his *Sira*, Ibn Kathir removes this entire article without giving any reason. It may be noted that article 18 mentions the Jews of Banu al-Aws, while article 32 mentions the Jews of al-Aws. It may be that the Banu al-Aws are the allies of al-Aws, i.e., of a tribe actually different from one with the same name. Hence their special mention in the Charter, in view of their power and their alliance with the Banu Qurayza, a Jewish group of considerable standing in Yathrib. The article specifies everyone's responsibility and duties, and that each person is answerable for his actions – a recurrent theme in the Charter.

Article 33 concludes the Charter, though Ibn Kathir omits the final phrase 'Muhammad is the Messenger of Allah', again without giving a reason. The article recognizes previous agreements among the tribes of Yathrib, provided they abide by the new order. It also underlines, once more, the responsibility of everyone before a law that does not distinguish among the separate tribes now unified in the Medinan state. Anyone entering Medina is safe, provided he does not commit injustice or sin. Anyone leaving Medina is safe, provided he does not fight against the new faith, and provided he has permission from the supreme authority. Similarly, anyone staying in Medina is safe, and has the same rights and duties with regard to war expenses and fighting. This concluding article, then, emphasizes coexistence. Whoever stays in Medina acquires its nationality when granted political asylum.

II. History of the Charter

The Medina Charter represents a turning point in the history of Muslims. It was drawn up after the emigration from Mecca to Yathrib in order to regulate the relations between, on the one hand, the Meccan emigrants and Ansar (supporters) of Yathrib, and, on the other, between the Muslims, believers and all other groups living in Yathrib. The Charter is therefore considered the starting point for the establishment of the state, which began in Mecca and reached its final form in Yathrib.[3]

Historians agree that the Charter was drawn up in the first year of immigration, as a response to the need for regulating relations on clear bases. Hence, it was the second step after the establishment of the *masjid* (mosque) as the centre of the state.

Historians are not, however, agreed on the order of the articles in the Charter. Some have considered it an integrated document drawn up at a stroke, while others have seen it as more than one document, drawn up at various times and subsequently collated.[4] There are also differences over the name given to it. Some call it the 'Charter', others the 'Letter'. It has been accorded more significance by historians than by jurisprudents.

Historians treat the Charter as a temporal document, the formulation of which was supervised by the Messenger at a period when the Medinan *sura*s had not yet been revealed. This renders it of great importance, since it was the only framework regulating relations among the various groups, though jurisprudents see its importance as diminished by the very fact that it was temporal rather than revealed. When the Medinan *sura*s were revealed in Yathrib, the Charter was replaced in importance by these *sura*s, which regulated social life, the legal process and other relations; hence, jurisprudents do not consider it a source of legislation. For historians, though, regarding it as a temporal document, it is an event that cannot be ignored. Moreover, historians and jurisprudents alike agree on its validity and on its significance as a turning point in crystallizing a distinctive character for Muslims in the early years of the immigration.

Historians themselves differ in their approaches to the Charter. Some refer to it casually. Some summarize it, others refer to its main points, while still others quote it in full. Writers of *sira* differ from other historians in that they quote the Charter in full. The main source for the Charter is Abu Muhammad 'Abd al-Malik ibn Hisham (d. 215/830), who quotes the entire text of the Charter in his biography of the Messenger, known as the *Sira* of Ibn Hisham.

Ibn Hisham derives his information from Ziyad al-Bakka'i, who, in turn, derived his information from the first writer of a full *sira*, Muhammad ibn Ishaq (d. 150/767). The latter derived his information from his *shaykh*, Muhammad ibn Shihab al-Zahri (d. 124/742).

Time, negligence and wars that devastated the area caused most references to be lost, but Ibn Hisham's *Sira* was saved, and it is regarded as an edition of Ibn Ishaq's *Sira*. Thus, Ibn Hisham's book became a basic and reliable reference, because it adopts the method of attribution, and because the sources are clearly identified.

Most historians and writers of *sira* depend on Ibn Hisham and on other biographers like Abu 'Ubayd al-Qasim ibn Sallam (d. 224/839). With the multiplicity of references it became possible to identify details by comparing one *sira* with another.

These activities continued up to the eighth century after the emigration (fourteenth century AD), when the historian and exegete Imam Abu 'l-Fida' Isma'il ibn Kathir (701/1300–774/1373) composed his biography of the Prophet by reorganizing the various sources into a coherent contextual whole. Ibn Kathir discusses the Charter, quoting Muhammad ibn Ishaq. He also talks of the conclusion of an alliance between the emigrants and the Ansar (fraternization), quoting Imam Ahmad ibn Hanbal. 'Affan related to us, Hammad ibn Salama related to us, 'Asim al-Ahwal related to us, quoting Anas ibn Malik, that the Messenger of Allah (peace be upon him) allied the emigrants and Ansar in the house of Anas ibn Malik.' Ibn Kathir quotes what was related by Imam Ahmad, al-Bukhari, Muslim and Abu Dawud from various sources, 'quoting 'Asim ibn Sulayman al-Ahwal, quoting Anas ibn Malik, who said that the Messenger of Allah (peace be upon him) allied the Quraysh with the Ansar in his house.' Ibn Kathir adds: 'Imam Ahmad said: "We were informed by 'Abbad, quoting Hajjaj, who quoted 'Amr ibn Shu'ayb, who was informed by his father, who in turn was informed by his grandfather, that the Prophet (peace be upon him) concluded a contract between the emigrants and the Ansar to the effect that they were to retain their blood money customs and ransom their captives fairly, and to provide peace among Muslims."'

In his *Sahih*, Muslim quotes Jabir as having said: 'The Messenger of Allah (peace be upon him) confirmed the blood money customs of every sub-tribe. Muhammad ibn Ishaq reported that the Messenger of Allah (peace be upon him) concluded a contract between the emigrants and the Ansar whereby he was reconciled with the Jews, concluded a contract with them and recognized their religion and trade, stipulating conditions on and for them.' Ibn Kathir quotes the Charter in brief and concludes by saying: 'This was recorded by Ibn Ishaq to the letter. It was discussed by Abu 'Ubayd al-Qasim ibn Sallam (may he rest in God's mercy) in his book *Al-Gharib* and elsewhere, which takes long to relate.'[5]

Ibn Kathir attempted to coordinate reports by jurisprudents, compilers of *hadith* and writers of *sira* in order to document his sources. He mentions the Contract (fraternization between emigrant and Ansar in the house of the Companion Anas ibn Malik). He quotes the Charter in the version of Ibn Ishaq and Ibn Sallam, as Ibn Hisham had done. Then he cites the full text without any summarization.[6] This is the text cited in the present essay, as reported by Ibn

Hisham and adopted by contemporary historians and Orientalists studying the 'Medina Constitution', as it came to be called in the latter works.

Contemporary historians and Orientalists have divided the Charter into articles, dealing with each article as a constitutional item and studying the articles independently to explain the Charter's components. This division has led scholars to disagree over the number of items in the 'Medina Constitution'. Some have combined two or more items together if they give the same meaning. Others have kept the articles independent, considering each a separate constitutional item, with a view to rendering a clearer explanation. Khalid ibn Salih al-Hamidi, for instance, divides the Charter into 47 items, while 'Awn al-Sharif Qasim divides it into 52. I have adopted a happy medium of 33 independent items.

The Charter has undergone a number of adjustments. Some scholars have seen it as embodying more than one treaty by virtue of the repeated articles. In his *The Rise of the Islamic State at the Time of the Messenger of God*, 'Awn al-Sharif Qasim takes it as more than one document, concluded among the various groups of Yathrib, and 'which was collated at a later time'. The repetition of some articles he attempts to explain by saying that 'practical necessities called for a revision of certain parts of the Charter to suit the new conditions'.[7]

The Charter comprises a preamble, a number of articles and a conclusion. It has been given various names – Constitution, Document, Pact, Covenant, Contract, etc. – to denote its various implications.

Before reviewing the general concept of the articles, however, we need to address the question of why the Charter was drawn up at all.

III. Why the Charter?

Before the arrival of the Meccan emigrants in Yathrib, the town was composed of two large Arabian clans (with eight tribes), three Jewish tribes and five other tribes living near the other major clans. In addition to these clans and tribes, there were two groups, one Jewish, spread throughout other tribes and clans, the other Muslims, the Ansar, who were spread among the Aws and Khazraj only, along with certain alliances and friendships.

When the emigrant Meccan Muslims and their allies began arriving in Yathrib to escape Qurayshi injustice in Mecca, order had to be established and the need arose to regulate and organize relations according to a constitutional format (some kind of pact or contract) between the emigrants and the Yathrib residents of all tribes and groups.

Not all the people in Yathrib were Ansar. Those of the Aws and Khazraj who made a covenant with the Prophet in Mecca – the first 'Aqaba Pledge (the Pledge of Peace) and the second 'Aqaba Pledge (the Pledge of War) – were a minority not exceeding 90 persons. In addition there were some followers of the Call in Yathrib, who had been won to Islam when the Messenger sent some Muslims to Yathrib to explain the new religion to those who were interested.[8]

It was essential to regulate relations so as to be able to deal with the growing number of newcomers, and to avoid chaotic disorder between the Ansar and the immigrants. Yathrib, as we have seen, was divided into two large groups, the Arabian Aws and Khazraj, with smaller tribes living in their vicinity, and Jews (the Banu Qaynuqa', Banu al-Nadir and Banu Qurayza) who were said to have emigrated from Syria 600 years before and had adapted themselves to Peninsular customs and traditions.

In the course of time, conflicts erupted between the Jews and the two Arabian clans. Battles also broke out among the Arabian tribes (the 'Bu'ath war' between the Aws and Khazraj), and there was warfare and competition among the Jewish tribes themselves.

Yathrib underwent many battles and disturbances in a context of intricate power structures and alliances. The Aws allied itself with the Jewish tribes of Qurayza and Nadir against the Khazraj allied with the Jewish Qaynuqa' tribe. The battles lacked clear characteristics. They were not between Jews and Arabs only, but between Arabian tribes and other Arabian tribes, and between Jewish tribes and other Jewish tribes. There were also Arab-Jewish alliances against other Arab-Jewish ones. These conflicts exhausted all parties, especially the Yawm Bu'ath ('day of Bu'ath'), which devastated the two major Arabian tribes, the Aws and Khazraj.[9]

In such an atmosphere it was essential to regulate relations by recognizing previous traditions and adjusting them to the new conditions, with a view to guarding against local disruptions – against tribal conflicts and power struggles becoming dominant with a consequent loss of specificity for the new call for unity.

From the moment of his arrival the Messenger saw how each group wished to win him to its side so as to spite the other party. Each tribe wanted him on its side in order to gain power, in conjunction with the immigrants, against its local rivals. The Messenger refused the invitation of various tribal chieftains to stay with them, realizing this would be interpreted as showing a bias toward one party and against another. Accordingly he resolved, from the very start, to build the *masjid*, or mosque, as a temporary residence and centre for propagation of the Call – and of the subsequent Islamic state.[10]

Having made this decision, the Messenger now began to organize relations on two levels: the first between the Muslim immigrants and the Ansar; the second between Muslims and other believers or non-believers (Jews and other minor Arabian tribes).

To address the first question, the Messenger devised the system of 'fraternization', so as to spare embarrassment on the part of the Meccan immigrants, who had left their land and source of livelihood when they embraced the new message. According to this system, each immigrant was regarded as brother to a *nasir* with whom he shared residence, food, land, source of livelihood and inheritance on an equal basis. This system removed embarrassment on the basis of brotherhood in faith.[11]

To address the second question, the Messenger drew up the Charter between, on the one hand, the Muslims and their allies, and, on the other, the believers and allies, whereby 'he was reconciled with the Jews . . .' The Charter was, then, drafted in response to an urgent need for initial political organization of the Call, following permission to emigrate and fight against the Quraysh and the unbelievers.[12]

The Charter was eventually bypassed on account of the revelation of the Medinan *sura*s, which retained some of the articles though cancelling most. Caliphs and jurisprudents began to follow what was revealed and ignore those items of the Charter that ran counter to Shari'a. The Charter thus lost some of its significance, though it retained its value as a historical document.

IV. Various opinions

There are several readings of the Charter, mainly reflecting the writer's approach and methodology. Out of dozens of such readings we shall choose three:

1   In his book entitled *The Emigration: an Event That Changed the Course of History* (Al-Hijra: hadathun ghayyara majra 'l-tarikh), Shawqi Abu Khalil claims that the Charter achieved four objectives: unifying Muslims of all nations and tribes; establishing cooperation and solidarity among the members of a group on the basis of brotherhood in faith rather than family ties; placing Jews on a par with Muslims in the public interest, and opening the door to those wishing to embrace Islam by guaranteeing them the same rights as Muslims; and the Messenger of God's establishment of himself as the source of authority, while at the same time forestalling any sense of anxiety or any fear of violation of the recognized authority.[13]

2 Muhammad 'Abid al-Jabiri believes the Charter 'is basically a treaty between the Messenger and the Jews', with two parties involved. The first of these is the 'Muslims and believers', who are to retain their pre-Islamic law and traditions in the matters of blood money and the proper treatment and fair ransom of prisoners. With this in mind, the Charter specifically names all groups, calling them to solidarity and cooperation among believers. The second party is that of the Jews, who must bear their share of expenses for war in which they take part alongside believers, since in this respect they form one nation with the believers.

As a treaty between two parties, al-Jabiri says, the Charter proscribes fighting in Yathrib, calls for a joint defence of the town and forbids any polytheist or Jew of Yathrib to offer refuge or protection to the Quraysh. The Charter further specifies that any conflict among believers or Muslims, or between them and Jews, should be referred to the Messenger. Finally, the Charter stresses that relations in Yathrib must be based on fidelity, righteousness and keeping the peace.[14]

3 Dr 'Ali al-Hawwat refers to the Charter as a Constitution. In contrast to al-Jabiri, he regards it as a contract between three parties: the immigrants, the Ansar and the Jews of Yathrib. The Charter, he says, defined the constitutional form of society and accorded with the Quran in its general principles of unifying Muslims as a single nation apart from other people, characterized by a belief in Islam. The Charter cancelled tribal boundaries but retained the tradition of the tribes, and their former social structure was retained in support of Islam. The Charter imposed solidarity among tribes and cooperation against outside aggression, along with mutual protection among believers. The Jewish groups, as a special case, were required to respect the principles of society in return for protection for themselves and their property.[15]

A different approach to the articles of the Charter does not prevent division of it into independent items in order to study them as legal articles. This will help provide a realistic answer as to the Charter's underlying intention: why it includes penal articles while recognizing the 'other'; why it recognizes diversity within unity; why it gives equal rights to minorities while at the same time warning them against breaking of agreements, violation of the public interest and betrayal of Medinans. These are the general principles. Historically, the Charter represents a transitional period between the end of an old society and the beginning of a new, at a time when the text of Shari'a had not yet been revealed. It is a moment between two periods of time, and a starting point for establishing the state on the basis of creed. Coordination between the two times was the watchword for the moment the articles of the Charter were drawn up.

V. What Does the Charter Say?

The Charter comprises two parts. The first regulates the relation between immigrants and Ansar. The second regulates relations between Muslim immigrants and Ansar, and believers: Jews and others. This division is suggested by a distinction between the section comprising the first article (preamble) to article 16 and the section from article 17 to 33, which concludes the Charter. Generally speaking, the Charter makes a single whole, but it is divided into a number of articles, each dealing with a specific case or phenomenon.

Necessity seems to have dictated that every clan or tribe be mentioned by name (article 3), so as to avoid misunderstanding and preclude any attempt on the part of an unmentioned group to disclaim the Charter and its terms. Hence there are articles repeating the names of clans, tribes or groups addressed by the Charter.[16]

By virtue of these details, the Charter names all groups in Yathrib, so providing precise information about tribal distribution in Medina at the time, and about the relations among tribes. Nor did the Charter overlook intermarriages between Jewish and Arabian tribes, and their alliances of interest and friendship (article 18). It further mentions individuals from the two major tribes (Aws and Khazraj) who embraced Judaism, thereby acquiring a very special status as belonging to a tribe and following a certain creed at the same time (article 19).

Complications like these led the Charter to strive to include everybody without exception. This comprehensive nature has led some contemporary historians and Orientalists to claim the Charter was drawn up at different periods. Some scholars even say article 32 was an addendum intended to cover the Jews of Aws.

For all the various interpretations of the order and chronology of the Charter, scholars agree that it summarizes and captures all the data within one frame of reference. Historically, it is a highly significant document, politically comprehensive, socially detailed and legally clear. It is a record of the first year of immigration, and of the type of relations established by the call of Islam before the revelation of the Medinan *suras*, the imposition of *zakat* and *jizya* and the change of name from Yathrib to Medina, and before adjustment of the *qibla* Orientation toward Mecca (articles 22, 24).

In article 1 the Charter speaks of a 'contract' on the part of the Prophet Muhammad, as a source of authority, with the Medinans and Meccans (Qurayshi emigrants and their allies). In article 2, it speaks of believers, Muslims and a nation apart from other people, referring to people who do not believe in the call of Islam. The Charter also speaks of a creed as basis for the state, of equality in belonging to this creed for Meccans and Medinans alike. It speaks of a political group and of an open pluralistic society where all are equal. The articles of the Charter guarantee religious freedom and peaceful coexistence for all groups in Medina (articles 4, 5, 6, 7, 8). It calls for the regularization of relations in light of the new order; it recognizes agreements made before emigration; it prohibits sedition and revenge, demands the maintenance of internal security and the defence of Medina, and places the judicial process above all (articles 9, 10, 11, 12, 13, 14).

The Charter makes all groups subject to the same law, since the source of legislation and power is now the Messenger rather than the tribe or tribal chieftain. Finally, the Charter emphasizes the unity of Medina, its acquisition of a common identity, and prohibits any segregation among the identities of clans, tribes or religions. As such, the Charter emphasizes the new identity of Medina and the Covenant among its groups (articles 15, 16, 20, 21, 28, 33).

Some scholars see the Charter as akin to a political contract. As a political covenant or contract, it guarantees all groups their religious liberties and financial rights in return for certain commitments imposed on all (expenses of security and defence). It gives freedom of choice to individuals to take part in war and *jihad* (holy war), with the exception of Muslims, for whom this is a duty (article 22).

For contemporary scholars, exemption of non-Muslims from the duty of fighting against the Quraysh and the enemies of the call of Islam is the most important point vis-à-vis what, in modern times, is called human rights: the right of the individual to choose his creed, and to personal independence from the state provided he fulfils general commitments in the light of the common interest (articles 23, 24, 25, 26, 27).

The general order is common to all groups of clans, tribes, Jews or polytheists. Within this general sphere there are independent areas. These are concerned with financial relations, economic independence, allowing each group to keep its previous creed and customs (payment of blood money, ransoming of captives). This is to be done within a framework of cooperation among all groups, defending Medina against outside aggression and participating in ensuring security and preventing sedition and disturbances (articles 29, 30, 31).

VI. Objectives of the Charter

It is obvious that the Charter involves more than a mere organization of coexistence among the various groups in Yathrib. This is only one objective within the larger programme of establishing a legal state on a constitutional basis, so as to control relations within a new format. It was laying the ground for a later stage in which tribal friendships and alliances would be bypassed and a united society set up under one source of legislative, judicial and executive authority. The state in Islam came before the rise of the nation, which was originally based on legislative texts forming the infrastructure of the nation state. The Charter was drawn up at a decisive moment between two periods: one tribal and pre-Islamic, the other creed-based and Islamic.[17]

A review of the articles of the Charter will indicate the following constitutional areas:

1   The parties included in the project are defined as three major divisions of emigrants: the Quraysh, their allies, their supporters in *jihad*, their followers and other tribes; the Ansar (Aws and Khazraj); and the believers (Jews and their followers from major and minor tribes). To control relations the Charter added various groups, specifying the parties concerned by name. Thus three large tribes of Jews were mentioned; eight tribes of Aws and Khazraj; five groups other than the emigrants, Ansar and Jews (the Banu Tha'laba, Jufayna and Shuzayba, supporters of the Tha'laba, intimate followers of the Jews). The Charter further mentions the Judaized tribes among the Aws and Khazraj, and believers who embraced Islam and allied themselves with the Muslims in fighting the polytheists and Quraysh. These are related to the Jews and other tribes of Yathrib, other than the Aws and Khazraj.

2   The supreme reference is specified as the Charter and the party responsible for executing its articles. The Charter emphasizes the centrality of decision-making and the source of legislative and judicial powers, so as to prevent the law from fragmenting and tribal decisions from conflicting.

3   The Charter confirms its recognition of former customs, friendships and traditions, and stresses comprehensive equality among the various groups and tribes of Yathrib. It singles out the Jews in two articles. One is general, covering all Jewish tribes. The other is specific, covering the Jews as a group spread outside the tribal division, and giving this group, which is both religious and tribal in nature, equal rights with Medinans as a whole.

4   The Charter specifies duties and rights, spreading them across many fields where everyone is equal to everyone else, without distinction between one tribe and another, between emigrant and *nasir*, or between one group and another.

5   The Charter specifies penalties in a number of cases linked to internal and external security, defence, war, participation in expenses and shares in the division of wealth (booty). These cases cover many points related to sovereignty and duties applicable to all. They are: the sovereignty and independence of Medina, social cooperation, civil peace, prevention of sedition, ensuring of internal security, supremacy of law and the legal process, prevention of revenge (since the state is responsible for subjects), the right to political asylum, the right to leave Medina with permission, and the right of acquiring nationality status for anyone staying in Medina. The individual is responsible for his actions, not his clan, tribe or group. Protection is due to the wronged person or claimant of a right. Article 8, for instance, says that 'the Covenant of Allah is one and the same'; that is, it applies to everybody. The Charter speaks of mutual protection among believers. Article 9 specifies that Jews who follow Muslims will enjoy the same rights and protection as others. This indicates that non-Muslim believers are considered part of the state, as citizens who have the right to protection if they are wronged or in danger.

6   The Charter includes compulsory articles, albeit of a temporary nature. They may be invalidated when the reason behind them no longer exists. Boycotting the Quraysh, prohibiting contracts or relations with this tribe, is something that may change with a change in the situation. The state is the decision-maker in this case, whether in declaring war or in concluding peace. As such, the Charter prohibits the concluding of separate peace treaties or the breaking of contracts.

The spirit of toleration, openness and recognition of the other and his right to exercise his own different traditions meant that the Charter was able to unify Medina in the first year of immigration. The call of Islam won over many hesitant groups, and the minority of 90 Muslims grew to be a majority that enabled the Medinan state to overrun the Arabian Peninsula in the first eight years following the immigration.

PART 2

Human rights in contemporary Arab-Islamic thought

Chapter 9: The question of human rights in contemporary Islamic thought

Ridwan al-Sayyid

I. The problem of progress and civilization

In his work *The Best of Ways to Learn about Kingdoms*, Khayr al-Din al-Tunusi writes: 'The torrent of European civilization has burst into the land so that nothing trying to stand in its way will avoid being uprooted by the force of its rushing current. That torrent is a source of fear to states adjacent to Europe, except if they should follow suit in the *worldly organizations* [*tanzimat*], which may save them from drowning.'[1]

What Khayr al-Din says about *civilization* is similar to what was said by the majority of nineteenth-century revivalists.[2] This produced two points of agreement: that *civilization* or *progress* is the basis of the supremacy of the European West over the world of Islam; and that there is no other concept of this civilization or that progress outside the European sense. Therefore, it goes without saying that Muslims, if they were to be saved, should be called upon to follow the European concept, in the question of 'worldly organizations' in particular.

Writing about three decades before al-Tunusi, Rifaʻa al-Tahtawi shows a similar understanding of the nature and meaning of civilizational struggle, barring only a difference in emphasis on particularities and priorities. Al-Tahtawi was a man of education and culture, while al-Tunusi was a statesman of authority. According to al-Tunusi, the basis for deciding the question of civilization is the power and organization of the state, while, for al-Tahtawi, the prerequisite for 'achieving progress' is a coordination between society and the political system. Kingdoms were established, according to al-Tahtawi, 'to protect the rights of subjects' equally, with regard to rulings, liberty, protection of life, property, and honour, on the basis of legal judgements and recognized, precise principles.[3] Throughout the human race, *the issue of rights* is based on two concepts with which God has endowed human beings, namely, mind and freedom.

'Freedom is naturally impressed in the heart of man.[4] It is the factor which ensures the continuation of 'human society', which must characterize every member of that society 'in that man has the freedom to move from one abode to another, and from one area to another, without anyone to annoy or coerce him. Such a man is free to dispose of himself, his time and work with nothing to prevent him, except what is specified by Shari'a, politics or the principles of his just state.'[5] Based on an understanding derived from his French education, his long experience, and his understanding, as he says, of the principles of *human community*, al-Tahtawi divides freedom into five parts:[6] natural, behavioural, religious, civil and political. The concept itself, and its five aspects, he derives from an awareness of what he calls *public interests*, which place these liberties in their human, social and state frame of reference, without impinging on *Shari'a* or on *politics* required by *the principles of the just state*.

This system based on the two concepts of *public interests* and *organizations*, which crystallized fully in the second half of the nineteenth century, was permeated by an overwhelming sense that Islamic Shari'a, the basis of a worldwide civilization in the past, can, through its essence and rulings, provide the impetus for the new civil order. This is because scientific, political and economic organizations are based on interest and the endeavour to further it. This is not only permitted but actually encouraged by Shari'a. A quasi-coalition was therefore formed between the men of religion and science on the one hand, and the men of politics or public affairs on the other: in the *religious field*, to renovate Shari'a and its methods; in the *public field*, to renovate the political infrastructure of the Muslim world.

Al-Tahtawi and, subsequently, al-Tunusi, spoke of protecting life, property and honour in Islamic laws – probably with an eye on *The Gleaned* of al-Ghazali[7] and also on modern laws. But the revivalist *faqih*s of the 1860s and 1870s were soon to discover the great Maliki *faqih* al-Shatibi (d. 790/1388) and his book *The Agreements*. Under the title *The Intents of Shari'a*,[8] which the book celebrated, the organization of parts heralded in the previous decades came together. The Muslim innovators resorted to these earlier works to enrich the traditional criteria, or bypass them, in the interest of the general intents of legislation, with its higher ceiling, thus, permitting, in the name of *necessities of interest*, the adoption of modern military, political and educational organizations. In fact the great achievements of the nineteenth century – like the Ottoman organizations, the concepts of citizenship, the overriding of the question of 'the two abodes of war and peace', innovation in the issues of money, wealth and private property – were made possible under the banner of interest and the intents of Shari'a.[9]

By the same token, and by virtue of such writings by al-Tahtawi and al-Marsafi, along with the approaches of Muhammad 'Abduh, Rafiq al-'Azm and 'Abdallah al-'Alami, down to Qasim Amin and al-Kawakibi,[10] the idea took shape as an umbrella beneath which the issue of human rights in modern and contemporary Islamic thought was to operate. The intents of Shari'a as manifested by al-Shatibi (and we have recently come to learn that their origin lay in texts by Imam al-Haramayn al-Juwayni (d. 478/1085) in his work *The Proof*), were *to safeguard the necessities of human life*, this covering the protection of life, mind, faith, progeny and property.[11]

The revivalists, therefore, had four ideas which they handled in various ways for about a century – from the late 1830s to the late 1930s. These ideas were:

1   The relation between Europe and the Muslims is based on supremacy. The essence of that supremacy is the progress of Europeans and the backwardness of Muslims.

2   The way to rectify the balance in the struggle is to learn from Europeans and compete with them using the same methods. There is no concept of progress except that formulated by Europeans.

3   There is no contradiction between Islam and progress. In fact progress is the objective of Islam and the general intent of Shari'a. Muslims, and not Islam, are to blame in this respect.

4   Progress within the social and political framework lies in public interests and organizations.

II. Muslims and their special characteristics

This tendency to innovation and joining of the modern world reached its apex in the first decade of the twentieth century. A case in point is the answer given by Sayyid Muhammad Rashid Rida in his magazine *The Beacon* (Al-Manar) in 1907. A reader asked: 'Why don't we regard the *constitutional* system of government as a *consultation* [*shura*] system of government, since both mean the same thing?' Sayyid Rashid answered: 'Do not say, oh Muslim, that this system of government, which is bound by consultation, is one of the sources of religion, and that we learned it from the Holy Quran and from the life of Rashidi Caliphs, rather than through acquaintance with Europeans, and familiarity with Westerners. Had we not learned from these people, those like you would never have thought this comes from Islam . . .'[12] This implies that, even where a certain concept or organization is contained within Shari'a, awareness, and rediscovery of it will only come by learning from the culture and organizations of the West.

But this obvious endorsement of the notion of Western progress had its limits too. This is reflected in the polemics between Jamal al-Din and Muhammad 'Abduh with Renan and Hanotaux, and in the controversy between Muhammad 'Abduh and Farah Antun, about progress and its relation to Christianity, Islam and the West.[13] In the second and third decades of the twentieth century, certain events and variables came to unsettle the bases of this cultural and political coordination, leaving deep scars in modern and contemporary Islamic thought. Muslims were appalled by the Italian attack on Libya in 1911, and by the ensuing occupation, which brought no serious objections from the major European powers (powers that were themselves occupying most parts of the Muslim world). The dilapidated Ottoman Empire (dressed in the attire of an Islamic caliphate) was defeated, along with Germany, by the European alliance; upon which the European powers began, in various ways, to divide and colonize parts of this empire. Under the order forming after the First World War, and under the supervision of the European powers, the Muslim world began to witness the emergence of national states antagonistic to Islam (Albania, Turkey) or at least neutral in their stance toward it. This was soon to be reflected in culture, and in the writings of 'Abd al-Ghani Sani Beg (*The Separation between the Sultanate and the Caliphate*), Hasan Taqi Zada (*The Complete Westernization*), 'Ali 'Abd al-Razzaq (*Separation of Religion and State*) and Taha Hussein (*Re-examination of the Religious Heritage*).

The reformists and their disciples began to see, in the new culture and the new state, certain matters threatening to their cultural and social identity. Reactions were soon to appear in various forms. On the social/religious side, there emerged societies and organizations for the protection of identity, involved in propagation and education in that field, such as Muslim Youth (1927), the Muslim Brothers (1928), the Upholders of *Sunna*, the Shari'a Society (1931) and the Union of Islamic Youth (1933). On the cultural side, there were many reactions to the writings of 'Abd al-Ghani Sani Beg, 'Ali 'Abd al-Razzaq, and Taha Hussein. Some members of the Arab and Islamic intelligentsia began to treat major Islamic figures and topics in their cultural writings. The 1920s and 1930s witnessed a kind of process of 'disengagement' between the Islamist elite and the upcoming state. A gradual shift away from the West was taking place in the cultural arena, while Islamist reformists began to make a habitual distinction between politics and culture in relations with the West.[14] Perhaps the best example of this shift among the Islamist elite is found in the life of one man, Sayyid Muhammad Rashid Rida himself, quoted above in the context of *learning from the Europeans* in order to rediscover genuine Islamic values. Sayyid Rashid had formerly praised the two books by Qasim Amin, *The Liberation of Woman* (1899) and *The New Woman* (1900), when they first appeared. But, in his *Call to the Fair Sex* (1932), he attacked these claims, calling on Muslim women to abide by the rulings of Shari'a. He had published texts by 'Abd al-Ghani Sani Beg on the separation of the sultanate from the caliphate, only to attack them later (1922–3). Then he published his book on *The Great Religious Leadership* (1923), rebutting calls to abolish the caliphate. His attitude to Mustafa Kamal Ataturk radically changed when the latter abolished the caliphate (1924). In the 1920s the news pages of his *Manar* magazine were filled with complaints about the French and the English. In 1927, he claimed that 'constitutional rule', which he celebrated along with other reformists, did not stop Europeans and Western-educated Zionists from exercising tyranny and enslaving nations, motivated by material gain and hunger for power.[15]

In the 1940s, a clear connection was made between missionary activities, imperialism and orientalism. Attacks were made on the materialism of the West, on its vicious war against itself and the world.[16] Then clearer voices began to echo an attitude broached back in the 1930s: that the West had good social and political systems, but that Islamic systems were better.[17] Then came the severance between Islamic and nationalistic currents in the 1950s. The West and its protégés (systems and rulers) became a model of evil rule, along with its culture and values. In the 1960s and thereafter, there was considerable discussion about cultural invasion, and about international conspiracy against Islam. Dogmatism prevailed in Arab-Islamic circles, even among the non-religious, and it was directed against the culture of the West and its policies in general. The new culture of identity and severance put an end to the last traces of reformist discourse, paving the way for a fierce cultural-specific campaign which, according to Sayyid Qutb, Muhammad Qutb, Muhammad Muhammad Husayn and others, placed the 'system of heaven' in opposition to the 'system of the earth', and the 'light of Islam' in conflict with the gloom of *jahiliyya* (the age of ignorance, before Islam).[18]

III. The specific Islamic view of man and his rights

Parallel to this development or shift toward the idea of separate identity and cultural specificity among Muslims, the International Declaration of Human Rights was issued on 10 December 1948, following the proclamation of the United Nations Charter of 1945. Although some Islamic countries were present and active in the promulgation of the two charters, and some had reservations about certain articles of the Declaration of the Human Rights in particular,[19] the Muslim intelligentsia expressed views which went far beyond the attitudes of states and organizations. Such reactions varied between initial rejection of the charter, reservation expressed against some of its articles, and a criticism of double standards in its application. The latter attitude has remained the most popular to the present day.[20]

In fact the 1980s witnessed, in Islamic thought, a partial return to sober reflection and balance on a number of issues, including that of human rights. But the return to moderation implied no starry-eyed celebration of the idea of progress, as seen among some reformists early in the twentieth century. What emerged was the adoption of a *third stance*, different from the absolute acceptance or absolute rejection known during the 1960s and 1970s. Rather, in the past two decades, Islamists have begun talking about an Islamic establishment of human rights within the parameter of specificity and equality. They have also expressed some tolerance in the area of specificity, as in not recognizing any contradiction between the Islamic concept of mutual consultation (*shura*) and democracy, or by way of accepting political plurality, participating in government without giving priority to the application of Shari'a laws, etc.[21]

The groundwork for an Islamic establishment of human rights had actually begun in the late 1940s, with a reinvestment in the Quranic concept of the *divine vicegerency* of man on earth, in contradiction to the concept of 'natural law', which was the basis of the Universal Declaration. The first writer to do so was, I believe, 'Abd al-Qadir 'Oda in his slender volume, *Islam and our Political Situations*, published in 1951.[22] The idea then became popular with writers on this theme, down to the present day. Dr Muhammad 'Abdallah Darraz has developed this idea of the divine honouring of man with reference to the Holy Quran. He contends that man was honoured by God in four ways: the honour of humanity (17, *Al-Isra'*, 7); the honour of vicegerency (several *suras*); the honour of faith (63, *Al-Munafiqun*, 8); and the honour of work (9, *Al-Tawba*, 105).[23] After this groundwork, Islamists undertook completion of the structure, not, as was expected, by recourse to 'the intents of Shari'a' (used by the reformists), but by positing that the trust mentioned in the Holy Quran (33, *Al-Ahzab*, 72) means entrusting man with *duty*, and that there is no duty outside the worship of God; that is, the application of His law on earth, and the establishment of an Islamic state, which should realize complete justice, and *complete submission* to God.[24] The hardliners understand this to mean that authority to rule belongs to God alone, and that submission is similarly to God alone. When non-partisan Islamists abandoned this concept in the 1980s, they returned to al-Shatibi and his *Intents of Shari'a*, but within the two previous limits of vicegerency and duty. This informs their saying that the *rights* of man in Islam are in fact necessities (or duties), not rights as such.[25] This, they thought, would give those rights/duties a greater significance and more impressive credibility, since they stem from divine revelation rather than natural right. But al-Shatibi, on whom they rely, refers to these 'necessary interests'[26] by saying: 'they [earlier scholars] had said that these were recognized in every nation', which meant that realizing and recognizing those interests was general, universal and necessary for human welfare, and not necessarily confined to the Islamic faith.

IV. Human rights in contemporary Islamic thought: a comparative approach

In line with tendencies emphasizing cultural identity, specificity, integrity and originality, which have dominated over the last three decades, a number of Islamic constitutions, and dozens of declarations of human rights within Islam, were formulated by individuals, groups, official organizations or states. Ann Elizabeth Mayer has already studied a number of these declarations and proclamations in a book she published in 1991. She ran comparisons between these documents and the UN Charter, the International Declaration of Human Rights, and the documents and treaties which followed up to the early 1980s.[27] Sami al-Dib Abu Sihliyya similarly collected around 15 proclamations and declarations issued by individuals and Islamic organizations, translated them into French and published them, in 1994, under the title: *Muslims and Human Rights: Religion, Law and Politics*. I intend here to make a comparison between, on the one hand, the Declaration of Human Rights and the relevant charters and treaties, and, on the other, three proclamations issued by Islamic personalities and organizations. The first of two proclamations is entitled 'The International Islamic Declaration of Human Rights'.[28] Fifty Islamic intellectuals and dignitaries worked on this declaration, under the auspices of the Islamic Council in London, and it was announced at a meeting held at UNESCO Headquarters on 19 September 1981. The second proclamation, or declaration, was recommended for formulation by the Organization of the Islamic Conference in 1980. The committee entrusted with the task included 'Adnan al-Khatib, Shukri Faysal, Wahba al-Zuhayli, Rafiq Juwayjati and Isma'il al-Hamawy. But the Organization Board failed to follow up on the assignment, which led one of its authors, 'Adnan al-Khatib, to publish the work in Damascus in 1992, together with a commentary, under the title, *Human Rights in Islam*.[29] The third declaration was issued by the 19th Meeting of the Foreign Affairs Ministers (of the OIC States). The meeting was held in Cairo (31 July–5 August, 1990); hence its name: 'The Cairo Declaration of Human Rights in Islam' (I'lan al-Qahira 'an Huquq al-Insan fi 'l-Islam).

The subjects of comparison include various social, economic and cultural rights, such as the right to work, to education, family and child rights and the right of ownership. A detailed comparison between the international charters and the two declarations will come in the conclusion, where I discuss the Cairo Declaration, and append it to this article, as it has assumed an official character through the Organization of the Islamic Conference.

IV.1 The Right to Work

• The International Covenant: economic, social and cultural rights

1   The states which are party to this covenant recognize the right to work, which covers the right of every person to have the opportunity to make his living from the work he chooses or accepts freely; and the states concerned must take the appropriate measures to protect this right.

2   All the states which are party to this covenant should take measures to secure the full exercise of this right by providing technical and vocational programmes of guidance and training. In this field, policies and techniques should be adopted which realize a steady economic, social and cultural development, and a full and productive labour force, under conditions ensuring the individual the basic political and economic liberties. (The International Covenant, III, 6).

• The International Islamic Declaration of Human Rights

Every person may work and produce to make a living in all lawful ways. 'There is no moving creature on earth but its sustenance depends on Allah.' [11, *Hud*, 6]. 'Traverse through its tracts and enjoy of the sustenance which He furnishes.' [67, *Al-Mulk*, 15]

(The International Islamic Declaration: 15–Economic Rights)

• Human Rights in Islam

a   Work is a right secured by the state and society for everyone capable of work. People have the liberty to choose the legitimate work that suits them.

b   The worker must do his work proficiently and honestly. He has the right to fair and sufficient wages for his work, and the right to full guarantees in respect of safety and security.

c   In the case of disagreement between workers and employer, workers have a right on the state to remove injustice and establish right, without discrimination.

(Human Rights in Islam:
6, The Rights of Work and Social Security, 14)

IV.2 The Right to Education

• The International Covenant

1   The states which are party to this covenant recognize the right of every individual to education and learning. They are agreed on the necessity of directing education and learning to the full development of the human personality and a sense of its dignity, and to establishing respect for human rights and basic liberties. The states are also agreed that education and learning should aim at enabling every person to perform a useful part in a free society, to strengthen the ties of understanding, tolerance and friendship among all nations and various racial, ethnic or religious groups, and to support UN activities in the maintenance of peace.

2   The states concerned in this covenant testify that ensuring the full implementation of this right demands:

a Making primary education compulsory and free for everybody.

b Popularizing secondary education of all kinds, including technical and vocational education, and making it available to everybody by all possible means, especially the gradual development to free education.

c Making higher education available to everybody, on equal basis and according to qualifications, by every means possible, especially the gradual development to free education.

d Encouraging and intensifying basic education, as far as possible, for the benefit of those who had no primary education or did not complete it.

e Trying actively to develop an interconnected school network on every level, and to initiate an adequate scholarship system, and to continue the improvement of the financial situation of the teaching staff.

3   The possibility of choosing non-governmental schools.

(The International Covenant, 13)

- The International Islamic Declaration

b   Education is a right for everyone, and the quest for knowledge is a duty
     enjoined on men and women alike, 'The quest for knowledge is a duty of
     every Muslim man and woman' [*Hadith*] Learning is a duty on the educated
     towards the uneducated. 'And remember Allah took a covenant from the
     People of the Book, to make it known and clear to mankind, and not to
     hide it; but they threw it away behind their backs, and purchased with it
     some miserable gain! And vile was the bargain they made!' [3, *Al 'Imran*,
     187] 'Let the ones who are present inform the ones who are absent.'
c   Society must provide everyone with an equal chance to learn and be
     enlightened. 'If Allah wills it to bestow His favour on a person, He will
     make that person versed in religion. I can only divide, and Allah gives'
     [*Hadith*] Every person may choose what suits his talents and skills. 'Each
     one is destined to what he was created for' [*Hadith*.]

                              (The International Islamic Declaration –
                                       The Right to Education, 21)

- Human Rights in Islam

a   The quest for knowledge is enjoined on every human being.
b   Education is a duty of society and the state. They must provide its ways and
     means, and ensure its variety for the benefit of the community, and for
     leading people to understand the religion of Allah, and the facts about the
     universe, and to direct nature to the benefit of humanity . . . [Such educa-
     tion] is compulsory in its early stages.

                              (Human Rights in Islam, 5 – The Right to Education, 12)

IV.3 Family and Child Rights

- The Universal Declaration

1   When reaching the age of puberty, men and women have the right to marry
     and form a family, without any restriction due to race, nationality, or reli-
     gion. They are equal in rights at the time of marriage, when marriage is
     holding and when it is no longer holding.
2   Marriage is not concluded without the full agreement of the uncoerced
     two parties.
3   The family is the basic and natural component of society, and has the right
     to enjoy the protection of society and state. (16)

• The International Covenant

3   Special measures of protection and help should be taken for the benefit of all children and adults, without segregation due to descent or any other reason. It is a duty to protect children and adults against social and economic exploitation. The law must punish those who employ such persons in any way that may corrupt their morals, harm their health, threaten their life or undermine their natural growth. The state has also to set an age limit beneath which the employment of children in paid labour is punishable by law. (10–3)

• The International Islamic Declaration

(The right to form a family)

a   Marriage *in the Islamic sense* is the right of every person. It is the legitimate way to build a family, beget a posterity, and preserve chastity. 'O mankind! Reverence your Lord who created you from a single person, created, of like nature, his mate, and from both of them scattered [like seeds] countless men and women.' [4, *Al-Nisa'*, 1]

b   Every child has the right on his parents to bring him up well, and give him a good education and cultivation. 'And say, "My Lord! bestow on them Your Mercy even as they cherished me in childhood".' [17, *Al-Isra'*, 24] It is not permitted to employ children at an early age, nor to burden them with work which may exhaust them, impede their growth or interfere with their right to play and learning.

c   If parents fail to fulfill their responsibilities toward the child, this responsibility reverts to society.

d   A young man or woman may not be obliged to marry one they do not like. 'A young virgin slave-girl came to the Prophet (peace be upon him) and said that her father forced her to marry against her will, so the Prophet (peace be upon him) gave her the choice [to decide for herself].' (The Right to Build a Family–19).

• Human Rights in Islam

a   The family is the basis of Muslim society. Marriage is the foundation of the family. *It is a duty on men* and women, which Islam encourages. There should be no restriction on the grounds of race, colour or nationality, except for what is necessitated by Shari'a.

b   The state and society must remove obstacles before marriage, and facilitate its means.

c   Mutual agreement is the basis of the marriage contract. Its annulment cannot be effected except in accordance with the rulings of Shari'a.

d   The man is the protector of the family and bears responsibility for it. The woman has her own civil personality and independent financial means, and she keeps her name and parentage.

e   Every child has, from his birth, a right on his parents, society and the state to nursing, education, and moral and financial care.

f   Society and the state must protect motherhood and devote special care to it.

g   The father has the right to choose for his child the suitable education *in the light of Islamic moral values*. (Family Rights, 7, 8, 9)

IV.4 The Right to Ownership

• The Universal Declaration

1   Every individual has a right to ownership, whether alone or in association with others.

2   It is not permitted to deprive anyone forcibly of what he owns. (Article 17)

• The International Islamic Declaration

b   Private ownership is legitimate, individually and jointly. Every person has the right to own what he has gained by his effort and work. 'It is He Who gave wealth and satisfaction.' [53, *Al-Najm*, 48] Public ownership is legitimate, and it should be employed in the interest of the entire nation. 'What Allah has bestowed on His Messenger [and taken away] from the people of the townships – belongs to Allah – to His Messenger and to kindred and orphans, the needy and the wayfarer; in order that it may not [merely] make a circuit between the wealthy among you.' [59, *Al-Hashr*, 7]

(Economic Rights–15)

• Human rights in Islam

Every person has the right to legitimate gain, provided he does not monopolize, cheat or harm an individual or a group.

(7. The Rights of Gain, Profit, and Moral Property – Article 16)

*   *   *

The above quotations from international texts and documents, and from two Islamic declarations, concerning the rights of work, education, family, the child and ownership, show points of agreement and points of difference. In fact the 'agenda' of the two international covenants forced itself on the two subsequent Islamic declarations, which were obliged to reiterate what was covered in the two previous declarations, with a few added details. But the differences are still visible beneath the similar titles. It is noticeable that the universal declarations mention several points as natural rights, whereas the International Islamic Declaration bases itself on the Quran and the *sunna*; the other on Shari'a. Hence the difference in accent. The international declarations remain as *rights*; the Islamic ones become *duties*. This difference becomes more significant in subsequent details. There is an emphasis, on the part of the authors of the two Islamic declarations, on abiding by rulings of Islam or referring to them in matters of marriage, protection of the family, rearing of children, etc. There is also an emphasis on the use of Quranic and jurisprudential terminology and expressions, such use being seen not as a mere distinctive feature but as an inevitable result of recourse to the use of Shari'a texts. In short, there is a tendency to fundamentalization (in the declaration of the Islamic Council more than in that of the Organization of the Islamic Conference). There is also further emphasis on the special characteristic of Shari'a, leading to a sense of independence from the types and models of the West. The two declarations are not an address to Muslims in the Muslim world, but to members of the international community, who should, according to these declarations, realize that Muslims insist on distinctiveness and equality alike, because of the special characteristics of their texts and traditions; and, consequently, on their integrity being respected. Hence, they cannot be absorbed into Western societies, as some of their ancestors had been before. Other than that, these two declarations do not present anything new, except in the 'codification', as we see in the Declaration of Human Rights in Islam. Codification is a tendency which began in the first half of the nineteenth century. It crystallized in the Gazette of the Ottoman Judicial Rulings and continued intermittently through the first half of the twentieth century. In recent years it has reappeared on the level of drawing up constitutions, human rights declarations and the codification of transaction rulings. This codification has three objectives: to give the Islamic texts (of the Quran, the *sunna*, and jurisprudence) a legal format; to prove the validity of Shari'a as being applicable in every time and place; and to prepare for the establishment of the Islamic state, a concept that gained momentum after the success of the Iranian revolution and the declaration of the Islamic Constitution there.

The Cairo Declaration comprises a long preamble and 25 articles. It draws its authority, as stated in its last two articles, from 'the rulings of Islamic Shari'a'. All 'rights and liberties specified in this declaration are bound by Islamic Shari'a rulings, which are the only reference for the interpretation of any article in the Declaration.' The expression of commitment to Shari'a rulings is repeated in several articles, such as item c of article 7: 'Parents have rights over their children; relatives have a right over their kindred in accordance with *Shari'a rulings.*' In article 19–d, we read, 'There is no crime or punishment except in accordance with *Shari'a rulings.*' In article 22–b, we find, 'Every human being has the right to call for the performance of good deeds, to enjoin what is right and to forbid what is wrong, in accordance with the controls of Islamic Shari'a.' In article 23–b, again, we find, 'Every person has the right to participate in the administration of public affairs in their country . . . in accordance with *Shari'a rulings.*' It is unfair, therefore, to claim, as Ahmad Mubarak al-Baghdadi has done, that those who drafted this declaration were not *faqih*s (jurists) but men of law.[30] The declaration is dominated by a conservative Islamic spirit, concerned with *fiqh* expressions and terminology. Some of its drafts were, in fact, prepared in Tehran. In June 1996 I personally witnessed, in Jeddah, a discussion about the declaration in the Jurisprudence Academy of the Organization of the Islamic Conference. Shaykh Muhammad 'Ali al-Taskhiri, the Iranian delegate, mentioned that jurists, including himself, had contributed to the drafting of that declaration. The Preamble is reminiscent of the Islamic revivalists of the 1960s and 1970s, when a tendency to isolate Muslims from the West and the world was most conspicuous. The Declaration, according to the Preamble, came 'to emphasize the role of the Muslim nation in civilization and history, a nation which Allah raised to be the best, a nation which bequeathed to humanity a balanced international civilization, connecting this world with the other world, and joining knowledge to faith; a nation which was given the wherewithal *to guide humanity out of its bewilderment among contending currents and schools of thought, and to provide the solutions for the chronic problems of materialist civilization.*' The Cairo Declaration was given further authority, as it was referred to in the Declaration of the Islamic Summit Conference in Tehran, in November 1997.

The nature of the Cairo Declaration is problematic. It was drafted by member states of the Organization of the Islamic Conference holding different opinions and following different schools of thought and laws. They have different attitudes toward the international declarations, on the one hand, and toward Islamic Shari'a on the other. This fact has at times led the authors to bypass certain sensitive issues, or resort to generalizations. But this did not deter some Islamic countries from objecting to certain of the articles in that

Declaration,[31] such as the right to life and the freedom to conduct it (which was not mentioned in the Cairo Declaration); the right to equal inheritance (which was not mentioned either); the right to adopt a faith (which was mentioned in a roundabout manner, suggesting, possibly, that only the Muslim is liable to aggression against his religion); the right to marriage and the freedom to choose a spouse (which was so formulated in the Declaration as to suggest that men and women should not be hindered from marriage on grounds of race, colour or nationality, but with no mention of religion).

*   *   *

The eminent scholar George Maqdisi[32] has noted that humanism and scholasticism appeared in the Muslim world first, then penetrated into the West through Italy and Muslim Spain. But the difference between the Muslim and European worlds is that Muslims experienced the humanistic movement first, then learned the scholastic system of teaching; while Europe experienced scholasticism first, then moved on to humanism. It seems to me that our cultural problems with the West stem from a pronounced similarity of origin rather than from difference. Nor am I completely convinced that cultural-specific criteria and specificity are the most suitable ways to protect or salvage identity. Yet the phenomenon of the Islamic declarations of human rights is not totally passive. There was a time when we used to reject the *international* and the *cosmic* completely.[33] But now we have come to say, through these declarations, that we agree to enter and participate, but on conditions we see in terms of needs and improvements, not impositions. There are, nowadays, intensive discussions and dialogues, societies and periodicals, throughout the Arab homeland, concerned with human rights and the problems they raise in our civilization.[34] The question now under discussion continues to involve a major existential and historical choice; and the basic prerequisite in confronting this choice or alternative is an awareness of place and time. Hence this critique of man's options and rights in our civilization.

Appendix

The Cairo Declaration[35]

Human Rights in Islam

To emphasize the historical and civilizational role of the Islamic nation, which was made the best nation to bequeath to humanity a balanced international

civilization, joining this world to the hereafter, and joining knowledge to
faith;

And in expectation of what this nation may do today, to guide humanity
which is perplexed in the midst of contending currents and schools of thought,
and to present solutions to the chronic problems of material civilization;

And to participate in human efforts with regard to human rights, which aim
at protecting man against exploitation and oppression, and at emphasizing his
liberty and rights to a dignified life compatible with Islamic Shari'a;

And, further, out of conviction that humanity, which has attained high levels of material knowledge, is still, and will always be, in dire need of a support
of faith to its civilization and an inner deterrent to protect its rights;

Finally, out of belief that basic rights and general liberties in Islam are part of
the religion of Islam, which no one can, in principle, suspend, completely or partially, or violate or ignore, as divine rulings and duties revealed by Allah in His
Books, and conveyed through His final Messenger, completing what was conveyed through heavenly messages, whose recognition became a form of worship, and whose disregard or violation is a reprehensible action, for which each
person is answerable individually, and the nation is responsible collectively;

The member states of the Organization of the Islamic Conference, based on
the aforesaid, declare the following:

Article One

a   Human beings are all one family, joined by submission to Allah and by fil-
     iation to Adam. All people are equal in their honourable origin, irrespec-
     tive of race, colour, language, sex, religious belief, political affiliation,
     social position, or any other consideration. It is sound doctrine to guaran-
     tee the growth of this honour and the progress of man toward integration.
b   All people are Allah's dependents. The nearest to Allah's heart are the
     most useful among His dependents. There is no preference for any over
     another except by piety and good deeds.

Article Two

a   Life is a gift from Allah. It is guaranteed to every man. Individuals, soci-
     eties and states must protect this right against any aggression. No life may
     be suppressed without a legitimate reason.
b   Resort to any means leading to the termination of the human source of life
     is proscribed.

c   Ensuring the continuation of human life until Allah wills is a Shari'a duty.
d   The safety of the human body is guaranteed; its violation is prohibited. It should not be interfered with except for a legitimate reason. The state must guarantee this.

Article Three

a   In the case of use of force or in armed conflicts, it is not permitted to kill those who had no part in the conflict, such as old men, women or children. The wounded and the sick have the right to medical care. Captured prisoners must be fed, clothed and sheltered. Mutilation of the dead is proscribed. Families divided by conflict must be exchanged and reunited.
b   It is not permitted to cut down trees, destroy crops and fields, or destroy enemy civil buildings and facilities by bombardment or similar means.

Article Four

Every person has a right to privacy and the protection of his reputation in his life and after his death. The state and society should protect his dead body and secure its burial.

Article Five

a   The family is the basis in the structure of society. Marriage is the basis of the family. Men and women have the right to marriage and there should be no obstacles to prevent them from enjoying that right on the grounds of race, colour or nationality.
b   Society and the state must remove obstacles to marriage, facilitate its means and protect the family.

Article Six

a   Woman is equal to man in human dignity. She has rights equal to her duties. She has her civil personality, independent financial means, and has the right to keep her name and descent.
b   The man is charged with the expense of his family, and he is responsible for its care and protection.

Article Seven

a   When a child is born, it has a right on parents, society and the state to nursing, upbringing, material health and moral care. The unborn baby and its mother should be protected and given special care.

b   Fathers, and others in a similar position, have the right to choose the type of education they desire for their children, considering their interest and future, in the light of Shari'a moral values and rulings.

c   Parents have rights on their children; and relatives have rights on their kindred in accordance with the rulings of Shari'a.

Article Eight

Every man has the right to enjoy his legitimate capacity in enforcing and commitment. When that capacity is lost or impaired, his guardian takes his place.

Article Nine

a   The quest for knowledge is a duty. Education is a duty on society and the state, which must ensure its means and methods, secure its variety to further the interest of society, and help man to understand the religion of Islam, and the facts of the universe, so as to deploy these for the good of humanity.

b   Every man has a right on the various providers of education and guidance, such as the family, the school, the university, the media and others, which must endeavour to educate man in religious and worldly affairs, in a balanced and integrated manner, in order to develop his character, and strengthen his faith in Allah and his respect for rights and duties and the protection thereof.

Article Ten

Islam is the religion of nature. No type of coercion may be exercised on man, nor may his poverty or ignorance be exploited to force him to convert to another religion or to become an atheist.

Article Eleven

a   Man is born free. No one may enslave, degrade, oppress or exploit him. No submission except to Allah (swt).

b   Colonialism of all sorts is considered enslavement of the worst kind and is unconditionally proscribed. Colonized nations have the full right to liberate themselves and they have the right to self-determination. All states and nations have a duty to support colonized nations in their struggle to liquidate every kind of imperialism or occupation. All nations have the right to preserve their independent personality and control their wealth and natural resources.

Article Twelve

Within the limits of Shari'a, every man has the right to move around and choose his place of residence inside or outside his country. When oppressed, he has the right to seek asylum in a different country, where he should be given protection as long as he remains in danger, except when he has committed a crime in the judgement of Shari'a.

Article Thirteen

Work is a right guaranteed by the state and society for everyone capable of work. Man has the right to choose the work that suits him and furthers his interest and the interest of society. The worker has the right to security and safety, and all other social guarantees. He should not be charged with anything that is beyond his capacity, or that will coerce, exploit or harm him. Without distinction between male or female, the worker has the right to fair wages for work, paid without delay. He has the right to days of leave, increments and differences in payment due to him, and he is expected to perform his work proficiently and honestly. In case of conflict between workers and employer, the state must intervene to settle the dispute, establish the right and enforce justice without bias.

Article Fourteen

Man has the right to legitimate profit, without monopoly, cheating, or harming self or others. Usury is strictly forbidden.

Article Fifteen

a   Every man has the right to ownership in the legitimate ways, and to enjoy the rights of ownership without harming himself or other individuals or

society. Expropriation is not permitted except when necessitated by public interest, and against a just and immediate compensation.

b   Every man has a right on his society and state for social and health care,
through provision of all necessary facilities, within available possibilities.

c   The state guarantees every man his right to a dignified living, suitable to his
needs and the needs of those under his charge. This covers food, clothing,
residence, education, health care and all other necessary considerations. . . .

Article Eighteen

a   Every man has the right to live in peace, with regard to himself, his religion,
family, honour and property.

b   Every man has the right to privacy with regard to his personal affairs,
home, family, property and communications. Spying or surveillance on
him, or undermining his reputation, is forbidden; and he should be safeguarded against any abusive interference.

c   The home is inviolable in all circumstances. It is not permitted to enter it
without leave or illegally. It cannot be demolished or confiscated or have
its occupants displaced.

Article Nineteen

a   All men are equal before the law, both the ruler and the ruled.

b   Recourse to the law is a right guaranteed to everybody.

c   Responsibility is fundamentally personal.

d   There is no crime or punishment except as specified by the rulings of
Shari‘a.

e   The defendant is innocent until convicted by a fair trial in which all means
to defend himself are provided.

Article Twenty:

It is not permitted to arrest a person, restrict his freedom, exile or punish
him without a legitimate reason. It is equally not permitted to expose a person to physical or psychological persecution, or any type of degrading,
cruel or insulting treatment that undermines human dignity. It is also not
permitted to subject any person to medical or scientific experiments without his consent, provided his health and life are not endangered. Enacting
exceptional laws to authorize the legislative powers to enforce the above is
not permitted.

Article Twenty-One

Taking a man hostage is proscribed in all circumstances and for any purpose.

Article Twenty-Two:

a   Every man has the right to express his opinion freely, without prejudice to legal principles.
b   Every man has the right to call for good deeds, enjoin the right and prohibit the wrong, in accordance with the rulings of Islamic Shari'a.
c   The media is a vital necessity for society. It is proscribed to exploit or misuse it, or undermine the sanctities or the dignity of prophets through the media. It is equally proscribed to exercise, through the media, anything that leads to the disruption of values or the disintegration of society, or that weakens, harms or undermines religious belief.
d   It is not permitted to incite to national or doctrinal hatred, or do anything that leads to any kind of racial discrimination.

Article Twenty-Three

a   Governorship is a trust. It is strictly proscribed to exercise it tyrannically or exploit or misuse it. This is necessary in order to guarantee the basic rights of man.
b   Every man has the right to take part in the management of the public affairs of his country, directly or indirectly. He also has the right to assume public office in accordance with the rulings of Shari'a.

Article Twenty-Four

All rights and liberties specified in this Declaration are bound by the rulings of Islamic Shari'a.

Article Twenty-Five

Islamic Shari'a is the only referable authority for the explanation or clarification of any of the articles in this document.

(Cairo, 14 Muharram, 1411 AH, 5 August 1990 AD)

Chapter 10: The problematic of freedom and human rights in Arab-Islamic thought

Yousef Salama

The concept of human rights is clearly bound up with that of freedom, to such an extent that consciousness of the first is regularly linked to awareness of the second; and awareness of freedom has, in turn, become a condition and standard prerequisite for the discovery, by individuals and nations alike, of the significance of the human rights concept. The European Enlightenment philosophers of the seventeenth and eighteenth centuries defended and advocated human freedom, above all in its natural aspect, and in this way they prepared the ground for the development of human rights. We are now witnessing a similar correlation in modern Arabic culture, with 'freedom' and 'human rights' being merged within a single intellectual structure employed in a variety of ways by numerous contemporary Arab intellectuals.

Towards the end of the nineteenth century, Adib Ishaq concluded that 'freedom is a single unified trinity embodying many relevant characteristics. In its essence it is called natural freedom; in society, it is civil freedom; and in terms of conclusive relations, it is described as political freedom.'[1] Adib Ishaq, then, distinguishes three basic aspects of freedom: natural, civil and political. He was, though, primarily concerned with natural freedom, the aspect which, he maintained, had been virtually suppressed by human association:

> Freedom has, by definition, been a natural trait whereby the individual is enabled to develop his physical and mental faculties, and to ascend in the hierarchy of complete existence. It is unfortunate for humans that the exercise of authority has obstructed their path, in all respects and at all times. A prime objective of human association has, one might think, been to prevent the development of individuals into human beings. Social assembly has done enormous harm to natural human freedom everywhere. If you look around, you will see how people wish their children to be moulded in the form of their parents. The Chinese bind the feet of baby girls with hard leather and iron to make them look like their grandmothers; Europeans weaken the child's left hand in order to strengthen his

right; easterners smother the infant in tight covers and wraps . . . They all impede the child's natural forces so as to make him a replica of others in the community. These customs, which block human existence off from its intended, natural condition, and strive to turn him into what others wish him to be, will eventually take away his natural freedom.[2]

According to Ishaq's argument, the re-forming of the natural individual into new moulds goes far beyond the mere selection or deformation of physical characteristics. The process subsequently involves the development of mental and psychological traits imposed by educators, in all societies, on the minds of the new generations. Education thus redirects the natural, spontaneous dispositions and tendencies:

> As soon as the child is turned over to educators, they begin to take over his simple and pure mind, moulding it like wax and stamping on it whatever instructions they wish; gearing it not to what is good but rather to what they think is good, turning it away not from what is evil but rather from what they think is evil. They deter him from exploring the unknown and persuade him to accept the things he does not know. In this way their ideas are inculcated in his mind, as the driving force of his life. In this way he lives, from swaddling clothes to coffin, as they have wished him to live and not as God created him.[3]

Having re-formed the bodily qualities, society has now completed the restructuring of the individual's mind and self according to its own objectives and orientations, so depriving humans of their psychological and physical dimensions: in other words, the freedom to be what they wish to be. Humans have been treated as a malleable substance with which educators work, so forestalling individuals' natural freedom.

The influence of the Enlightenment philosophers is obvious here, particularly the impact of Jean-Jacques Rousseau. As an Arab Renaissance intellectual, Ishaq adapted Rousseau, in his own way, to meet the specific requirements of the period.

> The teacher does not present his instruction as a matter of choice, but rather imposes it as something unquestionable and mandatory. As a result error and fallacy have become duplicated and entrenched, and ignorance has endured over the years. The method of teaching was formalized by Law and consolidated by custom, these coming to be taken as unquestioned premises. People began to move backwards, to descend from the heights of innovators' grand ideas to the abyss of triviality; from creative notions to harmful illusions and hallucinations; and so on and on.[4]

Ishaq believes, with Rousseau, that the natural, intrinsic, innocent human state was vitiated by a society of feudal burdens, and by the nobility and clergy, being reduced, as a result, to levels utterly inappropriate to human dignity. The process of human development became skewed. According to Ishaq, the ignorant and backward society of Turkish feudalism, sectarianism and tribalism had undermined human dignity. If Arabs had only been left to themselves, they would have developed and advanced like all other human beings. Their natural, instinctive tendencies had, however, been corrupted by society, all the more so when the Turkish power actively worked to move Arabs backwards, against the natural course of evolution and progress towards civilization. The Turkish presence entailed a whole series of obstacles and structures inimical to the progress which is a consequence of human freedom.

Ishaq is not, in fact, simply translating or adding a veneer. Rather he is applying French Enlightenment notions, critically and sensitively, with a view to assailing the obsolete composition and structure of his own society and advancing it towards freedom; and, more specifically, with a view to criticizing the ruling power for its opposition and hostility vis-à-vis every form of freedom. If the concept of freedom in nineteenth-century Arab society were ever to be developed on the political level, then the ruling powers – whether Turkish or European – would simply refuse to countenance any such progress. The events of 1882 and the preceding period provide ample evidence for this. Khedive Tawfiq of Egypt stood against the Egyptian national movement and allied himself with the British to protect his personal authority, which would, he suspected, be reduced by parliament and by people's representatives in the legislative assembly.

For all that, Ishaq remains sceptical as to the eventual prevalence of political freedom, for all individuals, in the society of his time.

> The freedom of the individual is subjected to constant tyranny. In saying this, we do not mean that total freedom should be maintained, beyond the confines of any definition or law . . . True law does not undermine freedom or destroy independence, but rather defines these things and protects them from deterioration or disappearance. The essential condition of freedom in law is concern for the rights of all and the preservation of the individual's rights so long as he does not harm the rights of others. Government is not legitimate when it takes away the freedom of the individual with a view to maintaining freedom for all.[5]

Freedom and law are, then, inseparably bound, with law supporting freedom rather than impeding it. To put it another way, freedom cannot exist in the absence of law, since legislation is a clear expression of reason, which is itself a prerequisite for freedom. The enforcement of law does not imply coercion; nor is law itself a limitation on freedom, but rather the rational necessity guiding the rational practice of freedom, without unnecessary restraint or forcible imposition.

The essential link between freedom on the one hand, and reason and law on the other led Ishaq to establish a correlation between freedom and equality, the latter springing naturally from the former.[6] The outcome of all of this now emerges:

> Political freedom is not an achievable end and cannot be fully attained. It is virtually impossible to realize because it is influenced by factors like customs, laws, morals and social conditions. Various forms of distinction and privilege will arise and spread. In principle every individual in the community should have commonly held privileges, as though all were noble, all being equal in the presence of true freedom.[7]

Thus freedom, in its true sense, is inseparable from equality. This is indeed the essence of the Declaration of the Rights of Man and Citizen, which was issued by the institutions of the French Revolution in 1789 and provided the basis for the Revolution's Constitution of 1792. In this light, Ishaq emerges as a liberal Enlightenment intellectual, whose ideas on freedom ultimately underlay his urging of a broadened institutional structure; an effort consolidated, subsequently, through the efforts of other intellectuals who moved on to new horizons and visions of various kinds, all of them demonstrating that Arabic thought had kept pace with the movement of events at the turn of the twentieth century. Ishaq's untimely death, while still in the prime of youth, deprived Arabic thought of his prolific and fruitful output.

Ahmad Lutfi al-Sayyid offered, by contrast, a conceptualization of freedom far broader and far more thorough, in its elaborate clarification of liberal elements, than that provided by Ishaq. His vision of freedom was, indeed, not that of a Renaissance intellectual concerned merely to criticize the status quo, but rather involved the experience of a 'mentor of a generation', able to understand a point in its generality and aware of the implications of political and cultural exposure. Al-Sayyid had familiarized himself with liberal thought at its source, having lived in European countries first as a student and then as an official, and he had visited capitalist countries. For him freedom was an a priori principle of first importance for human life, whether at the individual or social level – the springboard for all other things and the necessary condition for human life itself. Any harm produced by excessive freedom could not, he believed, be compared with the grave damage liable to stem from a tendency to despotism.[8]

His attitude to tyranny – given the subsequent oppression produced by various forms of military rule within the Arab world – was clearly justified; the real danger, to individual and society alike, comes not from freedom but from lack of freedom. The wretched plight of the present-day Arab world is largely the result of the absence of individuals' right to criticize, express opposition and take part in choosing the appropriate social and political system.

In the light of all this, al-Sayyid concluded that human beings lose their humanity when they lose their freedom:

> When the torch of freedom is extinguished in the soul of the individual, and his mind is darkened by its absence, he can no longer be considered a human being, and all life's responsibilities will be taken off his shoulders[9]

Freedom, he maintained,

> is the right of the individual on the day of his birth. People are born free, and the right to freedom would be enjoyed by all from the moment they were born, if this condition were not replaced by the power of arbitrary rule . . . Power does not acknowledge or recognize any right. The power that despoils freedom effectively despoils the life of individuals and nations alike.[10]

The existence of everything is founded on freedom: the existence of the individual, the community and the nation. There are countless examples in the Arab world today of people denied the right to live, or to be citizens, under the umbrella of certain systems of power that impose a wide range of limitations and constraints on freedom of action and thought, and on participation in political activity. In the final analysis, political freedom is the criterion for all other forms of freedom.

The citizen-individual is the pillar of liberal thought, and it is from this perspective that al-Sayyid calls for people to be provided with a larger measure of freedom, and for constraints on thought and movement to be lifted if social problems are to be solved. Only by enjoying freedom can citizen-individuals develop from subjects into true citizens. Liberty is the threshold of progress within a liberal society that gives its members all necessary guarantees of their freedom, through the institutions of civil society vis-à-vis policy, economy and culture:

> What we now need to do is to broaden the scope of development towards individual freedom, so that people can restore the conditions necessary for progress to civilization and competition in life. We must relieve ourselves of the dependence on government to manage the affairs of life, great and small, and we must transcend the sense, so clearly pervasive in the East, that a nation is a group of

subjects living beneath a shepherd ruler who governs according to his own lights. We seem to have taken this sense as a basis for our policies and as a mode of conduct in our national life. This state of mind has diverted us from the principles necessary for modern progress, has divided our ranks and blocked our way to advancement. It has crushed our confidence and our sense of self-reliance, undermining that virtue which is the basis for success in the lives of individuals and nations.[11]

In al-Sayyid's view, a liberal framework for life would allow members of society to move on from their status as subjects to a lord or master – to an absolute ruler, in other words – and become citizens who play their part in the election, appointment and removal of the ruler according to the principles of democracy. Arabs, though, are still subjects to their rulers, who are 'monarchs' under a variety of forms and disguises. Herein lies the significance of liberalism as a political and economic creed capable of taking Arabs out of the feudal era to a stage of capitalism and individual enterprise, under which citizens' rights are protected by law. Until this stage is attained, progress will always be sporadic or endlessly deferred – where indeed it is possible at all.[12]

As the rational medium for meeting the requirements of practical situations, law guarantees freedom for the individual and for society, so securing natural rights, or an approximation to natural rights, and raising these to the level of civil rights. In al-Sayyid's view:

> All people have natural rights that legislators may not impeach: rights that existed before human assembly, which is accidental rather than essential; rights that effectively override human assembly, or, as we believe, natural actions that have been associated with humans from creation onwards and will be sustained until God inherits the earth and those who live on it. If the legislator is permitted to trifle with these rights according to his wish, the benefits of human gathering and assembly will cease to exist, and social association will become a penalty and a punishment rather than a gain.[13]

The natural and inalienable rights in question are: individual freedom in the broad sense; freedom of thought and faith; freedom of speech and writing; and freedom of education and learning; provided, in all cases, that these cause no harm to others. These are 'rights for all, providing the ties that knit human assembly together'.[14] Al-Sayyid concludes that 'the legislator may not frame a law whereby the right of freedom is to be taken away from individuals, groups or the whole nation without justification on the grounds of guarding the public interest from specific harm'.[15] If a legislator takes away individual rights, he will

undermine the education of the individual and the individual's capacity to use his
faculties in the interest of society, by a measure proportionate to the amount of
freedom he has lost. When the legislator usurps the freedom of an individual,
totally or in part, there will come about an obstruction to the individual's development, and to the progress of the community for which he himself was given
the responsibility for protection and safety and advancement through lawful
means.[16]

Basically, then, the absence of freedom incapacitates the development of the
individual with regard to social progress; and freedom depends not on human
will but on the capacity for action that makes history and permits human beings
to use their innovative and creative powers.

Such was the point reached in the liberal Arab conceptualization of freedom
in the first half of the twentieth century. Clearly it represented an advanced
stage of development – in principle, at least. From such a concept of freedom
we can discern a specific viewpoint on human rights, all the more so in that
essential human rights principles remain linked to their historical development
from liberal thought and, specifically, from Enlightenment philosophy.
Human rights cannot, nevertheless, be derived from mere theoretical principles; they are, above all, a matter of concrete application in political life, of
actual respect for such rights and compliance with them. All theories and ideologies claim to respect human rights, but only practice can bear such claims
out – or fail to bear them out.

The preceding pages have outlined the stance of Arab liberalism towards the
issue of freedom, as reflected by Adib Ishaq and Ahmad Lutfi al-Sayyid. What
is the position of present-day Islamic intellectuals vis-à-vis a general liberal orientation in Arabic thought?

We shall now discuss the viewpoint of Islamist thinkers on a liberal notion
of freedom, so preparing the groundwork for an analysis of their own critical
conceptualization of freedom and human rights. How do Islamist intellectuals
view themselves and their opponents? Does the image of Islam they portray
allow for any common ground, or at least for a neutral medium whereby other
thinkers may put forward their views? And do Islamic thinkers show an inclination to listen to such views?

According to the Islamist thinker Yousef al-Qaradhawi, Islam has two characteristics that distinguish it from all other theories and ideologies, particularly
in the Arab context. These are the godliness of objective and orientation, and
the godliness of origin and means. The first Qardawi explains in the following
terms:

The deeply-rooted objective and ultimate goal of Islam is to enjoy a good relationship with Almighty God and to obtain His approval. This is the objective of Islam, and, as such, it is the objective and orientation of man and his highest aspiration, pursuit and labour in life. Islam does, of course, have other human and social objectives and aims, but these we shall find, on consideration, to be subsidiary to the ultimate aim, which is the approval of Almighty God and the pursuit of His good reward. This is the objective and the aim of aims.[17]

As for the second characteristic of Islam, the godliness of origin and means, this is explained as follows:

The means established by Islam to reach its objectives and aims are of a pure, godly nature, stemming as they do from the Revelation of Almighty God to the seal of His prophets. These means did not result from the will of an individual, or family, or class, or party, or particular people, but rather from the will of God, Who provided them as guidance, light, lucidity, enunciation, purity and mercy for His worshippers.[18]

Such are the grounds on which contemporary Islamist intellectuals base their portrayal of Islam; a conceptualization that replicates Islam in the early days of its mission, when the essence of divinity encompassed the source as well as the objective and goal. The Islamist intellectual has thus become a spokesman for Heaven, and the individual Muslim a tantalized individual torn, in his deep yet divided consciousness, between, on the one hand, his status as a human being, and, on the other, his obligation to deny his humanity and raise himself to the level of the divine, so as to fulfil the aims of religion in this human world. The process leads, inevitably, to a dehumanized world in which divine qualities have not as yet been realized.

In the light of all this, the Islamist intellectual's evaluation of other attitudes takes the form of a sharp and utterly self-assured criticism. Dialogue moves in one direction only, with advice and instructions passed down from top to bottom. The right of the other party to participate in his own way, and enrich the dialogue, is disregarded.

In al-Qardawi's view, liberalism, in its entirety, in all its various images and forms, is 'an alien trend the West takes as its focal point and key guide in most of the affairs of life'.[19] Here revealed is sufficient reason for ruling out liberalism or any other creed. Since this or that doctrine does not emanate from God, it is by definition alien, imported from outside and lacking in any value for Arab countries, or at least for Islamic countries.

According to al-Qardawi, the elements characterizing the Arab liberalism prevalent before the military coups were the following:

1   Secularism, i.e., the separation of religion from the state.
2   National and pan-national orientation.
3   A feudal capitalist economy.
4   Personal freedom in the Western sense, entailing women's freedom to beautify themselves and mix socially.
5   Enabling foreign and positivistic laws.
6   The emergence of parliamentary representation and the proclamation of the nation as the source of power.[20]

I shall not here discuss certain specific elements in al-Qardawi's argument, such as his tendency to limit women's freedom in terms of use of cosmetics and mixing with men. What he seems to favour most is the political aspect of liberalism:

> It is the establishment of a parliamentary life whereby people may elect their representatives in the source of legislative authority by free and direct public election of those candidates obtaining the majority of votes. This elected authority is the only legislator for the nation and the only monitor over the executive power ... through these elected authorities, people will hold their destiny in their own hands and the nation will be the source of power.[21]

Despite this enthusiastic admiration for liberalism and its democratic system, al-Qardawi is disinclined to follow the path of democracy to its end. He makes a number of observations and comments which, in effect, undermine the essence of the democracy he has idolized. In his discussion of the legislative power, he argues as follows:

> The elected authority cannot legislate beyond what God has authorized. It cannot validate the forbidden, or prohibit the permissible, or disable an obligation. The prime legislator is Almighty God, and humans can legislate for themselves only within the limits of what has been permitted to them; that is to say, on issues relating to those interests in their lives which have not been covered by stipulation, or which allow for different understandings and interpretations to be weighed according to the rules of Shariah ... It must be said, therefore, that the nation is the source of power only within the confines of Islamic Shariah. Within the legislative bodies there must also be a council of competent jurists who will interpret the laws presented to them and draw conclusions from them, with a view to establishing their legality or contravention.[22]

He goes on to add further conditions and limitations on those who present themselves as candidates for legislative councils. They must have religious and moral qualifications alongside such things as experience in public affairs. No one should be permitted to put himself forward, as a candidate to represent the nation, if he is a lecher or drunkard, or if he discards prayer or disregards religion.[23] It is clear enough that al-Qardawi is effectively annulling liberalism and democratic life, especially in the constraints and limitations he imposes on the principle that the nation is the source of power; such power exists only within the framework of Islamic Shariah. This modification shifts things away from a view of man as focus – a democratic vision of the world – towards a theological vision whereby God is taken as the centre of the world and man as a creature whose function is to meet objectives and targets not his own. As such the contemporary Islamist thinker is far from any discovery of the concept of man on which democratic life is founded. The modern state can assume a secular character only when it recognizes that its systems of law are based, in the final analysis, on one central concept: the concept of man.

All this is confirmation that present-day Islamic thought remains unable to form the basis of a modern state, in which the concepts of man, freedom and human rights occupy a central position vis-à-vis other ideas, both at the theoretical level and in concrete practice in the spheres of legislation and implementation.

In the absence of such concepts, even in the theoretical systems set forth by modern Islamic intellectuals, al-Qardawi is able to claim that 'the most serious defect of secular liberal democracy is the lack of, indeed the deliberate disregard of, the spiritual element; a turning away from God and rejection of His guidance'.[24] In his view, there is one prime cause for the failure of democracy in the Arab-Islamic context:

> We Muslims have no faith in it, nor do we believe in its legitimacy. For that reason we do not readily give it our loyalty and respect. We remain firmly convinced that liberal democracy, like all other systems made by human beings for themselves, apart from the guidance and the enlightenment of God, is a defective system.[25]

Secular liberal democracy fails to find acceptance with contemporary Islamist intellectuals because, quite simply, it is not a religion; and more specifically because it stands opposed to the Islamic religion on a number of issues and questions. What we are dealing with here, clearly, is a criticism of democracy from the outside; one that makes no attempt to discuss, in any depth, the viewpoint it opposes and rejects, or to study the internal elements of the theory against which it decides. This is the most fragile form of criticism.

Al-Qardawi further clarifies his rejection of liberalism by the argument that Eastern nations, in contrast to other peoples, have a natural disposition to accommodate only religious thought. The Western mind (he continues) is prepared to accept science and the disciplines and methodologies springing from it, whereas the nations of the East, especially Turks, Arabs, Berbers and some others, have a more intense need for religion, which, in Ibn Khaldoun's view, has a powerful hold on them.[26] Al-Qardawi thus reverts to the position of Renan over a century before, when the latter posited that the Semitic mentality was naturally inclined to religion, metaphysics and mythology, whereas Aryans and Europeans rather possessed a rational mentality capable, by nature, of understanding science and philosophy, benefiting from these, and taking them as sources of guidance for their lives.

Here, then, is the viewpoint of one of the most prominent contemporary Islamic thinkers on liberalism, and on Arab liberalism in particular. In order further to clarify the position of contemporary Islamist intellectuals vis-à-vis the problems of freedom and human rights, we shall now consider these two issues from a political viewpoint, since they have relevance both to the state and to civil society. The measure of democracy within the state is reflected in the strength, prosperity and effectiveness of its civil society. Similarly, the absence of democracy is associated with a weak or non-existent civil society. Freedom and human rights are, in consequence, prominent, obvious and strong in the first case, and weak, often perhaps lacking, in the second.

Let us, then, ask the following question. Is it possible for Islam to be a spiritual system, regulating the relation between man and God in a private fashion, while turning over the issues of politics and the state to policy-makers and political philosophers, and over and above them – to the people, who will decide for themselves and be accountable for the choice they make, rightly or wrongly, of their representatives in the legislative authority?

To this question modern Islamic thinkers answer unanimously in the negative. Islam, they underline, is at once a religion and a state – or rather, the state is an essential aspect of Islam. It is a function of the Islamic state to organize all the affairs of society, including the structure, form and competence of the state, and all the rights and duties of individuals within that society. On this issue, Muhammad Yousef Moussa makes the following observation:

> Islam has not simply introduced the true religious faith, nor has it simply introduced the ideal moral system upon which society must be founded. It has also introduced a just and tried Shariah that governs man and his conduct and transactions in all cases, both in relation to himself and in his relations with his family and society, and his relations with his state and other states. In this respect, it is

distinct from other revealed religions. By virtue of this quality, Islam has organized all these various relationships, has laid down the principles and general tenets upon which they are founded, and has clarified – albeit in a broad sense – every kind of governing legislation. In consequence, Islam has introduced legislative measures indispensable for founding the nation and the state, on grounds that are reasonable, acceptable and sufficient for meeting the needs of any society and any nation, at all times and in all places. Because Islam was the final, decisive religion to come to the whole world, it has not left its nation to take what it wished from the legislation and laws, but has rather supplied them with what both society and nation can be founded upon, in all the aspects and affairs of life, in the case of peace and the case of war alike.[27]

Rashid al-Ghanoushi, the leader of the Tunisian Islamic Renaissance movement, takes the same position:

> Discussion of public freedoms is an integral part of the discussion of the Islamic political system. It presupposes the comprehensive nature of the Islamic system in relation to the life of mankind both on the individual and communal level, and the inter-relatedness of all its components, in terms of faith, rituals, morals and intentions, inseparably. This we take as an unquestionable starting point, decisively established by all those concerning themselves with the Islamic faith – Muslims and non-Muslims alike . . . The proof of reality has been more eloquent than any argument in refuting the claims of secularists. It has confirmed that Islam is a religion and a state, or that the religion of the state is one of its aspects.[28]

In the understanding of contemporary Islamist thinkers, then, Islam is at once a religion and a state, and any separation of religious and secular authorities will, in the light of this, be viewed as a form of rebellion against the requirements of divine rule. This implies condemnation of anyone who advocates such a separation between religion and the state, or between this world and the hereafter, or between the political and civil on one hand and religion and the sacred on the other.

For al-Ghanoushi, as for almost all Islamist thinkers, the notion of vicegerency – that man is God's vicegerent on earth – is the bedrock on which the Islamic political philosophy of government is based. The theory entails two essential elements.

It entails, first, acknowledgement of the singular oneness of God and that the Almighty is God and King and Ruler of all, with no successor or partner and no rival to the law He ordains.

Man, for his part, is a creature dignified with reason, freedom, responsibility and a message. Holding such dignity, he has been accorded rights upon which no one can encroach. He also bears burdens he cannot relinquish. The rights represent a pact or contract: 'Men must worship God, Who has no rival, according to His Shariah. In return, they will merit from their God blessings and satisfaction, and gain in this life and the life to come.'[29]

The first consequence of the contract of vicegerency so conceived is, naturally, the absolute predominance of Shariah over any other authority. This may be briefly summarized in a single text: 'The text of Revelation, as a Book and as a Sunna, is definitive in its source and signification. It is the supreme constitution of the Islamic state.'[30]

The second constitutional consequence of the vicegerency agreement is that 'the general organization of the Islamic government may likewise be summarized in a single word: shura'.[31] Text and shura are, according to al-Ghanoushi, 'the two prime principles upon which the Islamic state is founded, and the two necessary fruits of the theory of vicegerency which is the cornerstone of political ideology'.[32] If we view shura as a form of political practice involving a measure of consultation and resort to the views of certain people able to provide advice to guide the ruler, the system is seen to be governed by an authority higher than its own, i.e., the text of Revelation as represented by the Book and the Sunna. Shura does not, in fact, entail any absolute power, or any sense of self-sufficiency, as a source of legislative power. It is fundamentally constrained by a divine text above humanity, and by the interpretation of those who hold power, or those who are delegated to explain the text to the ruler, or to the group or class to which he belongs. In other words, the efficacy of shura, already subject to constraint, descends progressively to still further inefficacy and reduction of power. In interpreting the Text, the ruler resorts to narrow, attenuated ideological foundations, which suit the interests of a certain sector of society and serve certain biased visions of government and politics.

Under the auspices of the Islamic state so conceived, the legislative powers are consistently limited and finite, regardless of any interpretative attempt to enhance them and broaden them into different areas. The interpreter is faced, in the final analysis, with an ahistorical text that must be recognized and kept intact, as a sacred text. For such a state, private faith or individual certainty, as a hidden constitution, is subsumed into a sacred text that may not be approached, whether by believers or non-believers, with a view to any form of amendment, development or change. This is how Islamist thinkers understand the meaning of the text: 'It is the ultimate ruler and the unrivalled authority; and this is the solid base upon which Islamic society is built, the power that institutionalizes and organizes community, state and culture. It is the source from which Islamic government draws its philosophy, values, forms, legislation, objectives and ultimate goals, the supreme governor . . . to whom everyone and everything belongs and subscribes. The Text is the constant, unchanging Shariah.'[33] This conclusive permanence and ahistorical tendency in thought and action do not simply create a political problem for Muslims. They also create a cultural problem, one that generates all kinds of political obstacles. It might be argued that the foundations of the tyranny now prevalent in most regions of the Arab and Islamic world stem from the core of this culture, a culture inherited from a definitive vision of history. According to this, the varied historical elements of life, for the individual and for society, can find their effective solution through a series of mental deductions whereby jurists move on to a new judgement supported by an old text. As such, fresh beginnings are impossible; the conclusive initial prescriptions of Shariah are sufficient for the needs of humanity at all times. Perpetuation of the despotic forms of government active in contemporary Arab and Islamic life – forms belonging, historically, to the pre-modern world era – emerges as reasonable, indeed positive and credible.

So it is that the Islamic community has been generally preserved and maintained, as firmly based and established as the text on whose foundation it has been institutionalized; and no development in political life can be entertained without a cultural change in the way the community understands and reads this text. Indeed, the very survival of the community can be explained only by reference to the text from which it has been miraculously produced.

> The divine text is therefore the essential fact within the community. The community could not have continued without the text, which is likewise its *raison d'être*. It is what gives its existence a sublime legitimacy. It is the path from which the Islamic community has stemmed and upon which the nation has been established.[34]

The very existence of the Islamic community is, then, characterized by sublimity and elevation. One can imagine the existence of transcendental or a priori ideas whereby the human mind works. Yet it is difficult, if not totally impossible, to imagine such sublime communities existing in reality. This sense of transcendentalism implies, on the one hand, ahistorical existence, and, on the other, the community's atrophy and seclusion within a dead culture. The community will only be resurrected when it has relinquished the culture of elevation al-Ghanoushi attaches to the Islamic community. Cultural development within Islamic thought is a necessary prerequisite for any serious transition from political despotism to democratic life and cultural pluralism.

Since the Text is the founder of the Islamic community and the elevator of its existence, al-Ghanoushi is able to argue as follows:

> Regardless of the occasional delinquency of government in Islamic history, Islamic Shariah has continued to provide the supreme legitimacy needed by all rulers, interpreters and thinkers to justify their actions and positions. The Islamic experience has not seen a theocratic ruler proclaim himself to be the actualized will of God, since Muslims know the will of God has been embodied in His Shariah. What was consistent with Shariah was right, and what violated it was wrong.[35]

Historical evidence points, however, to something else. The divine right of sovereigns has been a recurrent theme in the political life of Islamic communities. It has, indeed, perpetuated itself in new forms and images, like the authoritarian rule, supported by brutal security systems, of our own day. Even if we turn our eyes for a moment from the Umayyad power based on war and conquest, we might recall how the Commander of the Faithful during the Abbasid era was

> addressing people in his capacity as the shadow of God on Earth. God had placed in his hands the keys to His coffers, which he might open as he pleased and close as he wished. The theory of the divine right or sacred right of sovereigns was recognized during the Abbasid era and, at a later stage, among the Christian nations of Europe.[36]

This will suffice to refute any claim that the political life of Islamic societies has always been in a perfect and ideal state. Political life is a matter of concrete reality. These communities never existed in actual fact; they were only projected, in the light of an abstract mental image.

Al-Ghanoushi's conceptualization of the Text and its relation to the historical Islamic community leads, finally, to three conclusions:

> The government and dominance of Almighty God in the life of man was proclaimed in Revelation as a Book and as a Sunna. This is the source from which Shariah has derived. Islamic government merits obedience from its citizens only to the extent that the government in question demonstrates its total compliance with Shariah and commitment to it . . . The obedience of the Muslim to his government is not extended to the governor as a person but rather to the guardian of Shariah. He merits a reward for such obedience, and he will be a sinful person if he rebels against instructions that comply with the constitution of the state, that is, with Shariah.[37]

The first conclusion, then, is that governance belongs to God. Consequently, God is the centre of the universe and man enjoys only a secondary worth. This conclusion is sufficient in itself to form the basis of an undemocratic system within the community.

The second conclusion is that Shariah is a dual medium. On the one hand it is a medium between God and man, in that it involves the essential commandments directed from God to man. On the other hand, it is a criterion whereby man's conduct is evaluated and his nearness to or distance from the divine will is measured. In this sense, Islamic government becomes the bearer and guardian of Shariah as well as its prime interpreter.

This brings us to the third conclusion. Obedience to the government is not obedience to an individual human creature but rather submission to the guardian of Shariah – or else rebellion against him. The world of civil politics thus merges into a world of Shariah politics. The dimension of citizenship and humanity disappears from the individual, giving way to that of the worshipper or pious person, whose conduct is placed between two poles: those of poverty and taking for himself; in other words, of obedience and rebellion.

What is clearly set forth here is a sacred language upon which no social, economic or political system can be built; a language entailing old concepts inconsistent with the current requirements of modernization. In viewing the Text as the foundation and constitution of the state, and in drawing an analogy between, on the one hand, obedience and disobedience to the state and, on the other, the same two stances vis-à-vis the guardian of Shariah, al-Ghanoushi is effectively calling for the establishment of a theocratic government. In the light of this, he maintains that 'the gravest rebellion against the provisions of Islamic Shariah is the disregard of commitment to its commands'.[38] The political issue is thus resolved into a religious question, and the social issue – that is, the problem of government and the relationship between governor and governed – is reduced to a question of worship; in other words, to the relationship between man and his Creator. Individual and personal human affairs are thereby merged into the affairs of the citizen within the state and within civil society. The political aspect of Islamic government is, in the eyes of contemporary Islamist intellectuals, apolitical in practice, because such government does not conceptualize the state according to ideas of citizen and citizenship, but rather according to a personal and spiritual dimension relating to individual persons rather than to a system of relationships among individuals. Such systems can be observed, understood and evaluated on objective grounds, because associated with specific constitutional rights in the modern state.

Such a conceptualization has had a profound impact, among modern Islamic thinkers, on the development of views and outlooks vis-à-vis the issue of freedom and human rights, and vis-à-vis the implications of these concepts within the modern Islamic state. Whatever objective value their notions about the nature and function of freedom may have, these thinkers invariably conclude that the worship relationship between the Creator and the creature is, in the words of al-Ghazali, 'the highest authority in Islam, and the decisive distinction between Islam and atheism'. This relationship is the objective that must guide human beings in their lives, and be their road to gaining the blessings of Divine approval in the afterlife. This means that life, in the sense of 'this world', does not lie at the core of a Muslim's soul; for man is, quite simply, not the centre of the universe. In the final analysis, anything may be deferred till the promised day.

Modern life, which is based on reason, is also based on the concept of the citizen and on the concept of a right to be met here and now, through the agencies of the modern state – the legislative, executive and judicial institutions. In such a state, the separation of powers and the autonomy of law are fully observed and respected. This is the best model yet discovered by human society in organizing life. It protects the rights of individuals and communities alike, acknowledging that the rights of the community should not supersede those of the individual, and that the state should not overrule the distinctive aspirations of the individual citizen.

When we turn to the problem of freedom, we find contemporary Islamist thinkers handling the issue at various levels – all of them converging, in the final analysis, to entail a type of individual or personal relationship between God and man. These conceptualizations tend to lose their efficacy and value in any procedural definition, or in any useful or meaningful application within the social and political life of the state in a particular place at a particular time. The first of the various levels is the metaphysical one. Here we find al-Ghazali, for instance, presenting the question more or less within the traditional framework of the Ash'ari school and classical Islamic scholastic theology. In his view, questions relating to freedom are the same as questions relating to finality and preordained prescription, and to fatalism and choice. It is a question of somehow reconciling the two opposite extremes within a single unity encompassing positive and negative sides alike. It is the kind of unity whereby the human being merges and vanishes into the ultimate Divine Self. Politically, it is expressed in terms of the unitary quality of the governor and of the necessity of deferring everything for a promised day, since it is impossible to recognize intention, and because the intent of a ruler, who could well be a pious person, may be better than his actions.

Al-Ghazali draws a distinction between two kinds of action in connection with the theory of finality and prescription: one in which we are constrained and one in which our will is completely free:

> There are things that take place by the capacity of the Supreme Force, and in accordance with the Divine Will. They are imposed on people in a voluntary or obligatory manner, regardless of whether they are aware or unaware of them. These include conditions like life and death, health and sickness, affluence and hardship, all of which happen without intervention by man. It is the fingers of Fate that, explicitly or implicitly, move the event, and life is thus directed according to the wish of the Creator of life: 'From God, verily, nothing is hidden on earth or in the heavens. He it is Who shapes you in the wombs as He pleases. There is no god but He, the Exalted in Might, the Wise.' (3, *Al 'Imran*, 5–6.)[39]

The second components of this principle of finality and prescription – or Fate and Divine Decree – relate to acts contrary to those stated in the first part. In performing these acts:

> We feel the alertness of our minds, the motion of our tendencies and the control of our conscious ... We feel the independence of our will and ability in acts that we do within these two spheres. This feeling is sufficient to demonstrate the freedom of our will and our capacity. But some say that it may be a deceptive sensation. We therefore either believe or disbelieve this feeling by referring to the Holy Quran for interpretation and certainty. We find in the Quran a confirmation of this initial feeling and an exaltation of the freedom of human will. 'Say: "O ye men! Now Truth hath reached you from your Lord! Those who receive guidance, do so for the good of their own souls; those who stray, do so to their own loss: And I am not set over you to arrange your affairs."' (10, *Yunus*, 108.) In fact, the nature of a religion, which comprises both the assignment and the test, cannot be fulfilled at all if the will is enslaved and constrained.[40]

In response to this contradiction of extremes and sharp juxtaposition between obligation and choice – and these distinctions have burdened the Islamic consciousness, troubling it throughout its history – al-Ghazali resorts to the traditional Ash'ari argument on the issue of obligation. There is, he states, no conflict between the freedom of the way and the fact that our actions do not go outside the comprehensive and all–encompassing divine knowledge.

> The pages and the visions of the Divine Knowledge are not directly associated with actions in which our acts are administered and moved. The association is rather one of discovery and clarification. It follows rather than precedes the action. The ultimate characteristic of such knowledge is that it does not only

reveal the present, but also uncovers the past and the future, and reveals things
as they were and as they will be and as they are now.[41]

The question remains, then, unresolved. It is the same old metaphysical question that has been posed by Islamic culture since it first became self-aware:
What is the relationship between the accidental human action and the eternal
divine knowledge? When the intellectual presents the issue within the framework of traditional scholastic theology, he will find no answer to this question
other than al-Ghazali's. The alternative answer is the Mu'tazili solution, which
argues that man is the creator of his actions – a solution that was rejected by the
majority of Muslims.

Other solutions propounded by Islamic philosophy were never accepted
outside the narrow circles of philosophers. This explains why the method of
the scholastic theologians has exercised dominance even on modern Islamic
thinking. Modern Western civilization, and ancient Greek civilization before it,
cast aside all reservations on the matter, readily accepting that man is free; and
promotion of the idea of freedom led to the concept of democracy and the
democratic system, initially in Athens and more recently in the Western world
as a whole.

Al-Qardawi argues that freedom has many aspects without which man's
humanity cannot be fulfilled. It is an essential prerequisite for individual happiness, and security is one of its components. Al-Qardawi seems here to be
reflecting his own personal experience, when the Muslim Brothers were subjected to a long political repression in the modern history of Egypt. He says:

> Freedom is not a secondary issue at the margin of human life. It is a basic require-
> ment for human life . . . Individuals cannot enjoy their humanity, and their dig-
> nity, and their ability to design their own paths in life, outside an environment of
> freedom, which allows them to develop and mature. Freedom is a necessary
> condition for the attainment of happiness. People cannot be happy if they are
> forced to do things they do not accept, or to like things they do not agree with,
> and to swallow ideas and systems they do not like. Happiness, in turn, cannot be
> achieved without a sense of security. Individuals who do not enjoy freedom can-
> not enjoy security.[42]

It is true that freedom is a necessary condition for life and existence, giving
individuals their distinct identity and the ability to exercise choice and action.
The ability to act entails a freedom necessarily linked to responsibility, and this
al-Qardawi rightly points out: 'A mature person assumes full responsibility for
his action, and endeavours, to this end, to carry out his duties and shape his
life in co-operation with others.'[43] In addition to this personal and private

dimension of freedom, al-Qardawi draws attention to the decisive significance of freedom for society as a whole, since freedom is the only mechanism whereby social progress can be weaned from its errors:

> Freedom is necessary for society in order to amend the course of action, to root out corruption and to criticize exaggeration or inefficiency in planning and execution, and also in thought and conduct . . . Climates of repression, exhaustion and fear will tie up tongues and pens, and prevent them from pointing out mistakes or demonstrating error. Mistakes then multiply, felony worsens, and things move ever from bad to worse.[44]

Al-Qardawi speaks, finally, of another type of freedom, which he calls the freedom of the citizen and regards as the most significant form of freedom for individuals within modern society and the modern state. This directly involves the right of the individual to practise freedom, and to take part in building the political, economic and social world, within the state, that citizens set up in their country. In his discussion of the freedom of the citizen, he distinguishes between two aspects: the negative side, involving the removal of obstacles, and a positive component that relates directly to the practice of freedom in the state and in society. The negative aspect means:

> Removal of fetters and rescuing people from any domination that intimidates them, or obstructs their conduct, or governs their thought, consciousness, will or movement. In removing such domination, be this of a political, religious or social nature, individuals are enabled to lead their lives with a sense of peace, security and independence in what they take or leave.[45]

The positive element, on the other hand, is represented in the following:

> Intellectual and political freedom that allows the citizen to think and express his thoughts in legitimate ways, and to criticize situations, systems, trends and types of conducts . . . It is the freedom of the individual to deliver a public address, or conduct an open seminar, or write a book containing his opinion and criticism, or publish a newspaper free of the control of the government and its political party, or form an intellectual or political society opposing the government's ideological, political or economic line.[46]

One can only praise, and accept, what al-Qardawi says on the freedom of the citizen in both its negative and positive aspects. This does not mean, nevertheless, that we should be anything but hostile to his categorical judgement on the necessity of killing apostates and renegades. His position on this is hardly consistent, after all, with his call for citizens to be free to set up political assemblies and establish a free press through which citizens can express their opposition to official state policy in political and economic areas. Nor is the viewpoint in line with his demand that citizens should feel themselves safe from harm, imprisonment or exile by the state, or from other illegal constraints imposed on citizens by Arab and Islamic governments. Al-Qardawi is an ideologue and a theorist of the Islamic movement. He offers the following advice on what the movement should do to modernize itself for the future:

> It should not take a harsh view of individuals and the society around it. It should not rush to accuse individuals of heresy or expel them from Islam on controversial and questionable grounds. The benefit of the doubt must be given, and Muslims should, as far as possible, be given the opportunity to mend their ways and restore their pure state. Most of those accused are in fact ignorant people in need of teaching rather than apostates who should be killed. Their blood and property are protected by their testimony that 'there is no god but God and Muhammad is the Messenger of God'; and God will pass His judgement on them. Those who have proclaimed and propagated their blasphemy in public should be placed in the station they have chosen for themselves, and they should be judged accordingly.[47]

Is the killing of the so-called apostate, for his conflict with the state or the ruling party, consistent with advocacy of freedom for the citizen and of political freedoms of all kinds? The freedom of the citizen advocated by al-Qardawi will be incomplete unless the individual is granted freedom of thought, belief and faith, within any religion or without commitment to any religion. If a person should be denied such rights while in opposition, we can imagine his attitude easily enough when he becomes unrivalled ruler, exercising power in the state. Arab intellectuals are at present facing two grave threats. The first is the power of the state, which brooks no criticism, imprisoning or exiling them, or forcing them to seek human refuge. The second is the power of the opposition, especially the Islamist opposition, which threatens death to anyone who thinks in ways different from its own.

　　　　Another contemporary Islamist thinker, Rashid al-Ghanoushi, propounds a third position on the issue of freedom. He offers a selective and conciliatory approach, starting out from universal conventions on human rights and the rights of the citizen. Freedom, he says, is natural for human beings, without distinction. Subsequently he concludes that the individual is not originally free; rather freedom is a legal entitlement granted to people by virtue of prophecy and Revelation. In defining the essential rights and freedoms, al-Ghanoushi starts out from a clearly democratic and liberal viewpoint:

The nation is the source of all powers and the only institution having absolute predominance in the process of governance, either through selecting and monitoring the ruler, or by taking part with him and holding him accountable, or even by removing him from office.[48]

Essential freedoms he defines as 'the series of human rights that are recognized by the state for citizens, such as the right to take part in government and influence it by means of direct or indirect election, and the right of information, assembly, formation of parties and unionization'.[49]

He takes specific guidance from the Universal Declaration of Human Rights:

Every individual has the right to manage the public affairs of his country, either directly or through freely elected representatives . . . [and every person has the right] to take up public posts in his country . . . The will of the people is the source of the government's authority, and the expression of this will takes the form of periodic honest elections by means of a secret ballot in which all people have an equal voice, or by any comparable procedure that guarantees the freedom of voting.[50]

Clearly al-Ghanoushi is here citing the most recent liberal ideas about freedom, and about organizational procedures for ensuring its proper application. Al-Ghanoushi, with his knowledge of French culture, must have been thoroughly familiar with such notions, which will have influenced him via his association with the liberal system during his stay in Europe as an exile.

Soon, though, al-Ghanoushi, takes a step backwards, speaking of freedom in its Islamic origins, and distancing himself from all the liberal notions of freedom he had initially adopted and supported. In developing this (Islamic) freedom, he falls far below the liberal level with which he had started out. He also falls short of a modifying and authenticating liberalism in the context of traditional Islamic thought itself. His attempt to blend various elements leads not to a coherent system of components but rather to a mixture of disparate notions. He ends up, in fact, by standing against human rights declarations vis-à-vis freedom, considering these 'merely guarantees given to the bourgeoisie as a weapon against feudalism and the Pope. As such, they are an assortment of fragmented ideas which, in turn, were refuted by socialist systems that emphasized social rights and imposed a new form of tyranny.'[51]

In making this simplified assessment, he disregards a long process of human endeavour in which Muslims, unfortunately, played no part. For five centuries these endeavours have continued in the Western world, from the Renaissance up till today, in a progressive line culminating in the form of political democracy now mostly practised in the industrialized countries. Other ancient people – the Indians, for instance – are now attempting to proceed along the same lines. Nor do their culture and history present any obstacle on their road to the democratic system as a political mode and as a way of life.

For al-Ghanoushi, then, freedom in the Islamist sense means that 'we undertake our responsibilities in a positive manner, and fulfil our duties voluntarily by complying with commands, and avoiding things that are prohibited, and bringing ourselves to the level of the caliphs and God's holy persons'.[52] Whatever the value of this analysis of freedom, linked to duty and responsibility, al-Ghanoushi's definition overlooks the point that closeness to God is a relative, subjective and personal matter. Freedom in its original meaning is designed, on the one hand, to reflect human action through history, and, on the other, to organize relations between individuals in society in a rational fashion. This is what prompted the development of institutions and the setting up of constitutions, with a view to making social life practicable and possible, and enabling the individual to express himself, through these institutions, by carrying out his duties and winning his rights. In contrast, the pursuit of goodness makes freedom a subjective value, with no objective impact on the life of individuals and societies or on the institutions through which human existence can be fulfilled.

In an attempt to reinforce his stance, al-Ghanoushi approvingly cites the viewpoint of 'Allal al-Fasi, who views freedom as an integral element of worship. Freedom, according to al-Fasi, is a legal entitlement rather than a natural right. Humans could not have obtained freedom without Revelation. Man was not born free; he was rather born to become free.[53]

A similar viewpoint is cited from Hassan al-Turabi:

> Freedom is not an end in itself but rather a means for worshipping God. This sense of servitude does not call for any departure from faith. When the faithful worship God, their feelings and conduct are driven by love, reverence and gratitude for the blessings they receive. This makes freedom both the instrument for – and the fruit of – the love of God. If freedom is associated, in its legal aspect, with permission and allowance, it is, in its religious essence, a path to the worship of God. It is the duty of Man to liberate himself for his God, and to be sincere in the opinions and positions he holds. Freedom in the Islamic conceptualization is absolute, because it is a ceaseless pursuit of the absolute. The more faithful man is in worshipping God, the more liberated he becomes from all other creatures in the world, and the larger measure he attains of human perfection.[54]

According to al-Fasi, then, freedom is a divine gift linked to Revelation. This means that, no matter how high the level of freedom attained, no matter how long the road travelled towards it, none of this can go beyond what has been prescribed by Revelation. Without historical consciousness, it is impossible to imagine any concept beyond the infinite freedom that reflects human identity as manifested in history. Freedom will be manifested in a limitless variety of forms and images already delineated by Revelation in specific and concrete historical circumstances. But freedom, according to al-Turabi, is expressly a means to worship rather than an end in itself.

It is only partly true that freedom is a means. It is also an end per se. Indeed, it is actually impossible to draw a line between the means and the end regarding the concept of freedom, since the whole of human existence manifests itself through this medium. The point to be contested in al-Turabi's argument is that turning freedom into a means for worship effectively reduces the concept to a poor skeletal instrument used to alienate the human being from himself; man becomes, thereby, a dependent rather than a creative, action-oriented human being whose existence develops and flourishes through freedom alone. Freedom has, in fact, become a mere instrument for denying and abnegating individuals' privacy and creative capacity. For al-Turabi, human perfection is proportionate to a person's devotion to worship and detachment from nature and other creatures, including individuals and colleagues. This situation of virtual solitude prepares the grounds for mystical and subjective Sufi experience – for the death of the human dimension. Clearly, state and society cannot be dealt with on the basis of such a conceptualization of freedom. It is, moreover, inconceivable that experience of this kind can serve as an alternative to political democracy, and to public participation by the members of society with a view to modernizing state and community.

The preceding discussion shows how freedom, according to such prominent representatives of contemporary Islamic thought as al-Ghazali, al-Qardawi, al-Fasi, al-Turabi and al-Ghanoushi, is to be viewed as a form of religious faith or an instrument for worship; as a means whereby freedom is cancelled and annulled. The end of this process is, in effect, sublimation at a level above nature and all its beings and creatures (as advocated, for instance, by al-Turabi); in other words, sublimation in the form of personal spiritual experience. Freedom is only fulfilled when the individual departs from the very component qualities essential for establishing a modern state or civil society: community, citizenship, the state, modernity and historical process.

Al-Ghanoushi, who combines all these contradictions within a single position, comes up with a surprising statement. Islam, he argues, can absorb the Western democratic system and preserve its positive elements and genuine contribution to political thought, for Muslims and for humanity, through introducing the principle of *shura*, that is, the participation of the nation in government by its own will and through its guardianship and control of the ruler. Islam can develop its ethics and general principles into a system of government in much the same way that the Western mind dealt with our heritage in engineering and algebra, in developing them into an advanced technology. This is a feature of the scientific revolution and genius of the West: the capacity to turn ideas and values into machinery. Are we to reject these industrial and political technologies simply because they have been manufactured by the West? Or shall we rather say that this is our own commodity coming back to us? Wisdom is the end of the faithful's quest, and wherever there is interest there will be God's jurisprudence.[55]

We may set aside the rhetoric – a rhetoric that reduces the achievement of five centuries of Western civilisation to the return of an Islamic commodity Muslims have the right to take back in compliance with the ordinance of God. We should note, though, the puzzling and self-contradictory aim inherent in the propositions he puts forward. Al-Ghanoushi wishes Islam to encompass the Western democratic system; but he wishes simultaneously to develop the *shura* principle, which is an assemblage of ethics and moral tenets, into a model similar to Western political democracy but under a new Islamic label which he himself calls *shura*. Such an endeavour should not surprise us, for *shura* is, after all, the applied form of the Islamic theory of freedom. For al-Ghanoushi, Islam in general and the system of *shura* in particular is the only means of preserving political democracy while avoiding its defects.

> The mechanisms of democracy, like those of industry, are a human heritage that can be operated in various cultural environments and with different intellectual backgrounds ... These mechanisms are not necessarily inconsistent with the values of Islam, from which democracy can draw its best driving force and energy and efficacy. The values and philosophy of Islam will also preserve the democratic system from pitfalls and catastrophes, from imperialist wars, human impoverishment, social plagues, brutal epidemics, environmental pollution, the collapse of the family and social relations, the fatal isolation of the individual, the crisis of conscience and dominance of the strong over the weak ... This, against the chaos, tyranny and underdevelopment manifested at all levels in the world of backwardness – which includes the Islamic world.[56]

This text in fact encapsulates al-Ghanoushi's most heartfelt dream – one representative of the contemporary liberal democratic intellectual. It is, though, a dream that tends to oversimplify realities in an almost naive fashion, ignoring all the essential differences between the categories in question, between democracy and industrial mechanisms. Since planes are produced in America and Europe, and used in the Islamic world, why (he asks) should we not apply the same principle to democracy? He draws a further artificial analogy when he claims that introducing Islamic values into democracy would save the present democratic system from the disasters and wars it has undergone, and that the merger of democracy and the Islamic *shura* system will take the Islamic world out of backwardness. Al-Ghanoushi barely seems aware that dealing with machinery and technology is less complex and elaborate than a transfer and exchange of cultures. If things were really that simple, there would have been no need for the countless seminars and conferences about the transfer of technology to the Third World. Cultural action clearly involves cultural interaction of considerable complexity.

Al-Ghanoushi sustains and complements his first dream with a second, also relating to democracy and *shura*; the dream of an intellectual whose mind teems with conflicting cultures. He wishes to project a concrete culture, but the variegated forms of his discourse contain a subtext that reveals what he actually wishes to hide. He makes the following proposition:

> The democratic system has worked within the framework of Christian values, producing Christian democracies; and in the context of socialist philosophies, producing socialist democracies; and within the ambit of Judaism, producing Jewish democracy. Is it not possible for the system to be operated within the framework of Islamic values, to produce Islamic democracy?[57]

What induces al-Ghanoushi to expend so much effort in attempting to harmonize what is, by definition, a cluster of incompatible ideas?

There are two reasons. First, al-Ghanoushi does not wish Islam to entail 'a severance with the contemporary cultural heritage, but rather an extension that keeps the best and avoids the destructive negative elements in the tradition'.[58] He is well enough aware that the current of contemporary civilization is unstoppable, that globalization is inevitable even for strong nations, let alone for weak states and cultures. His language here is a form of precautionary warning. Without revealing the facts and realities openly, it is nonetheless aware of them. The second reason is that al-Ghanoushi's faith in democracy alerts him to the risks of becoming enclosed and of trying to ignore concrete realities. 'Even the form of Islamic rule,' he cautions, 'would not provide sufficient guarantees in the absence of the democratic system.'[59] He then proceeds to paint a rosy picture of Islamic *shura* as the applied model for the Islamic theory of freedom, especially in its political aspects. The picture is in fact weak and altogether unconvincing. Advocating *shura* as a basis for democratic political procedures is merely ideological in the negative sense of the term. Those wishing to place *shura* at the centre of Islamic political theory commonly build their argument on a number of Quranic verses and *hadith*s which they interpret in their own way, to support their argument for a specific kind of political organization within state and society. Two of the Quranic quotations are: 'Their affairs by mutual Consultation' (42, *Al-Shura*, 38); and 'And consult them in affairs of moment' (3, *Al 'Imran*, 159). Interpretation of these verses differs, as to whether *shura* is a principle to be used in organizing political life or whether its application is general and non-political.

The prime argument against those putting forward *shura* as a political process equivalent to Western democracy is that Islamic Shariah is divine in nature, with God as the one and only Legislator. The proposition reflects an unconscious tendency among ordinary Muslims and the Muslim elite alike. If the proposition is correct, what is there left for people to do in the legislative sphere? Islamic *fiqh* was, it would seem, fully aware of this issue, and did not assign a special section for *shura* in the many and varied chapters and doctrinal writings on jurisprudence. In contrast, jurists did restrict the interpretation they applied in drawing judgements from the texts of the Holy Book and the *hadith*. Muslims had no need of a legislative authority because the nation was not the source of powers. God, Muslims believed, was the Great Legislator and the source of any legitimacy and legality enjoyed by men in this world, regardless of their rank or competence, even in the field of politics and legislation.

Modern Islamic thinkers are generally inclined to define *shura* in broad terms as 'accepting the right of the "successor" nation to public participation in the affairs of governance which is, indeed, one of its legitimate obligations'.[60] According to al-Turabi, *shura* is

> one of the principles of religion and a prerequisite for succession, i.e., the transfer of divine power to the faithful people who have given their pledge to worship God. *Shura* is, therefore, the backbone of the nation's power and the pillar of its faithful performance of government on the basis of participation, cooperation and responsibility. It is a participation that God has delegated to His nation on the level of legislation, of establishing government and drawing up the necessary laws for it, and safeguarding it and enjoying its fruits.[61]

Al-Turabi is here returning to his definition of authority as being essentially divine in nature. He enjoins people, through the *shura* system, to play their part in implementing the authority of Shariah within their society. The religious character, and especially the worship element, is thus fully maintained with respect to *shura*, as opposed to its role as a strictly political and civil process.

From the perspective of the Islamic *shura* system, we may envisage authority – in which the political and the juristic are inseparable – as a hierarchical pyramid headed by God, followed by the Prophet, then by the guardian rulers, and finally by the faithful in general. This is the implication of the Quranic verse: 'O ye who believe! Obey God and obey the Apostle and those charged with authority among you.' (4, *Al-Nisa'*, 59.) In other words, the supreme authority within Islamic society is God. As a result:

No creature shall be obeyed in things against Him. Obedience to the Messenger (may God pray upon him) is the practical form of submission to God. These are followed in rank by the authority of the nation, whose legitimate influence is confined within God's Shariah as laid down in the Book and the Sunna. Any Muslim holding authority . . . must be obeyed within his area of competence as long as he delivers that with which he was entrusted, within the limits of Shariah. Any dispute between individuals or authorities must find its conclusive resolution in the Book and the Sunna. The Quran and the Sunna embody the ultimate Law that governs the conduct, alike, of those charged with authority and of Muslims in general. The former are the evaluators of any new judgemental interpretation, and will assure themselves that such interpretations do not contradict the Text and are such as to fulfil the objectives and the general principles of Shariah.[62]

This analysis leads us to two conclusions. The first is that *shura* differs from democracy and that the two systems absolutely cannot be reconciled one with another. One modern Arab analyst makes the following observation:

Thinkers in the traditional heritage camp, who make *shura* equivalent to democracy, can offer only the model of Caliph 'Umar ibn al-Khattab, whose way of rule was a blend of justice and despotism . . . *Shura*, in its traditional Arab-Islamic content, is an alternative not to absolute despotism but rather to one brand of despotism, practised by the unjust ruler till God gives him guidance by leading him to *shura*, or consultation. *Shura* entails seeking the opinion of wise and mature jurists and knowledgeable people and notables before carrying out any action. Consultation in this sense does not correct or constrain the ruler. He may ask for consultation, but he it is who takes the final decision, whether or not it accords with the consultation he has received.[63]

This makes clear the limited scope of action that is possible in practice, within the framework of the *shura* principle.

The second conclusion is that the common people exercise no power in practice, because they do not elect people to represent them in the legislative councils. According to some scholars, a body of experts may be set up to monitor actions by referring them to God and His Prophet, or by establishing 'an influential council which draws conclusions. It may consist of senior judges and learned people, standing supreme and functioning as a high court.'[64] Its judgement may be accepted, rejected or modified by Muslims, because the interpretation in question is personal, to be assessed against the texts of the Book and the Sunna with a view to establishing correspondence or contradiction.

There is another significant issue vis-à-vis the Islamic theory of freedom and its applications. *Shura*, which embodies the sole form of participation in political power, also involves the participation of a few members of the nation only, that is, of learned and knowledgeable individuals. These limitations mean that the majority of people will be totally deprived of any kind of participation in determining their future and the future of their society.

Shariah imposes a further constraint, on all Muslims. They are not permitted to change their faith by choosing another creed over that of Islam. If they do, they will be regarded as apostate and may, in the eyes of most jurists, and even in the eyes of intellectuals and legists generally, be killed. Apostasy does not only mean conversion from Islam to another religion, but also a shift to atheism or adoption of any of the philosophical and ideological disciplines that Islamic scholars and doctrinaires view as a form of heresy or aberrance, like existentialism, or Marxism, or even democracy.

Clearly, the challenges facing the true intellectual in the Arab and Islamic world are becoming ever more difficult; all the more so in view of the undeclared alliance between state and opposition – especially the Islamist opposition – against the genuine culture of rejection and the bearers of this culture. State and opposition are essentially fighting a single battle: the former to maintain a substantially corrupt power, the latter to attain power with an equally backward, often still more degenerate content. The only opposition in either case is the true or organic intellectual, facing two brutal authorities that do not recognize human freedom or human rights. So it is that state and opposition are brought together against the authentic culture that defends human freedom and rights, and promotes an open future in the face of those who consider themselves the final, ultimate authority in human history.

Chapter 11: The issue of government in modern Islamic thought

Ahmad Barqawi

Introduction

Islam remains a basic constituent of present-day Arabic culture and a source of notably influential political movements and ideologies. As a culture, Islam has a presence both in the spiritual and the practical lives of individuals. There is indeed hardly any aspect of life where it has no say, explicitly or implicitly, from matters of marriage, divorce and inheritance to selling, buying, contracts, penalties, diet, conversation, and, finally, the overall issues of government, authority and moral values. Since most Arabs are Muslims, the presence of Islam remains, despite all intervention by European modernism and its universal tendencies, a force unmatched by any other. Nor is Islam a channel for the cultural awareness of ordinary people only. Such awareness is shared by many of the elite; it has become comprehensive, constantly reproducing itself.

It is difficult, even so, to speak of a homogeneous Islamic identity encompassing the whole Islamic world. On a purely religious level, concerning metaphysical issues having their basis in the Book and the *sunna*, we do indeed find more homogeneity than difference. Such things as belief in one God, Who is the Creator of the universe; in human beings and angels; in revelation, the prophethood of Muhammad, Heaven, Hell, and the hereafter; in *salat*, fasting, Ramadan, *zakat*, pilgrimage, attestation – in all these things there is consensus among Muslims, Sunni and Shi'ite alike.

Such homogeneity, though, becomes harder to find once we move away from these parameters. Legislation, for instance, though based on the Quranic text, is open to types of interpretation so varied that they sometimes border on the contradictory. In Islamic theology, where the human interpretation of texts is involved, we find ourselves amid extensive disagreement.

The further Islam moves from the period of revelation, the greater the differences and divergent tendencies become. This is due, basically, to the

different perspectives on reality that arise, and from the desire to find some
way in which the text can address the new reality, with all the moral, political,
and social changes it entails.

This may explain why modern Islamic theology has found itself oscillating
between strict conservatism and modernization; the trend either to reconcile
the achievements of universal civilization with Islam or to reject them outright
is a key factor here. Although every contemporary theological movement
claims the text as its source, such claims need in practice to be treated with care.
Conservative Islamic theology, stemming ostensibly from the original text, the
Quran, actually springs from an older theology in which it finds ready answers
to present-day queries. Correspondingly, innovative theology, while again
claiming kinship with the text, adheres to a tradition of intellectual reading and
interpretation of that text. Each party claims a merely formal relation to the
text, when the true area of conflict is the nature of reality itself. As such, theology is actually a matter of ideology, with moral, political and metaphysical elements; and the political element stands out by virtue of its direct relation with
the issue of government. The stance of Islamic ideology – or theology – vis-à-
vis government is very much a central topic of discussion at present, both
within Islamic currents of thought and within opposing secular trends. The
topic has gained special prominence since the era of the Arab Renaissance.

We shall examine, in this essay, the two basic currents dominating present-
day Islamic thought: reform based on wisdom, and traditional thought
informed by ideas of governance.

I. Secularist elements in the thought of Muhammad Abduh

The issue of government in the context of religious reform, as viewed by
'Abdu, is inseparable from the framework of his religious reform movement as
a whole. To understand this framework we need to understand the network of
concepts informing his reform discourse: text, history, reason and interpretation. The very issue of government is effectively defined by these concepts in a
discourse designed to address reality. Islam is, above all else, a text and a history. The text is the Quran and the *hadith*; the history is the history of Islam
based on these two texts. If the text is a structure implying what is constant, history is the field of change and progress; the relation between history and text is
not one of correspondence but of difference. History has always been against
Islam as divine revelation. Islamic fact becomes weaker as history progresses.
If it did not, after all, religious reform would be unable to describe the reality

rejected; and if the religious reformer could view history as corresponding to the text, he would not oppose the reality in the first place. However, the best way to acquit the text of its responsibility vis-à-vis reality is to make a distinction between the divine and the worldly, the latter being the product of man's industry.

Man, in all his worldly affairs, is an 'industrial' world, clearly separated from nature and standing apart from its effects. His need for nature is the need of the workman for his tools. Such is man in his matters of eating and drinking, in his living conditions, and in the matters of his mind and soul. Religion is a divine state called for by human beings, received by minds through bearers of good tidings and warnings. It is acquired by those who have not been endowed with divine revelation, and transmitted through information and education.[1] The divine intervenes in the 'industrial' in order to elevate mankind's condition. Muhammad 'Abdu is profoundly struck by the ironic situation regarding Islam and Christianity. Islam calls for the assumption of power, yet Muslims are made subject to opponents not of their religion. And his astonishment grows greater still as he considers the following question: How could the Christian nations, who proclaim peace, subjugate those very Muslim nations who call for supremacy?

The divine cannot be held responsible for the present situation. This is the message of *Shaykh* Muhammad 'Abdu. For, if the divine were responsible, the modern West would not be so advanced, or the East so backward and weak. Therefore, there must be some contradiction between text and history; between the divine text and human history. But what, for 'Abdu, was the source of this contradiction? At a certain moment in Arab history, Islam was a source of progress – the prime force indeed. That moment passed, however, when certain people assumed religious robes and ascribed to religion such alien aspects as predestination, which became deeply rooted in people's minds and so disrupted healthy progress. In view of all this, the relation of past to present proves, for the religious reformer, to entail a deviation from genuine Islam.

Yet the current history of Muslims, in all its weakness and humiliation, cannot be explained solely by pointing to deviation from the text, or by making comparisons with the Muslim past. The backward state of Arabs and Muslims is only identified in the first place by comparison with European progress. This is a point agreed on by all reformers, Muslims and non-Muslims alike.

Europe stands for science, constitution, justice, economics, trade and armaments; and Europe, by reminding the reformer of the text itself, spurs him on to try and discover Europe within his text. The whole process has the feel of a historical irony.

The text and the East are contradictory, whereas the text and Europe correspond to one another. European concepts like science, democracy, justice and
reason are all recorded in the text; indeed, the text has called for them. What is
needed is to apply reason to the text itself. A religious reformer like 'Abdu has
no problem in finding textual proof for the importance of reason. The text is
full of calls to use the mind. Reason, for 'Abdu, is a basis for Islam. Moreover,
the concept of reason stands opposed to the habit of imitation. The latter may
be rightly or wrongly employed, usefully or harmfully. Animals may be excused
if they go astray for such a reason, but not human beings.[2]

'Abdu rejects imitation by reference to Islam itself. Precedence in time does
not, he believes, entail precedence in knowledge. Indeed, the one who comes
later has more knowledge of what went before, and is in a better position to
learn from past experience, a privilege denied to the one who came earlier.
Reason provides the means of interpreting the text in accordance with reality;
and reason does not assume its full power till it is able to exercise an unrestricted right to investigate all terrestrial and celestial affairs. How, then, can we
resolve the problem of government in 'Abdu's thought by reference to such
concepts, which are intellectual tools of reform?

To begin with, 'Abdu had to face the reality and nature of the actual state, in
Egypt and in the Ottoman state generally. On the theoretical level, then, we
have a confrontation between the state as it is and the state as it should be;
between the real, historical state as it stands opposed to the spirit of the age, and
the spirit of the text itself. The contrast with the spirit of the age is reflected in
one basic factor, historically applicable on the universal level: namely the
means by which authority is exercised. The West has arrived at the democratic
means, expressing the spirit of the people. This highly attractive notion
emerged as the ideal solution to the problem of Egyptian and Ottoman authority. The complexities of Egyptian authority went, however, far beyond the matter of Ottoman authority over the country. In Egypt itself there was a royal
authority, arrogant and allied with an occupying power. To reject the relation
between the two authorities was only possible if authority could proceed from
the people, in the teeth of the occupying power. In a highly significant text,
Shaykh Muhammad 'Abdu says:

> The one thing we have learned from the British is that we need to unite if we wish
> them to leave. Before and during [the First World War] we fought to do away
> with the tyranny of our rulers. We complained of the Turks and regarded them
> as foreigners. We hoped to improve ourselves politically and advance along the
> path of freedom, like the European nations. But now we know there is a worse
> tyranny and enmity than that of the Turks, who are our brothers in religion if not

in race. If we were left alone with them, we should know how to advance in peace. We want just one thing from you [the British]: leave us in peace, now and for ever.[3]

When asked about Khedive Tawfiq, the *Shaykh* said: 'We do not want traitors with Egyptian faces and English hearts.'[4] This clearly indicates the basic trend in 'Abdu's thought: an end to tyranny, promotion of political reform, advance along the road of freedom like Europe, and resistance to European hegemony. The despotic authority is of two kinds, Ottoman and Egyptian, the latter a client of the British. In fighting the despotic Ottoman authority, the question of government remains within the same household; but fighting the Egyptian also involves fighting the foreign British enemy. And yet this foreign enemy represents the path of progress, towards freedom; and, as such, we have to advance along the same lines. No irony is intended here. This is the point at which the patriotic and the historical meet. A sense of patriotism does not mean refusal to accept the experience of the other, only to reject enslavement by that other. Nor does the historical sense entail blind acceptance of foreign authority, but rather resistance to it. In sum, rejection of tyranny is coupled with rejection of a form of government supported by a foreign power.

But why should tyranny be rejected? Simply because it contradicts the logic of history? No. Tyranny contradicts the bases of Islam itself. For 'Abdu, the historical sense is part of the structure of Islamic thought; to change judgements as conditions change is a recognized measure in Islam. In this light, it might be said that the logic of history is identical to the logic of authentic Islam. Any nation – even a non-Muslim one – that actively possesses the means of progress is a nation following the course of guidance prescribed by Islam.

This is not placing words in 'Abdu's mouth. He wrote as follows in his *Message of Monotheism*:

> Then the nations of Europe began to rid themselves of their bondage and improve their state, until their affairs became settled in a manner similar to that called for by Islam. They were inattentive to their leader, oblivious to their guide. And so the principles of modern civilization were established, to be the pride of generations influenced by earlier times and peoples.[5]

There is, then, no contradiction between the spirit of Islam and the spirit or logic of the age. But what is dominant in Islam now is not its spirit or truth. This truth *Shaykh* Muhammad 'Abdu, the religious reformer, has to uncover by returning to what he calls the 'principles of Islam'. These are the principles absent in the present forms of Islam, so far removed from the origin; and it is the origins and bases of Islam that inform Islamic judgements. For 'Abdu, the principles are eight in number:

1   Rational reflection in the attainment of belief. The bedrock of Islam is rationality.
2   Preferring reason over the letter of Shariah where the two conflict. When reason and revelation are in conflict, we are faced by two alternatives. One is to accept revelation, admitting to a failure to comprehend it. The other is to interpret revelation within the confines of language, so that meaning accords with what is established by reason.
3   Avoiding charges of unbelief. If someone should utter a speech which might be interpreted as unbelief on a hundred grounds, but as belief on one ground, the latter interpretation should be unconditionally adopted.
4   Learning from the laws of other nations. God has unchangeable laws among nations. These fixed laws inform the 'affairs' that lead to laws.
5   Overthrowing religious authority. After God and His Prophet, Islam permitted no one to have authority or control over man's creed or faith. The Messenger was enjoined to inform and remind, not to control or dominate. Any Muslim may reflect on the words of God or His Messenger without mediation from anyone. Islam has no such thing as 'religious authority'. Even so, Islam is a religion and a source of law. It has delineated limits and rights. Wisdom in prescribing rules is not complete unless a judge has power to establish the right and protect order within the community. This power cannot be arbitrary, involving a number of people. It must be in the hands of a single person, a sultan or a caliph. Nevertheless, this person is not God's representative on earth. He is simply a man, characterized, primarily, by the power of *ijtihad* (interpretation). When, however, this person deviates from the path established by religious scholars, and moves away from the Book and the *sunna* in his conduct, he must be removed and replaced by another person. It is for the nation, or the nation's representatives, to install the ruler. The nation has the right to control this ruler, and to depose him if this is shown to be in the nation's interest. As such, he is a civil ruler in every sense.
6   Protecting the call to Islam in order to prevent sedition. Killing is not in the nature of Islam. Its nature is to forgive and pardon. Any fighting, in Islam, is to prevent aggression against people's rights. It was never meant to enforce the faith of Islam or take revenge on opponents.
7   Friendliness towards those of opposing creeds.
8   Combining the interests of this world with those of the hereafter.[6]

Clearly, all these principles are interrelated. But the fifth basic element, the overthrowing of religious authority, requires further treatment here, since it is linked to the issue of government.

For Abduh, overthrowing religious authority does not mean merely changing it but uprooting it altogether. The fundamental source of authority within Islam, if we investigate the matter closely, is consensus and the choice of the nation; and, since the nation is the party that installs the ruler, the nation has the right to depose him. Thus the ruler is civil in every sense.

However, since Islam is the religion of the state, the laws of the state are those set out by Shariah. Islam has delineated limits and rights, and the duty of those in authority is to put these into effect. The ruler is basically an interpreter (*mujtahid*) and not an imitator. He is a religious scholar employing *ijtihad*. Perhaps, though, he will show a tendency to deviate from the path established by a consensus of religious scholars. In such a case he may be deposed. Yet taking this fifth fundamental in isolation, without considering its relation to other fundamentals, may easily lead to an impasse. Is it enough, for instance, that the nation should choose a strictly civil ruler when his responsibility is to apply the rules of Islam itself – which are the rules of the state? And what exactly is meant by overthrowing, uprooting the religious authority, when this authority is there specifically to apply the rules of Shariah. Does confirmation of such a role not imply support for the religious authority?

This fifth principle is, in fact, somewhat ambiguous. Nevertheless, we soon discover that these principles of Islam, taken together, result in a type of civil authority based not on selection of the ruler but on the promulgation of laws. In the second principle, 'Abdu underlines that reason should be preferred over the letter of Shariah when the two conflict. But in what circumstances does such a conflict occur? It occurs only when the letter of Shariah fails to provide answers to questions raised by real situations; and reality then introduces answers from outside Shariah laws. Since reality and its laws are changeable, then judging this changeable reality by old religious considerations becomes a form of imitation, which 'Abdu deplores. Hence a return to the essence of Shariah is a necessary prerequisite for reconciling Shariah and reality. The intervention of reason has thus become a basis of Islam, and the question of authority is seen to entail a contradiction between authority and the reality by which life is governed. This, in turn, leads to a conflict between authority and the essence of Shariah, and it becomes essential to show that the desired authority imposed by reality actually implies no such conflict. The solution lies in interpretation, which is expected to demonstrate that the constitutional state is an Islamic state in essence, i.e., that it has no conflict with true Islam, since

Islam gave human beings the freedom to choose their political system in accordance with the principle of reality itself.

Clearly, there is a difference between saying that the *ruler* is civil in every sense, and saying that the *rule* is civil in every sense. But has Abduh thereby moved from the ruler to civil rule?

In fact, 'Abdu's theoretical basis on this issue becomes clear in the light of his proposed Egyptian constitution. In his view:

1   All government affairs should be entrusted to one of the following authorities:

    a   A legislative authority to promulgate administrative and juridical laws.
    b   An executive authority to implement these laws.

    The legislative authority should be restricted to a parliament, which should have more members than the present Council of *Shura* (Consultation). The recommendations of this parliament are to be applied. The Council of Ministers should recognize the recommendations under all circumstances. Parliament is the authority for the promulgation of all laws, and the Cabinet is to be chosen from among its members. As for the executive authority, this should be limited to the Cabinet, which is to be given the right to present draft laws only, not to promulgate laws, this latter right belonging to Parliament.

2   The Cabinet is to be entrusted with all government affairs not related to the promulgation of laws, including the granting of decorations and ranks. No governmental affairs should be left to the Khedive. The Cabinet should also be in charge of religious education, and of Shariah and civil courts, without however intervening directly in the activities of these.

3   All consultant posts should be abolished, with Cabinet ministers assuming the functions in question. Under these circumstances, the Prime Minister should be a Muslim, with his official authority limited to the Prime Ministerial post; he should not occupy any other position of governmental power. All other employees in the government – directors, deputies and judges in all courts and in all the legal professions – should be Egyptians

Close inspection of such a constitution will make it clear that 'Abdu wished to have an authority civil in every respect. There is the legislative authority of Parliament. There is the executive authority answerable to the legislative authority. There are Shariah and civil courts, religious and civil education. The employees are to be 'Egyptian', regardless of their religious persuasion. The Prime Minister must be a Muslim (though other ministers need not be) because there are certain religious issues on which he must decide.

Islam being the majority religion, it is necessary for the Prime Minister to be a Muslim. Nevertheless, his position is not a religious one. He is a civil servant, and the Cabinet and Parliament are likewise civil in nature – the government and the whole type of rule are civil in every respect. That a religious leader like *Shaykh* Muhammad 'Abdu should have said all this indicates a germ of secularism in the Egyptian and Arab mind, providing a potential for development, in this respect, within later Islamic thought. In my view, 'Ali 'Abd al-Razzaq's book *Islam and the Principles of Government* is the final product of a seed planted in Islamic thought by Muhammad 'Abdu. In other words, secularism, though the term itself is not used by religious reformists, emerges as a genuine viewpoint of these reformists – which refutes any claim that it was merely the vision of a few intellectuals alienated from their own world.

II. The disciples of Muhammad Abduh

It might be said that the enlightened Azhari *Shaykh* 'Ali 'Abd al-Razzaq was the first to set out, in a clear manner, the relations between state, history and society. His conclusion was a radical one: that government is a human institution, and nothing else. This very much chimed in with 'Abdu's reforming thought.

According to 'Abd al-Razzaq:

> The religion of Islam has nothing to do with the caliphate known to Muslims, or with religious plans, judiciary or government and state functions. All these are Islamic creations in which religion actually has no hand. Islam itself is unaware of such creations; it has not mentioned, commanded or forestalled them. Islam has left these arrangements to us, left us to use our rational judgement in benefiting from the experience of other nations, and in applying the principles of politics.[7]

This brief statement raises a number of important contentions:

1   The caliphate is a historical, civil phenomenon, and may be described as a form of government unspecified by any religious text. As such, its historical status transforms it from a system sanctified absolutely by the majority, as the highest possible system of government, to an incidental system made necessary by specific historical circumstances.

2   Since government is a historical human phenomenon, the attitude towards
     it must be based on rational judgement, the experience of nations and the
     principles of politics.
3   Since government follows the principles of politics, which entail a struggle
     for power, government is the outcome of such a struggle for power.

The enlightened *Shaykh* Khalid Muhammad Khalid, a contemporary of 'Ali
'Abd al-Razzaq and author of *Citizens not Subjects: You do not Plough the Sea, it is
Man,* developed 'Abd al-Razzaq's theses further. *Shaykh* Khalid directly con-
fronts the dominant state of tyranny and despotism, and offers the democratic
alternative:

> Suppose you ask an Egyptian, an Iraqi, a Yemeni or a Saudi: 'From which of
> Gdulod's lands are you?' Do not trouble yourself to wait for an answer. You can
> provide it yourself: 'Your humble servant is from the land of listen and obey.'
> Rulers laying claim to divinity have long since vanished from the world. But
> there are still those who lay claim to infallibility . . . We are not alone in this
> respect. The whole of human society has travelled this path, with listening and
> obeying their law and their programme. Perhaps man has devised democracy
> only in answer to his dire need to be rid of this indignity and helplessness.[8]

Tyranny is not a matter of rule only; it is also a matter of discourse. *Shaykh*
Khalid realizes the spell cast on people by religious discourse, and so he strives
to overcome it by denying it any worthwhile religious content. This enlightened Islamist will not allow religion to justify tyranny. When society was
Christian (he observes), the teachings said: 'Servants, be obedient to them that
are your masters, with fear and trembling. Let as many servants as are under the
yoke count their own masters worthy of all honour.' When Islam was revealed
in our valley, there were people in the land, speaking in the name of Islam and
falsely claiming to the people that the Messenger of God had said: 'Listen to
your prince and obey him, even if he lashes your back and seizes your money';
or: 'Be conquered and not a conqueror.'[9] In this manner (he concludes), the
land of listening and obedience became an enclosure where people lived in a
fashion below the standards demanded by human rights.

    This is not the place to detail all the ideas of this enlightened *shaykh* con-
cerning the authority he rejects or the one he calls for. Let us note, though, how
this man had begun to speak the very language of the age: tyranny, democracy,
human rights, homeland, citizen, constitution, liberty, and so on. Quite simply,
he rejects tyranny as a historical state, and calls for democracy as a vital human
need. Tyranny is rejected not merely because it is, as a form of government, no

longer appropriate to society and the times, but because it blocks the incentive
to morally acceptable conduct. Both moral incentive and decent conduct
improve with the improvement of the mind.[10] Khalid makes a clear distinction
between a tyrannical state and a democratic one. The former is a state of listening and obedience and despotism; a state of immorality, of confiscating freedom and the rights of man. The latter is a state of free will, of morality and
rationality; a state of human rights.

The model of Khalid Muhammad Khalid recurs whenever the intellectual
concerned with history is an advocate of change, reason and liberty. The outstanding characteristic of such an enlightened Islamic intellectual is his inclu-
sion of religion within history; that is, the way he puts forward a historical view
of religion. His interpretation thereby becomes a matter of historical requirement, imposed by historical change itself.

These Islamic reformers, 'Abdu, 'Abd al-Razzaq and Khalid, treated the
issue of government from a civil viewpoint, but without using the specific term
'secularism'. In contrast, the contemporary Syrian reformer Muhammad
Shahrour poses the direct question: Is the Islamic state secular?[11] He provides
the following answer:

> The secular state, as I see it, is the state that receives its legitimacy not from the
> men of religion, but from the people. It is, therefore, a civil state, neither sectar-
> ian nor denominational. Since Islam does not recognize the men of religion to
> begin with, and does not need them to acquire legitimacy (the men of religion
> being self-appointed guardians of the faith, and supervisors of its application),
> those truly holding authority in Islam are the representatives of the people, who
> are elected by free ballot and thus form the modern *shura*. The secular state is a
> state where there is a multiplicity of opinion, together with freedom of opinion
> and dissent.[12]

In his new reading, Shahrour distinguishes between liberal and conservative
Islam. Liberal Islam: first, recognizes the traditions and conventions of all peoples of the world, so long as these do not overstep the limits set by God; and
second, believes that Islamic legislation on marriage, divorce, inheritance and
the law of personal status is a matter of civil legislation within the limits set by
God.

Shahrour sees despotism, and the lack of democracy in politics, as a serious
flaw and a chronic ill within Arab-Islamic societies, from the end of the Rashidi
caliphate up to the present day.[13] He takes a clear stand on all types of tyranny,
such as the tyranny of belief, by which he means the belief that man's deeds and
his sustenance are both pre-ordained from time everlasting. This should be

radically rejected. Intellectual tyranny began with the age of writing, and came full circle with the deadening of the Arab-Islamic mind at the hands of al-Ghazali and Ibn 'Izzi. The tyranny of knowledge is that of the subject, the method, the means and the system. Social tyranny covers all the social relations inherited from the ages of decadence, and similar elements – the prime issue being that of 'deviation', where the notion of prescribed and proscribed matters tends to be prominent. Then, there is economic tyranny, political tyranny, and so on.

Clearly, when a religious reformer comes to defend secularism and democracy not as something contravening Islam but as a system derived from Islam itself, then reform discourse has become radical in the highest degree.

III. The return of God's governance

At the time an Islamic intellectual like Khalid Muhammad Khalid was writing in defence of democracy, Arab political life was witnessing the rise of political systems described as secular or quasi-secular. Nasserism became established in the popular mind as a nationalist and natural liberation movement. The Arab nationalist trend dominated political consciousness, and there was high expectation that nationalist aspirations would be realized. As for the Islamic religious current, this now seemed to belong to the past.

Some time before *Shaykh* 'Ali 'Abd al-Razzaq's death, a publisher approached him for permission to bring out a new edition of his book *Islam and the Principles of Government*. This was in 1966, and the dialogue between publisher and *shaykh* went something like this:

'Would you allow us to reprint your great book, *Islam and the Principles of Government?*'

'No, sir. No!'

'Why is that? Are you renouncing your book and your views?'

'Not in the least. But I've had enough problems from that book. I can't take any more of them. I've had enough. Did you know they almost arranged for me to be divorced?'

'They went as far as that?'

'Yes, they did. Luckily I wasn't married at the time. So they missed their chance!'

'But that wretched period's over now. This is 1966. You're not going to suffer the way you did then. Your book won't find anything but honour and appreciation. Intellectuals will praise you, and so will the state.'

'How can I be sure of that? I want an assurance from the state. I want a
   guarantee.'
'Our new social, intellectual reality – that's the best guarantee.'[14]

Reality, the publisher firmly believed, was different now. 1966 belonged to the
years of upsurge, of secular, socialist, nationalist liberation; surely there was no
comparison between the Egypts of the 1960s and 1930s. He could hardly have
expected that, barely three decades later, conflict would flare up once more
between al-Azhar and innovative books; that Nasr Hamid Abu Zayd would
appear before the court on charges of apostasy, and that the court would issue
the following judgement:

> The defendant has renounced Islam and become an apostate. The consequence
> of apostasy, according to the consensus of jurisprudential and juristic opinion, is
> separation between husband and wife. It is also ruled that the apostate may never
> marry either Muslim or non-Muslim. Apostasy is akin to death in meaning and
> status. Since the defendant has renounced Islam, his marriage with the second
> defendant is annulled on the grounds of this apostasy, and they should be sepa-
> rated as soon as possible.[15]

The publisher could never have conceived that history would repeat itself in
such a ludicrous manner. Murderous hands have reached out to a number of
journalists and intellectuals in Egypt. Algeria wades in a morass of violence
from underground Islamic movements. Sudan is ruled by the military in the
name of Shariah.

On the practical level, political Islam is represented, in one of its many
forms, by violent movements seeking to establish a purely Islamic state and to
kill all intellectuals of contrary opinion, on the grounds that the state, society
and most intellectuals stand outside Islam. Since Muslims cannot be governed
by laws contrary to the teachings of Islam and the rulings of the Quran and
sunna, every measure needs to be taken to realize the Shariah state.

This practical stance rests on verses from the Quran: 'Do they then seek
after a judgement of [the Days of] Ignorance? But who, for a people whose
faith is assured, can give better judgement than Allah?' (5, *Al-Ma'ida*, 50);
'Therefore, do not listen to the unbelievers, but strive against them with [the
Quran] to the utmost [level of strife]' (25, *Al-Furqan*, 52); 'If any do fail to judge
by [the light of] what Allah has revealed, they are [no better than] unbelievers .
. . the wrongdoers . . . the rebels' (5, *Al-Ma'ida*, 44, 45, 47).

On these and similar verses the idea of God's governance is based. Such a
concept of governance was, it is well known, advanced in India by Abu 'l-A'la

al-Mawdoudi, then adopted by Sayyid Qutb in Egypt; in my view, supporters of the governance concept generally identify especially with Sayyid Qutb. For Qutb, the idea of governance is based on two contrasting concepts: *jahiliyya* (the age of pre-Islamic ignorance) and the governance of God. *Jahiliyya* involves the notion of human rule, governance the rule of God. When human beings become powerful actors capable of promulgating laws and regulations independent of the law of God, the result is *jahiliyya*, or human rule; this is an open violation of the rule of God. In contrast, God's governance means submission to the laws of God. There is no governance except God's, no law except God's, and no authority except God's.[16]

For Qutb – and, with minor differences, for all strict Islamists – the idea of governance became the cornerstone of the whole issue of government. According to Qutb, 'people are very much in need of Islam today to save them from tyrants and despots, as it did thirteen centuries ago'. Hence, the current function of Islam is the same as that in the early days of the call. Since Islam does not rule in this country, and since these people are Muslims in name only, they fall under the holy verse, 'If any do fail to judge by [the light of] what Allah has revealed, they are [no better than] unbelievers' (6, *Al-An'am*, 44). The Islam for which Muhammad Qutb calls is the one that shakes thrones and overthrows despots, or blows up the ground beneath their feet:

> When Islam rules – and it will rule by the permission and with the support of God – there will be no despot in the land of Islam, since Islam does not sanction despots, and allows no one on earth to rule in his own name, but only in the name of God and His Messenger. God rules with justice and good will. When Islam rules, the ruler can only execute the law of God.[17]

'Abbasi Madani believes that divine providence has marked out the Islamic state by establishing the governance of God, and the necessary divine legislation, binding on ruler and ruled alike.[18]

Muhammad Sa'id al-Buti joins with Qutb in maintaining that governance belongs to God alone. He is the legislator for His worshippers in their worldly and other-worldly affairs, and the point of reference in solving all their problems and in setting up every command and law in their lives. Whoever denies this is an unbeliever renouncing God and His Messenger, even if he performs *salat*, pilgrimage and the Ramadan fast.

All this (the argument runs) is supported by the evidence of reason and revelation, the Book and *sunna*, and the consensus of all Muslims.[19] 'What, then,' al-Buti asks, 'is the duty of man?' He answers:

The duty of man is to execute only . . . He is responsible for carrying out every word in the law revealed by God, Who made it binding on man. Man cannot interpret except where interpretation is commanded by God. Consultation (*shura*) for opinion and judgement is resorted to only where there is no clear text in the Book or *sunna*, or where there is no consensus.[20]

As to whether history has ever known such a state, al-Buti says:

Whoever objects to God's governance on the pretext that history witnessed its realization in Islamic society for a short period only, in the few years towards the end of the Prophet's life, the closing years of 'Umar ibn al-Khattab's caliphate, and a few years during the reign of 'Umar ibn 'Abd al-'Aziz, is in fact claiming a false pretext with no foundation in truth or reality . . . Government and society have always been Islamic, in the age of the Companions, the Followers, the Umayyads, the Abbasids and up to the early decades of the Ottoman caliphate. But a rise of Islamic society is one thing and infallibility is another.[21]

In fact, the return of the idea of governance, with Madani, Buti and others, along with the charge that whoever repudiates this is an unbeliever, has led to the idea of revolt against the 'unjust' ruler; unjust rule being that of the human ruler who does not abide by the idea of God's governance. It has also resulted in a degree of hostility towards the society ruled by an authority other than 'governance'; this has become a civil society and, as such, a deviation from the true path and the absolute divine truth. The democratic or secular state is thus considered one of unbelief and conspiracy against divine rule. According to Yusuf al-Badri, the prime exponent of this trend, 'Shariah regards democracy as contrary to Islam, since the source of democracy is the people. They say the people is the source of power, but we say rule belongs to God.'[22] In connection with this refutation of secularism, Dr Muhammad Yahya says:

Secularism is the forearm of crusading evangelism, its chosen tool to defeat Islam and wipe it out. Secularism is the main weapon in the hands of imperialism, thriving under the protection of imperialism and through its agents.[23]

According to Sa'd al-Hajj Hasan:

As the Lebanese experiment has shown, secularism can succeed only by exploiting sectarianism, racism or narrow provincialism. Therefore it cannot unify or be a means of unity.[24]

Rashid al-Ghanoushi explains the spread of secularism from his own Islamic point of view.

Clearly, those among the Muslims whose belief was shaken and depraved, who were lured by the secular and Communist parties, were the victims of futile training, fruitless conventional education, rigid Islamic culture, decadent religiosity, and an intellectual invasion armed with modern culture, charged with values of unbelief and revolt to wash away this human wreckage. These are more victims than criminals, victims of degraded culture, futile education and foreign domination . . . The Islamic movement has succeeded in marginalizing the secular programme, despite the latter's access to the vast mechanics of the state.[25]

Al-Ghanoushi's stance towards democracy is a positive one. For him the defect lies not in the democratic system itself, which he considers supreme, but in its specific content: in its materialistic secular philosophy which distances God from the organization of society, and in its deification of man.[26]

The Islamic criticism of secularism is part of a religious viewpoint whereby human beings are divided into believers and unbelievers, and the world is divided into a Muslim East and an atheist West bent on the defeat of Islam; and whereby, in addition, people are divided into the party of righteous forefathers – that is, the party of God – over against the degenerate party of modernity. Such a viewpoint is, ultimately, making a division between one world of closed privacy and another which is open and different; and, in the light of this, Islamic critics view secularism as the embodiment of a conspiracy concocted by the West, an aspect of diversity in mind and faith, a relapse from the true path and a new form of unbelief.[27]

Contemporary political Islamic theology starts out from a belief that the law suitable for mankind has already achieved completion in the divine law represented by revelation, text and experience. Such a law is, therefore, not open to change; it is appropriate for every time and place. How, this theology asks, can fallible human beings contrive a law superior to the law revealed by the Perfect One? If they make such an attempt, they are not creating a law but devising a heresy. In such a theology man has no place. As for defending human reason and the role of human reason, this theology limits itself to quoting Quranic verses and *hadith*s that honour reason. In fact the function of reason here goes no further than to justify belief and defend the idea of governance; and such a defence of this idea, asserting its absolute validity, merely confirms the insufficiency of man and his failure to know what is suitable for him. Thus, the idea of governance becomes a multifaceted means of coercion. This is a forfeiture of freedom of belief, of the social contract, of the promulgation of laws appropriate for human development, of human rights – a forfeiture of progress itself.

From the perspective of God's governance, the old not only contains the best of all possible worlds, it also acts as a check on the birth of what is possible. This is the essence of governance from Abu 'l-A'la al-Mawdoudi, to Sayyid Qutb and 'Abbas Madani, and on to Muhammad Sa'id Ramadan al-Buti.

The question that now arises is this. Why did the idea of governance reappear, so boldly and so effectively, within political Islamic movements? In my view, the reason behind the powerful return of this religious current was the series of defeats suffered by the Arab liberation movements, with all their slogans of unity, liberation and justice, and all their inability, in practice, to avoid the defeats in question. Conservative political systems in the region have tightened their grip on the Arab homeland, employing degenerate forms of traditional policies and arming themselves with a sham revolution. The attack on constitutional democracy led merely to despotic political systems which prevented man from building a civil society for himself. The severe repression this involved produced a quite unprecedented state of accumulated inhibition and psychological damage. Development reached a dead end. The national debts of Arab states, especially the non-oil-producing countries, reached such levels that settlement became well-nigh impossible. Hope of a united Arab state, or states, dwindled – even died. Israel became increasingly powerful and despotic, with hardly any effective Arab reaction.

In such an atmosphere of devastation, amid such grave problems, the political Islamic phenomenon developed, setting Islam forward, once more, as a comprehensive divine system, the best of all possible worlds, and the only way out of the present situation.

After the 1952 revolution in Egypt, the agrarian reform, the Aswan dam and the Hulwan industrial complex, the Nasserite phenomenon dwindled, and its achievements were lost under a free market policy. The policy of Anwar Sadat merely reintroduced poverty and economic breakdown, and turned the previous ambience of learning and faith into one of bribery and excessive wealth for a tiny minority of people, while the great majority, notably the middle classes, found its standard of living plummet.

The Islamic phenomenon, used by the Sadat regime to fight Nasserism and communism, emerged as the power to promote the future of Islamic Egypt once more, through change by force. The idea of God's governance reappeared. From the perspective of the new Islamic groups, Egyptian society is a *jahili,* Westernized society. Democracy is a European phenomenon (*shura* being the alternative), and secularism likewise an imported idea. And since Islam is a religion and a state, and laws are, in view of their divine origin, of absolute validity, governance is in the hands of God.

Algeria is the clearest example of an emerging Islamic current and of the idea of God's governance. Once the political and economic crisis within the

Algerian system began to make itself felt (when the bureaucratic groups began plundering the public sector, to the extent of 25 billion dollars, equal to the size of foreign debts), the alternative was ready and waiting. Islam was propounded once more as a means of escape from despotic power and economic crisis.

To sum up, there are Arab reasons behind the return of an Islamic discourse based on governance: in the main, the absence of democracy and increasing plundering of the public sector. To gain a clearer picture of the situation, we need to consider the following question: Is it possible to separate the return of Islamic movements and their ideology from the structure of the dominant culture? As a religion, Islam is in fact deeply concerned with political, social, economic and moral life; it does not limit itself to spiritual relations between man and God. For this reason it is easy for Islamic ideologues to advance an Islamic discourse with worldly solutions to people's problems: Islamic economics, an Islamic theory of equality, of government, and so on. Indeed, Islam has itself been introduced as a way of bypassing the worlds of capitalism and socialism, and their economic, political and moral systems – all this in tandem with the basic reality that Islam is the Arab majority religion. This introduces a cultural factor with regard to conduct, customs and values; Islamic ideology is addressing people who are, to a large extent, ready to believe. At a time of grave crisis, Islam becomes the only worldly solution. To move on, at such a time, from Islam as a religion and cultural component to Islam as a political ideology requires no great effort, for, if the Muslim masses wish to express their rejection of a reality whereby the state exerts authority without democracy, they have no refuge but the mosque, which the state authority cannot control. In the mosque, the Muslim believer is impelled through a discourse of identity, tradition and salvation. There he can be indoctrinated, emerging filled with every kind of rancour against his world, and so becoming a conductor for all the violent religious currents raising the banner of God's governance.

The question of rule in Islamic thought, be that thought reformist or conservative, cannot be separated from the attitude towards man. This is because rule is basically to be viewed as a relationship between people, directly defining the two poles of the issue: the ruler and the ruled. Where, then, does man belong in these two types of Islamic thought?

In Islamic religious reform, from Muhammad 'Abdu to Muhammad Shahrour, man has a significant place as a free being. Such freedom is viewed from two perspectives: of God, and of history and society. God has created man such that he himself may decide his future destiny. Since the relationship between man and God is limited to the worship of God – according to individual practices which bring man closer to God, like attestation, *salat*, the

Ramadan fast, pilgrimage, and prescribing and proscribing – the relation between Creator and created becomes individual and personal. The above rites, in practice, decide the closeness or distance of man from God; consequently, man is directly responsible before God, and the hereafter decides his destiny of reward or punishment. This results in an annulment of any mediation between the worshipper and his Lord; there should be no human intermediary between the two. As such, belief and unbelief become individual attitudes based on human choice. On the historical level, history is viewed in terms of situational change, which entails a change in judgement. Those judgements that were valid in one particular age may no longer be valid in another, and so man, changing and developing as he is, can hardly be made subject to legislation originally tailored for men at a specific stage of their social, economic and cultural development. Man is thus free to choose what he finds appropriate to a particular situation. Islam does, it is true, recognize certain rules and limits, but these stand in direct relation to historical movement. Historical awareness changes man from a mere passive being, unable to reflect on his world, to an active being capable of formulating laws and limits relevant to his interests, which are, in turn, defined by the historical conditions underlying them. In reforming Islam, then, historical awareness underpins rejection of the religious state. The concept of interest leads on to that of variation of interests, which, in its turn, leads on to various human approaches towards achieving those interests. The state is merely an expression of that variety of interests, its power no longer a matter of divine commission. Since it is purely human as an institution, no one has the right to claim that he is ruling in God's name.

At the underlying level, human governance confirms the historicity of rule itself. Since humanity has succeeded in establishing forms of rule based on various forms of human contract, the religious reformer was encouraged to appeal to such human experience. This is not contrary to Islam, for Islam never laid down a particular form of government or a particular means of establishing it. This has greatly lessened any trend towards specificity, in favour of a broader human trend whereby human experience becomes intrinsically profitable and cannot be ignored. From this springs the religious reformer's insistence that the nation should be free to choose its ruler, that democracy or the legislative power do not contravene Islam, that human beings are free to organize themselves, that secularism, in its upholding of citizenship irrespective of religious persuasion, is suitable for our times. The reformer has liberated himself from old, traditional terms like 'subject', 'allegiance', 'caliph', 'punishment', etc. He speaks, now, of 'state', 'constitution', 'citizenship', 'elections' and 'rights'.

By contrast, reactionary Islamic thought, still calling for God's governance, remains a slave to the cosmic image of man's relation to God. Man is strictly incapable of deciding his destiny, since the relation between God and man, from the governance perspective, is a relation between Perfect and imperfect. The Perfect wished man to achieve perfection, and so He designed the totally, absolutely ideal way for man to fulfil the will of the Perfect on earth. How, then, can the imperfect being produce anything better than what the Perfect has produced? Any deviation from what is specified by Shariah and text is necessarily a human violation of God's will; and such violation is unbelief itself, and a return to *jahiliyya*, or pre-Islamic ignorance.

Under governance, God alone has the will to decide what should be. Man has no role beyond that of realizing God's will on earth. Heaven decides; earth executes. Since revelation came to an end with the death of the Prophet, legislation was complete, and there is now no room for interpretation in the presence of the text.

Historically speaking, there is absolutely nothing new under the sun. Nothing demands innovation, because the Perfect has decided everything irrespective of what may occur subsequently. Otherwise, He would have given a clear indication of what was to be done. In other words, God has decided everything, up to the Day of Judgement. Since, however, God does not rule directly, He must have agents on earth to constrain people, especially those who distance themselves from the divine law, to submit to the will of God. If man is given the freedom to choose the systems and laws he likes, then the truth revealed by God will disappear – all the more so as the spirit of man is prone to evil. And what is this power able to mediate between God and man? It is the community of believers, who struggle ceaselessly in the cause of God. Under governance, people are returned to the true path by force.

For indeed, the concept of struggle, under governance, has come to work in tandem with violence. Punishment in this world has become fundamental. With these notions of *jahiliyya*, the present-day Arab is exposed to charges of apostasy and deviation, and is exposed to coercion. The alternative offered is a decisive return to God, applying God's rule, revolting against the unjust ruler, remaining within the precincts of faith and fighting for the cause of God.

I believe that the contemporary Arab world, in the absence of democracy, is engaged in a futile struggle between, on the one hand, fundamentalist movements proclaiming governance, and, on the other, despotic states. Such a struggle can lead only to destructive forces within society. The sole answer is to realize a free civil society that permits social, political and economic contradictions to find expression in the context of peaceful civil action. It might well be claimed that the various fundamentalist movements are the only elements to gain from the absence of democracy. Only the fundamentalist tendency is accorded the right to advocate change, through the institution of the mosque which provides the basic publicity. Democratic, secular or enlightened trends of thought find all possibility of different means of expression slammed in their faces. The despotic states are, one might say, creating an opposition in their own image. As a result, any fundamentalist success will merely replace one despotism with another – and in still more unambiguous fashion.

Chapter 12: The Islamic intellectual Mahmoud Muhammad Taha on the impasse of human rights in Islamic legislation

Al-Nour Hamad

Introduction

As Muslims and Arabs, we are often vexed and offended by the way the Western media speak of the human rights situation in the Arab-Islamic world. Even so, an objective and unbiased look will show us that hardly a single country in the Arab world is free from violation of human rights.[1] Nor is there any wonder in this, since the distinguishing characteristic of Arab countries to date is the absence of a democracy serving to monitor the state's conduct and ensure its compliance with constitutional law, binding on state and citizens alike. No scrupulous intellectual, surely, can fail to see a connection between, on the one hand, the numerous violations of human rights in the Arab region and, on the other, the realities of thought, historical formation and political reality, and the ramifications of these, in the region in question.

Some people might ascribe the recurrent violations of human rights in the Arab world to the poor quality of rulers and governmental systems, with no consideration of the realities of Arab-Islamic culture or of the historical framework informing the culture's characteristics. I can find no better description of the framework of this culture, dormant for so many centuries now, than the words of Muhammad 'Abid al-Jabiri in his book, *The Formation of the Arab Mind.* 'The fact is,' al-Jabiri says, 'that current Arab cultural history is a mere repetition, a paltry reproduction, of the cultural history written by our forefathers under the pressure of the ages through which they lived and within the limits of knowledge and means available in those ages. Consequently, we remain prisoners of the old vision, concepts and methods that guided our forefathers. This leads us, unconsciously, to partake in the problems and conflicts of the past, to make our present preoccupied with our past, and, ultimately, to view the future in the light of the problems and conflicts of the past.'[2]

It is obvious, on the other hand, that the centuries of intellectual stagnation through which our Arab region has lived have produced a culture characterized, in some aspects, by a hypocritical support for state power and for keeping within the red lines marked out by this power. As such, those among our people who are intellectual and enlightened have often preferred to make peace with the state, accepting whatever transient gains they may be offered. A confrontation with the power of the state has never, after all, been an attractive alternative. The returns and gains are not immediate; in fact, such a confrontation will result, at best, in dire poverty, while ideological opposition will often lead to the gallows.

This argument applies to intellectuals in general, but particularly to those involved in religious issues. Repeatedly, throughout Islamic history past and present, our so-called men of religion have found justifications for the conduct of rulers.[3] It is also clear, nevertheless, that the behaviour of these rulers is simply one more natural outcome of a state of backwardness, intellectual, cultural, social and economic.

In short, when seeking to know why we are living on the margin of current civilization, we should look no further than the chronic disorder in the structure of our thought and culture. All too often we have blamed our deficient state of affairs exclusively on the rapacious schemes of the West. All too often we have blamed our intellectual deficiency, and our victimization, on a deficient sense of justice in current Western civilization – a sense that has continued to decline vis-à-vis other nations since the rise of this civilization at the dawn of the industrial revolution.

Our efforts must be directed at triggering a comprehensive intellectual awakening, based on a critical view of the Islamic tradition: a real awakening, liberating minds from the constraints of ancient methods, and the ways in which our forefathers dealt with the problems and challenges of their societies, issues that were in no way similar to what we are facing in our current cosmic reality. In other words, we have to strip the robe of holiness from the contributions of our forefathers and give these contributions their proper place in the structure of our history. We are facing a civilizational challenge; and the first thing we have to do in confronting this is to admit that we are living on the margin of current civilization. We are, in fact, 'living on a few husks of Western civilization and a few others from Islam'. These are the words of Mahmoud Muhammad Taha, the Muslim intellectual who is the subject of this essay.[4]

Though some might take offence at the statement, the fact is that, in all God's creation, we are among the people furthest from the values of democracy and freedom. This applies to us as individuals and nations alike. Moreover, we had no part in the creation of the current machine-based civilization. We do not make machines or tools; indeed, we can neither properly maintain tools or machines, nor use them properly.[5] Similarly, we are making no significant contribution to the intellectual and cultural output of present-day civilization. Our record in human rights is notoriously poor. In some of our countries there is no way of knowing what goes on in the dark, damp dungeons and prison cellars; and, consequently, there is no way of knowing how many prisoners of conscience have perished at the hands of rulers in these countries, or how they have perished. It should be pointed out, nonetheless, that we are still not the absolute worst in the field of human rights violation, though we are often in the limelight. We should remember that the West, that self-appointed defender and guardian of human rights, has a long history of blatant human rights violations on its own account. All the welfare nowadays enjoyed by Western countries is based on the blood, exploitation and oppression of other nations of the world.

This preamble is intended to prepare the reader for consideration of a Sudanese Islamic intellectual who took it on himself to stand up to the civilizational challenge currently facing Muslims; to put forward ideas which, in my view, provide the most original and coherent way out of the impasse of human rights in the Islamic state. Moreover, the ideas of this thinker are no mere immature, intellectual attempt to apply cosmetic treatment to the face of contemporary Islamic thought before the challenges of contemporary cosmic thought and culture. On the contrary, his ideas move clearly toward delineating a new, cosmic Islamic civilization. Such is Master[6] Mahmoud Muhammad Taha, an intellectual worthy of the closest scrutiny.

I. Mahmoud Muhammad Taha

In view of the blackout imposed on the thought and life of Master Mahmoud Muhammad Taha, it may be proper to start by introducing the man to the reader. We shall then present his original and pioneering contribution[7] with a view to taking innovative Islamic thought out of its impasse and divesting it of its chronic historical problems. Special attention will be given to the contradiction between traditional Islamic Shariah and what twentieth-century humanism calls the Universal Declaration of Human Rights – a declaration that stresses, among other things, equality among human beings irrespective of colour, religion, race or gender.

Mahmoud Muhammad Taha was born in Hijelij, a village near Rufa'a, to the East of the Blue Nile. He graduated as a civil engineer at Gordon College,

Khartoum, in 1936. In 1945, with the support of some other educated Sudanese, he formed the Republican Party, which called for an end to the British occupation of the Sudan and the founding of a Sudanese Republic independent of both Egypt and Britain. Master Mahmoud was the first political prisoner in the movement against British occupation. He was tried for leading a demonstration by the people of Rufa'a, who crossed the Nile and besieged the office of the British Commissioner at the nearby town of Hasahisa, demanding the release of a Sudanese woman who had been imprisoned by the British authorities for having a Pharaonic circumcision performed on her daughter. Traditions, Master Mahmoud declared, should be fought not by laws but by education, and the British authorities had no right to punish those who knew nothing beyond such traditions. He succeeded in using this incident to incite citizens against the British authorities. In the face of the demonstrators' insistence, the authorities were obliged to release the woman. In the early 1950s the Republican Party was transformed into a religious call, adopting the ideas of Master Mahmoud on Islamic renaissance and on the development of legislation to suit the spirit of the age.

If the name of Master Mahmoud became linked with the human rights issue in general, and with human rights in the Arab world in particular, it was because he lost his life in defence of such rights and of the right of others to a religious belief and to the expression of their beliefs. This led the Arab Organization of Human Rights to mark the day of his martyrdom as the Day of Human Rights in the Arab world. Master Mahmoud was seventy-six years old when, on 18 January 1985,[8] he was publicly hanged in the Cober prison in Khartoum on charges of apostasy. The court ordered that his books be burned and his home and possessions considered a booty for Muslims.[9] All this followed a sham trial, during which judges were guided by the practices of decadent periods of Islamic history and those of the notorious Inquisition of medieval Europe. Master Mahmoud had published a pamphlet rejecting the application of what was then referred to as the laws of Islamic Shariah in Sudan, laws promulgated by Sudanese Islamists represented by the leaders of the Islamic Charter Front (headed by Dr Hasan al-Turabi), which at the time shared power with the former Sudanese president Ja'far Numairy.[10] The group contrived to put these laws into practice, touring the country with President Numairy to secure allegiance to him as a Muslim imam, exploiting the state of religious mania that took hold of him toward the end of his reign. They encouraged and lured him with the so-called Shariah laws, including an article on apostasy listed as number 3 of the Principles of Judicial Rulings.[11] The measure led, in its calculated aftermath, to the crime of executing this true intellectual, who faced death for

the sake of his belief with a courage recognized by all those witnessing the out-
rageously brutal sentence. The American journalist Judith Miller, then a *New
York Times* Middle East correspondent, masqueraded as a man and witnessed
the execution, subsequently writing a moving description of what she saw.[12] It
is worth mentioning that Master Mahmoud was given the chance to retract his
claims and be granted a pardon, but that he rejected this with dignity.[13]

Master Mahmoud refused to cooperate with the court from the very start,
because he knew they were contemplating a verdict prepared in advance. In his
defence before the court he stated as follows: 'I have, on a number of occasions, made clear my views on the September 1983 laws, saying that they run
contrary to Shariah and to Islam; and that, moreover, they have distorted both
Shariah and Islam, estranging people from both. These laws were promulgated
and implemented to terrorize the people, to subjugate and degrade them, and
they threaten the unity of the country. So much for the principle. As for the
practical side, the judges in this court are technically unqualified and too
morally weak to refuse to put themselves at the service of the executive authority, and so be exploited for the forfeiture of rights and the humiliation of political opponents. For these reasons, I am not prepared to cooperate with any
court that has no respect for the independent judiciary, and has accepted the
role of tool for degrading the people, humiliating free thought and persecuting
political opponents.'[14]

It is lamentable indeed to picture the trial of an intellectual, near the end of
the twentieth century, on a charge of apostasy, and his subsequent execution by
public hanging, and to reflect that this would happen nowhere but in the Arab-
Islamic world. The strange, stunning thing about this is that we fail to learn
from our experience. It was said by the old sages that 'any experience that does
not teach a lesson repeats itself'. Master Mahmoud was charged with apostasy
and executed in 1985, but the sages of the Arab and Muslim nations budged
hardly at all. Perhaps many people found his plight a natural consequence.
There were even those who supported the execution and made no effort to hide
their feelings. This man had laboured in areas normally unconsidered by people
in the Middle East. Indeed, one doubts whether most people in the Arab and
Islamic nations know the name of Master Mahmoud, even since his execution.

II. The innovative project

Propagators of innovative, enlightening projects in contemporary Islamic
thought have often chosen to withdraw them under pressure from traditional

Islamic institutions. Such innovators might have been expected to help divest traditional contributions of their sanctity, then suggest ways out of the impasse of human rights in Islamic legislation. But Taha Hussein withdrew, and so did 'Ali 'Abd al-Razzaq, Khalid Muhammad Khalid, and many others.[15] Generally speaking, intellectual confrontations springing from the impasse of human rights in Islamic Shariah have been characterized by an indiscreet distortion of crucial Quranic texts, or else by a distortion of crucial historical facts.[16] Hence, it is commonly difficult to conduct a systematic and coherent discourse on human rights in Islamic legislation, and under the Islamic state, without discussing the development of Islamic legislation itself.

'The basic concept in Islam,' says Master Mahmoud, 'is that everyone is free until he is found unable, in practice, to commit himself to the duty of freedom. Freedom is a natural right balanced by the duty of performance, which is the sound use of freedom. When a free person is found unable to abide by the duty of freedom, his freedom is accordingly confiscated by constitutional law. Constitutional law, as previously explained, is the law that balances the need of the individual for absolute individual freedom with the need of the community for comprehensive social justice. This we have called the law of reciprocity . . . Some Islamic scholars have believed that the wars of Islam were purely defensive in nature. This is a lapse springing from their concern to refute the vilification, made by some orientalists, that Islam spread solely by the sword. The fact is that the sword was used when it was found necessary to confiscate a misused freedom. For its first thirteen years, Islam was clear in delineating the rights of the individual and the community. When many Muslims failed to fulfil the duties of their freedom, or misused that freedom, they were denied the right to manage their own affairs, and the Prophet was appointed as a guardian over them until they reached maturity. If they embraced the new religion, and fulfilled the divine directives on proscriptions and prescriptions, the sword was no longer needed in their case. A violation of the new law brought a forfeiture of freedom. Islamic Shariah legislation followed suit; so did the new government . . . This leads us on to a crucial point, namely that most of the legislation we have now was not originally intended by Islam. It comprises measures dictated by the times and by human capacity . . .'[17]

The essence of Master Mahmoud's notion here is that some aspects of Islamic Shariah are of a temporary nature. Examples of this are *ikrah*, or coercion, which was the basis for combating non-believers and for the system of slavery, and the idea of consultation. The concept of consultation is not, Master Mahmoud believes, necessarily democratic. It rather represents the rule of the mature individual over the minor. In the final analysis, it is a matter of guardianship, although informed by a consultation between the ruler and the ruled, so as to listen to the latter's opinion and show respect for his human dignity. But the ruler has the right to disagree with the opinion of the ruled. 'And consult them in affairs [of moment]. Then when you have made a decision, put your trust in Allah, for Allah loves those who put their trust [in Him].' (3, *Al 'Imran*, 159.) The system of guardianship led on to the judgement of apostasy, and to regarding the 'People of the Book' as second-class citizens.

Then there are the rights of women, which put the woman under the guardianship of the man. 'Men are protectors and maintainers of women, because Allah has given the one more [strength] than the other, and because they support them from their means. Therefore the righteous women are devoutly obedient, and guard in [the husband's] absence what Allah would have them guard. As to those women on whose part you fear disloyalty and ill conduct, admonish them [first], next, refuse to share their beds, [and last] beat them [lightly]: but if they return to obedience, do not seek against them means [of annoyance]: for Allah is Most High and Great.'(4, *Al-Nisa'*, 34.) The testimony of the woman was valued as half that of the man. 'And get two witnesses, out of your men. And if there are not two men, then a man and two women such as you choose for witnesses, so that if one of them errs, the other can remind her.' (2, *Al-Baqara*, 282.) The woman was given half of the man's share of inheritance. 'To the male, a portion equal to that of two females.' (4, *Al-Nisa'*, 11.) The woman could be a fourth wife. 'Marry women of your choice, two, or three, or four: but if you fear that you shall not be able to deal justly [with them], then only one.' (4, *Al-Nisa'*, 3.) Furthermore, the woman was placed below the man in religious and worldly affairs.

Master Mahmoud, however, views the seventh-century Shariah as a transitional one, based on certain branches of the Quranic text. Grounded as they are in historical origins that had been abrogated for seventh-century Muslims, *jihad* is not fundamental to Islam, nor is slavery, nor veiling, nor a society where men are separated from women, nor polygamy. Nor, he believes, is capitalism fundamental to Islam. In other words, Master Mahmoud believes the original Meccan verses were grounded in leniency, equality, liberty and democracy. When, though, it became evident in practice that those addressed were not up to such a high level of discourse, these verses were abrogated by the subsidiary Medinan verses, which inform present-day Shariah. However, the Master believed that the original Meccan verses, albeit abrogated by the Medinan ones, did not vanish for good. They were saved for the proper time. Such a time, the Master believes, has come with the advent of contemporary global society, which is connected by modern means of communications and is thus prepared for the universal banner of the call of Islam.[18]

The outstanding characteristics of Master Mahmoud's thought are clarity and courage. This is seen in his admission that Islamic Shariah, applied in the seventh century AD, was based on coercion. It did not give the unbeliever the basic right to life; he had either to accept Islam or be fought until he did accept, or else perished. Even the Muslim had no right to change his religion. The judgement of apostasy is a strong indication of coercion within Islamic Shariah. This is among the challenges facing those who claim that Islamic Shariah is suitable for every time and place. One *hadith* reads, 'Whoever changes his religion, kill him.' Abu Bakr fought the apostates after the death of the Prophet. Some were killed, others returned to Islam against their will. Some may argue that these apostates renounced Islam because they did not wish to pay the *zakat* tax. This is true, but refusing payment of *zakat* is a violation of religious principles, which is cause for execution. It is reported of Abu Bakr that he said, 'I will fight anyone who separates *salat* from *zakat*. If they deny me a mere binding rope for a camel, which they used to yield to the Messenger of Allah, I will fight them for it.' The 'People of the Book', of other religions, are under the protection of the Islamic state in return for a *jizya* tax they reluctantly pay. They do not enjoy the same rights as Muslims.

III. The impasse of human rights

The proponents of the Islamic state undoubtedly find themselves in a serious impasse today, especially in connection with equal rights for non-Muslim citizens in the Islamic state, and with the right of women to equality with men. Some Arab countries, of course, still do not allow women to assume positions of leadership, nor do they permit co-education even in university lecture halls. Work opportunities for women, when available, are probably limited to teaching, in a set-up where women are separated from men. Moreover, a single woman is only allowed to travel in the company of a male relative whom she is not legally allowed to marry. In some of these countries, a woman is not even allowed to drive a car! Most Arab-Islamic countries do not accept the testimony of a woman alone, even if she happens to be a university professor, yet a man's testimony is accepted, even if he is illiterate and ignorant. The right to divorce is exclusively in the hands of men. Followers of the Hanafi school do indeed claim that a woman may be a partner in exercising the right to divorce, but only if permitted by the man; in other words, divorce is basically the man's right, but he may allow his wife to be a partner in this right if she demands it and he accepts.[19] Some men in our countries are still polygamists. And all the above is quite compatible with traditional Shariah: 'Men are the protectors and maintainers of women, because Allah has given the one more [strength] than the other . . .' (4, *Al- Nisa'*, 34); 'And stay quietly in your houses . . .' (33, *Al-Ahzab*, 33); or in the reported *hadith*, 'No people will ever prosper if it has a woman as its leader'; and 'Marry women of your choice . . .' (4, *Al-Nisa'*, 3).

What is noteworthy, according to Master Mahmoud, is that modern life, with its training and teaching opportunities, has provided the woman with unprecedented powers. Seventh-century legislation no longer suits her new status; hence the contradictions which have led courts to accept the testimony of ignorant, illiterate men, while finding no religious or intellectual justification to accept the testimony of a woman even if she is a university professor of law or Shariah. Master Mahmoud gives a formidable portrayal of these contradictions. He goes through the stages of education for girls and boys, together, until girls too pass their examinations competently, then go on through law school until they become lawyers and even judges. Yet a female judge, whom we have prepared and trained to sit in judgement and consider the testimonies of men and women, accepting some and rejecting others, would have no right to be a witness without the presence of another woman witness, if she herself were to appear before the court in the role of witness.[20] It is of course clear that the position of witness can in no way be compared to that of a judge or attorney in respect of the need to be versed in law.

Master Mahmoud sees that the way out of this impasse lies not in distorting the old bases of Shariah, or diverting the crucial texts in a new direction; it rather lies in the knowledge that the Quran has two messages. One message is informed by subordinate verses suitable to the society and capacity of the seventh century, while a second is informed by the original verses, which were kept until the proper time – a time Master Mahmoud believes has now arrived.

IV. The impasse of contradictory texts

In fact, the idea of a developing Islamic legislation, as set out by Master Mahmoud, and the idea of alternating the use of Quranic verses – with discerning judgement – to suit changing times and to grasp the flow of present-day life, practicing redirection in an Islamic perspective, represents a coherent way out of textual contradictions found in the Quran and *hadith*. We read, for instance: 'Say, "The truth is from your Lord:" Let him who will, believe, and him who will, reject.' (18, *Al-Kahf*, 29.) Also: 'Therefore, give admonition, for you are one to admonish, you are not to control them.' (88, *Al-Ghashiya*, 1–2.) But we also read: 'But when the forbidden months are past, then fight and slay the pagans wherever you find them, and seize them, beleaguer them, and lie in wait for them in every stratagem [of war]: But if they repent and establish regular *salat* and practise regular charity, then open the way for them, for Allah is Oft-Forgiving, Most Merciful.' (9, *Al-Tawba*, 5.) Then: 'O Prophet! Strive hard against the unbelievers and the hypocrites, and be firm against them, their abode is Hell, an evil refuge indeed.' (9, *Al-Tawba*, 73.) This is parallel to the *hadith*: 'I was commanded to fight people until they declare that there is no God but Allah, and that Muhammad is the Messenger of Allah.' Jurisprudents of the past found a way out of this contradiction in the divine text through recourse to the existence of abrogating and abrogated verses in the Quran. 'None of Our revelations do We abrogate or cause to be forgotten, but We substitute something better or similar.' (2, *Al-Baqara*, 106.) However, there is a consensus among jurisprudents that the latter verse abrogates the former, not the other way around.[21] The knowledge of abrogating and abrogated verses helped these jurisprudents answer the question: 'How could a holy book contain contradictory and conflicting texts?' Nevertheless, what served as a solution in the past is insufficient for the present, especially when we take into account that the abrogating verses replaced a standard of discourse informed by liberty, responsibility and equality with a less congenial discourse, informed by *jihad*, guardianship and inequality. This is found in the command to fight unbelievers, establish slavery, execute apostates, enforce *jizya* on non-Muslims – which they have to pay 'with willing submission' – and implement guardianship over women. Master Mahmoud offers a new, enlightened reading of this situation. He says that the more congenial verses on leniency and equality are the ones quoted first above, which were abrogated by the less congenial verses, which are the latter ones on coercion and inequality. If we say abrogation is a cancellation, then this would imply a change of opinion – as if to say that the Legislator originally presupposed maturity and responsibility in the people addressed, but, surprised by their incapacity, He changed His mind, and introduced other verses, in a less congenial discourse. This, Master Mahmoud asserts, cannot be said of the divine knowledge. The alternative is to say that the Legislator was aware from the first of the incapacity of addressees to appreciate the original verses, but nevertheless revealed them first to prove to the addressees their incapacity, in practice, to realize the verses' objectives. When this had been proved, after 13 years of the call to leniency, they were abrogated and replaced by other verses in a less congenial discourse, because these latter were more suitable for application at that stage of history. The original verses were postponed for use until the present time, when emerging contradictions made it necessary to choose one of two alternatives: either to forgo the religious legislation completely and look for solutions in positive law, or to abrogate the subordinate verses that had been in force in the past and adopt the judgement of the abrogated, original verses.

'The perfection of Islamic Shariah,' says Master Muhammad, 'lies in its being a living body, growing and developing along with life. It directs life in its progress toward God, a progress that never halts. "O you man! You are ever painfully toiling on towards your Lord, but you shall meet Him." (84, *Al-Inshiqaq*, 6.) This meeting is effected by the grace of God, then by that of Islamic Shariah on its three levels: Shariah, method and truth. The development of Shariah, as we have said, lies in moving from one text to another; from a text that suited a seventh-century judgement to another text that was too great for the time, and was hence abrogated. 'None of our revelations do We abrogate or cause to be forgotten, but We substitute something better or similar, did you not know that Allah has power over all things?!' (2, *Al-Baqara*, 106.) The divine words 'None do We abrogate' mean, We do not cancel, nor remove as a verse of judgement; 'Or cause to be forgotten' means, We postpone its power of judgement; 'We substitute something better' means, closer to the understanding of men, and more in keeping with their times than the forgotten one; 'Or similar' means, We repeat the same verse so that it has the power of judgement when the time comes. In other words, the abrogated verses were so abrogated to suit the times. When the proper time comes, these verses assume control of the times, apply judgement, thus becoming 'categorical'; and the verse that was categorical in the seventh century becomes 'abrogated'.

Such is the meaning of the judgement of times. The seventh century had the subordinate verses; modern times have the original ones. Such is the point of abrogation. It is not a complete cancellation, but a postponement until the proper time. In our suggested development, we look at the wisdom behind the text. If a subsequent verse, which abrogated an original verse in the seventh century, has now served its purpose and has proved inadequate for our modern times, it is time for this subsequent verse to be abrogated in turn, and to restore the original abrogated verse, allowing it to assume judgement in modern times and so become a basis for legislation. Such is the meaning of the development of legislation: a move from one text that has served its purpose to another text saved for a more suitable time. It is no mere leap in the dark, or immature viewpoint.

The Master adds: 'But the Messenger of Allah died and left what was abrogated or categorical as it was. Can anyone now be permitted to introduce such a drastically essential change, restoring the abrogated and abrogating the categorical?' Such a question presses itself on the reader. In fact, though, many of those who object to our call for a message of Islam may not object to the content of the call, or even care much about that content. They object to the idea that a message is in need of a messenger endowed with prophethood, and that prophethood was concluded with a categorically clear text. It is true that prophethood was concluded, but the message was not. 'Muhammad is not the father of any of your men, but [he is] the Messenger of Allah, and the Seal of the Prophets, and Allah has full knowledge of all things.' (33, *Al-Ahzab*, 40.) The first thing to realize is that prophethood was not concluded until all that heaven wished to reveal to those on earth had been settled and concluded. All this revelation came by instalments, and with consideration for time, from Adam down to Muhammad. This revelation is the Quran, and its establishment on earth is the reason for the conclusion of prophethood. The wisdom behind the conclusion of prophethood is that people should receive divine inspiration by rational ideation, not through the Archangel Gabriel. This may sound curious at first, but it is the truth, emerging by a process of reason.'[22]

The foregoing demonstrates the coherence of the notion of development as conceived by Master Mahmoud. He sees that all revealed religions represent the Islamic idea in its various stages. They are revealed by instalments across the ages, in an attempt to become established on earth; each of the monotheistic prophets brought a fresh part of this comprehensive idea. 'The best that I brought, as the prophets before me, is that there is no god but Allah,' said Muhammad. Though this testimony is the same with all prophets of monotheism, the level of its application is different for various prophets and nations.[23] This led to different legislation in different times. Master Mahmoud gives an example of this by saying that marriage of brother and sister was an Islamic Shariah for Adam, whereas the present Islamic Shariah has proscribed marriage with relatives far more distant than sister.[24] Master Mahmoud explains difference in legislation for the different prophets, even though they issued from the same source, by the necessities of time, the needs and drives of society in a specific historical situation. 'God,' he says, 'does not legislate for His perfection, but for our imperfection.'

And yet, another question presents itself repeatedly: since we have opened the door for a second message, is it not possible to have a third, a fourth, or even a fifth message? Master Mahmoud does not, though, consider the question formally or logically, but from the perspective of the historical development of societies. Current human society has, he says, attained the highest levels of technical and scientific development, but its spiritual development bears no comparison with its material development. He further believes that the golden age of Islam is not, as many might think, behind us in the folds of history; rather, it is still before us. The golden age will, he thinks, dawn when the original verses, which fundamentally embody the divine intention, are applied; for the subsidiary verses were only the divine intention as alternative. On the original verses is based the social democratic society that endeavours to erase distinctions of religion, race, gender, and so on. He also believes that the course toward full democracy and socialism begins with constitutional law, a law that can only be realized through restoration of the original Meccan verses. He makes a distinction, in the light of this, between the law of man and the law of the jungle, the final stages of which, he believes, we are now experiencing. The first and lowest step of the law of man is constitutional law, which is a ramification of the constitution. The latter is the basic law, so called because it specifies basic rights. These rights are called basic because they are not offered or denied, in the law of man, without right: the right to life and freedom, and the basic ramifications of these that complete and guard the whole body of rights.

The essence of constitutional law is that it removes guardianship over mature men and women. Guardianship should apply only in the case of children. All human beings, men or women, are an end in themselves, and under no circumstances should any human being be used as a means for another individual. This fundamental view derives from the very foundation of the Quran, which is individuality. Basically, responsibility in Islam is an individual issue. 'No sinful soul may carry the sin of another. If such [soul] laden [with sin] should call for its burden [to be shared] none of it will be borne even by a next of kin. You may only admonish those who fear their Lord unseen and establish regular *salat*. And whoever purifies himself does so for the benefit of his own soul; and the destination [of all] is Allah.' (35, *Fatir*, 18.) Moreover: 'The day when no soul shall have power over another, for everything, that day, will be [wholly] with Allah.' (82, *Al-Infitar*, 19.) No man may bear responsibility for a woman, and no woman may bear responsibility for a man. So, why was it necessary for the principle of complete personal responsibility to be reduced to the level of guardianship, which implies incomplete personal responsibility? The answer is: the exigencies of time.[25]

There is, therefore, no need for a third or fourth message. Government may be either democratic or totalitarian. Law may be based either on individual responsibility or on guardianship. For democracy is secured by the legislation of the second message – inherent in the original verses. Democracy begins, but it never ends. It begins by allowing the president broad prerogatives at the beginning, and this keeps the shadow of guardianship on the people and their representatives. But in the long run education will help prepare mature individuals and bring about a homogenous public opinion, while adaptation of laws, with a view to breaking up monolithic authority and weakening the central domination of the state, will serve to restore rights to individuals.[26]

Socialism, he believes, begins by giving the poor their due rights rather than charity, and by managing the means of production through cooperation. Such an application of socialism will serve to guard against state capitalism, whereby the state, itself playing the capitalist role, becomes the exploiter of workers under the pretext of knowing what is best for them, as happened in the former Eastern bloc. This kind of applied socialism follows a path of reform by narrowing the gap between higher and lower incomes, so that a life of dignity becomes a right for every citizen,[27] and the fear of losing one's livelihood disappears. Some may think socialism is gone forever with the fall of the Communist bloc, that the market economy has achieved a final historic victory; but all this is now debatable. Economic experts in some major Western educational institutions have already voiced their doubts and ridiculed this so-called final victory.[28]

In addition to all this, Master Mahmoud believes the subordinate verses will be applied twice. The first time was in the seventh century. Now, in our current times, the original verses will be applied once more, as he had called for and expected. When this application takes place, it will lead to what he calls the 'golden age' of Islam. Then peace will prevail throughout the world, suffering will come to an end, and the divine promise to the people of the earth will be fulfilled. On other occasions, Master Mahmoud has called this the 'millennial age', an age that will last a thousand years. A gradual descent, he says, will follow that age, until the application of the subordinate verses becomes mandatory, once more. And the descent will continue till life returns once more to the jungle whence it originated.[29] He further believes that the 'hour' mentioned in the Quran is actually two hours: one is an hour of prosperity, following the application of the original verses, the other the hour of destruction, coming long after the second application of the subordinate verses.[30]

Conclusion

Master Mahmoud's thought is characterized by a coherent methodology, a comprehensive view, and an integral, critical epistemology informed by an

Islamic philosophy, one that adopts a new, enlightened understanding of the texts. In my modest opinion, his ideas are undoubtedly capable of laying a solid foundation for an Islamic renaissance, through which contemporary Muslims might leave the margins of history to become, once more, makers of history. We should not forget that secularism and positivism, having offered humanity much good since their rise following the fall of church authority, have now run their course. Moreover, our Muslim East is not obliged, in moving toward any future renaissance, to follow the same course taken by the West. There are two reasons for this. First, the course of the West is now under review by the people of the West themselves, especially with regard to human aspects and the guarantee of rights. This course has, after all, had fearful repercussions in terms of family disintegration, a constantly rising crime rate, accelerating drug abuse and other phenomena of alienation and loss leading to a sense of futility and pointlessness – things which cannot be fully covered here. The second reason is that our cultural heritage and viewpoint rests on bases that are still religious in nature, even if, it must be said, we have presently departed from the spirit and values of religion. The serious point here is that such an excessive concern for religion may lead our peoples, in their present bewilderment, to embrace traditional Islamic concepts, along with their disseminators, who are not aware of the current civilizational challenge – who believe, indeed, that current civilization is merely the work of the devil.

The challenge now facing humanity is a global one confronting man as man, irrespective of colour, religion or race. Master Mahmoud sees this challenge in terms of the ability to establish a harmony between man and this 'old-new' atmosphere, which he finds to be a spiritual one with a material aspect.[31] As such, his thought does not defend Islam simply by placing a good image of it before the West, in the context of human rights. He is rather saying that Western civilization itself, whether capitalist or communist, has insufficient knowledge to ensure these rights. Indeed, it is not even following the path that will lead to the securing and safeguarding of these rights. This is because Western civilization is materialistic, based on a severing of the relations between man and the unseen world, elevating material values and enhancing individuality in the narrow, egoistical sense of the word. At the same time, Master Mahmoud affirms categorically that Islamic Shariah based on the subordinate Quranic verses, as applied since the seventh century, does not ensure these rights either. He further stresses that human rights cannot be ensured in any social system unless socialism is combined with democracy. Many people, as noted earlier, believe socialism is gone forever with the dramatic breakdown of Communism. Master Mahmoud, in contrast, believes the challenge represented by the necessity to combine socialism with democracy will remain in force. The claim of freedom within capitalism will remain hollow so long as wealth, and therefore power, is in the hands of rich proprietors. Moreover, he was always of the view that Marxism would fail to apply socialism, let alone communism – [32] because, he said, Marxism lacks the spiritual element informing education, which might in turn replace the drive of capitalist production by enhancing a vigilant conscience.

In sum, we may say that the issue of human rights in Islamic Shariah will continue to represent a serious impasse if we insist on confronting it by contradicting proven historical fact, and by ignoring the evidence of abrogated texts that were not the bases of Shariah in the first place. The coherence of Master Mahmoud's ideas lies in his proposal of a harmonious, coherent and logical programme to confront these two very issues. It must be pointed out, even so, that this essay has not dealt with all the basic aspects of Master Mahmoud's thought. It has concerned itself exclusively with his unique solution for exiting from the impasse of human rights in Islamic Shariah.

PART 3

The concept of human rights in modern social and political Arabic thought

Chapter 13: Human rights in contemporary Arabic thought

Burhan Ghalyoun

I. Arab preludes to human rights

It may be argued that human rights, as a series of pragmatic programmes separate from constitutions, laws and guarantees – in other words, as a distinct
movement and an intrinsic activity – existed nowhere in the world before the
end of the Second World War. The references to human rights and those of citizens that we find in British, American and French declarations or constitutions were simply attempts to identify the new framework for organizing civil
policy; they were not rights imposing specific commitments on the public
authority and allowing for the presence of an organized civil force that would
call for the implementation of these rights. The old declarations expressed the
limits of individual liberties and freedoms, or called for the lifting of such constraints, rather than constructing a series of duties due from the state or the
public authority. In other words, they were an expression of the will or the
determination to achieve liberty, rather than a moral or political commitment
to develop all individuals into free citizens. Later the critical liberal trend would
highlight this phenomenon, arguing that such claims related only to nominal
freedoms and ended, ultimately, in a form of bourgeois democracy that concealed social dictatorship. Perhaps the best evidence for this argument was the
fact that the General Assembly of the United Nations, when discussing the
issue of human rights for the first time, elected to adopt a draft declaration of
general principles and values that failed to commit anyone except in a moral
capacity that could be neither confirmed nor ascertained. The declaration held
back from signing a human rights agreement or convention that would impose
procedural mechanism and create material implements for the mandatory
enforcement of these rights. This explains why states and political authorities
all over the world still treat human rights declarations with great negligence,
despite occasional vocal media coverage in the West as well as in developing

countries. These pronouncements are treated with a measure of gravity only when the powers in question employ them in their political manoeuvres. Human rights have thus become a theme in the context of struggle by private organizations and non-government bodies.

It may be argued accordingly that the genesis of human rights occurred in the late 1960s and early 1970s with the formation of the first societies for defence against the violation of individual rights by the political authority. Amnesty International has played a pivotal role in advocating action against such violations and in sharpening perception of the urgent importance of the concept of human rights to communities suffering such repression and stricture.

The promulgation of the idea was further assisted by the political and social transformations experienced in all human societies during the first half of the twentieth century, and then in the era of major transitions after the Second World War and independence. These transformations released the masses from behind their medieval curtains and developed them into citizens or semi-citizens, or else planted the seeds of citizenship in their minds without necessarily providing the conditions for achieving it. The trend was also given some emphasis by changes to the concept of democracy, which had, since the beginning of the century, emerged from its crises and turned to adopting the social issue as an integral part of its ideology. The disintegration of the Soviet block and its totalitarian experience, along with the collapse of the national development projects of progressive movements in most developing countries, came to consolidate faith in social democracy as the only single alternative; and this, in turn, was given a new driving force, one never before enjoyed by any political or ideological system.

In Arab countries, as in other parts of the Third World, interest in human rights started at both the official and popular levels following the great liberal crisis in the 1970s. This preoccupation was certainly generated under the umbrella of what would later develop as an international ideology of human rights promoted by the United Nations. Arab constitutions still in force clearly reflect this interest. Their provisions show unequivocal commitment to human rights, and their introductions carry statements that are generally in line with the articles of the International Declaration of Human Rights and the two agreements attached to it.[1]

The most recent of these 'constitutions', the Palestinian Declaration of Independence (1988), further manifested this trend toward recognizing the value of human rights, and was, as such, more elaborate and detailed in emphasizing commitment to public freedoms and human rights.[2]

The situation would not, however, remain static. The next two decades were to witness further practical development and further concerted focus on the issue of human rights. Currently, we can identify four types of distinct discourse within contemporary Arab thought on human rights, reflecting the various main approaches toward this theme. The first is expediency discourse, in which the social actors use the idea to present a positive image of themselves and of their behaviour, without having any genuine relationship to its content, or without awareness that such views involve an implicit commitment to achieve its objectives. This discourse looks at human rights from a technical angle, and takes the concept as part of the ideological equipment employed by the states. It does not necessarily have a clear or practical content, nor does it imply any concrete commitment. It is rather a form of speech, or the language commonly circulated in international relations with no visible returns in actual practice. It is the sort of discourse that is prevalent in the transactions of official authorities and United Nations agencies. The second approach is a pragmatic political discourse that believes in human rights and their objectives and values, but handles them as groundwork for more significant issues, such as development, national liberation, strategies to manage national ineptness, etc. The third approach is emanation discourse, which aims at merging and incorporating human rights as a concept and as a value in an ideological context that will maintain the credibility of the local and national heritage and culture. This discourse is interested, primarily, in retaining, maintaining and sustaining a positive presentation of identity; it is prevalent largely in the context of nationalistic and religious national trends. The fourth discourse is critical discourse, which develops side by side with an increase in practical activity. It aims at monitoring, evaluating, and enhancing the effectiveness of these activities, and, as such, is constantly reviewing the nature and objectives of human rights and examining the problem of how these can be realized in tangible and practical terms.

II. Expediency discourse on human rights

It is worthy of note that all Arab constitutions pledge, in their texts, their respect for basic freedoms and human rights. These stipulations concerning all or part of human rights do not, however, involve any political value, nor do they cover any actual legal obligation. These provisions have been incorporated since the 1950s and 1960s as a routine or decorative procedure. As such, they have not prevented governments from disregarding these rights in their entirety. The main incentive for maintaining the idea of human rights in Arab constitutions was perhaps the desire to give these conventions a semblance of modernity, but the Arab League Charter, signed on 22 March 1945, completely ignored the issue, and did not decide to set up a special human rights committee until 1966, in order to take part in the international programme for the Year of Human Rights. On 3 September 1968, and under pressure from certain international and legal circles, the League council issued resolution No. 2443, which recommended setting up a permanent regional Arab human rights committee.[3] The Regional Arab Human Rights Conference, held in Beirut between 2–10 December 1968, called for active cooperation between the committee and the human rights agencies and authorities in other countries with a view to implementing special programmes for these rights, especially those relating to people in the Occupied Territories. The conference also invited member countries to establish national human rights committees that would cooperate with the permanent human rights committee within the Arab League.

On 10 December 1970, in its resolution No. 2668, the Arab League Council established a committee of experts for the purpose of preparing a draft Arab human rights declaration. The committee met at the headquarters of the Arab League Secretariat between 24 April 1971 and 10 July 1971, and endorsed a draft, which was to be reviewed by the member states.[4] Only nine Arab states took the trouble to respond to the draft. Moreover, the positions of these states showed drastic contrasts: some countries gave their full support to it, without any reservation, others rejected it in both form and content, and a third group requested amendments from formal and substantive modifications downward.[5] The project was eventually relegated to total neglect. The situation prompted the League Secretariat, after the provisional transfer of the League, to commission new Arab consultants to draw up a draft for a new Arab human rights charter.[6]

In fact, the Arab League managed to agree on the text of what came to be called the Arab Human Rights Charter only in its plenary session No. 102 on 15 September 1994. Notwithstanding the delay, the Charter is still awaiting ratification by the Arab League member states. The text of the new Charter reflects the negative climate that still characterizes the attitude of official political circles toward human rights. The nominal recognition it accords the conventional rights of individuals and citizens is undermined, if not rendered altogether void, by other provisions and articles. It starts with a confirmation of the right of peoples to their wealth and to the freedom to choose their political system, then moves on to spell out the rights of individuals. The aim here is to emphasize the legitimacy of the regimes of the day, and to prioritize their right to existence over other rights; indeed, by making one dependant on the other. The first article reads as follows:

1a All peoples have the right to self-determination and control of their wealth and natural resources, and, on the basis of this right, they are entitled to freely determine the pattern of their political entity, and to freely carry through their economic, social and cultural development.

1b Racism, Zionism, and foreign occupation and control are a transgression against human dignity, and a principal obstruction to the realization of peoples' essential rights, and it is imperative to condemn all their practices and work to eliminate them.

The following articles are then stated in an attempt to emulate the special international conventions on human rights:

2 Every state partaking in this Charter pledges to guarantee the right to enjoy all the rights and freedoms stated therein for every individual who lives on its territory and adheres to its authority without any discrimination based on race, colour, sex, language, religion, political opinion, national or social or wealth or birth origin, or on any other position, and without any differentiation between men and women.

3a Essential human rights that are established or extant in any state partaking in this Charter in accordance with law, agreements, or convention may not be restricted. Nor can they be parried or depreciated on the grounds that these rights have not been established in this Charter.

3b States partaking in this Charter may not disengage themselves from the basic freedoms that are stated therein when another state gives a lesser measure of such freedoms to its citizens.

4a No constraints may be imposed on the rights and freedoms secured in accordance with this Charter, save those stipulated by law and deemed necessary for the protection of national security and economy, public order, public health, morals, or the rights and freedoms of others.

4b Partaking states, at times of general emergencies that threaten the life of the nation, may take measures that absolve them from their commitment according to this Charter to the necessary extent as strictly dictated by the requirements of the situation.

4c These constraints and such disengagement may not under any circumstance infringe or cover the rights and guarantees relating to the prohibition of torture, offence, repatriation, political asylum, illegitimacy of retrial for the same action, and the legality of crimes and penalties.

As for capital punishment, the Charter provides for the following:

10 Capital punishment shall be confined to extremely grave crimes, and any-
    one condemned to death has the right to request pardon or commuted
    punishment.
11 Capital punishment may not be imposed in all cases for a political crime.
12 The death penalty may not be executed on people below the age of eight-
    een years, on a pregnant woman until she has delivered, or on a nursing
    mother before two years have passed after the date of delivery.

Other articles stipulate that:

26 Freedom of faith, thought, and opinion is guaranteed for every individual.
27 Members of every religion have the right to exercise their religious rituals,
    and the right to express their ideas through worship, practice, or teaching,
    provided that they do not infringe the rights of others. No restrictions may
    be imposed on the practice of the freedom of faith, thought, and opinion,
    save instances stipulated by law.
28 Citizens have the freedom of peaceful meeting and gathering, and no
    restrictions may be imposed on the practice of these two freedoms except
    in consideration for national security, public safety, or the protection of
    the rights and freedoms of others.
29 The state guarantees the right to establish unions, and the right to strike
    within the limits stipulated by law.
30 The state guarantees for every citizen the right to work that secures a stan-
    dard of living which would meet the basic requirements of life, and the
    right to comprehensive social security.

Article No. 37 states that:

> Minorities may not be deprived of their right to enjoy their cultures or comply
> with the tenets of their religion.[7]

In the words of Eric Goldstein, executive director of the New York-based
Human Rights Watch for the Middle East, the long-awaited Arab Human
Rights Charter endorsed by the Arab League is a 'flimsy document. While it
emphasizes a series of human rights for the individual, it gives governments
immense authority to suspend these rights in order to maintain national, economic, or public security, or in cases of emergency. Worse still is the fact that
the Charter – despite its innate frailty – appears to be too exacting in the eyes of
the member states of the League. Of the twenty-two member states, seven

have voted against the Charter since its presentation three years ago, and only one country, namely Iraq, has endorsed it.'[8]

Similarly, as one researcher observes, no reference is made to citizens' right to election as a significant channel for political participation and power circulation, unless such rights are promoted by governments intent on maintaining their stay in power. This is also evidenced by the ambiguity and generality of the references made in the Charter to political and civil rights and freedoms that are closely related to participation and election, such as the freedom of faith, thought, and opinion, and the freedom of peaceful meeting and gathering.[9] This practice is no cause for surprise. Arab authorities constantly argue that the depth of their concern over human rights is reflected in the special councils set up to observe the application of these rights, as in Morocco, Algeria and Tunisia. Arab and international human rights organizations, however, still maintain that no genuine change has been introduced to the conventional practices.[10]

Arab constitutions are rich in principles that guarantee rights and freedoms and secure human rights. Practice, however, is impeded by many obstructions. Most Arab constitutions refer the regulation of various rights to the laws, and some of them include qualifications to the provisions and political constraints that, in effect, undermine the guarantees previously endorsed.

These constraints are stated as main premises and truisms in some of the constitutions in question. They include qualifications added to the principle of transparency of laws, or conditions that jeopardize the principle of equality. This does not apply only to the Arab constitutions of the previous generation. It has even aggravated the situation in some of the constitutions that were proposed in 1990 as part of reform programmes in certain Arab countries.

Foremost among the impediments obstructing the observance of legal provisions are the emergency and martial laws, which give wide powers to governing bodies that default on human rights guarantees. They permit the martial governor, by decree, to detain suspects or persons considered to be dangerous to public law and order, and to search and inspect people and places irrespective of the provisions of penal procedure law. They also give him the authority to impose penalties for actions and abstentions, penalties that are not consistent with legal principles.

Similarly, Arab legislation is crammed with exceptions put forward as regular laws, whose provisions, in effect, infringe the guarantees established for human rights at regional and international conventions, and often blow away the guarantees laid down in the national constitutions themselves. Notable among these is law No. 95 for the year 1980, known in Egypt as 'the law for the protection of values from shame.'[11]

The first and most important of these guarantees lacking in Arab conventions and constitutions is the absence of an independent constitutional quote system, without which no constitution can claim validity. As Shibli Mallatt observes:

> Governments usually disregard rights and constitutions that are not protected by autonomous institutions which have the right, and indeed the legal duty, to remind the negligent authority of its constitutional limits.[12]

The independence of the judiciary system is stressed in the constitutions. Yet Arab governments, while thus underscoring their respect for the principle, deprive it of substantive content by giving the legislative and executive authorities the necessary means to ensure their precedence over the judiciary, and the ability to subdue it in one way or another. In the words of Ahmad al-Rashidi:

> Contravention of the principle of independence for courts is represented in many Arab countries by such actions as interference in the proceedings of the judiciary process, holding back the execution of court judgement, permitting wide judiciary powers to the executive bodies in exceptional circumstances, intervention in the formation of judiciary bodies, delegating a wide range of authorities to martial courts, etc.'[13]

As clearly pointed out in the annual report of the Arab Organization for Human Rights for 1997, authorities in Arab countries continue to violate guarantees to fair trial by extensive referral of civilians to military courts and by applying various forms of exceptional judiciary administration. There are still supreme state security and emergency courts in Egypt, Syria and Iraq. The role and powers of security courts have also been enhanced in Jordan and Bahrain. Special courts in Sudan and martial courts in Somalia are still active. Committees and observers of human rights still highlight the absence of the conditions for justice and fair trial in scores of cases, along with the withholding of defendants' rights and the obtaining of confessions under duress and coercion, the infringement of the rights of defence, and the disregard shown by security authorities in releasing decisions taken by courts. The treatment of prisoners and other detainees is still a general issue in most Arab countries, and there are increasing complaints of torture, which has become a systematic practice in detention centres. In some Arab countries large numbers of victims have died in prison, leading to condemnation by United Nations agencies.

The report also states that more than a third of Arab countries suffer from strict restraint on freedom of opinion and expression in its various forms. Although these countries follow different political or ideological disciplines, they share the policy of prohibiting opposing views and banning all forms of protest and peaceful gathering. 'They all impose on people with different opinions such heavy and varied sanctions as dismissal from service, detention, trial, imprisonment, or persecution of political opponents.'[14]

Arab human rights groups have requested the conclusion of an Arab human rights agreement similar to the European and American human rights conventions signed in the Costa Rican capital San José on 22 November 1969, and many advocates of human rights, led by Hussein Jamil, have called for the creation of a practical instrument for the protection and proper application of Arab human rights, including the setting up of an Arab Court of Human Rights, similar to the European Court of Human Rights, which was the prime protection mechanism stipulated in the European agreement on human rights.

Jamil has suggested that the Arab agreement should include provisions for the establishment of the court and for its competence and procedure in connection with the protection of human rights and essential freedoms, and has recommended that the agreement should call for the formation of an Arab human rights committee with each participating state represented by one member. Complaints against any violation of the provisions of the Arab human rights agreement would be presented to this committee. The general panel of the court would include a number of judges equal to the number of the states endorsing the agreement. Each state would nominate three judges, two of whom would be citizens of the state in question, and the political committee of the Arab League would then select one for membership within the court. The assignment of judges to the court should be discontinued only when they had reached a particular age. The court would elect a president and a number of vice-presidents as required. A number of judges representing the participating states would be selected by the court panel to look into certain cases. The provisions of this agreement are generally similar to those of the European convention, with some differences of detail.[15]

None of these demands has been accommodated in the Arab League Charter on Human Rights. Arab states still, in practice, elect to apply human rights only in the interests of publicity. Many of them will set up higher councils to supervise the proper observance of human rights, or form subsidiary bodies to forestall independent organizations – their main objective in thus raising the banner of human rights, within this discourse of publicity, is to turn the legal instrument which targets systems and regimes practicing human rights violations into a mask to cover such violations, and also to give the violators themselves a liberal and humane image.

III. Political discourse: human rights as a means of
redeeming the national regeneration Project

In reality, any actual movement for the defence of human rights in the Arab world would wait until the 1970s, with the deepening of the crisis in Arab ruling regimes, and the increasing demands this crisis had imposed on non-government organizations in the various fields of social activity. Unlike other organizations, this movement witnessed a swift and strong development, despite the historical opposition of those of progressive tendency toward the idea of democracy, plurality and human rights, which was portrayed as a romantic utopian notion lacking scientific perspective on the reality of social and class conflict throughout the world.

Reality would soon introduce the theme of human rights into Arab political thought of every tendency, just as it did in the context of intellectual currents all over the world. What had been projected, a few decades earlier, as one of the features of liberal divisionism would now become the common claim of all leftist, nationalist and socialist forces through the world, against increasing racist trends in the West, and against fundamentalist Islamic trends, or ethnic orientations, in the developing world. In the Arab world, the concept of human rights would, as an ideological benchmark, become the resort and refuge of those social forces which, following the collapse of progressive national and socialist ideologies, were left defenceless in the face of assaults from the rising Islamic and radical current. Soon, however, these same groupings, or at least large numbers of the intellectual elite within them, would find themselves obliged to fall back on the ideology of human rights in an attempt to defend themselves, this time, against the powers of repression that had now entered a life or death struggle with the Islamic movement. In less than two decades, many human rights organizations would provide a refuge for former militants now grown frustrated at the deterioration in the quality of political practice in the Arab world. Human rights would be promoted as an indemnification for – and an alternative to – hopes of democratic and peaceful change, and would be taken as the focal point for meeting and convergence of the various political forces. The new reality would play a major role in representing the subject of human rights at the widest possible level in contemporary Arab intellectual and social circles.

What entrenched the cause of human rights in Arab consciousness so firmly, and in less than two decades, was the conviction that current political regimes had reached a point of bankruptcy. It then became necessary to return to a natural state of affairs that would eliminate the exceptional political conditions established in the name of national liberation, together with all the attendant hopes for unity and social justice, and for confrontation with Zionism and Israeli expansionism. The call for human rights, and the parallel advocacy of democracy, came to confirm this strong orientation toward the return to law as a concrete materialization of the condition of a natural social life, and as an expression of the dissipation of revolutionary illusions or the anticipation of extraordinary historical transformations. In short, serious contemplation of human rights in the Arab world started only after the credits of politics had been exhausted, and only when progressive and revolutionary political practitioners had reached a political deadlock.

Such was the context which characterized, and would continue to characterize, the approach adopted by contemporary Arab nationalist and leftist thought, irrespective of its orientation, toward human rights. The primary objective of this approach was to consolidate the idea of human rights as a leverage for political nationalist and national work, both as an instrument for building democracy and as a weapon in the struggle against existing totalitarianism. Arab nationalist and leftist thought had undoubtedly been distant from the idea of human rights. The reservations raised by this school of thought, which was dominant in the 1960s, were in fact no different from those posited by progressive camps elsewhere in the world. There were two important reservations in this respect.

The first pointed out that any discussion of these rights, and of work to defend them, meant, in effect, a recognition of the legitimacy of the ruling bourgeois political system, and of the possibility of work within its framework. In the light of this, any such discussion would give the masses seeking change an illusory impression that the desired objectives could be reached through the legal battle and through a revival of civil and political rights. This meant relinquishing the demand for changing the material, social and political conditions within society, and hence forsaking the strategy of comprehensive social change in favour of fragmentary solutions. Workers in the field of human rights were thus accused of and indicted for liberalist pollution and supporting the current bourgeois rule instead of combating it.

The second reservation focused on the position of human rights organizations during the period, most of them being seen as instruments of imperialist policy for intervention in the internal affairs of independent countries to which they were opposed.[16] Apparent in this intervention was a double standards policy, which deprived the large powers of any validity or credibility in their practices.

With regard to the Arab world, we might add a third reservation to the two important apprehensions noted above. The organizations active in the field of human rights often favoured the policies of the Zionist state, and thus concentrated their criticism on Arab countries – to the credit and benefit of the Israeli side. In the eyes, therefore, of a large sector of public opinion in the Arab world, dealing with human rights organizations and their ideologies was perceived as a risky form of conscious or unconscious collusion and cooperation with the enemies of the nation and the national movement, whether these enemies were functionaries within the defeated conventional bourgeois systems or else sympathizers with international imperialism and its anti-independence policies, or with the Jewish state – the enemy and occupation force.[17]

In the light of these reservations, the pioneers would not emphasize the autonomy of the concept of human rights. Nor would they seek to deny that it subscribed to liberal ideology, or that it lent itself to exploitation by the enemies of the Arab nation. Instead they would stress one central idea: namely the role of freedoms in saving Arab societies from the risk of losing their battle and their national objectives at both the social and local levels. Human rights activities would thus focus on exposing constraints that had been imposed on freedoms and would indicate their support for political action or party affiliation. At other times, they would present themselves as alternative courses of action. This explains why the first generation of pioneers came largely from the broad ranks of Arab nationalist, progressive and leftist trends alike. They were prompted primarily by their hope of saving the national regeneration project, which appeared on the verge of collapse.

Perhaps the best representative of this trend, in both thought and action, was Mundhir 'Anabtawi, who was one of the early activists and theorists working to launch the movement for Arab human rights. His thinking on the subject of human rights stemmed, he affirmed, from a solid conviction perhaps shared by large numbers of people interested in public affairs: that the military and political defeats which had stricken the nation, which had stunted its national objectives and driven the people into moral sterility if not pervasive desperation, sprang largely from depriving citizens of a multitude of rights and basic freedoms, or else of inculcating in them the fear that they might lose even such minimal rights as they enjoyed. Contemplation of human rights also stemmed from the belief that such conditions would hamper fulfillment of the minimum level of national and pan-Arab hopes within each small country and in the larger Arab homeland. The persistence of this situation would also present a threat to what might be described, by some, as a personal or public achievement here and there.

'Anabtawi declares in no uncertain terms that his thinking on human rights is driven by:

utter amazement not only at the position taken by régimes vis-à-vis the tumultuous events in Lebanon, especially after the Israeli invasion in early June 1982, but also at the complete silence that enveloped the Arab masses everywhere with regard to this catastrophe, and the absence of any spontaneous popular demonstration against it. In the grip of this amazement – or shock rather – many people started to wonder: if the régimes have been so spineless, what will happen to the nation from the Ocean to the Gulf?

In an attempt to identify the causes of these events, 'Anabtawi begins with the following proposition:

What happened was a natural result of the way the Arab citizen continues to be deprived of his rights and essential freedoms through new and advanced techniques guided by a policy of distraction, intimidation and attraction, i.e. a stick-and-carrot policy, aimed at taming and subjugating citizens, disabling their public interests, and, subsequently, downsizing their national and pan-Arab objectives.

He then goes on to say:

What this study suggests is to invite some among the intellectual elite to leave their towers; to ask them to dedicate some of their intellectual, professional and scientific capabilities to supporting the cause of human rights and basic freedoms for their citizens, and to give a proper example in the field of public service without expecting any returns, even when some small sacrifices have to be made. Until such pressure has been brought into being, specialized groups must rise in all Arab countries and address this issue in action and thought by conducting scientific studies, organizing seminars, and adopting practical proposals that would be circulated and discussed amongst them, and with the official authorities, without their becoming involved in the periodic conflicts of the régimes. In this way they will insure their credibility and enhance their effectiveness.'[18]

Another Arab intellectual points in the same direction:

In the history of societies there are defining moments at which events and catastrophes interact and lead to the presentation of issues in an urgent and pressing fashion. This is our situation today with democracy and human rights. Over the last fifteen years, the issue of democracy has knocked at the doors of the Arab mind, and imposed itself twice on the concerns of Arab intellectuals and thinkers. The first instance came in the wake of the battle of June 1967, and the second in June 1982 after the Israeli invasion of Lebanon, which had passed without invoking any deep reactions at the popular or governmental levels. The question was: why did we not witness any popular reaction . . . and why did Arab

citizens not raise their voices as they had done tens of times in the 1940s and
the 1950s? The answer this time lay in systematic repression, and the strutting
powers of the state in the absence of constitutional or popular government, and
the constant violation of human rights.'[19]

In an attempt to define the interests and motives that drive human rights militants into political action, Munsif al-Marzouqi, former president of the
Tunisian League for Human Rights identifies an enormous hidden force:
namely patriotism.[20]

It may be argued that, for the first time in Arab political thought, democracy
and the liberation of citizens from the tyranny of authoritarian systems were
perceived as affiliates or as necessary conditions for initiating or reactivating
national action. According to 'Anabtawi, the collapse of the nationalist Arab
project has stripped the monolithic political regime of its credibility, legitimacy
and raison d'être, following the systems' failure to provide external means of
protection and achieve industrial take off and national integration, and the
attendant deterioration in the structure and traditions of the national authority.

> People now started to hold a different view of the system and the means of reg-
> ulating authority and government. The system, which, in the eyes of the large
> majority of people, reflected the youthful, living and open national and nation-
> alistic will for innovation and change, had now turned into a symbol of deterio-
> ration and corruption. The politics of the single party, which once signified
> effectiveness and achievement, had now become merely symptomatic of sense-
> less violence and usurpation of power, of rejection of participation and natural
> transaction with the rest of the people.
>
> Since the 1970s, the radical turn around in social orientation has manifested
> itself in a general change in the Arab ideological climate. The retreat from total-
> itarian thought has begun to take a stronger and more violent character since the
> early 1980s, which saw a vigorous return to the values of democratic thought.
> This was represented in writings, seminars and political meetings, and reflected
> in the deep, almost terminal crisis experienced by the political parties in general
> and by leftist parties in particular.'[21]

The clear political motives that inspired the first generation of active nationalist intellectuals, and provided blueprints for their conceptualization of the
issue of human rights, were projected in the establishment of the 'Arab
Organization for Human Rights' as a pan-Arab institution.[22]

The theoretical framework for these rights, and the mode of their application, were also manifested in the project for a 'Charter on Human and Peoples'
Rights in the Arab World.'[23]

A comparison of the introduction to this project with that of the Arab League will show the width of the gap between the two propositions. The introduction to the Charter on Human and Peoples' Rights in the Arab World states as follows:

Whereas the recognition of the natural dignity of all members of the human community, and of their equal and inalienable rights, represent the foundation of freedom, justice, and peace in government,

and owing to the strong and indivisible ties that combine the members of the Arab nation, as represented in the unity of values, heritage, history, civilization, and interests, in all its states, whose land was blessed by Allah the Almighty who made it a cradle of messages from heaven, and in view of the hopes they have for resuming participation in the development and advancement of human civilization, and since neglect of the collective rights of the Arab nation and the rights of people on its territories, has led to countless catastrophes that started with the occupation of Palestine and the establishment of an alien racial entity in it, and in the expulsion of its people, and ended with violating all the Arab land and wasting its human and material resources and binding its capabilities and destiny with external forces, thus incapacitating it from maintaining its development and independence and from fulfilling its legitimate expectations. And since exit out of this tragic reality can be achieved only through a common understanding of these rights and of the means necessary for securing them under the principle of the autonomy of law if the Arab nation were to avoid resorting to revolt against tyranny and prosecution,

and in confirmation of their belief in the principles of the United Nations and in the legitimacy of international human rights, a number of experts, intellectuals, and jurists committed to the causes of the Arab nation and concerned about its future and destiny, met in Syracuse – Italy, in the period 5–12 December 1987, at an invitation from the high international institute of criminology,

these representatives now declare the following project for an Arab Charter on Human Rights and the Rights of the Arab People, and turn to the members of the Arab nation in all its states, to adopt it as an ideal model to be reached, and to make it the starting point for the pan-Arab project in order to contribute to the development and restoration of the nation.

They also turn to the Arab countries, individually and collectively, and to their joint bodies, primarily the Arab League, to study it with a view to affecting its adoption and implementation.[24]

The Charter begins with article No. 1, which states: 'Every human being, wherever he may be found, has the right to have his legal character recognized.'

The draft consists of 65 articles, divided into two sections; the first comprises articles relating to human rights and the formation of the Arab Human

Rights Committee; the second covers the procedural aspects for human rights protection and the Arab Human Rights Court.

These concepts, merging human rights with the pursuit of achieving national objectives and securing the future of the Arab nation and defending its rights and destiny, were reflected in a more expressive and mature statement, namely the final declaration of the general conference of the Union of Arab Lawyers.[25]

After discussing social and political conditions, the conference members explicitly emphasized 'the unity and indivisibility of human rights, and that reaching a condition whereby some of these rights may be fully enjoyed cannot be achieved by neglect or disregard for the other rights, and that the venue for facing the current crisis in democracy in our countries calls for wide participation, as well as for implementing economic, social and cultural rights in addition to civil and political rights.'

The conference also made the following points:

> [It stresses] the necessity to implement the right to comprehensive development as an integral part of the system of human rights and democracy. It also calls on competent parties not to comply with the demands of international lending institutions, primarily the International Monetary Fund and the World Bank, which damage economic, social and cultural rights belonging primarily to the disadvantaged social sectors.
>
> It also calls for the activation of other rights, including the right to possession of a clean environment.
>
> It also calls upon Arab governments to remove all obstacles impeding the enjoyment by women of all their rights in society, and for the annulment of all legislation depriving her or constraining the practice of her civil and political rights. The conference also calls upon Arab countries to consider the rights of children and the family, and, in this respect, it expresses high appreciation for the endorsement by Arab governments of the charter for children's rights, and calls upon the governments to implement the pledges and commitments stated therein.

The conference further called upon Arab governments to endorse international agreements relating to the plight of refugees, and to cooperate with the United Nations High Commission for Refugees to find effective solutions to refugee problems. It noted the effective role played by the Union of Arab Lawyers in drafting an Arab agreement on refugees, and requested the General Secretariat of the Union to exert optimal efforts to insure the Arab League Council would adopt and endorse these agreements. It also called on the General Secretariat to continue its cooperation with the High Commission for Refugees in Geneva on issues relating to refuge and refugees.

At the national level, the conference stressed its condemnation of all violations against the rights of the Palestinian people by the Israeli occupation forces, particularly in issues relating to murder, provisions for capital punishment outside the law, arbitrary and administrative arrests, detention without charge or trial, restrictions on movement, the besieging of the Palestinian people in its homeland, expatriation of citizens from their homeland, violation of their economic, social and cultural rights, especially in cases of expropriation, replacing of rightful citizens by immigrants from outside, demolishing of houses and uprooting of trees and plants, and recurrent closure of educational institutions. The conference appealed to the international organizations concerned to work to halt these repressive procedures, and to secure the guarantees and special rights relating to the conditions of the population in occupied territories as expressed in the fourth Geneva convention. The conference called for the provision of international legal protection for the Palestinian people, and urged all Arab countries and the Arab League to face Israeli violations in the Occupied Territories, and to condemn them at the international level, and to work toward the provision of the necessary legal guarantees. The conference cautioned against pressure to accept the idea of the divisibility of United Nations resolutions, particularly in cases of expulsion. It also called upon all Arab countries to lift restrictions on the movement and stay of Palestinians.[26]

The stress on the importance of human rights in alleviating the impact of the failure of national development and liberation projects was articulated more forcefully in the final report issued by the seminar – 'For a Better Arab Tomorrow: Current Arab Situations and Ways to Resolve the Crisis'[27] – where discussions and themes were reminiscent of elaborations made prior to the establishment of the Arab Organization. The report states as follows:

> [It emphasizes the need to] consolidate the struggle to instate democratic rights and human rights, and to face the obstacles standing in the way of this end. In this respect, a number of simple yet practical recommendations have been made for achieving the necessary gradual accumulation:

- Members of this seminar and of the Arab National Conference will join the Arab Human Rights Organization, and pledge to persuade others to join as well;
- Through our associations with parties, institutions and media, we intend to make the issue of human rights a prime cause;
- We intend to devote the utmost attention to supporting the institutions of civil society. This struggle includes an entrenchment of democratic values

within these institutions, given that some of them do not establish their internal ties on democratic grounds;

• We, as intellectuals, must present, more forcefully, issues relating to national non-Arab communities living within Arab territories and speaking a language other than Arabic. The trend toward neglecting these communities must be resisted, and we, as Arab intellectuals, must show an unequivocal attitude toward recognizing these communities and their national rights, especially in view of obvious excesses in connection with this question. On the one hand, there are parties that wish to exclude these communities on grounds of equality, whereas other parties, conversely, fail to show due regard for the unity of Arab countries in their claims for national rights for these communities. This issue must be viewed from a democratic and human perspective. These communities are there, and must achieve their rights within the framework of unity of Arab countries.[28]

IV. Emanation Discourse: Islam and human rights

In the words of Muhammad 'Asfour, who was commissioned by the General Secretariat of the Arab League to draw up a draft for the Arab Human Rights Charter,

> In the Arab scene, a significant issue has arisen regarding the manner of issuing the Arab Human Rights Charter: would the Charter be an attempt to project a purely Arab point of view, or a distinctly Arab concept of human rights that would take into consideration the special characteristics of the Arab social reality and its underlying intellectual and philosophical origins; or should it rather be a reiteration of the International Declaration and a confirmation by the Arab homeland of its support and adoption of the western heritage expressed in the International Declaration?
>
> In fact, the two aspects of the controversy relate to questions of peculiarity and universality: there is a clear position in some Arab countries that the principles of Islamic Shariah should be the exclusive basis for defining human rights. This position is supported by the writings of a number of jurists who argue that the history of human rights is not the history prescribed in the West ...
>
> I have taken these considerations and disputes into account in submitting the draft for the Charter. I was clear that the issue of human rights must not be merely an international matter, but an issue of local concern as well. This local characteristic, however, cannot be inconsistent or contradictory with the achievements and gains made by the human rights cause at the international

level, as expressed in the Charter of the United Nations, or the International Declaration of Human Rights, or in subsequent conventions. Within this understanding, the objectives of issuing an Arab Human Rights Charter are – indeed must be – more modest than a projection of special Arab characteristics or a distinct concept of human rights. As such, it is far from being a clear and specific Arab vision of the human rights issue as a manifestation of the contribution of Arab culture to international heritage. There is no room here for rivalry or competition or even confrontation between Arab Islamic civilization and Western Christian civilization. Accordingly, when we stress the special or national aspect of human rights, we emphasize, at the same time and with the same force, the universality of human rights. The principles that guarantee these rights go beyond cultural distinctiveness because they express common human meanings and values, whether of a heavenly nature through what God revealed to His prophets, or of a secular nature as established in the human soul and conscience throughout cultural evolution.'[29]

Most of those advocating respect for Arab Islamic distinctiveness in the area of human rights come from the Islamic camps, regardless of their orientations and tendencies. This is, perhaps, what differentiates these from their colleagues. The various trends in Islamic thought have kept pace with the track of Arabic thought in addressing the human rights issue, and Muslim thinkers have felt the need to highlight the presence of this concept in Islamic heritage. Three trends may be outlined within these orientations. There is a humanist liberal trend that continues the spirit of revival initiated by Islamic reformist thought under the influence of Jamal al-Din al-Afghani and Muhammad 'Abduh. This trend treats international gains as part of the common heritage of humanity, without labelling it as alien or as a foreign expression exclusive to the spirit of western culture. While seeking to ground these concepts in Islamic frameworks, this camp makes no attempt to stress their precedence in Islam, or to stress the superiority of the guarantees for implementation offered by Islam. The second camp is the neo-fundamentalist trend, which accepts the notion of human rights but criticizes its western frame of reference, and attempts to reconstruct the concept on Islamic grounds that would make it consistent with the provisions of Islamic Shariah. This camp emphasizes the precedence of Islam in discussing the issue of human rights, and the mandatory character of these rights as part of the requirements of faith, although it often treats these rights in accordance with the prescriptions of Shariah. The third orientation is the radical conservative camp that rejects all idea of thinking from western perspectives, and calls for adherence to Islamic terms and principles, which provide guarantees for the protection of the rights of humans – the heirs of

God on earth – better than those provided by secular rights. The common denominator among all these, however, is the wish to take the concept out of its western framework and modify it in line with the values of Arab Islamic culture.

One proponent of the first camp is Ahmad Kamal Abu 'l-Majd who argues as follows:

> Respect for human rights everywhere, and defending the freedom of those who are, politically and socially, victims of injustice, must occupy a prominent position in the interests of the new Islamic trend . . . it is surprising that Muslims do not have a very powerful presence in all formal and popular international organizations that are preoccupied with the protection and defence of the freedoms and the rights of the victims of justice everywhere.[30]

Similar notions are put forward by Muhammad Ahmad Khalafallah:

> When Shariah is associated with faith, it is the right of God exclusively. In this case, Shariah will be taken into account and science will have no bearing on the matter. On the other hand, when Shariah relates to human rights, or, in the language of jurists, to transactions, humans may then take guidance from science, especially in areas not provided for by the text . . .
>
> Some religious scholars, like the *imam* al-Toufi, contend that when contradiction arises within science, i.e. reason and interpretation/tradition, i.e. the text, one may take the course of action that serves one's interests in either of them . . .
>
> And Almighty God has given us the tracks on which we can habitually recognize our interests. We must not therefore move away from this road into an ambiguous objective which may or may not lead us to our interest.
>
> The road that fulfills interests is the way of human knowledge, at which reason arrives through trial, according to what is described as scientific principle or social theory.[31]

This trend encompasses the thoughts of the Algerian intellectual Malik ibn Nabi, who stresses that, in calling for the liberation of man and the rejection of tyranny, Islam, by necessity, involves a model of democracy.[32]

The interpretation of Shaykh Mahmoud Taha, the leader of the Republican Brothers, also falls in this category. He calls for the establishment of a new judicial system based on a rejection of the principles and systems of traditional jurisprudence, and for a return to the spirit of the message expressed in the Meccan *sura*s. His disciple 'Abdallah al-Na'im interprets this further.[33]

The neo-fundamentalist trend, on the other hand, acknowledges the consistency between these rights and Islamic Shariah, but refuses absolute acceptance and calls for the reconciling and modifying of these rights to the principles and limitations of Shariah. Some of these limitations relate to issues on which there are explicit texts, whereas others relate to legal reference points and to issues of equality between man and woman, as well as certain religious freedoms.

This trend is summed up by Yusuf al-Qaradawi, who stresses that:

> all principles and values upon which democracy has been built, such as freedom, dignity, the protection of human rights, are Islamic principles. They regard them as rights, but for us they are an obligation and a religious duty. What is considered a right in democracy is taken in Islam as an obligation. There is a difference between the two, because human beings can relinquish their rights.

In his critique of conservative Islamic trends, al-Qaradawi says:

> Some people take democracy to mean the rule of the people, and view this as inconsistent with Islam, which calls for faith in the government of God. In this view, democracy runs counter to the rule of God.

This view, however, is incorrect:

> Those who call for democracy do not necessarily argue against the rule of God, but rather oppose the absolute rule of individuals. The argument here relates to the rule of the people against the rule of tyrannical individuals, and not the rule of the people against the government of God. We Muslims do not wish the nation to be governed by an individual despot, who would impose his will on it and lead it by force against its will. We, therefore, call for democracy within an Islamic society, in which the constitution stipulates that the religion of the state is Islam, and that Islam is the prime source of government or the single source of legislation.'[34]

Muhammad 'Amara argues similarly, as follows:

> In Islam we find faith in man and sanctification of his rights reaching far beyond the extent of considering them as rights; rather we establish them as duties to be incorporated within the framework of duties. Food, clothing, housing, security, freedom of thought, belief, expression, science, education, and participation in forming the general order and control of society, calling to account the guardians of social affairs, revolution to change régimes of disablement, repression, promiscuity and corruption, etc. – all these matters are not simply rights for man in the Islamic perspective, rights that he should claim, work for, and persevere in achieving, without being barred from demanding them. They are rather necessities imposed on man, and duties that he has to perform . . .

These obligatory human necessities are so sacred in Islam that they are considered the foundation without which religion cannot be instituted for men. It is upon these obligations that faith and, subsequently, religiosity are built.

In our Shariah, the health of the body is given precedence over the health of religion, because it is sound bodies that are prerequisites for religiosity and faith, hence the subjugation of human needs to religious prohibition. Significant as they are as the core of our conviction and commitment to our great faith, our beliefs in the Oneness of God and in the subservience of man to God are rights that we owe to Almighty God for the blessings bestowed on humans in terms of the necessities of life, such as security and moral and material benefits. Religiosity, in this case, stems from our enjoyment of these human necessities, and it is but a manifestation of our gratitude for the grace of God and the flow of these necessities from His generous beneficence. Man's religiosity here is based on his enjoyment of these necessities. And Almighty God says:

'For Quraysh's customary journey,
The journey of the winter and summer,
Let them worship the Lord of this House,
Who has fed them when they were hungry and secured them
against fear.'

(Holy Quran, Surat Quraish, 1–4)

The soundness of the affairs of religion is dependent on, and subject to, the soundness of the affairs of this world, and the condition of religion cannot be amended unless the worldly situation has been ameliorated, that is to say unless man enjoys these necessities that have been stipulated by Islam.

The absence of these human necessities deprives humans of their capacities and facilities. Jurists have thus agreed that the worship of the hungry and the fearful is not valid because it has not been preceded by the appropriate elements of prayer. Similarly, Islam has elevated the status of humans by establishing as obligatory human necessities what other civilizations have considered only rights.[35]

'Amara draws further evidence for this argument from a quotation by Ibn Qayyim al-Jawziyya (691/1292–751/1350):[36]

God has sent His messengers and revealed His books so that people may establish equality, which is justice as supported by heavens and by the earth. When the signs of truth are obvious, and the glowing evidence of justice is dawning in any direction, God's Shariah, religion, consent and command will be shown. Almighty God has not confined the road, the evidence and the signs of justice to one type, and has not annulled other routes that might be stronger and more visible. He has shown in the roads He established that His objective is to institute rights and justice and to enable people to induct equality. Any road that leads to the right and to the knowledge of justice must therefore be used and applied. Roads and ways are only instruments and facilities, which are not used for their own sake, but rather for attaining the objectives and aims to which they lead. But God, in whatever roads He has designed, has shown their justification as well as their resemblances.

This position is also defended by Salim al-'Awwa[37] and Rashid al-Ghanoushi:

Many contemporary Islamic thinkers believe that:

1   The principles of human rights are not as genuine and original in any ideology as they are in Islam, because Islam established them as obligations and religious worships rather than interests as they are in the West.
2   Western declarations on human rights represent a significant development toward the universality of Islam. Recognizing that man, on grounds of his humanity, enjoys rights and dignities is a commendable human development welcomed by Islam, whose human discourse has been unprecedented . . . this declaration, and any other document to the same effect, is acceptable by Islam as a general improvable framework for rights and relations among people.'[38]

This trend, which represents the dominant force in current Islamic thinking, is further represented by Muhammad al-Ghazali,[39] Taha Jaber al-'Alwani and many intellectuals in the camps of the Muslim Brotherhood in different Arab countries. It lay behind the issue of the Islamic International Human Rights Statement which was published in the same year in London and Paris.[40] Authors of this declaration placed these rights in the context of Islamic Shariah as derived from the Quran, or the *sunna*. This could not be achieved without moulding the concept of human rights and establishing its status and the limits of its application. The introduction contains the following statement:

Fourteen centuries ago, Islam instituted human rights in a comprehensive and thorough manner, provided them with sufficient protection guaranty, and developed society on principles that consolidate and support these rights.

The declaration gives human rights the character of religious obligations, rather than allowances or licences for human action as is the case among many partisans of this trend. The rights of minorities and the right to equality between women and men, and the issue of defection as well as other Islamic judiciary provisions, are also pointed out in the statement, with restrictions consistent with Islamic Shariah.

The statement reflects the predominant theme on human rights in this camp, as best expressed by Dr. Yusuf al-Qaradawi:

> We therefore call for democracy in an Islamic society in which the constitution stipulates that Islam is the religion of the state, and that Islam is the major source of government or the only source of legislation. We must not follow the experience of the West in democracy, with all its strengths and weaknesses, its good and evil sides, and its bitter and sweet tastes. We must take this experience within restrictions dictated by Islam's ultimate principles. It must be articulated in the text of the constitution of the Islamic state that Islam and Islamic Shariah are the sources of laws, or that any law or system or situation that contradicts Islamic principles is null and void.[41]

Muhammad Fat-hi 'Uthman refers, in his critical remarks, to some of the issues relating to human rights that are still under review by the proponents of this trend.

> I do not think there is a disagreement over the principles. The discussion occasionally centres on an Islamic human rights perceptive. Here there is a renewal of what has been established in Islamic jurisdiction, that rights are determined first and foremost by the legislator. It is my belief that the statement by Almighty God: We have bestowed dignity upon the children of Adam, refers to honour determined or destined for man at birth. It can be achieved in legislation only by enacting the provisions of Islam.

'Uthman then calls on Islamic movements to take liberal positions in this respect by developing a new concept of rights in which humans are part of the decision.

> In the political field, human rights are manifested especially in the right to opinion, expression, and criticism, as well as in the right to gathering and formation of associations on a permanent basis, and supporting these rights with guaranties for any individual or community without discrimination, and taking positions of support and opposition on these grounds. This attitude needs to be consistent and clear in order to remove contradiction between what the movement recognizes in principle and its practical stands in implementation.[42]

In contrast to this camp, proponents of the conservative Islamic trend, particularly the activists, concentrate on the Western and nationalistic character of these rights, and some of them reject the whole idea as a matter of imported and alien systems which, like democracy, are distant from the traditions and teachings of Islam. The first to promote these ideas was Sayyid Qutb (1906–1966), who was imprisoned in Egypt in 1954, and prosecuted in 1966.

Qutb stood in opposition to trends aimed at introducing Western political ideas into Islamic thought. He made a sharp distinction between, on the one hand, the society of *al-jahiliyya* (darkness and ignorance), which is dominated by positive and secular values, principles and systems, and, on the other, Islamic society, which is subject to the government of God and implements His tenets as stipulated in the Quran. Sayyid Qutb himself embarked on an elaborate interpretation of the verses in the Holy Quran that call for revolution to build the Islamic society.[43]

Qutb's hostility to democracy and liberal ideas was associated with enmity toward the West and the ruling regimes. His conservative ideas on religion and his radical political orientations played a major role in forming the political culture of Islamic groups in the 1980s. They all stress the precedence of divine laws over positive laws, the supremacy of Shariah over human rights, and the originality of the systems and political institutions on which the Islamic state is founded – principles that must not be confused with their modern Western counterparts.

Like their counterparts in other Islamic trends, protagonists of this trend on the whole emphasize the centrality of *shura* (consultation) in Islam, but reject translation of it as 'democracy'. They tend to highlight the contrast between the rule of God and the rule of people, between the law of God and the law of man, and between the rights of God and the rights of man. According to 'Ali ibn Hajj:

> *Shura* is a political ordinance, and, as such, has been placed between two other obligations: one relating to worship, and the other pertaining to society. Almighty God says:
>
> > 'And those who answer their Lord, perform the prayer – their affair being a counsel among themselves, and of what We provided them with, they spend.' (Holy Quran, *Sura* 42 [*Al-Shura*], 36)
>
> It is therefore a mandatory duty when the ruler is chosen, and without it there is no legitimacy for anyone who attains the seat of government.[44]

Ibn Hajj affirms, however:

> It is a sign of naked tergiversation, prohibited by the Wise Legislator, to seek judgement and conciliation in a faith other than the True Religion. Almighty God says:
>
> > 'But no, by your Lord, they will not believe until they call you to arbitrate in their dispute; then they will not be embarrassed regarding your verdict and will submit fully.'
> >
> > (Holy Quran, *Sura* 4 [*Al-Nisa'*], verse 65)[45]

As for individual freedoms, Ibn Hajj continues:

> . . . Military régimes increase restrictions on political freedom in particular,
> although they have the gates wide open to individual and material freedoms.
> They promote promiscuous liberties under the pretence of encouraging per-
> sonal and individual freedom, and the freedom to run off the trail of religion
> under the pretence of liberating opinion and thought, support usury and
> monopoly as economic freedom and freedom of property. These régimes, how-
> ever, intensify constraints on political freedom because it is the only freedom by
> which society expresses, in a collective fashion, its preference for a particular
> system of government. This is the difference between traditional democracy and
> modern democracy.[46]

V. Critical Discourse: the future of human rights in Arab countries

It may be said that confirmation of the importance of human rights, largely by
former activists in the nationalist and leftist current, and attempts by activists
in the liberal Islamic trend to accommodate international discourse on human
rights within the cultural heritage of Arab society, have assisted in launching an
effective movement for defending human rights in Arab countries. The movement today encompasses a wide network of organizations, institutes and periodicals, and conducts various activities in information, intellectual and legal
fields. It is also supported by enthusiastic activists and well-known experts in
many countries. The birth of the Arab Human Rights Organization in
December 1983 came to project this increasing activity in the field of human
rights, and to give considerable drive to the movement. The Organization
played an active role in regional coordination among the various Arab activities, and in consolidating the role of existing regional organizations and the
development of new subsidiary organizations for them, such as the Moroccan
Human Rights Organization (1988), the Algerian Human Rights League
(1987), the Mauritanian Human Rights League (1987), the Egyptian Human
Rights Organization (1985) and the Lebanese Human Rights Association
(1985). The Tunisian Human Rights League has been active since its establishment in 1975.[47]

Parallel to the growing strength of Arab human rights organizations, intellectual and media activity would be enhanced through seminars, statements
and reports, and special media channels would be established. Along with the
development of this movement, a special human rights problematic would
emerge in Arab political thought. Those interested in public affairs, and

students of Arab thought and of transformation in Arab societies, will feel urgently bound to give serious attention to this problematic, and to identify the status and the position of human rights within this general activity.

The problematic revolves around three major focal points. One group of human rights activists argues for the distinct specialty of this movement, while another emphasizes the universality of its character and criteria. Still others contend that action within human rights organizations must necessarily be carried out by experienced practitioners who are familiar with its principles and procedures, and some of them look to transform it into a popular movement that is open and capable of making a mark on governments and public opinion. There are some in the third group who argue either for maintaining the legal character of the movement or for giving it a political colour to enable it to achieve reasonable results.

The former president of the Tunisian Human Rights League, Munsif al-Marzouqi, believes that the tension is not between universality and exclusiveness, but between the liberal and totalitarian aspects within the framework of specialty in each culture. He also rejects any separation between human rights and politics. Human rights is essentially a political project, provided we understand politics in a manner different from the prevailing Machiavellianism.[48]

Human rights activists do not approach the issue of universality and specialty from an ideological angle only, but also move to discuss the question from a practical point of view. The theme is, in fact, relevant to the strategy of Arab organizations, and to their association in terms of material and moral support, and their viability, with international organizations. A large number of human rights activists criticize Arab organizations for their growing dependence on external funding – with the attendant risk of creating organizational bureaucracies that depend in their activities and modes of work on international organizations, and of separating them, increasingly, from the society in which and for which they work. Some critics of these organizations contend that human rights activists are merely engaged in profitable business, drawing in abundant funds from foreign parties whose aim is to ruin the reputation and the people of the country concerned, and that they spare no effort to distort the image of their country overseas. They are working, consciously or unconsciously, to serve the foreign parties that contribute to their funding. Human rights activists do not rule out the dangers of external financing, but they argue that 'these problems can be solved by adopting the principles of financial transparency and control of account'. Such solutions will minimize the likelihood of corruption. The major problems, however, relate to the future of civil work as a whole.[49]

In the view of Muhammad al-Sayyid Saʿid, the human rights movement, like the international movement, faces many dilemmas. In contrast to political action, the movement presents itself as a moral rather than a material force. It hinges on moral appeals directed toward the same forces that violate human rights, and, as such, faces a crisis when authorities disregard these appeals, or when public opinion is feeble or indifferent to the values of human rights. The politicization of the human rights movements poses one of the major problems facing these movements in the Arab world. This predicament goes back to the circumstances under which these movements emerged, and it has a destructive effect on human rights movements. In Saʿid's view:

> [The process of politicization has long involved] virtual monopoly of the Arab Human Rights Organization by proponents of the Arab nationalist trend, which has cost the Organization a high measure of its credibility. In certain countries, the protagonists of the extreme nationalistic trend have practised a measure of monopoly and control that is in total contradiction with the values of the human rights movement.

Other manifestations of this politicization are the tensions relating to political Islam. The problems also entail the philosophical and cultural gap between the commitments of the human rights principles on the one hand, and the programmes and fields presented in the current political culture on the other. This gap originated in the dominant political culture within the Arab world today, which is one overwhelmed by extremist religious visions.

> Legal problems, the relative poverty of political legitimacy and the politicization of the activities of human rights have all combined to weaken the material and human resources available to the human rights movement, and consequently contributed to the deterioration of the institutional capacity of human rights organizations in the Arab world.[50]

According to Bahiy al-Din Hasan, former secretary-general of the Egyptian Human Rights Organization and supervisor of the Cairo Centre for Studies on Human Rights, the activities of Arab human rights organizations must strike a skillful balance between avoiding the language of political confrontation and, at the same time, paying due attention to the social and cultural realities of society.[51]

Hani Migalli, former director of the Middle East Research Department at Amnesty International, points out that representatives of secular political opposition always raise the banner of human rights and subscribe to the principle established by the Universal Declaration of Human Rights, but devalue these principles by allowing precedence and priority to political ideology. Human rights is thus transformed into politics by proxy.[52]

A critical assessment is given by Hani Shukrallah, former member of the board of trustees of the Egyptian Human Rights Organization, concerning both the model of the experienced professional organization, such as Amnesty International, which includes human rights specialists and is concerned with strict monitoring of human rights and with following up their application, and the politicized model which transforms the organization into a front for opposition parties to defend democracy. He then suggests a third democratic and popular model to deal with the contradictions experienced by Arab human rights organizations. It is an option which, in his words, aims at maintaining the autonomy of the organization, not by raising fences around it but through driving its popular and democratic character to its optimal limits. It is an option that does not stem from depoliticized human rights, but attempts to crystallize human rights policy into an effective and influential current within society. It is an option that does not fear membership, but launches its initiative and frees the organization and the principles of human rights from partisan bargaining and tactics, and challenges party forces to demonstrate their consistency and breadth of focus in defending human rights. It is, in the final analysis, an alternative that refuses to submit to the bloody polarization of the forces of totalitarianism, rather taking up the challenge to pave a third road that can be a human substitute for both of them.[53]

The human rights organizations and movement in the Arab world, like those in all countries suffering political repression and the absence of an independent arena of legal and social civil action, are obliged to live with the variety of tensions created through their being drawn to political, moral, professional, popular, local and international tendencies. These organizations are now expected to manage such tensions, and to eschew the kind of profoundly hazardous venture whereby the balance is lost and one tendency takes absolute control of the other. It must be realized, nonetheless, that human rights organizations cannot avoid collision, in one way or another, with government authority and policy; cannot avoid appearing like political organizations in the context of political systems that set their face against freedoms and political pluralism, often prohibiting political life and even independent civil activities, such as forming associations in any form. The strong tendency to politicize these organizations has emerged only when they were joined by large numbers of political militants deprived of the proper framework for political action. In all circumstances, however, the issue of human rights will be a theme of conflict between the political authorities, who are determined to cover up their anti-freedom policies, and their political opponents, who seek protection within human rights organizations enjoying relative international dimensions

and support. The actual bone of contention in this conflict lies, in fact, in identifying the nature of the political systems that exercise governments in these
countries, that is to say, in maintaining the status quo for the ruling elite, and,
for the opposition, driving through democratic changes and imposing them on
political regimes that are bent on maintaining total political initiative in all
fields, and reject any form of political participation or submission of their
authority and decisions to any effective national control.

This explains the continuous antagonism Arab authorities have shown
toward these organizations since their establishment. Many human rights
activists are arrested and banned from legitimate action in many countries.
Most notable among the institutions in question is the Arab Human Rights
Organization, which was obliged to hold its first conference in Limassol,
Cyprus, outside the Arab world. It still awaits legal recognition and formal
licensing from the official authorities in its host country. This antagonism was
manifested in its strongest form on the occasion of the International Human
Rights Conference in Vienna in June 1993, when Arab governments did everything possible to prevent the Arab non-government organizations from participation in the meeting. The governments succeeded in their efforts, and so
thwarted all efforts to record violations of these rights. Consequently, 'Arab
performance turned out to be a shaky and incoherent one. Coordination and
ability to carry out unified action was absent and the scope was enhanced for
illegitimate competition.'[54]

Activists in the area of human rights have recognized this reality from the
very beginning. They have been aware of the difficulty of finding an independent space for civil society and human rights without expanding the scope of
free political and civil action, and without rebuilding politics on more democratic foundations. Effective action in the field of human rights has, therefore,
called for changing the bases of political practice as a necessary condition. In
that sense also, the need for a strong human rights movement has appeared and
imposed itself forcefully only as part of a course of action aimed at re-estab-
lishing politics in its noblest sense after traditional forms of political action
have been exhausted. This could take place only by going back to society and
supporting it with new material and moral forces that would restore its balance
in facing the state system, and by reinstating social ethics without which no
political action can be initiated.

> From this alienation of Arab policy, and from the subsequent apathy in relations
> between state and society, the need arises in the Arab world to re-emphasize
> the prime importance of two sources: the will to face the state, and the ethics
> of regulating politics by sublime principles (serving society and man). This is a

double-faced revival of the essence of legislation and rights as the sources of law. The majority of Arab policies lost their legitimacy when maintaining power became the first and last objective. The perpetuation and survival of this power, with the concomitant repression of any social and political alternative, became a source of destruction for society and of disintegration for its unity.[55]

In conclusion, the Arab world is witnessing a keen awareness of the significance and urgency of human rights. However, the stagnation of the political structure and the frustration felt by human rights activists over the difficulty of achieving concrete and permanent results, combine to add a sense of tension, violence and crisis to this awareness, which makes practice more sporadic, if not altogether deadlocked.

The question now presenting itself in the Arab world is this: can the human rights movement sustain development and carry meaning without the development of law, and without arriving at a situation wherein law commands respect and right has a dignified place?

The issue of Arab human rights will continue to be posed in Arab countries as part of a programme and a framework for democratic transformations, and of a quest to impose law as the foundation of the relationship between the citizen and the state, and, looking wider, to establish citizenship and the citizen as the focal point of reference for this relationship.

For the defence of freedoms to be both meaningful and effective, law must be institutionalized or reinstated in the light of the values and moral criteria expressed in human rights charters. It is therefore necessary

> to exert rigorous efforts – collectively and in solidarity – to define systems and procedures that would alert any ruler or executive to think a thousand times before committing any transgression against the freedoms of the people and the dignity of the Arab individual.[56]

Chapter 14: Human rights and social problematic in the Arab world

Fahmiyya Sharafuddin

Introduction

The issues of democracy and human rights are currently in the foreground of most critical analyses of social and political thought, being considered, chiefly, in terms of their presence or absence, with a view to understanding the crises marking the present turbulent political and economic state of the Arab world. Some analysts take the argument still further, treating these issues as a major factor, often the primary cause, underlying the backwardness of Arab societies[1] and the inability and inefficiency of these communities' attempts to achieve the quality changes prerequisite for crossing the threshold of underdevelopment and entering the modern age.

This study will make no attempt to reiterate the abundant literature on the obstruction of human rights in the Arab world,[2] or the countless inquiries into Arab history, and into the related problems of imperialism and liberation, which have been the subject of research, discussion, exploration and criticism over three centuries.[3] We shall rather move directly to a range of current questions which, in our view, cover the more recent past along with the present, and scan, as far as possible, the horizons of the foreseeable future.

The term 'recent past' refers here to post-independence history, during which tremendous sacrifices have been made in the pursuit of political and economic liberation. It is, in effect, the transitional 'virtual' history during which we were supposed, by international criteria and definitions, to be in control of our affairs and to exercise the power to determine the directions our development should take. Questions have been often asked about the absence of such concepts as democracy and human rights from the political and social practices marking this post-independence stage, and about the position of silence adopted, vis-à-vis this situation, by the cultural and political elites. What should be of equally pressing concern, however, is the absence of such concepts from sociological research. Some Arab sociologists[4] attribute this to objective factors pertaining to the Arab social and political situation, and to the consequent priorities imposed by such circumstances. Others relate it to the concentration of social and other research on projects carried out by independent states and to a faith in the priorities these projects reflect. This state of affairs has, according to some analysts, produced a paradoxical situation and a tragic dichotomy between ideology and scientific research, leading to a concentration of scholarship in fields which may have been relevant and meaningful but which have nevertheless proved inadequate to cover the problems of societies emerging from periods of chronic backwardness under colonial rule. One social analyst[5] argues that social research should have explored the following five main areas:

the entrenchment of the Arab–Israeli conflict;
the consolidation of ideological and economic development;
the absence of genuine democracy;
the dominance of forces of backwardness and division and the deepening of social conflicts; and
the perpetuation of social stagnation and political apathy.

The same analyst notes the argument of Qazzaz: that social researches have marginalized these issues, regarding them as sensitive areas, or as politically taboo, or as part of a negligible sociological area. Researchers have turned their attention to methodological and instrumental topics instead, and, as such, have formalized Western problems within their frozen framework in industrial societies. The problematic of our social research has been confined, in consequence, to behavioural patterns, delinquent actions, pathological values or observable phenomena.[6]

In his assessment of the work of the National Centre for Social Research in Egypt, Ahmad Muhammad Khalifa has made a statement to this effect, noting that the theoretical frameworks thus far adopted by the Centre have failed to provide an appropriate interpretation of the given empirical data,[7] since sociology, in the words of 'Izzat Hijazi, has kept its distance from any critical sociological analysis of such major social concerns and problems as poverty, illiteracy, sickness and class exploitation.[8] Arab sociology has also been indifferent to the formulation of problems prevalent in Arab sociology. Arab sociologists, in the view of Sa'd al-Din Ibrahim, have not contributed sufficiently to the presentation and interpretation of the problems of Arab society or, for that matter, to the suggestion of appropriate solutions.[9]

At a time when many observers relate this crisis to the absence of democracy in the Arab world,[10] the delay in undertaking serious research on democracy, human rights and women's rights remains a valid and urgent consideration. What emerging developments in Arab social thought have made these two related areas, i.e. democracy and human rights, a major preoccupation for thinkers, researchers and intellectual elites? Why have these issues been marginalized from research and discussion, and also from advocacy and struggle? Why should these issues be focal points for social and political reform, and why should these human rights demands embody a claim singled out by the elites rather than by the mass of the people?

Does this transformation of interest relate to changes in the quality of thought and policies witnessed by the world toward the end of the twentieth century, or to changing political forms within Arab societies? Are these developments a logical conclusion to deep-seated changes within social structures and frameworks in the Arab world?

The present study will approach these pressing questions with great caution. Such concepts are still charged with teasing emotions and sentiments for individuals and groups living beneath the shadow of political and social powers that have abrogated individual and political and social liberties, sometimes in the name of national and nationalist interest, at other times, as in our own period, in the name of cultural and ideological distinctiveness.

These questions are still the subject of an ideological debate that refer the whole issue back to external circumstances and determinants. One camp maintains that such questions arise spontaneously in societies which have been subjected to tyranny over long decades; that they are, effectively, a logical response to the failure of general political, economic, social and cultural policies. Analysts from this camp argue that the correspondence of these issues with the new circumstances of globalization confirms their universal quality and their significance for human beings anywhere and everywhere.

It is difficult to avoid the risks inherent in rejecting or accepting the various propositions on the subject. We shall, however, reposit the problematic as a primarily social one. Our interpretation of the social problematic is that it involves all aspects of Arab life – economic, political and cultural. We might also argue that the human being is the focal point, the *lieu géométrique*, at which all these dimensions converge and manifest themselves.

This study will therefore approach the complex and sophisticated relationship between human rights and social problematic in the Arab world as a starting point for drawing a distinction between human rights as a concept and human rights as a matter of moral value and advocacy, both of these stemming from a number of profound crises in the economy, culture, politics and society of the Arab world.

The choice of this particular research course does not mean we are espousing an ideological option that makes human rights a distinct value for specific societies. Nevertheless, we shall distance ourselves equally from the monopolist media stir that tends to eliminate the essential elements of the issue, and tends, especially, to obscure the need for social development in the so-called underdeveloped countries if these are to secure the requirements necessary for dignified human life – requirements encompassing a political and military security that still remains a remote objective for whole continents of the world.

We are, then, approaching this issue by posing questions rather than by positing ready-made answers. And our first question is this: Why has the human rights issue not occupied the position it merits in Arab societies?

I. A return to history

History is not only a vessel for events. It is also a locus for ideas and memories which are formed by human beings and through which people are influenced. The reading of history is, therefore, a controversial matter. From what perspective should we approach history? Should we start out from a sense of grievance and injustice, and adopt a hostile attitude toward the 'Other', the aggressive imperialist intruder? Or should we begin from a sense of superiority and add to previous elements a new defensive dimension inspired by the ingredients and priorities of the past? Or should we, from yet another perspective, read history with a critical eye, aiming to understand the events of the past and coming, perhaps, to control the tempo of transformation and change?

In our reading of recent Arab history, contemporary with the propagation, declaration and application of human rights principles in the West – in our reading, in other words, of Arab post-independence history – we may pose the following question: How exactly would things have turned out if the Arab world had not been colonized over a long period? Would we have taken a course identical to the one we are now pursuing, or would we have had a different history altogether?[11] The question might be asked in more direct fashion. Could Arab social structures have changed by adopting a new course, by transforming the position of family, individuals and power structures? Would the concept of human rights and democracy have had a better chance of realization and achievement? The question may be extended. Are the traits and characteristics of the Arab personality, as we see it today, the result of this history, or are they, as some Western and Arab theorists claim,[12] permanent features of the Arab psyche, features that correlate with Arab history and political geography in conjunction with Islamic culture?

We are aware that virtual history has no place in reality. Modern theories have, nevertheless, permitted the concept of probability to be set in operation. Even if we avoid sweeping generalizations and focus on tiny details and fragments, our social analysis of the absence or presence of human rights concepts cannot exclude consideration of the part played by imperialist rule with regard to the continuation of traditional forms of life, in societies suffering foreign intervention over a long period of time.[13]

This is confirmed by simple empirical observation. Human rights concepts, statements and applications are still confined to imperialist centres – both old and new. The appearance of particular democratic phenomena or legal forms of human rights, in particular regions that were subject to imperialist rule, can be viewed only as a transient and artificial superimposition, since the objective prerequisites for consolidation within the social structures have not been present in actual reality.[14]

Such objective elements include, along with other ingredients, political independence, the building of a modern state – 'the State of Law' – and social development in all areas. Rights cannot be maintained in the absence of law, which, in turn, can be sustained only within a state that enjoys the essential measure of political and economic independence. In other words, human rights have no content or meaning in the shadow of poverty, unemployment and marginalization.

The recent history of Arab countries testifies to these circumstances. While the failure of projects for state building and social development might be attributed to external factors – the urgent need to protect independence and national autonomy following the introduction of the state of Israel at the heart of the Arab world and the emergence of Arab–Israel conflict – the lack of popular participation and democratic practice has also, nevertheless, led to the failure of modernization and development projects. This is not a controversial or debatable point among Arab scholars today. Causes and effects reinforce one another, and no amount of discussion can find a way out of this vicious circle of antecedent and consequence. The situation is aggravated by the fact that gradual transition toward the concept of human rights in Europe and other advanced Western centres has been closely associated with economic and political developments that have arranged and rearranged social forces and their economic and political priorities. The individual produced by the scientific revolution, and by the various systems and forms of industrialization, has been made the focus of priority and interest. 'Arrival at those values which are prioritized in the practice of democracy, human rights and social justice, was not a matter of sheer mental conceptualization or intellectual compromise, or of a peaceful agreement by mutual consent among the members of the nation. It was rather the result of a long struggle and a series of social conflicts which reached levels of bloody violence in these countries'.[15] According to Isma'il Sabri 'Abdallah's analysis of Western democracy and human rights: 'The resolution of these contradictions and the arrival at this advanced democratic situation cannot be understood without the introduction of an important dimension. Western countries were imperialist powers, exploiting their Third World empires. Consequently there was transfer of a huge economic surplus from all over the world to Western countries. Such a surplus allowed the ruling capitalists to make great concessions to the popular masses without incurring large losses to their profits or their living standards.'[16] In other words, the peoples of the Third World have effectively borne the cost of liberation and democratization in Western societies.

This does not apply to our history alone; it might also explain the absence of democracy within societies of the former socialist countries. The economic situation in this region may not have become sufficiently developed to permit transition to the complete liberation of the individual.

Recognition of these facts does not necessarily provide a solution to the problem. We agree with most scholars that the series of defeats and failures, along with the absence of democracy and human rights, are simply a result of the deprivation of Arab individual freedom in the light of imperialist rule. We must realize, too, that such deprivation is not yet over. The growing external political pressures, as a result of the transplantation of the Zionist entity into the heart of the Arab world, have paved the way for the exercise of a more stringently despotic control on the domestic front, on the pretext that all internal forces must be marshalled for the conflict against external powers and all energies devoted to the struggle. 'Any advocacy of human rights will therefore be looked at with suspicion and apprehension.'[17]

Can these concepts be introduced within dependent societies that have had no right to direct their economic and social policies?[18] There is, it is true, a growing consensus among all elites on issues relating to human rights, and there are clear trends emphasizing the importance of a climate of democracy and respect for human rights, with a view to releasing creative energies and breaking the vicious circle of the causes and consequences of backwardness. Nevertheless, these currents have not developed into an objective social concern or a preoccupying claim on the part of all social categories. This area calls, in our view, for close study. Why has the concept of man not developed into a collective demand? What are the obstacles, subjective and objective, hindering realization of this concept?

If the objective obstacles return us to the 'I' and 'Other' debate that dominates Arabic thought nowadays, a move to discuss the subjective obstacles will bring us back to a social problematic interrelated, in a complex and sophisticated manner, with culture, history and anthropology.

II. Human rights: The 'I' and 'Other' debate

The Other here is, quite simply, the West, which began its assault with the Crusades and remoulded its instruments from the guns of Napoleon, which signalled the beginning of a new imperialism in the Arab region. It has also assumed all the fascinating colours of a spectrum of ideas on justice and fraternity derived from the French Revolution. The image of this Other has been maintained in the Arab imagination. The Other is still the imperialist, exploiting conqueror. It is also the superior model imposed by the economic transformations springing from the Industrial Revolution, and by the liberal ideas propagated by the French Revolution. The model is, at once, fearful and entrancing. The perplexed view of the Other has likewise been maintained. At times the perplexity would clear and the attitude of enmity recede, as happened at the beginning of the nineteenth century. At other times matters would become still further confused, and antagonistic sentiments would be intensified in moments of defeat, as happened after the Second World War with the emergence of the Zionist state in the Arab land. Neither feelings of popular solidarity in the West nor supportive socialist policies coming into force in socialist states could amend the image of the Other within Arab societies; and the situation was exacerbated by the way all ruling regimes have since employed the contradiction to establish their national legitimacy. This attitude toward the Other reached a point of final no return after the loss of Palestine, the failure of regimes to fulfil their promises[19] and the series of Arab–Israeli wars somehow lost by the Arab camp. Arab regimes have also used the situation as a weapon and a defence mechanism to justify their losses in these battles. Despite modifications to the image of the Other in the 1960s, and the distinction drawn between a supportive socialist Other and an exploiting imperialist Other, any differentiation in measures and colours has vanished in the face of continued defeats and debacles. Sometimes the distinction would be dropped on the grounds of safeguarding the national entity; at other times, as we see today, for the purposes of defending the faith, or religious, historical and cultural identity.

From this initial and early political stance, the focus changed. First it was a civilization, then a religion, and finally an Other that incorporated all these positions beneath the umbrella of 'cultural difference'. The human rights issue was then located in the centre of a cultural controversy that has eliminated or suppressed all other differences. It was natural such a situation should arise within this particular value and culture framework. The study of concepts cannot be conducted outside the relevant social context. It would be quite immaterial to discuss the rights of Arab individuals located in specific Arab times and places that teem with elements of a strict fundamentalist culture. We are talking of human rights, at the beginning of the third millennium, in a region that has had great civilizations throughout its history. It is therefore not strange, in this paradoxical situation, to witness the plight of human rights in tangible form within Arab societies. Arab jails are still crowded with prisoners of conscience, Arab authorities refuse to tolerate difference, or conflict, or even opposition, and laws to protect the rights of individuals and groups are either suspended or non-existent.[20] Where opposition individuals or groups are not in prison, they are either in exile or *persona non grata*, regarded as criminals fleeing from justice. Disappearance or arrest without trial is an ongoing fact of Arab life.[21] Such circumstances do not simply eliminate the basic criteria for democracy and human rights; they go still further in the face of an escalating fundamentalist rejection of all 'alien' Others. Parallel to these developments is the general sense of malaise in Arab life, whereby the masses are growing ever more passive and apathetic vis-à-vis public and national issues, involved merely in the pursuit of daily bread and basic needs. The masses have thus been moving into the margins of politics; away, that is, from the role they are supposed to play in observing and monitoring developments – and from other roles that comprise the basic ingredients of democracy.

The concept of human rights has recently recovered a measure of vitality among Arab elites as a result of changes introduced by the telecommunications revolution and by the world becoming, effectively, a 'global village'. Interest in this subject is still, however, very weak, and below the level required within the structures of Arab societies. This lassitude remains prevalent both at the social level, where the concept has not as yet found issue in a demand by the popular majority, and at the political level, where the authorities continue to neglect the concept. Nor, all things considered, do the local media in the various Arab societies contribute to the dissemination of the concept or support it.

As a result, it is impossible to note any widespread interest in this issue, though we may come across scattered islands of interest, in the form of societies and clubs here and there.

This situation springs, we believe, from two main factors:

The first relates to the origins and sources of the concept. The original principles refer this concept to the West, tracing its progress through the philosophy of the Enlightenment and through the slogans of the French Revolution, along with subsequent constitutions, declarations and positions. The concept's principles, routes and stages of development are all associated with the Other, whose image was moulded in the Arab mind at an early stage of history. Debate on the matter is, in consequence, linked to the controversy between the 'I' and the 'Other'. Sometimes it is not compatible with our socio-cultural structures, and in some other instances it is perceived as an instrument for dominating and controlling our cultural values. In all cases it is Western in origin, sources and development, and judgement against the West is generalized as a verdict against the concept itself. Individuals thus relinquish their right and surrender to the blackmail of political regimes. The actual reality experienced by citizens in different Arab societies confirms this view. The arguments of human rights advocates and supporters are shattered by the Western practice of human rights in the Third World – a practice contrasted with attitudes toward human rights within Western countries, vis-à-vis such categories as immigrants, residents and political refugees. Very little need be said about the way the West handles human rights inside the Arab world. The violated rights of Palestinians to their land and life, and the rights of Lebanese detained for decades in Israeli prisons, are concrete examples of the disregard shown by the West to human rights. Many other situations might be cited, concerning the support given by the West to terrorist regimes in South America and Africa, as witnessed, for instance, by the military dictatorships of Pinochet and Mobutu.

Such positions and views are used by Arab regimes to relieve any pressure of the human rights concept on themselves and to justify their aversion to such basic rights in the face of the masses. In so doing they augment the arguments of strict fundamentalists, who are basically opposed to the concept on cultural grounds. They help them tighten their control, reinforce their call for a totally closed culture, special and distinct, based on the freezing of history at particular periods.

The second reason for the prevalent apathy toward human rights is linked to the failure, in the Arab world, of development and modernization projects – two essential prerequisites for the institutionalization of such an epistemological concept. The process of change has ended in failure because, on the one hand, the national social project was never realized, and, on the other, the historical and imperialist heritage proved so decisive. The attention of the Arab masses was therefore diverted from the tremendous developments that accompanied cultural advance in the West. When Arab intellectuals proclaimed the crisis in the early 1970s, ordinary Arabs were, in view of their particular material and moral condition, themselves the embodiment of the crisis. Discussions of the crisis, mainly descriptive and analytic (and, on occasion, critical), failed to prescribe in concrete and complex detail the necessary systems of ideas and policies. This failed initiative gave sufficient reason for a loss of confidence in Arab regimes and authorities. Judging strictly by an evaluation of results in this area, the legal and legislative context of the national state, or so-called modern state, was brought into question. The value systems adopted by these states as the foundation of Arab modernity were rejected in their totality. The hard line fundamentalist came back to resume the intense 'I' and 'Other' debate, seizing the favourable conditions created by a series of Arab defeats and failures in which the Other proved superior in all fields.

In the prevailing controversy, the concept and application of human rights had no chance to assert itself. No attention was paid to the intrinsic elements of social structures and their cultural historical ingredients. What, in fact, does restructuring imply? How is it to be implemented and what is its guardian value system?

III. Human rights and social dimensions

Sociologists argue that knowledge cannot be separated from its social context. For a better understanding of concepts and their implications, one must depict the social realities that entail such notions. We have attempted, in the preceding pages, to establish the precise nature of those aspects and elements of the current Arab reality that determine the standpoint taken toward human rights as a new incoming concept. In the following pages, we shall pinpoint a series of conceptualizations and corresponding modes of conduct, both actual and potential, which regulate the attitude in question. This analysis will perhaps help us in identifying other factors, primarily in the social area, that relate to the different visions governing Arab mental structures within a specific political and economic framework.[22]

These conceptualizations may be depicted on three levels: authority and power; value systems; and the level on which the two previous disciplines manifest themselves, i.e. the position adopted toward the 'Other'.

IV. Authority

Authority implies the social conceptualization of the origins and hierarchy of strength that infiltrate and penetrate the various segments of society and prevail in the social culture as a whole. These begin with the primary circle of family, moving up from there toward the strata of political authority. Social researchers believe such notions to be strongly instrumental in shaping social conduct, which is, in turn, articulated in certain patterns of social and political relationship. According to most analysts, the concepts of authority and its hierarchies may be traced back to primary family relations, namely 'patriarchal authority'.[23] They contend that patriarchy, in this sense, finds itself reflected in all social structures and is, as such, responsible for the backwardness of Arab society.[24] Social scientists attribute hegemony and dependency relations specifically to the early anthropological structure of the Arab family. From this spring the concepts of obedience, loyalty and dependency which are the essential educational starting points from which patriarchal authority is constantly reproduced in society, and which stand, consequently, as deterrents to the emergence of the individual who is the essential unit in modern society. In his analysis of the Arab family, Ali Zei'our underscores the 'loss' of the individual in the Arab family, which is dominated by the father and by patriarchy-based society generally. The patriarchal family thus prevents self-fulfilment. In his book *Psychoanalysis of the Arab Self,* Zei'our argues that the Arab family imposes a heavy weight and dominant burden, and, as such, gears the young child toward obedience alone. Many of our traditional educational methods fail to prepare him for discussion and argument, promoting, rather, a tendency to twisted double standards and duplicity, along with dependence on the 'boss' – father, older brother, family executive, employer or chief.[25] The father here, according to Sharabi, is a form of the original model of 'neo-patriarchy'. Obedience, on the other hand, is the primary concept upon which education is founded and based. What concerns and interests the Arab is to have an obedient child who will be prized by relatives and wanted by the family.

In another analysis of the structure of the contemporary Arab family, Halim Barakat suggests that the family in Arabic culture connotes a sense of mutual dependence and support, and perhaps a sense of identity. This situation ends up by generating a family member rather than an independent individual. Within these parameters, the father occupies the centre of power within the authority hierarchy of the family. He issues orders, advice, instructions and warnings to other family members, who can respond to him only with obedience, respect, reports, demands, supplications and petitions. Barakat adds that this image has remained unmodified by perceived contrast or by exposure to the ideas of modernity. Indeed, the image of the father has become still further deepened and entrenched in society. People now adopt the same perspective in viewing the teacher, the employer, and the leaders and rulers, who in turn conduct themselves as fathers or patriarchs.[26] It may be argued that the system of patriarchy has recently been modified in the light of certain structural changes within society and by the emergence of the nuclear family, along with the expansion of education, immigration and women's involvement in paid work. The role of the father remains, nevertheless, central and omnipresent. It is constantly associated with obedience, punishment and firm authority, even within societies like those of Tunisia and Lebanon, which have made considerable progress in these directions. The family still moves and revolves in a patriarchal cycle characterized by 'the father's absolute power, the mother's suspicion, the distinct role of the older brother and finally the inferior status of girls'.[27]

In his detailed study *Contemporary Arab Society*, Barakat agrees with other Arab sociologists that the focal point of relations in the Arab family – which remains an extended family – is the group rather than the individual.[28]

Sharabi suggests that the particular details of this situation are visible in our lives and experiences,[29] although we cannot and should not generalize these traits as representing permanent and distinctive characteristics of the Arab psyche. The concepts of obedience and dependence may not allow for the development of the individual, but the continuation and dominance of such concepts must be viewed in the light of the specific economic and political circumstances interrupting and slowing the tempo and pace of social life in Arab countries. The failure of social and economic liberation projects in the independent countries has perhaps been the main cause of social immobility and the key obstacle to the development and modernization of social structures. There is no point in harking back to the actual reasons for the failure of modernization. Researchers have been exploring or discussing this issue for more than two decades. We must point out, nevertheless, that failure to modernize these structures, and so liberate social relations, particularly family ties, was not merely a result of the abortive policies in question; it was also, as we argued earlier, one of its essential antecedents. This is perhaps the key factor underlying the difference between European and Arab histories. The industrial societies of Europe undermined traditional family structures, whereas these same structures have only been shaken and fractured in our societies, which remain in a transitional stage vis-à-vis industrialization. In our case these structures have been impeded without actually disappearing or even undergoing drastic change. Now we are on the threshold of a new revolution in all aspects of life.

These issues call for further discussion and examination in future research. We shall, however, turn now to the value system of Arab societies, examining the capacity of such a system to embody human rights, together with the underlying ideas and concepts involved.

V. The value system and the relation to the other

According to Barakat, values are 'beliefs in preferred issues, objectives and patterns of behaviour that direct people's emotions, thoughts, attitudes, conduct and choice, and regulate and organize their relations with reality as well as with institutions, and with others as well as with themselves in relation to space and time'.[30]

Sharabi, on the other hand, argues that the prevalent system of values which, in Arab society, generates obedience and submission within the family represents a set of intrinsic mechanisms for the reproduction of Arab family structures, including the regeneration of the patriarchal power structure. In this view, the values in question lead inevitably to dependence. Dependence, like independence and autonomy, is embodied in a system of values and social formations. The former hinges on submission and compliance and is founded on differential power, whereas the latter depends on mutual respect and justice together with the freedom ethic.[31] The social sciences make a distinction between instrumental values and objective values. The first are beliefs that differentiate between one pattern of behaviour and the other, preferring the good to the bad and diligence to idleness. Objective values, on the other hand, delineate our direction and our aims and targets. In both cases, values direct human behaviour and regulate people's relationships with others as well as with reality and time.

According to Barakat's analysis, the Arab value system entails five trends of direct relevance to family life and to education:

> A tendency to emphasize membership of the family rather than individual independence;
> A disposition to over-dependence and obedience rather than self-reliance;
> Reliance on punishment rather than persuasion as an educational instrument;
> Inclination to egotism and selfishness; and
> The domination and subjugation of women by men.[32]

The correlation between submission, obedience and over-dependence on the one hand and self-centred domination on the other is self-evident. According to Ghassan Salama, these values regulate not only family relations but political relations too. He argues, accordingly, that anthropological power structures are the most powerful impediments to the realization of human rights in the Arab world.[33]

The Arab individual, then, is suppressed by a single system based, in a variety of forms, on one authority and a single will that finds its structural and historical model in the patriarchal system. The ruler, according to Barakat, conducts himself as patriarch in much the same way as a father governs his family as ruler. Sharabi, on the other hand, believes that the precedence of group over individual is but one outcome of this value system, which has been consolidated by religions in various forms, so making it a natural ingredient of Arab culture.

This is not, however, a natural given, something to be taken for granted. It is rather a historical given that has emerged from a series of economic and social developments.[34] A dependent economic structure in the Arab world has failed, for these and other reasons, to change the patriarchal family structure to any significant extent.[35] In the wake of modernization policies, this patriarchy structure has developed into 'neo-patriarchy'[36] as a social value system; one which, according to Sharabi, is responsible for what is presently taking place in the Arab world. Neo-patriarchy is a social, intellectual and value system concomitant with the dependent mode of production and development. In the words of Taher Labib, this system has aborted attempts to fulfil social demands. The absence of democracy and human rights is associated with this mode of production, and also with the instrumental role of foreign powers, not in the intellectual sense but in the imperialist dimension.[37]

From a blend of all these elements there has emerged an equivocal attitude toward the Other configured either as a patriarch or a neo-patriarch. This Other has assumed different roles. Sometimes he is a stranger from outside the family, at others he is someone who does not belong to the same sect or category, or an alien from a different race or from another geographical location. At all times he is, in the final analysis, the foreigner.

The attitude toward the Other is not a value in itself but rather a mode of social conduct reflecting a set of values which regulate our behaviour, such as our compliance with the value of submission, obedience and dependence on the father or the boss. It presupposes a priori judgements that neither recognize nor accept the Other. The patriarchal system may have been largely responsible for the generation of this perplexed attitude toward the Other but historical developments within the Arab world have consolidated an enduring and negative position vis-à-vis this Other. Since the Crusades the relationship between Arab and foreigner has been one between victim and conqueror. The trend of incomplete modernization has given this Other the role of a model, but the model has turned out to be an aggressive and belligerent one.

Nor has the domestic situation been much better. The image of the superior Other, which penetrated traditional political structures and systems, has prevailed. It was natural, as Ghassan Salama argues, that despotism and oppression should find fertile soil under the aegis of systems governed by families, sects and creeds.

The overall attitude of passivity, fragmented into related and inter-dependent values of submission, obedience and lack of autonomy, is only one extreme position in the binary perspective that divides the world into the good and the bad, the strong and the weak. This pattern of thinking may be traced in the origins of classical idealist cultural structures; and, as such, it is not a characteristic exclusive to the Arab world. It is a historical structure that has its roots in a series of economic and political conditions.[38]

In his book *Towards a Theory of Culture*, Samir Amin suggests that this value system pertains to a specific mode of historical development,[39] and is not peculiar to Arab culture. We may add that the attitude toward the Other has suffered domestic tensions and disruptions. Even successive revolutions have failed to introduce essential changes to this attitude in the face of a residual traditional heritage, acting in conjunction with external pressures exerted by imperialist powers.

Can these moves toward democracy and human rights make any genuine advance now, assisted by a network of superior values disseminated by the media and by information systems? Can the international stance on human rights, which treats human beings differently – as we see in the attitude toward the rights of Palestinians – in the light of particular interest and benefit, change people's concept of the Other, which is still perceived as an admirable and superior model yet also as a hateful and aggressive entity? What are the ultimate prospects for human rights in the Arab world under current economic and political conditions?

VI. The prospects for human rights

Our sociological analysis has shown that Arab mental structures and value systems are not necessarily incapable of accommodating the concept of human rights and making it a distinct value in social behaviour. Social structures are developed through dynamic processes influenced by economic and political change. Accordingly, human rights, which at present exist as mere notions and ideas in the minds of intellectual elites, must be developed into a public social concern for which all social segments struggle and fight.

There are many problems and impediments. The objective obstacles relate to the location of the Arab world and to economic, social and political conditions. The subjective obstruction stems from the domestic situation and from the attitudes of political powers within Arab societies. Jurists attribute such impediments to defects in the Arab constitutions, or to loopholes in legislation that fails to spell out rights and freedoms explicitly, or to the prevalence of exceptional legislation, especially emergency and martial laws.[40] Social researchers, on the other hand, believe that people's apathy toward public issues and interests is a result of the economic condition and growing impoverishment of the majority of Arabs.

The concept of social development is currently under review in different parts of the world, and world organizations argue that such development is, at once, a product of and a prerequisite for such progress.[41] A new balance must be established between domestic requirements and external intervention on the one hand, and, on the other, facilitating participation, among the various internal social categories, in taking decisions and drawing up policies. The status of women is perhaps the prime element in the process of building the new balance. One of the salient features of backwardness in the Arab world is, as Sharabi confirms, the way the feminist movement has up to now been confined to women. 'The position of women has thus far been only a marginal and minor issue for male intellectuals and critics.'[42] The risks involved in the position and future of women in society may be depicted in the light of present situations and practices. The Arab woman is still far from exercising her natural rights: the rights to enjoy equitable opportunities in education, work and health, together with the exercise of political rights. The road to liberating Arab individuals may have to pass through the gates of woman's liberation because the two processes are complementary.[43] On the other hand, the practices of political powers, especially in areas relating to civil and political rights, must be reviewed and revised, with a view to releasing energetic and creative social forces and ensuring a more equitable distribution of wealth and power.

These two processes – internal equilibrium and external balance – are the starting points in removing obstacles to the establishment of democracy and human rights. The mechanisms and instruments are well known: they comprise, primarily, political independence and control of natural and human resources, non-interference in the affairs of other states, and the balanced and fair application of international conventions for all peoples. In this age of globalization, of turning the world into a global village, a new international order must be developed to protect the interests of societies under a more forceful and just arrangement of power relations. In view of the large gaps between wealth and poverty, the United Nations Organization will have a vital role to play, under more appropriate conditions.

The concept of human rights is not a geographical one. It is an epistemological international body of knowledge and principles. It is the outcome of a series of human struggles to achieve happiness, and, as such, all societies in the world are eligible to espouse it and capable of doing so. The adoption of human rights must take place under objective and subjective conditions that integrate and converge to produce the relevant future structures and institutions. This was in fact the case in Western centres. Detailed and comprehensive research needs to be undertaken with a view to understanding how and why it happened there and not in our own countries.

Chapter 15: The rights of Palestinian refugees

Salman Abu Sitta

Introduction

The twentieth century witnessed a series of momentous events which, quite apart from two world wars, saw the rise and fall of a variety of totalitarian or racist political systems and, in consequence, a change in the lives of almost a third of the human race. Nazi Germany and Fascist Italy were defeated, the communist system collapsed and the Soviet Union disintegrated. The colonial era ended in most Asian and African countries, with British colonialism folding, for example, in India, Pakistan, Cyprus and Hong Kong. The racist segregation system of apartheid was defeated in South Africa. In the course of the last century, the Arabs turned from a dependent geopolitical unit under the auspices of the Ottoman state to become more than 20 independent Arab states, fragmented and separated both politically and geographically.

On the level of human knowledge, the century witnessed enormous advance in the fields of telecommunication and transport, and in other areas of science. These developments transformed people's lives, providing access to things and ideas, and giving world cultures the chance to become acquainted with one another and familiar with the viewpoints and achievements of different parts of the world.

Amid this overwhelming global trend towards liberation, the establishment of Israel as a fortress of Zionism, built on foundations of colonization and occupation that had vanished elsewhere, stood as a stubborn obstacle to progress. Underlying it was a blend of aggression and racism that amounted, in principle, to Nazism and apartheid; to exploitation of others' natural resources, to the suppression of a people and the blocking of their advancement.

The above is a necessary introduction if we are to comprehend the dimensions of the Palestine disaster and the subsequent shock waves. Modern history provides no other example of a foreign minority driving out the native majority of people, usurping their lands and preventing their return, depriving them of identity and homeland, and practising against them various forms of racism, colonization, occupation and exploitation. All this took place, more-over, with the material, moral and political support of the West, a support that continues to this day. It is ironic that the actions of usurpers should have been described as a victory for civilization, a divine miracle, while, simultaneously, the disaster of the victim should be ignored – that this victim should, indeed, be branded as terrorist, fanatical and backward, and that the countries of the Western world should be marshalled to eliminate or suppress him.

The sheer scale of the *nakba* (disaster) speaks for itself. In 1948, the Palestinians were driven out from 531 of their villages, towns and other places. The people of Palestine represent 85 per cent of the population of the Palestinian land occupied by Israel, and their land accounts for 92 per cent of Israel. As a consequence of the *nakba*, crowns toppled, heads of state were assassinated and regimes were changed in all the Arab states surrounding Palestine. More than a quarter of a million martyrs have fallen, and, up to now, around five million Palestinian refugees have been driven out, together with millions of other Arabs in Egypt, Syria and Lebanon. Cultural and economic progress has simply ground to a halt, and billions of dollars have been wasted on futile armament.

The rights of the Arabs have been lost on account of their political and mil-itary weakness. They have been left, nevertheless, with a solid and persistent attachment to Palestinian rights. Although the Palestinian nation has been dis-persed into five regions served by the United Nations Relief and Work Agency (UNRWA) and 30 other states, the determination of refugees to implement their rightful return to their homeland has kept solidarity and unity intact. Such implementation was the objective of the *fida'iyyin* in the 1950s, of the Palestine Liberation Organization (PLO) in the 1960s, of the Palestinian revolution in the 1970s and of the Intifada in the 1980s. For Palestinians, the right to return is a sacred, legitimate and – we might add – feasible one.

I. The word and the gun

In the 1950s, the horror of the tragedy engulfed the consciousness and con-science of the Arab world. 'Arif al-'Arif,[1] who actually coined the apt term *nakba*, portrayed the disaster in a work of six volumes, so producing the first comprehensive, encyclopaedic treatment of the loss of Palestine. It was called 'the disaster', because 'for us, Arabs in general and Palestinians in particular, it was the first such historical experience for generations and centuries: our country was taken away; we were driven from our homeland; we lost our children and suffered a deep injury to our dignity.' There followed a series of books by eyewitnesses or fighters who had taken part in defending the homeland. Shaykh Muhammad Nimr al-Khatib,[2] the militant imam from Haifa, described the issue of Palestine as 'the issue of struggle between right and wrong, the issue of evicting landowners by the force of injustice and by the gun'. Similarly, Kamil al-Sharif,[3] one of the leaders of the Muslim Brotherhood whose members had put up a stern fight, set down his experiences in the Palestine war. 'It is no disgrace,' he said, 'for nations to be defeated. Shame lies only in submission to defeat.' Dr Hasan Hathout,[4] an Egyptian physician who fought as a volunteer in Palestine in the spring of 1948, described the courage of the combatants and the scarcity of their resources, along with the trickery of the Jews and the frailty of the Arab governments. Perhaps the most painful and poignant testimony on this period was that provided by 'Abdallah al-Tall,[5] the commander in the battle for Jerusalem, who described the secret negotiations of King Abdullah with the Jews, the conspiracy of the British and the way Lydda and Ramleh were evacuated to face their tragic end at the hands of Yitzhak Rabin's forces.

The prime attitude of Palestinians in the 1950s was one of resolution to return to their homeland. No one had reconciled himself to an end to battle in the form of an armistice wrapped in barbed wire. The problem was not to convince people – apart, that is, from those imperialists gathered at the United Nations and in the corridors of Western governments – of the justice of the cause; and, as such, the commando organizations began to prepare for return – often spontaneously, at other times coordinating with the army of Nasser following its overthrow of the regime of King Farouq. The refugees had no understanding of the concept of 'infiltrator', propagated by the Jews and accepted by the Mixed Armistice Commission, as a label for those returning home.

It was obvious in the 1960s that sporadic, scattered efforts would be powerless to liberate the homeland. The period was marked by the establishment, under the auspices of the Arab League, of the Palestine Liberation Organization, which developed over time into a Palestinian organization in essence, content and origin. It was characterized, too, by the fiery speeches delivered at the United Nations by Ahmad al-Shuqayri,[6] representing first a number of Arab countries, then the masses of the Palestinian people.

Al-Shuqayri took part in all the phases of the Palestinian struggle, guiding this national endeavour in the 1960s until Yasser Arafat became Chairman of the PLO. He had worked at the Arab Office in Washington in 1945, and had helped prepare a report submitted to the Anglo-American Commission of Inquiry in Jerusalem. He joined the Syrian delegation in 1947, was a member of the Arab League delegation that met Count Bernadotte (1948), of the Syrian delegation at the Conciliation Commission on Palestine (1949–51) and the United Nations (1955), and of the Saudi delegation at the United Nations (1960). Then he represented Palestine at the Arab League (1963). His efforts were crowned, in 1964, with the establishment of the Palestine Liberation Organization, followed by the Palestine Research Centre.

Al-Shuqayri was a prolific writer and speaker, the focus of his effective public speaking being to invoke a sense of dignity, to raise morale, to demand an end to injustice and to advocate the liberation of Palestine. He wrote and delivered his addresses with an unabashed fervour that went, at times, beyond accepted diplomatic practice, something that led to considerable problems for him. His influence on the Arab masses was far more powerful than his impact in international circles, where only diplomatic manoeuvres and the language of power counted for anything. His message was clear: Palestine was an Arab country and must be returned to its people. As for Zionism, this was a movement of racial expansion that could be neither tolerated nor recognized.

The 1967 setback, however, once more moved verbal polemics on the Palestine question from the battlefield to the United Nations, which had not at that point recognized the presence of the Palestinian people except by confirming Resolution 194, which gave refugees the right to return. The Security Council issued its Resolution 242, which confirmed the inadmissibility of occupying territories by force but surrounded the measure with elusive interpretations.

The resolution made reference to refugees calling for a 'just solution' to their problem. The years following saw a war of attrition and the emergence of the Palestinian resistance movement. As may be seen in the memoirs of one participant in this campaign, the Jordanian Ambassador to the UN, Dr Muhammad al-Farra,[7] a ferocious diplomatic battle was launched at the United Nations to endorse recognition of the legitimate rights of the Palestinian people.

In 1969, the United Nations acknowledged the principle of self-determination. The principle had been applied to the Palestinians, in an unprecedented decision on the part of an international organization, in 1974. Resolution 3236 confirmed the 'inalienable' rights of the Palestinians, explicitly regarded return as a 'right', and, for the first time, associated the right to self-determination with the right to return. It even called on states to assist the Palestinians in achieving these rights by all means, including armed struggle.

The 1970s were a golden period indeed in the history of the Palestine resistance movement, one associated with a unique cultural and political momentum. The Institute for Palestine Studies,[8] under Walid al-Khalidi, and the Palestine Research Centre,[9] under Anis al-Sayigh, produced many significant works in Arabic and English on all the historical, legal and political aspects of the Palestine problem. Memories of Palestine, and of Palestinians and their lives, were revived in the plastic arts, notably in the celebrated paintings of Isma'il Shammout,[10] and also in other forms of art like music, folk dancing and theatre.

II. The return of the phoenix

The Palestine issue was not, by this stage, confined to deliberations at the Arab League and the United Nations. The refugees (who had now become revolutionaries, artists, economists and engineers) had reconstituted and rebuilt Palestine in exile, with text and spirit and an integrated history, but simply with a displaced geographical location, a hundred miles away in the host country. Rosemary Sayigh provides a brilliant and eloquent portrayal of the imaging process in her English-language book *From Peasants to Revolutionaries*.

The issue is no longer one of a refugee problem. The Palestinians wish to return to their native soil, while others wish them only to have a sufficiency of food and accommodation (anywhere except in their homeland), so as to evade the problem and bury the issue for ever. The concrete image projected to the world has been one of a distinct and integrated nation, one that has been exposed to unprecedented injustice by racial Zionism; a nation that has internationally recognized rights. This nation has, moreover, persisted, has insisted on realizing its return to its motherland. Acceptance of Palestinian rights is evidenced by the fact that twice as many countries accredited the offices of the PLO as recognized the state of Israel. Conferences and forums were held in various parts of the world in support of Palestinian rights. Scores of legal,[11] economic, historical, political and cultural studies were published to explain these rights, and organizations and associations were established in many countries in support of the Palestinian cause.

Soon, though, this momentum dwindled into atrophy, for the same reasons that led to the 1948 defeat in Palestine. In both cases enthusiasm and passion proved more powerful than organization and efficiency; words resounded more than deeds, and were less influential. The management of crises emerging on the Lebanese scene, or initiated there, whether from domestic or external sources, led to exit from Lebanon and to dispersion once more, in countries far more distant from Palestine, such as Iraq, Yemen, Sudan, Tunisia and Algeria.

The sad 1980s culminated in the Intifada, which took everyone by surprise. When the militant fighters laid down their arms in exile, and Israel had begun to feel sure the new generation of young Palestinians, born and raised under occupation, would never revolt, the fire beneath the ashes was aglow once more, in the largest cities and the smallest villages. The end result of the Intifada may be subject to controversy, but the uprising has unquestionably moved the Palestine question into every home throughout the world, and the particular images conveyed to the world showed clearly enough who was the persecutor and who the victim; Israel could no longer go on deceiving the Western world. The most significant achievement for the Palestinians during this period was the marshalling of data in the ever-expanding and increasingly influential human rights organizations in the 1990s, especially after the spread of the Internet. The NGOs, which defended human rights and opposed repression, torture and racism, provided strong forces of popular pressure, within parallel parliaments that democratic governments could not ignore. The swift transmission of information led to prompt reaction and feedback. Within hours of the arrest of a political activist or the destruction of a home, or the enclosure of a whole people by sealing off access to cities and villages, the news would spread and expand in different directions. Even when the occupation forces remained undeterred, they, together with their supporters, could not pretend ignorance of what had actually happened.

For all these reasons, Palestinian political discourse took on an international character in its outreach and presentation. Then, while the Palestinians were awaiting the fruition of these efforts, they were struck by a third tragedy called 'Oslo', which came to save their leadership from its dilemma but not to restore the rights of the people. In the face of this the Palestinians had to return to their books and reiterate the enduring principles of their struggle.

III. Reminiscences of the Nakba

The *nakba*, whose effects are still burningly alive before our eyes, cannot be forgotten. Half a century after the disaster, the Palestinian people remains steadfast, albeit deeply wounded, still wavering between hope and despair. The memory of Palestinians is alive and active. We have sufficient evidence of this living memory in the writings of historians, scholars, veteran soldiers and ordinary people who were traumatized by the event and later reflected their pain, hope and determination to restore their lost rights.[12] The city or village where these people lived, raised families and died, had the lion's share vis-à-vis the documentation of memories.[13]

Such recollections were no mere nostalgia for a past growing still more beautiful over time. They were rather the visualization of a promised future. The past became an image of the future pursued, and called, as such, for a documentation and reconfirmation of the rights in question by eye-witnesses who had lived and experienced the realities and were conveying these to their children and grandchildren. As one of those eye-witnesses, I myself wrote *A Letter to my Daughter* – for the daughter who had never seen her homeland. I wrote the book after extensive efforts to document the past I knew. I researched the history of my family in European libraries that housed the chronicles of the European conquest and the histories of their expeditions, spies, travellers and pilgrims to the Holy Land. In the library of the Royal Geographical Society, I found the papers of Jenning Bramly on south Palestine and its tribes, and the volumes of Alois Musil, who worked for the Austrian Emperor at the end of the nineteenth century. I also found the volumes of Oppenheim, who worked for the German Emperor. All these documents recorded the region and more precise location of my family. In the library of the British Ministry of Defence, I came across the Allenby maps, in which my home town is mentioned. The reference is also found in the military records of the Australian War Museum. At the British Public Record Office, I found papers of Herbert Samuel recording Churchill's meeting with my father and other Palestinian notables in 1921. At the National Library in Paris, I found Jacotin's maps and the reports of French scholars on the tribes of Palestine in 1799.

I almost jumped with joy when I read that Victor Guerin, the French traveller who visited all parts of Palestine, had, on 13 June 1863, met my great-grandfather, who was with a group of his horsemen and asked the Frenchman why he was wandering in his country. I also found the writings of Father Jaussen, the priest who turned spy and moved from Jerusalem to Transjordan, and thence to 'Aqaba and 'Arish, before returning to Jerusalem bearing the names, numbers and history of tribes in the First World War. At the German War Museum in Munich (Kriegmuseum), I found the first aerial photograph of Palestine, taken in 1917. In the Turkish central archive, attached to the office of the Prime Minister in Istanbul, I found the Turkish correspondence from and to the administrator in Jerusalem, who had complained of my tribe's power over the country and of its rebellion against the state in 1800.

Over ten years, I methodically compiled references, maps and data for the purposes of confirming my right to a small piece of territory[14] I had known as a child, as part of Palestine, my homeland. I brought in witnesses and items of evidence, and put them forward to play their part in documenting an unforgettable past before an imagined Court of Rights. I even ventured on a futile attempt to confront my enemy with his crimes: I sent excerpts from the documents to the kibbutzim that were occupying my land, reminding them the territory was mine, and that one day I should return!

In addition to personal documentation of this kind, efforts were made to document the nation's folk heritage. Many books were written on Palestinian tales, proverbs and customs.[15] This was one area that had attracted certain orientalists, who for many years lived in Palestine to record and document the life of the people of the Holy Land. Although they wrote in foreign languages, and had not yet been translated, I found in these books decisive testimony to the rights of the Palestinian. Notable among the authors were the German scholar Gustav Dahlmann, who produced a comprehensive encyclopaedia on the lives of Palestinians, Baldwin Burger, who was born in Palestine, and Miss Grankvist, who lived in the village of Ertas for a number of years. All these authors wrote their books at the end of the nineteenth century and the beginning of the twentieth.

Notable among the early Palestinian writings on heritage are the works of the talented physician Tawfiq Kan'an.[16] He was well versed in Turkish, German and English, and, for almost 40 years from 1914 on, he wrote in European languages and in Arabic on folklore, anthropology, women's rights and Palestinian rights. As a particularly distinctive aspect of Palestinian life, the journalist and former Jordanian Minister of Culture, Jum'a Hammad, wrote of Bedouin life in Palestine. Is-haq al Diqs wrote *The Childhood of a Bedouin*, which was later serialized in English in the London *Times* newspaper.[17]

Nor should we overlook the role of the novel in documenting Palestinian rights, notably the works of Ghassan Kanafani (especially *Men in the Sun*) and Emile Habiby's *Pessoptimist*. This literature has, however, been sufficiently considered by more specialized critics, and has been fully surveyed by Salma Khadra Jayyusi in her encyclopaedic works.[18]

The writings of a number of figures active in the national Palestinian movement provide vivid treatments of Palestinian rights as they saw them. Such writings are few when compared in number with the number of those who fought against the colonial and occupation forces, but the combatants possessed the special advantage of authentic and accurate documentation to supplement their stylistic gifts. Prominent among them were 'Arif al-'Arif, referred to earlier, and Muhammad 'Izzat Darwaza, whose eventful life spanned a period from the 'Urabi Revolution to the Israeli invasion of Lebanon. He authored over 50 books on the Palestinian heritage and the active political life of the region.[19] This host of writers further includes 'Ajaj Nuwayhid, who was at once a witness and an active participant in political life before and during the nakba,[20] 'Izzat Tannous, who worked at the Arab Office in London, Beirut and New York,[21] and Akram Zu'aytir, a prominent Palestinian leader during the Mandate.[22]

In the wake of the nakba that astounded the Arab nation, and following the collapse of crowns and governments, loyal patriots began their pursuit of causes and solutions, with many providing diagnoses. In their view, salvation lay, variously, in democracy, in Arab unity, in armed struggle and in the pursuit of regional alliances.[23]

At the beginning of the struggle, Arab states recognized the important role of Western countries in creating and directing the conflict, and acknowledged the need to influence Western culture and communicate with it. Modest attempts were made, broadening and growing stronger with time, to explain the Palestinian issue to the West, in the English language. First among such attempts were the writings of the lawyer Henri Cattan and of the land expert Sami Hadawi. The most prominent advocates of Palestinian rights in the 1960s were undoubtedly Fayiz Sayigh and George Tu'meh, both of whom worked with Arab delegations at the United Nations.

The prominent Palestinian historian Walid al-Khalidi published important studies of Palestinian history in both Arabic and English. The key feature of his research was, perhaps, his refutation of the Zionist propaganda that Arabs had been responsible for instructing the Palestinians to leave their country. He demonstrated, with ample evidence, that the exodus of Palestinians had in fact been forced by a Zionist plan called DALET, initiated in April 1948 to implement the Israeli project to occupy Palestine. The works of the Institute for Palestine Studies, directed by al-Khalidi, continue to provide historical documentation and expose false claims, the most recent of the works in question being an encyclopaedia in English called *All That Remains* – a chronicle of abandoned and depopulated Palestinian villages.

The Palestine Research Centre, under Anis Sayigh, has published a large number of pamphlets and research documents on all aspects of the Palestinian question; the Centre exerted a strong influence on Arab political thought in the 1970s. Abdul-Wahhab al-Kayyali, before his assassination in the prime of youth, published his *Modern History of Palestine*,[24] one of the first Arabic reference works to draw directly on British documents. The period provided a suitable climate for the production of numerous works exploring the identity of the Palestinian people, defending its heritage and advocating its national rights. Nevertheless, the strong need remained to identify permanent principles and to explain these within a legal scientific framework comprehensible to the West and capable of eliciting approval in international circles.

IV. Modern writings

The most important Palestinian right is the right to return to the homeland. This is a sacred, legal and feasible right, on which many studies have been written.[25] It is sacred because it is carried in the conscience and the consciousness of every Palestinian wherever he moves. Eloquent testimony to this is provided by an Israeli writer: 'Very strange people, those Palestinians. All over the world, people live in a place. As for the Palestinians, the place lives in them.'

The legality and legitimacy of this right has been established by an unprecedented international consensus. Resolution 194, issued on 11 December 1948 and confirming the right to return on the basis of international law, has been underlined 110 times in 50 years by the world community. It resolved

> 'that refugees wishing to return to their homes and live at peace with their neighbours should be permitted to do so at the earliest practicable date, and that compensation should be paid for the property of those choosing not to return and for loss of or damage to property which under principles of international law or in equity, should be made good by the governments or authorities responsible'.

Even if Israel were, by a miracle, to succeed in abrogating it, the right to return remains guaranteed by Article 13 of the Universal Declaration of Human Rights – a declaration that has been recognized by European countries as an integral part of their legislation, taking precedence over local laws even when these latter contradict it.

The right to return is also guaranteed by the right to benefit and possess and own property, which cannot ever be abrogated by occupation or by change in sovereignty. It is guaranteed for individuals by virtue of human rights, and for communities by virtue of the right to self-determination. It cannot fall into obsolescence or be cancelled by agreements or conventions. It is a *right*, not a tourist visa that expires after a certain period. It is applicable at any time, and the desire or lack of desire to return is irrelevant in this regard.

The groundless Israeli myth that Palestinians left their homeland voluntarily has been undermined and exposed by Israeli historians like Benny Morris,

Ilan Pappe' and Tom Segev, and by the Jewish-American scholar Norman Finkelstein. In any case, the right to return is guaranteed regardless of the reasons for leaving. Israel is, moreover, accountable for the damages caused to Palestinians by depriving them of citizenship and expelling them from their homeland. International law stipulates that Palestinians retain the right to national citizenship irrespective of which state imposes its sovereignty over their land. Specifically, it stipulates that 'land and people go together, and whoever rules one guarantees the other'.

International law also provides for the right of Palestinians to compensation, by the principle requiring that 'damages must be made good'. Accordingly, Palestinians are entitled to receive indemnities for material damage incurred by individuals, such as having their homes destroyed and their land exploited over 50 years, and also for the loss sustained by the community in relation to its rights to water, minerals, quarries, woods, roads, seaports, airports, beaches and other assets. They are further entitled to receive recompense for individual moral impairment, such as psychological suffering and loss of family, and for collective damages such as loss of identity and dispersion. They similarly merit compensation in respect of war crimes and crimes against humanity and peace, like murder, destruction, torture, imprisonment and ethnic cleansing. Above all, they have the right to have their property returned and regained, as well as receiving compensation for it. A homeland cannot be sold, and, contrary to the common perception, such right covers *both* return and compensation. Many sectors of Western society, even those that sympathize with the Palestinians and endorse their legal rights, are inclined to fall prey to the misleading Israeli argument: that return is impracticable because village boundaries have been lost and the territory is now heavily populated by Jewish people.

In the 1990s, I demonstrated the fallacy of such claims on the basis of geography, demography, water and agriculture. Palestinian discourse to the world has changed in recent times, moving away from sentimental and emotional argument in favour of the use of figures, maps and analysis. This new line of argument has taken the Israelis by surprise, silencing any possible response.

Present-day geographical techniques enable us to determine and identify every single hectare of land, to trace its location and recent changes to it. The misfortune of Palestine, as a target for colonialists, has not been without its positive aspect. No country anywhere in the East can match Palestine in terms of documentation and studies. We have maps going back to the days of Napoleon's expedition of 1799 and to the British 'Palestine Exploration Fund' of 1871, along with the maps of the British Mandate and the registers of property inherited – or rather looted – by Israel.

To say there is no more room in the country is another fallacy, both in principle and in practical application. The underlying implication is that Palestinians should disappear from Palestine, giving way to any Russian or Ethiopian who holds papers indicating his Jewish religion. This is objectionable both legally and morally, and any thought of its application reveals ignorance and carelessness of the facts. We have demonstrated that 80 per cent of Jews live in 15 per cent of Israel, and that a further 18 per cent beyond this live in a number of Palestinian towns such as Isdud, Beer Sheba and Nazareth. The remaining 2 per cent comprise the population of the kibbutzim and the moshav. In other words, around 150,000 Israeli farmers control more than 18 million *dunum*s, which are the inheritance, and the heritage, of 5 million refugees. No human principle or just, legal and civilized form of conduct can find such a crime acceptable.

The return of the refugees and the restoration of their land would not in fact be to the detriment of Israeli Jews. This is a strictly practical point. As for the legal or moral perspective, Palestinians cannot be obliged to remain dispersed through the world, with no identity or homeland, simply in order for a Russian or Ethiopian Jew to enjoy a home that is not his at all, but rather the home of an expelled Palestinian. One of the great ironies of the situation is that the kibbutz, in which early Zionists were raised as a symbol of the new Jews' attachment to the land and their 'return' to its soil, has reached the point of ideological and economic bankruptcy. Early 'pioneers' were depicted, in the West, as holding a gun in one hand and driving a tractor with the other, towards a distant horizon from which the sun rose on a barren, unpopulated land – a land awaiting the Zionist saviour who would restore it to lush greenness. Those images are shabby and discredited now.

The moment the new immigrant arrives, he is sent to a kibbutz in some remote part of the country or near the frontiers. Soon, though, he will find his way to the heart of the country, where he can lead the kind of city life to which Jews have been accustomed, engaged in business and financial activity. The Zionists have failed to make a profession for themselves out of agriculture; they have abandoned countless colonies in the kibbutzim. Statistics show that 26 per cent of these settlements produce 75 per cent of the crops, and the yield of three quarters is of poor quality. For the first time hired workers in the kibbutz exceed the original workers, and those who have stayed on the kibbutz are unable to cope with the burden of agricultural work. Although the Israeli national domestic product has increased substantially since 1948, the proportion contributed by agriculture has declined from 8 per cent in 1983 to 2.4 per cent in 1993. Agricultural produce accounts for just 4 per cent of exports.

The situation is aggravated by the fact that this flawed Israeli agriculture consumes and wastes 80 per cent of the water – of which three quarters comes from plundered Arab water. The kibbutzim are flooded with water, subsidized at prices as low as a fifth, or even a tenth, of the prices imposed on people in Tel Aviv. Should this situation continue, with the increase in the number of Russian refugees, the need for additional water will almost certainly lead to a new war; for the water resources of Palestine and the neighbouring Arab countries have become exhausted and can only be replenished through the occupation of new Arab territory.

It is clear that the ground water table has declined, that the quality has deteriorated with salinity, and that the use of recycled sewage water now presents a serious hazard. Over time, and with the increase in the number of refugees, the situation is bound to deteriorate further.

The objective of Israel's persistent spoliation of the environment, wasting of water resources and control of such vast tracts of refugees' land is to prevent Palestinians from returning, by handing over these spoils of war to the early Zionist elites who have exerted such significant political influence in the army and the Knesset. Were refugees to return to their land and cultivate it – something they have mastered over the centuries – they would produce better crops at less cost. This has in fact been demonstrated in Gaza, despite the restricted space for agriculture, and the salty water, and all the restrictions imposed on their freedom.

These and similar studies are not commonly found in earlier Arabic texts. Such texts were rather designed to arouse enthusiasm and raise morale; and, vis-à-vis the West, to draw attention to legitimate rights and to the mandatory requirements of international law. There have, though, been changes since Oslo. America and Europe have become actively engaged in one form or another; and their involvement has gone beyond conventional, ongoing practices, in favour of opening up dialogue, holding conferences and providing assistance. On our side, it has become necessary to substantiate our arguments, and, in the wake of the tremendous advance in communications, to use a language that can be understood by the world. The need has grown still more pressing as we have come to realize how modest – notwithstanding the sacrifice of so many innocent lives – the result of armed action, by the various brigades, has been in practice.

V. The post-Oslo political discourse

As hopes pinned on reinstating Palestinian rights through the Oslo Agreement
faded away, most people felt a sense of frustration. The failure of the Oslo
negotiations was, however, hardly unexpected, considering the capacities,
instruments and objectives of the Palestinian party involved. Committed
Palestinians returned to an insistence on basic principles; few of them accepted
this situation as a mode of 'political realism'. Acceptance by the negotiators
themselves was one more expression of this small group's failure to achieve
its objectives, to find a means of salvation from the predicament to which
their own poor performance had led. The members of this elite believed
they could salvage their political future by watering down their objectives
rather than raising their sights. This was precisely what Israel desired and
worked for, with the full support of an America that, by turns, wielded the
sword of power and waved the notes of money. All of a sudden, the 'terrorists'
were transformed into moderates, and the freedom fighters became brilliant
politicians aware of 'the balance of power'. This elite, which retained control of
the situation, gained world respect and financial support, together with an
influence now exercised over those Palestinian people who came under its
control.

The other set of people, who remained firm to basic principles, resorted to
the written word – the only weapon left to them – to articulate Palestinian
rights. They wrote on the various aspects of refugees' rights of return and compensation, and on the life of refugees in Lebanon. They also explained the
rights of Palestinians within Israel, including those evicted communities which
are still, in so many respects, the country's forgotten refugees.[26]

The Institute for Palestine Studies made its own contribution to clarifying
Palestinian rights in terms of legal, historical, political and statistical documentation. It published books on the Conciliation Commission on Palestine, on
the right to return, and on the negotiations of multilateral committees which
discussed marginal issues.[27]

The United Nations Economic and Social Commission for West Asia
(ESCWA),[28] based in Beirut, published studies on democracy and statistics
with regard to the Palestinians, and on their rights according to United Nations
resolutions. There were also publications by the United Nations Relief and
Works Agency (UNRWA) on the Palestinian refugees, in terms of their standard of living, health and education, on their numbers, distribution and rights
as established by the United Nations. Although the UNRWA took a neutral
position in its writings, the documents it produced served to convey the

tragedy of Palestinians to the world, all the more so as the Agency routinely avoided exaggeration and rhetoric. This led Israel to launch a virulent campaign against the UNRWA, resorting to every possible device to liquidate its functions and activities.

Nor was writing confined to specialists or professionals. Some of those who simply felt for the refugees' plight were prompted to take up their pens.[29] 'Political realism' infected some writers, who found the appropriate environment to express their views; they were driven to embrace this tendency by the celebratory atmosphere surrounding the signing of the first and the subsequent series of Oslo-related agreements. They favoured a Middle East Market that would provide them with ample funds. The manufacturers of 'political culture' were part and parcel of the scene. The flow of funds, in the new climate of peace, led to the setting up of numerous NGOs, which interested themselves in human rights and the rights of refugees, and undertook studies of the latter's situation. Many of these institutions played a significant and noble role in this respect, through their information and their scholarly efforts. A review of their research, whether published or circulated on the Internet, will provide evidence enough of the significant positive impact of their efforts and the valuable benefits they brought. On the negative side, some of these institutions called for dilution of the rights involved, or proposed a reinterpretation that effectively emptied them of content. A flurry of wide-ranging, well-financed intellectual battles ensued, with a series of conferences, seminars and joint dialogues between Israelis and Palestinians, who gathered for discussions in areas where their interests joined. Both parties believed in peace, and for both this entailed acceptance of an improved status quo and of the necessity of coexistence. Both supported the premise that bygones should be bygones, that the two parties should now move together, hand in hand, towards the bright sun of the future. What this meant, quite simply, was that the murderer should be exonerated of his crime, the looter given permission to run off with his spoils. It also meant, correspondingly, that the victim should not receive indemnity or the dispossessed regain his usurped property. If the killing and looting had taken place without any systematic criminal intent, then tolerance and forgiveness might well have been offered in a spirit of magnanimity. The crucial point, though, is that murder and usurpation were not a matter of historical coincidence, but rather integral parts of an ideology; and that victims did not fall on one particular day in 1948, but continued, constantly, to lose their lives till this day. Meanwhile, the murderer and the usurper felt no remorse for the crime he had committed the day before and would commit again next day. How could the whole matter end in exculpation?

This is why the writing of a handful of Palestinians, on 'realism', is a mere voice in the wilderness, with an odd and hollow ring for those who hear it. Being written in English, it often escapes attention. In a few instances, it continues to attract praise and tribute, being periodically quoted or cited as reflecting the voice of 'moderate' Palestinians.

What is this voice saying in effect? It is saying that what happened belongs to the past, that the ordeal and the agony of refugees over half a century can be relieved by a word of apology from Israel, with no subsequent moral, legal or financial liability. Over against this, Palestinians should sacrifice and relinquish their right to return, because it is, their opponents maintain, 'impossible in practice'. The Palestinians would accordingly concur with Israel in the promotion of a new United Nations resolution calling for an annulment of resolution 194, which guarantees the right to return.

And how would the refugee problem then be resolved? Pressure would need to be exerted on host countries to naturalize and absorb refugees where they currently were. Refugee camps would become a homeland, where pupils, standing in early morning rows in their schools, would applaud and cheer and pledge themselves to sacrifice 'soul and blood' for this homeland's sake. Should the host countries decline, another solution would have to be found, similar to the one devised by the American Jewish lawyer Donna Arzt, who strove to resettle Russian Jews in Israel. This was her solution published by the American Foreign Relations Committee, which tried to persuade Arab countries to accept the absorption of refugees – anywhere in the world except in their homeland. The Jewish American lawyer was effectively replacing the Nazi trains bearing Jews off to the holocaust with modern planes bearing Palestinian refugees off to their final destination in Alaska or Australia.

Needless to say, such ideas have, like earlier projects for settlement, ended in total failure. The nation that has sacrificed 50 years of its life in exile, and under oppression, will not perish or die. A refugee child of the third generation, who regards himself, still, as a native of this or that village in Palestine, will never cease to claim his right of return to his homeland.

Chapter 16: Human rights in the heritage of the Yemeni National Movement

Ahmad Qayid al-Sa'idi

Introduction

Man's struggle to institute and justify his rights is as old as human history, however the specific content of these rights may have varied at different times and in different societies, according to the development of political and economic life, the various systems of government and the differentiation in the value systems. It goes without saying that the *raison d'être* of all religions and human doctrines, however simple, is the imbuing of human life on earth with greater justice, security, ease and freedom. The legacy of known rules and laws, as experienced by ancient human societies, aimed at regulating and organizing relations among the members of society, so as to ensure their coexistence and cooperation and to free their lives from injustice, despotism and exploitation, in so far as this was permitted by the legacy of human mental development, and by the measure of advancement in the form of political, economic and social systems. We may, for example, cite Hammurabi's laws in the eighteenth century BC. The subtle themes and elaborate structure of these laws suggest that the codes in question did not originate in a vacuum or emerge suddenly without any antecedent. They were rather the outcome of a long history of development in human societies prior to Hammurabi, and the result of man's ongoing struggle to establish laws and principles aimed at introducing to life larger measures of acceptability, security and fairness.

A review of the two authoritative frames of reference in Islam, i.e. the Holy Quran and the *sunna*, will provide ample assertive evidence for this argument. Islam paid an extraordinarily detailed attention to human rights, for individuals as well as for society, for the rulers and the ruled, ranging widely over the family, the neighbour, the worker, the needy, the deprived and poor, the passer-by, the ally, the friend and the enemy, through to the entire Islamic community, and then on to human society as a whole.

This brief reference is sufficient to highlight the centrality of the issue we now call 'human rights' both in overall human history and, specifically, in Islamic history. We have no intention here of involving ourselves in distracting details. Our objective is rather to shed some light on human rights as witnessed in the texts available to us from the heritage of the Yemeni National Movement, since it took the form of an organized political movement.

For a proper understanding of the content and implications of our excerpts from the texts produced by the National Movement, the following considerations must be taken into account:

1   The Yemeni National Movement emerged in an Islamic environment which left its mark on the Movement's characteristics, influenced the formation of its objectives and claims, defined its perspective on the existing system of government, and shaped its concept of the ruling system for which it was struggling, as well as moulding its images of human rights. These concepts and images were largely derived from the Islamic heritage. We shall nevertheless see clearly, in the selected texts, that the Movement did not draw upon the Islamic heritage only, but also drew heavily on modern culture and on the knowledge and influences of the day. The Movement lived through what we might describe as a transition period, i.e.

> a historical era that witnessed an interaction between the old ways of life and thought and modern life with its facilities and new modes of thought. The Movement thus lived through the interactive stage between two historical eras, one belonging to the old and the other committed to the requirements of the modern age.[1]

Its struggle, writings and demands represented an ambition to keep pace with the modern age. This ambition was, however, constrained by the reality and context of the old life within which it lived and interacted.

2   The human rights demands made by the militants of the North (known as the Yemeni Liberals or Constitutional Liberals) in these early years of their struggle may nowadays seem ordinary, even astonishingly commonplace; yet in those days they were not so very simple or modest. At a time when the essential demands of the citizen were centred on providing food, retaining a house or a piece of land from which to make a living, and the right of the enlightened social elite to suffer natural death rather than persecution and execution without fair trial, any discussion of rights regarding expression, organization, gathering and public freedoms, or the right of people to elect their representatives and choose their rulers, would have

appeared a far-fetched ambition. Nevertheless, the demands of the Liberals in the early periods of their struggle did embody a wide range of such expectations. Tardy as they may now seem in proposing them, the Liberals were in fact playing a pioneer role in raising these claims in their time, striving to fulfill a noble dream in the face of the reality and constraints of their situation. For this dream they were expelled, imprisoned, impoverished and persecuted.[2]

3 A sense of the relativity of human rights is underscored in the more recent demands made by the National Movement in the South at an early stage of its development – demands made only at a later stage in the struggle of the National Movement in the North. In the South, the Movement was initiated in a more liberal and enlightened environment, allowing a broad measure of freedom not experienced in the North. Given the presence of an organized administration and a modern code system, of schools, hospitals, roads, transport and communication facilities, newspapers, libraries, organizations, recognized unions, etc., their demands were necessarily different, and the rights in question inevitably assumed a more advanced and sophisticated quality. They included the right to work and to improve wage levels and working conditions, along with legitimate political and civil rights, such as the right to election, the right to hold senior administrative posts, freedom to work in unions and to work toward improving the level of public services such as health and education, the right of Northerners staying in Aden to contribute to political life and to participate, like their brothers in the South, in the election of the legislative and the municipal council, etc.

Bearing in mind these necessary considerations for understanding the demands of the National Movement for human rights, we shall now provide a glimpse of the development of the modern Yemeni National Movement in both North and South, and the circumstances surrounding its activity. We shall then review some of the texts generated by the National Movement in the North with respect to certain aspects of human rights. Given the very distinct and special circumstances in the North, and the limited scope of this essay, we shall not cover the activities of the Movement in the South.

I. The general development of the National Movement

As may be seen from our preceding discussion, the National Movement in the North and the National Movement in the South evolved against the background of different political, social and economic characteristics. The social structure in Yemen consisted largely of tribes and peasants, together with merchants and businessmen who represented a smaller category with little influence. The Aden colony, however, had a social setup that was different from the social structure in all regions of Yemen (the kingdom of the Imam and the Aden protectorate), and from other cities as well. In Aden a tribal and rural character gave way to a commercial and labour presence. This differentiation originated in the different qualities of economic activity in the Aden colony and in the other regions of Yemen. In the other Yemeni territories the growth of agricultural activity overwhelmed business enterprises and professional activity, whereas business enterprises flourished in the colony, which, for all its limited space, contained an area for export and free export to the protectorates and the northern areas. Aden had the advantage of a seaport and the presence of organized management, modern law and an advanced banking system, all operating in an environment of stable security. An active commercial bourgeois class was developed, and large sectors of the population were involved in service activities, while an active working class developed its sizeable base in the petroleum refinery and at the Aden seaport. This contrast between the Aden colony and the other regions in Yemen left its mark on the structure of the National Movement and on the mode of its activity and demands. The presence of the entrepreneurial bourgeoisie and the workers, the spread of schools and the provision of law and order and press in Aden, all assisted in enhancing a relatively advanced political awareness and consciousness. This situation provided the conditions necessary for the development of parties and organizations with modern outlooks. Such conditions were not available in Northern Yemen, where the National Movement was, from its inception, clandestine in nature and subjected to a constant repression forestalling the presence of public organizations or mass activity as witnessed in the South. The National Movement in the North found some space for its public activity only in Aden city, where the leaders of the Movement sought refuge from the tyranny of the Imam and, in 1944, formed the party of Free (Liberal) Yemenis, *hizb al-ahrar al-Yamaniyyin*, in cooperation with their brothers in the South.[3] The National Movement, in its broad features, had been initiated in Northern Yemen at the end of the nineteenth century as a movement of armed struggle against the Turkish presence, and it continued during the reign of Imam Yahya ibn Muhammad Hamid al-Din, who took over from the Turks in 1918 in the wake of their defeat in the First World War. It was a movement of armed struggle against his rule, but it developed as a national movement only in the 1930s, when it assumed a clear political character and specific objectives and programmes. Unlike its predecessors, the Movement in its early stages of development manifested a broad orientation toward political and national reform, and reflected the character of the new social forces providing the Movement with its leaders, who came largely from educated and business circles. Some of the factors contributing to the development of the National Movement in the 1930s may be characterized as follows:[4]

- The despotic character of the regime, which placed power exclusively in the hands of the Imam and his children;
- The general repression exercised by the Imam, which targeted not only peasants, merchants and the educated sectors, but even the instruments of his authority, such as government functionaries and soldiers;
- Financial and economic policies leading to a general impoverishment and frugality, from which all categories of the people suffered;
- A policy of seclusion and preservation of backwardness, and of resistance to all features of modernization. The country had no modern management and no service facilities or financial and economic institutions. Nor did it have schools, hospitals, roads or modern communication facilities. Life in Yemen in the twentieth century was not very different from what it had been centuries before;
- Modern influences seeping into Yemen from the outside world, albeit in a meager way, were nevertheless sufficient to induce change in the minds of the representatives of opposition. A category of enlightened and educated people emerged, bearing the promise of a modern-day life, defining the content of the entire National Movement and shaping its new form;
- The Saudi–Yemeni war, which broke out in 1934, led to the defeat of the Imam, who was then obliged to sign the treaty of al-Ta'if. The war revealed the fragile nature of the ruling system and exposed its feebleness in the face of foreign forces, for all its apparent strength and harshness in suppressing opponents within the country.

The National Movement in the North consisted of different social forces that had suffered under the regime. Nevertheless, they agreed unanimously on a general national objective, namely changing the system of government by establishing an imamate governed by a constitution and parliament, rather than unconstrained rule by an imam, and introducing changes that would enable Yemen to keep pace with the other, relatively more advanced Arab countries.

The thinking, objectives and demands of the Movement evolved side by side with the development of a struggle against the enemy system – a struggle reaching its peak in two unsuccessful coup attempts in 1948 and 1965, in which a large number of its leaders were slaughtered and even larger numbers imprisoned. The Movement was also influenced by developments and events elsewhere in the Arab world, notably the 1952 July revolution in Egypt, the nationalization of the Suez Canal in 1956, the subsequent tripartite British-French-Israeli attack on Egypt, the 1958 revolution in Iraq, the Algerian revolution (1954–1962), and the enhancement of the rising Arab revolution movements. These developments left their mark on the political awareness of all Arabs.[5]

With the development of the National Movement in the North and the evolution of its political thinking, its objectives grew more concrete and its demands clearer and more specific.[6] Its demands, for all their apparent simplicity, focused from the very beginning on what we now describe as human rights. This feature will become apparent in our examination of the selected texts. By contrast, the National Movement in the South, especially in Aden, emerged in circumstances that were less rigorous and more open and tolerant. Britain had occupied the city of Aden in 1839, turning it into a station for fuelling vessels and a transport link with its major colony in India. The city was also developed as a military base and a major commercial centre, separated from the kingdom of the Imam by a series of sultanates and sheikhdoms known as the Aden protectorate, and bound to the British administration in Aden by protection treaties making them, in effect, a British zone of influence.[7]

Britain was determined to maintain the state of backwardness in the protectorates, whose people, as such, continued to live in conditions not much better than those in the kingdom of the Imam. In the Aden colony, however, Britain developed a system of modern administration, a network of paved roads and a series of hospitals and elementary and preparatory schools that provided the administrative system with clerks and employees. The presence of the British base, the seaport and the old refinery provided employment opportunities, and the colony, with its seaport and modern administration and liberal environment, became the prime commercial centre in Yemen and in Arabia as a whole. Aden therefore became a major urban centre and a focus for job seekers from the protectorate regions in Northern and Southern Yemen.

The service sector played a leading role in the economic activity of Aden, especially in such important areas as marine services (shipping and vessel handling), import and export agencies, banks, restaurants and hotels, aviation and land transport, communication and telecommunication, and contracting and insurance companies. On this economic foundation, a new class of labourers and employees began to take shape and gradually organize itself; and, over time, this class came to exercise considerable weight in the National Movement, especially in the early 1950s after the establishment of the oil refinery, which absorbed large numbers of workers coming from different regions in Northern and Southern Yemen. In addition to workers, a new class of local commercial bourgeoisie appeared alongside the foreign bourgeoisie.

Society in the Aden colony thus assumed a composition and character different from the traditional social set-up in Yemen, both in the Aden protectorate and in the North. The emerging social system in Aden included various categories of administrators and managers, upper, middle and lower categories of merchants, and employees and workers, in addition to school teachers and small numbers of journalists, writers, lawyers, physicians, contractors, soldiers, policemen, etc.

The British colonial administration encouraged foreign immigration into Aden, with a view to furthering its interests through the subsequent demographic shift. Non-Arab migrants, sensing their stay would be guaranteed by a continued British presence, expressed a stronger loyalty to the British and enjoyed better positions in administration, commerce and security services. The combination of British support and immigrant monopoly was one of the early reasons for the growth of national feeling, and for the gradual development of this into national organizations that later took the form of an influential national movement; one whose impact stretched beyond the borders of the colony into the protectorates and Northern Yemen. The Greater Islamic Association (al-jami'a 'l-Islamiyya 'l-kubra), established in Aden in 1949, was one of the early organizations to embody a social outlook. It was characterized, among other things, by an interest in the teaching of religious subjects and the Arabic language, and by its efforts to formalize Arabic rather than English as the language of official transaction.[8] Many other associations and societies followed, such as: the Aden Association (jami'at 'Adan, 1950), which called for self-rule in Aden within the framework of the British Commonwealth and under the motto of 'Aden for the Adenis',[9] then the League of the Children of the South (rabitat abna' al-janoub, 1951), which, in contrast with the Aden Association, represented an advanced stage in national political consciousness, and called for the union of the Arabian South, i.e. Southern Yemen.[10] In the mid-1950s, first the United National Front (al-jabha 'l-wataniyya 'l-muttahida), then the Labour Federation (al-mu'tamar al-'ummali), were established, advocating the unity of Yemen and Arab unity as the main platform for their struggle, thus presenting a more advanced framework for their programme, which would encompass all Yemenis without any discrimination.[11] From the mid-1950s to the explosion of the armed revolution in the South in 1963, the political scene in Aden would see the emergence of ideological parties with Arabist, Islamist and international orientations.[12]

II. Selected texts from the writings of the National Movement in North Yemen; Images of Situations Incompatible with Human Rights

The struggle of Yemenis for human rights has largely taken the form of explanation and exposition of the inhuman situations they experienced under the Imamate. Their presentation has, in effect, implied a rejection of the situation and an attempt to change it for new conditions under which human rights might be observed and maintained. It is therefore important to present these explicatory texts, in which, as will be seen, images and themes tend to interchange and blend with one another, in the writings of the Yemeni Liberals, on this tragic situation. This will make it difficult to present complete texts on any one single subject or aspect. We have therefore made an arrangement of texts from those available to us, with possible intermingling of the various themes. This arrangement is, we must admit, broad and potentially misleading, and may, inevitably, involve the repetition of themes and concerns. The texts will, however, provide a fair perception of the significance of these themes in the eyes of the Yemeni Liberal.

II.1 The character of government

Yemen is an Arab country with a deep-rooted civilization, known in the histories of the Greeks and the Romans as Felix Arabia, and in the chronicles of Arab historians as *al-Yaman al-khadra* ('Green Yemen'). It is a large country with many different regions: high mountain peaks and wide expanses of coastal area. Both the mountains and the coastal areas, which are known as *Tihama*, are rich and affluent in wealth and blessings. This Arab country has been afflicted by a very strange and cumbersome system of government, namely the rule of the Imamate, which governs all its regions today. This powerful Imamate, with its authoritarian creed, has subjugated the population of all these regions, enforcing full compliance and blind obedience. It has thus maintained its control up to the present day, with no prospects for development or advancement over time. The population has been secluded and segregated from whatever is going on in the outside world in terms of progress and upheaval, and, as such, the people have not been given the scope to request or claim their fundamental human rights. This Imamate, i.e. the ruling dynasty in Sanaa, has, over time, maintained a deliberate policy of stagnation, permitting no political development which might keep pace with the outside world or be in line with the spirit of the age. This current general stagnation does not even match the minimum level of development achieved in the Arab scene generally, or the progress evidenced by the neighbouring Arab countries, such as the Kingdom of Saudi Arabia or the young Hashemite Kingdom of Jordan.

Under the circumstances, the Imamate must bear the major historical consequences and responsibilities with respect to the current conditions. The régime has spent a period of about three decades without introducing any changes to its position *vis-à-vis* history. It has not performed its obligations toward an Arab people which it subjects to its control and administration, while not, itself, being subject to any kind of accountability or monitoring.[13]

The reality of the present situation is that the catastrophe, the misery and the deprivation of Yemen, over half a century, has not been some curse descending on it from heaven, nor has it been a misfortune imposed by the devil, or the bankruptcy of the state or the lack of able men. Nor has it, for that matter, sprung from the ignorance of the rulers, or the fanaticism of religion, or concern over the independence of the country. The essence of the catastrophe is the deliberate plan ingrained in the rulers, and their insistence on continuing the policies they are pursuing now . . . This deliberate plan has been devised for the purpose of maintaining control over an ignorant, impoverished, fragmented, enslaved and broken people, and keeping it down to a level befitting only animals.

The extent of this catastrophe basically reflects a determination to keep the entire people, as individuals and as a community, deprived of its right to life and survival on this earth. This is because an absolute ruler can eliminate the life of individuals without any trial or explanation, either by execution or, in part, by imprisonment. This does not simply mean that the people are deprived of the right to life, which is something the possessor may strive or struggle to maintain. Our real calamity is that the people themselves have neither the right to live nor the freedom to obtain this right.

Our people know that, when some of their children spoke the sacred words of life – 'It is my right not to be beheaded without a trial' – the rulers would wilfully execute those who pronounced this phrase, or save themselves by making an alliance with the devil and joining the Baghdad Pact . . .

Yet even this is not the full story. The rulers who usurp the life of the people, and deny them the freedom to pursue this right, might at least admit that they have, in practical terms, imposed themselves on the people and deprived them, by force and by the edge of the sword, of their sacred right to life. Our particular situation, though, is entirely different. The usurpers of our right to life wish us to accept them as messengers sent down from heaven to earth to accomplish this great assignment. They expect people to believe that the powers of our rulers are a sacred right bestowed upon them by God – and that any denial or disbelief in such a right will invoke the wrath of God from above.

Such is the delineation of our catastrophe at its base and foundation. As for the details of the calamity, they are represented in concrete terms in life itself, with no limits and no end. Like the devil, it runs in the blood of Yemenis . . .

This is the will that seeks to keep possession of the people, to degrade us to the level of cattle, which remains resolved to govern the people with no principles or rules or organization, and, particularly, with no participation from among its children. This is the main cause and the prime mover of all other causes, explanations and phenomena, by which people try to explain the backwardness of Yemen throughout its long history.[14]

As it stands today, the Imamate has failed entirely in achieving the welfare and fulfilling the hopes built on its system, such as applying the Islamic principle of *shura* (consultation), or else by improving overall conditions in the country, retaining efficient and capable functionaries experienced in skills, arts and science, and using their talents for the progress of the country, or by recruiting people who are their equals or superiors, so that the rulers themselves can be at the forefront of the caravan rather than straggling at its back. The ruling system has maintained obsolete and outworn modes of government which, far from doing any good, have regressed to more degenerate actions still, sent the country back to the old days, completely eliminated all forms of order and organization practised in the departments of local government, and turned the country upside down. The Imamate has regulated and bound the affairs of the country, in matters great and small, to its will and personal whims, has replaced capable, conscientious and organized people wthin the government with people combining ignorance and mediocrity, enlisting the latter for a modest remuneration that can barely cover their basic needs – so prompting them, in their turn, to crimes of bribery and abuse of authority so as to obtain illegal and prohibited benefits. The system has encumbered the people with various kinds of injustice, and enabled crooked opportunists, who view themselves as prospective ministers and rulers, to embezzle the money of citizens. It has totally blocked every avenue to modern culture and education, and deliberately confined people to ignorance, poverty and sickness. It has confiscated the sums in the state treasury, has excluded the possibility of using people's money in public expenditure for the benefit and welfare of the country's children, has regarded people's money as the personal property of the rulers – a situation neither Shariah nor law can possibly tolerate in the lives of governments or states.

What is worse and more bitter still is that the Imamate, in order to perpetuate its cruelty against the aggrieved people, and to maintain its children in their current painful situation, has isolated the country from the rest of the world, exerted the strongest efforts to sever its communication with the outside world, so as to maintain a hegemony over the population . . .

The rule of the Imamate has not been a proper system of government over all its long history. Indeed, and in all frankness and clarity, we say boldly that it has been a catastrophe imposed upon a glorious Arab people, whose children have been afflicted with a curious and criminal style of government, suffering grievous losses in their personalities, mentalities, morals, characteristics and traits. Nor, furthermore, have they benefited from the Imamate in terms of religious belief. The system has spoiled and corrupted the very tenets of their religion and tradition, leaving them plunged in a misery no human mind can imagine.[15]

The excerpts relating to prisons will be taken from texts produced by Qasm Ghalib Ahmad, one of the *'ulama'* (religious scholars) of Yemen, and a minister of education following the revolution of September 1962. They reflect his own experience of the prisons in which, during the rule of the Imam, he spent 14 years of the prime of his life, without ever being advised of the reasons for his imprisonment.

II.2 *Prisoners, jailers and prisons*

In the outside world, prison is a matter of punishment and discipline, but in Yemen it is a grave into which the unfortunate person is thrust by the sharp blades of swords and daggers and by the barrels of guns. In their funerals, the victims have curses and blame and garbage heaped upon them, and the eulogies are delivered in derogatory terms, understood by Yemenis as meaning 'the crooked one, the devil, the one who is ungrateful to his parents, the enemy of God who must be beheaded'. The victim's possessions are impounded by the treasury, or by the royal guards who have buried him in what they call the 'graveyard of virtue'. His coffin is made of worn cloth and with fetters and handcuffs. The adjectives applied to him are known only by the jailers and those who have experienced prison before. Prison in Yemen is the sin that no human forgiveness can tolerate. It is a chasm that extends from the gates of life into the abyss of the dead, where the victim bids farewell to all his dreams and vanishing happiness, and encounters constant tragedy, constant doubt and little certainty . . . At the threshold of their execution and death, the victims, their heads bowed, are told by their jailers to take out whatever they have in their pockets, to say farewell to all the blessings of life, and to prepare themselves to face the agony of death. The death of the prisoner will be ascertained when the jailer cauterizes him with fire for a full day.[16]

The prisons of Yemen house living persons, men of science, literature, poetry, old and young, who are condemned to death for unexplained reasons or crimes. They may have been sent to prison because they were reported as expressing anger at the worsening situation, something Yemenis are forbidden to do, and could not keep silent about what they saw. The expression of anger is, in the eyes of the rulers of Yemen, an unforgivable crime that deserves prison or death.[17]

The jailer is a noxious plant that springs in Yemen when God's faithful ones raise their voices. The man himself believes that torture and punishment in the afterlife come from God, and that he is simply the prosecutor and persecutor. He believes himself infallible, a mere instrument executing God's command; and when the sword, by mistake, severs the head of some person or even some young child, as it did once with one of the children of the Wazir family, then the Imam should take responsibility for this, since he could not send these victims to paradise or request God to grant them forgiveness.[18]

The jailer is never far from you. You face him the moment you step into the jailhouse. He receives you with handcuffs that he presents to you as if they were medals or gifts, then sends you in only after you have, quite literally, paid him the price of these cuffs, which is called the *qat* price or the price of *ibn hadi*. The warden hammers the steel onto your head with one hand, and receives the money with the other. He may even deliberately knock your leg with the hammer until you faint; and when you come to and cry out for help or relief, the jailer will denounce you as a coward and people outside the prison walls will shout, telling you to stop, to hold on and be patient. How can God reward this warden who knocks the legs and feet with one hand and receives his wage in the other?[19]

My brother in faith, where can the imprisoned victim find mercy or comfort, when he is believed to have sold his religion and stolen the money of God, when the prosecutor considers himself the legitimate agent of God and the prosecutor of His orders? The prosecutor will continue the torture, the thieving and despoiling, expecting God to bestow rewards on him for what he does.[20]

And what is the Nafi' [prison]? Do you know why His Majesty King Ahmad has chosen this name for the prison? Because some people told him how they had read, in some dubious history book, that Imam 'Ali (may God bless his soul) prepared a prison he called Nafi' for those who rebelled against him. Reader, please tell me this. If prophets had had prisons for jailing their followers, would there have been religions in the first place, and would these religions have continued to this day? Would Abu Bakr and 'Umar and 'Uthman have adopted such a religion? And even if 'Ali ibn Abi Talib had had this Nafi' prison, as they allege, could he have had followers like 'Abdallah ibn 'Abbas, and 'Abd al-Rahman ibn Abi Bakr, and al-Ashtar al-Nakha'i? And why did 'Ali not imprison 'A'isha, Talhah, al-Zubayr, 'Amr ibn al-'As, and al-Ash'ath?

> Would any prison be established in the name of religion
> after all these years and months . . .
> During which the Prophet had built people's souls on
> foundations of justice and piety,
> and led his nation to the heights of glory?

No, with prisons they have done a great injustice
to the Shariah which was, in the eyes of believers,
purer and more sublime.

And Nafi', what is Nafi'? It is hell in life, it is a house of which one half, or two
thirds maybe, is founded deep in the ground, and only the remaining third is visible to people's eyes ... [21]

II.3 Hostages

The Imam was mistrustful of some of the country's tribal *shaykh*s and dignitaries, suspecting they planned to revolt against him. He would therefore take
one child from each of these and place him in one of his prisons, as a hostage
to secure his father's loyalty. This hostage system was one of the major anti-
human rights landmarks of Imamate rule, and a cause for grievance and anger
in the circles of the National Movement. The following texts shed some light
on this system:[22]

> This is the worst mode of government, and the ugliest innovation among the
> means of injustice, which takes Yemen back to the darkness of primitive ages.
> Such is the practice pursued by the *Mutawakkili* government [the Imamate] in
> this age of enlightenment. The world has never heard the like of what is taking
> place at the hands of an Arab Islamic government that was supposed to be the
> first in observing and implementing Islamic Shariah in all transactions, and in
> demonstrating respect for the lofty ideals of Islam that call for kindness to sub-
> jects and the implementation of good rational government for them. Will peo-
> ple accept that little children should be taken from the arms and bosoms of
> fathers and mothers by force, and be flung into the darkness of prisons in castles
> on mountain tops? This is a vicious mode of government, the invention of
> unjust rulers who take the children of their subjects as hostages; and so these
> tyrants maintain their control over the tribes and their branches, clans and fam-
> ilies, in both Bedouin and urban areas. What is most outrageous in these shame-
> ful practices is that they are conducted in the name of the religion of Muhammad
> and the Shariah of the benevolent God ... The castles of Sanaa and the fortresses
> of Shihara and Hijja, the prisons of Ta'az and al-Hudayda, and such like graves
> for the living, overflow enough already with free and innocent people, let alone
> children and youngsters taken hostage. Their bodies have been plagued by star-
> vation, sickness, pain, torture and foul air. They live in excruciating and miser-
> able conditions; and some of them have been detained and confined for
> twenty-five years or more, their hands and feet fettered in steel. Some of them
> have spent the first twenty years of their lives as hostages, living in humiliation
> and degradation, with no one who will look into their case or listen to their

grievance or complaint. Their future is unknown, their imprisonment unlimited
... It is, by God, one of the greatest and most abominable of crimes, practised
under the eyes and ears of the Arab world in a significant region on God's earth,
in a country where the benefits and advantages of independence have been used
by the government to implement these unspeakable procedures and savage
modes of conduct, to the disgust of upright souls and the abhorrence of free and
noble consciences.

Awake then, you people, and respond to the call of humanity for justice in this
country, whose people are subjected to injustice and dehumanization, though
blessed by God on land and sea.[23]

II.4 Emigration and its causes

A lengthy letter addressed by some of the Yemeni expatriates to Crown Prince
Sayf al-Islam Ahmad ibn Yahya, who became Imam of Yemen after the failure
of the 1948 coup, explains the reasons for emigration from the country. The
letter was later published in a small booklet titled *The First Moan*. The following
excerpts are taken from this publication:

> Can anyone deny that our country today suffers grievances that must be elimi-
> nated, abject poverty that must be addressed, unemployment, spreading through
> our plains and mountains, that must be forcefully resisted, grave sickness in
> morals and souls, neglected and unused wealth, a monopoly in posts and offices,
> along with savage competition for these, until senior functionaries became direc-
> tors of commercial companies, and job are offered as goods to be sold and
> bought? Can anyone deny that the drive to emigration has taken over men, chil-
> dren and youngsters, who are being thrust into dispersion and revulsion by
> hunger and injustice? Where is the canopy of mercy, compassion and justice,
> beneath which the people can rest? The state of affairs remains still unchanged,
> and unjust men are still in their positions ... We have not opted for exile as a mat-
> ter of satisfaction and choice, but have rather been prompted to it by a profound
> necessity threatening our very lives. The doors of justice have been closed in our
> faces, the roads of fair dealing have been blocked, and solid barriers have been
> raised between us and His Majesty our Imam, the successor of our Prophet, may
> God pray upon him and upon his chaste and good family. Crowds of functionar-
> ies, rulers, and their puppets and lackeys, are watching us as wolves do sheep. We
> look left and right, and see only injustice and darkness, as a cruel government
> employee takes away our money with one hand and tortures us with the other. He
> drives us to starvation to satisfy himself, humiliates us to raise his position,
> impoverishes us to grow rich, and closes all the avenues of knowledge before us,
> while he himself follows the path of injustice. For this reason it was that we saw
> emigration, from our homeland and children, as our sole salvation.

The letter gives a detailed account of the various injustices suffered by people, such as *khutat*. The letter explains that

> the meaning of the word *khutat* may be unknown to many, since it is not men-
> tioned in dictionaries of the Arabic language. It exists only in the dictionary of
> workers and the public, who now understand well enough what it denotes.
> *Khutat* means the occupation by the military of the homes of subjects, who are
> then obliged to offer services and even meet the expenditure of the soldiers.
> This, in brief, is the meaning of *khutat*.[24]

The letter also explains the conditions of the peasant:

> The peasant has no profession or work or resource except his farm, which is
> about to vanish because of his neglect and lack of interest in it and his desire to
> emigrate. The government functionaries are concerned only with taking things
> from the rural and pastoral peasant, and are not at all inclined to give him any
> work or relieve him from his burdens.[25]

II.5 Other situations and problems incompatible with human rights

Muhammad Ahmad Nu'man, a young activist influential, within liberal circles, in drawing up the objectives and programmes of the Liberal Movement, points out a number of ways in which human rights are contravened:

> Meetings are banned, spying is widespread, the mail service is unreliable, the
> press does not exist, and there is fierce conflict of interest and savage competi-
> tion for government posts in view of the limited opportunities citizens have to
> obtain resources.[26]

One statement encapsulating aspects of this miserable reality is an appeal sent to the Yemeni people by Sayf al-Haq Ibrahim, the son of Imam Yahya.[27] It was made after his escape, in 1947, to Aden, where he joined the Yemeni Liberals and was given the leading role in their party, the Greater Yemeni Association. The appeal contains the following paragraphs:

> Children of my dear country: you are all aware of the conditions suffered by our
> stricken land as a result of the cruel injustice and savage actions of despotic
> tyrants, who have strayed from the road of freedom and rationality, followed the
> path of delinquent corruption and whim, and have turned their backs on the
> commands and instructions of the Quran and discarded the *sunna* of the
> Prophet, may God pray upon him and his family. These rulers have adopted
> devious means of rule and committed abominable crimes, plundering and pil-
> laging the property of Muslims, humiliating religious scholars, turning their

faces from the advice and prudence of honest advisers, withholding money in areas vital to the good of country and people, neglecting measures to secure welfare and success for the nation, along with like deeds that have angered Almighty God and made the outraged people pray to God to save them from this distress and relieve them through the removal of this hateful and despotic regime.

You all know the dreadful crimes the tyrants have committed: how they have enslaved the people and persecuted the men of the nation; have driven all those seeking the country's welfare into dark, secluded prisons, where they are presently suffering the most fearful agony and ill-treatment . . .

Wise men of the nation: the situation in Yemen has grown intolerable; it would be a crime to keep a tight-lipped silence at what we hear and see. You are the wise men and the heirs of prophets. God has singled you out as leaders to call for what is good, warn against vice, caution unjust rulers, and explain to the people the provisions of this orthodox religion bestowed upon the human race to institute justice, mercy and equality in all things . . . Should you perform just a part of your religious duty, unjust rulers will curb their actions, the people will find relief from their tyranny and excessive cruelty, and you will be the beacon, men leading the nation into the paths of well-being and success.

You government workers and administrators: you have been used by the tyrants neither to set justice and charity among the people, nor to maintain law and order in the country. They have exploited you as cruel tax collectors, to place at the service of these rulers the property of Muslims and the subjugated necks of your brother citizens. They have deprived you of every right, stripped you of every authority, giving no heed to your opinion or to any just action you might take. Given all this, people have come to believe you are good only for vicious deeds and capable only of doing harm. How can you then accept this status for yourselves among your Muslim citizens, and how will you face Almighty God, the Lord of the whole human race? . . .

Tribal *shaykh*s and dignitaries of the country: you had a beneficent station among your tribes. You would support your words by deeds, and your orders were met with obedience. The tyrants knew your position and status when they wanted your help and sought your assistance. Yet no sooner had they secured their interest than they denied your presence, deprived you of your rights and revenues, humiliated you among your tribes, and drove you into poverty after wealth and into humiliation after glory. What will you do, then, and how long will you accept these things?

As for you, toiling peasants and farmers: your plight is dire, your condition grievous. You have long borne patiently the tyranny of government administrators and workers, the arbitrary repression of embezzlers, the baneful conduct of military and other personnel who occupy your houses and violate the privacy of your homes. They have used you as subjugated serfs and slaves: you plant and they eat; you starve and they feed; you suffer and they enjoy. They never feel for you in times of drought, or assist you in time of poverty, or treat you in time of illness. Your state has worsened. You have sold your land and some of you have emigrated from the country, seeking to flee injustice and tyranny and pursue the life of which you were deprived in your own land . . .

And you, distressed tradesmen: you are victims of this fearful, deceitful régime, which has crippled your hands, paralysed your business, destroyed your commerce. You compete in vain with the merchant rulers, who are dazzled at the sight of money and have used their influence and powers to flourish in business with their subjects; have left you, amid the present misfortune and confusion, to scratch a living for yourselves and for your families and children.

Patient and dutiful employees: you are the diligent workers, the unknown soldiers, used by the tyrants to serve their interests and objectives, and not to contribute to the good of the country or the interests of the nation. They have taken away your rights, given you frugal wages and negligible means and resources, forced you to stretch out your hands and seize others' money illegally, stripped you of the dignity that marks the conduct of state functionaries in all other governments of the world. You work day and night, and yet receive no reward for your work. You spend your lives in service, then leave your children in poverty, without support from the government or custody from guardians. You, I know very well, are the most aware and conscientious category in the nation, the group best prepared to contribute to the welfare of the people, and yet those most in need of protection and fair treatment.

Brave Yemeni soldiers: you are the children of Qahtan and 'Adnan, the grandchildren of Himyar and Kahlan. The nations of the old world spare no effort to treat their soldiers worthily, spending large sums of money on training them and providing them with arms, paying every attention to their comfort and well-being, because they are the protectors of the homeland and guardians of the sacred country, who spill their blood in defence of its independence and interests, and offer their lives to protect its children. But unjust rulers and tyrants consider you, Yemeni soldiers, as mere hired servants employed to protect them and further their personal objectives. You wake at night so they can sleep in peace and tranquility. You sleep on straw mats beneath the sky to let them find happiness in their mansions and vast palaces. You wear rough clothes, while they parade in silk and fine brocade. You walk barefoot, and they ride well-equipped horses. You eat dry bread, while they enjoy delicate tasty meals. They do not even appreciate what you do, or recognize your special character. They use you in menial tasks and services, and insult you with harsh phrases and foul words. They do not even leave you such slender pay as you receive, but rather take it back in installments and reductions, treating you as the meanest of slaves. They attend to their animals in sickness, but care nothing for you when you fall ill. Your family meets with hardship if you pass away, for all they find passed on to them is the remains of your shabby groundcovers and worn-out clothes. By

God, you are the betrayed victims of injustice! Soldiers of the homeland, if you knew your value and claimed your right, the final say, the conclusive decision would be yours.

Yemenis in all walks of life: I wish you to know that the Arab and Islamic world has heard your voice and is awake to your cause, is angered at the disasters of this ugly régime. All Arabs and Muslims now recognize the situation in Yemen is too grave, too serious to be tolerated or accepted . . . My sole appeal to you today is to close your ranks, to cease assisting the tyrants against your own selves, and to work with me, as one, to save our country. May God be with us. He has pledged to help the righteous win victory over the tyrants and bring about their abject downfall. And may peace and God's mercy and blessings be upon you.[28]

This provocative appeal clearly demonstrates the rights usurped from citizens of all categories, and underscores their duty to pursue the struggle to retrieve these rights from the clutches of despotic and unjust rulers. The appeal may serve as a prelude for discussing the demands of the people, which would later be set out and projected by the Liberal Movement, notably the demands relating directly to human rights as we understand them today.

III. Human rights underlined in the writings and political programmes of the liberals

The writings and public programmes of the Liberals involved priority demands, representing the essence of human rights vital in their particular time and circumstances (i.e. the first half of the twentieth century), and also, in our own days, for many Arab countries and other regions of the world. The Liberals viewed these demands as imperative necessities in handling the worsening situation reviewed in the preceding texts, a situation they strove to change for the benefit, happiness, dignity, freedom, safety and security of the people. These demands included: the right of people to choose their rulers; the right to opinion and expression, and the citizen's right to dignity and the protection of his property and home; relief from grievances of all types; the right to education, health, security, equality, justice and work; reform of prison conditions; protection from sanctions, including prison and execution, unless preceded by trial, etc.

These and other demands were gradually projected in the writings of the Liberals, especially those relating to focused programmes (political programmes – a national charter – requests presented to the Imam or addressed to the people). We shall, as far as possible, highlight or review some of these texts, without, however, undertaking a close analysis of the vast content of the publications, essays and booklets in question, which explain these rights in considerable detail and were issued first by enlightened Yemenis, then by the Liberal Movement from its formation up to the revolution of September 1962. The first text of a programmatic nature is the programme of *Hizb al-Ahrar al-Yamani* (the Party of Yemeni Liberals), which saw its commencement, according to many documented sources, in Sanaa in 1938, that is to say a few years before the establishment of the Party of Yemeni Liberals in Aden. The party did not in fact undertake any activity apart from this programme, which was subsequently published in 1944. The programme included a number of paragraphs specifically relevant to human rights, such as: those dealing with disseminating culture and education, supporting victims of injustice in Yemen and defending those imprisoned without trial.[29]

In 1944, the Party of Yemeni Liberals in Aden published a list of demands that were presented to the government for fulfillment, including: annulment of implementation (the call by a soldier on a citizen, who would be obliged to feed and pay the soldier in return for the soldier's summoning of the citizen), cancellation of the *khutat* (see above), the provision of public health, the building of schools, the spreading of education, alleviating the hardship suffered by peasants, helping them with loans and assistance, relieving them of serf work, providing guarantees against arrest without trial, and reforming courts so that people's cases would not be subject merely to the will of the judges.[30]

In the mid-1940s, the Council of Senior Religious Scholars of Sanaa submitted a written memorandum to Imam Yahya, requesting, among other things: the placing of the *zakat* (the prescribed charitable donation) in trust like other religious obligations, so as to save citizens from the arrogance of the *kharrasin* (the government inspectors appointed to evaluate the *zakat*) and the tyranny of the *kashafin* (the officers charged with the duty of reviewing and verifying the estimates made by the *kharras*, for collection by the state); rescuing people from the tyranny of military personnel; lifting the illegal taxes levied by employees on citizens; cancelling arrears due from them (i.e. the balance of exaggerated and enlarged taxes which citizens could not pay, leaving them no option but to evade the tax authorities by fleeing the country); releasing those who had been arrested, 'since they have received sufficient punishment and been reduced to a wretched state'; and improving the conditions and raising the salaries of employees, 'in order to prevent them from seeking bribes and making errors against helpless people'.[31]

In 1947, the Sacred National Charter was drawn up as part of the prepara-
tions made by the Liberals for effecting the desired political change in Yemen.
It was presented as a provisional constitution with which the new Imam
should comply following the death of Imam Yahya, being published before the
coup of February 1948. Almost all the articles and clauses have a direct or indirect relevance to human rights. The Charter included the notion of a social
contract between the people and the new Imam, by which people's representatives pledged support to the Imam on behalf of the people – support that
would be

> a fulfilled religious pledge to a legitimate constitutional and *shura*-grounded
> Imam, acting in a manner consistent with procedures followed by advanced
> nations in the civilized world, and in a fashion that in no way contradicts the
> magnanimous teachings of Islam.

The Charter makes the pledge of loyalty dependent on a number of sacred conditions, including

> working, in word and action, in accordance with the contents of the Holy Quran
> and the *sunna* of the Prophet, may God pray upon him and upon his family, and
> in consistency with the actions of good predecessors, may God bless them.

According to this pledge of support, the Imam will have

> the ears and the obedience, in times of prosperity and hardship alike, of every
> individual within this system of expressed loyalty . . . as long as he conforms to
> the requirements of this pledge, and commits himself to this Charter, in pursuit
> of the desired objectives, with every possible dispatch.[32]

We shall present here, by way of illustration, a number of articles and clauses of
direct relevance to human rights:

- Article (27): The injustice and tyranny imposed on subjects shall be lifted
  by correct collection of dues and by cancelling the balance of false arrears.
- Article (29): Property, honour and lives of all people shall be protected,
  except in legitimate cases or legitimate law, and all members of the Yemeni
  people shall enjoy absolute equality, save cases where talents and actions
  may be differently rewarded, and all shall be under the rule of the just and
  magnanimous Shariah, whose provisions shall apply to great and small
  without any distinction.
- Article (30): Freedom of opinion, speech and assembly shall be guaranteed
  within the limits of security and law.

- Article (32): Efforts shall be exerted for the fighting of ignorance, poverty and sickness, unrelentingly and with all the methods available to the state, and for a speedy facilitation of the means of transport and improvement of the state of agriculture which is the basis of the economy in Yemen.[33]

In 1956, one year after the failure of the second coup aimed at removing Imam Ahmad and replacing him with his brother Abdallah, the Liberal Movement issued a National Charter that included a summary of the objectives of the Movement, along with the demands of the people for which Yemenis had struggled since the 1930s. The Charter also outlined the form of the desired political system. The introduction to the text of the National Charter expressed the main demands of the people:

1   The monarch rules but does not govern.
2   A transitional government will be formed from the people and will conduct elections for a general assembly.
3   The transitional government shall be committed to the attached National Charter as a provisional constitution before the people who are represented in the general assembly.

The text of the Charter consists of 40 articles that included almost all the issues of direct relevance to human rights.

In view of its brevity, and its concentration on human rights for which Yemenis have struggled, our discussion will conclude with the complete text of the Charter:

1   Yemen is an independent and sovereign parliamentary state; no region of Yemen may be divided or relinquished. The Yemeni people – as a sovereign entity – has the right to determine its own destiny.
2   The Yemeni homeland is part of the larger Arab homeland, and the Yemeni people is part of the great Arab nation and shall struggle to achieve the desired Arab unity.
3   People are born free and shall live free, combined by national brotherhood in the homeland.
4   Every Yemeni individual has the right to all inalienable rights and freedoms stated in this Charter, to equality in dignity, rights, and duties, and to the availability of all types of opportunities for life without any distinction based on creed, region, tribe, descent, or any social, economic, or political position.

5 Every individual has the right to life, freedom, security, tranquility, and safety for himself, his family, and his property, and no person may be suppressed, tortured, or subjected to a harsh, savage, or undignifying penalty.

6 All people are equal before the court, and they have the right to have equality in protection without any distinction and to have equality in protection against any distinction that may contravene this Charter and against any provocation for such distinction.

7 An individual cannot be accused, detained, or arrested, except in cases stipulated by law, provided that lawful procedures be followed. Anyone implementing a despotic command that contradicts with the law, or ordering it, or giving instructions for its implementation shall deserve punishment. Any person summoned or arrested in accordance with the law must show instant obedience and, in the event that he disobeys or resists, he shall be subjected to punishment.

8 Every person has the right to resort to national courts for fair treatment against all actions that may involve a transgression against his rights or his dignity.

9 Every person has the right – on equal grounds – to have his case reviewed by an independent and honest court, in a fair and public manner, whether this review covers resolutions on his rights, obligations or criminal accusations against him.

10 No person may be sanctioned for any action or for abstaining from any action, unless it is considered a crime in the eyes of the law at the time such action has been made. He may not receive a punishment harder than what he should have received when the crime was committed.

11 A person accused of a crime shall be considered innocent until his indictment has been legally confirmed in a public trial that must provide him with all the guaranties necessary for self-defence. Should it be necessary to detain a person before his indictment, any force used against him without justification shall be punished.

12 No person shall be subjected to arbitrary intervention in his private life, family, house, correspondence, or to assault against his honour and reputation. Every person has the right to be protected by law against such intervention or assault.

13 Houses are protected sanctuaries that no person and no government authority has the right to enter, except in certain conditions and in a form stipulated by the law.

14 Every Yemeni has the freedom to move and choose his place of abode within the Yemeni state, and has the freedom to exit from and return to

its territory as he wishes, without limitations except those stipulated by the law.

15 No Yemeni may be exiled from the territory of Yemen.

16 The right to enjoy Yemeni citizenship shall be defined by a special legislation, provided that Yemenis born outside the country enjoy Yemeni citizenship.

17 Every Yemeni has the right to own property, individually or in partnership with others, and he may not be dispossessed of his property except by reason of public interest, and upon payment of sufficient compensation, and in exceptional circumstances specified by the law.

18 Individual liberty is observed, secured by the law, and allowable for actions that do not cause harm to others. Every person shall enjoy his natural rights.

19 The Yemeni State shall guarantee the freedom to practise worship by different faiths.

20 Every person has the right to freedom of thought, opinion, and expression, verbally and in writing, or in other media.

21 Newspapers and other kinds of publication are free and their censorship is prohibited. Newspapers may not be discontinued, confiscated, or unlicensed, except by a judiciary judgement given by a competent court.

22 In times of war, the security of the state and public interest, and the defence of the country, calls for drawing up a special legislation for censorship of publications, newspapers, and broadcasting, only within the limits of defence.

23 Censorship on publications and broadcasting, and the modes and the means for such censorship, shall be clarified and specified by legislation.

24 Yemenis have the right to hold meetings and peaceful demonstrations, and to form associations and unions within the limits of the constitution.

25 Every Yemeni has the right to free participation in associations, and no person may be forced to participate in any society.

26 The association law shall specify the methods by which associations may be formed, and define the means for monitoring their resources.

27 Yemenis have absolute freedom to discuss with the authority matters relating to their private and public affairs.

28 All media for telephone, telegraph, or postal communication shall be confidential and accessible to every individual. They may not be censored, cancelled, or deleted, except in circumstances of war and only within limits relating to defence.

29 Every individual or community has the freedom to open and manage schools for teaching, provided they are consistent with the principles of public education and are under the supervision of the Ministry of Education.
30 Political refugees, who hold political opinions and principles, or defend freedom and independence, may not be repatriated to their countries.
31 Special legislation shall be drawn up for the receipt or delivery of normal criminals.
32 Every person has the right to participate in the management of public affairs of his country, either directly or through representatives who are elected in freedom. Every person has the same rights that are enjoyed by others to hold public office in his country.
33 Appointment to government offices, to institutions that are government subsidiaries, or to municipalities, whether these positions are permanent or temporary, shall be made on grounds of eligibility, personal competence, and academic qualifications – if available – according to a special legislation for civil service.
34 Every citizen has the right to work. One of the duties of the state is to provide people with opportunities for work by managing the national economy and by raising their material and moral standards.
35 The state protects work and institutes for it legislation that entails the following principles:

   1 The workers' wages shall be consistent with quantity and quality, and may not be lower than the minimal amounts stipulated by the legislation.
   2 Hours of work during the week shall be specified, and weekly and annual paid holidays for workers shall be given.
   3 Rewards shall be determined for heads of families, and guaranties given in the case of sickness, old age, and injury at work.
   4 Freedom for forming labour unions shall be guaranteed.

36 Every person has the right to enjoy a standard of living sufficient for preserving health and welfare for him and for his family, including food, clothing, housing, and medical care. He has the right to secure a living in the case of unemployment, sickness, inability, widowhood, old age, and in other cases where the means for livelihood are lacking in circumstances beyond his control.
37 There shall be no taxes except what is established by the representatives of the people. Movable or immovable assets cannot be confiscated except in accordance with the provisions of the law.

38 There shall be no mortgage, serf work, or obligatory work. However, services that may be necessary for the country can be commissioned to individuals or communities within the following limits:

1 When there is a threat of war, or in the case of fire, floods, famines, earthquakes, the spreading of epidemic diseases, or in other similar circumstances.

2 The circumstances and the necessity for these works shall be determined by the local political agencies, and supervised by competent employees.

39 The people are the source of all power. No individual or group has the right to issue orders or warnings, unless they derive power from the people.[34]

Conclusion

The above presents texts selected from the writings of the Yemeni National Movement and relevant to human rights, as published in newspapers and booklets covering the national issue in general and, specifically, the injustice, repression, backwardness and ignorance experienced in Yemen. The nationalist authors who published these texts were saved from the tyranny of the Imam only by their escape from local repression and establishment of their residence in the Aden colony or in Egypt. Human rights have, nevertheless, remained a pivotal issue in the struggle of Yemenis, and a vital theme in their writings, since the commencement of their newspapers, publications and public activity; that is to say, from the time their leaders fled to the Aden colony and formed the party of Liberal Yemenis in 1948 up to the present day.

[I should like to express my sincere thanks to the American Institute for Yemeni Studies for the help and practical kindness they showed me in the course of initial research for this article. – EDITOR]

PART 4

Human rights in modern Arabic thought: specialized studies

Chapter 17: Human rights in the historical texts of the modern Arab world

Bayan Nuwayhid al-Hout

Introduction

Modern writers have termed the nineteenth century in Europe the era of nationalism and colonialism, whereas the twentieth century, in both East and West, might fittingly be called the era of world wars and human rights.

The principles of natural human rights, as set out by world religions, by the codes of great historical civilizations and by modern international charters, do not differ at their core. However, these principles are incapable of providing for the happiness of the individual so long as he or she remains part and parcel of an oppressed people. The absolute separation of human rights from the rights of peoples is an instrument that can only serve the political goals of superpowers – who impose their hegemony in the name of defending noble principles! All the nations today considered among the most civilized and advanced in implementing human rights have known historical periods akin to those experienced by Arabs in this present era: periods, that is, of struggle against foreign hegemony or occupation.

The main problem facing a search for treatments of human rights in the historical texts of the modern Arab world lies in the fact that Arabs confronted four major challenges in the course of the twentieth century. Three of these, the Turkish, the colonial European and the Zionist/Israeli challenges, made no pretence of disguise, while the American challenge mounted toward the end of the twentieth century has been a veiled one, made in the name of friendship and the defence of human rights. How, then, have Arab historians, concerned with their nation's cause in the midst of all these challenges, viewed human rights?

At the outset of this research, my wish was to interview some of those Arab historians of outstanding maturity, impact and humanity. I knew, from reading their works, how they had given pride of place to the people's dignity and its rights, believing that, once this had been achieved, the human being would be liberated. This knowledge of their writings led me to expect that, even if the nature of the present era led them to be circumspect, they would welcome the idea. Even so, my interviews with Constantine Zurayq and Nicola Ziyada exceeded my expectations.

'Human rights as understood today?' Dr Zurayq said. 'No. Historians were not concerned with them – although this alleged "oversight" is not a specifically Arab affliction, but one affecting all voiceless peoples. No constitution has ever emerged, following a revolution or an independence movement, that did not place the rights of the citizen ahead of human rights . . . Palestinians have remained at the stage of citizens' rights to this day.' As for the question of personal freedoms during the reign of Egyptian President Gamal Abdul Nasser, Zurayq's reply showed his enthusiasm and spirit of activism to be intact. 'People gave up their freedoms, agreed to suspend them till some later time. We had been conquered at every stage of our political life, and such is the history we have documented; there are issues and problems more important than the freedom of individuals . . . Our concern is this vanquished, patriotic human being of ours . . . '

Zurayq's conclusion was decisive: 'Historians are not the ones to consult on this matter.'[1]

More like an advocate than a historian, and with the spontaneity of a child rather than the wariness of an elder, Dr Ziyada said emphatically: 'I never wrote a thing on human rights . . . I challenge you to show me anything I ever wrote on the subject!' Then, abruptly calm, Ziyada the historian plunged into an exposition of causes and of the modern historical eras, summarizing the battle for freedom in the Arab world, from the demand for freedom of the citizen – freedom from foreign domination – through to internal freedom. When I inquired about personal freedoms under Nasser, he maintained that no one had dared say 'No', and that the 1967 defeat might have been avoided had it been possible to do so. Nevertheless, he made a positive assessment of Egypt's distinctive experience in its struggle for freedom and for participation in forming political opinion, and insisted repeatedly, till the end of the interview, that he had written nothing on human rights. But his ardour was closer to that of a lover sublimating the story he had not yet written; perhaps just hinting at it, intentionally or not.[2]

Our first question is: Why did Zurayq and Ziyada speak as they did?

Our second question is: Is their stand typical of that of contemporary Arab historians as a whole? These are the two issues this essay will endeavour to address.

Most early nationalist writing on the challenges facing Arabs during the first quarter of the twentieth century focused on the Arab inhabitants of so-called Greater Syria; more broadly of the Fertile Crescent. However, from the outbreak of the Great Arab Revolt in Mecca in 1916, the Hijaz had also been viewed as part of this greater whole.[3] Hence, this region today includes six Arab countries: Syria, Iraq, Lebanon, Palestine, Jordan and Saudi Arabia.

This 'division' or 'selection' is not intended to detract in any way from the political experiences of the peoples of the Nile valley, the Maghreb or the Arabian Gulf, from their struggle for freedom from colonialism and its minions, and for human rights. It was simply necessary to limit the scope of the research by considering a single, cohesive experience. Most Arabs of the Mashriq, or eastern Arab world, have, it should be emphasized, studied the preoccupations of all Arabs no matter where they lived.

This essay focuses on the natural human rights most fully stressed by these historians, along with their views on them. As such, the subtitles for the human rights dealt with below are not of my own choosing, but rather dictated by the historians' own writings in the light of the prominence they gave to the categories in question. These subtitles are: public rights, 'democracy and justice'; the right to political representation; the right to freedom; women's rights; the right to religious belief; the right to work; and violations of human rights.

My criteria for selecting historians were as follows:

1   They should be contemporary historians of the Mashriq, who studied the history of this region in the twentieth century.
2   They should be historians of deep insight who witnessed and documented the nation's struggle.
3   They should be of various politico-philosophical affiliations, so as to represent the main schools of thought within the Arab world – such as the Islamist, Arab Nationalist, Marxist and Socialist currents.
4   There should be a variation in age, so as to cover more than one generation of historians.
5   Each should, by virtue of birth and 'nationality', represent one of the six Arab countries mentioned above.

The number of historians had, moreover, to be restricted on account of the limited length of this study. We might perhaps have restricted ourselves to ten historians, but for the fact that the search for human rights in this era is akin to searching for wild flowers ahead of spring – indeed amid the blustery chill of winter. I have been able, or so I believe, to gather a bunch of blooming wild flowers from among the writings of 14 historians – which is not to say these are the only Arab historians to mention human rights.

Initially I chose six distinguished historians, one from each of the six Arab countries in question. Yet equalizing the number of historians and countries turned out to be futile, not only because many were born in one country and raised in another, but also because the interests of some extended to encompass the whole of their nation, the Arab homeland, whereas others were concerned with the Islamic world at large. As such, grouping by nation state, while technically feasible and even scientifically desirable, failed to correspond to these historians' beliefs, to their true moorings and their philosophical and activist struggle. Once each nation-state had been covered by choosing one distinguished historian, the next step was to select other historians, each according to his status and oeuvre. In some cases where one historian was quoted over another, it was not a matter of one being a better scholar, but simply of achieving a coherent synthesis of the work of 14 integrated historians.

The six main historians are: Muhammad Kurd 'Ali (1876–1953) from Syria; 'Abd al-Razzaq al-Hasani (1903–1997) from Iraq; Yousef Yezbek (1901–1982) from Lebanon; 'Arif al-'Arif (1892–1973) from Palestine; 'Ali Mahafza (born 1938) from Jordan; and 'Abd al-'Aziz Ben 'Abd al-Muhsin al-Tuwayjiri (born 1915) from Saudi Arabia.

As for the remaining eight historians from the eastern Arab world, I chose, in the order of their birth: Prince Shakib Arsalan (1869–1946); Muhammad 'Izzat Darwaza (1887–1984); Mustafa al-Dabbagh (1897–1989); Nicola Ziyada (born 1907); Constantine Zurayq (born 1909); Shaykh 'Abdallah al-'Alayli (1914–1996); 'Abd al-'Aziz al-Duri (born 1919); and Anis Sayigh.

I. Public Rights, 'Democracy' and 'Justice'

The term 'human rights' was neither alien nor condemned in the Mashriq of the early twentieth century, or indeed of the nineteenth. The historian Philip Hitti, who has written the history of the Arabs of Syria, the Middle East and Lebanon from the earliest times, states unequivocally that the term was familiar and in common use in the last third of the nineteenth century, all the more so following the intellectual awakening at the century's mid-point. As for the accompanying political awakening, its leaders began casting about for some refuge after the Ottoman authorities had started to pursue them more virulently in the last three decades of the century; and Cairo, enjoying as it did greater freedom than other cities in the Mashriq, became the destination of these leaders, with Syrian and Lebanese journalists foremost among them. Cairo was, therefore, the site where new idioms such as 'human rights' appeared for the first time, then spread widely. Hitti has taken pains to introduce his foreign readers to the Arabic appellation, in the Lebanese dialect, transliterating it into Latin script as *huquq al-insan*.[4]

In truth, though, matters had been initiated a very long time before the nineteenth century. To say, as many historians constantly reiterate, that Arab thought embarked on the discussion of human rights only in response to Western thought, is in itself a gross injustice toward Arab thought, which had always been among the first to take in human inclinations, individual rights and the values of justice and democracy. Even though that distant history is beyond the focus of this essay, a brief survey is necessary to prevent fragmentation in the presentation of twentieth-century idioms. The Arab Iraqi scholar, 'Abd al-'Aziz al-Duri, may be taken as 'the historian' in this instance, for he followed the entire course of Arab history from early times through to the twentieth century from the standpoint of these concepts and values. Commencing with the comprehensive revolution brought about by Islam, he expounds such matters as how Islam stressed nation over tribe and unity over factionalism, implementing law/Shariah rather than tribal custom, as well as spreading the social justice for which Abu Dharr al-Ghafari and others fought. 'Their voices,' al-Duri comments, 'did not fall on deaf ears; they made a huge difference.'[5] He analyses the relevant societal values, without which individuals cannot possess rights, in the following terms:

> Arab-Islamic society had basic values and humanitarian views. Its main principle was justice.
>
> The spirit of justice manifested itself in Arab civilization and its manifold aspects, such as politics and legislation, socio-economic relations, but especially and most powerfully in the intellectual foundation.
>
> The notion of justice is embodied in the dominion of Shariah over both rulers and ruled. Shariah rests upon the texts of the Quran and the *hadith*, and upon the opinions of theologians and experts in *fiqh* [jurisprudence]. Shariah affirms justice and disavows tyranny.
>
> The notion of justice is also apparent in the emphasis on *shura* [consultation], and on the sanctity of the nation's views ... Since the nation is the foundation of society in general, those who dissolve and resolve, *ahl al-hall wa 'l-'aqd*, must represent all its diverse groups.

There is also the general view of the nation, as represented in the principle of *ijma'*, or consensus. Once the nation, or its jurist theologians, have agreed on a certain matter, thus creating a consensus, it becomes mandatory. However, al-Duri does not view the mandate resulting from such a consensus as a shackle; rather, it opens up the possibility for the nation 'to face its problems with an open mind once the public good is protected'. He also points to the separation of the judicial system from the executive branch as a main feature of the concept of justice.[6]

The significance of Islam's view of the human being's true nature, of his intellectual capabilities and his free will, has been discussed by al-Duri and other historians. Of course, actual implementation of Shariah was a matter for rulers, who are only human, and it was natural that this implementation should wax and wane over the course of fourteen centuries of Arab-Islamic history.

The dawn of the twentieth century saw a period of oppression, and it was 1908, the year of the Ottoman Constitution, that marked the Arabs' starting point for achieving their political aims and acquiring their rights within the Ottoman Parliament. But it is wrong to think that Arabs' awareness of their rights sprang solely from the move of the 'Unionists' to restore dignity to the Constitution and implement it. Already, in 1907, the historian Muhammad Kurd 'Ali had published an article entitled 'The Freedom of Nations'. He was one of the few who related the meaning of freedom to human rights and understood the significance of human rights and knowledge. He wrote:

> People are progressing along the road of order and freedom, approaching maturity, building their national life in a way different from the way of *jahiliyya* [pre-Islamic times], believing that eternal bliss is achieved through respect for individuals and universal rights and through sustaining the material and emotional means of life.
>
> People have never seen such a time as this, one in which their interests are subject to specific laws and liberal principles. Nor has knowledge known such a presence, encompassing land and sea, the profligate and the devout, white and black, even flora and inanimate objects, as has this strange and mysterious century. It is as though the spirit of progress were made up of enlivening, not deadly, breezes, permeating air and matter, entering all people, old and young.
>
> Knowledge is akin to a light that can dawn on some people and not others, or on one country and not another. Such is its power that the oppressors will be powerless to perpetrate further injustices against the weakened and vanquished.[7]

Al-Duri followed the interest of political thinkers in universal human rights at the start of the twentieth century, especially the work of 'Abd al-Ghani al-'Uraisi, publisher of the journal *Al-Mufid*. Al-'Uraisi defined his journal's character and goals as 'Arab, Ottoman, the protection of Arabs against harm and struggle for their rights'.[8] Al-Duri also alluded to al-'Uraisi's endeavour to translate Paul Domer's book in 1911, with a view to encouraging the young to be aware of their, and their countrymen's, freedom and rights,[9] and he further underlined the philosophy of Rafiq al-'Azm, leader of the Decentralization Party, who 'called on non-Muslims to work with Muslims within the framework of nationalism, and to strengthen national brotherhood to achieve democracy'; who believed in the Arab Nation and its historic role, defending its rights and demanding that it be a full partner in government.[10]

The Paris Conference of 1913 was the first in which Arabs demanded their political and individual rights. It never occurred to the conferees that a number of them would, in another three years, become martyrs at the hands of Jamal Pasha. One of these speaker-'martyrs' was al-'Uraisi. Various Arab thinkers and historians, such as al-Duri, Yezbek, and al-Husari, are unanimous in holding his speech in high esteem.[11] Of course, al-'Uraisi was not unique in comprehending constitutional principles and human rights. His fellow-students, dubbed the 'Paris Group', were marching alongside him. It has been said of this group that 'they were filled with the principles of human and citizens' rights, living in a free environment where the freedoms of thought, speech and belief were utterly sacrosanct'.[12] The main points al-'Uraisi stressed in his speech at the Paris Conference on 20 June 1913 were as follows:

> In every political system rights are of two kinds: the rights of the individual and those of the group. There are many groups, but the most prominent among them are the groups of peoples; for peoples' rights are distinct from those of individuals.

He proved the rights of Arabs as a people to a nationality and a political existence, and to what springs from these in the way of legislative and executive powers. He then demonstrated the absence of these rights even though the Ottoman Arabs numbered 13 million, more than half 'the kingdom's people'. 'As long,' he declared, 'as our rights are not safeguarded, we regard the Constantinople government as having failed to fulfil the conditions of justice. From the standpoint of the "Declaration of Human Rights", a government has no legitimacy unless it respects the rights of groups and peoples.' His main demands were for a partnership with the state in both the legislative and executive powers and in general administration. 'As for the internal issues of our lands, we must be our own partners in funding education, public works and *waqf* (religious endowment), in furthering the freedom to congregate and freedom of the press, none of which is possible without expanding the powers of the Public Councils.'[13]

Al-'Uraisi built up his *Mufid* journal, in his homeland of Lebanon, on his
return from Paris. In 1913 he published an article on the concept of universal
rights, the relation of the individual to the state and the significance of the
individual. He wrote:

> It is incumbent on every young Arab to believe that life is a tragic tale in which
> the state and the people fight on behalf of rights, and he must work to support
> the nation. Either the tale leads to oppression and hatred, and so to misery and
> suffering, or it leads to justice and brotherhood, and so to honour and pride. If
> the young Arab desires to live a life of honour and nobility, he must believe this:
> that the nation is a compact made on earth between the living, the dead and pos-
> terity; that the state is an end for the individual and not a means for its own ends;
> that the individual is an end for himself, his people and his progeny; and that
> without the nation there would be no individual, and vice versa, for they form a
> never-ending cycle. Therefore, this young Arab must adopt a stance of 'individ-
> ualism' vis-à-vis the state and of 'solidarity' vis-à-vis the nation, and play his part
> in this drama. We guarantee that he, his people and his offspring will acquire all
> their rights.[14]

At the height of the colonial ascendancy, many writers and thinkers devoted
themselves to exposing its goals and methods in oppressing peoples and individuals. Unique among them was Shakib Arsalan, the Prince of Eloquence, for
he was a fighter both in thought and deed. It was he who joined the Libyan
resistance against the Italian colonial occupation of 1911 and wrote of the col-
onizers' utter disregard for national and human rights:

> Islam in Tripoli and Barqa has begun to fade into oblivion ever since the Fascist
> party under Mussolini seized power in Italy.
>   It is well known that Fascists are concerned with nothing but achieving their
> goals by any means, and without the slightest consideration for what is called
> 'nations' rights' or 'humanity's rights', or any similar rights to which the rest of
> the world adheres. Moreover, they declare, without equivocation, that they nei-
> ther recognize freedom nor sanctify universal rights, and that anything bringing
> glory and hegemony to Italy and reinforcing the fascist state is permissible,
> whether it accords with the rights of nations and humanity or not. Mussolini has
> made many speeches and published numerous pamphlets to this effect, with the
> result that there is now, in Italy, neither freedom of speech nor freedom of the
> press, and anything that goes against the wish of the Fascists is prohibited . . .[15]

One of the most famous freedom fighters of Tripoli, if not of the whole twentieth-century world, was Shaykh 'Umar al-Mukhtar, a martyr who was executed
by hanging in 1931. Even his opponent, the Italian Commander-in-Chief

Graziani, attested that al-Mukhtar had fought 263 battles against him, in a mere 20 months. In Syria, Sultan Pasha al-Atrash had been leading a revolution against the French mandate since 1925. Al-Hajj Muhammad Amin al-Husaini of Jerusalem was providing his Syrian brethren with all possible aid, while also supporting the Buraq Revolution in Palestine in 1929. All these are examples of the various revolutions of the 1920s, which were breaking out even as life went on and many young Arabs were travelling in search of knowledge. One such, from Syria, was Constantine Zurayq, who studied in the United States at the close of this decade, became one of the main founders of the first comprehensive Arab nationalist movement,[16] and was to produce a substantial and pioneering body of work over the next 60 years, reprinted in its entirety in 1994. Recalling these early years, Zurayq wrote how:

> ... it was a time when responsibilities grew larger, during which individuals and groups were called upon to make great efforts in confronting external and internal dangers to the national entity, and a period in which droves of Arab freedom-fighters sacrificed their lives or were subjected to the worst torture and persecution in defence of their land, their heritage and their future, against the foreign powers of usurpation; or in defence of their national and human rights, which the authorities violated constantly.[17]

Zurayq then clarified the evolution in his understanding of democracy and human rights, and the effect on this of his US educational experience:

> I had not quite comprehended at the time that the intellectual liveliness I thrilled to, and whose participants thrilled me, was organically connected to the democratic trend in public life and its freedom of thought. For I perceived in those years and immediately thereafter that centralized rule was more adept than decentralized, democratic rule at creating the desired climate for learning and research, through sponsorship and by supporting it with human and financial resources. But I soon learned through observation and experience that all these attempts are inadequate, if not downright depraved and degrading, unless accompanied by respect for the intellectual process and for citizens' rights in a liberal democratic milieu. And so I reverted to the democratic inclinations that were a part of my earlier upbringing in Damascus and Beirut, and these took root owing to my later experiences during my studies in the US.[18]

Zurayq continued to write on citizens' rights – not human rights. He sometimes called them citizens' and human rights, rather than the other way around, in the way made famous by the French Revolution. In this respect he was in harmony with his compatriots in the nationalist movement, whose world-view took the foreign occupation of their country as its point of departure, and who therefore placed their country's independence and their nation's freedom ahead of the rights of individuals.

There were, in addition to the nationalist movement, a few Arab historians and thinkers who wrote on the rights of the human being as such, and not just of the Arabs. A pioneer among these was the man of knowledge and *fiqh*, Shaykh 'Abdallah al-'Alayli, a son of Beirut and a citizen of the world – for he saw the human being as the ultimate purpose of all religions and codes. For all his deep-rooted Arab affiliation, he distinguished plainly between nationalism and human rights:

> The essence of the Arabs' code of conduct is to be aware of their rights and not to ignore the rights of others; to know their responsibilities and not to neglect everyone else's. Their nationality can never be the foundation of their humanity; such an attitude has never displayed itself anywhere without undermining a people's essential humanity and allowing brute force to gain the upper hand.[19]

In his book *The Arabs' National Constitution* (1949), al-'Alayli authored an elaborate document that can only be compared to the United Nations Declaration of Human Rights, though it preceded it by seven years:

> Individuals have rights which society must respect and indeed sanctify, otherwise society would be transgressing against the individual's independence, negating his individualism and dissolving it into the greater body in such a way as to deprive this body of its organs' specialized efficiency. For no body can move ahead unless each of its organs is autonomous in its function and distinct from the function of other organs yet complementary to them.[20]

Al-'Alayli explained natural rights, which he called 'main rights', in great detail in some cases, in lesser detail in others, listing them as follows: the right to life, the right to seek one's livelihood, the right to freedom, the right to equality, the right to political representation, the right to an education, the right of ownership, the right of effecting contract, and the right to a childhood. On the latter he wrote as follows:

> Children preparing to enter society as useful, full-fledged members have certain rights. Foremost among these is the right to an education, to which the whole of society is committed. Education for youngsters has therefore been made mandatory and exempt from fees. Children also have the right to protection from exhaustion before reaching adulthood; it is therefore prohibited that they be put to work, thereby robbing them of their strength and impeding their growth.[21]

He then proceeded to 'the rights of the public vis-à-vis society', writing:

> A public that yields to a social order has general rights, such as the right to expect that its health be protected. The government is therefore obliged to protect the public from epidemics by various means. Aside from that, it is expected to organize urban life and encourage construction.[22]

He concluded with responsibilities, which he enumerated as follows: to respect public order; to respect the majority; to be concerned with the success of society; to respect other persons; and to be truthful in one's dealings. His definition of 'majority' was marked by a depth exceeding the common democratic concept:

> 'Majority' is not simply a matter of greater numbers, for a majority that is led by a single person's views negates the concept of a societal majority. As far as I am concerned, a proper majority is one that can participate in forming public opinion and expressing criticism, otherwise it is devoid of its meaning and no respect is due to it, nor does it become anyone's duty to yield to it when it is erroneous to do so. For the majority then turns into a minority because it is led by an individual who has manipulated and controlled the public with ulterior motives.[23]

The issues of freedom and democracy remained the concern of various Arab thinkers. Dozens of lectures and forums were held on the subject throughout the second half of the twentieth century, and many books written about them too. An outstanding book published in 1995 by the Centre for Arab Unity Studies, one of the most important institutes in the Arab world, focuses on the concerns of the Arab intellectual. It contains contributions by a few selected persons and an introduction by Anis Sayigh, a thinker and historian of Syrian origin, Palestinian birth and upbringing, and pan-Arab affiliation. Sayigh wrote of the human being's value, and of the challenge of democracy as the most pressing one facing the Arab intellectual:

Today's Arab intellectual, no matter the magnitude of his concern or the extent of his contribution, faces challenges unknown to his Arab predecessors in the fields of knowledge and culture.

There is, for example, the challenge of the scientific and technological revolution the world over, from which our countries should not be barred and which they cannot ignore. Were our countries to do so, they would be left behind in these areas of knowledge and precluded from playing their part in present and future civilizational action.

There is also the challenge of the intrinsic value of the human being, without whom neither awakenings and revolts, nor progress and development, would be possible, and for whom codes, laws and charters have been written. If the individual does not achieve his individuality except vis-à-vis society, then a society remains devoid of meaning, failing as it does to work for the good of the individual and for the presentation of human values.

And then there is the challenge of democracy. People have experimented, over millennia and with hundreds of systems, to find certain methods of inter-action within society, whether among individuals, groups or between the indi-vidual and authority. Only one method has succeeded in aiding the individual to achieve his individuality, and in aiding society to provide the most appropri-ate atmosphere for its citizens; and that is the democratic method in its numer-ous shapes and forms.[24]

The historian 'Ali Mahafza stands out among the selected group of histori-ans for his constant contributions to the cause of human rights, and for his dili-gent endeavours to introduce Universal Freedoms and Human Rights as courses in graduate programmes at the universities of Jordan. His writings are conspicuous for their modernism, and they take the experience of his country as their point of departure. In a lecture on the future of democracy in Jordan, he spoke of the conditions for strengthening democracy. The three years fol-lowing the 1989 parliamentary elections (the first in nearly two decades) had, he asserted, overflowed with swift changes and radical moves toward democ-racy, whereas the three years after that had been marked by stagnation and even by a reversal of the democratic process. He proposed a number of necessary criteria: that there should be a true balance among the political powers in the country; that the institutions of Jordanian society (political parties, labour unions, etc.) should be restored; that a nationalist movement should be cre-ated; and that links with international organizations and institutions concerned with the spread of democracy and the defence of human rights should be strengthened.[25]

II. The right to political representation

Modern constitutional theory had been spreading through the Ottoman state since the nineteenth century as a consequence of the diffusion of progressive ideas among intellectuals and some military officers. This led to the Period of Reform or *Tanzimat*, during which the Ottoman state attempted to make con-stitutional theory a basis for its rule, influenced partly by the reformist camp under the leadership of Rashid Pasha[26] and partly by its wish to placate the Western powers. In order to ward off any accusation of heresy, the Ottoman state based its reforms on Islamic Shariah law, and it did the same when it first promulgated the Constitution in 1876, under the influence of the reformer Medhat Pasha.[27] It appeared, ostensibly, as if the state had brought about a reconciliation between the two ways: those of the religious state and the constitutional state. The accommodation was, however, one of style rather than content, and the constitutional experiment under Sultan Abdul-Hamid was accordingly short-lived.[28]

Arab intellectuals were ahead of others under Ottoman rule in recognizing the significance of the constitution in the modern state. Foremost among these Arab thinkers was Najib 'Azuri, of Lebanese origin, of French education and of Palestinian experience through his work in the Ottoman state offices at Jerusalem. He is remarkable for having been the first to alert people to the imminent Zionist threat, in his book *The Awakening of the Arab Nation* (Yaqazat al-umma al-'Arabiyya) published in 1905; the work underlined the inevitability of a clash between pan-Arabism and Zionism, and called for the revival of the Arab Nation. But the greatest intellectual value of 'Azuri's writing lies in his espousal of modern constitutional principles; his party, which he named 'The League of the Arab Homeland', was established as a foundation for constitutional rule and the principle of equality before the law.[29]

In 1908, the year of the constitution, no fewer than 35 journals were being published in Syrian cities, in which Western political concepts and modern constitutional interpretations were discussed. Often journals would reprint the main articles published in other cities' journals, and this led to the diffusion of a good many writers' opinions and the spreading of their fame. Personal testimony – no less important than theoretical analysis – was widely set down by Arab historians, indicating their deep awareness of political representation.

Shakib Arsalan, the Prince of Eloquence, described how his first homeland, Lebanon, had moved into the constitutional age. This, he said, was the age of freedom:

> When freedom was proclaimed in the Ottoman Kingdom and rule by *shura* [advisory council] restored, and all this was being celebrated with relish throughout the Sultanate, Lebanon was also moved. Many realized that the Lebanese should benefit from the new order, for they felt that authoritarian rule at the hands of the *mutasarrif* [provincial governor] no longer expressed the spirit of the times.[30]

An educator and intellectual of Jerusalem, Khalil al-Sakakini, described in his diary the farewell procession for the representatives on their way to the 'Emissaries' Council' in Constantinople, on 16 November 1908; it was as though they were marching to celebrate an assured victory, not a mere 'parliamentary' session.

> We went to the city centre, and, lo and behold, there were the young Muslims, parading through the markets, dancing with their sabres, shooting their pistols into the air. The young Christians joined them, and they formed a grand parade marching toward the train station, which overflowed with well-wishers. Speeches were made and poems declaimed. The young people danced on, while patriotic songs were chanted and women ululated.[31]

The historian of Arab nationalism Sati' al-Husari, who also witnessed the period in question, had this to say:

> Proclaiming the constitution, putting an end to authoritarian rule and adopting a system of consensus in the Ottoman Sultanate . . . produced an extraordinary sense of happiness and rejoicing throughout the Arab states, and indeed in all the other Ottoman states. People began to hail freedom and equality, on every front and on every occasion. Clerics of all religions and denominations forgot their differences and embraced one another, rejoicing in the dawn of a new age. Turbans and hoods representing every creed mingled to the chants of the crowds. In sum, all the Ottoman states surged with euphoria.

The joy was, however, short-lived. Before long the same quarrels, among the various members of the Sultanate, were reawakened in many guises. Racial disturbances between Turks and Balkans resurfaced first, and eventually engulfed the Arabs as well . . .[32]

Time proved al-Husari right, but this did not prevent the Arab representatives uniting their efforts through their 'Arab Parliamentary Bloc' and presenting their main demands, for Arab rights. The historian Muhammad 'Izzat Darwaza was one of the few to give this bloc its rightful place in history,[33] writing of the first constitutional experience worked through by the Arabs: preparation of the Constitution of the Arab Kingdom of Syria. His diary, as secretary of the committee entrusted with drawing up the Constitution,[34] documented vociferous discussion, reflecting the intellectual conflicts among the multifarious generations and trends. Finally, though, this Constitution had been in force a bare matter of months when General Gouraud triumphed at the Battle of Maysalun on 24 July 1920, paving the way for a French mandate over Syria.

In Iraq, over which Faisal was subsequently crowned king, the first constitution was promulgated in 1925 under the title 'The Text of the Basic Iraqi Law'. Its importance, and the circumstances of its promulgation, were emphasized by the historian 'Abd Al-Razzaq al-Hasani, who set down an analysis and critique, pausing over its restrictions, or 'reservations' as he termed them; these he viewed as having been established with the aim of lessening the authority of the legislative power, and consequently the people's rights, in favour of the executive power, where the British High Commission (not the King or the Prime Minister) held the upper hand.[35] Nevertheless, the first chapter of the Constitution, entitled "People's Rights", embodied human rights formulated into a good text and at a superior level.[36]

There is near consensus among historians and constitutional scholars that human rights are covered in the Basic Laws and Constitutions of the Arab world, for there is certainly no scarcity of texts in this area.

How, then, do the historians of Saudi Arabia, where no constitution even exists, view human rights?

The Saudi author al-Tuwayjari showed himself very keen on collecting every piece of available documentation, and the testimonies of others, on the founder of the Kingdom, King Abdul-Aziz (Ibn Saud), with respect to the man himself and to his reign; he deserves to be called a historian in his own right, even though he did not view himself as such. In the matter of the Kingdom's constitution, he adapted the words of the historian 'Abdallah al-Qusaymi on the occasion of the King's visit to Egypt in 1946:

> Many people believe this king rules his country and his people in a despotic man-
> ner. However, one ought not to be swayed by such a claim, for he has restricted
> himself by a law in which he believes and which he respects, as do his compatri-
> ots. This law is the Islamic Shariah, which he upholds and does not invade. And
> if a person bound by a constitution of a people's making – and subject to this
> people's modifications, substitutions and annulments – is called a constitutional
> monarch, what does one call a person bound by an unchangeable law of God's
> making?[37]

III. The right to freedom

Nicola Ziyada differentiated between two kinds of freedom; one religious, the other personal. He wrote:

> The word 'freedom' appears frequently in Arabic literature, and especially in
> Islamic literature. In religious discourse it was discussed in terms of coercion and
> choice, the human's freedom in his life and God's judgement on him. The same
> may be said of 'equality', which permeated religious texts, in that all believers are
> equal before God, save in piety. The novel sense that came to attach to 'freedom'

through interaction with the West applied to secular life: to people's freedom in their political and civil life, their equality before the law and their access to various opportunities. People's freedom vis-à-vis one another, and their relationships, became a focus of research and reflection; and, even though studies barely scratched the surface initially, they began to go deeper into these issues toward the end of the nineteenth and beginning of the twentieth centuries.[38]

Al-Duri stressed how individual freedom and public opinion played a prominent role in the history of the Arab-Islamic nation,[39] while at the same time making a distinction between the first and second halves of the nineteenth century, noting the change in the concept of freedom and the relation of the Islamic concept to the Western one. The first half of the century was marked, simultaneously, by a sense of the superiority of Islam and its values, and by a feeling of admiration for the West's superiority in the sciences. Freedom and parliamentary rule were associated with such Islamic concepts as *shura*, choice and clarifying the evil of authoritarianism.[40] Citizenship was associated with universal rights from the time of Rifa'a al-Tahtawi, the *éminence grise* of Arab reformers. The individual's affiliation with a homeland is defined as 'enjoying his country's rights, the greatest of which is complete freedom in society'. But in the second half of the century, when the first stirrings of fear arose of the exposure of the Islamic heritage and entity to the danger of Western permeation, al-Afghani strove to raise political awareness within the Islamic nation and to embolden the East to combat European invasion.[41] Nevertheless, this stand does not, in and of itself, negate al-Afghani's greater sense of belonging to humanity as a whole, especially in view of his explanation that the human being belongs to three congruent spheres: starting from the smallest, the sphere of the nation, then moving on first to the sphere of the creed, then to the sphere of the human race.[42]

The dawn of the twentieth century saw Shaykh 'Abd al-Rahman al-Kawakibi hailing freedom: 'Let us agree on this motto: long live the nation; long live the homeland; and long may we all live in freedom and dignity.'[43] His first precept for lifting authoritarianism was: 'The nation that does not feel the pain of authoritarian rule does not deserve freedom.'[44]

After al-Kawakibi's call for action came the calls of the first group of martyrs executed by Jamal Pasha, midway through the First World War, in the public squares of Beirut, Damascus and Jerusalem. Numerous historians referred to the concept of freedom as defined in 1911 by al-'Uraisi, who analyzed it thoroughly in an original landmark essay. He envisaged 13 'stages' toward freedom: freedom to settle and work; freedom to unrestricted movement; freedom of speech; freedom to write; freedom to publish; freedom of the press; freedom of assembly; freedom to perform the rites of any religion whatever; freedom to enjoy possessions; freedom to form associations; one's right to feel secure (which is the essential backbone of freedom); freedom to hold philosophical beliefs; and freedom to have political representation.[45] In 1912 al-'Uraisi also called for freedom of conscience,[46] not knowing he was destined to become a martyr in the cause of freedom at the hand of 'the butcher', Jamal Pasha.

The testimonies of these martyrs, and their speeches in the last moments of their lives, overflowed with love of freedom, which they defined as the freedom of the homeland and the human being.

Most of their words would have been lost had it not been for that great man and historian Yezbek, who, in the mid-1950s, published in his journal *Lebanese Papers* (Awraq lubnaniyya) the testimonies of eyewitnesses such as officials, prison guards or comrades spared the death sentence. His documentary approach made his journal indispensable for those researching the history of Lebanon and its martyrs. One eyewitness quoted 'Abd al-Karim al-Khalil, as he approached the gallows, addressing his hangman, Rida Pasha:

> The laws of the civilized world allow a convict to speak his mind before he is executed. Does your law allow me a final word before you place the rope around my neck?

Rida Pasha was perplexed for some moments, his head bowed in reflection. Then, ashamed and embarrassed, he raised his head and said to al-Khalil: 'Very well. Speak!' The bold martyr leaped onto the scaffold and declaimed as follows:

> Sons of my nation and my homeland! The Turks wish to strangle the voice of freedom within our breasts! They wish to keep us from speaking, but we will not remain silent . . . We will proclaim to one and all: we are a nation that seeks independence . . . A nation struggling to be rid of the Turkish yoke . . .
>
> O you sky of my homeland! Greet every Arab for us martyrs . . . Tell our people of our tragedy and our words . . . Tell them we lived for independence, and here we are now, dying in the name of independence!

His words were interrupted as the gallows stool slipped from beneath his feet. He convulsed a little, then died for his nation and for history.[47]

The word 'freedom' also exercised its magic in the leaflets of the Great Arab Revolt. The leaflets dropped by British pilots over the Ottoman forces in Palestine at the end of 1917 contained a letter 'to all Arabs and other officers and men of the Ottoman army', signed and sealed by ''al-Husain ibn 'Ali, Sharif of Mecca and King of the Arab Countries'. Among other things it said: 'We believe the plain truth has not yet reached you, and so we are sending you this leaflet, sealed by us, to make it clear to you that we are fighting for two noble causes: to protect Islam and to achieve freedom for all Arabs.'[48]

The above leaflet was reprinted in a communiqué by the Arab Independence Party in Palestine on 12 September 1932, the fifteenth anniversary of the British invasion, with the aim of raising awareness and reviving the spirit of freedom.[49] Most of this party's founders had also been active in the Revolt. The party president, 'Awni 'Abd al-Hadi, for example, had been a secretary to King Faisal; Subhi al-Khadra had been a military leader in the Revolt; and 'Izzat Darwaza, 'Ajaj Nuwayhid and Akram Zu'aytir had been three of the Revolt's historians.

'Freedom' was hailed not only by martyrs and freedom fighters, but also by kings. Al-Tuwayjiri followed the speeches of King Abdul-Aziz in Riyadh. The King said, on 30 April 1930:

> They talk of 'freedom', and some claim the Europeans devised the notion. The truth is that the Holy Quran provides for utter freedom, guaranteeing everyone's rights. It provides for brotherhood and total equality, which no nation has ever dreamed of. It brings people together; great and small, strong and weak, rich and poor, and makes them all equal.[50]

Al-Tuwayjiri wrote as follows in connection with King Abdul-Aziz and freedom of speech:

> He receives people of knowledge weekly to hear from them every last detail, large and small. They never hesitate to offer their counsel, which the King welcomes and encourages. He has said publicly: 'If you do not say it and we do not accept it, then – as Caliph 'Umar said – right is lost for ever and evil takes its place. Give me all the advice you have!'[51]

Al-Hasani followed King Faisal's words in Baghdad. He reports how Faisal kept diaries at various times before his death in 1933. 'Evil hands took hold of them immediately after his departure, on the night of 8 September 1933 . . . His Majesty King 'Ali had kindly given me one of the salvaged notebooks dealing with the formation of the Iraqi state and its administration..'[52] On 12 December 1932, Faisal wrote the following concerning freedom of speech: 'To ignore an opinion totally, no matter how insignificant it may be, is an unforgivable sin.'[53]

One of the most prominent historians to deal with the topic of freedom, at all stages of his life, has been Constantine Zurayq. Analyzing Zurayq's focus on freedom, Anis Sayigh wrote: 'Freedom is the essence of history, as a philosophy and series of events. If one were to reduce the essence of the history of people and communities down to one word, that word, according to Zurayq, would be "freedom".[54]

Zurayq first wrote on freedom in his book *Nationalist Awareness* (Al-Wa'i al-qawmi) of 1939. In it he dealt with interpersonal struggle, enumerating a number of characteristics. The first is discipline, premised on disciplined thinking, followed by disciplined work whereby 'discipline' is related to 'freedom'. He added:

> I do not mean by that the external freedom provided from above, but that which grows from within; not solely the freedom that gives a person the space to contemplate and work toward the breaking of his socio-political chains, but that which evokes in him the content of his philosophy and action by striking off his intellectual and spiritual chains; not the freedom that enables people to satisfy their urges, but that which teaches them what their urges are. For inner chains are every bit as powerful and dangerous as outward ones, and no freedom is complete unless they have been broken.[55]

Having defined these 'inner chains' as ignorance, bias, materialism and egotism, and having conceded the importance of 'the individualistic tendency, which has contributed greatly to progress in civilization', he specified his priority in working to reach the level of advanced peoples. In his view, this cannot be achieved unless the individualistic tendency can be purified from envy, greed and vanity; 'this is a painstaking process of purification, and only those who understand its complexity can withstand it ...' Further: 'If a person wishes to achieve his goal and create an entity for himself, he must destroy these chains through unrelenting inner struggle and through acquisition of the second characteristic, that of "freedom".' By the latter he means, essentially, freedom from egoism.[56]

The third characteristic Zurayq enumerates is 'a sense of responsibility' in thought, speech and action:

> But what I want to stress in myself, and to find in the souls of all Arabs, is that these characteristics, as is the case with independence, cannot be accorded; they must be acquired. No external source will grant them. Only inner struggle will achieve them. This inner struggle is intimately linked to our national struggle in the cause of freedom, independence and unity; it is the proper basis upon which to build a national struggle and the strongest factor for its success ... and so no one need be concerned over our smaller struggle for freedom and independence, for we will have won the greater struggle, that of the soul.[57]

In 1964, in his book *The Battle of Culture* (Ma'rakat al-hadara), he wrote as follows on freedom of thought:

> The intellect acts and produces in proportion to the freedom granted to it. Its development, represented by its level of applied and theoretical knowledge, is conditioned by the development of intellectual freedom at large. Moreover, it would not be erroneous to see these two types of struggle as one. By the same token, creative, artistic work does not truly thrive unless it is taking place in an atmosphere of intellectual freedom . . . A culture's level of intellectual freedom is a criterion of its civilization . . .[58]

In his book *The Meaning of Catastrophe Revisited* (1967), Zurayq returned to the importance, even in times of war, of political and intellectual freedom, 'without which the people cannot actively participate, in war or in building society'. He also voices fear of the gulf between people and rulers, and of the natural contradiction between husbanding resources and demanding sacrifices. This leads to 'restricting freedom and democracy and broadening the government's authority', and to a fundamental need for freedom of thought and for the highlighting of human dignity, which he described as 'the paramount value that must be defended above all else'. He goes on to concede the difficulty of reconciling the two sides, but says, finally, that if a choice has to be made, then freedom must take priority:

> For, despite our call for swift progress, we still place the necessity for freedom and participation ahead of it, if for no other reason than to preserve the progress itself. There is no alternative to freedom; and if it slows down progress, then one must remember that a people's work is measured not by years but by generations . . .[59]

Nicola Ziyada wrote on his concept of freedom in scattered publications, focusing more on others' concepts of it; his writings are replete with the spirit of freedom. His views were adopted by the Lebanese philosopher and politician Kamal Jumblat in his keynote address to the African and Asian Writers' Conference of 1967 in Beirut:

> The issue of freedom, which we are meeting to discuss, and whose repercussions on the literature of Asia and Africa we are assessing, is an age-old question for man. It attracts him. He possesses it. He then proceeds to exhaust, restrict or abuse it, refuse to give it its due, apply it without insight and without the framework of a physical system, emotional sanctity, or social responsibility; and so it recoils and takes its revenge on him, whereupon he re-emerges to knock at its door.[60]

In answer to the question on how this mutual attraction affects man and freedom, Jumblat says:

> Man reverts to his possessiveness and abuse, and freedom returns to wreak vengeance on him in the name of permanent human values, and so forth . . . as if all history were a dialectic contradiction coloured by this conflict between man's reality and freedom . . .[61]

The freedom of academics fared no better than that of poets and men of letters. 'Ali Mahafza spoke of the main problem facing research in the Arab world:

> Foremost among these stumbling blocks is the violation of citizens' rights and freedom and the imposing of restrictions on freedom of opinion and research. Such restrictions are increased when it comes to sensitive sociological, economic or political topics, where study and research are prohibited by the government. These restrictions have struck such deep roots that researchers have taken to practicing self-censorship – realizing that, should they venture beyond these well-known limits, they will certainly clash with the authorities . . . Providing academic freedom is undoubtedly an essential condition for this sought-after reform.[62]

IV. The rights of women

All our selected historians have spoken of the rights and suffering of women. A good example is M.K. 'Ali, head of the Arab Academy in Damascus, who throughout his life emphasized the re-emergence of civilization. He commented on the worsening condition of women, under successive governments, since the fall of al-Andalus (Muslim Spain):

> With a view to holding on to wealth, families took to pairing close relatives in marriage, which resulted in weakened progeny and a growth of idiocy . . . People may even have prevented their daughters from marrying altogether, so as to keep the inheritance in the male line. Many families deprived females of their rightful inheritance, which locked a large part of society out from enterprise. Men have so oppressed women that they have not even bothered with their schooling or their true happiness, as though woman had been born (as some ancient Europeans believed) without a soul.[63]

The first manifestly equitable treatment of women was a legal one harking back to the first modern Arab constitution in the Mashriq (referred to in section two above). At the end of March 1920, the Arab government in Damascus appealed to the General Syrian Convention, which was acting as a constituent assembly, to expedite discussion of the proposed Constitution. The Convention proceeded to debate the draft articles one by one, and approved many of them. There was, however, insufficient opportunity to discuss the remaining articles due to the French demand that the Arab government accede to its mandate and halt discussion of the draft. Even in these sensitive circumstances, however, a hot debate continued, resulting in the provision of equality before the law for women. Darwaza, the Convention secretary, wrote in his dairy that the progressives wished to spell out the political, civil, electoral and parliamentary equality of women and men. The debate between progressives and traditionalists became very heated indeed. Darwaza saw no religious or social reason against the wording, but fear of angering extremist traditionalists and the general public, combined with concern at being forced to approve the Constitution on account of the French demand, obliged them to maintain the text of the version proposed earlier, which stated: 'all Syrians are equal in rights and duties.' This, Darwaza observed, indicated equality for all Syrians irrespective of their religion, ethnicity or gender.[64]

The Constitution did not long survive, but Darwaza's historical legal testimony remains the first of its kind. Yezbek also provided a personal testimony, based on his struggle to found and reinforce the Lebanese labour movement. He relates, in connection with the first celebration of Labour Day in Beirut on 1 May 1925, how Khayr Allah Khayr Allah, Middle Eastern editor of the Parisian daily *Le Temps*,[65] had been the first to stress a woman's right to work.

After the celebration, Yezbek, along with Fu'ad al-Shimali, devoted himself to laying down the principles of the Lebanese People's Party, which included the liberation of women and working toward reclaiming their violated rights.[66]

The Arab Lebanese historian Muhammad Jamil Bayhum went beyond simply writing about women. He also became their steadfast ally, to the point of being nicknamed the 'Qasim Amin'[67] of the Arab Mashriq. In 1919 he said: 'The Eastern Question[68] occupied the minds of the political world before World War One, but no sooner had this evil war come to an end last year than it was replaced by the "Woman Question", to the point that some have taken to calling this the era of woman.'[69] But this 'era of woman' was, for him, neither revolutionary nor liberated in the literal sense, but one of reform in certain instances and of pseudo-progress in others; for, while he recognized woman's right to equality with men, he nevertheless had reservations about certain other rights, such as her right to work. He did in fact believe this to be an absolute right, and a matter of historical inevitability, but he preferred – from a realistic viewpoint – that women should remain at home for the sake of their husband and children. Bayhum published four books on women, and a fifth was brought out posthumously, but he never established a supportive trend.[70] Hasan Hallaq, the Beiruti historian *par excellence*, admits that Bayhum had a dual view of woman: he 'respected and appreciated her as long as she demonstrated high moral values, but viewed her askance when she attempted to make use of her freedom and look critically on others'.[71]

Ziyada realistically recorded the condition of women in Palestine in 1939, the year he graduated from London with a degree in history and returned to his homeland. He found that most people looked askance at the notion of women attending universities, and that the issue of women had not been seriously raised in Palestine, even though it had resurfaced in Egypt and Beirut, especially when Nazira Zain al-Din published her books *The Veiling and Unveiling* (Al-Sufur wa 'l-hijab) (1928) and *The Young Woman and the Old Men* (Al-Fatat wa 'l-shuyukh) (1929). The women of Jerusalem made great strides during the Second World War, only to be blocked once more by the catastrophic events of 1948.[72]

Shaykh 'Abdallah al-'Alayli was a historian who wrote about women from a modern, innovative and humanitarian perspective. In 1941 he wrote:

> The antiquated individualistic notion – even though we live now in the age of community – still informs law, behaviour and ethics. The keeping of women at home, along with favouring the primacy of fathers within the family and treating the adulteress more harshly than the adulterer . . . is inspired by this notion of enslavement.[73]

In his famous book *Where is the Wrong in That?*, which was banned by most Arab censors, al-'Alayli had this to say about the marriage of a Muslim woman to a man 'from the People of the Book':

> The religious and national arenas reel from time to time with arguments over cross-religious marriage, which then boil over into charges of deviation, unbelief and apostasy. But, stop, you people! The matter is far simpler than you think. Firstly, it is limited, and therefore one of *ijtihad* [legal opinion] . . . I make no claim to outdo noted theologians . . . I merely wish to arrive at the truth of the matter at hand, by referring to the basic document of judgement, upon which all agree; especially since the matter, in some of its aspects, relates to that which is vital and communal. This matter, though it be theological, translates into a national impasse; in other words, it is a hindrance to broad national brotherhood . . .[74]

V. Freedom of religious creed

The twentieth century inherited from the age of religious reform a sense of toleration, affinity and equality among religions. The best-known reformer,
Imam al-Afghani, did not discriminate between the people of the Mashriq on
account of their religious affiliations. He took to addressing them as 'Muslims'
not out of fanaticism but because Muslims formed the majority in fact, and
everyone understood his speeches in this sense. Equality among believers in
heavenly religions was one of the bases on which he built his thought and his
world view.[75] Other scholars and reformers took the same view, like al-
Kawakibi who addressed all his Arab brothers, in their various groups and religions, as 'speakers of Arabic]':

> O people – you, I mean, who speak the Arabic language and are non-Muslim – I
> call upon you to put aside insult and hatred, and that which our forefathers
> committed . . . Let us manage our daily lives on earth, and let religions alone judge
> our other lives . . .[76]

Yezbek researched every event or announcement calling for freedom of religious belief and the unity of Muslims and Christians. Here is a historian telling
us how a group of free Lebanese and Syrian men founded in Europe, in 1881,
'The Society for the Protection of Arab Religious Rights', and issued a communiqué appealing to Arabs, and especially to their countrymen, 'to unite as
Muslims and Christians, and remember the good qualities of their forefathers,
their dignity and their honour; to awake and save their lands from the foreign
yoke, before they are sold out to western countries . . .'[77]

In his history of the first group of Arab politicians seeking independence, al-
Duri notes how 'Abd al-Hamid al-Zahrawi of Syria, (the president of the first
Arab Conference in Paris in 1913, who was executed by Jamal Pasha along with
his comrades in Damascus) stressed citizenship in combination with toleration, explaining that Islam supported freedom of religious beliefs. He appeals
to Muslims, accordingly, to hold fast to the worthy rule that 'non-Muslims
enjoy the same rights as Muslims and have the same duties as they do'.[78]

The worst kind of religious oppression experienced by Muslims of the
Maghreb took the form of the 'Berber Decree', issued by the French governor
Lucien Saint on 16 May 1930, with the full co-operation of General Noguès.
This decree sought forcibly to christianize the Berbers of the Maghreb, the first
experiment of its kind in the French colonies, and one destined to be repeated
in further of their colonies. This led to waves of Arab and Muslim protest, raging over several years. Arsalan was one of the most prominent thinkers to fight

against this tyrannical decree, not only from a religious viewpoint, but from a humanitarian and national one too. He viewed the freedom of the human being as paramount. Christianization was not, in his view, the point at issue; the true issue was the process of forcing someone to adopt another faith. In an essay in the spring of 1933, he wrote:

> All the misrepresentations attempted by Lucien Saint, the French governor of the Maghreb, and his aides to re-interpret this decree through legal reforms and judicial retouches are worthless and doomed to failure, one and all . . . A few Berber chieftains travelled to Rabat to protest against the repeal of Muslim Shariah courts and were jailed. A few other chieftains had sent their sons to study Arabic in Fez. They were told that, unless they withdrew these boys, their salaries from the French governorate would be stopped . . . Even if we suppose the Berbers will be christianized by force, a faint possibility indeed, still the Berbers are not going to turn suddenly French as some Frenchmen believe. The Berbers will remain patriots insistent on the independence of their country. We wrote, in our magazine *La Nation Arabe*, a number of chapters on this issue and brought to the attention of the French the case of the Ethiopians, who are zealously Christian and fanatically anti-French. We gave as a further example the people of central Africa, some of whom have been christianized for a hundred or even two hundred years, others for a few years only, but who all hate the Europeans. So, even if we were to suppose some Berbers did in fact become Christian, they will not become malleable in the hands of the French. The christianized Chinese are patriots too, and they hate Europeans, just as the Buddhists and Muslims of China do. The christianized people of India also seek independence for their country, just like all other Indians. Nor will the French profit by forcing the Berbers to partake of French culture. Thousands of young Muslims in Algeria speak no Arabic, speak French as fluently as the French themselves do, and yet they are more zealously patriotic and more enthusiastically pro-independence than Muslims who speak no French.[79]

Arsalan had taken the same humanitarian stance, during the First World War, against the Ottoman Turks, when they attempted to force the Christian Armenians to adopt Islam:

> Defence of the freedom of religious belief, language and culture is a sacred principle that should be observed by all people. I would go so far, indeed, as to say that if a Muslim government anywhere in the world were to seek to force a group of Christians to adopt Islam, then Muslims everywhere should rise up as one to prevent such an attempt. This is in accordance with Almighty God's words: 'Let there be no compulsion in religion: Truth stands out clear from Error.' (2, *Al-Baqara*, 256.) I was a representative of Syria in the Ottoman National Assembly

during World War One, and the arrival of the Armenians in Syria coincided with a visit of mine to Damascus. A whisper reached me to the effect that certain Ottoman officials were placing pressure on some of these immigrants to adopt Islam. The moment I heard of this, I went to the Ottoman Governor, Khalus Bek, and relayed the news to him, saying that such an action was not only against Islamic law but also ran counter to international law and the interest of the Ottoman state. He immediately telegraphed to all provinces that any such attempt should be severely punished.[80]

Arsalan went beyond merely respecting freedom of religious belief and choice; he also admired Sanusi thought, which called for respecting the unbeliever exactly like the believer. He extolled the founders and activists of this movement for their values, their understanding and their struggle, quoting Ahmad al-Sharif al-Sunusi, who was in turn quoting his uncle al-Sayyid al-Mehdi: 'Do not denigrate anyone: neither Muslim, nor Christian, nor Jew, nor an unbeliever, for in his heart he may be a better person than you in the eyes of God. You cannot know how this person will finally end.'[81]

Al-Hasani, alone among the historians under study, undertook research on religious minorities, about whom little is known. For most, such people are linked to unbelief and to abandonment of the essence of religion. Al-Hasani's intention was not merely to uncover the curious aspects of those minorities, nor was he motivated only by a love of knowledge and history. His approach was suffused by his respect for the human being irrespective of religious creed, and for the conscience that stands alongside the human being in his belief. From the late 1920s on he researched these religions exhaustively, also visiting the various religionists in their homes and living among them, seeking to understand their thoughts and motives and recording all this in a scientific, objective and humanitarian way. He wrote of the Baha'is,[82] the Yazidis[83] and the Sabaeans,[84] constantly adding and revising information as he published successive books about them over half a century. He also compared his conclusions with those of orientalists, for very few Arab historians concerned themselves with these minorities. It was all this, perhaps, that persuaded two of the most prominent Islamic religious scholars, Imam al-Sayyid Muhammad al-Husain Kashif al-Ghata' and Ahmed Zaki Pasha,[85] to write introductions for his books. Al-Hasani set out his opinion on the nature of religious multiplicity in the introduction to his book on the Yazidis:

> The natural surroundings and social ambience no doubt have their influence on people's mentality, thinking and emotions. People feel, through their natural surroundings, certain things about the universe and about life, and the differing notions, opinions and beliefs spring simply from the differences of culture and

national heritage. This is why various nations differ in their understanding of the universe, in defining its origin and destiny in a manner congruent with the environment in which each of them lives, and in the extent to which they interpret it. People have an image of the Creator, and of their relation to Him, according to their notion of universal phenomena and their interpretation of these. Multiplicity of religion results, then, from the multiplicity of people's notions, tastes and the environments in which they live.[86]

VI. The right to work

No detailed research is necessary to demonstrate historians' interest in the right to work. We shall limit ourselves here to a single quotation from a religious scholar and historian, Shaykh 'Abdallah al-'Alayli, who wrote, in 1941, on the 'Right to Make a Living':

Economic progress led to the concentration of capital; that is to say, it allowed one group of people to seize the financial initiative, while the other group toiled at their beck and call. Disequilibrium was the order of the day, and equality, or fairness in rights and responsibilities, was annulled. Slavery disappeared as a form, but was renewed in content. Economic slavery became more horrendous than personal slavery. The worker who laboured of his own free will became a slave to the financier who controlled the labour projects. The labourer even became vulnerable to starvation, in contrast to the old system of slavery, whereby the master guaranteed his survival, so making him less vulnerable.

Even though democracy became politically rooted in society, an aristocracy of wealth sprang up alongside. Economic power was concentrated in the hands of the few . . . and so one group acquired numerous rights and very few duties, while another was left with the opposite. The economic system needs to undergo radical change with a view to restoring the higher ideal, namely the balance in rights and duties, to its previous state. In order to rebuild society on a basis of fairness, economic democracy must be allowed to take root in society, just as political democracy had taken a degree of root previously. This is the main fault of modern society; it is primarily a defect in its economic system . . . [87]

VII. Violations of human rights

Much contemporary Arab historical writing focuses on the core content of the reports made by modern human rights committees, on such matters as the various violations in this country or that. This is especially the case with those

historians who have dealt with this nation's history during the age of colonialism. Here the writings of Arsalan, Darwaza, al-'Arif, and al-Dabbagh may suffice. This is not to say their writings are like carbon copies of modern reports;
on the contrary, they surpass such reports because they contain more than
mere data and statistics. These historians wrote out of their depth of conscience and from a profound sense of responsibility. Each saw himself as the
one entrusted with his nation's history. If he did not write it, then it would be
lost forever!

It is almost impossible to separate Arsalan's life from his struggle and his
writings. From Geneva he wrote to his spiritual teacher and close friend Rashid
Rida, in Cairo, on the atrocities of the Italians in Libya:

> As for the eighty thousand Arabs whose lands in al-Jabal al-Akhdar they pil-
> laged, and whom they evacuated to the wastelands of Sirte, all their animals have
> perished from scarcity of water and pasture. The Italians have calculated two
> francs per Libyan family per day, while Libyans are dying of hunger and from
> exposure in the cold weather. The Italians' objective is to annihilate them so that
> they can never return to al-Jabal al-Akhdar, where the aim is to house hundreds
> of thousands of Italians.
>
> The Italians have also conscripted all the men aged fifteen to forty, and they
> have taken all male children aged three to fourteen to Italy, despite their parents'
> protests, under the pretext of educating them . . . Why to Italy? Forcible seizure
> of these boys raised a scream to the heavens and made for a scene fit to split
> rocks, but no one budged . . . We spoke to the Human Rights Commission in
> Geneva about these atrocities two months ago . . . and they promised to hold a
> meeting . . . But then they delayed it, and my suspicion is the Italians heard of it
> and sought to prevent it – there are many of them in Geneva.[88]

In February 1940 Arsalan wrote an essay entitled 'The allies are Distorting the
Facts', defending the rights of the individual and the community, especially
against beating, torture, and murder during torture. He enumerated France's
atrocities in the vast Maghreb, ranging from appropriation of water, to suppressing demonstrations, to firing on and killing peaceable demonstrators, to
annulling the League of National Action and arresting seven thousand accused
of 'unrest'. About the end of these latter, he wrote:

> They tried two thousand five hundred of them, sentencing some to two years'
> imprisonment with hard labour, others to one year's imprisonment. They drove
> the cream of the literati of Fez and the pupils of the Qurawiyun Mosque into the
> desert, and there, under the pretext of hard labour, they tortured them horribly,
> beating them severely each day, and insulting and cursing them too, for a whole

month until Shaykh Muhammad al-Qurri died of his wounds from beating and others fell unconscious. All this was committed by French officers under the command of General Noguès himself, about whom a detailed report has reached us. This report we published in translation in our magazine *La Nation Arabe*. We also published it in the newspaper *Al-Shura* in Egypt . . .

The leaders of the League for National Action were exiled to distant lands. Their anger was greatest against Muhammad 'Allal al-Fasi, whose ability, maturity and efficiency are known to them, and in whom they see a danger to French colonialism. They took him without informing even his family, who only found out later, first by plane to Saint Louis, Senegal, then to some other place on the Atlantic, and finally by ship to Gabon on the Equator. They sent him there deliberately, so as to destroy him without having to shoot him or beat him to death – for Gabon is one of the hottest countries in the world. Even some of the French themselves tried to persuade the authorities to transfer him to some more liveable place, but they refused, resolved to torture him till he died, what with his frail body and his physical inability to tolerate extreme conditions.

All the other leaders of the League for National Action they exiled to the desert: leaders such as Muhammad ibn al-Hasan al-Wazini, 'Umar ibn 'Abd al-'Aziz 'Abd al-Jalil, Muhammad al-Yazidi, Ahmad Makwar and others, all highly educated scholars . . .[89]

In the same article he wrote as follows on French colonialism in Algeria:

There is no stratum lower than that of Muslims in Algeria, except that of animals, even though Muslim Algerians are the noblest people on earth. In fact a sign has been noted at the entrance to some of the French clubs there that reads: 'Entry Forbidden to Dog Arabs'. Moreover, one European murdered another in Algeria, but the court acquitted him on his plea that he thought him Arab when he killed him. It is as though killing an Arab were permissible according to their law, calling for no punishment . . .[90]

Darwaza, a son of Nablus, also wrote on the oppression of British and French colonialism in the Mashriq, both of which he had experienced at first hand. His writings on the Palestinian cause in all its phases are essential reading. On British atrocities during the second phase of the Great Revolution in Palestine (1937–9), he wrote:

Emergency Law has been amended so that possession of a few bullets or a firearm, no matter what the type or how usable, is grounds for execution, or for imprisonment lengthy or for life. Every building in a city or village, every orchard or field, has become subject to expropriation, blowing up or other destruction, on the mere grounds that some bullet was fired from its direction or some incident occurred in its vicinity. The number of those hanged has reached forty-six, while more than two thousand have been sentenced either to life imprisonment or to lengthy prison sentences, among them elderly people and adolescent boys, to say nothing of the number of homes and shops – now five thousand – that have been blown up, torn down and split open . . . A number of villages have lost more than half their houses. Investigations and searches have been accompanied by extreme cruelty, such as destroying, burning, striking, kicking, whipping, torturing, looting, destroying of personal effects and supplies, raping and violation of holy sites . . .

The number of those arrested for short or long periods has reached fifty thousand . . . arrests have been made, by administrative order and under the crime prevention law, for certain renewable periods and without a specific charge . . . arrests in cities and villages were individual at first, but then they were made by the dozen . . . It was not unusual for all the males in a village, perhaps more than a thousand in number, to be driven to the British governor's office . . . Among the various kinds of torture perpetrated on people like these was the practice of tying them with rope, then having tanks or patrol cars drive in front of them and behind them, forcing them to run in between to keep themselves from being run over![91]

We ought to consider the suffering of the Palestinian people at length here, since it was the most enduring through the course of the twentieth century, not just among Arab peoples but among the peoples of the world at large. The century has ended now, and Palestinians have been under threat in their homeland since the end of the First World War, whether through mandate or occupation. A great many Palestinian and Arab historians have written on this topic, both before and since the *nakba* (catastrophe) of 1948, in Palestine and throughout the Diaspora, but the most prominent among them all is undoubtedly 'Arif al-'Arif. In his famous five-part work, *The Nakba*, and his *'Arif al-'Arif Papers*, he has performed the work of a historian scrutinizing human rights. Not content with recounting generalities, or establishing the numbers or even names of the arrested or exiled, he published all he was able to collect on the tragedy of each individual, whether executed, martyred, jailed, tortured or exiled, or whose home had been destroyed, or who had been deprived of any natural human right. Al-'Arif worked alone between the ages of 75 and 80, without support from any government or from any research or humanitarian institution. Explaining his methodology in documenting the lists of Palestinian homes torn down by the Israelis, he addressed himself to the reader as follows:

I wish . . . to emphasize to you that the figures you find in this document are not the result of cautious guesswork, but are true figures supported by names, places and dates, and, in many cases, by telling photographs . . . Never have I contented

myself with hearsay . . . On the contrary, I visited the place in question personally in many cases, saw the torn-down home with my own eyes and questioned
its owner. If he had been arrested, I asked his neighbour . . . and if unable to visit
the scene of the crime myself because of the long distance or my frail health, I
relied, having no other option, on available news from journals, radio stations
and news agencies that are above suspicion . . .[92]

The number of those arrested during the first five years following the June
1967 war reached 10,000 people, of whom 13 young men died of torture while
in prison. 3,373 people were killed by Israeli soldiers, and al-'Arif documented
the names, dates and places of martyrdom for 1,088 of them. 1,448 people
were exiled from their homes in the West Bank and Gaza Strip, and 16,212
Arab homes were torn down.[93]

Take the following example appearing in his 'Register of Immortality' for
the 1967 war as Case No. 214:

Husain Muhammad Salim, an old paralyzed man from the village of Yalo was
martyred on 11 June 1967. He had been pushed against his door sill, whereupon
he fell to the ground. They then tore down the house and door sill on top of him
and he died.[94]

In the same 'Register', the following appears in Case No. 853a:

Muhammad 'Abdallah Jaffal. From the village of Abu Dis. Martyred in Jericho
on 11 June 1967. Killed by the Israelis along with his wife and four children. For
no reason except that when they heard of the ceasefire, they wished to return to
their village which they had left during the fighting.[95]

The historian Mustafa al-Dabbagh did not write separately on the 'last' oppression visited on his Palestinian people; he was not 'another 'Arif'. His starting
point was disproving of the main Zionist claims against his people and its history past and present, foremost among them: the Zionist denial of Arab-
Islamic civilization in Palestine; their denial of the very existence of the
Palestinian people; and the claim that Palestine was a wasteland without a people. How is one to defend the rights of the Palestinian as an individual when the
rights of the people as a whole, along with country and land, have been sum-
marily made off with? Al-Dabbagh spent his life writing his ten-volume encyclopaedia entitled *Palestine, Our Country*, following this with his six-part
Filastiniyyat. These two works complement one another through geography,
history, civilization and various human sciences, arriving, finally, at the reality
of a city or village and the plight of its inhabitants. Let us take as an example one

particular village called Farradiya, in Safad province in the north of Palestine. Farradiya was only one of 292 villages completely destroyed by Israel, a figure that represents seventy per cent of the 418 villages it occupied during the *Nakba* war.[96]

Al-Dabbagh wrote on the history of this village (which the Romans called 'Barud'): on its site, agriculture, inhabitants, schools and ruins. The reader feels as though he has become intimately acquainted with the village and its people – only to be shocked at the end upon reading of its fate: 'The enemy destroyed Farradiya and drove its people into the Diaspora, after they had lost a hundred of their young men in defence of their country against the enemy.'[97]

Al-Dabbagh's works are considered the standard reference for researchers and for other Palestinian encyclopaedias, as, for instance, in the reference volume on the Palestinian villages destroyed by Israel during the *Nakba* war, and the names of their martyrs. This extensive volume was prepared by a huge team of researchers, headed by Walid al-Khalidi, Secretary-General of the pioneering Institute of Palestine Studies, and the man entrusted with documenting Palestine's history and cause. Al-Khalidi goes into considerable detail on the two Israeli settlements built on the site of Farradiya, and on the forcible exile of its inhabitants. Under 'The Village Today', he writes:

> The site is abandoned and covered with thorny vegetation, trees and piles of torn-down homes. Cacti abound in the land surrounding it, which is used mainly as pasture. Parts of it have been planted with trees and made into parks for the Israelis.[98]

These historians' links with the violations of human rights, possessions and homeland were not limited to writing on the subject; a number of them were subjected to arrest, exile or attempted assassination, among them 'Arif al-'Arif, who was accused, along with Mufti al-Hajj Amin al-Husaini, of organizing the unrest of April 1920 in Jerusalem in protest against the Balfour Declaration. Each was sentenced to ten years with hard labour.[99] 'Izzat Darwaza was twice arrested: once during the British mandate of Palestine, and again during the French mandate of Syria during Second World War, and the French further exiled him to Turkey until just before the end of this war. Shakib Arsalan chose to remain in exile; he was, he said, staying in Geneva rather than returning to his homeland for fear the French would humiliate him and because he preferred a life of freedom. 'He says whatever he wishes in defence of his nation and homeland. His speech and his pen remain free, only his body bears exile and age. This is better than having his body live in plenty while his mind and pen are constrained by the prison the mandate represents.'[100] Anis Sayigh, director of the pioneering Centre for Palestine Studies, funded by the Palestine Liberation Organization, was one of the victims of Israeli terrorism; in 1972 Israel attempted to assassinate him by means of a booby-trapped letter, leading to amputation of some of his fingers and a weakness in his eyes. However, he persevered in his intellectual struggle, editing, among other things, the *Palestinian Encyclopedia* in the 1980s.[101] Mustafa al-Dabbagh was himself a victim of forcible uprooting. He recounted, in his introduction to *Palestine Our Country*, how he had been forced to leave Jaffa in 1948 after the Zionists managed to occupy the al-Manshiyya quarter, cutting off the electricity and starving its people. He went out to sea in a small boat, carrying nothing but the manuscript of his book on Palestine and its geography, in 6,000 pages. But the sea was surging and rough, and the captain ordered all passengers to rid themselves of excess baggage for fear of capsizing. 'I held on to the bag containing my manuscript,' al-Dabbagh said, 'but a pair of strong sailor's hands, aided by a wave that leaped onto deck, whisked my bag away and hurled it into the water. And so the book was lost, along with the effort of all the long years I spent collecting and organizing its material.'[102]

Conclusion

Contemporary Arab historians have clearly treated two essential aspects of human rights: the theoretical-philosophical aspect concerning the principles of these rights, their essence, nature and objectives; and the practical aspect, dealing with the subject in the light of these natural principles.

The theoretical-philosophical aspect

If we take a comprehensive overview of the oeuvres of Arab historians and thinkers at the turn of the twentieth century, we find their awareness of human rights to have sources both Eastern and Western, i.e. both traditional and acquired. In the minds of some the acquired Western principles were combined with tradition, while others adhered more closely to the source itself. Those known as the 'Paris Group', for example, along with others who lived and studied in Europe in general and France in particular, were sincere in their expression of the principles of the mother French Revolution, and of human rights according to the Western concept. Their vocabulary was quite clearly translated from Western sources. Najib al-'Azuri and 'Abd al-Ghani al-'Uraisi were representatives of this trend, while Yezbek, Ziyada and al-Duri are among the most prominent historians to have adopted their view of human rights and stressed its importance.

As for those who took as their starting point the eastern tradition and history, namely Islamic principles and civilization in all their dimensions, most were deeply cognizant of Western thought as well, and they read several languages. They had a comprehensive view of the human being, one not restricted to East or West, even though their writings contained Quranic verses or historical examples, and even though they addressed themselves to the people of the East or to the Arab nation. Shaykh al-Afghani, the foremost among these reformers, is the best representative of the trend, while Shakib Arsalan and others like him are its spiritual inheritors.

If we go beyond source of knowledge and awareness to deal with the concept of human rights as viewed by the historians themselves, we shall find that many of them expounded certain human rights, or a single right, in a distinctive way, or treated such rights from a novel angle. However, two among the group of historians chosen for this essay stand out, each in his own way, for their attempts at a comprehensive presentation of the issue and dignity of man. These are Zurayq and al-'Alayli, both from the cultural elite that synthesized the civilizations of East and West in thought and spirit.

Zurayq dealt in most of his writings with the issue of man's freedom and dignity, along with the issue of the people's liberation, of their freedom and dignity. His analysis of peoples' and citizens' rights usually takes as its starting point the reality of the Arab nation. This makes his writings a prime example for nations similarly under foreign hegemony. His assured belief in the nation's liberation before all else was second to none. At times, indeed, it seemed as though he made no distinction between the two issues of individual and nation; for the individual's objectives are achieved through the nation's liberation and through the acquisition of all its rights. Nevertheless, when he is obliged to separate the two issues, he accords unequivocal priority to the interest of the nation, secondary consideration to that of the individual; the interest of the individual must be sacrificed whenever it conflicts with that of the nation. With respect to the individual's rights and duties, the latter, according to him, come first. As for human rights, he was still mentioning them (having first mentioned citizens' rights) in his last book in early 1998.[103]

Zurayq could easily have leaped onto today's human rights bandwagon, of American origin and worldwide dimension: the bandwagon that sets human rights over and above all other considerations, that even ignores all other considerations. He could have revised his opinions and analyses, yet he did not regress, and this truly marks him out. He continued to believe in national rights ahead of individual rights, and to hold that no individual can acquire his rights as long as he is part and parcel of an oppressed people. A day may come, in the course of the twenty-first century, when a charter for human and peoples' rights is issued, inspired by peoples' struggles, for man himself and for humanity as a whole. Should this day come, it would bring honour once again to this great thinker, this pioneering scholar in nationalist philosophy and peoples' freedom.

'Abdallah al-'Alayli set forth an integrated philosophy for human rights in 1941. It appeared rather modestly as an addendum to one of his books entitled *Personal Rights* – although it is, in fact, a comprehensive charter on the subject of human rights and duties, and on the relation between the individual and society, appropriate for any time or place. As such it surpasses the Human Rights Charter issued by the United Nations only in 1948, in that it preceded it chronologically, and in that it was issued by an individual scholar and not an international institution. It also surpasses charters specific to human rights in connection with a certain continent, nation or creed, because it addresses man wherever he may be.

This is also the case with the other historians chosen for this study, such as Ziyada, al-Duri, and Sayigh, all of whom set forth explications of a certain human right, or rights. All of them mostly tower above their colleagues in the West because they were informed not by a monoculture, but by a deep awareness and comprehensive understanding of numerous civilizations, which may be summed up as those of West and East. Western scholars and thinkers, by contrast, are informed by Western civilization alone. Even where, in some cases, they read or learn about Eastern philosophy, such knowledge is rarely reflected in their oeuvre; the only exceptions are a few orientalists and a minority of great historians, such as Gustave Le Bon and Toynbee.

To illustrate this state of affairs let us compare the work of Arab historians with that of the university professors and writers who edited the encyclopaedia entitled *Great Books of the Western World*. This is a fifty-four volume collection containing writings by 74 philosophers, scientists, novelists and poets from among the West's geniuses, from Homer, Herodotus and Plato to Dostoyevsky, William James and Freud. The goal of the *Encyclopaedia Britannica* in selecting and reprinting these classics was to search in them for the main ideas and concepts of human philosophy. Yet not a single Eastern classic is included in this collection of 'great' books. Robert Hutchins, the general editor, admitted this weakness in his introduction to the encyclopaedia, stating his belief that all people, Easterners and Westerners alike, should have this chosen collection of Western works available to them, not because it was better than what had been produced by the East, but because it was of the highest importance for all to understand the West. Scholars specializing in the East and its tradition would, he expected, publish a similar encyclopaedia, one that would enable a finding of common threads in human tradition and philosophy, through an immense encyclopaedia to be titled *Great Books of the World*.[104]

Hutchins' wish has yet to be fulfilled in any grand encyclopaedic project, or in, say, a joint East–West cultural venture. First of all, however, we may say that the goal of which he dreamed has been achieved through individual efforts. Many Arab historians have read the chief classics of both East and West, synthesizing the essence of both sets of civilizations and identifying their common threads; foremost among these is al-'Alayli who set forth an integrated human rights charter emanating from a synthesis of human experiences.

Our second observation concerns the 102 human scientific and social concepts covered by the editor of *Great Books of the Western World*: the concept of existence, art, education, logic, beauty, freedom, justice, wisdom, etc. No mention is made of 'human rights', even though this collection came out in 1952, long after these ideas had been raised by the great revolutions of the late eighteenth century, and four years after the proclamation of the Human Rights Charter by the United Nations in 1948. The charter of al-'Alayli, a lone individual, pre-dated the international charter by seven years, and the encyclopaedia by more than ten years!

Natural principles of human rights: the practical aspect

Historians have dealt mostly with the practical rather than the theoretical aspect. Many, indeed, have devoted their lives to the cause of implementing the principles of human rights, and to uncovering blatant injustice wherever it occurred. Arsalan, Darwaza, al-'Arif, and Dabbagh represent this trend, and they have been quoted extensively throughout this essay. However, it may be said that the violations of human rights documented by historians hark back to the age of colonialism: an indication of how their pursuit of such violations, and their reporting on them, demonstrate an imbalance between the age of colonialism – which ate up the first half of the twentieth century – and the age of independence – which characterized the second half. We might venture to say, in fact, that historians' efforts in this area have been directed at colonial times alone and rarely been in evidence during the time of independence, except when aggression has been perpetrated against the Palestinian or other

Arab by the Israeli enemy. This case is treated with precision, courage and clarity, as was the case with colonialism.

It is strange how this coincides with amazing media advances for the benefit of the age of independence, but without any benefit for the human being. Under colonialism, the nature of the media made acquiring information a slow process, while publication of it exposed the writer to aggressive pursuit by the colonial authorities. Press, old-fashioned radio and word of mouth dominated the media for the first half of the century, whereas transistor radio, television and now even the Internet are available to the Arab historian. Yet for all this, no advances are being made in uncovering human rights violations in a fashion consistent with the ease of acquiring information. Why?

Historians themselves refer back to the increasingly flourishing nationalism of the 1950s and 60s, the time of the revolutions in Egypt, Algeria, Iraq and Yemen. The nation as a whole looked upon these revolutions with the pride and dignity it had missed under colonialism. No one disputed that the nationalist goals of unity, freedom and socialism, along with the liberation of Palestine and Iskenderun, should come first. The Arab individual would acquire all his rights as soon as his nationalist goals were achieved. Historians regarded the aggravation of political imprisonment in their recently independent countries, and the poor state of the prisons themselves, as a temporary problem. But these temporary problems turned into chronic diseases.

When both Zurayq and Ziyada told me, as I mentioned at the beginning of this essay, that Arab historians in general did not address human rights, they were doubtless referring to the failure of those times – not to be confused with our current times, when the words 'human rights' echo in US State Department reports more than they do in Sunday sermons!

Where does historians' responsibility lie?

Some historians, it need hardly be said, did not write on the practical aspect; nor need it be pointed out that fear is a human instinct, or that such a dangerous responsibility as this is a public issue, wherein historians form merely one of the groups supposed to rise to the occasion, advance the civilizational process, achieve total liberation and protect human rights. It is evident that contemporary historians contributed in more ways than one to the issue of human rights, in terms of intellectual work, analysis and documentation, when they were quite alone in the arena, combating the colonialists. In the last three decades of the twentieth century – in the time, that is, of human rights committees – this became their regular duty. If we were to compare the 1990s in Arab Palestine to the 1950s or 60s, we should find numerous active and productive committees concerned with human rights, prominent among them 'The Citizen's Rights Committee', which publishes an extensive annual report on human rights. The registered social and cultural committees number in the dozens, headed by such well known university professors as Hanan 'Ashrawi and Ibrahim Abu Lughd, whereas only al-'Arif and a few others were to be found earlier.

It will be the responsibility of twenty-first century historians to write on this current phase, but the likes of al-'Arif, Darwaza and al-Dabbagh will continue to be beacons and examples, no matter what the shortfalls in their works, or their overly individualistic style. Suffice it to say that they stood alone.

Chapter 18: Patriarchy and human rights

'Abd al-Razzaq 'Eid

Introduction

From the time Arabs began defining and identifying themselves as a distinct pan-national entity, the theme of human rights has been the weakest link in their ambitious dream and their pursuit of freedom and democracy. The Arab order has now defined itself as a self-contained system. At the domestic level, it has swallowed, indeed devoured civil society from within, and now pays no attention to the meaning or connotation of democracy, except in terms of human rights as propagated and promoted by independent international organizations and bodies not specifically connected to the foreign Realpolitik of Western countries, which bring the human rights issue into play only when they wish the patrons and guardians of the Arab order to be more disciplined and 'better mannered' vis-à-vis the 'supreme patriarchy' in the West.

Indeed, it is the relative independence of the international agencies promoting human rights that arouses fear within the Arab patriarchal system, since such agencies can lend support to dissident and outlawed Arab intellectuals. The family patriarch nevertheless tolerates the behaviour of these naughty children – they are, after all, backed up and shielded by a degree of international support. The world bodies provide some kind of refuge for dissenters, after the patriarchal rulers have turned their countries into silent prisons and voiceless graveyards; a development that came about following a period in which Arab regimes had the blessing of Interpol and obediently designed their message and their political centres to serve the interests of their arch-patriarch, at a time when the structure of patriarchal relations created a world order based largely on authoritarian hierarchy.

There are patriarchal Arab rulers who believe they have a sacred right to govern their peoples, and even offer up some of them as scapegoats to perpetuate their regime and authority. They have an innate predilection, within their collective cultural mindset, for the primitive notion of the father willing to offer his son as a sacrifice. By virtue of this mythic ritual, each one is transformed, psychologically, from an unyielding hereditary ruler into a benign, malleable creature. He becomes akin to the dog described by Chekhov in his portrayal of the spiritual bankruptcy and moral corruption of Russia under the tyrannical Tsarist patriarchy. When kicked by its owner, the dog would wag its tail, begging for more, lying head down and whining in supplication.

The pattern of a despotic patriarchal system, with all the ensuing consequences for the cultural and spiritual structure, conscious or unconscious, of relations with the Western metropolis, has emerged as a pivotal theme of the Arabic novel dealing with East–West acculturation. The prototypical Arab father of the family, tribe and political body, the ruler dwarfed by the West, is vividly portrayed by 'Abd al-Rahman Munif in his five-volume *Cities of Salt*.[1]

The relationship between the patriarchal system and human rights is implicitly contradictory. Where patriarchy steers the recipient's consciousness directly towards a set of inherited traditional and cultural relations, the human rights perspective belongs to the modern age; to the age, that is, of the liberal democratic and nationalist European revolution. Whatever the psychological elements involved, the dichotomy of patriarchy and human rights creates a situation of conflict: old versus new, backwardness versus modernity. However, before discussing this relationship further, we should first perhaps define the two concepts in question.

I. The patriarchal system

Historically speaking, the patriarchal system emerged in the wake of matriarchy; in fact, the development of the single patriarchal family heralded the beginning of human culture proper. This family system was based on male control, and it aimed primarily to produce offspring of unquestionable descent so that the male children, as natural heirs, could inherit their father's property.[2] Engels argued that the ties in such a household would strengthen so long as the father retained the right to untie this bond and release his wife, while still enjoying the privilege of adultery out of wedlock – at least as a normal option. (The Napoleonic Code specifically accorded such a right, as long as the husband did not bring his mistress into his home.)

According to Marx, women's status began to deteriorate with the Greek heroic age, from a far more elevated position as goddesses in the old mythology. In this new heroic age, they were overruled by men and rivalled and outdone by concubines. We see how Telemachus, in Homer's *Odyssey*, reproves his mother, commanding her to remain silent. In the *Iliad*, female captives were the targets of men's sexual lust. Indeed, a central subject of the *Iliad*, as we all know, is the rivalry over one of these captives between Achilles and Agamemnon.[3]

The patriarchal family was thus the outcome of monogamous marriage, and it involved the concentration of substantial fortunes in the hands of one individual – the husband – and the need to pass property down to the male children of this particular man, and to no one else. This underlying theme was to continue, despite the disintegration of the patriarchal system in the West, with the advance of capitalism and the advent of industrialization and modernization. These more recent developments did indeed force women to leave the home and become involved in economic and social life. Nevertheless, post-patriarchy capitalism was, by virtue of its constituent components, powerless to undermine the hegemonic structure of family relations. The man of the family became the 'bourgeois', the woman the 'proletarian'.[4]

The decisive element in conceptualizing the socio-cultural construct of patriarchy is, therefore, the central role of the paterfamilias as master, lord and sovereign, who both owns and fully controls the economic, social and cultural assets. This is consistent with the ancient mythic belief that the father may offer his son as a sacrifice to God; and it is also in line with the organic concept of fatherhood that gives power, authority and superiority to male virility. This notion blends well with the practice of eating whereby the man is figuratively envisioned as the 'eater' and the woman as the 'eaten'. Sex, according to Lévi-Strauss, equates with eating.[5] In this series of mythic invocations, the woman is an organic extension of nature, while the man enters as a cultivator and an actor upon nature. Foucault takes the metaphor further in his analysis of the patriarchy culture, by interpreting the sex act as one of penetration, incursion, control and superiority.[6]

The patriarchal relationship within the household thus instituted a form of natural organic cohesion, which sociology would later term 'blood ties'; and these ties, in their turn, laid the foundation for the kinship structure, and for a system of hierarchical stratification within which the household is the cornerstone of clannish society, and the family set-up its nucleus and the model for the social formation first of the clan, then of the tribe. In a society governed by patriarchal relations, blood ties become the vital bond shaping the organic characteristics of the community. Loyalty to the family and the ethnic group supersedes affiliation to society, country, land and class. All these latter terms appear alien to the field of signification in patriarchal grammatology.

I.1 Patriarchal discourse

Jacobson draws a fine distinction between the philological perspective, which
sees speech as a system allowing us to say, and modern semiotic analysis, which
views language not merely as a passive transmitter of ideas but as an active
instrument for moulding thought. For Jacobson, speech is what the system
'compels' us to say. Accordingly, as a system closed by virtue of blood ties,
patriarchal discourse is based on inculcation, obedience, compliance, memo-
rization, repetition, worship of the past and idolization of the text. These are
the elements constituting the signification field of such a discourse. They have
been held in great esteem by the West, but only as something to be exported to
Arabs and Muslims, for the exercise of sovereignty in their mythic rituals. This
was the view held by a wide range of Westerners: by the British Foreign
Secretary Palmerston, for instance, who was angered by Muhammad Ali's vigorous modernization, and by Cromer, who wished the curriculum of the
Egyptian university to be grounded on the distinctiveness of an Arab and
Muslim mind captured by the past and captivated by the text; and it was
reflected, too, in the collusion between the British and al-Azhar against 'Ali
'Abd al-Razzaq's book *Islam and the Principles of Government*. The strategy has
now culminated in a canonization of the past as a patriarchal idol, without
which no project for renaissance can be initiated or even contemplated.

The patriarchal Arab speech system takes its prime inspiration from the
exemplary model of the classical Arabic language, with its enchanting,
powerful eloquence and rhetoric. Speech takes its starting point, in Jacobson's
view, from what is allowable; more specifically, from what is both permissible
and open-ended, since room is in fact left for the candid, forthright and out-
spoken. The Arabic speech formula, however, follows a close-ended modus
operandi: from the 'Master of Heaven and Earth' down to the 'master of the
household'.[7]

The magic of Arabic eloquence is the miracle of the Arab Prophet and the
marvel of the Quranic message, which exercises an enormous, and indeed irresistible influence on minds and hearts. According to Barthes, this linguistic
authority allows the classical original, the prime prototype, to work its patriarchal spell on speech – not only to shape the speech itself, figuratively and sym-
bolically, but also to mould our thought, our consciousness and our
knowledge. The classical Arabic language is thus decisive for the formation of
Arabic thought; not only because of its ideological nature, or its stringent religious and patriarchal attributes, but because of its capacity to 'think in its own
right'. It can impose its patterns and structures on all linguistic applications. It

is the ready-made language that 'prefers literary writing to scientific writing, rhetoric to the written text, and speech to writing'.[8]

Patriarchal relations exercise power, through the speech system, by ideologizing mythology in the man's favour. Political patriarchal power goes far beyond rescinding two important clauses of the Universal Declaration of Human Rights: that individuals shall not be persecuted for their opinions, and that the freedom to disseminate ideas should be respected.[9] It generalizes a mode of discourse teeming with a luxuriant, eloquent rhetoric, but flimsy in signification and inclined to thrust dialogue into a maze of abstract generalities. Everything descends vertically, down a hierarchy that begins in the heavens and ends in the underworld of other people – worshippers, subjects, and the family. This is a world of compliance and acquiescence, of lending the ear. The hallmark of courtesy and good manners, in a patriarchal upbringing, is 'listening to the word'; listening is the keyword used in describing well-mannered children: 'They listen to the word.' According to Sharabi, the dominant discourse at home is the father's; at school it is the teacher's; in the religious congregation or tribal gathering it is the *shaykh*'s; in the religious institution it is the learned man's; and in society at large it is the discourse of the ruler. Such discourse derives its powers from the structure of the language; and this structure implicitly leads on to various forms of opposition, such as gossip, telling tales, vilification and falling silent in the face of wrongdoing. In such an overall ambience, there can be no public discussion or opposition; debate can take place only in secret, away from the authority.[10]

A patriarchal discourse of this nature is incapable of instituting a rational, dialogic and critical system. The critical mind is replaced by a mind well-equipped for backbiting, spite, squabbling, indictment and internal strife. The analytical mind, which can examine, understand, interpret and apply judgement, is absent. In European society, the invention of the printing press played its part in the spread of the Protestant Revolution, which turned the speech system away from moulded rhetoric and towards critical reading, explanation and interpretation of the sacred text. The patriarchal system, deep-seated within the Arab social, historical and cultural structure, has impeded such a process. The Quran is quoted and memorized but seldom read. Interpretation has been monopolized by specialists and religious men whose interpretations draw heavily on classical explanations.[11]

By contrast, modern writing that has been freed from the inherited patriarchy can produce a rewritable text, and this in turn can generate a variety of discourses. The capacity for dialogue with the text, by reading and rewriting, turns the reader or critic from a consumer into a producer. His is the text capable of rebellion against the patriarchy of authority. In his work *Le plaisir du texte* (1973), Roland Barthes argues that the intellectual can find refuge for his right to protect his human freedom only in a writing capable of producing a new text – a text free from the patriarchal heritage.

The response to the terror of patriarchal social institutions lies in 'writing', or in reading akin to writing. It is the last uncolonized spot where a thinker can play, enjoying the generous luxury of the 'signified' and disregarding what goes on at the Elysée Palace or the Renault plants. In writing, and through the interplay of language, a person can tear apart the structural tyranny and free the writing self/reader from its straitjacket, transforming it into an intoxicated, joyous self. This is because, in Barthes' words, 'the liberated text turns its back on the political patriarch'.[12]

So where does it come from – this patriarchal authority which underlies the structure of social, cultural and political repression? Here the neo-Freudian school steps in, to explain that the authority in question is the natural product of household relations. The father poses as the representative of law, which, according to Lacan, is the taboo prohibiting incest and the factor disrupting the child's libido tendency towards his mother. The child comes to realize there is a larger network of family ties, of which he is a part; and he becomes aware, too, that he has to play a specific role devised for him by the practices of his society. The presence of the father separates the child from the mother's body, and the child's desire for the mother is thereby driven down into his subconscious. The appearance of law and the emergence of desire take place simultaneously; the child suppresses his illicit desire only when he recognizes the taboo or prohibition symbolized by the father. This desire is itself identical with the subconscious.[13]

I.2 Patriarchy, women and human rights

What gives conceptual legitimacy to the term patriarchy is the latter's stance vis-à-vis women, as the historical culmination of a conflict between the two polar elements of human existence, female and male – a stance in favour of the male following a long period of dominant matriarchy. This triumph coincided with a step forward for human society, from the oral to the written stage. The writing of male-centred epics and myths signals the successive defeats of the woman goddess in the face of the man god.

Written civilization signals the decisive triumph of culture over nature; and since this point in human history coincided with the victory of man over woman, it is possibly valid to relate the binary relation of woman-man to that of culture-nature. Such a link may be considered on three levels of analysis:

1 Woman's body and reproductive functions place her physiologically closer to nature, when compared with man, who has been given full freedom to handle cultural projects.

2 Woman's traditional roles, as imposed on her by her body and its functions, have given her a different psychological make-up, one akin to her physiological characteristics and social roles.

3 In terms of the cultural process, woman's body and its functions have forced her into roles inferior to those of men.[14]

Industrial society has given women the chance to work and leave the home to carry on an active social and cultural life. Yet, despite these achievements, industrial society has kept for men the privilege of male dominance and control. Western anthropology recognizes the continuing domination of men, and throughout Western society a variance between the sexes – albeit with a varying degree of lowliness on women's part – has been regarded as an established fact of human social history.[15]

The Freudian school has, in the person of Lacan, provided some explanatory notes on a perspective that emphasizes male superiority in transcendence and sublimation, while the phallic libido condemns the female to a semi-eternal inferior status. Indeed, Freudianism goes still further, underlining the male–female binary as the ultimate original frame:

Manhood = Action – Positive – Transcendence – Sadism.
Womanhood = Reaction – Passivity – Induction – Masochism.

Sadism here equates to the male tendency to act, and to dominate and transcend subject matter, whereas masochism is a female activity characterized by submissiveness and passive reliance. In the interpretation of dreams, this ontological binary is symbolized figuratively by associating the male phallus with sharp, solid and long instruments, and with tree trunks and bamboos, and the female genitalia with closets, cans, carriages and fireplaces.[16]

As a socio-cultural construct, patriarchy, even in its moderate, diluted forms, can be sustained at the expense of human rights thanks to the system's structural incapacity to transcend the male–female binary and embrace an essential element of human rights: that men and women are born free and remain free and equal in rights. This incapacity applies to all peoples, so that women would seem to be victims of species and culture on a worldwide level. How, in this context, should we view the specifically Arab patriarchal system, within the cultural framework of Arab-Islamic civilization?

I.3 Patriarchy, Islam and human rights

Hisham Sharabi is perhaps the most sophisticated scholar to have treated the issue of patriarchy and backwardness in Arab society. The theme has also, however, been tackled in other Arabic texts, from a variety of socio-cultural and intellectual perspectives. Sometimes 'patriarchal structure' is considered in the light of the father's dominance, or the patriarchal propensity, or the socio-logical derivatives of these. Kinship systems or blood ties are viewed as the decisive factors, within traditional societies, in shaping communities like tribes, clans and families. Such an approach removes the focus from the investigation of society from a social stratification viewpoint. Yassin al-Hafiz had earlier viewed Arab society as one governed by conflicting and confused relations, and by Bedouin class structures penetrated by vertical blood and kinship ties; and, in the light of this, he provided a perceptive analysis of the civil war in Lebanon as a squalid sectarian war. In his view, a class perspective has no appli-cation to the consciousness of a pre-class pre-modern society – a patriarchal, familial and sectarian society.[17]

The prevalence of ideological and political discourse in the Arab intellectual and cultural arena may explain the absence of any conceptualization instru-ment for analysing the internal structure of Arab society – this despite the pre-dominance of Marxist grammatology, as represented by Engels' viewpoint on family, private property and the state. As a result, texts dealing with patriarchy concentrate largely on the issue of women, and patriarchy is treated as one of the apparatuses of repression used against women. This is exemplified in the writings of Nawal al-Sa'dawi, who argues that the essence, in this respect, is the tragic quality of the female body.

> The woman's body, the medium for reproduction and intermarriage, is the cen-tre of her value, and her honour is symbolized by her sexual chastity as repre-sented by her hymen. Her honour is reduced to an anatomical feature that may or may not be in her when she is born.[18]

For another analyst, correlating a girl's honour with her hymen, and a man's honour with his daughter's chastity, is a clear indication of the flimsy – indeed precarious – nature of the criterion by which a man's status is judged by oth-ers.[19] In some sociological and anthropological literature, patriarchy stands opposed to human rights in condemning the woman's body to sin and feelings of guilt. 'The free sexual movement of the woman is associated with shame and disgrace, and the canonization of such a notion is the essence of honour.' A woman's body is thus historically shackled and institutionalized, and the function of all the taboos and inhibitions is to contain and confine this body, and pass the keys on to men.[20] This sense of patriarchy as enforced repression has been well-circulated in contemporary Arab discourse. With Sharabi, however, it is discussed as a social construct that produces its own intellectual and cultural equivalent; and this latter, in turn, articulates within a primordial world view of reality and history.

As with all pioneer endeavours, this approach is marked by a slight imbalance. The flaw lies in his identification of the historical beginnings of patriarchy, its roots and its relationship to Islam. Up to the twentieth century, he maintains,

> Arab society has seen only two major social movements that have gone beyond the identity and aspirations of the family-clan: the revolution of the Arab Prophet in the seventh century, which advocated the institution of the Muslim Community as a replacement for the family relation; and the Arab nationalist movement which called for twentieth-century Arabs to gather beneath the banner of a secular ideology, as a nation state with clear geographical borders . . .

This judgement is inconsistent with earlier arguments in the same book, where the author speaks of the 'impediment of the patriarchal mode in the era of the Prophet and the orthodox caliphs'. Nor, for that matter, does it correspond with another statement made by Sharabi on the same page:

> From its beginnings, patriarchy demonstrated its innate resistance to change and maintained its presence as an essential component in the structure of the nation in both the religious and the secular sense. This was the case during the Prophet's revolution. In the twentieth century, the second social movement combined both the Islamic and the tribal dimensions as promoted by Arab nationalism.

The author here comes close to Samir Amin's thesis: that the Arab world came to know the feudal system only towards the end of the nineteenth century, as a result of European imperialism. In contrast with feudal Europe, however, where blood and kinship ties were replaced by social and political relations, kinship ties were maintained as essential elements within Arab society, and the family and the clan continued to be the crucial unit for social and political relations.[21]

This confused reading of Islam's role would appear to derive from the paradox experienced at other major turning points in history, when a discrepancy emerges between the new ideal model and the weighty anchors of the past. The ambition of Islam to create and realize universal humanistic ideals was on a collision course with a reality based on smaller units (tribes, clans, branches or offshoots). Historically, the old tribal society simply developed into a centralized state that was effectively a greater unified Arab-Islamic tribal society, and not a global tribe according to the ideological ideal propounded – this latter not being then embedded in the consciousness of the Muslim community. Islam, in Weber's view, maintained its political nature in its early stages, assuming its ideological dimension only after the appearance of sects, trends and factions.

The argument that patriarchy coincided with the rise of Islam has some validity; and patriarchy was indeed to find its equivalent in the emergence of the Islamic state. There is some validity, too, in the interpretation of Fatima al-Mernisi, who likewise linked patriarchy to the rise of the Islamic state, especially during the time of the second caliph, 'Umar ibn al-Khattab.[22] The latter (she maintained) ruled over a community still influenced by pre-Islamic factors, and thought it best to establish patriarchy in people's minds (as the main element of Islam) with all possible speed. Al-Mernisi's argument finds no support in the Caliph's sayings. Nor is a tendency to patriarchy clearly identifiable in the sayings or actions of the first caliph, Abu Bakr, other than his citation of the Prophet's saying that 'a people will not succeed if ruled by a woman'.[23] Her aim is to free the essence of Islam from a propensity to patriarchy, and so she takes the latter to derive incidentally from 'Umar ibn al-Khattab, who was one of the Prophet's closest advisers. In fact, any responsible research methodology, in the context of Islamic ideology and its stance vis-à-vis women, must lead to acceptance of 'Umar as the founder of what was subsequently called the Islamic state; and 'Umar must have realized that the new-born state called, among other things, for monogamous marriage and a single patriarchal family, as a necessary social unit within an increasingly centralized society.

Women had, in the circumstances, to lose some of the freedom they had enjoyed before Islam; before, that is to say, the establishment of an ideologically-grounded and Shariah-governed state. A more convincing approach towards this historic junction is that of the Iraqi heritage scholar Hadi 'l-'Alawi (1932–1998), who streamlined the emergence of patriarchy through the concept of the society state. Before Islam, he maintained, women and men had enjoyed almost equal rights within a stateless society. The pre-Islamic era and the early period of Islam provide historically significant examples: Queen al-Zabba' (Zenobia) of the fourth century before the Hegira; Sijah, the prophetess of the Tamim tribe; Hind, the wife of Abu Sufyan; and Khadija, the businesswoman and first wife of the Prophet. Under Islam women lost much of their freedom, being constrained by various limitations unknown before as Arab society moved closer to a patriarchal system and a state structure based on male-centred private property.[24] One such limitation was the prohibition on mixing between women and men. During the time of the Prophet, women said their prayers in the mosque and performed the ritual of ablution along with men. They also circumambulated the Kaaba together with men, and this continued until Kahlid al-Qasri, the ruler of Mecca during the reign of the Umayyad caliph al-Walid ibn 'Abd al-Malik, ordered the practice to be discontinued. This was after he had heard a poet recite the following lines:

> Delightful is the season [of Pilgrimage],
> And beautiful is the Kaaba as a prayer place,
> When those [lovely women] flock with us, shoulder to shoulder,
> To [kiss the] Black Stone!

After al-Qasri, mixed assembly around the Kaaba was resumed until al-Ghazali introduced the restriction once more. He acknowledged, even so, that the Prophet had permitted such a joint practice. 'The Messenger of God,' he wrote, in his *Revival of the Sciences of Religion*, 'permitted women to be present in the Mosque. But prohibition is now the correct thing, except for old women.' Women were also prevented from travelling unless accompanied by a male guardian, and men's custodianship over women was formalized in accordance with the Quranic verse: 'Men are the Protectors and maintainers of women because God has given one more than the other.' Such custodianship entailed permission for a man to beat his wife should she become disobedient.[25] Women's subordination was obligatory. Some jurists, indeed, went still further. 'Marriage,' al-Ghazali wrote, in *The Conduct of Marriage*, 'is a type of slavery; she is his slave and must obey her husband wholly, in whatever he asks of her, apart from wrongdoing.' Such male-centred concepts were examples of women's severely diminished human rights.

Another implication of custodianship, al-'Alawi argues, is women's unfitness to rule. The *hadith* to this effect cannot be denied or questioned, since it is quoted in six of the authoritative books of the Prophet's sayings, and it is consistent with the requirements of custodianship.[26]

1.4 The viewpoint on sexuality

Islamic jurisprudence has accorded men a host of rights in terms of sexual relations and possession of a woman's body. There have, accordingly, been many interpretations and explanations of the Quranic verse: 'Your wives are as a tilth unto you; so approach your tilth when or how ye will.'[27] Al-Tabari examined 41 testimonies, opinions and suggestions, coming, finally, to a moderate conclusion: the verse, he says, permits a man to have sexual intercourse with his wife as and when he pleases. The essence is penetration of the vagina, the only bodily place whereby the cultivation (semen) and sowing of the offspring can be secured.[28] Shi'ites have enhanced the provisions relating to sexuality and elaborated on the areas of sexual intercourse.

The patriarchal system in Arab society is, then, based not on a mode of socially conscious values and norms but rather on a religious ideology amenable to modification and adaptation through the actual experience of life. This experience is not, though, open-ended, as was the case before the advent of Islam. The discourse here produces and reproduces its necessities, and it contributes to the nature of subsequent steps. The ideology and the creed remain, at all times, the centre of gravity.[29]

The credo, as an ideology and a revelation from Heaven, must necessarily generate a discourse with a touch of the sacred – however human or sensual it might be. Nor does the patriarchal discourse that reduces a woman to a body stop here; it goes still further by acquiring the right to possess the body in question and confiscate it from its owner. The title-holder and proprietor is the man, who owns and controls that body's response and means of expression. Al-Tabari produces a conclave of 41 witnesses confirming a man's right to handle the body of the woman, who has no right to speak on behalf of something she no longer possesses in any case, either physically or spiritually; her body has been transferred and reassigned to male patriarchy. The new owner has the full right to restructure and control the property as he pleases, according to his own instincts, desires and impulses, which are now enshrined in a sacred cause. Even Heaven can be invoked to help him on occasion, as was the case with the *ifk*/untruth episode.[30]

Any attempt to achieve democracy and enhance its human rights implications must, therefore, embark on a deconstruction of the deep-seated theoretical and ideological structure of patriarchy in Arab-Islamic culture. The process of developing human rights into an integral part of the inner constitution of society is twofold: the modernization of overall social policy through democratization must be paralleled by a modernization of culture through secularization. All other attempts, made under the name of heritage exploration or cultural criticism, will merely provide a superficial, ornamental gloss for patriarchy. Left-wing Arab forces have failed to show the necessary intellectual liberation from the dominant social patriarchy; rather they have produced a modernized patriarchy under a variety of names. Despotism and tyranny are the ultimate signifier to which all Arab discourses, old and new, finally lead.[31]

In the same vein (and in contrast to Sharabi's approach), a modernized heritage discourse falls short of any drastic criticism of the new cultural patriarchy. Al-Jabiri, for instance, bestows legitimacy on the patriarchal system by making heritage itself a father, to be consulted on every new step – in much the same way that modern traditionalists expect us to search out the legitimacy for any new idea by seeking the response of the heritage-father.[32] This amounts to appointing traditional heritage as one's point of reference – which is merely the equivalent of the old system of blood and kinship ties. From this viewpoint, the Arab mind can never be rational according to the perspectives of Descartes, Spinoza, Kant, Hegel or Marx. It must return to the rationalism of the 'father', beginning with Ibn Hazm and moving on to Ibn Rushd (Averroes), Ibn Baja and Ibn Khaldoun – to the Maghrebi branch of the rationality of the greater Arab tribe. As a result, and in the name of authenticity, heritage criticism and cultural criticism, distinctiveness becomes idolized and human rights are downgraded and unsupported. In this way, backwardness is modernized and cultural lag becomes legitimized by reference to the legitimacy of the father – the sole legislator.

II. Human rights in modern Arabic texts

The enormous effect of the inherited patriarchal system on the Arab individual and society no doubt explains Hegel's observation: that the Eastern state entails absolute freedom for one individual and enslavement for everyone else. We have shown how the patriarchal power of this individual takes a multitude of shapes: head of household and family; employer; ruler; and shadow of God on earth. This crushing weight may also explain the overwhelming presence and circulation of the term 'freedom' in cultural circles, and in the language, slogans and programmes of all Arab political parties. The other face of this passion for freedom is deprivation and absence of freedom. The entrenched patriarchal system has nibbled at freedom little by little, before chewing it, devouring it and gulping it down, in the fields of economy, society, culture and politics, until the very banner of freedom has lost all point. There is a tendency nowadays to revive and rehabilitate Arab Renaissance thought, which promoters of patriarchy and modern-day fundamentalists accuse of being Westernized and Europeanized. 'Abdallah al-'Aroui, who initially discerned Western origins in Renaissance thought, is now withdrawing his thesis, saying that the call for freedom in the Arab world was not, after all, a translation of Western notions and a reflection of European liberal thought.[33] He now underlines that 'the call for freedom originated primarily from an innate need within Arab society'.[34]

The first Arab author to provide a text making reference to a 'declaration of human rights' was al-Tahtawi (1801–1873), in his celebrated book *Extracting Gold in Summarizing Paris*. Considering the rights enjoyed by the French, he lists the provisions of the constitution during the time of Louis XVIII: Article (1): 'All French people are equal before the law'; Article (2), which stipulates that all persons must pay taxes according to their wealth; Article (3), which entitles all qualified French individuals to assume public office; and Article (4), which guarantees individuals' independence and freedom, a right that can be violated only in cases specified by law.[35] Al-Tahtawi's pioneering role went, however, beyond the simple promotion of human rights. He also pointed out the organic connection between the absence of such rights and the backwardness and ignorance of women within patriarchal society. He was the first to defend and advocate the right of women to education, and he succeeded, in the time of Khedive Isma'il, in establishing the first Egyptian school for girls.[36]

The 'declaration of human rights' would subsequently emerge in many versions, according to particular political circumstances – a reminder of the necessity of the proper 'historical moment'. After the revolution of 1908, and the return to the constitution of 1876 in the Ottoman state, Jamil Ma'luf translated the 'Declaration of Human Rights and Citizen', with a view to pointing out the essentially chauvinistic nature of the new regime and exposing the defects of the constitutional monarchy proclaimed in the Ottoman empire. Monarchy would, he showed, remain despotic in its nature so long as the constitution accorded the Sultan the rights of an absolute ruler.[37] Anton Thabit also provided a faithful translation of the Declaration, in an attempt to defend human rights in the face of the rising Nazi and fascist ideologies.

In his matchless book about the impact of the French Revolution on modern Arab political and social thought, Ra'if Khoury thoroughly examines the liberal and democratic content of the texts of the Arab Renaissance writers.[38] The idea of human rights was, he argues, not the brainchild of a few political parties or groups, or of a few enthusiastic intellectuals and writers. It was rather an underlying theme in the motivational structure of modern Arabic thought. This is attested by the writings of such early advocates of democracy, freedom and human rights as al-Shidyaq (1804–1887), al-Tahtawi (1801–1873), al-Afghani (1830–1897), al-Kawakibi (1854–1908), al-Shumayyel (1860–1916), Adib Ishaq (1856–1885), Farah Antun (1871–1922), Amin al-Raihani (1876–1940), Mustafa Lutfi 'l-Manfaluti (1876–1924), Gibran (1883–1931), Shaykh Rashid Rida (1865–1935), Muhammad Kurd 'Ali (1873–1921),

Mustafa al-Ghalayini (1885–1944), Ma'rouf al-Rasafi (1875–1941), Bishara al-Khoury (al-Akhtal al-Saghir) (1884–1968) and Elias Abu Shabaka (1903–1947). The human rights issue was, it should be noted, closely associated with the struggle for national and political liberation. The social dimension was evident only in areas relating to the issue of women's rights, which, for the Renaissance writers, was a secondary question in the face of the tremendous challenges posed by the superior West. Furthermore, the excessive Arab and Muslim backwardness of the time gave neither Renaissance intellectuals nor women the chance to look beyond the religious rationale for educating women, removing the veil, demanding their right to divorce and denouncing polygamy. This was the case even with Qasim Amin (1865–1908), author of *The Liberation of Woman* (1889) and *The New Woman* (1906), who was concerned throughout his life to further the cause of women.

> Qasim Amin felt constrained to return to the 'correct' Islam of the Prophet's days, when the status of women was far more respected than it came to be at the end of the nineteenth century. As a follower of Muhammad 'Abduh, he called for a return to the roots: to the Prophet (Muhammed) and to the Quran, which did not prescribe the veil, or indicate that a woman with her face uncovered contravened the principles of religion, or anything else of the kind.[39]

The revolutionary Arab human rights document was in fact 'Abd al-Rahman al-Kawakibi's *The Features of Oppression*, a book that not only denounced tyranny but spoke out firmly against the whole intellectual and spiritual thrust of the patriarchal system. The work echoes the ideas of the Italian writer Vittorio Alfieri (1749–1803), the 'Declaration of Human Rights', the concepts of revolutionary French philosophers like Montesquieu, Rousseau and Holbach, and even the Enlightenment philosophy of the eighteenth century. Yet for all these reverberations, and for all his openness to the culture of the times, al-Kawakibi specifically addresses the Eastern patriarchal despotism that combines the monolithic powers of the patriarch in family, religion and political life. Ignorant peoples, he believes, borrow their notions of a despotic ruler from their concepts of the Omnipotent God, to whom is due adulation, glorification and worship.[40] From this he proceeds to touch on one of the essential tenets of human rights with regard to freedom and equality. 'Why,' he asks, addressing his people in his inimitable fiery style, 'should there be so much differentiation among you? God has created you equal in power, equal in nature, equal in needs. There should be no divine superiority or servitude among you. I swear by God that the distinction between the smallest and the greatest among you is a mere thin line of illusion.'[41]

The Features of Oppression remains, still, a source of concern to the new Arab patriarchal system, embodying anew the call for an 'Arab Declaration of Human Rights'. His prophetic protest against the patriarchal system will again, in his words, be a resounding 'word of truth and a cry in the wilderness. If today it flies off on the wind, it may uproot the foundations tomorrow.'

Chapter 19: Civil and political rights in Arab constitutions[1]

Fateh Samih 'Azzam

Introduction

It is beyond doubt that Arab civilization has, over thousands of years, exerted no less effort than any other at organizing its societies on a basis of justice and fairness, and at striving to strike a fair and adequate balance between its security and stability and the rights and duties of members of society. At the beginning of the twenty-first century, nevertheless, a quick perusal of the reports of Arab and international human rights organizations reveals a sorry state indeed for the Arab citizen's human rights. Violations of human rights in the Arab world have become the norm: torture is prevalent, as is detention without charge, unfair trial, heavy-handed control and censorship over freedom of expression, assembly and association, and much more.[2] These reports beg the question, 'Why?', and the answer would no doubt need numerous volumes of studies, in all fields, before we could begin to understand the complex cluster of political, economic, cultural and historical reasons behind this state of affairs. A modest research paper such as this can only hope to provide a glimpse.

Arab states, for all their cultural and political particularities, follow the same model of the modern nation-state as is found in most of the world: the nation-state governed by law, at least in form and structure. It is necessary, as a first step, to discover how such states have translated their values into their constitutions, which organize the relations of individuals to state and authority, and, especially, to see how human rights have been recognized and guaranteed in these constitutions, in principle at least. We can also acquire a better understanding of the human rights situation by briefly examining how these guarantees are implemented on the ground, or whether their implementation is in fact being prevented. This study aims, briefly, at examining how the texts of Arab constitutions recognize civil and political rights, and questions or seeks to understand the various structural and legal factors that affect citizens' actual enjoyment of those rights.

I. The historical/legal background

Since the death of the Prophet (Muhammed), the Arab nation has been striving to find an appropriate balance between, on the one hand, the religious concepts and values of Islam, and, on the other, the struggles of political and economic power and authority to control the destiny of the nation.[3] For a thousand years, caliphates followed one another, each governing the Arab-Islamic World in accordance with its own particular synthesis of the spiritual and the temporal, interpreting matters in a manner appropriate to its perspectives and interests, and seeking the necessary credibility and legitimacy. This legitimacy found its source, as it still finds it today, in terms of a tight balance between the religious and temporal sources of law. We note, for example, that only the Lebanese Constitution fails to identify Islam as the state religion. Islamic Shariah and law continue to be the most important, or the first, source of legislation in the Arab world.

Early in the sixteenth century, the Ottoman Empire conquered most of the Arab world; and, in the mid-nineteenth century, the Empire made a decisive move towards secularism under the impetus of European reform. In 1839, the first constitutional document, inspired by the Napoleonic Code, was adopted in the region, and it contained the first recognition of certain rights such as personal liberty, equality before the law, non-discrimination and the sanctity of private property. A number of new laws, such as the Ottoman Penal Code of 1840, were based on a combination of Islamic Shariah and French and Italian legal principles. These legal developments were implemented in most of the Arab regions subject to the Ottoman Empire at the time, and the new laws formed the basis upon which contemporary Arab legal systems were built.[4] Today we can still see the influence of Ottoman law, the European family of laws and Islamic Shariah on the structures of Arab legal systems.

The introduction of the Egyptian Civil Code was widely welcomed: 'heralded as a harbinger of a uniform Arab Civil Code' and acclaimed for containing nothing 'un-Islamic'.[5] Indeed, it has been adopted with little variation by a number of Arab countries. However, Arab legal systems today are not uniform, nor are they identical. Rather, they are the result of each country's search for the appropriate synthesis of modern secular law (required to meet the needs of modern society) and divinely inspired Islamic Shariah law (closely intertwined with the very identity and sense of being of the Arab world). Today we find that the legal system in some Arab states is quite advanced in form, very closely resembling European law — especially French law. Other states have steered a more traditionalist course, closer to Islamic Shariah and its principles; interpreting these principles in their own way in accordance with their purposes. Such is the case, for example, in the monarchical Gulf States.

II. Rights in Arab constitutions

With the exception of the Sultanate of Oman, all Arab states are organized in accordance with constitutions or basic laws that determine, with varying degrees of detail and clarity, the basic principles and attitudes of these states, regardless of their differing political systems. These constitutions define the ordering of governance and authorities as well as the rights, freedoms and duties of their citizens. Normally, rights and duties are defined under specific chapters or sections, the exceptions being Morocco and Tunisia, which place civil and political rights at the beginning of their constitutions under 'General Provisions'.

More general exceptions do exist. Mention has already been made of the Sultanate of Oman, which takes the Quran as the source of all rights and duties as defined in Shariah. The definition of civil and political rights, and the degree to which these are guaranteed, naturally depends on the regime's own interpretation of the rules and provisions of Shariah. The situation of Saudi Arabia is not drastically different, even since the promulgation there, in March 1992, of the Basic Law, Article 26 of which provides that the State protects human rights in accordance with Islamic Shariah. In 1991, Mauritania promulgated its first constitution; the first in the region to include in its preamble clear commitments to the Universal Declaration of Human Rights (UDHR). Djibouti has put into effect Constitutional Law No. 1; here again, Article 2 commits the State to the UDHR, and the law affirms the importance of establishing a political system guaranteeing rights and liberties with full force. This was followed, in 1992, by ratification of the new constitution, which, in principle at least, confirmed political pluralism, separation of powers and respect for the rights of citizens.

The Libyan *jamahiriyya*, by contrast, approached Islamic Shariah from a political perspective different to any hitherto known system or approach. In March 1977, the state exchanged its 1969 constitution for a Declaration on the Establishment of the People's Authority, which declared the Quran to be 'the

Constitution of the Land' and vowed the people's 'total commitment to block-ing the way in face of all forms of traditional instruments of government'.[6] In 1988, the People's Council issued the 'Great Green Charter for Human Rights in the Era of the Masses'. This document is unique in the annals of human rights covenants and protective instruments, and is deserving of a special study. For our purposes here, it is important to note that the Green Charter clarifies the obligation to implement the principles mentioned therein by force of law, but does so in unfamiliar language. For example, Article 26 states, in rather general terms, that 'the sons of the *Jamahiriyya* are committed to this Charter . . . and do not encourage its violation . . . and "criminalize" all violations'.[7]

The civil and political rights selected for examination below illustrate the approach to rights and the broad general treatment of rights in Arab constitu-tions. The late Mundher 'Anabtawi focused on freedom of opinion and expres-sion and the right to peaceful assembly as the most important rights needed by the Arab citizen to live a life of dignity.[8] We have chosen here to add the rights of association and personal security and integrity, including the right to life and the prohibition of torture. Also included in this review are a number of legal rights, such as the right to defence and fair trial, that are essential in guarantee-ing equality and proper citizenship in any society.

II.1 *The Right to Life*

Article 6 of the International Covenant for Civil and Political Rights (ICCPR) regards the right to life as 'inherent'. While capital punishment is not expressly prohibited as a violation of the right to life, it is to be reserved only for the most serious of crimes (para. 2), and a number of restrictions and limitations are placed on its use (para. 5); and, finally, its abolition is encouraged in paragraph 6 of the article.

Not a single Arab constitution guarantees the right to life in general, even in principle; nor is there anywhere a prohibition of the death penalty. This would suggest that the drafters of these constitutions considered the death penalty a given. The constitutions are, moreover, devoid of any provisions that limit the use of capital punishment, such as prohibiting the execution of minors under 18, or of pregnant women (article 6, para. 5 of the ICCPR). Arab constitutions only hint at the death penalty, and they do this in two ways. First, they articulate a right to seek pardon, or a stay of execution, or a right to seek an alternative penalty. In nearly all instances, Arab constitutions give the power of amnesty or pardon to the president or other head of state. The Libyan Green Charter is unique in giving the convicted person the right to seek a mitigation of his sentence, or to offer *fidya* (monetary compensation) in lieu of his life (Article 8). No other Arab constitution makes any mention of the concept of *fidya*. We do find prohibition of what are considered 'illegitimate' penalties; a case in point is the Yemeni Constitution in Article 33, though it is not clear whether this includes the death penalty. Article 8 of the Green Charter is much clearer in prohibiting 'execution by inhuman means such as the electric chair, injections and poisonous gases' – a clear reference to, and condemnation of, the means of execution used in the United States of America.

A review of Arab and international human rights reports on Arab countries will show capital punishment to be in effect in almost all the states of the region. It is, moreover, prescribed for quite a wide range of crimes. In Iraq, for example, execution is the penalty for around 29 different crimes, including the 'crime' of membership of the Masons or propagation of their principles, or of insulting 'in an inciteful fashion' the president of the republic or government, or the ruling Ba'th Party; and many others.[9]

II.2 *Freedom of opinion and expression*

We should, to begin with, note the distinction between the right to hold an opinion and the right to express it. Only four Arab constitutions provide guarantees of freedom of opinion or thought, without clear limitations in the texts. Most others subject enjoyment of this right to definition in the law, without supplying any clear criteria for the definition. This is sharply at odds with the first paragraph of Article 19 of the ICCPR, which prescribes the right to hold an opinion without limitations or corresponding duties or other considerations. In other words, the right to hold an opinion should be absolute and not subject to restriction.

Nevertheless, the right to express such an opinion carries with it, according to Article 19, paragraph 3, of the ICCPR, 'special duties and responsibilities'; and these duties translate into restrictions that should be provided for by law and are necessary for respect of the rights of others, or for the protection of national security or public order, health or morals. Arab constitutions generally do guarantee freedom of expression, but use broad, simplified language largely devoid of detail or clarity in defining the scope of the right. The interesting thing here is that Arab constitutions do not clearly subject freedom of expression to any of the restrictions in question; rather, they prefer it to be organized in terms of law, using a variety of terms to this end. For example, we see freedom of expression guaranteed 'in law' (i.e., not necessarily in the constitution), or 'within the limits of the law', or 'in accordance with the law', or 'according to conditions set by law'. There is, of course, the risk of an over-wide interpretation in the light of the law of 'national security', 'public morals', etc. In some constitutions, enjoyment of freedom of expression would appear to be wholly dependent on political opinion. For example, Article 38 of the Syrian Constitution guarantees every citizen's right to express himself 'freely and publicly in speech and writing and all other means of expression'. The phraseology seems splendid – until we read that each citizen has a duty 'to participate in oversight and constructive criticism in order to safeguard the security of the national structure and support for the Socialist system'. Similarly, Article 26 of the Iraqi Constitution guarantees a number of liberties 'that are harmonious with the nationalist and progressive line of the revolution'.

The Libyan *jamahiriyya* once again breaks new ground. Article 5 of the Green Charter affirms 'the sovereignty of the individual in the Main People's Congress, guaranteeing him the right to express his opinion publicly and in the open air'. It is not clear from the language used whether the individual has any 'sovereignty', or freedom of expression 'in the open air', *outside* the Main People's Congress. Everything is liable to Libyan legal and political interpretation with respect to the article.

II.3 The Right to Association

All Arab constitutions guarantee the freedom to form associations, except for the Qatari Constitution and the Saudi Basic Law, which are completely silent on the matter. Definitions of 'forming' associations, and perhaps the very concept of association, differ from one constitution to the next. For example, we find in constitutions a general reference to the right to form or establish 'societies and associations'; and some add a reference to forming political parties or parties 'of a political nature' as part of the freedom of association. Eleven constitutions specifically include reference to the right to form professional associations, trade or labour unions, or both.

It is important, in this connection, to note that the right to form associations, in the straightforward sense expressed in Article 22 of the International Covenant, includes societies, professional associations, labour unions and political parties. The International Covenant adds, in Article 25 (a), the right of every citizen 'to take part in the conduct of public affairs, directly or through freely chosen representatives' and to do so 'without unreasonable restrictions'.

Arab constitutional provisions tend towards greater detail in defining freedom of association, adding a number of restrictions which, taken together, effectively represent a sharp narrowing of the scope of this right, even though the original text may be quite liberal. We may note, for example, Article 16 of the Jordanian Constitution, which states: 'Jordanians have the right to form associations and political parties, as long as their aims are legitimate, the means are legal and they contain regulations that do not violate their constitutional rules.' Similarly, the Bahraini Constitution guarantees freedom of association on condition that associations are 'patriotic' and have 'legitimate' aims. Clearly, no constitution or law will permit the establishment of groups that set out to threaten national security, since society has the right to protect itself. Nevertheless, the use of broad terms like 'legitimate goals' and 'patriotic basis' leaves the authorities too much leeway in interpreting their precise meaning and scope. While some constitutions are clearer on this point, they nonetheless arrive at the same conclusions. The Iraqi Constitution, for example, adds to its Article 26, which guarantees a number of freedoms including that of association, a dangerously explicit qualification: that 'the State ensures the considerations necessary for the exercise of those liberties which are in harmony with the nationalist and progressive line of the revolution'.[10] The Egyptian Constitution also guarantees this right, but prohibits the establishment of associations whose activities are 'hostile to the social system' (Article 55). This constitution places a further onus on trade and labour unions, charging them with participating in implementing the social programmes and plans . . . [and] consolidating socialist behaviour among their members' (Article 56).

We may surmise from the above that Arab constitutions guarantee the right to form groups or associations of a social or professional character, but with many reservations and restrictions. The nearer these associations approach to political action, broadly defined, the more restrictions there are. The language used in defining this right is open to wide interpretation. It is not precise or legally specific enough to express, in clear language, the conceptual framework or scope of the right in such a way as to aid adjudication. We should, though, remember that the language of the International Covenant on Civil and Political Rights is itself not absolutely clear; especially the phrase that allowable restrictions on freedom will be 'necessary in a democratic society' (Article 22, para. 2) – a rather elastic concept, open to debate. In order not to lose ourselves in interpretation, we need to refer to the law that organizes enjoyment of this right, since all constitutions defer to the law to fine-tune the right of association, in all its forms.

II.4 Arrest and detention

All Arab constitutions, with the exception of the Qatari, contain provisions dealing with arrest and detention, but few are in adequate harmony with the standards required by the International Covenant. A number of constitutions speak of 'personal freedom' in general as guaranteed, while others add that such freedom is 'a natural, inalienable and protected right' (Egypt, Article 41), or a 'sacrosanct' right (Syria, Article 25 para. 1). According to these constitutions, no person may be denied the right to personal freedom and security except in accordance with law. This does not in fact differ too fundamentally from the presentation in the ICCPR, where it is stated that 'no one shall be subjected to arbitrary arrest or detention' (Article 9, para. 1). Yet a clear problem emerges even so, in that the concept of arbitrariness is entirely absent in Arab constitutions. This concept is not to be taken lightly; for the purpose of using the word in the Universal Declaration of Human Rights, and in the Covenant, was to 'protect individuals from both "illegal" and "unjust" acts'.[11] Had the purpose been to protect persons from "illegal" acts alone, it would be self-evidently impossible to appeal against repressive or illegitimate acts by a government authority where such acts were consistent with domestic laws.

We may note, in the way Arab constitutions deal with fundamental rights in cases of arrest and detention, many further variations that demand a far sharper look at the domestic laws of each country, so as to determine the adequacy of provisions for the protection of personal security. Normally, indeed, the constitutions in the region do protect this right, but in terms so general as to be ambiguous; only a study of the actual practice can produce a proper evaluation in this respect. There is, it should be added, a ray of hope in some constitutions: those of Algeria, Bahrain, Egypt and Yemen are consistent with Article 9, paragraph 3, of the ICCPR in providing broader and some more detailed guarantees. Some, like the Egyptian Constitution, for example, provide a role for the judicial authority, in making an order for arrest conditional on the necessity for interrogation and the 'protection of societal security', issued by a judge who has jurisdiction or by the Prosecutor General, in accordance with the law (Article 41). Article 34 (b) of the Yemeni Constitution is similar, and is further supported by the preceding paragraph that refers to the inadmissibility of 'restricting anyone's freedom except by judicial order'. Some other constitutions give the judiciary further power by prohibiting the extension of periods of detention except by judicial order; for example, the Yemeni Constitution, Article 32 (c), and the Algerian Constitution, Article 45.

A number of constitutions (those of Tunisia, Jordan, Lebanon, Morocco and Qatar) make no reference to torture or cruel, inhuman or degrading treatment, and torture is only explicitly proscribed, with varying degrees of clarity or detail, by half the Arab constitutions. In some constitutions, torture includes 'bodily harm', or 'maltreatment', or 'treatment' in general that may be considered torture of a 'bodily', 'physical', 'moral' or 'psychological' kind. Kuwaiti and Bahraini constitutional provisions add a prohibition of 'degrading treatment', while such treatment is treated as 'humiliating' in Article 28 of the Syrian Constitution. Some constitutions approach the entire matter from a perspective of positive rights rather than proscription, providing for the treatment of detainees or defendants in such a manner as to 'preserve dignity', or by the simple assurance that 'human dignity is guaranteed' (Iraq). This is an opposite approach to a number of constitutions that specifically order criminal penalties for those who commit the crime of torture or violate the prohibition on this (Syria, Article 28, para. 3, and Bahrain, Article 19 (d)). Perhaps the strongest deterrent against torture is that found in Articles 19 and 42 of the Egyptian Constitution, which state that, where confession can be shown to have been extracted under various forms of coercion, threat or torture, then such confession is null and void.

Of special note is the text of Article 45 of the Algerian Constitution, which states that, at the end of the initial detention period, the detainee must undergo a medical examination should he request one; and that he must be informed of such a possibility. This text, it would seem, has been used as an alternative to a clear proscription of torture. Nevertheless, although medical examination is indeed one of the more important deterrents to torture, it must be seriously open to doubt whether this particular text provides adequate protection, in that it places the onus of demanding such an examination on the detainee, and that only at the end of the detention period. The state's responsibility extends only to informing the detainee of his right in this respect.

II.5 Non-discrimination and equality before the law

All Arab constitutions include the principle of equality before the law in clear and straightforward language, saying that all 'people' or 'citizens' are equal before the law. Article 40 of the Egyptian Constitution is representative of the kind of language used in almost all the constitutions:

> All citizens are equal before the law. They are equal in public rights and duties with no discrimination between them as to sex, ethnic origins, language, religion or creed.

The only constitutions that do not include the phrase 'public rights and duties' are those of Iraq, Morocco, the United Arab Emirates and the Saudi Basic Law. Most constitutions are, therefore, consistent with the International Covenant on Civil and Political Rights, albeit with minor differences of expression. An exception is the ICCPR's prohibition of discrimination on the basis of 'political or other opinion', and 'property, birth or other status', which are missing. These are replaced in some constitutions by 'social status' or 'place of residence', and the Yemeni Constitution includes 'occupation'. The Lebanese Constitution, on the other hand, simplifies the whole matter by stating: 'All Lebanese are equal before the law ... without any distinction' (Article 7).

The Saudi Basic Law makes no mention of equality before the law, and does not proscribe discrimination, and the Libyan Green Charter also makes no mention of non-discrimination before the law. The Charter is, however, of particular interest in that Article 17 includes expressions that seem more spiritual and proselytic than constitutional, referring to the equal right of members of society:

> to share in the benefits, advantages, values and principles which are the fruit of
> harmony, cohesion, unity, affinity and affection among the family, the tribe, the
> nation and mankind.[12]

A judge would be in no enviable position trying to interpret these phrases, which seem very much like a two-edged sword; protecting from discrimination on the one hand, and, on the other, severely restricting the right to be different. The Green Charter also contains a firm text regarding the protection of minorities:

> All nations, all peoples and all national communities have the right to live freely,
> according to their own choices and the principles of self-determination. They
> have the right to establish their national identity. Minorities have the right to
> safeguard their own entity and heritage. The legitimate aspirations of those
> minorities may not be repressed. Minorities may not be forcibly assimilated
> either within one or several nations or national communities. (Article 16.)

Despite the trap laid in the phrase 'legitimate aspirations', this article remains one of the strongest expressions vis-à-vis minority protection in Arab constitutions and other documents.

II.6 Legal rights: presumption of innocence and the right to defence

As in the previous case, most Arab constitutions contain guarantees for a fair trial and for presumption of innocence until conviction by a 'trial' or a 'legal trial'. There are, however, some exceptions. The constitutions of Jordan and Morocco are entirely silent on presumption of innocence, as are the Libyan Green Charter and the Saudi Basic Law. The Lebanese Constitution, on the other hand, includes in its provisions that the law determines the 'conditions and limits of judicial guarantees' (Article 20) – which in reality is no guarantee at all.

As for the right to defend oneself, we find this, constitutionally, either included in provisions detailing a number of other rights, as in the constitutions of Kuwait, Bahrain and others, or in separate articles, independently or as a subsidiary. It is covered quite extensively, and in clear language, in a number of constitutions, such as those of Algeria, Egypt, Qatar and Syria. For example, Article 20 (b) of the Iraqi Constitution defines the right to defend oneself as 'a sacrosanct right in all stages of interrogation and trial in accordance with the law'. Some constitutions focus on the role of lawyers and guarantee the right to representation; the Bahraini Constitution does so in Article 20 (c), which states that anyone accused of a crime must have a lawyer of his choosing for his defence. The Egyptian Constitution goes a step further, in its Article 69, in providing for financial assistance to facilitate access to justice. The Yemeni Constitution provides anyone 'whose freedom is restricted' an additional right that seems to be adopted from the American experience: namely, 'the right to remain silent and to speak only in the presence of a lawyer' (Article 32). With one hand, the Emirates Constitution gives the accused the right 'to engage a competent person to defend him during trial', while taking this right away with the other hand: it is for the law to determine 'the situations where a lawyer should be present on behalf of a client' (Article 28). Thus it leaves ample room for trial without defence.

It is worth noting that most constitutions discuss 'necessary guarantees' and the 'conditions and limits of judicial guarantees', referring them to the law for specification without providing sufficient constitutional determination of the scope of these guarantees and conditions. This leaves a very wide margin for interpretation vis-à-vis the actual details of penal and criminal laws, with a clear potential for totally undermining the effectiveness of the guarantees in question.

II.7   Right to a fair trial and other judicial guarantees

The first observation to make is that we find only minimal mention of the right to a fair trial in constitutional provisions under the chapters related to citizens' rights and fundamental freedoms. We need to read these provisions together with others, under the chapters related to the judicial authority, or judicial 'system' or 'rule of law'. These provisions are mostly of a general character, aimed at organizing and defining the role of the judiciary and its responsibilities, and not designed to provide a definition of citizens' rights. As such, we must read these combinations of provisions if we seek a clear picture of the extent of protection in the constitutions.

The right to fair trial has five essential components, as articulated by Article 14, paragraph 1, of the International Covenant:

> ... In the determination of any criminal charge against him, or of his rights and obligations in a suit of law, everyone shall be entitled to a *fair* and *public* hearing by a *competent*, *independent* and *impartial* tribunal established by law. [My italics.]

When we examine Arab constitutions in the light of these five elements, we find them sorely lacking, unable to provide an individual on trial with more than minimal effective guarantees. A clear declaration or guarantee of a fair or impartial trial is exceptionally found in the Constitution of the United Arab Emirates, under Article 28, which speaks of presumption of innocence in a trial which is 'legal and fair'; and a similar provision is found in Article 11 of the Qatari Constitution. Only six constitutions (Algeria, Bahrain, Egypt, Iraq, Jordan and Kuwait) require that trials be public.

Nearly all constitutions allow for secret trials under exceptional circumstances (e.g., Kuwait, Article 165), or if the court decides to make the trial secret (Iraq, Article 20 (c)). Some constitutions define the purpose of secrecy more specifically: for example, for the protection of public order (Egypt, Article 169, and Jordan, Article 101 (2)). These are the only restrictions consistent with the standards laid down by Article 14 of the International Covenant. Moreover, there are no Arab constitutional provisions guaranteeing accused individuals the right to appear before a 'competent, independent and impartial' tribunal.

There are broad guarantees for the independence of the judiciary in all Arab constitutions, without exception. We find these provisions stating that judges are subject 'only to the law' and that 'interference by any authority' in the work of the judiciary is impermissible; and sometimes simply that 'the judicial authority is independent'. These texts are general, and would seem to point to the principle as a principle, with no serious effort made to put in place effective guarantees capable of implementation; especially when we recall that all constitutions leave principles and guarantees to the law for definition and enforcement. Some constitutions tie the general principle of judicial independence to individuals' rights, through a text such as the following: 'The honour and conscience and impartiality of judges is a guarantee of people's rights and freedoms' (Syria, Article 133 (2)); or: 'The honour and integrity of judges and their justice is the basis of authority and a guarantee of rights and liberties' (Kuwait, Article 162).

Most constitutions guarantee access to justice and the right to litigate, but in brief, almost cryptic language that essentially refers to access to adjudication in civil matters arising between citizens. It is not clear that this includes access to justice against the authorities. Only four constitutions (Yemen, Emirates, Algeria and Egypt) specifically guarantee the protection of individuals from the authorities' abuse of their rights, but still in rather loose language. For example, Article 34 of the Yemeni Constitution guarantees a citizen's right 'to appeal to the judiciary for the protection of his *legitimate* rights and interest. He has the right to present complaints, criticisms and suggestions to the state apparatus directly or indirectly'. [My italics.] Only two constitutions bolster this right by providing the right of compensation for damage resulting from abuse of rights, and the Egyptian Constitution, in Article 57, is clearer than the Algerian in the specificity of its language:

> Any assault upon personal freedom or the sanctity of citizens' private lives and other rights and public freedoms guaranteed by the Constitution and the law is a crime, where the civil or criminal case resultant therefrom is not ameliorated by statutes of limitation. The State shall grant a fair compensation to the victims of such an assault.

III. Implementation of (and obstacles to) constitutional guarantees

As stated earlier, one cannot gain a clear and complete understanding of the role of Arab constitutions in the protection of guaranteed rights without examining the implementation of such guarantees and the factors affecting this. As we shall see in the following section, the situation in the Arab world, in this regard, is so denigrated that constitutional protection of citizens' rights in the Arab states can barely be said to exist. This is for a variety of reasons.

III.1 Judicial supervision

Independent judicial supervision over the constitutionality of laws, and over the legality of administrative and executive action, is a necessary prerequisite for the proper functioning of the rule of law in any society.[13] In the case of most Arab countries, this is one of the weaker links vis-à-vis the effective implementation of constitutional guarantees of civil and political rights.

Some constitutions expressly provide for the establishment of a high court or constitutional court with authority to review the constitutionality of laws and administrative orders made by government. Few, however, contain provisions for citizens seeking redress from violations. Article 124 (a) of the Yemeni Constitution does in fact establish a Supreme Court whose competence includes, *inter alia,* verification of the constitutionality of 'laws, statutes, regulations and decrees'. In the Egyptian Constitution, Article 174 describes the Supreme Constitutional Court as 'an independent judicial body'; and Article 175 charges the court with 'sole judicial control in respect of the constitutionality of laws and regulations' as well as 'interpretation of legislative texts'. The Egyptian Constitution may indeed be the most effective of all at the present day, for the Egyptian Supreme Constitutional Court has recently ruled a number of laws unconstitutional, including Association Law 153 (1999), now cancelled. In 2001, the SCC declared recent elections unconstitutional on the grounds that they had been undertaken without judicial supervision.

The new Sudanese Constitution (1998) establishes a constitutional court that must be 'the guardian of the Constitution' (Article 105), and it is at present the only Arab constitution that gives authority for its Constitutional Court to review 'cases brought by those claiming abuse of freedoms or rights guaranteed by the Constitution'. This court has, however, yet to be constituted. The Sudan is still in the midst of political crisis, and it is debatable whether the Sudanese judiciary remains capable in practice of protecting rights or constitutional guarantees.[14]

A number of constitutions provide for a high court of one kind or another, or for a 'judicial body' with functions or responsibilities related to the constitutions. The competence, jurisdiction and organization of these bodies are, however, subject to the law for clarification. Article 173 of the Kuwaiti Constitution simply states that the 'law shall specify the judicial body competent to decide upon disputes relating to the constitutionality of laws and regulations and shall determine its jurisdiction and procedures', making no reference to citizens' rights. Article 100 of the Jordanian Constitution mentions a 'special law' that details the formation of courts, and provides for 'the establishment of a High Court of Justice'.

Three constitutions (Iraq, Qatar and Lebanon) do not establish a constitutional or other court of this order, and consequently no judicial body has authority to adjudicate on conflicts of a constitutional nature. A number of constitutions provide for judicial supervision over the actions of ministers or government employees, but it would seem that these are aimed at administrative abuses and misuse of authority rather than designed to deal with violations of citizens' rights. For example, Chapter Six of the Moroccan Constitution discusses a constitutional council with authority to inspect the constitutionality of laws and the conduct of elections (Article 81). However, the authority to investigate the matter of criminal responsibility by government functionaries 'for felonies and misdemeanours committed in the course of performing their duties' is referred to a high court (Article 88). This is as close as the Moroccan Constitution gets to the protection of citizens' rights.

The crucial point is that independent judicial watch over citizens' enjoyment of their constitutional rights is very weak in the Arab states. Only a few countries, like Egypt and Sudan, are exceptions, in theory at least. Perhaps the best example is that provided by the Syrian Constitution, where we find the most numerous articles, and the widest scope, for formation and definition of the authority of a constitutional court, but with the opposite effect on the rule of law. Article 139, for example, provides for a constitutional court composed of five members, appointed by the President by decree. This seems unremarkable, until we note that membership of the court is for four years only, renewable (Article 141). A number of procedural provisions forestall the consideration of cases: only the President, or a percentage of People's Assembly members, can bring cases before the court (Article 147). Also, Article 146 undermines the authority of the court by the following provision:

> The Supreme Constitutional Court shall have no authority to examine those laws which the President of the Republic submits to public referendum and which are approved by the People's Assembly.

The implication is that the President has the right to add to or take away from the constitution through a popular referendum. It is clear, in fact, from the foregoing, that the work of the Syrian constitutional court is totally at the mercy of the President of the Republic.

The Syrian example perhaps best sums up how weak constitutional supervision is over the legislative or executive authorities in the Arab world. It is the law itself that is supervised, rather than the constitution, or the president or head of state. The situation has inspired one Arab lawyer to say as follows:

> There is no supervision of any kind to stand watch, and where some forms of supervision (constitutional and administrative courts) are found in some Arab countries, their judgments are most often not adhered to; or [we find that] the legislative authority – always supportive of the executive that created it – will enact new legislation to circumvent judicial rulings.[15]

III.2 The executive authority

According to Dr 'Abd al-Ghani al-Mani': 'Most constitutions were framed in accordance with the wishes of a ruler, or one part of society, or foreigners. Rare are the constitutions springing from a collective will on the part of all sectors of society.'[16]

Arab constitutions, whether the states are monarchies, socialist, or parliamentary pluralist, clearly state that sovereignty belongs to the people, or that the people are the source of all authority. Yet monarchies, socialist republics, one-party states, those based on political pluralism – all are largely alike with respect to the rights and authority of their president or monarch. Arab constitutions give the head of state a number of authorities and privileges that allow him absolute or near-absolute control in the affairs of the state or its citizenry. These authorities include:

- An executive power exercised personally, or through a cabinet of ministers or ministerial committee, which in turn appoints and dismisses by personal decision of the head of state.
- Participation in the legislative process, and, in some cases, the right to legislate by decree. Usually (though not always), presidential legislation requires ratification by a parliament or a people's assembly, which is normally under the total control of the President/King/Emir, either personally or through the ruling party. Sometimes a constitution may require the approval of presidential legislation through a public referendum.
- Extraordinary powers in the appointment and dismissal of major state functionaries, including administrative, judicial and military authorities. In some cases this even includes members of parliament or consultative (*shura*) councils and others.

How do constitutions define the accession to power of a head of state? First of all, we should recall that eight of the Arab states are monarchies, headed by a King, or Sultan, or Emir, who accedes to power by heredity. There are only four republics with constitutional texts requiring direct election of the president by the people, albeit with varying degrees of guarantee for freedom of candidature or election. In Tunisia, for example, the President is to be chosen through 'general, free and direct elections' (Article 39), while Article 36 of the Sudanese Constitution states, more briefly, that 'the President is elected by the people'. The President of Yemen is chosen through 'competitive elections' (Article 107 (a)), and in Algeria through 'general, direct and secret ballot' (Article 71). Significantly, three of these four constitutions (the exception being the Tunisian) have been adopted only within the past six years. In other Arab states, the head of government is elected indirectly through a council of representatives (Lebanon, Articles 73–75), or else he can be nominated by a people's assembly, with the nomination confirmed by public referendum thereafter (Egypt, Iraq, Algeria and Syria). In these cases, governments follow a one-party system, or are controlled by one party for several decades, despite the formal existence of a multi-party system. In all these cases, the single party and its president exercise total control over parliaments or people's assemblies, thereby assuring the party's successive choice of the president. The citizenry as a whole has only one choice, which is to confirm the sole candidate for the office, usually by near total consensus or more than 90 per cent of the votes.

Finally, we should note the five constitutions that prevent the president from enjoying more than two consecutive terms in office: those of Algeria, Lebanon, Yemen, Sudan and Tunisia. The Tunisian regime is in fact currently seeking out a loophole in the country's constitution or law to allow President Zein El-Abedeen Ben Ali to continue his rule. We should also note that most Arab constitutions grant the president legal immunity in the performance of his duties, cases of high treason or constitutional violation excepted. The president's near-absolute authority makes his trial or conviction next door to impossible.

III.3 States of Emergency: declared and undeclared

The powers and competence of the executive include the declaration of states of emergency. Article 4 of the International Covenant on Civil and Political Rights recognizes temporary circumstances which 'threaten the life of the nation', and which may require the declaration of a state of emergency whereby some civil and political rights are suspended. Nevertheless, the Covenant regards states of emergency as quite exceptional; and it provides that such measures should be taken 'to the extent strictly required by the exigencies of the situation', and should be declared and annulled within a specified period of time. The Covenant also lists the rights and freedoms that cannot be derogated from or violated during the period of emergency, even under the most difficult conditions.

For all that, states of emergency in the Arab world have become so widespread that, far from being the exception, they have actually become the rule, with normalcy itself exceptional. States commonly declare a state of emergency as a temporary measure, to deal with some political crisis, instability, social disturbance or natural disaster. This practice has become more frequent with the

rise of Islamic fundamentalism, especially its armed variety. States of emergency have been repeatedly declared in Algeria since 1988, and are continuing
with the continuation of the brutal massacres in that sad country. In Syria, a
state of emergency has been in force since 1967, as it also has in Egypt apart
from one brief respite between May 1980 and October 1981, when President
Anwar Sadat was assassinated; it has been renewed every three years since.
Such declaration of emergency has been automatically followed by the promulgation of emergency laws, like Law 162 (1958),[17] which undermines numerous rights and liberties. Article 3 of this law, for instance, imposes a number of
restrictions on freedom of opinion and expression, including the imposition of
censorship over the media and correspondence, authority to close print shops,
authority to confiscate books, and other forms of media control. A number
of these restrictions are still on the books, albeit used only in exceptional cases.
As such, the human rights and citizens' rights guaranteed in the Egyptian
Constitution are actually hostages to government whim.[18]

Yet in some states it is not necessary to declare a formal state of emergency,
by presidential or royal decree, for the constitution or certain of its provisions
to be suspended. Armed conflict and civil wars have conflagrated in Lebanon,
Somalia, Sudan, Iraq, Kuwait, Algeria, Yemen, Mauritania and Djibouti, and
have enforced effective suspension of their constitutions following the total
collapse of government authority; Lebanon and Somalia are potent examples.
It might be said that more than half the Arab constitutions – or significant por-
tions of them at least, relating to the protection of civil and political rights – are
inoperable as a result of declared and undeclared states of emergency.

III.4 Exceptional courts

States of emergency also endow the head of state with extraordinary powers,
notably that of issuing 'temporary' decisions that usually include the establishment of exceptional emergency courts. Arab jurists and human rights activists
regard these courts as one of the primary violators of human rights in the
region.[19] In most Arab states, cases having to do with state security – and state
security has rather broad interpretations that include the criminalization of
many acts deemed to be of a political nature – are handed over to a parallel judiciary taking different forms: 'state security', 'exceptional' or 'military' courts.
Mostly these courts are formed by emergency regulations issued under a state
of emergency. At other times, they are established by special laws that do not
require a state of emergency to exist or to be formally declared. In Iraq, for
example, the Revolutionary Court was established in Baghdad by law, with

competence to adjudicate political and security crimes directly submitted by the President's office. The judgements of the Revolutionary Courts are final and not subject to appeal or other judicial review.[20]

When the Jordanian National Concordance was ratified in 1991, after the cancellation of the state of emergency in force there since 1967, the Jordanian judiciary did acquire a semblance of independence. Nevertheless, the exceptional courts were not disbanded and still investigate cases of a political nature. Such courts have also been in operation in Tunisia since the conspiracy trials of August 1992. In Egypt, similarly, civilians periodically appear before military courts under the consistently renewed state of emergency. In Syria, Presidential Decree No. 6 of 1965 established an exceptional military court charged with political crimes. These courts were replaced by what are called 'Field Courts' in August 1986 (Decree 109), a few months after the formation of the State Security Court in accordance with Decree No. 47. Strangest of all, even the Palestinian Authority, elected under the Oslo interim agreements, established a State Security Court before the state itself was established![21] This court, like other exceptional courts of its ilk in the region, is gravely lacking in fair trial procedures.

Finally, we should note that these exceptional courts work very closely with the office of the head of state. Cases are referred to it either by presidential or royal decree, or by informal decision through a law that defines the authorities and establishes 'political crimes', meaning that the accused may be automatically referred to such a court. In most states, there are presidential or royal authorities to ratify these courts' decisions, reduce the penalties or issue an amnesty.

Conclusions and recommendations

This brief study is not intended to provide a comprehensive picture of Arab constitutional guarantees of civil and political rights. Rather, it attempts to focus on the crucial issues relevant to strengthening the enjoyment of those rights. In the light of the points made above, we may summarize the salient issues as follows:

*   Arab constitutions, with few exceptions and with varying degrees of detail and specificity, generally guarantee most human rights and fundamental freedoms. While they differ from one another in how they specifically guarantee civil and political rights, they are fundamentally similar in that

the guarantees are not adequate for safety, and are inconsistent with the spirit of the International Covenant on Civil and Political Rights, if not with the text itself.

- There are severe restrictions on Arab citizens' enjoyment of their rights in reality. The first restriction is found in the language of the constitutional provisions, which is generally rather loose and imprecise, and consequently subject to a broad range of interpretation. In any case, the chances for exploring interpretations – before the courts, for example – are minimal.

- The most important undermining factor is that most Arab constitutional provisions concerning the rights and duties of citizens refer their further interpretation, and the manner in which citizens may enjoy them, to the law. While this brief study has not been able to cover criminal or civil laws, it should nevertheless be said that rights in these cases are interpreted so narrowly as to render them devoid of substantive content.

- There is a severe absenting of the role of the courts and the judiciary in most constitutions, and a near total lack of independent judicial review of administrative and executive decisions. Moreover, in some countries access for citizens seeking redress for violations of their constitutional rights is severely limited or non-existent.

- Absolute or near absolute scope for the power of the head of state, emir or king is one of the most important factors restricting Arab citizens' enjoyment of their civil and political rights. This in turn restricts the fundamental role of the legislative and judicial authorities, and places insurmountable obstacles before citizens' right to participate in the conduct of public affairs.

- The phenomenon of declared states of emergency in the Arab world has created a most difficult situation for implementing constitutional guarantees of civil and political rights. Most of these rights are suspended in a state of emergency; such a state has been in force in seven Arab countries for decades, and will probably continue. Thus, the exception has become the rule and vice-versa.

- Exceptional and state security courts, created under powers of emergency but continuing even after these have been lifted, are the greatest danger for the independence of the judiciary and for human rights. They create a shadow judiciary that undermines normal courts and the rule of law. In this shadow, the Arab citizen is liable at any moment to trials lacking in necessary fair trial standards. The executive authority has maximum influence and the final decision in dragging citizens before those courts for entirely political reasons. Consequently, these courts become a political tool in the hands of the ruling authorities.

We must conclude that Arab constitutions, as they exist at the present day, express the vision and will of the ruling elites in these countries and are designed to guarantee the security of these elites. They do not express the will of the peoples of the countries in question, nor do they guarantee these people's rights. They may claim to respect human rights theoretically and in principle, but they more accurately express the lack of confidence executive authorities have in the citizenry. Restrictions on the enjoyment of human rights and fundamental freedoms are such that, in practice, the rights are rendered devoid of content.

Chapter 20: Arab political parties and human rights

Muhammad al-Sayyid Saʻid

Introduction

Why should we be interested in identifying the status of Arab political parties within the juristic arena, and in their position vis-à-vis international legal instruments and human rights systems in general? The need for such an inquiry springs from three main and broadly distinct considerations.

The first consideration is historical. A number of Arab countries, notably Egypt, Syria, Iraq, Sudan, Tunisia and Morocco, underwent an early phase of constitutional development before falling prey to European imperialism, or in the course of their struggle for and subsequent achievement of independence. This dimension is of particular significance, rebutting as it does conclusions drawn from a cultural perspective that condemns Arab culture as intrinsically anti-democratic and anti-modernistic. Arab political culture has developed its own model for drawing on modernistic achievements consistent with its aspirations, and has succeeded, at least in part, in accommodating and modifying a number of salient achievements, including the constitutional movement and the democratic model of government within which the political party plays a vital role. These developments had in fact been initiated long before some countries in Eastern and Central Europe, and in Asia, began to follow the democratic option.

At the same time, these facts pose a new question about the actual reasons for the failure of constitutional democratic development and for the abrupt interruption of these moves shortly after the realization of independence. The many answers commonly given to this question seem both insufficient and shallow. The importance of the question itself, however, goes far beyond an interest in history; it is also capable of shedding some light on the road to the future.

The second dimension covers the current situation. Since the actual achievement of independence, a curtain has fallen on the issue of democracy in the direct and valid sense of the term. Although a number of countries have introduced certain political and constitutional reforms leading, eventually, to a transition to multi-party systems, we have not in reality left the stage of the authoritarian despotic state with its family, religious, sectarian or conservative variations.[1] Under the circumstances, we cannot talk about actual parties, whether in power or in opposition. As long as the essence of the democratic concept is absent and there is no genuine organization and peaceful competition for higher political offices and government posts, and as long as channels for the circulation of power remain blocked, it will be impossible for true parties to emerge.[2]

In this context, our inquiry into position and attitude vis-à-vis the human rights system is not a matter of the impact of these parties on the state regime, and, consequently, on the legislation and practice of human rights. The significance lies rather in helping us appreciate the degree to which human rights have been accepted in the political formation of Arab countries, this providing one measure for an assessment of the human rights issue in the Arab world.

The third dimension relates to the conceptualization of future strategies aimed at consolidating the democratic and legal struggle, and at identifying the optimum venues for achieving the objectives of this struggle in the Arab context. This dimension delineates the position and attitude of the parties as focal points for cultural, economic and social arrangements and results, and also demonstrates the outcome of negative and positive forces vis-à-vis the adoption of the human rights system in the Arab world.

This study will concentrate primarily on the second dimension, leaving the first for another form of historical examination, and confining itself, as far as the third is concerned, to pointing out some essential conclusions. As such, our analysis will fall into three main parts. The first will discuss the state of Arab 'political parties' in the context of authoritarian regimes. The second will cover the actual and changing positions of the current parties in relation to the human rights system. The last part represents an attempt to understand the patterns and significance of transformation in the system of the Arab state, and their underlying legal implications, in the light of potential future development.

I. The state of Arab political parties

The notion of 'the political party' faces serious challenges at the international level, and within western democracies in particular. These challenges stem from deep-seated changes within political formations in the more highly developed societies as a result of the current technological revolution, and from subsequent changes in the international division of labour and the nature of social work processes, and, in turn, in class and partisan formations and in modes of communication and political thought.[3]

For all the growing depreciation of its significance, the political party remains an integral and inseparable mechanism for political action within the democratic system. Still more important is the fact that the development of a political party, in the strict sense of the term, is inconceivable outside a democratic system.[4] In other words, the essential foundations of a political party cannot be set in place in the absence of democracy, irrespective of the position of the party vis-à-vis the power of the state, or of its location within the ruling regime or in the opposition camp.

It goes without saying that the Arab world continues to strive within the limitations and constraints of authoritarian patterns of government, whereby power generates power and where rulers are not elected to their offices through popular, free and open elections under the umbrella of democratic constitutional law.

The limited political reforms undertaken, at various times in the 1980s and 1990s, in 13 Arab countries have not led to any transition to democratic systems, being rather confined to 'relative political relaxation or rapprochement but without democracy'. The circulation of power is virtually ruled out. The exception seen in Morocco after the 1997 elections does not significantly change this conclusion.[5]

Given the continuation of the authoritarian state, the absence of any circulation of power and the sustained power of a legislative structure opposed to essential freedoms and rights, party formations have developed a range of common basic characteristics. The first of these traits is the nominal dependence of the political authority on the state party to provide a democratic justification for consolidating powers in the hands of the state bureaucracy, and particularly within the security and military systems. There is no rational justification whatever for describing these formations as 'ruling parties', since they are not actually ruling parties or even formations with the characteristics of parties as known in democratic societies. Perhaps the only common denominator with respect to these 'parties' is the preference shown to a variety of social segments, for various reasons, so as to allow them to approach and support the centre of power without necessarily enjoying popular approval or obtaining votes in their electoral constituencies – without, indeed, exerting any serious effort to gain support and votes in non-competitive elections. This dichotomy has turned parties into lifeless structures, called to action only for ceremonial functions outside election seasons in which the electoral process is often in any case rigged.

Accordingly, these parties may be dismantled, or inclined to shift their loyalty from one power centre to another; or they may be prepared to reconcile and accommodate themselves to drastic changes in overall state policy. Parties nevertheless fulfil specific objective roles within the framework of the authoritarian state. They represent channels for distribution and redistribution, and a reserve camp from which nominations are drawn for essential political offices. At certain times they entrench the authority of the state deep into the social structure, through such sophisticated mechanisms as buying the loyalty of certain sectors, or taking the government's side (especially in the context of powerful tribal and clan alliances), or, above all, providing a deceptive nominal democratic cover for state actions.

The second characteristic is the presence of a strong tendency to excessive and continuous multi-party development. In most Arab countries that adopt political liberalization without real democracy, formal parties may number more than ten – a situation that cannot be justified by the level of voting or of general political interest. The cause of this extravagant plurality is the lack of any requirement for concluding major alliances or initiating party mergers. The situation also reflects the absence of any genuine opportunity for circulating authority or competing with the 'ruling' party and pushing it from its dominant position. This excessive plurality may also provide formal cover for regional, sectarian or tribal agglomerations. In the final analysis, the parties in question are all competing for the loyalty of the middle classes and rarely find their way into the structures of the higher social class.

The third of these features is a marked and growing loss of weight in political opposition parties – whether civil or secular in character – and a recession in mass support, together with a disintegration of organized political structures over time. This trait is closely associated with the blockage of power circulation, the systemic rigging of public elections (in both legislation and practice) and the propensity of the state bureaucracy to place its weighty influence behind government candidates, against political opposition.

The deteriorating position of most opposition parties in Arab countries that have adopted this model for the electoral system has led to the last support drifting away from these parties. The result is severe crisis, both domestic and external.[6]

All this has led, significantly, to the development of a further and highly important feature in Arab political formations. Their structures have come to embody a 'bi-polarity' between the 'state party' on the one hand and the

'Islamic parties and movements' on the other. At a time when non-religious opposition parties seem suspended in mid air, the Islamist opposition has taken root in social reality, and on the political scene, irrespective of whether or not it enjoys legitimacy. At other times this bi-polarity has taken the form of an aggregation of civil parties opposing an authoritarian regime acting in the name of Islamic rule, as in Sudan.[7]

The fourth feature is the growing social tendency away from party politics. This sense of political apathy is coupled with a recession in the social bloc that has embodied political or party communities with all their categories and elements, and with a decrease in the social volume of interest in party life. This bloc is composed of different social categories that have their agenda in terms of daily life, civil affairs and local reality, and are, as such, inclined to vote for individual rather than party candidates. These categories may give a measure of encouragement to pro-Islamic candidates but do not generally attach much weight to their political affiliations. Such groups and categories form the ever-expanding basis for a lack of mobility in the political scene, regardless of its precise nature.[8]

The apparent formal stability of the party structure can barely conceal the violent changes actually taking place within; changes, it might be argued, that have led to a marginalization of the concept of political parties in the Arab world. Such political structures are becoming, increasingly, empty and abandoned formations. This tendency is linked to a lack of confidence in their ability to work change through party mechanisms as opposed to bureaucratic channels or other venues of civil society.

In the light of all these features and characteristics, one might conceptualize a general theory of political and party life in the shadow of late authoritarian regimes. Assuming authoritarian rule to be passing through its final stages – marked by a measure of relative political liberalization without actual democratic transition or even restricted pluralism – we might discern some general tendencies in most Arab societies: indications that political and party life is losing its vitality, with a growing hostility toward party politics in general.

It may be necessary to carry out some theoretical and field investigation to support this conclusion or that theory in general. We cannot state, decisively and conclusively, that authoritarian regimes are now in their last phases. Such forms of government may implode in civil wars, as is the case in Algeria. This possibility, in itself, represents an adverse model or a counter argument against such theorization.

We do, however, need to explore the correlation between, on the one hand, the development of informal policies (clandestine or non-legalized activity and non-party or non-legalized activities such as family relationships, and sectarian or tribal politics), and, on the other, the formal legal positions involved.

As a preparation for such a coherent theory, to explain the current nature of political and party life in the Arab world, it may be sufficient to point out the present, acute crisis that exists in the domestic and external context alike.

II. Party positions and human rights

The attitudes of Arab political parties to the issue of human rights may be considered from different viewpoints. Here we shall first explore these positions at the level of ideology and political discourse, then in terms of actual practice. We shall consider the specific positions of different party and ideological formations, bringing out some of the consequences of interaction among these formations on the political scene in a number of Arab countries. An attempt will then be made to draw some general conclusions from this analysis.

II.1 Patterns of ideological and party formation

As noted earlier, we shall not here be providing a strict technical definition of a political party, or of its legal form, in accordance with prescriptions adopted in democratic societies. Similarly, we shall not be making any distinction between forums for current political movements and groupings and parties in the strict sense of the term, or between clandestine, public, legalized or non-legalized parties, so long as these stem from a relatively concrete political and ideological position.

From this perspective, it may be argued that the Arab world has seen a relative materialization of five political/party formations: bureaucratic/technocratic parties; radical/pan-national parties; Islamist parties; communist parties; and liberal parties. The basic positions of these vis-à-vis the human rights issue, at the levels of ideology/political programmes and actual practice, may be identified as follows.

II.1.1 Technocratic parties

Unlike the political party that develops around a certain ideological discourse and a political programme, and also around certain class, sectarian and perhaps ethnic interests, technocratic and functional groups have their origin, in the first instance, as unions, scientific societies and NGOs. Bureaucratic and technological parties may spring up even in western democracies. One might, indeed, argue that this pattern of party formation is becoming increasingly pervasive in some European democracies.

This situation arises when certain interest groups move away from the current ideology and present themselves to society as a grouping of technocrats, professionals and scientists with no clear political affiliation to any particular ideology. Parties marked, in the past, by specific ideological orientations have developed into techno-parties; and, in the interim, differences and conflicts among various major ideologies have gradually disappeared. As such, essential points of distinction among the political programmes of these parties have tended to become a matter of technical and technological definition rather than ideological differentiation.[9]

In the Arab world, however, the rise of techno-bureaucratic parties has sprung from factors and causes quite different from those in Western democracies. The prototypes for these parties go back to the crisis of the semi-liberal political period before actual independence, which was characterized by frequent constitutional and political transformations and, on occasion, by military coups. In the course of this crisis, Egypt saw the emergence of what were called 'administrative parties' supporting the regime during these critical periods. They were supposed to run and operate the administrative state apparatus until government was formed through general elections. These parties had short-term functions in preparing for elections after the resignation or dismissal of a particular government that had enjoyed a parliamentary majority.[10]

Following independence, these administrative–technocratic–bureaucratic parties merged under the auspices of – and as an integral element of – the overwhelming umbrella of the authoritarian regime in some Arab countries.[11]

These parties emerge, then swiftly disintegrate unnoticed, as transient and provisional structures, often exercising a form of 'nominal' rule to provide a civilian cover for military rule and to give a government of this type the character and characteristics of a natural and normal permanency. The head of state may resort to such structures to consolidate his power against opposing ideologies and parties, perhaps with additional support from a seemingly parliamentarian system.

In either case, the political regime deals strictly and rigorously with party or ideological opposition, even when such a legislative and political approach is in direct violation of democratic requirements. There is also a third mode whereby techno-bureaucratic parties are born: within the framework of the 'liberalization without democracy' model where the authoritarian regime shows a conspicuous interest in democratic appearance, legalizing party pluralism and heralding parliamentary elections. The bureau-technocratic formation then turns into a 'state party', exercising nominal rule and failing to observe the restrictions or considerations that regulate parliamentary systems.

There are many models for all these patterns. One prominent model of the first type was the socialist union during the strict military rule of former president Ja'far Numeiry in the Sudan. Of the second type, we see an example in Morocco, where many parties were established in the name of, and with the support of, King Hassan II, including the Shura and al-Istiqlal parties, the popular movement (*Al-Haraka al-Sha'biyya al-Dusturiyya wa 'l-Dimuqratiyya*), the national liberal grouping, the National Democratic Party, etc.

The third type, which operates within a 'liberalization without democracy' framework, is currently represented in Egypt, by the National Democratic Party which has been in nominal power since 1978, and in Tunisia, where the Destour Party has been in government since independence.[12]

The discourses of the techno-bureaucratic parties and their positions in relation to democracy and human rights vary with the overall attitudes of actual power and of the existing head of state. Often they reconcile themselves, accommodating and justifying the status quo. More often still, they establish their discourse on the basis of an ideological 'medium' or centre, between right and left, or between the traditional and liberal parties on the one hand and the radical and socialist/leftist parties on the other. In this sense, such parties have no problem with democracy in principle, but they often introduce the concept of national distinctiveness and cultural peculiarity to justify the absence of actual democracy, and to help bring into being exceptional and extraordinary legislation which, in effect, annuls or constrains essential liberties and rights.[13]

Under the circumstances, these groups and political formations ruling in symbolic fashion only, under an authoritarian regime, can hardly qualify as techno-bureaucratic parties. They simply accommodate and justify the existing or changing positions of the head of state. They may be given that name only if we consider the actual or potential ideology of the groups that constitute the middle or higher leaderships in these parties.

Such ideologies can be envisaged in terms of mental profiles that part ways with the major ideologies prevailing in the world, and especially in the Arab world. These profiles involve a common belief that 'politics' in general and 'party politics' in particular are the direct causes of confusion, chaos and poor performance in public life. The problems of the country can, in their view, be resolved only through scientific and technical venues, i.e. through techno-bureaucratic channels. 'Political stability' tends to be idolized as the 'mind of the state'. This belief drives these groups, objectively and not merely out of moral or political opportunism, to extend their cooperation toward the current political system irrespective of its nature or orientation. Members of these groups often occupy high positions within the state machinery and attract elements that have left major 'ideological' parties. As such, they regard themselves as the true elite of society and the real guardians of the public interest, which is based on the stability of the state. They are consequently eligible to exercise and enjoy their role in governance, albeit in a nominal fashion.

In practice these groups and functionaries launch their political careers with a marked moderation and pragmatism, and, in this respect, may not be opponents of the government of man system or the rule of law principle. In the underlying principles of their original political discourse, they may have been inspired by the Western model of modernization, and bedazzled by its achievements. However, the actual and concrete course of action they take is often subject to the political powers of an authority that is itself largely arbitrary and opposed to the essential constitutional principles of the democratic system. This situation invariably leads them to supply a sustained justification and rationalization for the violation, by the authority, of the values of democracy and human rights. Indeed, they may often be directly involved as instruments of such violations. Such groups, so far from displaying political aversion to violation, end up by positively sanctioning it.

When co-opted by techno-bureaucratic parties, these elements and groups tend to colour their political career with a blend of discourses based on the manipulation of terms and concepts, and on the moulding of themes and sophisticated rationalizations, which, in the final analysis, lack logical integrity and moral honesty. They always maintain a 'democratic' façade, which is adorned with attractive terminology but is geared in practice to justifying every form of violation of public freedoms and human rights. They resort to a hybrid intellectual mishmash based on pretensions of cultural originality and fragments of Marxist, fascist and liberal ideologies, all moulded within a 'neutral' scientific or functional frameworks. Such characteristics have come to stamp formal Arab political thinking. Some Arab intellectuals have described this trend as the conciliatory school.[14]

At the individual level, these categories may be represented by former university professors who entertain the ambition to occupy high positions, with or without past achievements. The general ideological framework for these parties is a blend of folk nationalism and empty scientism (which is different from a sense of Arab nationalism, though not necessarily separate from it).

II.1.2 Pan-national parties

Belief in an immemorial Arab nation, in reunifying this nation by bringing down barriers and frontiers among Arab states, and in opposing all factors of fragmentation and division created by imperialism, are central, focal concepts in pan-national thinking and in the ideology of nationalist parties. Beyond this concept, we see the expanding development of nationalist thought, along with nationalist party programmes, at various stages of modern Arab history.

The Arab nationalist idea emerged in Syria in opposition to the Turanic movement and in direct confrontation with the colonial Ottoman heritage. It was later projected as a political movement supporting the Great Arab Revolt in 1916, but soon lost its impetus in the debacle of the upheaval that followed, when the dynasty of Sharif Hussein and his children allied itself with the British – who subsequently broke their wartime promises to the rebels and themselves replaced the Ottomans as the new colonial power in the Arab East. In the period between the two wars, the Ba'ath party geared itself to take power in Syria, where it had considerable influence among the military personnel, and it took actual control in the 1960s. The Ba'ath party and the Arab Nationalist Movement led the nationalist call. The emergence in Egypt of Nasserism, and its presentation of a radical nationalist discourse, divided the nationalist movement into two major blocs, Nasserite and Ba'athist, and for some time created intense rivalry between them, especially after the Ba'ath party assumed full power in both Syria and Iraq.[15]

The 1967 defeat and the death of Nasser dealt a severe blow to lofty nationalist discourse in Egypt, and Nasserites could develop only minor political parties existing side by side with other opposition parties. The authority of pan-national thought was subsequently centred on the two ruling Ba'ath parties in Syria and Iraq, although the overall nationalist trend went far beyond the influence of these two regimes.

The two parties established brutal political regimes that have since maintained abominable records in the flagrant violation of human rights, both in legislation and in practice. Of all ruling Arab systems, they now represent the two regimes most antagonistic to democracy and human rights and most opposed to the universal human rights system.

Nevertheless, this record of tyranny and repression does not warrant any categorical judgment against nationalist discourse. The Ba'ath parties of Syria and Iraq have not in fact ruled as political parties, except for a short period after the coups that gave them exclusive powers in the two countries. In both cases authority and power swiftly became concentrated in the hands of one person, and implementation, in its broader sense, was actually transferred from the party to the state bureaucracy and to security systems in particular. In the meantime, the two parties underwent two interrelated yet separate processes.

In the first process, and during the critical stages in the development of the two parties, the ideological and political leadership fell victim to the despotism of the system it had struggled to establish. The parties were finally subjected to purges that removed the majority of their intellectual elements at the upper and medium levels. Some members who found themselves outside the party were able to set up small structures of political opposition in exile, under modified party names.[16]

These provided an element of 'democratic' criticism of the arbitrary intellectual and political practices of the party, the state and the higher leadership exercising effective power. Such criticism was a mixture of fragmented commentary and statements of justification, lacking any thorough and comprehensive review of the institutional intellectual and political heritage. It did, however, contain one genuine and original ingredient. Practical and direct experience of the moral, human and political ordeal, and of the brutal and savage political repression of all opposition, deeply shocked enlightened and more honest elements, and prompted them to make a genuine review of the institutional discourse of the nationalist movement and of the Ba'ath party in particular, especially in connection with its disregard and disrespect for democracy and its practical opposition to it.

Some of the more remarkable forms of democratic criticism levelled against violent authoritarian repression, as practised by the Ba'ath party, has in fact issued from prominent intellectual leaderships maintaining a commitment to nationalist thought.

Furthermore, a strong tendency within Arab nationalism presented democracy as a strategic option and defended essential human rights, thus distinguishing itself in sufficiently clear terms from the current thinking and practices of the Ba'ath party in both Syria and Iraq.[17] This tendency converges around the 'Centre for Arab Unity Studies' in Beirut, and around the 'Arab Nationalist Conference', which was developed through an initiative of the Centre as an expression of the framework of Nasserite and other nationalist tendencies outside power in the Arab world.

This school of thought has exerted a remarkable pluralistic effort through its journal *Al-Mustaqbal al-'Arabi* (The Arab Future), and has been a pioneering enterprise in founding the Arab human rights movement. Within this school, we may note many intellectual interpretations of the issue of democracy and the human rights system. Some of these initiatives accept the Universal

Declaration of Human Rights, including international legislation, without reservation. Others express reservation on many of the juristic formulations and emphasize the concept of particularism in the application of some of these rights, while still others accept the overall legal principles but express apprehension or criticism over specific details.[18]

By merging the concept of democracy and the legal idea within the intellectual framework of Arab unity, this salient trend is making a significant contribution to Arab national thought. There are, however, two distinct limitations. On the one hand, this critical trend has little political impact, perhaps in view of the profound changes that have led to abandonment of the nationalist dream of unity in the policies of different Arab countries. The negative impact of Ba'th party practices in Syria and Iraq, together with the widespread political repression in both countries, has, in effect, overshadowed and overruled the positive contributions of the critical trend within the current nationalist movement.

The second limitation lies in the fact that the critical democratic trend within the nationalist movement is still concentrating most of its effort on nationalist struggle rather than on a militant interest in the issue of democracy and human rights. There is, it is true, direct criticism of domestic situations in other Arab countries, but this does not entail any specific and direct commentary on the internal problems in Syria and Iraq. Where there is temporary contradiction between the issue of democracy and what this current views as struggle against the West (as seen, for instance, with the explosion of the second crisis in the Gulf), the final stand has been taken, unhesitatingly, in favour of the latter rather than the former position.

II.1.3 Islamist parties

In the 1980s and 1990s, Islamist political currents, in legalized or non-legalised party structures, rose within the political scene as the most popular and deep-seated opposition movement in many Arab countries. Such countries include Egypt, Algeria, Tunisia, Syria, Yemen, Iraq and even the Gulf States, notably Kuwait, while Sudan is actually ruled by the National Islamic Party, one of the fundamentalist trends within the Islamic movement. Some ruling dynasties in the Gulf also exercise powers in the name of religious legitimacy.

The central concept of the powerful Islamic currents within the Arab world is a return to literal commitment to the Quran, the *sunna* and the tradition of orthodox predecessors, as crystalized in the Sunni or Shi'a schools of thought. Only these are regarded as providing a sound resolution of the current cultural and political crisis of the Islamic world as a whole.

Parallel to this concept is a forceful belief, implicit or explicit, that the world is divided between Muslims and non-Muslims, that the primary objective of the Western-led world system is the destruction of Islam and its civilization and autonomy, and that *jihad* – in peace as well as in war – is an obligation on all Muslims so as to convey the message of the Prophet to the whole world.[19]

This concept entails total rejection of a system of modernization that calls, as one of its important elements, for the division of state and religion, i.e., for secularization. This does not, however, necessarily mean a rejection of all western achievements in science and technology. Theorists in this camp draw attention to the fact that Islamic civilization drew on previous and contemporary achievements of all other peoples and cultures – achievements that were then merged within a coherent and distinct framework, and on a superior epistemological and moral foundation, which distinguishes Islam from other religions and cultures. It is, then, possible to take what does not contradict Islam and reject what is inconsistent with it. Islamists express different views on what might, according to Shariah, be adopted or rejected. Originally most so-called Islamist intellectual and political thinkers rejected the democratic concept, or expressed reservation or rejection in relation to the human rights concept. Some more recent representatives of the trend have partly developed a more advanced conceptualization of this attitude. Similarly, the position that initially rejected the human rights system and the democratic political process is not unanimously adopted by modern theorists, who take Islam as both the platform and framework for their political thought.[20]

This issue is a major point of controversy and a significant subject for political and scientific research in the outside world and the Arab world alike. Democratic and progressive trends used to describe the Islamist trend as fascist, and certain Islamist elements are still labelled as such. More recently, however, some attitudes have changed, bringing about concomitant changes in the positions of certain currents and parties within the Islamic movement. Some theorists on the left of the Islamist movement argue that modern democracy is the political system closest to the Islamic concept of government, state and politics. The gap between Islam and human rights is, they believe, a very narrow one and may be confined to specific and limited issues.[21]

The Muslim Brothers movement in Egypt has issued statements and declarations revealing an acceptance of democracy and basic human rights for women and minorities. These positions are but one indication of maturity in the political thought of the movement, and of the presence, in intellectual trends within the Islamic current, of domestic pressures for modernization and for coordinating Islamist positions with the legal achievements realized in the Universal Declaration of Human Rights.[22]

At the heart of the body of academic research that articulates Islamic political thought, or expresses sympathetic attitudes toward the movement, we find particular emphasis on the superiority of the juristic theories produced by the *sunna* over current international human rights legislation. There are now hundreds of such studies by jurists working at different Arab universities. The scholarly works in question range from outright rejection of certain aspects of human rights legislation to attempts to resolve controversial issues and work out a moderate solution with regard to them.

On the far right, we find the Islamist movement characterized by strict and rigorous positions. Here we find such parties as the Salvation Front in Algeria, the Mujahidin Movement and the Justice and Charity Jama'a in Morocco and the National Islamic Front in Sudan, various terrorist movements in a number of Arab countries, such as al-Jama'a al-Islamiyya and the Jihad Movement in Egypt, and the propositions of Wahhabi institutions in Saudi Arabia. These movements, in varying degrees, express an outright rejection of the democratic concept, along with the international legal system, and espouse an extreme interpretation of Islamic *fiqh* (jurisprudence) and, consequently, of Islamic Shariah.[23]

The extremist movements, which employ terrorism in the name of Islam, are undoubtedly a major source of the outrageous violation of essential human rights. Although they still take their positions in the opposition camp, they do not hesitate to use violent civil and political action in the widest possible way. These violations are evident in the actions of al-Jama'a al-Islamiyya in Egypt and Algeria.

The Islamist political trend entails, therefore, variegated positions in relation to democracy and the human rights system. A small minority of intellectuals seek reconciliation, and a group of moderate theorists, supported by large movements like the Muslim Brothers, underscore the superiority and precedence of Shariah, while tending, in practice, to opt for certain democratic concepts and human rights formulations. On the other hand, the formal sector of the Islamist movement, as represented by Saudi jurisprudence, along with the fundamentalist movements, still directly opposes the whole concept of democracy and the international system of legal rights.

Points of conflict between attempts to reconcile political and Islamic thought on the one hand and international human rights law on the other turn primarily on the following areas.[24]

First: There are restrictions and constraints on the essential and principal concept in the system of human rights, namely the principle of absolute equality before the law, without any distinction on the basis of religion, gender, colour or any other consideration. The Islamic current accepts the principle of equality irrespective of colour, race or language, but refuses to accept it with respect to the equality of men and women. There are some Islamists who also reject equality of Muslims and non-Muslims in 'Islamic' countries.[25]

Second: The Islamic Movement tends to restrict all other rights on the basis of Shariah, and to narrow down or even abrogate the application of freedom of expression, meeting, organizing or participating in public life.[26]

Third: The application of penalties or physical punishments is, from the perspective of the Universal Declaration of Human Rights, a brutal form of torture rather than a mode of sanction.[27]

Fourth: There is also a total rejection, by the Islamic current, of any interpretation of equality or of individual rights, such as the right to adopt a certain faith – which implies permission to convert from Islam to other religions – or the rights of children.

Fifth: As an extension of the dispute on the preceding issue, there is a further obvious conflict relating to the issue of punishment that may be imposed on persons branded as renegades or apostates from Islam.[28]

Furthermore, the largest sector within the Islamic movement still expresses reservation on, or outright rejection of, the democratic system, which in effect provides the only secure guarantee for applying minimal human rights.

In actual reality, the self-proclaimed Islamic political systems stand in direct contradiction to the essential prerequisites for democracy and commit flagrant human rights violations in both legislation and practice. The cases of Iran, Saudi Arabia and Sudan exhibit variations of a wide range of obnoxious impeachments and transgressions against essential rights and against private and public freedoms alike.[29]

These conclusions do not rule out the possible emergence of democratic Islamic parties in the future, especially in Egypt, Tunisia and Lebanon. According to François Borja, the relationship between Islamic currents and democracy is defined by four dimensions: We must consider the mode of the historical relationship with the West, the cultural policies adopted by elites toward the religious issue, and the role of internal factors. The fourth dimension depends on the moderate policies of ruling elites in appreciating the role of religion in public life, and in resolving the contradictions between Shariah on one hand and the gains from modernization on the other. The outcome of these interrelated factors may be a concrete and positive disposition, within Islamic currents, to respect and observe the principles of democracy and to raise fewer reservations with respect to the human rights system.[30]

II.1.4 Communist parties and socialism

The emergence of communist parties or other Marxist-Leninist movements stems from fairly distinct historical contexts in different Arab countries. The 1940s, however, saw the development of communist movements of considerable significance in Iraq, Syria, Lebanon, Palestine, Egypt, Sudan, Tunisia and Morocco. The movement has since maintained its position in the opposition camp, playing different roles according to the particular country. Only in two Arab countries, Iraq and Sudan, has the performance of the communists carried sustained political weight, but all such parties have played significant roles at the cultural and intellectual levels, and also in the sphere of national struggle. The Lebanese Communist Party, for instance, played a pivotal role in building the national alliance that led the struggle against Israeli occupation of southern Lebanon and supported the military Palestinian resistance movement.[31]

Some communist parties undertook a nominal participation with the ruling powers, notably in Syria, Iraq and Sudan, and for short periods in alliance with other radical parties, particularly the Ba'ath party. Egyptian Marxists also participated as individuals in carrying out certain state functions during Nasser's regime and during the rule of the late President Sadat. The historical experience of the Arab communist parties has, by and large, been a tragic one, marked by tyranny, torture, lengthy arrest and continual pursuit. The party rank and file, who have been the main victims, have suffered a variety of brutal persecutions and serious human rights violations in the Arab world.[32]

Arab Marxists have, in consequence, set a high value on democracy, and their struggle to this end has been the main item on the agenda of their political programmes, along with their struggle on national and social issues. For all the loyalty expressed by the communist parties and groups to Marxism and Leninism, and their self-denying role as leaders of the labour movement, their programmes and practices have centred on these two major issues, especially in Lebanon, Egypt, Sudan and Morocco. The Iraqi communist party, on the other hand, was given no opportunity to comprehend and absorb the necessity for democracy until the late stages of its long and arduous political career, following the end of the Iraq–Iran war and military action in the mountains.[33]

This broad conclusion may be a valid one. It should be noted, even so, that harmony between Arab Marxism and the democratic and legal concept has been powerfully constrained by three essential considerations.

The first is that Arab Marxists – like their counterparts world-wide following the establishment of the 'Comintern' and standardized 'Cominform' in Moscow, the headquarters of the international communist movement – have inherited Lenin's contemptuous depreciation of democracy as a mere transitional stage on the road to a proletarian revolution leading to socialism. Their belief in Lenin's theory of the two stages, of democracy and revolutionary socialism, has undermined their faith in the value of democracy as a permanent goal to be pursued for its own sake. This belief has impaired the credibility of the democratic struggle of the Arab communist parties, which were, at times, quite close to assuming or participating in actual political power (as in the case of the Iraqi communist party in 1958, and the Sudanese communist party in 1971).[34]

Second, Arab Marxist parties and some communist parties have played tangible and concrete roles, during their actual or nominal participation in power, in the ideological system that endeavoured to justify grave violations of human rights and law in more than one Arab country. This is the case in Syria and, to a lesser degree, in Iraq. During these short periods, Arab Marxists expressed a preference for social gains over the general principles of democracy, rule of law and human rights. This preference was an underlying assumption of Marxist-Leninist thought.[35]

The third and final consideration relates to the cultural role of Arab Marxists and communists. Specific reference may be made here to the active contradiction and tension experienced in the thought and discourse of Arab Marxists, between a true and genuine struggle for democracy on the one hand, and, on the other, the publicized spirit of degrading these principles.

There is sufficient evidence to acknowledge Arab Marxists' genuine struggle for democracy and the rule of law. The other, negative aspect of their efforts remains to be documented. There is, however, no lack of testimony and proof that Arab Marxists, like their colleagues elsewhere, have generally undermined aspirations toward law and legality, which they have seen as a mere superstructure, to be placed in the second rank behind progressive social gain. The more serious aspect of this political culture was the success of Arab Marxists in propagating a series of fallacies and inconsistent concepts relating to democracy and human rights. In their uncritical adoption of the experiences of Eastern European countries, they employed such terms as 'popular democracy' and 'democratic republic' (as opposed to parliamentary democracy) to identify the desired political system. Such ideological camouflage could hardly hide the widespread tyranny practised by the so-called socialist Eastern European regimes up to 1989. On the other hand, the Soviet Union's adoption of Cold War discourse had promoted a misconceived notion of the nature of social and democratic systems in the Western world. The prevalence of this misconception, among elites and people alike, served to erect firm psychological and social barriers against any appreciation of the concept and modes of democracy, and against a proper understanding of the West. In certain cases, Soviet and Marxist arguments and terminology constituted a political as well as a cognitive framework, which established itself in many currents of Arab political culture. The salient element of this discourse was its total partitioning off from actual reality and its re-employment by the masses; this allowing it to be applied by and for a number of repressive Arab regimes with radical ideologies, such as the Ba'ath systems in Syria and Iraq, and indeed by other regimes that were conservative or right wing.[36]

These bitter historical experiences were scrupulously reviewed by many Arab Marxist in the 1990s, either because they themselves had been victims of serious human rights violations or in the aftermath of revolutions and drastic democratic reforms in Eastern Europe and within the European communist parties there. Even so, significant segments of Arab Marxism have maintained traditional attitudes to Cold War discourse as disseminated by the Soviets in the 1960s, and a traditional faith in it.

II.1.5 Arab liberal parties

The term liberalism is very hard to define. Liberal attitudes, in life and in politics, have been developed and moulded in various directions and over many generations. In this sense, a very broad distinction may be drawn between nineteenth-century and twentieth-century liberalism within the Western capitalist framework. The former promoted market freedom and expected the state to refrain from interfering in matters of economy and business. The latter called upon the state to intervene so as to maintain a pattern of balance the market was incapable of maintaining alone, and so as to protect the disadvantaged social sector which was constantly vulnerable to the forces of the free market. A liberal party may, then, be broadly defined as one that advocates economic, social and political balance through the forces of the market, and calls for the sustaining or restoring of such balance through limited government intervention. The rule-of-thumb principle of liberalism is that of economic, political and cultural freedom, guaranteed by law and protected by state institutions.[37]

The liberal current in modern politics is the origin for formulating and cherishing civil and political rights – wheras the socialist current places more emphasis on drawing up and implementing economic and social rights.

The beginning of the twentieth century saw the birth of the Arab liberal tendency, notably in Egypt, and the parties that governed a number of Arab countries before independence – such as Egypt (1922–1952) and to a lesser extent

Syria and Iraq – might be described as liberal parties. The discourses of these parties focused predominantly on constitutional and political rights on the one hand and market freedom on the other. The Egyptian Wafd party, which had formed all elected governments in the country since 1924, may be taken as a model for the liberal party in its twentieth-century sense. Another model may be found in the Istiqlal Party, which won the majority of votes in immediate post-independence Morocco. Similar examples may be found in such countries as Tunisia, Sudan and Lebanon.[38]

The final prominent feature of Arab liberalism is its immediate and total collapse following the military and political coups that took place in the 1950s and 1960s in most Arab countries. The history of liberalism thus suffered disruption and discontinuity in these countries, with the possible exception of Morocco and, to a lesser degree, Tunisia and Sudan. No sooner had the authoritarian Arab state adopted the restricted multi-party pluralism model than some traditional parties began to re-emerge, especially in Egypt and Jordan, but the returning parties were nevertheless very different from their historical forerunners. The New Wafd in Egypt is significantly altered from the intellectual and practical nature of its predecessor, as is testified by the position now occupied by the present party in the political scene.[39] The old Wafd was the centre of actual and popular political life, and it was a vital and generally progressive force encompassing all issues. The New Wafd, in contrast, has exerted most of its energy and concentration on restoring the symbols of the past – and has striven in vain. The party soon lost the glamour and mass following of the original Wafd, turning, ultimately, into a 'newspaper party' like all the other legalized formations.

Despite some non-liberal positions and practices, however, the New Wafd may still be taken as the focal point of liberal economic and political tendencies. The party still advocates constitutional democracy as the ideal system of government and promotes essential constitutional reforms. It supports the universal human rights system, calls for the annulment of extraordinary legislation and martial law and rejects grave violations of human rights.[40]

The Istiqlal Party in Morocco was the 'objective equivalent' of the Wafd in Egypt during the struggle for independence, and is still the cornerstone of constitutional and democratic struggle. It started as a liberal party in the sense of the term prevalent after the Second World War, and has since been the most transparent and principled Arab party in the pursuit of constitutional reform and the development of economic and social policies. The party line was further consolidated by its support for state intervention in the economy to achieve social and moral objectives, along with the policies of neo-liberalism advocated by US President Roosevelt in his 'New Deal' and by the Liberal Party in Britain. The party nevertheless projected Arab distinctiveness as promoted by its founder Allal al-Fasi and his supporters, who believed in what is generally described as 'equilibrium'. In present times, however, the Destour Union Party in Morocco, which took part in post-independence governments and came second in the 1997 elections, seems to have come closer to the meaning and concept of 'Western' liberalism in the 1990s.[41]

In addition to these models, the Arab cultural and political scene has known towering figures in the liberalist camp, including personalities whose political and cultural appeal has turned them into distinct institutions in a number of Arab countries. Groups of believers in liberal thought, and activists for parliamentary democracy and civil and political rights, have surrounded these figures in such quasi-party cultural forums as the 'New Appeal' society, headed by the well-known Egyptian economic theorist Sa'id al-Najjar. This society espouses the entire human rights programme in its civil, political, economic, social and cultural aspects and rejects the use of the distinctiveness or peculiarity concept to justify attack on the universality, integrity and indivisibility of human rights.[42]

II.2 Party interactions and their influence

II.2.1 The juristic field

The position and attitude of Arab parties vis-à-vis human rights cannot be discerned in their public ideas as individual entities. It must rather be viewed in the context of current interactions in the political arena in each particular Arab country.

This reality has become self-evident. Arab communists, for instance, have taken contradictory positions depending on their interaction with salient events and developments in both the regional and the pan-national fields. Iraqi communists declared their opposition to their country's ruling system in principle and in detail, whereas communists in Egypt and the Arab Maghreb gave unhesitating support to Saddam Hussein's regime during its confrontation with what was described as the American-led international alliance in the second Gulf crisis. In the course of this crisis, the Muslim Brothers in other Arab countries adopted positions opposed to those of their counterparts in the Gulf in general and in Kuwait in particular. We can find the same pattern of political conduct in other major crises at both the regional and the pan-national levels in the Arab world.[43]

Since the state and its apparatus form the focal point in the political scene, the assortment of party positions depends upon the state's strategies and stances in each individual country. For Arab countries that have laid a good deal of groundwork in their political liberalization, the different state strategies toward, say, the Islamist orientation will be highly influential in fixing the positions of the parties in the various countries – positions that may reflect major inconsistency if not outright contradiction.

The intensity of a given position vis-à-vis the issue of democracy may also depend on the urgency of other issues in the political arena in different Arab countries. Thus, the position of political parties regarding the issue of democracy and human rights cannot be studied separately from their position regarding other major issues.

At the Arab level, the issue of democracy relates, in various and often contradictory forms, to such further issues as relationship to the world order and relevant major national problems and economic and social transitions in key Arab countries. Similarly, the position of the Islamic current displayed a new point of polarity in a number of countries in the 1980s and 1990s. Since the position of each party may vary with each of these issues, interaction both between the parties themselves and between the parties and the current government may prompt different and differential arrangements in relation to the question of democracy and basic rights in the political scene as a whole. A clear manifestation of this influence may be seen in political and party alliances. The Muslim Brothers' support for the market economy and privatization leads to an objective alliance with the government, but the movement is often forced to coordinate with nationalist and Marxist/socialist parties on issues relating to democracy. A reverse process may also take place when nationalist and Marxist/socialist parties take the side of the state against Islamic movements, as seen in the case of the Islamic Nahda party in Tunisia and, to a lesser extent, with the Salvation Front in Algeria.[44]

In pan-national issues, we may find an entirely different pattern of alliance. Islamists may, on occasion at least, form an objective alliance with the nationalists and Marxists/socialists against the government. In all circumstances, the government/state is the central power in the regional political arena, and, in this capacity, can manipulate such patterns of alliance together with specific party positions on major issues. The state can align the liberal current on its side in the process of economic and social transformation – which may reduce the liberals' opposition to the state in the areas of democracy and human rights. The state can, on occasion, marshal the support of the Marxists and the nationalists against the Islamic current, and, in the meantime, undermine the opposition party alliance in relation to democratic and juristic issues. As mentioned above, these tactics have been employed at one point against the Islamic trend, then used by the state, at a later stage, against its former allies. This was the case in Tunisia, where the state started with the Nahda party and ended up with a strike against the Democratic Socialist Party that was its former ally.

The assessment of party attitudes to democracy becomes more difficult when we consider occasional and periodic changes in these alliances. In the second half of the 1970s and the beginning of the 1980s, for instance, Syrian communists changed their political tactics toward the Muslim Brothers. Their positions ranged from condemnation, silence on the conflict between the government/state and the Brothers, and proposing alliance with the latter. The same pattern of oscillation and hesitancy characterized the stance of the Brothers toward the communists, though constrained, in this case, by a deeper and more forceful hostility to communism.[45]

These alliances and animosities need to be studied in closer detail, to allow us to reread and understand true attitudes to democracy and human rights. Broadly and generally, however, the trends of these alliances may be depicted as follows:

1 The complete record of interaction and conflict shows very clearly the feeble spirit behind Arab parties' struggle for democracy and human rights – a struggle that has been subdued by their concern over other priority issues in their political discourse. This low-key attitude is reflected in the scant interest in democracy shown by the literature of most parties when compared with their pursuit of other major issues.

2 The current state/government can manipulate the positions of parties and set them one against the other in questions relating to democracy, to constitutional and political reform and to essential rights. In a number of countries, such as Egypt and Tunisia, this process has weakened the parties, decreased their impact in political and civil life and reduced their credibility with the masses. Cumulative manipulation has, in substance, led to retrogression for the plural, multi-party system, and to restoration and consolidation of a shaky form of the one-party system – a pattern identical to that seen with the bureaucratic party that rules only in a nominal symbolic sense.

3 Consequently, party alliances for democracy and political and constitutional reform are now extinct in a number of countries, notably Egypt. There have been active attempts, in many Arab countries, to build such broad opposition alliances following initial transition to multi-party

systems, but these moves have collapsed, leaving a large vacuum in the realm of democracy in most Arab countries.

4   With very few exceptions, actual practice has been consistent with the attitude expressed toward democracy. The few liberal parties, such as the Wafd in Egypt, seem to be the most consistent and faithful in the pursuit of democracy and of constitutional and legal rights, followed in this respect by the communist parties. Similarly worthy of note and appreciation is the performance of certain 'national parties' like the Algerian National Liberation Front. When removed from power after the December 1991 elections, the Front did not take an exclusionary or destructive attitude toward the Islamic Salvation Front, which was, however, then dissolved and declared illegitimate by the military-backed government.

5   Nevertheless, it may be argued that the different Arab parties are learning over time, and are beginning to value democracy and essential rights and freedoms. Despite mutual suspicion, they are still expected to form a broad alliance with a view to introducing constitutional and political reform and to incorporating basic human rights, especially in civil and political areas.

III. The parties and the future of legal struggle

From the preceding analysis and assessment, which we have tried to make as objective as possible, a varied picture emerges. Most Arab parties seem, at best, to have placed the issue of democracy and respect for human rights low down their list of priorities. Some have been antagonistic to democracy and apathetic to the human philosophy underlying international legitimacy. Most seem prepared, in actual practice, to sacrifice their belief in democracy in favour of tactical manoeuvres, or the interest of their causes, or objectives with a higher priority.

Yet, for all this, it is the principal contention of the present study that any harsh judgement on Arab parties, and on their positions vis-à-vis the issues of democracy and human rights, will be unequivocally harmful and liable to produce results counter-productive for the legal struggle.

We also find, whatever the conclusions noted above, significant indications strongly favourable to democracy and human rights in the main Arab party formations. The main criterion is a sufficient measure of respect for the democratic idea and the legal system. This is not only the case with the liberal parties but also applies to pan-national parties like the Ba'ath party, to Marxist trends and even to the Muslim Brothers movement.

Some of these parties were, in the 1950s and 1960s, involved in anti-democratic practices contrary to the international legitimacy of human rights, and some are even now moving timidly toward the democratic idea and the legal system. These characteristics cannot, nevertheless, be divorced from the general context of political, social and global thinking in pre-independence times. The old political and social system was not as enchanting or attractive as some people are inclined to think, even in the democratic and legal field. In the Arab world, we had no liberal or democratic/juristic system that was consistent and coherent even in the civil and political spheres. When we take into account the factors of social stagnation and the system of privilege, coupled with intensive and increasing deprivation of the poor peasant and labouring masses, it will be evident that a strong justification existed for rebellion and revolution against the semi-liberal system inherited from the pre-independence era. It was historically legitimate for various parties to seek solutions to the social, economic and cultural problems experienced by Arab societies at the beginning of the second half of the twentieth century, even at the cost of effecting a 'temporary' interruption or relinquishment of modern constitutional and legal democracy.

This brings us to a second criterion of special significance for the purposes of this study, namely learning and education. Most Arab political formations in the opposition camp have suffered painful and bitter experiences, marked by brutal forms of repression and tyranny. A considerable sector among the party rank and file appears to have 'graduated' from the school of ordeal through discovering or rediscovering the values of democracy and of strict compliance with the legal and human principles and foundations of modern society.

It was, then, no coincidence or mere hypocrisy that the Arab Parties Conference should issue resolutions calling for the application of modern democratic and constitutional rules.[46] Despite the failure or ineffectiveness of the various forms of coordination between the parties at the regional level, party interactions revolve essentially around genuine democratic and constitutional demands. At times of political tension and disintegration, as in Algeria and Yemen, even political authorities with exceptional powers admit that the only way out of the crisis is by a democratic or at least a semi-democratic route.[47]

A third indicator of this tendency to learn and advance is the state of public opinion in different Arab countries. This indicator has been the subject of considerable controversy. Some believe the status quo in Arab societies actually represents the main obstacle to democratic transformation. However, the few

field surveys and public opinion polls conducted, in a number of Arab countries, confirm that the democratic model enjoys the support of a large majority
within society.[48]

We are perhaps in need of further research and theorization to resolve the
contradiction between, on the one hand, the rise of popular support for
democracy and, on the other, the recession of participation and the increase in
political apathy among the masses. We can nonetheless speak with some confidence about what is described as the 'Arab exception' in the area of democratic consciousness and awareness. We can also argue that there has been
enough groundwork laid now for the development of a constitutional, democratic and legal system in most Arab countries.

The position of Arab parties in this respect cannot in fact be resolved outside the democratic process itself. As argued above, the emergence of true parties cannot conceivably be discussed unless the channels of serious
competition for political power have been opened by securing the circulation
of power in the wake of open and credible elections.

Seen from this perspective, it is too early to reach any firm conclusion concerning the positions of Arab parties vis-à-vis human rights and democracy. It
is sufficient to point out that most Arab parties are capable of adapting themselves and accommodating the requirements of the democratic system if the
state itself espouses such a system.

This may sound a problematic formulation. Our hopes for democratic transition depend on the parties themselves, who have to be flexible, adaptive and
willing to embrace such a transition. At the same time, they must be qualified
to launch an effective and successful democratic struggle.

In fact this does not seem to be the case with Arab parties, especially those
in the opposition camp. Given their domestic situations and their political and
ideological residues, they are still incapable of streamlining their efforts and
launching a successful struggle for democratic transition within society.

A plausible way out of this dilemma, this situation of ambiguity and confusion, might be found in the formation of a democratic and juristic bloc among
the parties.[49] The parties themselves will lack the strength necessary to initiate
a successful democratic and legal struggle unless they lay down deep roots in
society, forming alliances, in particular, with democratic and juristic forces in
civil society.

Human rights organizations can play a leading role in this respect, not simply in the juristic field but also in providing support for such a struggle by
paving the way and preparing the appropriate environment for the building of
a democratic party–civil bloc.

There are noteworthy models for a dialogue between juristic and human rights organizations and representatives of the major party and political currents in the Arab world, undertaken with a view to bridging the gaps and establishing harmony and conciliation for a constitutional, democratic and human resolution of the current Arab predicament.[50] It is our duty to intensify and promote the pursuance of such dialogue.

Chapter 21: Labour laws and human rights

Asma Khader

Preamble

Labour is as old as human existence, and man, through labour, has moved from the primitive stage to civilization and progress. At a time when nature governed his life, man contrived to make use of his resources both for his own well-being and to serve the world around him. This mastery has led to the development of communities and civilizations through the ages.

Nor has man stopped there, but has toiled to broaden the sphere of his activities. His discoveries have enabled him to reach outer space, and he is still striving to further the development of human civilization and the welfare of all human communities.

Despite all this, however, certain societies have witnessed the violation of man's right to work. The reasons for this have varied through the ages, and the violations in question have affected different social classes and various intellectual, cultural and social movements. Such violation has aroused strong and vigorous reaction within the international community, leading to extensive conflicts that have resulted, specifically, in a declaration of the right to work as one of the basic human rights.

Arab states have been part and parcel of such events within this community; all Arab states protect the right of individuals to undertake every type of work. There are, nevertheless, differences over some of the fundamental issues involved, and these differences will be considered in the course of this essay.

The essay focuses on the issue of Arab labour laws and human rights, illustrating the extent to which Arab labour legislation respects and conforms to the principles of human rights with regard to work. The essay is divided into three sections. First, an Introductory Section considers the right to work as set out in Arab and international charters and national legislation. Next, Section One considers such issues as equality in all its forms, the implementation of labour laws, individuals liable to their provisions, social care, occupational safety, rest, social security, the right to form trade unions and the right to hold strikes. Finally, Section Two looks into the rights of certain social categories, such as children, women and individuals with special needs.

Introduction: The concept of human rights in the field of work

'Every person has the right to work.' This is an indisputable truth, for human existence has no meaning without work and production. Without work, life cannot be sustained.

I. *The right to work in Arab and international charters*

'Human rights are those rights related to humans regardless of their nationality, sex, religion, race or social or economic class.'[1] 'The right to work is one of these rights and falls within the framework of economic and social rights.'[2]

The right to work, in its broad sense, implies: the elimination of all obstacles standing in the way of an individual and the work he does or wishes to do; not forcing an individual to do a specific job; and the individual's right to strike and hold back from working.

The international community has felt the need to proclaim human rights and guarantee respect for them. As a result, these rights have been transformed from mere general principles into laws, in the form of international conventions and of legislative provision at state level. As such, most basic state laws have guaranteed and protected human rights.[3]

I.1 *The Universal Declaration of Human Rights (1948)*

In 1948, in the wake of considerable and prolonged efforts by human rights activists and supporters through the world, especially in Western countries, the United Nations issued the Universal Declaration of Human Rights; and the various nations found no difficulty in endorsing this Declaration, given that all the stipulated rights were in fact ideals that states have striven to attain. Among these rights was the right to work, stated under the article on economic, social and cultural rights.

Article (23) of the Declaration stipulates that:

1   Everyone has the right to work, to free choice of employment, to just and favourable conditions of work and to protection against unemployment.

2   Everyone, without any discrimination, has the right to equal pay for equal work.
3   Everyone who works has the right to just and favourable remuneration ensuring for himself and his family an existence worthy of human dignity, and supplemented, if necessary, by other means of social protection.
4   Everyone has the right to form and to join trade unions for the protection of his interests.

Article (24) of the Declaration stipulates that:

> Everyone has the right to rest and leisure, including reasonable limitation of working hours and periodic holidays with pay.

This declaration, which subsequently came to be regarded as a historical document of the first importance, covered the general human rights aspects in the labour field, leaving details to be determined by international charters[4] and national laws.[5] It was also the document to which states referred in connection with raising man's status and respecting his rights.

The Universal Declaration of Human Rights is considered to be the main and most important source for the enrichment of national and international efforts aimed at determining and protecting human rights and basic freedoms. It has also provided a frame of reference for many international conventions relating to human rights. These include:

> The International Convention against Torture;
> The UN Declaration on the Elimination of all Forms of Racial Discrimination;
> The Convention on the Political Rights of Women;
> The Convention on the Rights of the Child; and
> The Convention Relating to the Status of Refugees.

1.2 The International Covenant on Economic, Social and Cultural Rights

With a view to deepening the emphasis and international assurance regarding man's right to work, the international community has specified this right in the International Covenant on Economic, Social and Cultural Rights (1966).

As a means of emphasizing the principles of equality vis-à-vis implementation regarding rights stipulated in the Covenant, including the right to work, the second paragraph of article (2) of the Covenant stipulates that:

The states parties to the present Covenant undertake to guarantee that the rights enacted in the present Covenant will be exercised without discrimination of any kind as to race, colour, sex, language, religion, political or other position, national or social origin, property, birth, or other status.

The actual right to work is stipulated in paragraph 1 of article (6):

The states parties to the present Covenant recognize the right to work, which includes the right of everyone to the opportunity to gain his living by work which he has freely chosen or accepts, and will take appropriate steps to safeguard this right.

In the second paragraph of the previous article, the Covenant further urges the imperative to take all necessary legal measures, be they legislative or executive, such as technical and vocational training programmes, and to ensure equal opportunities for all, depending on expertise and qualifications without discrimination of any kind.

Article (7) also underlines every individual's right, without discrimination, to just and favourable conditions of work, through the determination of fair and equal remuneration for work of equal value without discrimination. In particular, this article guarantees to women conditions of work which are not inferior to those enjoyed by men, with equal remuneration for equal work.[6]

I.3 Conventions and Recommendations of the International Labour Organization (ILO)

The 'right to work' has, it should be stressed, received considerable national, international and regional attention. Within the framework of international efforts, and in light of the need to determine special provisions for work, the International Labour Organization (ILO) was founded in 1919, following the First World War, with the aim of raising the conditions of the work force without discrimination of any kind.

The ILO, whose members include most countries of the world, is regarded as the only international authority specializing in labour issues. It is also the authority to which all countries refer for the enactment, update or amendment of their national labour legislation and social security laws. It has issued numerous conventions and recommendations on labour issues at all levels, with emphasis on those cases where protection is most needed, such as those involving women,[7] children and individuals with special needs.

In Arab countries, legislative intervention to regulate labour and workers' affairs can be justified by many different factors.

On the economic level, the vast expansion of industry and trade, and the intertwining, sometimes conflict, of interests have made intervention necessary to solve disputes through labour legislation, and to preserve the rights of the weaker party, i.e., the worker in conflict with his employer.

On the social level, workers have become aware of the increase in demand for labour, and of the urgent need for them to unite in the face of exploitation by employers, through the establishment of labour unions that will defend and respect their rights, especially those regarding the right to work within favourable conditions.

On the political level, finally, most Arab countries have attained independence following a period of occupation, and are thus able to enact legislation without external interference. Pressure groups (within parliament, for instance) have also come into existence, and these continually demand the organization and improvement of the status of workers, who make up a large proportion of the voters. Another factor is the existence of the International Labour Organization, of which Arab countries became a part with a view to keeping up with the progress taking place in the sphere of labour legislation.[8]

I.4 Conventions and Recommendations of the Arab Labour Organization

In 1965, the prime ministers of 13 Arab countries met in Baghdad. Their meeting brought about the Arab Labour Charter and the Constitution of the Arab Labour Organization.[9]

The Arab Labour Organization (ALO) was established in accordance with article (15) of the Charter, which stipulates that: 'Arab countries agree to the establishment of an Arab Labour Organization, which implements the tripartite representation system based on the participation of workers, employees and governments in all the activities of the organization, and in accordance with the constitution appended to this charter.'

This charter might be regarded as a declaration of principles. Our main concern here, however, is to note the actual establishment of the Arab Labour Organization and the agreement of Arab countries to work towards achieving similar Arab working levels and social securities.[10]

The constitution of the Arab Labour Organization, in article (3), stipulates that:

The Arab Labour Organization aims at the following:

1 To co-ordinate Arab efforts in the field of labour.
2 To develop and preserve union rights and freedom.

3 To unify labour legislation and working conditions in Arab countries wherever possible.

4 To conduct studies and researches on various labour issues, and in particular:
   - Labour force planning.
   - Working conditions for women and juveniles.
   - Problems relating to work in the fields of industry, trade and services.
   - Problems of agricultural workers.
   - Industrial safety and occupational health.
   - Small and rural industries.
   - Occupational categorization.
   - Cooperatives.
   - Production sufficiency and its relation to operation and production.

5 To offer technical aid in the field of labour to Arab countries which require it.

6 To set up social security schemes for the protection of workers and their families.

7 To set up technical training schemes and seminars for workers.

8 To compile an Arab labour dictionary.

Since its establishment, the Arab Labour Organization has issued numerous covenants and recommendations, and has striven to guarantee the right of the Arab individual to a decent life based on social justice, and his right to work in just and favourable conditions.[11]

The legal value of such covenants and recommendations has nevertheless differed from one country to another, and this has led to contradiction over legal application and to dispute as to which kind of law should be implemented. In Tunisia, for instance, these covenants, following their ratification, have been accorded greater importance than local law.[12] In Jordan, by contrast, implementation of the covenants requires that they should pass initially through all the legislative stages required for issuing local legislation, after which they become equal to local laws.[13]

II. The Right to Work in National Legislation

The initial date for regulating labour in Arab countries, from 1904 on, differs from one country to another. In Jordan,[14] for example, the first labour law was issued in 1960, under Law No. (21) for that year. It included training contracts, a system for determining minimum wages, group agreements, health, safety, welfare, working hours, annual leaves, and provisions regarding women and maternity leave. Laws implemented in Jordan prior to this labour law had not included provisions regarding women. These laws were the Labour Unions Law No. (35) for 1953 and Compensation Law No. (17) for 1955.

Although women had played no effective role before the issuance of the 1960 Labour Law, we nevertheless find certain constitutional provisions were being implemented. It is also worth noting that, before the 1960 Labour Law and for a few years after it was issued, women were still working without pay, their work being limited to work for a single family.

II.1 The Right to Work in Arab Constitutions

Most modern states are states of law and institutions, deriving their legitimacy from the basic law in each case. This basic law is regarded as a constitutional document, and all provisions and principles stipulated in it are regarded as constitutional principles.[15] Typically, a constitution comprises a group of subjects deemed constitutional in their essential nature, whether included in the constitutional document or not.

Regardless of all the above definitions, the constitution is considered to override all other laws and regulations. Even changing or amending articles in the constitution requires procedures different from those required when changing ordinary laws. As such, the constitution is the law dealing with the formation of the state and the establishment of a ruling system within it.[16]

Article (23) of the Jordanian Constitution for 1952 stipulates that:

1   Work is the right of every citizen, and the state shall provide opportunities for work to all citizens by directing the national economy and raising its standards.
2   The state shall protect labour and enact legislation accordingly, based on the following principles:

   a Every worker shall receive wages commensurate with the quantity and quality of his work.
   b The number of working hours per week shall be laid down. Workers shall be given weekly and annual days of paid rest.
   c Special compensation shall be given to workers supporting families and on dismissal, illness, old age, and emergencies arising out of the nature of their work.

d Special conditions shall be made for the employment of women and juveniles.

e Factories and workshops shall be subject to health safeguards.

f Free trade unions may be formed within the limits of the law.[17]

It is noteworthy that the Jordanian Constitution refers not only to the right to work in general but determines the principles to be included in the labour law, such as special provisions regarding the work of women and juveniles.[18]

All this leads us to conclude that a labour law that fails to specify the working conditions for women and juveniles, wages, weekly working hours, the right to form free trade unions, leaves, compensations, and health safeguards, is a law that contravenes the constitution. For example, Jordanian Labour Law No. (8) for 1996 contained provisions regarding the work of women and juveniles. This was commensurate with the provisions of the constitution and the rights of women and the role they play in society at different levels.

II.2 The Right to Work in Arab Labour Legislation

As noted above, the right to work, which has been guaranteed by international human rights conventions, has received Arab attention. Legislative measures have been enacted to protect this right, though the dates of enactment differ from one Arab state to another; differences springing principally from differing dates of independence.

In Egypt, civil laws were the vehicle for regulating work contracts, using brief articles. This was before the issuance of a decree regulating individual work contracts under Law No. (317) for 1952. This law was amended by Law No. (165) for 1953, after which the Unified Labour Law was issued under No. (91) for 1959. This replaced all previous labour legislation and also Social Security Law No. (92) for 1959, which in turn was annulled in accordance with Law No. (63) for 1964.

In Syria, the first labour legislation was issued in 1964. After that, and throughout the period of union with Egypt, the laws implemented were Law No. (91) for 1959 and Social Security Law No. (92) for 1959. After the union was dissolved, both legislations remained valid with a few amendments.

In Iraq, the first labour legislation was issued in 1963. It was later replaced by Law No. (1) for 1958. In 1946, the first labour law was issued in Lebanon, being amended a number of times thereafter.

In Saudi Arabia, the first labour law was issued in 1947. It remained valid until 1969, when it was replaced by the new Labour Law, and, in the same year, the Social Security Law was also issued.

In Kuwait, the first Labour Law for the government sector was issued in 1959. This law was derived from the Egyptian Labour Law. As for Bahrain, the first Labour Law was issued in 1957, and its provisions were derived from the principles of English Public Law. In Libya, the first Labour Law was issued in 1957, and was later replaced by the Labour Law for 1962.

Tunisia and Sudan also issued legislation regarding labour. The first labour law in Sudan was issued in 1908, under the name of the 'Progressive Workers' Law'. This was followed by the Law of Servants in 1921. By 1948 most labour legislation had been issued. As for Tunisia, the first Labour Law was issued in 1904, the Unified Labour Law being finally adopted in 1960.

III. Human Rights in Arab Labour Legislation

The right to work is clearly linked to a number of other, equally important rights. There are also many distinctive features surrounding man's right to work, such as equality between men and women, equality in pay and equality in promotion and training. Another feature is the definition of categories of individuals who are subject to labour legislation provision, those who are not, and the reasons for the latter's exclusion. This is known as the scope of implementation. Other features include social care, the right to form trade unions and the right to take strike action.

III.1 Equality

Unlike the provisional law, the new Jordanian Labour Law No. (8) for 1996 explicitly stipulates equality between men and women in the field of work. In article (2), the Jordanian Labour Law defines a worker as: 'Any person, be they male or female, who performs a job in return for pay, and who is under the authority of their employer. This includes juveniles and individuals under probation or rehabilitation.' The same article defines a juvenile as: 'Any person who is seven years of age or above but has not yet reached eighteen years of age.'

III.1.1 Equal Opportunities

The law's unequivocal and detailed assertion of equality between men and women shows the legislator's intention to underscore this point. To take the issue a step further, we might view equality between men and women as being relative rather than absolute.[19] Relative equality means that a woman's right to work and equal opportunity requires that she should join the workforce and depend on the commensurability of her academic and practical abilities with the nature of the work she performs.

The provision regarding equality between men and women in the Jordanian Labour Law is commensurate with Arab and international covenants. For example, article (23) of the Universal Declaration of Human Rights (1948) stipulates that: 'Everyone has the right to work, to free choice of employment, to just and favourable conditions of work, and to protection against unemployment.'

Thus, the right to work is considered a basic right for both men and women, without any discrimination. However, this right is never complete until a person, whether male or female, is granted all accompanying rights, such as the right to rest and to periodic leaves.[20]

To emphasize the international legal guarantees to women's right to work and their equality with men, the right to work was also included in the International Covenant on Economic, Social and Cultural Rights (1966); for the second paragraph of article (2) of the Covenant stipulates that: 'The states parties in the present Covenant undertake to guarantee that the right enunciated in the present Covenant will be exercised without discrimination of any kind as to race, colour, sex, language, religion, political or other opinion, national or social origin, property, birth, or other status.'

The Convention on the Elimination of all Forms of Discrimination Against Women (1979), in articles (11), (12), (13) and (14), also included provisions regarding the work of women, especially in respect of their equality to men in the field of work.

The conventions and recommendations of the International Labour Organization have laid down general principles applicable to working women regarding work relationships and conditions. The ILO has shown a special interest in working women in view of their nature and the various responsibilities they undertake. As such, the ILO underscores the principle of equality between men and women in the field of work.

For example, the ILO issued Discrimination in Employment and Occupation Convention No. (111) for 1958. Article (2) of this convention stipulates that: 'Each member for which this Convention is in force undertakes to declare and pursue a national policy designed to promote, by methods appropriate in natural conditions and practice, equality of opportunity and treatment in respect of employment and occupation, with a view to eliminating any discrimination in respect thereof.' Hence, this convention lays down the fundamental principles of equality between men and women in employment and occupation.[21]

On the Arab level, the Arab Labour Organization, through the various conventions it has issued, also stresses the principle of equality in treatment between men and women. Convention No. (10) for 1966 stipulates that: 'Protection determined by levels of work should be the same, and there should be no discrimination among workers based on sex.' Article No. (1) of Convention No. (5) for 1976 stipulates that: 'Equality between men and women should be observed in all Labour Legislation.'

Some Arab countries have even derived their own laws from Convention No. (5) above, with regard to equality between men and women. This is the case with the new Jordanian Labour Law No. (8) for 1996.

It is also worth pointing out that, in Arab labour law, equality between men and women should not remain implied but should be explicitly stated. This requires a strenuous, ongoing effort on the part of all the parties concerned, especially non-governmental feminist organizations and movements.

III.1.2 Remuneration

Remuneration[22] is the subject most closely linked to the issue of equality between men and women in the field of work. It also constitutes fertile ground for child exploitation. In view of this, the international community has striven to emphasize equality in remuneration for work of equal value.

This principle was clearly stated and stressed in the Universal Declaration of Human Rights (1948), where article (23) stipulates that: 'Everyone, without any discrimination, has the right to equal pay for equal work.'[23] It was further stressed in the International Convention on Economic, Social and Cultural Rights (1966), article (7) of which stipulates that: 'The states parties to the present Covenant recognize the right of everyone to the employment of just and favourable conditions of work, which ensure, in particular, a remuneration which provides all workers, as a minimum, with fair wages and equal remuneration for work of equal value, without discrimination of any kind, in particular women being guaranteed conditions of work not inferior to those enjoyed by men, with equal pay for equal work.'

This principle was topped off by the UN Convention for the Elimination of All Forms of Discrimination Against Women (1979), article (1) of which stipulates the rights of women in the field of work, including their right to equal remuneration for work of equal value.[24]

It is worth noting that equality in remuneration was one of the main aims of the International Labour Organization in 1919; workers in fact share a history of constant struggle in this field. To implement this principle, the ILO issued numerous conventions regarding the protection of women at work and the elimination of discrimination against women with regard to equal opportunity and treatment.[25] Equal Remuneration Convention No. (100), issued by the ILO in 1951, stipulates, in article (1), that: 'Each member shall, by means appropriate to methods in operation for determining rates of remuneration, promote and in so far as is consistent with such methods ensure the application to all workers of the principle of equal remuneration for men and women workers for work of equal value.'

On the Arab level, the Arab Labour Organization has played a vital role in including and stressing this principle in its conventions and recommendations. Article (3) of Arab Convention No. (5) for 1976 stipulates that: 'Equal remuneration for men and women workers shall be guaranteed for work of equal value.'

Arab Convention No. (1) for 1966, regarding Arab labour levels, and the amended Arab Labour Convention No. (6) for 1976, both stipulated equality of remuneration between men and women for work of equal value.[26]

Clearly, therefore, there is no dispute, either on the international or the Arab level, regarding equality between men and women for work of equal value. All previous conventions urged states to emphasize this principle in their national legislation, and this encouraged many Arab countries to include provisions regarding equality of remuneration within their labour legislation.[27]

Arab states whose legislation includes provision regarding equality of remuneration include Kuwait. National sector Labour Law No. (38) for 1946, in article (27), stipulates that: 'Working women shall receive remuneration equal to that received by men for work of equal value.'

In Algeria, with regard to individuals' work relations, Article (8) of Law No. (6/82) for 1982, stipulates that: 'All workers benefit from the same rights and are subject to the same duties, regardless of sex or age; as long as their positions, qualifications and revenue are similar, then they shall receive equal remuneration for work of equal value and they shall enjoy the same privileges.'

In the United Arab Emirates, article (23) of Law No. (8) for 1980 stipulates that: 'Women shall receive remuneration equal to that of men in the event that these charitable or educational institutions aim at providing rehabilitation or vocational training for juveniles or women, on the condition that the internal systems of these institutes stipulate the nature of work and working hours which do not stand in contradiction to the true abilities of juveniles and women.'

In Egypt, article (161) of the Egyptian Labour Law[28] stipulates that: 'Working women are liable to all provisions which apply to workers, without any discrimination, in the same type of work.'

While labour legislation in Arab countries is characterized by the prohibition of discrimination between men and women, there are nevertheless individual differences of approach. Some states expressly stipulate equality in remuneration between men and women for work of equal value, while others mention this indirectly. The latter do not refer to equality explicitly, but rather recommend it in provisions that remuneration should be equal between men and women. Nevertheless, given the crucial importance of equality in remuneration, the Jordanian legislature should have allocated a special provision stipulating equality of remuneration for work of equal value.

The presence of such provisions helps women demand equal remuneration from employers. Thus the Jordanian legislature ought to respond to the numerous recommendations of Jordanian non-governmental organizations to include special stipulations regarding this issue within new labour law.

Jordanian Labour Law No. (8) for 1996 includes a provision specifying the minimum wage, for the protection of workers, be they male or female. This provision may be used to minimize abuse on the part of employers, manifested in the paying of extremely low wages to women. Paragraph (a) of article (52) stipulates that: 'The Cabinet, upon the recommendation of the Minister, shall form a committee made up of an equal number of representatives from ministers, workers and employers. The Cabinet shall appoint a Head of the Committee from its members. This Committee shall undertake the responsibility for determining minimum wages in the Jordanian *dinar,* either in general or within a specified area or field of work. Membership of this committee is for two years renewable.'

Even countries with special provisions for equality in remuneration face the problem of employers who do not abide by these provisions, basically for reasons of profit.

It is also noticeable that equality in training and promotion differs from what is stipulated in labour legislation. This legislation does not differentiate between male and female workers in their right to receive training courses. However, discrimination in such areas does exist, especially in Arab countries.

III.2 Scope of Implementation

Labour legislation should originally apply to all workers performing jobs for other parties, without any exceptions. For a number of reasons, however, many types of worker do not fall within the scope of implementation of labour laws. Government employees, for example, are subject to Civil Service regulations, while others are outside the scope of implementation for various reasons to be considered below.

It is worth pointing out, though, that an issue of this kind requires a careful study of those categories of workers including a high percentage of women, juveniles and individuals in need of protection. There is also a need to investigate the reasons why such individuals are excluded from labour laws and to demand a reversal of such exceptions where possible.

Arab labour legislation tends to eliminate and exclude certain groups of individuals,[29] and does not list or specify those to which the legislation applies. Some of those excluded are subject to certain general principles, which include less care and fewer privileges than for those stipulated in labour laws. Others are subject to other laws.[30]

The categories of workers excluded or eliminated from the new Jordanian Labour Law and other Arab labour laws may be categorized as follows:

First: government and municipal employees. These are excluded from the labour laws of Jordan, the United Arab Emirates, Bahrain, Syria, Qatar, Kuwait, Lebanon, Libya, Egypt and Yemen. Thus, government and municipal employees are not subject to the provisions of labour law, but rather to Civil Service Law No. (1) for 1988. A detailed consideration of how to secure rights for this category of worker would, however, need to be the subject of a separate research paper.

Second: family members of the employer who work in his project without remuneration. These categories of worker have been excluded from the labour laws of Jordan, the United Arab Emirates, Bahrain, Qatar, Lebanon and Libya.

'Family members' refers here to those related to the employer and whom he is legally obliged to support. Those advocating the exclusion of such individuals believe family ties to override those imposed by the law. Since the employer supports his family members, their relationship tends to be highly personal and extremely sensitive. If these advocates believe that making such individuals subject to the provisions of labour law will lead to the dissolution of family ties, then how are we to protect family members, especially women, whose rights, provided and protected by the law and the constitution, are being totally ignored?

We believe a woman should choose to work or not to work for a supporting family member, and hope all family members working together will become subject to the provisions of labour law, with no exceptions whatever. The justification for this is that strong family ties will not in any case be destroyed simply by making family members subject to the provisions of labour law, all the more so as many of these regulations, such as the Law of Personal Status, apply to each and every member.

Third: house servants, gardeners, cooks and similar workers. The labour laws of ten countries exclude these: namely, Jordan, the United Arab Emirates, Bahrain, Syria, Qatar, Kuwait, Lebanon, Libya, Egypt and Yemen.

Also included within these exceptions are those who work in a private residence.[31] Those advocating the exclusion argue that such a worker enjoys a direct and personal relationship with his employer, and that, as such, retaining or terminating the individual's services should be left to the employer.[32]

From a human rights perspective, most of these workers receive low wages, be they nationals or expatriates, who usually come from Eastern Asia. Most of them, moreover, are women, who also need protection from sexual harassment through penal laws.[33] If we take into consideration the economic circumstances that lead women to work in private residences, we shall realize the urgent need to place them within the protection of labour laws, or at least to specify and control their working environment and the employer-employee relationship by means of regulations issued by the concerned official parties.

Fourth: agricultural workers, apart from those who, on the recommendation of the Minister, are covered by the provisions of the Council of Ministers. This exclusion is present in Jordan, the United Arab Emirates, Bahrain, Lebanon and the Arab Republic of Yemen.[34] Those in favour of such exclusion maintain that agricultural work is by nature different from that in other areas. Agricultural work has its own rules and is usually seasonal.

Arab society in general, and the Jordanian community in particular, depends on agriculture. Many of those working in this area are women, who are subject to exception either because they come under the category of workers within the same family or come under this specific category of agricultural workers. Arab interest, especially that of the Arab Labour Organization, in laying down certain principles for workers in this sector, is based on a number of considerations:

1   The inability of labour legislation to meet the needs and solve the problems of agricultural workers.
2   The presence of Arab labour laws that have specifically excluded this category of worker.
3   Agricultural work has its own nature, conditions and rules, which set it apart from work in other sectors.
4   The volume of the labour force in agriculture, especially women, and the size and depth of its problems, which require special attention.

In view of these highly important considerations, the Arab Labour Organization issued Arab Convention No. (12) for 1980, regarding agricultural workers, and Arab Recommendation No. (4) for 1980, regarding the development and protection of the agricultural labour force.

Some Arab countries in north-west Africa[35] have made considerable strides in protecting workers in this sector by issuing special laws and provisions for agricultural workers, based on the conventions and recommendations of the Arab Labour Organization.

We hope that the Jordanian legislature will similarly seek to guarantee and protect the rights of agricultural workers, especially women, by issuing laws and regulations that will reorganize their affairs, taking into consideration that this type of work requires special conventions and relations between them and their employers.[36]

III.3 The Right to Social Welfare

There is no longer any disagreement over the importance of providing workers with social services and welfare. A worker has the right to preserve his health and safety, to be protected from dangers which might result from the nature of his work, to enjoy sufficient hours of rest by virtue of specified working hours, to receive compensation at the end of his service, and to receive regular pay on retirement or by virtue of any other reason or injury which may prevent him from working, such as an occupational accident.

If all these rights were guaranteed, workers would feel secure, and this, in turn, would reflect positively on their performance, quality of work and loyalty to their employers.

III.3.1 Occupational Safety and the Right to Rest

In addition to international conventions dealing with occupational health and safety, the Arab Labour Organization has played an important role in this field, issuing Arab Convention No. (7) for 1977 and Recommendation No. (1) for 1977, which included special provisions regarding the issue.

Article (1) of the Convention stipulates that Arab legislation should include provisions regarding occupational health and safety in all working fields and sectors. It also stipulates that they should include special provisions regarding insurance against occupational accidents and diseases.

The Convention also specifies the means of ensuring occupational health and safety,[37] and leaves the door fully open for Arab legislation to carry out whatever measures it finds necessary in this regard. For example, Jordanian Labour Law No. (8) for 1996 includes a whole section on occupational health and safety, in which it deals with the duties of employers,[38] the guidelines for public safety,[39] the prevention of dangerous materials,[40] a prohibition on introducing mental stimulants into the workplace,[41] workers' observance of prevention guidelines,[42] health prevention guidelines,[43] and regulations regarding occupational health and safety.[44]

The Jordanian Labour Law devotes special attention to occupational health and safety, imposing penalties on any employer violating the relevant provisions. Such penalties might extend to a partial or total closing down of the institution or workplace, or a halt to the use of equipment or machinery liable to endanger workers, or the institution, or even other machinery.[45]

Other Arab countries have likewise devoted attention to the issue. Over the past few years they have issued special legislation specifying the duties of all working parties and governments. However, information on practical implementation of this is scarce, due to the unavailability of statistics and a lack of experience in those responsible for controlling and supervising the implementation in question.[46]

As a result of various international and Arab conventions, most Arab legislation sets the standard working day at six hours. Overtime may be either optional or compulsory thereafter.[47] Where overtime work is optional, a worker is paid more than his usual wages. Jordanian law sets overtime payment at 125 per cent during weekdays and 150 per cent at weekends and on public holidays.

III.3.2 Social Securities

Legislation regarding social securities has been limited to certain types of security such as insurance against sickness and old age, maternity leave and end of service remuneration.

Social securities are, however, new to the Arab world, and legislation has witnessed numerous amendments and alterations. This is mainly, as said, because it represents a new experience in this part of the world, and the practical implementation sheds light on the gaps and imperfections involved. These are due, too, to the expansion of the fields covered in the legislation.[48] While many Arab countries do use modern and developed systems regarding social securities, the scope of implementation varies from one country to another.

Arab countries do not contribute to the financing of social securities, with the exception of the state of Kuwait, whose government contributes almost

40 per cent of old age, incapacity and life insurance, and the government in Lebanon, which contributes in financing health insurance, up to the equivalent of 25 per cent of wages.[49]

Arab countries vary in their specification of the amount of pension salaries, or the option of paying pensions all at once. They also differ over the bases on which retirement salaries are calculated. Some Arab countries, such as Saudi Arabia, Morocco, Bahrain, Kuwait and Lebanon, have issued special provisions regarding optional insurances.

The issue of social securities is, it should be noted, linked directly to workers' rights, especially in respect of providing a decent life. There is, within the Arab world, social security legislation representative of all forms of security and insurance stipulated in Arab Convention No. (5) for 1971 regarding the minimum level of social securities, including insurance against occupational accidents and sickness, health insurance, maternity insurance, insurance against incapacity, old age, unemployment, death and family facilities.[50]

IV. The Rights of Certain Working Categories

The international community has devoted special attention to certain working categories, with a view to protecting these on account of considerations like sex, and physical and emotional state. Women, children and persons with special needs are the focus of this attention.

Many international conventions and recommendations, and many enactments of local legislation, have emerged to provide more comprehensive and detailed protection and help for such categories. International criteria have also been established in respect of the work such persons undertake, taking into account the special circumstances under which each category functions. Nowadays, protecting the rights of children, women and those with special needs has become a prime indicator of respect for human rights, especially in the field of work.

IV.1 The Rights of Working Children

Paragraph (3) of the International Covenant on Economic, Social and Cultural Rights stipulates that: 'Children and young persons should be protected from economic and social exploitation. Their employment in work harmful to their morals or health or dangerous to life or likely to hamper their normal development should be punishable by law. States should also set age limits below which the paid employment of child labour should be prohibited and punishable by law.'[51]

It is also evident that the International Labour Organization has devoted much attention to the matter of child labour, issuing many conventions in this regard.[52]

Focus has been set on many aspects of child labour, such as medical examinations qualifying children to enter the field of work, the protection of children against exploitation and immorality, the prohibition of their employment at night and the specification of minimum wages for children, apart from other aspects they might have in common with older workers.

Jordanian Labour Law No. (8) for 1996 tackles the issue of juvenile employment. Article (73) stipulates that, taking into consideration the provisions regarding vocational training, under no circumstances shall juveniles below the age of 16 be employed in any capacity whatever.

It is also prohibited to employ juveniles who have not completed their 17th year in any form of work which is dangerous, exhausting or harmful to health. Such forms of work are to be determined by decisions issued by the Minister following consultation with the concerned authorities.[53]

Article (75) of the same law specifies the working hours of juveniles. It prohibits their employment for more than six hours a day, during which there shall be a rest period of at least one hour after four consecutive hours of work. It also prohibits the employment of juveniles at night, defined as the period between 8 pm. and 6 am., and during religious feasts, public holidays and weekends.[54]

Before an employer employs any juvenile, the law requires him to ask the juvenile, or his parents, for a certified copy of the birth certificate, a certificate of good health, and written consent from the parents for their child to be employed in the institution in question. The law also imposes penalties on any employer who violates the provisions of the law or of the regulations issued in accordance with it.

The Arab Labour Convention[55] also contains articles regarding the employment of juveniles, and provisions supervising their work, including minimum wages, working hours, the prohibition of night work, and occupational health and safety.

All Arab labour legislation has included provisions regarding the employment of juveniles. There are, however, variations in the different cases involved.

With regard to minimum age, some Arab legislation sets this at 12 years,[56] while Saudi labour law sets it at 13.[57] Iraqi and United Arab Emirates law stipulate that juveniles must be 15, this corresponding to the international specification.[58]

Arab legislation also lays down special provisions for a full medical examination to be undertaken before employment, to be sure the juvenile's health qualifies him to undertake the tasks and duties assigned.[59] They also stipulate the consent of the parents to his employment,[60] and prohibit the hiring of juveniles to perform work which is exhausting or harmful to health. Legislation has also prohibited the employment of juveniles at night,[61] for overtime work, or during holidays and feasts.[62] It has also limited the working day to six hours.[63]

IV.2 The Right to Work for people with special needs

From the beginning of the twentieth century on, international interest in individuals with special needs has grown, this being crowned by the United Nations declaration (1971) regarding the rights of the mentally disabled.

One of the most important articles of this declaration embodied a recognition that the mentally disabled individual has the same rights as those specified for other individuals, as well as the right to suitable medical care and treatment, education, training, rehabilitation and the right to enjoy economic security and a suitable standard of living. He also has, in accordance with his abilities, the right to work or carry on any other beneficial profession.

Initial emphasis was placed on the mentally disabled. In 1975, however, the United Nations issued a further declaration regarding those with all forms of disability. This declaration stipulated that: 'Disabled persons have the same civil and political rights as other human beings. Disabled persons have the right to medical, psychological and functional treatment including prosthetic and orthetic appliances, to medical and social rehabilitation aid, counselling placement services and other services which will enable them to develop their capabilities and skills to the maximum and will hasten the processes of their social integration or reintegration. They have the right, according to their capabilities, to secure and retain employment or to engage in a useful, productive, and remunerative occupation and to join trade unions.'[64]

We may note that this declaration underlines the right of the disabled to work according to their physical and mental capabilities, and no human being has the right to take this right away. Disabled persons should be helped to be integrated and rehabilitated, to enable them to live with their health or mental state.[65]

The International Labour Organization has also involved itself with the rights of the disabled, especially in respect of their work. It issued Recommendation No. (99) for 1955, regarding the vocational habilitation and rehabilitation of the disabled. It also issued Convention No. (159) for 1983, regarding the vocational habilitation and employment of the disabled. The principal points included in this Convention are:

1   It is necessary for every state to establish a national policy for the habilitation and employment of the disabled.
2   The policy should include all forms of disability and should take into consideration the principle of equal opportunity between disabled and ordinary workers on the one hand and male and female disabled persons on the other.
3   To provide adequate services for the disabled in the fields of training, development and employment.

This convention had a major impact on Arab labour legislation, in Jordan as elsewhere. The Jordanian legislature made it compulsory to employ disabled persons in major establishments, subject to certain conditions and circumstances.

Article (13) of Jordanian Labour Law No. (8) for 1996 stipulates that: 'Any employer with 50 or more employees and the nature of whose work permits the employment of disabled persons who have been vocationally habilitated through vocational habilitation programmes and institutions accredited by the Ministry or establishments in cooperation with official or private institutions shall employ disabled persons which make up not less than 2 per cent of the total number of employees, and shall send to the Ministry a detailed account of jobs being occupied by disabled persons who have been habilitated vocationally, in addition to a detailed account of their wages.'

IV.3 The Rights of Working Women

The special nature of women has led the international community to exert its efforts to provide them with the necessary protection within the framework of their natural reproductive function. On the other hand, recognition of the principle of equality between men and women has obliged the Jordanian legislature to accord women the same privileges as men in respect of all forms of leave from work.

The Universal Declaration of Human Rights contains a specific provision on the issue of motherhood. Article (25) of the Declaration stipulates that: 'Motherhood and childhood are entitled to special care and assistance.'

This principle was translated into legal commitments in the International Covenant on Economic, Social and Cultural Rights. Paragraph 2 of article (10) stipulates that: 'Special protection should be accorded to mothers during a reasonable period before and after childbirth. During such period, working mothers should be accorded paid leave or leave with adequate social security benefits.'

This has also been stated in the UN Convention for the Elimination of All Forms of Discrimination Against Women, which subsequently became known as the Declaration of the Rights of Women.

As for the International Labour Organization, its interest in protecting the motherhood of working women has been quite comprehensive. It issued International Labour Convention No. (3) for 1919, which was amended in accordance with ILO Convention No. (103) for 1952, according to which the total number of maternity leave days should be not less than twelve weeks (subject to extension) and financial aid should be given to mothers during this period.[66]

As for the Arab world, Arab Labour Convention No. (3) for 1971, regarding minimum social securities, stipulates that national legislation should include two branches of the eight social securities, including maternity insurance (pregnancy and childbirth).

As for paid study leave, Arab Convention No. (10) for 1979 stipulates that: 'The principles and provisions of the policy regarding paid study leave stipulate that every male and female worker shall be entitled to paid study leave with equal opportunity.'[67]

Article (13) of Convention No. (5) for 1976, regarding working women, stipulates that a woman may obtain an unpaid leave to accompany her husband whose work has been transferred to another location, inside or outside the country. The maximum duration of this leave is left to the discretion of each country's legislation.

Article (14) of the same Convention stipulates that a working woman may obtain an unpaid leave to devote herself entirely to raising her children. This may be granted in accordance with the conditions and duration specified by legislation in each country. During this period of leave, a working woman has the right to retain her job.

In the case of sickness resulting from pregnancy or childbirth, working women have the right to seek sick leave in accordance with what is specified by the legislation of the particular country concerned, this leave is not to affect any other sick leave stipulated by law.

In addition to leaves regarding women, leaves granted to both men and women by the new Jordanian Labour Law No. (8) for 1996 are clearly different from those granted by the annulled labour law.[68]

IV.3.1 Maternity Leave

Article (70) of the new Jordanian Labour Law stipulates that: 'Working women have the right to a fully paid maternity leave before and after childbirth. It is prohibited for a woman to be employed during this period.'

In the previous Labour Law, the duration of this leave had been only six weeks.[69] This changing attitude on the part of the Jordanian legislature was in harmony with Convention No. (103) for 1952, issued by the International Labour Organization. In one of its provisions, this convention set the duration of maternity leave as not less than twelve weeks.

This is in total agreement with article (10) of Arab Convention No. (5) for 1976,[70] in respect of the duration before and after childbirth, the prohibition on employing women within this period, and not linking the use of maternity leaves to previous years of service or specifying a period of time for workers in the institution.

On the level of labour laws in the Arab world, we may note that all stipulate a woman's right to maternity leave except Libyan Law No. (58) for 1970, with regard to work. Differences between these Arab laws basically entail the period after which a woman is entitled to leave,[71] plus the fact that some countries do not define this period.

The duration of maternity leave varies from one country to another, as does a woman's right to unpaid sick leave due to illness after childbirth. Some laws specify, in detail, the duration of sick leave from which a woman may benefit and the relation between these sick leaves on the one hand and annual and maternity leaves on the other.

The Lebanese Labour Law, issued in 1946, with all its amendments, stipulates in article (28) a woman's right to a maternity leave of 40 days. Thirty days of this are to be taken after the birth with full pay from her employer.

In Kuwait, Civil Sector Labour Law No. (38) for 1964, in article (25), grants a working woman 30 days before childbirth if needed.

In Egypt, article (154) of Labour Law No. (137) for 1981 stipulates that a woman is entitled to maternity leave six months after commencing work. This leave shall be 50 days, 40 to be granted after childbirth. The total number of maternity leaves shall not exceed three during her period of service. If this number is exceeded, a woman shall be granted unpaid leave.[72]

In Somalia, article (91) of Labour Law No. (65) for 1972 stipulates that, after six months of service, she has the right to a maternity leave of fourteen weeks, at least six to be taken after childbirth.

In Algeria, article (29) of Law No. (83) for 1963, regarding child birth insurance, stipulates that a woman is due daily compensation for maternity leave, for a period of fourteen consecutive weeks.[73]

After reviewing the previous provisions of Arab labour laws, we may note that some of these contravene the duration of maternity leave stipulated in Arab conventions regarding working women. These states include Tunisia, Oman, Syria, the United Arab Emirates and Bahrain.

Other labour laws have granted women maternity leave, but have required a specific previous period of service in order to implement the full-pay leave system or the half-pay leave system. These states include Oman, Somalia, Sudan and the United Arab Emirates. Others have introduced a maternity leave whose duration exceeds that stipulated in the Arab Convention. These include Algeria and Mauritania.

IV.3.2 Nursing Leave

Article (71) of Jordanian Labour Law No. (8) for 1996 stipulates that: 'At the end of the maternity leave stipulated in article (70) of this law, a working woman has the right, and within one year of the date of childbirth, to one or more paid nursing leaves in order to nurse her new-born baby, not exceeding one hour each day.'[74]

Jordanian Labour Law sets nursing leave at one hour each day, within one year only after the date of childbirth. This leave may be taken all at once or divided up. This is in accordance with Arab and international conventions. It does, however, raise questions of implementation, which cannot be considered here for reasons of space.

Arab countries such as Iraq, Kuwait, Sudan, Algeria and Oman have not referred to this type of leave in their labour laws. Other countries have set the duration of this leave at between one and one and a half years, and the daily duration of nursing time at between one and two hours.

Somalia, for example, has granted a working woman two hours per day within the first year after childbirth. The same applies to Tunisia, which has granted the working woman, within the first year after childbirth, two periods of rest for nursing her child, each of half an hour.

IV.3.3 Employment and Working Hours

The international community has devoted particular attention to the protection of the working woman against harsh working conditions, whether in the nature of the work performed or in respect of working hours. This has been designed to help women avoid health and social hazards arising from their work, and enable them to care for their families.

The physical nature of women, differing as it does from that of men, increases the possibility of sickness in women.[75] Protective measures set in place by the International Labour Organization have been highly detailed, especially with regard to night work by women,[76] underground work by women,[77] protection from the dangers of lead poisoning[78] and gasoline poisoning,[79] protection from radiation[80] and determination of the maximum weight to be carried.[81]

The importance of these protective measures should not be undermined by the fact that they have not formed the subject of a particular convention or recommendation. They have in fact been stressed in many conventions and recommendations issued by the International Labour Organization, and these testify to the extent of the international community's vigilance in protecting women from harsh working conditions.

The ILO has taken a firm stand on the issues of working hours and rest days for women,[82] taking into consideration the danger of overtime work for the working woman and nursing mother, and the need to guarantee time off for the working woman to nurse her infant.

The Arab Labour Organization has, in more than one convention, also prohibited the employment of women for night work, but has given national legislation the freedom to exclude certain jobs, and flexibility in defining 'night time', in accordance with conditions, geographical nature and the customs observed in each country.

The same convention[83] has prohibited the employment of women in jobs that are dangerous, difficult or harmful to the health and morals determined by legislation in each country.

Arab Convention No. (7) for 1977, regarding vocational health and safety, has likewise prohibited the employment of women in jobs that are difficult or harmful to the health or morals determined by legislation in each country.

Article (69) of Arab Convention No. (1) for 1996, regarding Arab levels of work,[84] stipulates that: 'Women shall not be employed for night work, and the concerned authorities in each state shall define what is meant by night time, in accordance with the weather, location and customs of each state, excluding jobs defined by the legislation, rules and regulations of each state.'

The same principle was stressed in article (7) of Arab Convention No. (5) for 1976, regarding working women.

At the level of national legislation, article (69) of Jordanian Labour Law No. (8) for 1996 stipulates that: 'After consulting with the concerned official authorities, the Minister shall issue a decree laying down the following:

a   Industries and jobs in which the work of women is prohibited.
b   Periods of time during which the employment of women shall be prohibited in addition to exceptions.

A similar provision was stipulated in article (46) of the previous Jordanian Labour Law No. (21) for 1960.

It should be noted that the Jordanian legislature, in both the old and new labour laws, left the determination of dangerous industries and jobs and the working hours during which the employment of women is prohibited to the discretion of the Minister of Labour. In accordance with the provisions of article (69) of Labour Law No. (8) for 1996, a decree was issued by the Minister of Labour, and was published in the Official Gazette of Jordan, Issue No. (4201), dated 30 April 1997.

We may note, in this brief review, that the issue of night work for women is handled with considerable sensitivity, in view of social traditions and conditions, and because of the major impact a woman's night work has on her family.

Most Arab legislation has prohibited the employment of women between 8 p.m. and 9 a.m. However, some countries, like Lebanon, have taken into consideration the difference in summer and winter time when determining these hours. Other countries have laid down a period between sunset and sunrise, while still others, like Mauritania, have laid down a continuous period of rest extending to eleven hours, ending between 6–8 a.m.

Most Arab countries have defined the jobs women may be employed to do at night, in accordance with the executive decisions attached to their labour laws, with the exception of Mauritania, which has defined these within its Labour Law. It is also noteworthy that all Arab countries tend to specify and list prohibited jobs, but leave the door open to permissible ones.

Chapter 22: Child rights in Arabic culture

Violette Dagher

Introduction

Every human civilization that has ever existed has emphasized the duties of adults toward children, informed by the notion that the relationship between child and adult involves the continuity of self, race and life. As such, many ancient societies took pains to provide children with the essentials for survival and to ensure that they were raised within a human community. This has been the case even in the absence of any concept of child rights, which more powerful societies established as a negative concept to distinguish themselves from less powerful ones.

The first kinds of right – or rather commitment – toward children were those arising from kinship or value systems: the first granting the child the right of inheritance and bequeathing the burden of family commitment, and the second giving him affection, education, care and protection against adult violence. This primeval concept of rights was, however, far more advanced among undeveloped Indian and African societies, which did not discriminate between adults and minors. Hence, these societies dealt with such rights, where they were granted, as privileges common to parents and children alike. Disparities abounded even so, chiefly due to gender, affinity or the legacy of inter-personal violence.

The proscription of child sacrifice, a practice derived from a belief system that sought to dispel the forces of evil by offering up that which humans valued most, marked a radical change in the history of child rights. The story of Ishmael in the Eastern religious narrative remains a symbol of the end of child sacrifice as an ordained practice. Jesus of Nazareth prohibited all forms of infanticide. Sa'sa'a ibn Naji ibn 'Iqal (grandfather of the poet al-Farazdaq), regarded by Munsif al-Marzouqi as the spiritual father of the Arab human rights movement,[1] went far beyond condemnation of infanticide. He fought against the pre-Islamic *wa'd* custom of burying female newborns alive by pioneering a tradition, in the absence of a tribal regulation, of payment of a *fidya*, or ransom, to parents intending to commit *wa'd* for fear of starvation; and he himself was known for paying this ransom to save any female infant no matter what her tribe's affinity or proximity to his own. Numerous Arabs followed in Sa'sa'a's footsteps, giving rise to the title 'Resurrector of Murdered Girls'. Al-Farazdaq (d. 110/728) boasted of his grandfather in this connection:

> My grandfather, who prevented child murder
> And saved the child so she might not perish . . .

Caring for orphans was an early form of protection for children in general.

'Arabs in pre-Islamic times had orphan homes for those who lost their father due to illness or war. Tribal chieftains were in charge of raising them, and supported them out of a large cooperative fund, made up of donations from tribes and tribal elders, and from war booties. The most famous of these was the Ghatfan orphan home.'[2]

Al-Ahnaf ibn Qays is one of several sages living closer to the Islamic era who devoted much of his attention to the issue of caring for children:

> Children are the apples of our eyes and the pillars of our lives; we are their pliable land and shady sky. If they ask, give them, and if they be upset, appease them, for they give you their affection and extend to you their love. Be not cruel to them, lest they be burdened with you and pray for your death.[3]

Islam prohibited infanticide, which was practised out of a sense of shame or from fear of starvation. The Quran says: 'Do not kill your children for fear of want. We shall provide sustenance for them as well as for you. Truly the killing of them is a great sin.' (17, *Al-Isra'*, 31.)

It may be said that, since infanticide was interdicted at various times in history, a child's right to life became one of the first of all child rights. It also initiated the process of shielding children from whatever might put their lives at risk in times of peace or war.

For all their attempts to ameliorate children's conditions and improve their relationship with adults, Abrahamic religions did not proscribe taking children into captivity and enslaving them. Yet, notwithstanding this failure, they emphasized the right to life itself. Whereas Greek philosophers had a predilection for euthanasia in the case of disabled children, early Muslims, along with Arab philosophers and physicians (Muslims, Christians, Jews and non-religionists alike), categorically denounced this notion, reaffirming a child's right to life, regardless of the nature or gravity of its physical or mental disability.

I. Patterns of child rearing and education

Islamic tradition represents the richest source of religious education for children. There may not be an abundance of Quranic verses on the topic, but those concerning parents' duties toward their child are of the deepest significance:

> Do not say to them a word of displeasure, nor repel them, but address them in terms of honour. And, out of kindness, lower to them the wing of humility and say, 'My Lord! Bestow on them Your Mercy even as they cherished me in child-hood.' (17, *Al-Isra'*, 24.)

Also:

> We have enjoined on man kindness to his parents: in pain did his mother bear him; and in pain did she give him birth. (46, *Al-Ahqaf*, 15.)

The most specific verse concerns breastfeeding:

> The mothers shall give suck to their offspring for two whole years, if the father desires to complete the term. But he shall bear the cost of their food and cloth-ing on equitable terms. No soul shall have a burden laid on it greater than it can bear. No mother shall be treated unfairly on account of her child. No father on account of his child. An heir shall be chargeable in the same way. If they both decide on weaning, by mutual consent, and after due consultation, there is no blame on them. If you decide on a foster-mother for your offspring, there is no blame on you. (2, *Al-Baqara*, 233.)

This verse calls on parents to breastfeed their children for two full years. Numerous interpreters say that the period may be shortened by approval of both parents. The verse also emphasizes the notion of *nafaqa* (alimony) and permits the mother to arrange for a foster-mother to breastfeed.

With regard to *hadith*, we find two approaches, although numerous scholars of *fiqh* (jurisprudence), or theologians, combine them into one.

The first approach is embodied in *hadith*s that stress good manners and fairness, for example:

- 'Never did a parent give a child a better gift than that of good manners.'
- 'Be generous to your children and teach them good manners.'
- 'Teach your children and families goodness, righteousness and good manners.'[4]

This emphasis on good manners is accompanied by a call to approach the child gently in speech and deed and to play with him so as to fill his heart with happiness.

There are famous anecdotes about 'Umar ibn al-Khattab that tell of his dismissing an official for not treating his children with kindness. Also, 'Ali ibn Abi Talib gave children a wide latitude for learning by their own initiative: 'Teach not your children to follow in your footsteps, for they are created for a time other than your own.'

The 'Ajarida, a sub-group within the Khawarij sect, reaffirmed this notion:

Every child who reaches adulthood is called upon to enter Islam, preferably well before reaching adulthood; he may not be judged a Muslim during childhood. Moreover, the early *sunni* and *shi'ite* theologians saw that children are not to be required to pray nor may they be punished.[5]

'Ali ibn al-Husayn, grandson to 'Ali ibn Abi Talib, in his *Treatise on Rights*, writes as follows on the child's right to an education:

As for your duty toward your child, you know that he is of you, and a continuation of you beyond this ephemeral life, be he good or evil. You are responsible for what you taught him in the way of good manners, referring to God in all things, and obeying Him, for which you shall either be punished or rewarded. So do for him that which would enhance the grace of His effect upon him in this ephemeral life, and that which would justify your relationship in the eyes of God by raising him well and teaching him God's way.[6]

Numerous enlightened Muslims adopted this approach, among them al-Hasan al-Basri, the Mu'tazilis, the Isma'ilis and the Druze Muwahhidin. Moreover, Christian Arab theologians followed suit. The approach found its greatest ally in the secular physician and philosopher Abu Bakr al-Razi, who also emphasized good manners and deeds over strict religious education during childhood. The *Explication of Clarification* (Sharh al-tawdih li 'l-tanqih) defines this concept of *taklif*, or 'charging', in Islam:

Childhood is extrinsic even though it is an essential condition for humans by birth. Childhood is not a prerequisite for the essence of a human, for this essence does not require childhood *per se* . . . Childhood is God's means to achieving His goal of creating an intelligent, skillful and powerful human being . . .[7]

This education, appropriate for everyone and not just for religious families, includes sports ('Teach your children archery, swimming and horse-back riding'), as well as mingling with other children and with people in general.

The second approach, in contrast, stresses early religious teaching, and leading the child on to pray – even forcing him to do so. This approach finds support in other *hadith*s, such as those that reproach the child so that he will learn to pray. Other *hadith*s even recommend beating him into submission. However, the ages recommended for teaching and compelling differ from one *hadith* to another, for example:

> A boy is to be protected from evil, God's name is to be pronounced upon him, and a sheep is to be sacrificed for him when he is seven days old; upon reaching six years of age he is to be taught good manners; upon reaching seven he is to sleep alone; upon reaching thirteen he is to be beaten into praying and fasting Ramadan; and upon reaching sixteen his father is to arrange for his marriage and support him financially.[8]

Traditional *fiqh* institutes advocating early learning and prayer for children also had numerous followers of their own, such as physicians and philosophers. ʻUrayb ibn Saʻd al-Katib al-Qurtubi, a physician and contemporary of al-Hakam II (known as al-Mustansir bi-Llah, caliph in Cordoba, 350/961–366/976) writes in his book on children[9] that the teaching of good manners must be combined with the forcible teaching of religious codes and prayer. Ibn Sina (Avicenna) insists on teaching children the Quran first:

> One must begin by teaching the Quran as soon as the child is physically and mentally fitted for this, and thereby teach him the alphabet and the basics of Islam. The boy is then to recite poetry starting with rajaz, or short, light poems, and move on to the qasida, or long, lyrical poems . . . Once the boy has completed memorizing the Quran and mastered Arabic grammar, it is then time to direct him toward that which suits his nature and abilities.[10]

Ibn Miskawayh, a philosopher with humanist tendencies, took a highly ironic stance: while supporting the teaching of good manners, he nevertheless insisted on strict religious instruction – in contrast to his own upbringing. In his *Cultivating Good Manners*, he has the following to say:

> Islamic Shariah law sets minors right, inures them to good deeds, and prepares them to appreciate wisdom, seek virtue and achieve human happiness through

proper thinking and virtuous example. Parents must therefore raise them according to the Shariah, using all means, such as beating them, if necessary; scolding them, if [this is] successful; enticing them with various rewards; or threatening them with various punishments. And if they grow accustomed to this method over time, it will become second nature to them, and they will become aware of the ways to virtue.[11]

He strongly attacked 'raising children on ribald poetry, sanctioning abominations, and playmates who instruct them in exploring physical pleasures while eating, drinking and primping to excess'. Many Islamists ascribe this stance to Ibn Miskawayh's own upbringing, but some historians rather attribute it to his times, during which it became common for adult men to practise pederasty. This led to the development of ribald poetry glorifying pederasty, then to a sharp reaction against anything that might lead adolescents astray. Hence, most people reverted to a strict, traditional, religious upbringing, which advocated the death penalty for any youth who willingly participated in homosexual practices.

Haytham Manna"s paper 'Child Rights in Arab-Islamic Culture' gives an overview of the various *fiqh* schools of thought on the issue of the child's responsibility concerning prayer and religious teaching. He quotes Ibn al-Jazzar's *Governing and Managing Boys* (Siyasat al-sibyan wa tadbiruhum), Ibn Miskawayh's *Cultivating Good Manners* and Ibn Sina's *The Canon of Medicine* (Al-Qanun fi 'l-tibb). 'All three,' he notes, 'agree that it is incumbent upon the parents to discipline and habituate the child to good manners from weaning onward. This is done to keep him from acquiring bad habits that are hard to break once they are inculcated. If it becomes necessary to apply punishment, caution and care must be used. One must not apply violence at first, but be gentle. Desire may then be combined with threats or frowns at times, while praise and encouragement may be more productive at other times. It all depends on the case in question. But if beating becomes absolutely necessary, the caretaker must not hesitate in making the first couple of beats painful.'[12]

The motto 'punishment as a last resort only' was a principle of child rearing for these three philosophers, and most Western philosophers of the Age of Enlightenment continued in this vein until very recently. However, corporal punishment, instituted in a law of 1860, was prohibited in British schools only in 1999, and a number of Islamic countries unfortunately took the 1860 law as their model when they were colonized by Britain. These countries have not as yet seen fit to do away with corporal punishment in their schools and through their court systems.

Arab philosophical and medical tradition underscored the cultivation of good manners in the young and precluded threats and coercion. Ibn Sina wrote:

> The focus of attention must be on the cultivation of a boy's manners. He must therefore be sheltered from extreme anger, fear, sadness or sleeplessness by contemplating that which he desires and offering it to him, and that which he loathes and keeping it away from him. There are two benefits in doing this. One is developing good manners to the point that they become a second nature in the boy's mind. The second relates to his body, for bad manners bring with them an ill temperament . . . Hence, teaching preserves health, for mind and body alike.[13]

Arab philosophers of the Middle Ages saw a connection between educational advice on the one hand, and mental and physical exercise on the other. They urge children to walk, ride horses, run, and sleep regularly and adequately, while also stressing communication among children. Conversation, says Ibn Sina,

> gladdens the mind and resolves questions, for each child speaks of the most delightful sight he has ever seen, or the strangest story he has ever heard. The strangeness of the conversation becomes, in and of itself, a reason for being curious about it, remembering it, and for inspiring more conversation about it. Furthermore, they are keeping each other company, which contributes to their edification, enlivens their spirit, and provides them with opportunities to test out their habits.[14]

Scholars have long differed on the age at which a child ought to begin his schooling. Some have said seven, others twelve, and still others have left it to the parents and the child himself. Scholars of *fiqh* have also differed on the age at which a child should begin praying. There are *hadith*s that allow compelling them to pray from the age of seven, and others from the age of twelve. However, none of these *hadith*s has any basis in the Quran.

Greek, Persian and Arab cultures all agree that the most important time in the raising of a child is the first seven years of his life.

II. From leniency to rights

It may be concluded from the above overview that there exists an enlightened view concerning the rearing of children, based on toleration (parents' and

others'), on allowing the child a wide latitude to learn, and on avoiding the placing of restrictions on the child's view of life, existence and belief. However, this
enlightened view has stood in contrast to repressive behaviour based on subjugation through the resort to violence first by the family, second by the school
and the environment, and third by oppressive government. 'Abd al-Rahman
al-Kawakibi denounced this state of affairs in 1902 in his book *Features of
Oppression*:

> Child rearing consists of nurturing the body alone until the age of two, which is up
> to the mother or the foster-mother; followed by nurturing the psyche until seven,
> which is up to both parents and the family at large; then developing the mind until
> the age of reason, which is up to the teachers and schools; then refinement by
> learning from the examples set by relatives and friends until marriage, which is
> ruled by chance; and edification by comparison, which is up to both spouses until
> death or separation. The education beyond the age of reason must be accompa-
> nied by an education of the environment, the social structure, the law or political
> process, and the education of the human being himself. Good governments facil-
> itate these matters by promulgating marriage laws; providing midwives, vaccina-
> tors and physicians; establishing orphanages and foster-homes; and building
> schools stretching from mandatory primary education to the highest levels.[15]

As for the effect of oppression on childhood, 'children are iron balls tied to the
parents with chains of injustice, disgrace, fear and harassment. Procreation
under oppression is folly, and taking pains to rear children is folly multiplied!'[16]

The Arab Renaissance witnessed a number of significant attempts focused
on children, although most of these concerned themselves with children and
mothers together.

Ethics dominated the scene, while laws concerning children were few and
far between. This is perhaps best captured by Ahmad Shawqi:

> Love the child even if it be not yours;
> For a child is an angel on earth.

The concept of child rights began, in various Arab countries, to re-enter legal
discussion about personal status laws. This led to an exploration of opinion, in
the *fiqh* and positive schools, of thought on certain essential matters, through
such encyclopaedic entries as 'Abd al-Razzaq al-Sanhuri's on law. International
changes doubtless had their effect on the Arab scene. Recent developments
have entailed the adoption of rights for children and regarding the child as
having a say in his life. This has led to a growing and significant move on the
part of Arab democrats and human rights advocates to protect child rights,

especially in the Arab world and Africa. Moreover, Arab children's journalism and literature have been strengthened and given the means to produce a special and distinctive art and culture.

Abu Bakr al-Razi was the first physician to separate pediatrics from gynecology. At the threshold of the third millennium, we are still waiting for the separation of the adult republic from that of the child and for attempts to explore the world of children, with its own logic, experience and judgement that require adults' respect and understanding. Dr Janusz Korsak[17] from Poland, a pioneer in reassessing concepts related to children, merits serious consideration. We also expect much from the United Nations Human Rights Commission, now that it has started paying attention to local concerns in its ambitious pursuit of universality.

The positive change in the concept of rights has led to a transformation in the theoretical and legalistic approach to child rights. Respect for human rights generally has now conditioned society to respect the rights of its children and young people as individuals in their own right, albeit requiring special care and attention in view of their vulnerability and lack of experience in dealing with life's problems and demands. The period since the proclamation of child rights in 1959 has witnessed a broad, concerted effort by the international community to consolidate these rights and establish binding international standards. These were embodied in the proclamation of the Charter of Child Rights, signed on 20 November 1989. By virtue of Korsak's experience, Poland played a notable role in promoting this treaty.

The importance of this Charter lies in the conceptual leap it embodies and in its commitment for the future. It covers all civil, political, economic, social and cultural aspects of the child's rights. The treaty also guarantees the child's basic right to live and prosper and protects him against neglect, maltreatment and abuse. The document also recognizes the child's right to take an active part in his growth, to express his opinions, and to have these opinions taken into consideration when decisions are made that affect his life. Since it was adopted into international law, it has committed signatory states to implement it and to incorporate it into the appropriate national legislation. Furthermore, signatory states are held accountable by the Child Rights Committee.

III. Obstacles and problems

Regrettably, the official adoption of such a powerful document[18] cannot wave away, as if by a magic wand, the legacy of the past and the complexities of the present. The gap is still very wide between principles and their actual translation in reality. If hundreds of millions of children under the age of five live in abject poverty in the developing countries, an incalculable number suffer negligence, maltreatment, sexual abuse, lack of education, emigration, expulsion, vagrancy, disability and illegal labour under exhausting and unhealthy conditions. Hundreds of thousands of children die every day through malnutrition, famine, treatable diseases, lack of medical care, environmental degradation, drug use, armed conflicts, economic blockades, racial discrimination, foreign occupation and other policies and economic conditions for which children pay the price ahead of others. It is incumbent on us to condemn, in this regard, the continuation in Mauritania and Sudan of various forms of slavery dating back to the Middle Ages.

In developing countries the problem of hunger and poverty, which forces children to work under harsh conditions, cannot be dealt with in an unfavourable international atmosphere. National efforts, where these exist, must be reinforced by international co-operation. However, the policies of developed countries, imposed to ensure their economic hegemony, remain the chief obstacle to any progress. It is necessary to arrive at a comprehensive, permanent resolution of the problem of foreign debt, to establish a more equitable trade system, and to meet the increasing requirements for development funding so that a portion of this may be devoted to social and economic programmes, especially for primary health and education.

Large numbers of children also fall victim to these policies, and lead a marginal existence, in the advanced countries themselves. It needs to be recognized, however, that 90 per cent of the world's children live in developing countries, where 1.3 billion of them live on the equivalent of one US dollar a day, and 3 billion on two US dollars a day. The population explosion in Africa and Asia is by far the most complex problem. The population of Africa doubles every 23 years. Besides, those countries at an early stage of development adopt savage capitalist policies that are essentially ineffective, or inefficient for implementing social laws protecting the more impoverished strata of society.

Various Arab states have promulgated laws based on the principles of the Arab Child Rights Charter, whereby the child's interest is placed above all else. Yet for all the efforts made, reality remains far grimmer than would appear from government presentations to the Child Rights Committee. International treaties and the proliferation of local and international non-governmental organizations cannot, in and of themselves, solve the problems of our times. Nor can legislation and commitment to implement treaties change the differing applications and interpretations made under various pretexts. These variations are subject to the dynamics of each society and culture. Furthermore, they are unrelated to the conditions and demands of the present. Traditions and customs assume a greater weight than legislation, especially when acting in conjunction with powerful reactionary currents. How can the lawmaker legislate when his laws are made subject to traditional norms?

The hegemony of patriarchy in traditional Arab societies, and the absence of a genuine democratic environment allowing for individuality and diversity, are not factors favourable to the establishment of good education and psychological well-being. Women have a decisive role to play in early childhood. What guarantees are there that mothers' relationships with their children will remain healthy; that mothers will not, consciously or unconsciously, reproduce the same cycle of violence, alienation and marginalization from which they themselves suffered?

A proper society is built on caring for the family and disadvantaged strata. Eradicating illiteracy, which touches 48 per cent across the Arab world, and educating the young – especially girls, who suffer a higher rate of illiteracy – are all extremely urgent matters. So is the issue of local non-governmental groups taking the initiative in planning and working toward dealing with these problems. But did the Child Rights Charter not take into account the customs and cultural values of each people (setting aside for the moment the ambiguity of these terms), in the wake of painstaking negotiations conducted over a number of years by representatives of countries with strongly differing cultures, ethics and religions? Herein lies its weakness and contradiction. Efforts to consolidate the Charter through a non-binding protocol and through international campaigns to put an end to the use of children in armed conflict, to trafficking in women and children as sexual objects, and to illegal labour – such efforts will need to be made within a framework of co-ordination between UNICEF, UNESCO and the High Commission for Human Rights, with a view to establishing a more comprehensive legal underpinning of child rights throughout the world.

In sum, the recognition of child rights is an existential issue for the destiny of every people, and the future of humanity depends upon it. Unless child rights are approached through the use of critical rationality, free speech, initiative and creativity, and are left untouched by oppressive customs, institutions, ideologies and regimes, then democratic and human rights activists are destined to find themselves mere witnesses of numerous tragedies. They can do little but issue condemnations. We are still very far from the spirit of these words by the Lebanese poet Gibran Khalil Gibran:

'Your children are not your own: They are the children of life, and life does not tarry in yesterday's abodes!'

Notes

Introduction

Salma Khadra Jayyusi

1. Translation by M. Modassir Ali. See *Islamic Studies*, 40, 3–4, (Autumn–Winter 1422/2001), p. 415.
2. That is not, of course, to deny that such 'communal patterning' is often found in other societies. Strong similarities can indeed be found in the modes of conduct, and patterns of response, within those countries that most pride themselves on their promotion of intellectual freedom and respect for individuality. These latter cases differ, even so, from the case of Arabs and Muslims. In Western countries a degree of public uniformity prevails because of the need, within any large society, to provide an ordered framework and to manage time and lifestyle in a coherent, economical manner. None of this, though, excludes the right of individuals to be different if they wish to disregard a pattern they find wearisome or inimical to the development of their particular talents. In Islamic society, by contrast, compliance with social norms is favoured for its own sake, while any major divergence, any singing out of tune with the community, is frowned upon. This results in a self-reinforcing environment, hostile alike to individual or group difference, even though some people may find the majority principles of conduct tedious. On the one hand, such uniformity waters down originality and desirable individuality, suppressing open difference; on the other hand, such a society does protect individuals from alienation, making them feel part of a coordinated collective arrangement with its own consistent and integrated principles and rituals. The weakness in Western society, with its stress on the importance of personal hard work, success and thrift (within an overall framework of typicality and order), is that a particular individual may be impelled into alienation and loneliness. The regularized tempo and pace draws him or her into a life of daily routine without providing any sense of the sociability of life – its warmth and harmony.

1 The concepts of rights and justice in Arab-Islamic texts

Muhammad 'Abid al-Jabiri

1. Taqiyy al-Din ibn Taymiyya, *Shariah Policy in Reforming the Ruler and the Ruled* (Al-Siyasa al-shariah fi islah al-ra'i wa 'l-ra'iyya) (Cairo: Dar al-Kitab al-'Arabi, 1969), 61.

2. Abu Ishaq al-Shatibi, *Correspondences in the Principles of Shariah* (Al-Muwafaqat fi usul al-shariah) (Cairo: Al-Tijariyya, n.d.), Vol. 2, 8–11.

3. Al-Qadi 'Abd al-Jabbar Ahmad, *Explaining the Five Principles* (Sharh al-usul al-khamsa) (Cairo: Wahba, 1965), 301–3.

4. Ibid., p. 313.

5. This 'circle' is mentioned in *The Book of Policies in the Management of Sovereignty* (Kitab al-siyasa fi tadbir al-riyasa), known as *The Secret of Secrets* (Sirr al-asrar), ascribed to Aristotle; edited by Abdul-Rahman Badawi in his *Greek Origins of Political Theories in Islam* (Al-Usul al-yunaniyya li' l-nazariyyat al-siyasiyya fi 'l-islam) (Cairo: Al-Nahda al-Misriyya, 1954), p. 127.

6. Abu 'Abd Allah ibn al-Azraq, *The Wonders of Texture in the Natures of Sovereignty* (Bada'i' al-silk fi taba'i al-mulk) (Baghdad: Ministry of Culture, Heritage Book Series), 1977), pp. 229–32.

7. Compare the Greek philosopher Anaxemander's concept of 'justice', which he considered a sublime criterion to which the universe is subject, giving it order and preserving it from chaos.

8. Abu 'l-Qasim al-Husayn ibn Muhammad ibn al-Fadl al-Raghib al-Asfahani, *The Way to the Dignities of Shariah* (Al-Dhari'a ila makarim al-shariah) (Beirut: Dar al-Kutub al-'Ilmiyya, 1980), pp. 241–8.

9. Abu 'l-Qasim Jarallah Mahmoud al-Zamakhshari, *The Unveiler of Facts about Obscurities of Revelation and the Choice of Sayings about the Aspects of Interpretation* (Al-Kashshaf 'an haqa'iq ghawamid al-tanzil wa 'uyun al-aqawil fi wujuh al-ta'wil) (Beirut: Dar al-Kutub al-'Ilmiyya, 1995).

10. Muhammad ibn Idris al-Shafi'i, *The Treatise* (Al-Risala), edited by Ahmad Shakir Cairo: Mustafa al-Halabi, 1939, pp. 79–81.

11. *The Crown in the Character of Kings* (Al-Taj fi akhlaq al-mulk), ascribed to al-Jahiz (Beirut: Lebanese Book Company, n.d.), pp. 10–11.

12. Shihab al-Din Muhammad ibn Ahmad al-Abshihi, *Selections from Every Fine Art* (Al-Mustatraf fi kulli fannin mustazraf) (Beirut: Hayat, 1990), Vol. 1, pp. 138–9.

13. Abu 'l-Hasan al-Ash'ari, *Islamists' Treatises* (Maqalat al-Islamiyyin) (Cairo: Al-Nahda, two parts in one volume, 1969), 1, pp. 219–21.

14. Ibid., p. 221.

15. Ibid., p. 228.

16. Abu 'l-Fat-h Muhammad ibn 'Abd al-Karim al-Shahrastani, *Sects and Denominations* (Al-Milal wa 'l-nihal), Cairo: Al-Halabi, two parts in one volume, 1968.

17. Abu Muhammad 'Abd Allah ibn Muslim al-Dinawari ibn Qutayba, *The Book of Knowledge* (Kitab al-ma'arif) (Cairo: Dar al-Ma'rifa, n.d.), p. 441.

18. Muhammad 'Abid al-Jabiri, *Critique of the Arab Mind* (Naqd al-'aql al-'Arabi); *III. The Arab Political Mind* (Al-'aql al-siyasi al-'Arabi) (Beirut: Centre for Arab Unity Studies).

19. There has recently been much talk of the necessity for an 'Arab sociology'. This, I believe, is where Arab sociologists should begin.

20. Paul Foulquié, *Dictionnaire de la langue philosophique* (Paris: P.U.F., 1969).

21. Al-Zamakhshari, op. cit.

22. Beirut: Centre for Arab Unity Studies, 1994.

23. Ibn Hazm, *The Ornamented* (Al-Muhalla) (Beirut: Dar al-Afaq al-Jadida, n.d.), Vol. 6, p. 156.

24. Quoted by Abu Yusuf in *The Book of Taxes* (Kitab al-kharaj), p. 144.

25. [Quotations from Plato's *Republic* are taken from the English translation by A. D. Lindsay (London: J. M. Dent & Sons Ltd. [Everyman's Library], 1940), pp. 143–4. Quotations in the original essay were taken from the Arabic translation by Fu'ad Zakariyya (Cairo, n.d.), No. 455–6 of the international system. – EDITOR]

26. Abu 'l-Walid Muhammad ibn Rushd (Averroes), *Compendium of Plato's Politics* (Jawami' siyasat Aflatun), based on the translation from Hebrew into English by Franz Rosenthal (Cambridge, 1969), pp. 164–5.

2 The concept of person in Islamic Tradition

Mohammed Arkoun

1. See my description of philosophical *adab* in the tenth century in *L'humanisme arabe au IV/X siècle* (Paris: J. Vrin, 2nd edition, 1982).

2. On the seminal importance of this vocabulary, see my study of the marvellous in the Quran in *Lectures du Coran* (Tunis, 2nd edition, 1991).

3. See 'De l'*ijtihad* à la critique de la raison Islamique', in my *Lectures du Coran*.

4. See 'Comment se présente la notion de personne dans la pensée islamique', in *Ouvertures sur l'islam* (Paris, 2nd edition, 1992).

3 Obedience and disagreement in the context of human rights in Islam

Fahmi Jad'an

1. Abu Hamid al-Ghazali, *The Book of the Just Mean in Belief* (Kitab al-iqtisad fi 'l-I'tiqad), edited by 'Adil al-'Awwa (Beirut: Dar al-Amana, 1969), pp. 214–5.

2. 'Abd al-Rahman ibn Khaldoun, *The Introduction* (Al-Muqqadima) (Dar al-Tunisiyya, 1989), Vol. I, pp. 78–9, 243–4.

3. *Sahih Muslim*, Vol. 6, p. 13; *Sahih al-Bukhari*, Vol. 4, p. 6; *Musnad Ahmad*, Vol. 2, p. 253; *Sunan al-Kubra*, Vol. 8, p. 175; *Sunan Ibn Maja*, Vol. 2, p. 954.

4. Malik ibn Anas, *The Compilation* (Al-Muwatta'), 2nd edition, (Beirut: Mu'assasat al-Risala, 1993), Vol. 1, pp. 345–6.

5. *Ibid.*, p. 347.

6. Abu 'l-Hasan al-Mawardi, *Statutes of Governance and Religious Jurisdiction* (Al-Ahkam al-sultaniyya wa 'l-wilayat al-diniyya), Kuwait, 1989, p. 24.

7. Abu Bakr al-Bayhaqi, *Faith and Guidance to the Right Path* (Al-I'tiqad wa 'l-hidaya ila sabil al-rashad) (Beirut: Al-Afaq al-Jadida, 1981), p. 245. This is quoted by al-Bukhari under 'Discord' (Al-Fitna) and by Muslim under 'Governance' (Al-Imara). See also, regarding obedience of the 'people of religion' to the caliphal state, Fahmi Jad'an, *The Crisis: a Study of Religious and Political Dialectics in Islam* (Al-Mihna: bahth fi jadaliyyat al-dini wa 'l-siyasi fi 'l-Islam) (Amman: Al-Shurouq, 1989), p. 341.

8. Al-Ya'qoubi, *History* (Al-Tarikh) (Beirut: Dar Sadir), Vol. 2, p. 222; al-Ghazali, *The Revival of the Religious Sciences* (Ihya' 'ulum al-din) (Beirut: Dar al-Ma'rifa), Vol. 4, p. 99.

9. *Sahih al-Bukhari*, Vol. 16, p. 228.

10. Ibn Abi Ya'la, *Genealogies of Hanbali Scholars* (Tabaqatul al-Hanabila), Vol. 1, pp. 294–5; Vol. 2, pp. 130–1.

11. Hanbal ibn Ishaq, *An Account of the Ordeal of Imam Ahmad ibn Hanbal* (Zikr mihnat al-imam Ahmad ibn Hanbal), pp. 89–99.

12. *The Tahawiyya Doctrine Explained* (Sharh al-'aqida al-tahawiyya) (Beirut-Damascus, 1984), pp. 427–37. See also Jad'an, op. cit., pp. 343–4.

13. Abu 'l-Hasan al-Ash'ari, *Discourses of Jurists and Disagreements of Worshippers* (Maqalat al-Islamiyyin wa ikhtilaf al-musallin), 3rd edition, (Helmut Ritter, 1980), p. 451.

14. Ibid., pp. 451–2.

15. Muhammad Sa'id Ramadan al-Bouti, *The Road Back to Islam* ('Ala tariq al-'awda ila 'l-Islam), 6th ed., (Beirut: Al-Risala, 1992), pp. 64–5.

16. Ibn al-Ikhwa (Muhammad ibn M. ibn Ahmad al-Qarashi), *Clear Guide to the Rules of Accounting* (Ma'alim al-qurba fi ahkam al-hisba) (Cairo: Al-Hay'a al-Misriyya al-Amma li 'l-Kitab, 1976), pp. 67–8.

17. [Translation taken from *The Forty Hadith of al-Nawawi*, translated by 'Izzedin Ibrahim and Denys Johnson-Davies (Kuwait: Al-Sahaba, 1985), p. 111. – EDITOR]

18. Al-Mawardi, op. cit., pp. 22–3; Abu Ya'la al-Farra', *Statutes of Governance* (Al-Ahkam al-sultaniyya) (Beirut: Dar al-Kutub, 1983), pp. 27–8; Ibn al-Ikhwa, op. cit., pp. 73–83.

19. Al-Ash'ari, op. cit., pp. 1–2.

20. Abu Hamid al-Ghazali, *Criterion of Distinction Between Islam and Atheism* (Faysal al-tafriqa bayna 'l-islam wa 'l-zandaqa) (Beirut-Damascus: Dar al-Hikma, 1986), p. 104.

21. Muhammad ibn Jarir al-Tabari, *Compendium of Quranic Interpretations* (Al-Jami' al-bayan 'an ta'wil aay al-qu'ran), Vol. 30, p. 331; Fakhr al-Din al-Razi, *The Comprehensive Explication* (Al-Tafsir al-kabir), Vol. 32, p. 147; al-Qurtubi, *Compendium of Quranic Rules* (Al-Jami' li ahkam al-qur'an), Vol. 20, p. 229.

22. Abu Mansour al-Baghdadi, *Science of Religion* (Usul al-din) (Beirut: Dar al-Afaq al-Jadida, 1981), pp. 318–24.

23. Ibid., pp. 326–7.

24. 'Ali Umlil, *Legitimacy of Disagreement* (Shar'iyyat al-ikhtilaf), 2nd edition (Beirut: Dar al-Tali'a, 1993), pp. 12–55.

25. 'Abdul-'Aziz Jawish, *Islam: Creed of Fitra and Freedom* (Al-Islam: din al-fitra wa 'l-hurriyya) (Cairo, n.d.), pp. 160–2.

26. Mahmoud Shaltout, *Islamic Belief and Law* (Al-Islam 'aqida wa shariah), 17th edition (Cairo: Al-Shurouq, 1997), pp. 280–1.

27. Rashid al-Ghanoushi, *Public Freedoms in the Islamic State* (Al-Hurriyyat al-'amma fi 'l-dawla al-Islamiyya) (Beirut: Centre for Arab Unity Studies, 1993), pp. 42–5.

28. Ibid., p. 47.

29. Ibid., p. 48.

30. Ibid. pp. 48–50.

31. Ibn al-Ikhwa, op. cit., pp. 48–50.

32. 'Abdul-Jabbar bin Ahmad, *Explication of the Five Principles* (Sharh al-usul al-khamsa) (Cairo: Maktabat Wahba, 1965), p. 144.

33. For further details, see Jada'n, op. cit., pp. 58–62.

34. Ibid., pp. 161–73.

35. Ibn Taymiyya, *Legal Policy for Reforming Ruler and Subjects* (Al-Siyasa al-shar'iyya fi islah al-ra'i wa 'l-ra'iyya) (Beirut: Al-Ma'rifa, n.d.), p. 24.

36. Ibn Taymiyya, *Accounting* (Al-Hisba) (Cairo: Al-Matba'a al-Salafiyya, 1387 AH), p. 42.

37. See Fahmi Jad'an, 'Orthodoxy: Its Limits and Transformations' (Al-Salafiyya: hudouduha wa tahawwulatuha), *'Alam al-Fikr* (Kuwait), 3 and 4, 1998, pp. 88–90.

4 Human rights in the *hadith*

Husni Mahmoud

1. Al-Bukhari (Abu 'Abdallah Muhammad Abi 'l-Hasan), *Sahih al-Bukhari* (Dar al-Fikr, 1401/1981), III, 6, p. 116.

2. Ibid., II, 3, p. 107.

3. Ibid., IV, 7, p. 193.

4. Ibid., IV, 7, p. 10.

5. Ibid.

6. Ibid., III, 5, pp. 74–5.

7. Ibid., I, 2, p. 238.

8. Ibid., I, 1, p. 90; on 'Amr ibn al-'As, p. 90; on 'Ammar, p. 91.

9. Ibid., III, 5, p. 107.

10. Ibid., II, 4, pp. 7–8; IV, 8, p. 105.

11. Al-Ghazali (Abu Hamid Muhammad), *The Just Mean in Belief* (Al-Iqtisad fi 'l-I'tiqad) (Beirut: Dar al-Kutub al-'Ilmiyya, 1st edition, 1403/1983), p. 148.

12. *Sahih*, II, 3, p. 9.

13. Ibid.

14. Ibid., I, 2, p. 132. He also said: 'Wealth is not in the extent of property, but in the richness of the soul.' See III, 7, p. 178.

15. Ibid., I, 1, p. 17.

16. Ibid., I, 2, p. 108.

17. Ibid., I, 2, pp. 88, 89, 92.

18. Ibid., I, 2, p. 87.

19. Ibid.

20. Ibid.

21. Ibid., I, 1, pp. 8, 9.

22. Ibid.

23. Ibid., IV, 7, pp. 88, 91.

24. Ibid.

25. Ibid., II, 3, p. 98.

26. Ibid., IV, 7, p. 84.

27. Ibid., I, 1, p. 13.

28. Ibid., IV, 7, p. 81.

29. Ibid., II, 3, p. 117.

30. Ibid., IV, 7, p. 138.

31. Ibid., IV, 7, p. 69.

32. Ibid.

33. Ibid.

34. Ibid., IV, 7, p. 70.

35. Ibid., IV, 7, p. 71.

36. Ibid., IV, 7, p. 69.

37. Ibid., II, 4, p. 276.

38. Ibid., I, 2, p. 117.

39. Ibid., III, 5, pp. 123–34.

40. Ibid., IV, 7, p. 72.

41. Ibid.

42. Ibid., IV, 7, p. 73.

43. Ibid., IV, 7, p. 104.

44. Ibid., II, 4, pp. 166–7.

45. Ibid., IV, 7, pp. 78–9; III, 6, p. 145.

46. Ibid., IV, 7, p. 78.

47. Ibid.

48. Ibid.

49. Ibid., IV, 8, p. 21.

50. Ibid., IV, 7, p. 4; III, 6, p. 143.

51. Ibid., III, 5, p. 178; IV, 7, p. 76.

52. Ibid., III, 5, p. 189; IV, 7, p. 76.

53. Ibid., I, 2, p. 114.

54. Ibid., I, 2, p. 121; II, 3, p. 117.

55. Ibid., I, 2, p. 117.

56. Ibid.

57. Ibid., I, 1, p. 20.

58. Ibid., I, 2, p. 119.

59. Ibid., II, 3, p. 9.

60. Ibid., II, 3, p. 25.

61. Ibid.

62. Ibid., II, 3, p. 24.

63. Ibid., II, 3, pp. 160, 78.

64. Ibid., II, 3, p. 10.

65. Ibid., II, 4, p. 152.

66. Ibid., II, 3, p. 103.

67. Ibid., I, 1, p. 109.

68. Ibid., IV, 7, pp. 129–30.

69. Ibid., IV, 7, p. 142.

70. Ibid., I, 1, p. 172.

71. Ibid., IV, 8, p. 109; I, 1, p. 173.

72. Ibid., I, 1, p. 173.

73. Ibid., IV, 7, p. 75.

74. Ibid.

75. Ibid., II, 3, p. 186.

76. Ibid., II, 7, p. 65.

77. Ibid.

78. Ibid., II, 7, p. 177.

79. Ibid., II, 4, p. 150.

80. Ibid., IV, 7, pp. 77–8.

81. Ibid., IV, 7, p. 46.

82. Ibid., III, 6, p. 145.

83. Ibid., IV, 7, p. 68.

84. Ibid., I, 6, p. 218.

85. Ibid., II, 3, p. 191.

86. Ibid., I, 2, p. 245.

87. Ibid., III, 5, p. 159.

88. Ibid., III, 5, p. 189.

89. Ibid., III, 5, p. 153.

90. Ibid., III, 6, p. 23.

91. Ibid., III, 5, p. 135.

92. Ibid.

93. Ibid., III, 5, pp. 136–7.

94. Ibid., III, 5, p. 136.

95. Ibid., II, 3, p. 24.

96. Ibid., II, 4, p. 21.

97. Ibid., II, 3, p. 124.

98. Ibid., III, 6, p. 214.

99. Ibid., I, 1, p. 13.

100. Ibid., I, 8, p. 15.

101. Ibid., I, 1, pp. 102–3.

102. Ibid., IV, 8, p. 35.

103. Ibid., IV, 8, p. 118.

104. Ibid., I, 1, p. 13.

105. Ibid., II, 3, pp. 27, 29.

106. Ibid., III, 6, p. 120; II, 4, p. 19; I, 1, p. 33.; II, 3, pp. 123–4.

107. See Muhammad Fu'ad 'Abd al-Baqi, *Pearls and Corals* (Al-Lu'lu' wa 'l-murjan) ([Beirut-Amman]: Al-Maktaba 'l-Islamiyya, n.d.), Vol.II, 131, quoted by al-Bukhari, op.cit., *The Book of Manumission* (Kitab al-'itq), p. 49.

108. *Sahih*, IV, 7, p. 27.

109. Ibid., III, 5, p. 194.

110. Ibid., II, 3, pp. 113, 111.

111. Ibid., II, 3, p. 123.

112. Ibid., I, 1, p. 170.

113. Ibid., II, 3, p. 124.

114. Ibid., II, 3, p. 99.

115. Ibid., II, 3, p. 100.

116. Ibid., II, 3, p. 134.

117. Ibid.

118. Ibid., II, 3, p. 99.

119. Ibid., II, 3, p. 98.

120. Ibid., II, 3, p. 99.

121. Ibid., IV, 8, p. 109.

122. Ibid., II, 3, pp. 61, 62.

123. Ibid., II, 4, p. 150.

124. Ibid., III, 5, p. 154.

125. Ibid., II, 3, pp. 187–8.

126. Ibid., II, 3, p. 101.

127. Ibid., II, 4, p. 7; IV, 8, p. 104.

128. Ibid., IV, 8, p. 104; II, 4, p. 8.

129. Ibid., II, 4, pp. 42–4.

130. Reported by al-Tirmidhi.

131. *Sahih*, II, 3, p. 27.

132. *Musnad Imam Ahmad.*

133. Ibn Maja, No. 3747.

134. *Sahih*, I, 1, p. 34.

135. Ibid.

136. Ibid., IV, 7, p. 215.

137. Ibid., II, 4, p. 150.

138. Ibid., II, 3, p. 77; I, 1, p. 51.

139. Ibid., II, 3, p. 77; II, 4, p. 100.

140. *The International Organization since 1945* (Al-Umam al-muttahida fi nisf qarn: dirasa fi tatawwur al-ta Shariah nazim al-duwali mundhu 1945), Kuwait: 'Alam al-Ma'rifa Series 202, 1995, pp. 208, 212, 378.

5 'Man' and 'the Rights of Woman' in Islamic discourse

Nasr Hamid Abu Zayd

1. The scope and conditions of *jizya* are quite clear: it is not levied from children, women, old men or men of religion. See Ibn Rushd, *The Beginning of the Scholar and the End of the Mean* (Bidayat al-mujtahid wa nihayat al-muqtasid), edited by 'Abd al-Halim Muhammad 'Abd al-Halim and 'Abd al-Rahman Hasan Mahmoud (Cairo: Dar al-Kutub al-Haditha, 1975), Vol. 1, p. 436.

2. See, for instance, Fahmi Huwaydi, *So That There Will Be No Sedition* (Hatta la takuna fitna) (Cairo: Dar al-Shurouq, 1st edition, 1989), p. 275. On 14 June 1995, however, the Egyptian Judiciary witnessed a judgment issued by the Cairo Court of Appeal, Dept. 14, Personal Status, and confirmed by the Court of Cassation on 5 August 1966, ruling the 'apostasy' of the present writer. One of the reasons for the ruling was the writer's interpretation of *jizya*. The court quoted what the writer had said in his book *Critique of Religious Discourse* (Naqd al-fikr al-dini), p. 205: 'Now that the principle of equality in rights and duties is settled, irrespective of religion, colour or gender, it is not right to cling to the historical significance of *jizya*. Adherence to the literal significance of the relevant texts in this connection not only runs counter to the interest of the community, but also grievously harms the national fabric. What harm could be more serious than to drag society backward, to a stage bypassed by humanity in the long struggle for a better world, based on equality, liberty and justice?'

In condemning this interpretation, whose novelty lay in the method of interpretation and deduction, the court noted as follows: 'The defendant states here that attachment to the literal significance of texts drags society backward, when a better world has been attained [!] In his view, attachment to the literal significance of texts represents backwardness and a relapse into backwardness, after humanity has progressed to what is better [!!] This is a *rejection of the verses of God (swt) concerning* jizya *and a description thereof in terms that one would hesitate to use in describing human speech and judgments. Indeed, it contravenes the rulings specified by the* Quran *and the sunna . . . As for the verse on* jizya *which the defendant rejected (?!), it is No. 29 of* surat Al-Tawba.' (Italics mine.) Despite this ruling, the interpretation is sound and legitimate in a considerable degree.

3. See: Ibn Hisham, *Biography of the Prophet*, edited by Majdi Fathi al-Sayyid (Tanta: Dar al-Sahaba li 'l-Turath, n.d.), Vol. 3, 215–18, 221–9.

4. See: 'Abd al-Mun'im Majid, *The First Abbasid Age* (Al-'Asr al-'Abbasi al-awwal), Anglo-Egyptian Bookshop, 1973, Vol. 1, p. 67; also, O'Leary, *Arab Thought and its Place in History* (Al-Fikr al-'Arabi wa markazuhu fi 'l- tarikh), translated by Isma'il al-Baytar (Beirut: Dar al-Kitab al-Lubnani, 1972), pp. 60–1.

5. See: Mahmoud Isma'il, *Secret Movements in Islam* (Al-Harakat al-sirriyya fi 'l-Islam) (Cairo: Mu'assasat Rose al-Yusuf, 1973), p. 135.

6. *The Adequate Chapters on Monotheism and Justice* (Al-Mughni fi abwab al-tawhid wa 'l-'adl), Vol. 8, *The Creature* (Al-Makhluq), edited by Tawfiq al-Tawil and Sa'd Zayid (Cairo: Ministry of Culture and National Guidance, n.d.) p. 223.

7. Ibid., Vol. 11, *Duty* (Al-Taklif), edited by Muhammad 'Ali al-Najjar and 'Abd al-Halim al-Najjar, 1965, pp. 483–4.

8. Al-Qadi 'Abd al-Jabbar ascribes the dictum of 'determinism' to Mu'awiya ibn Abi Sufyan: 'The first to initiate and promote determinism was Mu'awiya. He claimed that the actions he performed were by the will and creation of God, in order to use that as a pretext for what he did, and to give the illusion that he was right and that God had made him an imam and entrusted him with authority. This became more marked with the Umayyads.' (Op. cit., Vol. 8, p. 4.)

9. Muhammad ibn Jarir al-Tabari, *Summa in the Exegesis of the* Quran (Jami' al-bayan 'an ta'wil al-Qur'an), edited by Mahmoud Muhammad Shakir (Cairo: Dar al-Ma'arif, 1969), Vol. 1, p. 512.

10. Jarallah Mahmoud ibn 'Umar al-Zamakhshari, *The Unveiler of Facts about the Ambiguities of Revelation and Choice Opinion about the Aspects of Interpretation* (Al-Kashshaf 'an haqa'iq ghawamid al-tanzil wa 'uyun al-aqawil fi wujuh al-ta'wil) (Cairo: Halabi, 1966), Vol. 3, p. 382.

11. Ibid., p. 383.

12. Ibid.

13. *The Appeal for Justice in Mu'tazili Doctrine Included in al-Kashshaf* (Al-Intisaf fima tadammanahu' l-kashshaf min al-i'tizal).

14. See: Agnus Goldzieher, 'Neo-Platonic and Gnostic Elements in *Hadith*', in 'Abd

al-Rahman Badawi, *The Greek Heritage in Arab Civilization* (Al-Turath al-Yunani fi
'l-hadara al-'Arabiyya) (Cairo, 2nd edition, 1965), p. 218.

15. See Ibrahim Bayyumi Madkour, *On Islamic Philosophy: Method and Practice*, (Fi 'l-fal-
safa al-Islamiyya: minhaj wa tatbiq) (Dar al-Ma'arif, 3rd edition, 1967), Vol. 1,
p. 40. See also Ibrahim Ibrahim Hilal, *Theory of Illuminism and its Influence on Thinking
of Prophethood* (Nazariyyat al-ma'rifa al-ishraqiyya wa atharuha fi 'l-nazar ila al-
nubuwwah) (Dar al-Nahda al-Misriyya, 1977), Vol. 1, pp. 38–9, 46–7.

16. Madkour, op. cit., pp. 66–7; Hilal, op. cit., p. 114; see also Joseph al-Hashim,
Al-Farabi (Beirut: Al-Maktab al-Tijari, 2nd edition, 1968), p. 140.

17. *Summa*, Vol. 16, *The Inimitability of the* Quran (I'jaz al-Qur'an), edited by Amin
al-Khouli, 1960, p. 403.

18. *The Final Word about the Connection between Wisdom and Shariah* (Fasl al-maqal fima
bayn al-hikma wa 'l- Shariah min al-ittisal), edited by Muhammad 'Amara (Cairo:
Dar al-Ma'arif, 1972), p. 32.

19. The question of the 'authority of the intellectual' is quite manifest in the political
and social Arab reality, and on more than one level, especially when the intellectual is involved in political 'action', ignoring the epistemological conditions for
the role of the intellectual. In the most extreme cases, he becomes a mouthpiece
for political authority, or, if he is more intelligent, an ideological 'apologist'; or,
again, he may – if he is reclusive by nature – exercise intellectual 'arrogance' over
the 'commoners' and the 'rabble'. One still remembers the slogan 'Egypt is for
the Egyptians', raised by intellectuals in the struggle against British occupation
and the authority of the Ottoman Empire, when the real 'Egyptians' were defined
as 'those who own the real interest,' and are 'rich in money and knowledge' –
completely ignoring the majority, who were 'rich in labour'.

20. Louis Massignon, *The Passion of al-Hallaj, Mystic and Martyr of Islam*, translated by
Herbert Mason (Princeton: Princeton University Press, 1982), Vol. 3, p. 34.

21. *Jewels of Wisdom* (Fusus al-hikam), edited by Abu 'l-A'la 'Afifi (Beirut: Dar al-Kitab
al-'Arabi, n.d.), p. 199.

22. See al-Tabari, *Summa* (Cairo: Dar al-Rayyan, fascimile edition, n.d.), Vol. 23,
p. 119.

23. See *Epistles of the Brethren of Purity and Companions of Sincerity* (Rasa'il ikhwan al-safa
wa khullan al-wafa) (Beirut: Dar Sadir, n.d.), Vol. 2, p. 457.

24. Abu 'l-A'la 'Afifi, *The Mystical Philosophy of Muhyiddin ibn 'Arabi* (Cambridge:
Cambridge University Press, 1939), p. 80.

25. Since the holy verse makes such a strong connection between the 'Life' of God
and His 'Knowledge', how can those who have no knowledge or insight insist
that the 'chair' spanning heaven and earth is anything but knowledge? See the
juristic sentence in note 2 above.

26. *Hayy Ibn Yaqzan*, edited by Albert Nasri Nadir (Beirut: Dar al-Mashriq, 4th edition), p. 29. It is also suggested in the tale that Hayy was the son of a secretly married princess who feared scandal and so placed him in a 'coffin' which she threw

into the sea for the tide to carry to the 'island'. This is a clear allusion to the story of the child Moses in the Quran, but it does not cover more than two paragraphs in the narrative, while the first opinion occupies the whole remainder of the first part of the novel.

27. Ibid., p. 39.
28. Ibid., pp. 26–7.
29. This sentence occurs once in the text when 'Hayy' compares his body to those of the animals and notices, among other things, that they are 'less obvious in their organs' (p. 34).
30. The grammar is slightly amended here.
31. Ibid., p. 64.
32. Ibid., p. 81. It was 'pantheism' for which al-Hallaj paid with his life. Al-Ghazali alludes to it in his books, which are 'jealously kept away from the common people'. Finally, it is the theory celebrated by Ibn 'Arabi a little after Ibn Tufayl. We therefore have to understand the narrator's 'emendation' as 'suspicious' with reference to the long description of unity as presented by the protagonist, p. 82.
33. Ibid., p. 90.
34. Ibid., p. 89.
35. Ibid., p. 90.
36. Ibid., p. 92, italics mine. The description invokes the Quranic 'text' on the process of teaching 'Adam' the names as explained by the books on exegesis.
37. Ibid., pp. 92–3.
38. Ibid., pp. 93–4.
39. I have treated this issue in my book: *The Intellectual Tendency in Exegesis: A Study of Metaphor in the* Quran *as Seen by the Mu'tazilis* (Al-Ittijah al 'aqli fi 'l-tafsir, dirasa fi qadiyyat al-majaz fi 'l-Qur'an 'inda al- Mu'tazila) (Beirut: Arab Cultural Centre, 4th edition, 1996), pp. 164–90.
40. I have treated this issue in my study 'The Discourse of Ibn Rushd and the Pressures of Counter-Discourse', in *Alif, A Review of Comparative Rhetoric*, (Cairo: AUC, 1996).
41. *Hayy ibn Yaqzan*, pp. 94–5.
42. Ibid., pp. 96–7.
43. Ibid., p. 97.
44. Reference may be made to my book, *Al-Imam al-Shaf'i and the Establishment of the Median Ideology* (Al-Imam al-Shafi'i wa ta'sis al-idyulujiyya al-wasatiyya) (Cairo: Madbuli, 2nd edition, 1996).
45. The title of al-Tabari's encyclopedia of history.
46. Isma'il, op. cit., p. 53.
47. The works of Abu Hamid al-Ghazali embody the intellectual formulations which have dominated most of the Islamic world from the sixth/twelfth century to the present. For all the vivacity of these works (especially when compared to similar later works), they effectively paved the way for the later closure of *ijtihad*. The

vivacity lies in the way al-Ghazali formulated a multi-intellectual discourse, within a political and social reality still capable of accepting intellectual plurality. Al-Ghazali's major works in the field of kalamology are: *The Just Mean in Belief* (Al-Iqtisad fi 'l-I'tiqad); *The Divide between Islam and Disbelief* (Faysal al-tafriqa bayna 'l-Islam wa 'l-zandaqa); *Silencing the Commoners from Kalamology* (Iljam al-'awam 'an 'ilm al-kalam). Other major works include: in philosophy, *The Incoherence of the Philosophers* (Tahafut al-falasifa); in mysticism, *The Revival of the Religious Sciences* (Ihya' 'ulum al-din) and *The Niche for Lights* (Mishkat al-anwar); and, in political thought, *A Refutation of the Batinis* (Al-Radd 'ala 'l-batiniyya). These are related to the fields discussed above.

48. See, for instance, 'A Failed Test in Human Rights' (Ikhtibar fashil fi huquq al-insan), in *Al-Ahram* daily, 16 July 1996.

49. *The Islamic Awakening between Stagnation and Extremism* (Al-Sahwa 'l-Islamiyya bayn al-jumud wa 'l-tatarruf) (Cairo: Dar al-Shurouq, 2nd edition, 1984), p. 40.

6 The body: its images and rights in Islam

Munsif al-Wahaybi

1. *Istibda'* is asking for intercourse. In pre-Islamic society a woman practised this kind of intercourse at the request of her own husband, who might ask her, when her monthly period is over, to have intercourse with another man known for his courage and physical power, in the hope of a better posterity.

Mudamada is when a woman lives with a man other than her husband. Pre-Islamic Arabs allowed this in years of drought, famine and economic hardship.

Mukhadana is when several men have intercourse with one woman. When she gives birth, she may choose the parentage from among any one of these men, who, in turn, cannot refuse.

Prostitution was practised in pre-Islamic times with slave girls brought from other countries.

Dayzan is the inheritance of the father's wife, by his eldest son from another wife, among other items of inheritance.

Shaghar is a kind of barter marriage, with no dowry involved. A man may give his daughter or sister in marriage to another man, provided the latter does the same for him.

Exchange of wives was a temporary measure popular in pre-Islamic society.

Pleasure Marriage: This type of marriage was known before Islam. Merchants on their travels and raiders in their raids would conclude a pleasure marriage for a specified period of time. See: 'Abd al-Salam al-Termanini, *Marriage among the Arabs* (Al-Zawaj 'inda 'l-'Arab); al-Alusi, *Achieving the Objective* (Bulugh al-arab); Jawad 'Ali, *A Detailed History of the Arabs before Islam* (Al-Mufassal fi tarikh al-'Arab qabla 'l-Islam); al-Maydani (Abu 'l-Fadl Ahmad ibn Muhammad), *Treasury of Proverbs* (Majma' al-amthal); Ibn Manzur (Abu 'l-Fadl Muhammad ibn Makram), *The Language of the Arabs* (Lisan al-'Arab), items: *damad, khadan.*

2. Adunis ('Ali Ahmad Sa'id), *The Static and the Dynamic* (Al-Thabit wa 'l-muta-hawwil) (Beirut: Dar al-'Awda, 1974–8), Vol. 1, 207.

3. Hegel, as quoted by Nayif Ballouz, *Aesthetics* ('Ilm al-jamal) (Damascus: Al-Ta'awuniyya Press, 1981), p. 87.

4. Adunis, loc. cit.

5. Ibid.

6. Ibid.

7. Ibn al-Kalbi (Abu Mundhir Hisham), *The Book of Idols* (Kitab al-asnam); al-Qazwini (Abu 'Abdallah Zakariyya), *Odd Creatures and Strange Beings* ('Aja'ib al-makhluqat wa ghara'ib al-mawjudat).

8. Ibrahim 'Abd al-Rahman, quoting from Muhammad al-Ghuzzi's article, 'The Celebration of the Body in the pre-Islamic Heritage' (Al-Ihtifal bi 'l-jasad fi 'l-turath al-jahili), in *Fikrun wa Fann*, Year 23, No. 43 (1986), p. 28. See also, al-Termanini, op. cit., p. 30.

9. Comment on a poem of Ibn Yamoun (see below) by Karam Idris, in *Anwal al-Maghrib* daily, March 1986.

10. Al-Ghazali (Abu Hamid Muhammad), *The Revival of the Religious Sciences* (Ihya' 'ulum al-din).

11. This variety may be illustrated by contrasting the Prophet's advice to cover the body during copulation with the advice of the *faqih* (religious teacher) Ibn Yamoun al-Maghribi in his poem:

Avoid copulation when in your clothes.
This is, certainly, an act of ignorance.

12. [It is of great interest to note that, from the early days of Islam, the right to phys-ical pleasure in marriage belonged also to the woman. The following anecdote about Caliph 'Umar ibn al-Khattab (586–644 AD) indicates a strong basis in social justice and respect for human nature in acknowledging and supporting the right of the wife to physical enjoyment. In the book on the *Life of the Companions* in *The Treasure* (Al-Kanz), by Shaikh Muhammad Yusuf al-Kandahluwi under *jihad* (reli-gious war): 'Going to fight for four months in the cause of God', Ibn Jurayj is reported as saying the following: 'I learned from a reliable source that 'Umar was walking in town one night when he heard a woman reciting:

"Night grows longer, its sides darker,
The lack of a beloved to embrace keeps me awake.
Were it not for the peerless fear of God,
The sides of my bed would have fallen apart."

"What's making you suffer so?" 'Umar asked. "For several months now," she answered, "my husband has been absent on your orders, and I yearn for him." "Have you committed any sin?" he asked. "God forbid!" she replied. Then 'Umar said: "Be patient for a while. It will only be the time length of the journey back." And he immediately sent for him. Then he asked his daughter, Hafsa. "I wish to ask you," he said, "about a matter giving me great anxiety. I hope you can bring me relief. How long can a woman endure before she begins to miss her husband?" She bowed her head in embarrassment. 'Umar said, "In the path of God, there is no shame to tell the truth." She made a gesture with her fingers to mean three or four months. Then 'Umar ordered the armies not to be kept away for more than four months.' *Life of the Companions,* produced by Abu 'l-Hasan al-Nadawi (Beirut, Dar al-Ma'rifa, 1968), Vol. 8, 308. – THE EDITOR. To my knowledge, this has not been preceded in any of the cultures I came to know.]

13. See Shafiq al-Balkhi, 'Rules of Worship' (Adab al-'ibadat) in Shafiq al-Balkhi and 'Abd al-Jabbar al-Nifari, *Unpublished Sufi Texts,* edited and introduced by Paulus Nwiyya the Jesuit, (Beirut, Dar al-Mashriq, [1973]), p. 17 et seq.

14. Abu Bakr Muhammad ibn Zakariyya al-Razi (c. 251/865–311/923 or 320/932), in *Selections from al-Razi,* edited by Paul Krauss (Cairo, 1939).

15. From *Self and Soul* of Fakhr al-Din al-Razi (544/1149–606/1209).

16. Op. cit., pp. 29, 35, 39.

17. For more information, see Salah al-Din al-Munajjid, *The Arabs and Female Beauty* (Jamal al-mar'a 'inda 'l-'Arab) (n.p., n.d.), p. 56 et seq; Termanini op. cit., pp. 119–48.

18. Al-Jahiz, 'The Bragging of Slaves and Singing Girls' (Mufakharat al-jawari wa 'l-ghilman) and 'The Epistle of Singing Girls' (Risalat al-qiyan) in *Collected Epistles of al-Jahiz* (Majmu'at rasa'il al-Jahiz), quoted by Termanini, op. cit., p. 138.

19. 'Ali Zai'ur, *Popular Versions on Knowledge, Fertility and Destiny* (Siyaghat sha'biyya hawla 'l-ma'rifa wa 'l-khusuba wa 'l-qadar), a psychological analysis of the Arab soul (Beirut: ar al-Andalus, 1984), p. 76.

20. Ibn 'Arabi, in his comment on the *hadith,* 'Three of your world were endeared to me: women, perfume, and the *salat,* my heart's desire', says that the Prophet used the feminine gender for the 'three', rather than the masculine, as he meant to enhance the love of women. Arabs usually prefer the use of the masculine gender, but the Prophet preferred the feminine.

21. Adunis, op. cit., Vol. 1, 233.

22. Al-Nazzam, was the woman Ibn 'Arabi loved and married.

23. Ibn 'Arabi, *Jewels of Wisdom* (Fusus al-hikam), p. 230 et seq.; Adunis, op. cit., Vol. 1, 232–3.

24. Henri Corbin, *Creative Imagination in Ibn 'Arabi's Mysticism* (Al-Khayal al-ibda'i fi tasawwuf Ibn 'Arabi), p. 159.

25. The original Arabic word is *sayasi,* which means a protective body. See Henri Corbin, Husain Nasr and 'Uthman Yahya, *Histoire de la philosophie islamique* (Tarikh

al-falsafa 'l-Islamiyya), Arabic translation by Naseer Muwuwwa and Hasan
Qubaisi (Beirut, Manshurat 'Uwaidat, 1966), p. 319.

26. Op. cit., pp. 309–20.

27. Al-Hallaj (Abu Mughith al-Hasan ibn Mansour), *Al-Tawasin*, p. 135; and al-
    Istakhri, (Abu Ishaq Ibrahim), *The Paths of Kingdoms* (Masalik al-mamalik), p. 90.

28. Mahmoud al-Munufi, *Pure Islamic Sufism* (Al-Tasawwuf al-Islami al-khalis) (Cairo:
    Dar Nahdat Misr, 1979), p. 184.

29. Op. cit., p. 184.

30. Corbin, op. cit., p. 149; 'Atif Jawda Nasr, *The Poetic Symbol of the Sufis* (Al-Ramz
    al-shi'ri 'inda 'l-sufiyya), (n.p., n.d.), p. 139.

31. The Poems of al-Hallaj (Ash'ar al-Hallaj) (Paris: Sindibad, 1985), p. 82.

32. Al-Qushayri (Abu 'l-Qasim 'Abd al-Karim), (Nahwa 'l-qulub al-saghir), p. 51;
    Al-Lata'if, I, 171.

33. Op. cit., p. 52.

34. Corbin, *Creative Imagination*, p. 157; Nasr, op. cit., p. 147.

35. Adunis, op. cit., Vol. 1, 230.
    [Consider also al-Shahrazuri's famous poem in *lam*:

    I said, greetings to you, people in love;
    I have a heart, away from you, busy with you. – EDITOR]

36. Abu Nasr al-Sarraj, *The Flash* (Al-Lam'), edited and introduced by 'Abd al-Halim
    Mahmoud and Taha Surur (Cairo: Dar al-Kutub al-Haditha, 1960), p. 437.

37. Corbin, *Creative Imagination*, p. 157.

7 Concepts of human rights in Islamic doctrines

Shamsuddin al-Kaylani

1. Hans Küng *et al, Islam and the Universality of Human Rights* (Al-Islam wa 'alamiyyat
   huquq al-insan), translated by Mahmoud Munqidh al-Hashimi, (Aleppo, 1995),
   pp. 83–4. See also Adunis, *The Static and the Dynamic* (Al-Thabit wa 'l-mutahawwil),
   Vol. 1, *The Origins* (Beirut: Dar al-'Awda, 1978), p. 43, where the writer distinguishes between the two contexts as follows: 'If the law consists of obligations
   and duties, the Legislator is God alone; therefore shirking duties is disobedience.'

2. Shaykh Rashid al-Ghanoushi, *Public Freedoms in the Islamic State* (Al-Hurriyyat al-
   'amma fi 'l-dawla 'l-Islamiyya) (Beirut: Centre for Arab Unity Studies, 1993), p.
   41. See also 'Ali 'Isa, *Man in Islamic Philosophy* (Falsafat al-Islam fi 'l-insan) (Beirut:
   Dar al-Adab, 1986), pp. 92–3; 'Abd al-Salam Tarmanini, *Human Rights in Islamic
   Jurisprudence* (Huquq al-insan fi nazar al-shariah 'l-Islamiyya) (Beirut: Dar al-Kitab
   al-Jadid, 1967), p. 19; Muhammad Asad, *The System of Government in Islam*,
   translated as (minhaj al-Islam fi l-hukm) by Mansour Madi (Beirut: Dar al-'Ilm

li 'l-Malayin, 1957), pp. 45–52; Ahmad Kamal Abu 'l-Majd, 'The Political Issue, Tradition and its Connection with this Age, and the Political System of the State' (Al-mas'ala 'l-siyasiyya wa silat al-turath bi 'l-'asr wa 'l-nizam al-siyasi li 'l-dawla), a paper submitted to the seminar on *The Heritage and the Challenge of the Age in the Arab World* (Al-Turath wa tahadiyyat al-'asr fi 'l-watan al-'Arabi) (Beirut: Centre for Arab Unity Studies, 1985), published by the Centre under the same title, 1985, p. 591, where he says that 'Islam commands that rights should be observed as a religious duty'.

3. Sami 'Awad al-Dhib Abu Sahliyya, 'Disputed Human Rights between East and West' (Huquq al-insan al-mutanaza' 'alayha baina 'l-gharb wa 'l-Islam), *Majallat Dirasat 'Arabiyya*, 5–6, March–April 1992, p. 7.

4. Mohammed Arkoun, *Islam, Europe and the West* (Al-Islam, Urubba, al-gharb), translated by Hashem Salih (Beirut: Dar al-Saqi, 1995), p. 135.

5. Mohammed Arkoun, *Islamic Thought (Criticism and Interpretation)* [Al-Fikr al-Islami (naqd wa ijtihad)], translated by Hashem Salih (Beirut: Dar al-Saqi, 1990), p. 321.

6. Ibid. p. 322.

7. 'Abd al-Hadi 'Abbas, *Human Rights* (Huquq al-insan), Vol. 1 (Damascus: Dar al-Fadil, 1995), p. 162.

8. Ibid., p. 16.

9. See Arkoun, *Islam, Europe and the West*, p. 136.

10. Muhammad 'Abid al-Jabiri, *Democracy and Human Rights* (Al-Dimuqratiyya wa huquq al-insan) (Beirut: Centre for Arab Unity Studies, Beirut, 1994), p. 147.

11. 'Abbas, op. cit., p. 172.

12. Hans Küng et al., op.cit., p. 45.

13. Burhan Ghalyoun, 'Rationalism and Rational Criticism' (Al-'Aqlaniyya wa naqd al-'aql) *Al-Wahda* (January 1988), pp. 19–20.

14. Mohammed Arkoun, *Islam, Morality and Politics* (Al-Islam wa 'l-akhlaq wa 'l-siyasa), translated by Hashem Salih (Beirut, 1990), pp. 98–9.

15. Mohammed Arkoun, 'Introduction to the Study of the Relations between Islam and Politics' (Madkhal li dirasat al-'alaqa baina 'l-Isam wa 'l-siyasa), *Al-Baheth*, year 2, No. 6, July–August 1980, p. 14.

16. Arkoun, *Islam, Morality and Politics*, p. 127.

17. Ibid., pp. 26–7.

18. *Human Rights in Islam* (Huquq al-insan fi 'l-Islam), which is the first legislation of the principles of the Islamic Shariah regarding human rights, introduced by Ibrahim Madkour (Damascus: Dar Tlas, 1992), p. 22.

19. Khalid Muhammad Khalid, *It Is Man* (Innahu 'l-insan) (Cairo: Dar al-Katib al-'Arabi, n.d.), p. 69.

20. 'Abd al-Rahman Badawi, *The Perfect Man in Islam* (Al-Insan al-kamil fi 'l-Islam) (Cairo, 1950), p. 137.

21. Husain Jamil, *Human Rights in the Arab Homeland* (Huquq al-insan fi 'l-watan al-'Arabi) (Beirut: Centre for Arab Unity Studies, 1986), pp. 26–7.

22. Quoted from Shaykh Mahmoud Shaltout, *Islam: Doctrine and Law* (Al-Islam: 'aqida wa shariah), 5th edition (Cairo: Dar al-Shurouq, n.d.), p. 346.

23. See Jamil, op. cit., pp. 26–7.

24. See al-Jabiri, *Democracy and Human Rights*, p. 209.

25. Muhammad 'Amara, *Islam and Human Rights: Requirements not Rights* (Al-Islam wa huquq al-insan: darurat la huquq) (Kuwait: 'Alam al-Ma'rifa, 1985), p. 34. See also Ibn Taymiyya (Taqiyyuddin Abu 'l-'Abbas Ahmad), *Juridical Policy in Reforming Ruler and Public* (Al-Siyasa 'l-shar'iyya fi islah al-ra'i wa 'l-ra'iyya) (Beirut: Dar al-Kutub al-'Arabiyya, n.d.), pp. 135–6.

26. See al-Suyouti (Jalal al-Din 'Abd al-Rahman ibn Abi Bakr) *History of the Caliphs* (Tarikh al-khulafa'), ed. Muhammad Muhyiddin 'Abd al-Hamid, (Cairo: Matba'at al-Sa'ada, 1952), p. 307.

27. 'Abd al-Karim Zaydan, *Rights of the Individual in Islam* (Huquq al-afrad fi dar 'l-Islam) (Beirut: Mu'assasat al-Risala, 1988), p. 49.

28. Ibn Taymiyya, op. cit., p. 65.

29. See Asad, op. cit., p. 70.

30. Ibid., p. 66.

31. Translation taken from *The Forty Hadiths of al-Nawawi*, translated by 'Izziddin Ibrahim and Denys Johnson-Davies (Kuwait: Al-Sahaba, 1985), p. 111.

32. Muhammad Sa'id al-'Ashmawi, *Political Islam* (Al-Islam al-siyasi) (Cairo: Sina' Publishers, 1989), p. 122.

33. See Jamil, op. cit., p. 25.

34. Zaydan, op. cit., p. 33.

35. Ibn 'Abd Rabbihi (Abu 'Umar Ahmad, d. 328/940), *Al-'Iqd al-Farid*, edited by Ahmad Amin *et al.*, Cairo, 1948–1953, Vol. 4, 7. See also Muhammad al-Khudari, *The Light of Certainty in the Life of the Chief Messenger* (Nour al-yaqin fi sirat sayid al-mursalin) (Cairo, 1910), p. 325.

36. Quoted by Madkour, *Human Rights in Islam*, p. 26.

37. Al-Jabiri, *Democracy and Human Rights*, pp. 233–4.

38. See 'Abd al-Salam al-Tarmanini, *Slavery, Past and Present* (Al-Riqq, madihi wa hadiruh) (Kuwait: 'Alam al-Ma'rifa Series, 23, 1985), p. 36. See also Shaykh 'Abd al-'Aziz Jawish, *Islam: The Religion of Instinct and Freedom* (Al-Islam: din al-fitra wa 'l-hurriyya), Dar al-Hilal Series, No. 18, 1952, p. 72.

39. See Madkour, op. cit., p. 74.

40. See al-Jabiri, *Democracy*, p. 233.

41. Karen Armstrong, *God and Man* (Allah wa 'l-insan), translated by Muhammad al-Joura (Damascus: Dar al-Hasad, 1996), p. 166.

42. Ibid.

43. Roger Garaudi, *Islam* (Al-Islam), translated by Wajih As'ad (Beirut: Dar 'Atiyya, 1996), p. 102. See also Roger Garaudi, *What Islam Promises* (Ma ya'idu bihi 'l-Islam), translated by Qusay Atasi and Michel Wakim (Damascus: Dar al-Wathba, 1981), p. 105; see also Jawish, op. cit., pp. 82–3.

44. Al-Jabiri, *Democracy*, pp. 242–243.
45. Hisham Juʿayt, *Sedition: The Controversy of Religion and Politics in Early Islam* (Al-Fitna: jadaliyyat al-din wa 'l-siyasa fi 'l-Islam al-mubakkir), translated by Khalil Ahmad Khalil (Beirut: Dar Al-Taliʿa, 1991), p. 33.
46. Ibid., p. 37; and see Muhammad ibn Jarir al-Tabari (d. 310/923), *History of Prophets and Kings* (Tarikh al-rusul wa 'l-muluk), edited by Muhammad Abu 'l-Fadl Ibrahim, Vol. 3, (Cairo: Dar al-Maʿarif, 1969), Vol. 3, 220 et seq. See also Ibn Qutaiba (Abu Muhammad ʿAbdullah ibn Muslim al-Dinawari), *The Imamate and Politics* (Al-Imama wa 'l-siyasa), edited by Taha al-Zayni, (Cairo: Matbaʿat Al-Halabi, 1967), Vol. 1, 21.
47. Juʿayt, op. cit., pp. 37–8.
48. Muhammad Saʿid Talib, *The Arab-Islamic State: the State and Religion: a Study in History and Concepts* (Al-Dawla 'l-ʿArabiyya 'l-Islamiyya: al-dawla wa 'l-din: bahth fi 'l-tarikh wa 'l-mafahim) (Damascus: Al-Ahali, 1997), p. 220.
49. See Juʿayt, op. cit., p. 55.
50. Ibid., p. 67.
51. Al-Tabari, op. cit., Vol. 4, 283.
52. Ibid., p. 284.
53. Ibid., p. 369.
54. Juʿayt, op. cit., p. 112.
55. Al-Tabari, op. cit., Vol. 4, 376.
56. Abu 'l-Fath al-Shahrastani [d. 548/1153], *Creeds and Sects* (Al-Milal wa 'l-nihal), edited by Husain Jumʿa (Beirut-Damascus: Dar Daniyya, 1990), p. 6.
57. ʿAli Mabrouk, *Prophethood: From Ideology to the Philosophy of History* (Al-Nubuwwa: min ʿilm al-ʿaqaʾid ila falsafat al-tarikh) (Beirut: Dar Al-Tanwir, 1993), p. 120.
58. Dorothea Kravolski, 'Authority and Legitimacy: a Study on the Mongul Crisis' (Al-Sulta wa 'l-sharʿiyya: dirasa fi 'l-maʾzaq al-maghuli), *Al-Ijtihad,* year 2, No. 3 (Beirut, Spring 1989), p. 114.
59. See Khayr al-Din Yuja Sawi, *Development of Political Thought in Sunna* (Tatawwur al-fikr al-siyasi ʿinda ahl al-sunna) (Amman: Dar al-Bashir, 1993), p. 83.
60. Muhammad Diaʾ al-Din al-Rayyis, *Islamic Political Theories* (Al-Nazariyyat al-siyasiyya 'l-Islamiyya), Anglo-Egyptian Publishers, 2nd edition, 1957, p. 66.
61. Muhammad ʿAbid al-Jabiri, *The Making of the Arab Mind* (Takwin al-ʿaql al-ʿArabi), 1 (Beirut: Dar al-Taliʿa, 1984), p. 110.
62. See al-Rayyis, op. cit., p. 87.
63. Mohammed Arkoun, *Window on Islam* (Nafidha ʿala 'l-Islam), translated by Sabah al-Juhaym (Beirut: Dar ʿAtiyya, 1996), p. 186.
64. Al-Imam al-Ghazali, *The Book of the Just Mean in Belief* (Kitab al-iqtisad fi 'l-Iʿtiqad), introduction by ʿAdil al-ʿAwwa (Beirut: Dar al-Amana, 1969) p. 214.
65. Ibid.
66. Al-Jabiri, *Democracy*, p. 258–9.
67. Al-Ghanoushi, op. cit., p. 43.

68. Shaykh Muhammad 'Abduh, *Islam and Christianity Accommodate Science and Civilization* (Al-Islam wa 'l-nasraniyya, ma'a 'l-'ilm wa 'l-madaniyya) (Beirut: Dar al-Hadatha, 1988), p. 57.

69. See Yuja Sawi, op. cit., p. 126. See also Abu 'l-Hasan al-Ash'ari, *Islamic Discourses* (Kitab maqalat al-Islamiyyin), 3rd edition (Beirut: Dar Ihya' al-Turath al-'Arabi), 3rd edition, pp. 454–8.

70. See Abu 'l-A'la 'al-Mawdoudi, *The Caliphate and Kingship* (Al-Khilafa wa 'l-mulk), translated by Ahmad Idris (Kuwait: Dar Al-Qalam, 1978), pp. 157–8.

71. 'Abd al-Rahman Badawi, *Islamic Sects* (Madhahib al-Islamiyyin), Vol. 1 (Beirut: Dar al-'Ilm li 'l-Malayin, 1971), p. 627.

72. Al-Shahrastani, op. cit., pp. 42–3.

73. See Sa'id Bensa'id al-'Alawi, *Al-Ash'ari's Address: an Attempt to Study the Arab-Islamic Mind* (Al-Khitab al-Ash'ari: musahama fi dirasat al-'aql al-'Arabi 'l-Islami) (Beirut: Dar al-Muntakhab al-'Arabi, 1993), p. 25.

74. Shaykh Rashid Rida, *Sunna, Shi'a, Wahabiyya and the Rejectionist* (Al-Sunna wa 'l-shi'a wa 'l-wahabiyya wa 'l-rafida), 1st Epistle, (Cairo: Al-Manar, 2nd edition, 1947), p. 46.

75. Sir Hamilton Gibb, *A Call for the Renewal of Islam* (Da'wa ila tajdid al-Islam) (Damascus: Al-Wathba, n.d.), pp. 23–4.

76. Ibid., p. 22.

77. Ibid., p. 26.

78. Mustafa 'l-Shak'a, *Islam Without Sects* (Islam bila madhahib), 5th edition, Al-Halabi, 1976, p. 414.

79. Al-Mawdoudi, op. cit., p. 177.

80. Ibid.

81. See Salwa 'Ali Milad, *Al-Dhimma Documents During the Ottoman Period and their Historical Importance* (Watha'iq ahl al-dhimma fi 'l-'asr al-'Uthmani wa ahammiyy-atuha 'l-tarikhiyya) (Cairo: Dar Al-Thaqafa, 1983), pp. 7–11.

82. Philip Hitti, *A Brief History of the Arabs* (A-'Arab: tarikh moujaz), 5th edition (Beirut: Dar al-'Ilm li 'l-Malayin), 1980, p. 142.

83. Garaudi, *What Islam Promises*, p. 105.

84. See al-Shak'a, op. cit., p. 394.

85. See Hadi 'l-'Alawi, *Undaunted Figures in Islam* (Shakhsiyyat ghayr qaliqa fi 'l-Islam) (Beirut: Dar al-Kunuz al-Adabiyya), 1995, p. 132.

86. Al-Shahrastani, op. cit., p. 44.

87. Badawi, *Islamic Sects,* Vol. 1, p. 629.

88. Ibn Khaldoun (fourteenth century), *The Introduction* (Muqaddimat Ibn Khaldoun) (Beirut: Al-Qalam, 1978), p. 91. See also Muhammad 'Abid al-Jabiri, *Religion, the State and the Implementation of Shariah law* (Al-Din wa 'l-dawla wa tatbiq al-shariah) (Beirut: Centre for Arab Unity Studies, 1996), p. 30.

89. 'Writings on *Islam and the Principles of Government* and on *The Caliphate and the State in Islam,*' in *The State and the Caliphate in Arab Discourse During the Kamalist Revolt in*

Turkey: Rashid Rida, 'Ali 'Abd al-Raziq, 'Abd al-Rahman al-Shahbandar (Nusus hawla 'l-Islam wa usul al-hukm, wa 'al-khilafa wa 'l-dawla fi 'l-khitab al-'Arabi ibban al-thawra 'l-kamaliyya fi Turkiyya: Rashid Rida, 'Ali 'Abd al-Raziq, 'Abd al-Rahman al-Shahbandar), introduction by Wajih Kawtharani (Beirut: Dar Al-Tali'a, 1996), p. 159.

90. See Muhammad Abu Zahra, *Islamic Sects* (Al-Mazahib al-Islamiyya), Cairo: One Thousand Books Series, No. 177, n.d., p. 144.

91. Abu Ya'la (Abu Muhammad ibn al-Husain) (d. 458/1065), *The Hanbali Genealogy* (Tabaqat al-Hanabila), edited by Muhammad al-Fiqi (Cairo: Matba'at al-Sunna 'l-Nabawiyya, 1952), Vol. 2, 305.

92. Al-Shak'a, op. cit., p. 391.

93. Al-Fadl Shalaq, *The Nation and the State* (Al-Umma wa 'l-dawla) (Beirut: Dar al-Muntakhab al-'Arabi, 1993), p. 37.

94. Ibn Khaldoun, op. cit., p. 208.

95. Arkoun, *Islam, Morality and Politics*, p. 134.

96. Wajih Kawtharani, *Authority, Society and Political Action* (Al-Sulta wa 'l-mujtama' wa 'l-'amal al-siyasi) (Beirut: Centre for Arab Unity Studies, 1988), p. 35.

97. 'Abdallah al-'Arawai, *The Concept of the State* (Mafhoum al-dawla) 2nd edition (Beirut: Dar al-Tanwir, 1983), p. 110.

98. See Wajih Kawtharani, 'Issues of Reform, Shari'a and the Constitution in Modern Islamic Thought' (Qadaya 'l-islah wa 'l-shariah wa 'l-dustour fi 'l-fikr al-Islami 'l-hadith), *Al-Ijtihad* (Beirut), Year 2, No. 3, 1989, p. 220.

99. Burhan Ghalyoun, *Dialogue of Religion and the State* (Hiwar al-Din wa 'l-dawla) (Casablanca: Arab Cultural Centre, 1996), p. 121.

100. 'Abduh, *Islam and Christianity*, op.cit., p. 82.

101. Muhammad Jamal Barout, 'Islamic Reform and Secularism' (Al-Islah al-Islami wa 'l-ilmaniyya), *Al-Tariq* (Beirut, Year 56, No. 1, 1997), pp. 66–8.

102. Arkoun, *Islam, Morality and Politics*, p. 132.

103. Arkoun, *Islamic Thought*, p. 282.

104. Marshal Hodgson, 'How Shi'ism Developed into a Creed' (Kayfa tatawwar al-tashayyu' ila madhhab), *Al-Ijtihad* (Beirut), Year 5, No.19, Spring, 1993, p. 143. See also Petrochovski, *Islam in Iran* (Al-Islam fi Iran), translated and introduced by Muhammad al-Siba'i (Cairo: Dar al-Thaqafa, 1982), p. 189, where he says: 'The Shi'a did not at first consider the concept of the Imamate and Caliphate a sacred issue.' See also Ju'ayt, op. cit., p. 127.

105. See Julius Wellhausen, *Skizzen und Vorarbeiten*, translated by 'Abd al-Rahman Badawi as (Ahzab al-mu'arada 'l-siyasiyya wa 'l-diniyya fi sadr al-Islam: al-Khawarij wa 'l-Shi'a) (Dar Al-Nahda 'l-Misriyya, 1958), p. 148.

106. See al-Tabari, op. cit., Vol. 5, 584 et seq.

107. See: Wellhausen, op. cit., p. 196; Mustafa 'l-Shak'a, *Islam Without Sects*, p. 186; 'Abd al-Hasib Taha Hamida, *Shi'a Literature to the End of the Second Century* AH (Adab

al-shiʻa ila nihayat al-qarn al-thani ʼl-hijri), 2nd edition (Cairo: Matbaʻat al-Saʻada, 1968), p. 48.

108. Adunis, op. cit., Vol. 1, 187.

109. Jan Richard, *Shiʻi Islam* (Al-Islam al-shiʻi), translated by Hafiz al-Jamali (Beirut: Dar ʻAliyya, 1996), p. 44.

110. Hodgson, op. cit., p. 143.

111. Wellhausen, op. cit., p. 211, where he says: ʻHis care for the "oppressed" was a central point in his programme; the term was understood to mean *al-mawali.*

112. See Hamida, op. cit., pp. 53–4.

113. See Muhammad ʻAmara, *Currents of Islamic Thought* (Tayyarat al-fikr al-Islami), Kitab al-Hilal, No. 376 (Cairo: Dar al-Hilal, 1982), pp. 317–8.

114. See Hodgson, op. cit., p. 155.

115. See Richard, op. cit., pp. 42–3, 70.

116. Ibn Khaldoun, op. cit., p. 196.

117. Muhsin al-Amin, *Prominent Shiʼites* (Aʻyan al-shiʻa), Part 1 (Beirut: Matbaʻat al-Insaf, n.d.), p. 68.

118. Hashim Maʻrouf, *Doctrine of Imamate Shiʼism* (ʻAqidat al-shiʻa ʼal-imamiyya) (Beirut, 2nd edition, n.d.), p. 21.

119. Al-Imam al-Akbar, Muhammad Husain ibn ʻAli Kashif al-Ghataʼ, *The Origins of Shʼism* (Asl al-shiʻa wa usuluha), 4th edition (Beirut: Muʼassast al-Aʻlami, 1982), p. 107.

120. Al-Amin, op. cit., p. 69. See also ʻAbdallah Fayad, *History of the Imamate and Its Shiʼa Predecessors* (Tarikh al-imamiyya wa aslafihim min al-Shiʻa) (Baghdad, 1970), p. 33.

121. Al-Shakʻa, *Islam without Sects*, p. 195.

122. Mabrouk, *Prophethood . . .*, p. 118.

123. Muhammad Rida ʼl-Muzaffar, *Imamate Doctrines* (ʻAqaʼid al-imamiyya) (Beirut, 1973), p. 74.

124. Quoted by Ahmad Amin, *The Forenoon of Islam* (Duha ʼl-Islam), Beirut, Vol. 3, 10th edition, n.d., p. 214.

125. Quoted by ʻAli Sami ʼl-Nashshar, *The Rise of Philosophic Thought in Islam: the Rise of and Development of Shiʻism* (Nashaʼat al-fikr al-falsafi fi ʼl-Islam: nashʼat al-tashayyuʻ wa tatawwuruh), (Cairo, 1964), Vol. 2, p. 224.

126. Adunis, op. cit., Vol. 1, p. 200.

127. Henry Corbin, Husain Nasr and ʻUthman Yahya, *History of Islamic Philosophy* (Tarikh al-falsafa ʼl-Islamiyya), translated by Nasir Muruwwa and Hasan Qubaisi (Beirut: Manshurat ʻUwaydat, 1966), p. 70.

128. Adunis, loc. cit.

129. Kashif al-Ghataʼ, op. cit., p. 67.

130. Husain Muruwwa, *Materialistic Tendencies in Arab-Islamic Philosophy* (Al-Nazaʻat al-maddiyya fi ʼl-falsafa ʼl-Arabiyya ʼl-Islamiyya) (Beirut: Al-Farabi, 1980) Vol. 1, 3rd edition.

131. Muhammad 'Abid al-Jabiri, *The Arab Political Mind* (Al-'Aql al-siyasi 'l-'Arabi) (Beirut: Centre for Arab Unity Studies, 1990), p. 222.

132. Mahmoud Isma'il, *Secret Movements in Islam* (Al-Harakat al-siriyya fi 'l-Islam) (Beirut: Al-Qalam, 1973), p. 67.

133. Ibid., p. 61.

134. Al-Jabiri, *Arab Political Mind*, p. 269.

135. See al-Tabari, op. cit., Vol. 3, p. 448.

136. Ibid., p. 405.

137. Richard, op. cit., p. 44.

138. *Nahj al-Balagha, Selected Sayings of 'Ali ibn Abi Talib*, chosen by the Shi'i poet, al-Sharif al-Radi, expounded by M. 'Abduh (Beirut: Dar Usama, 1986), Vol. 3, 83–4.

139. Kashif al-Ghata', op. cit., p. 91.

140. See Ahmad Amin, *Noontide Islam* (Zuhr al-Islam), Beirut: Al-Katib al-'Arabi, 1996, Vol. 4, 118.

141. Ma'rouf, op. cit., p. 61.

142. Al-Amin, op. cit., p. 257.

143. Kravolski, op. cit., pp. 119–20.

144. See Muhammad Jamal Barout, *The New Medina: Contemporar Islamic Movement* (Yathrib al-jadida: al-harakat al-Islamiyya 'l-rahina) (London: Riad Al-Rayyis Publishing, 1994), pp. 57, 72.

145. Kravolski, op. cit., p. 120.

146. Richard, op. cit., p. 73.

147. Ibid., p. 111.

148. Ahmad Kazim Musawi, 'The Rise of the Contexuality of Imitation in Twelver Shi'ism' (Zuhur marji'iyyat al-taqlid fi 'l-madhhab al-Shi'I al-ithna 'ashari'), Beirut: *Al-Ijtihad*, 4, Summer 1989, p. 202.

149. Kawtharani, *Issues*, p. 226.

150. Musawi, op.cit., p. 203.

151. See Radwan al-Sayyid's review 'The Relationships between the Jurist and the Ruler in Two Experiments: the Ottoman and the Safavid-Qajarid' on W. Kawtharan's book, *The Jurist and Ruler: a Study in Two Historical Experiments: The Ottoman and the Safavid-Qajarid*, (Al-faqih wa 'l-sultan, dirasa fi tajribtain tarikhiyy-atain: al-'Uthmaniyy wa 'l-Safawiyya-al-Qajariyya), *Al-Ijtihad* (Beirut), 4, 1989, p. 285.

152. Barout, *New Medina*, pp. 78–9.

153. Wajih Kawtharani, *The Jurist and the Ruler: a Study in Two Historical Experiments: The Ottoman and the Safavid-Qajarid* (Beirut: Dar al-Rashid, 1989), p. 147.

154. Ibid., p. 148.

155. Ibid., p. 163.

156. Musawi, op. cit., p. 207.

157. Kawtharani, *Jurist and Ruler*, p. 183.

158. Barout, *New Medina*, p. 65.

159. Kawtharani, op. cit., p. 189.

160. Barout, op. cit., p. 69.

161. Farhad Daftari, *The Isma'ilis: History and Beliefs* (Al-Isma'iliyyun: tarikhuhum wa 'aqa'iduhum), translated by Sayf al-Din al-Qasir (Damascus: Dar al-Yanabi', 1994), Vol. 1, p. 141. See also al-Nashshar, op. cit., Vol 2, p. 357.

162. Bernard Lewis, *The Origins of al-Ismailiyya* (Usul al-Isma'iliyya), translated by Jasim Rajab (Egypt, 1947), p. 50. See also al-Shahrastani, op. cit., p. 82.

163. See Daftari, op. cit., Vol. 1, p. 156. See also Hamid al-Din Karamani, *Peace of Mind* (Rahat al-'aql), edited and introduced by Mustafa Ghalib (Beirut: Dar al-Andalus, 1967), pp. 25–6; and al-Nashshar, op. cit., Vol. 2, where he says that 'the Sunnis claim that Muhammad ibn Isma'il did not leave any sons, and that Maymoun al-Qaddah claimed Muhammad to have been the father of 'Abdallah'.

164. See Daftari, op. cit., Vol. 1, 53–4.

165. Armstrong, *God and Man*, pp. 185–6.

166. 'Ali Nouh, *Isma'ili Discourse on the Renovation of Contemporary Islamic Thought* (Al-Khitab al-Isma'ili fi 'l-tajdid al-fikri 'l-Islami 'l-mu'asir) (Damascus: Dar al-Yanabi', 1994), p. 139.

167. Mustafa Ghalib, *History of the Isma'ili Mission* (Tarikh al-da'wa 'l-Isma'iliyya) (Beirut: Dar al-Andalus, 1965), p. 50.

168. Nouh, op. cit., p. 143.

169. Al-Karamini, op. cit., p. 23.

170. Ibid., p. 49.

171. Ibid., p. 240.

172. Badawi, *Islamic Sects*, Vol. 2, p. 264.

173. 'Ali ibn Muhammad al-Walid, *Nobility of the Mind* (Jalal al-'uqul); and 'Adil al-'Awwa, editor, *Isma'ili Selections* (Muntakhabat Isma'iliyya) (Damascus: Syrian University Press, 1958), p. 105.

174. *Epistles of the Brethren of Purity* (Rasa'il ikhwan al-safa') (Beirut: Sadir, 1957), Vol. 4, p. 374.

175. 'Abd al-Latif Muhammad al-'Abd, *Man in the Thought of the Brethren of Purity* (Al-Insan fi fikr ikhwan al-safa') (Cairo, Anglo-Egyptian Publications, 1976), p. 27.

176. Ibid., p. 151.

177. *Epistles of the Brethren of Purity*, Vol. 3, p. 152.

178. Ibid., p. 26.

179. Al-Walid, op. cit., p. 137.

180. *Epistles of the Brethren of Purity*, Vol. 2, pp. 59–60.

181. Ibid., p. 244.

182. Daftari, op. cit., Vol. 2, p. 44.

183. *Ibid.*, p. 140.

184. Milad, *Al-Dhimma Documents During the Ottoman Period*, p. 11.

185. Daftari, op. cit., Vol. 2, p. 59.

186. Isma'il, op. cit., p. 124. See also Badawi, *Islamic Sects*, Vol. 2, p. 107.

187. Amin, *Noontide Islam*, Vol. 4, p. 132.

188. Isma'il, op. cit., p. 124.

189. See Migal di Goeji, *Mémoire sur les Carmathes*, translated by H. Zayna, (Beirut: Dar Ibn Khaldoun, 2nd edition, 1980), p. 42.

190. Ibid., p. 157. See also Badawi, *Islamic Doctrines*, Vol. 2, p. 48.

191. See the introduction in Suhayl Zakkar, *News of the Qarmatians* (Akhbar al-Qaramita) (Damascus: Harsouni, n.d.), pp. 23–4.

192. Al-Shahrastani, op. cit., p. 84.

193. Al-Da'i 'l-Qurmuti 'Abdan, *The Book of the Tree of Faith* (Kitab shajarat al-yaqin), edited by 'Arif Tamir (Beirut: Dar al-Afaq al-Jadida, 1982), p. 14.

194. Muhammad 'Abd al-Fattah 'Ulayyan, *The Qarmatians of Iraq* (Qaramitat al-'Iraq) (Cairo: Al-Hay'a 'l-Misriyya 'l-'Amma li 'l-Kitab, 1970), p. 74.

195. Daftari, op. cit., Vol. 1, p. 199.

196. Ibid., p. 183. See also 'Arif Tamir, *The Qarmatians: Between Commitment and Denial* (Al-Qaramita bayna 'l-iltizam wa 'l-inkar), (Damascus: Dar al-Tali'a, 2nd edition, 1997), p. 38, where he says that 'during his [Abu 'Abdallah al-Mahdi's] rule, his imamate, which was concealed, was proclaimed, which led many Isma'ilis to doubt; these were later known as Qarmatians'.

197. Daftari, op. cit., Vol. 2, p. 179.

198. See Adunis, *op. cit.*, Vol. 1, p. 84. See also Maxim Rodinson, *Islam and Capitalism* (Al-Islam wa 'l-ra'asmaliyya), translated by Nazih al-Hakim (Beirut: Dar al-Tali'a, 1970), p. 52, where he speaks of the concept of justice in the thought of the Islamic opposition.

199. Daftari, op. cit., Vol. 2, p. 180.

200. Ja'far Ibn Mansour al-Yaman, *The Book of Revelation*, (Kitab al-Kashf), edited and introduced by Mustafa Ghalib (Beirut: Dar al-Andalus, 1984); and Zakkar, op. cit., p. 30.

201. 'Ulayyan, op. cit., p. 37.

202. Ibid., p. 109. See also Zakkar, op. cit., pp. 30–1.

203. De Goeji, op. cit., p. 36.

204. Muruwwa, *Materialistic Tendencies*, Vol. 2, p. 20.

205. Nasir Khosraw, *Safar Nameh*, translated by 'Ali 'l-Khashshab (Beirut, 1970), pp. 144–5.

206. De Goeji, op. cit., p. 123.

207. Khosraw, op. cit., pp. 144–5.

208. See Nouh, op. cit., p. 54.

209. Khosraw, op. cit., p. 145.

210. Ibid.

211. De Goeji, op. cit., p. 78.

212. Ghalyoun, *Dialogue of Religion and the State,* p. 116.

213. De Goeji, op. cit., p. 132.

214. Muruwwa, op. cit., Vol. 1, p. 633.

215. Ahmad Amin, *The Dawn of Islam* (Fajr al-Islam), 8th edition (Cairo: Maktabat al-Nahda 'l-Misriyya, 1961), p. 291.

216. Ahmad Amin *Forenoon Islam*, Vol. 3, pp. 6–7. See also Badawi, *Islamic Sects*, Vol. 1, p. 103.

217. Muruwwa, op. cit., Vol. 1, p. 642.

218. As Adunis suggests, op. cit., Vol. 1, p. 85.

219. Zuhdi Jarallah, *The Mu'tazilis* (Al-Mu'tazila) (Beirut: Al-Ahliyya li 'l-Nashr, 1974), p. 246.

220. Muruwwa, op. cit., Vol. 1, p. 822.

221. Jarallah, op. cit., p. 248.

222. Al-Jabiri, *Making of the Arab Mind*, p. 151.

223. Adunis, op. cit., Vol. 1, p. 86.

224. Ibn al-Khayyat (Abu 'l-Husain 'Abd al-Rahim ibn Muhammad) (ninth century), *Victory* (Al-Intisar) (Cairo, 1925), p. 126. See also Ahmad ibn Yahya ibn al-Murtada, the section on al-Mu'tazila in *The Wish and the Hope in Explaining the Book of Creeds and Sects,* (Kitab al-munya wa 'l-amal fi sharh kitab al-milal wa 'l-nihal), edited by Tuma Arnold (Beirut: Dar Sadir, 1316 AH/1898 AD), p. 6.

225. Al-Shahrastani, op. cit., p. 21.

226. Abu 'l-Hasan 'Abd al-Jabbar al-Mu'tazili, 'Summary of the Principles of Religion' (Al-Mukhtasar fi usul al-din), in al-Basri (Abu Sa'id al-Hasan) and others, *Epistles of Justice and Belief in God's Oneness* (Rasa'il al-'adl wa 'l-tawhid) edited by Muhammad 'Amara (Cairo: Dar al-Shurouq, 1988). See also Ibn al-Khayyat, op.cit., p. 61.

227. Badawi, *Islamic Sects*, Vol. 1, p. 343.

228. Amin, *Forenoon Islam*, Vol. 3, p. 34.

229. Al-Shahrastani, op. cit., p. 21.

230. Mohammed Arkoun, *Secularism and Religion: Islam, Christianity and the West* (Al-'Almana wa 'l-din: al-Islam, al-Masihiyya, al-gharb), translated by Hashim Salih (Beirut: Dar al-Saqi, 1990), p. 61.

231. Ibid., p. 60.

232. 'Abd al-Jabbar al-Mu'tazili, op. cit., p. 232.

233. Al-Shahrastani, op. cit., p. 21.

234. Amin, *Forenoon Islam*, Vol. 3, p. 45.

235. Ibid., p. 51.

236. 'Abd al-Jabbar al-Mu'tazili, op. cit., p. 239.

237. Al-Nashshar, op. cit., Vol. 2, p. 482.

238. Garaudi, *Islam*, p. 63.

239. Badawi, *Islamic Sects*, Vol. 1, p. 450. See also Abu Hamid al-Ghazali, *A Summary of the Religious Sciences* (Al-Mustasfa min 'ulum al-din) (Cairo: al-Matba'a 'l-Amiriyya, 1904), pp. 63–4.

240. Amin, *Forenoon Islam*, Vol. 3, pp. 47–8.

241. Arkoun, *Islam, Morality and Politics*, p. 103.

242. See Amin, *Noontide Islam*, Vol. 4, 20.

243. See al-Mawdoudi, *The Caliphate and Kingship*, p. 146.

244. Al-Jabiri, *Making of the Arab Mind*, p. 151.

245. Ibn Khaldoun, op. cit., p. 467.

246. Armstrong, op. cit., *God and Man*, p. 230.

247. I. Goldziher, *Vorlesungen über den Islam* (Al-'Aqida wa 'l-shariah fi 'l-Islam), translated by M.Y. Musa, (Baghdad-Cairo, 1959), p. 147.

248. Muruwwa, *Materialistic Tendencies*, Vol. 2, 152.

249. *Ibid.*, pp. 159–61.

250. Abu 'l-'Ula 'Afifi, *Sufism: Spiritual Revolution in Islam* (Al-Tasawwuf: al-thawra 'l-ruhiyya fi 'l-Islam) (Beirut: Dar al-Sha'b, n.d.), p. 85.

251. See ibid., pp. 89–91.

252. Armstrong, op. cit., p. 231.

253. Corbin, *History of Islamic Philosophy*, p. 67.

254. Ibid., p. 283.

255. 'Afifi, op. cit., pp. 256–7.

256. 'Abd al-Rahman Badawi, *Sufi Excesses* (Shatahat al-sufiyya) (Cairo, n.d.), p. 21.

257. 'Abd al-Rahman Badawi, *Restless Figures in Islam*, pp. 173–4. See also Muruwwa, *Materialistic Tendencies*, Vol. 2, 240–1.

258. As Adunis puts it, op. cit., Vol. 1, 98–9.

259. Muhammad 'Ali Abu Rayyan, *History of Philosophical Thought in Islam* (Tarikh al-fikr al-falsafi fi 'l-Islam) (Beirut: Dar al-Nahda 'l-'Arabiyya, 1970), Vol. 1, 296–7.

260. See 'Afifi, op. cit., p. 79.

261. See Muruwwa, *Materialistic Tendencies*, Vol. 2, 220. See also 'Afifi, op. cit., pp. 176–7.

262. Al-'Abd, *Man in the Thought of the Brethren of Purity*, p. 139.

263. Quoted by 'Abd al-Rahman Badawi, *Humanism and Existentialism in Arab Thought* (Al-Insaniyya wa 'l-wujudiyya fi 'l-fikr al-'Arabi) (Maktabat al-Nahda 'l-Misriyya, 1947), p. 36.

264. Ibid., pp. 43–4.

265. Al-'Abd, op. cit., p. 113.

266. 'Afifi, op. cit., p. 223.

267. Quoted by Muruwwa, *Materialistic Tendencies*, Vol. 2, 276–7.

268. Ibid., p. 278. See also 'Afifi, op. cit., p. 230.

269. 'Afifi, Ibid.

270. Badawi, *Restless Personalities*, p. 108.

271. Ibid., p. 117.

272. Armstrong, *God and Man*, p. 235.

273. 'Afifi, op. cit., p. 226.

274. Amina M. Nusayr, *Shaykh Muhammad 'Abduh and his Methodology in Doctrinal Issues*

(Al-Shaykh Muhammad 'Abduh wa minhajuhu fi mabahith al-'aqida) (Cairo: Shurouq, 1983), p. 224.

275. Albert Hourani, *Arabic Thought in the Liberal Age 1798–1939* (Al-Fikr al-'Arabi fi 'asr al-nahda 1798–1939), Translated into Arabic by Karim 'Azqoul (Beirut: Dar al-Nahar, 1977), p. 55.

276. Z. A. Levin, *Modern Social and Political Thought in Lebanon, Syria and Egypt* (Al-Fikr al-ijtima'i wa 'l-siyasi 'l-hadith fi Lubnan, Suriyya wa Misr), translated from Russian by Bashir al-Siba'i (Beirut: Dar Ibn Khaldoun, 1978), pp. 15–6.

277. *Al-Imam al-'Allama Muhammad 'Abd al-Wahhab* (Cairo: Matba'at A. A. Hanafi, 6th edition, 1377 AH/1957 AD), p. 10.

278. Ibid., p. 14.

279. Ibid., p. 31.

280. Ibid., pp. 14–5.

281. Ahmad Fawzi 'l-Sa'ati, *A Balanced Viewpoint on Wahhabism and its Opponents* (Al-Insaf fi da'wat al-Wahabiyya wa khusumihim) (Damacus, 1922), pp. 7–8.

282. Ibid., p. 10.

283. Abu Zahra, *Islamic Sects*, pp. 351–3.

284. Al-Shak'a *Islam Without Sects*, pp. 506–8.

285. Ibid., p. 510.

286. Armstrong, *God and Man,* p. 344.

8 The Medina Charter

Walid Nuwayhid

1. Abu 'l-Fida' ibn Kathir, *Biography of the Prophet* (Al-Sira 'l-nabawiyya), ed. Mustafa 'Abd al-Wahid (Beirut, 1976), Vol. 2, p. 321.

2. Abu Muhammad 'Abd al-Malik ibn Hisham, *Biography of the Prophet*, after Ziyad al-Bakka'i, following Muhammad ibn Ishaq, edited Shaykh Muhammad Muhyiddin 'Abd Al-Hamid, introduction by Muhammad Husain Haykal (Cairo, 1937), p. 120.

3. The first nucleus of Yathrib believers was formed in Mecca. 'Every season the Messenger of God would await people, go to meet them and call the tribes to Islam by presenting his case and the guidance and mercy he had received from the Almighty. Whenever he heard of an eminent Arab coming to Mecca, he would go to meet him and present to him what he had.' (Abu Ja'far Muhammad ibn Jarir al-Tabari, *History of Prophets and Kings* (Tarikh al-rusul wa 'l-muluk), edited by Muhammad Abu 'l-Fida' Ibrahim, Cairo, Vol. 2, p. 351.) Then he headed out 'during the season when he met a group of Ansar and presented himself and his case to the Arabian tribes as he would do each season. While he was near 'Aqaba, he met a group of Khazraj whom God meant for the good . . . They sat with him

and he called them to Islam and recited the Quran to them . . . They accepted what he presented to them and believed him . . . Then they went home, having accepted and believed.' (Ibid., Vol. 2, p. 354.)

4. In his study of the Charter, Khalid ibn Salih al-Hamidi quotes the views of Orientalists on what they called the Medina 'Constitution'. 'Some Orientalists, such as Wellhausen and Caitani, believe the Charter was drafted before the battle of Badr. Hubert Graham thinks it was drafted after Badr. Some think the document is not an integrated unit; hence it has different dates. Montgomery Watt thinks it was drafted at various times and collated later.' (Khalid ibn Salih al-Hamidi, *The Rise of the Islamic Political Thought: The Medina Charter* (Nushu' al-fikr al-siyasi 'l-Islami: *sahifat* al-Madina) (Beirut, Dar al-Fikr al-Lubnani, 1994), pp. 64, 66.)

5. Ibn Kathir al-Qurashi, op. cit., Vol. 2, 320–3.

6. Ibid., pp. 119–23.

7. Khalid ibn Salih al-Hamidi says: 'The document undoubtedly underwent several changes, and its articles were subject to rearrangement, deletion and addition, in whole or in part, as a result of being handled by various reporters. But this did not affect the general structure of the text, its integrity and unity.' (Al-Hamidi, op. cit., p. 71.) See also 'Awn al-Sharif Qasim, *The Rise of the Islamic State in the Time of the Messenger of God* (Nash'at al-dawla 'l-Islamiyya 'ala 'ahd Rasuli Allah), 3rd ed. (Khartoum-Beirut, 1991), pp. 25–37.

8. In his famous history, Ibn Khaldoun relates the names of the early Muslims from Yathrib. The Call began with six people from Khazraj. 'They returned to Medina and called for Islam until it became popular in Medina . . . In the following year twelve Ansar men came to Mecca, five of the six mentioned being among them . . . and seven others . . . Ten of them were from the Khazraj and two from the Aws . . . When they were due to return home, the Messenger sent Ibn Maktoum to accompany them, along with Mus'ab ibn 'Umayr, to call them to Islam . . . Many of the Ansar embraced Islam with his help . . . Then Mus'ab returned to Mecca. The next season, a group of Muslim Ansar headed out with him to meet with the Prophet, some of these were not Muslims yet . . . That night, seventy-three men and two women embraced Islam. The Messenger chose twelve of them to be in charge among their own people: nine from the Khazraj and three from the Aws.' 'Abd al-Rahman ibn Khaldoun, *Kitab al-'ibar* (Beirut, 1992), Vol. 2, pp. 404–6.

9. Ibn Kathir says, concerning the Bu'ath war of the Aws and Khazraj, that Bu'ath was the name of a place in Medina, 'where a great battle was fought and many people were killed, among them eminent men of both tribes. Very few of their elders were left alive'. Al-Bukhari reports 'A'isha as having said: 'Yawm Bu'ath was a day presented by God to His Messenger. The Messenger came to Medina when their tribes were disunited and their chieftains killed.' See, Abu 'l-Fida' ibn Kathir, *The Beginning and the End* (Al-Bidaya wa 'l-nihaya), edited by Ahmad 'Abd al-Wahhab Futayh (Riyadh-Cairo, 1994), Vol. 3, p. 192.

10. Al-Tabari relates as follows: 'The Messenger mounted his she-camel and loosened her reins. Whenever she passed by a house of the Ansar, the Messenger would be invited to stay with them . . . He would say to the Ansar, let her be, for she is guided in her movement. Then he stopped at the site of his present mosque.' (Al-Tabari, op. cit., Vol. 2, p. 396.) Al-Mas'udi relates a similar story in his *Meadows of Gold* (Muruj al-dhahab). 'He let his she-camel move at her will till she came to the site of his mosque, a place which then belonged to two orphan boys of the Banu 'l-Najjar. She knelt down, then rose again and moved away a little; then she came back to the former site, knelt and rested . . . He dismounted and walked to the house of Abu Ayyub al-Ansari, where he stayed for a month until he built the mosque, having first bought the site.' See Abu 'l-Hasan 'Ali ibn al-Husain al-Mas'udi, *Meadows of Gold and Ores of Jewels* (Muruj al-dhahab wa ma'adin al-jawhar), edited by 'Abd al-Amir 'Ali Muhanna (Beirut, Mu'assasat al-A'lami li 'l-Matbu'at, 1991), Vol. 2, p. 295.)

11. Historians and *Sira* writers are agreed that the mosque came first and the Charter second. The third step was fraternization between immigrants and Ansar. Ibn Hisham quotes Ibn Ishaq, in the *Sira*, to the effect that the Messenger of God encouraged fraternization between immigrants and Ansar, saying: '"Fraternize under the bond of Allah by twos." Then he took 'Ali ibn Abi Talib and said: "This is my brother."' (Ibn Hisham, op. cit., Vol. 2, 124.) Ibn Kathir, in his *Sira*, quotes Imam Ahmad as having said: 'It was reported of Sufyan: I heard 'Asim quoting Anas, who said: "The Prophet allied the immigrants with the Ansar in our house." Sufyan said: "As if he were saying that he caused them to fraternize."' (Ibn Kathir, *Sira*, Vol. 2, 324.) Books of *Sira* and history mention the names [list] of the 'two [fraternized] brothers', and Ibn Khaldoun arranged them after quoting Ibn Hisham and al-Tabari. See Ibn Khaldoun, op. cit., Vol. 2, 411.)

12. 'Charter' is my translation of the original Arabic word *kitab* (book) or *sahifa* (page), as the Charter is variably referred to. Al-Fayyumi's Arabic lexicon *Al-Misbah al-Munir* (Beirut, 1987), glosses *sahifa* as 'a piece of leather or paper on which something is written'. The other lexicon, al-Razi's *Mukhtar al-Sihah* (Beirut, 1992), says that *sahifa* also means 'book', which denotes 'duty, judgement, and destiny'. Al-Fayyumi adds: '"Book" is also used for the Revelation and for what a person writes and sends.'

13. Shawqi Abu Khalil, *The Emigration: an Event that Changed the Course of History* (Al-Hijra: hadath ghayyara majra 'l-tarikh) (Damascus, Dar al-Fikr, 1979, p. 111.

14. Muhammad 'Abid al-Jabiri, *The Arab Political Mind* (Al-'Aql al-siyasi 'l-'Arabi) (Beirut, 1990), p. 95.

15. 'Ali al-Hawwat, *Symposium on the Sira of the Prophet, Some Aspects of the Life of the Prophet*, (Nadwat al-Sira 'l-nabawiyya: ba'd al-jawanib fi hayat al-Rasoul salla Allahu 'alaihi wa sallam) (Tripoli, Libya, Manshurat al-Da'wa 'l-Islamiyya, 1986), pp. 194–7.

16. Ibn Kathir summarizes the Charter and only mentions the names of clans and tribes when the articles are repeated. In his two books *Biography of the Prophet* and his book of history, *The Beginning and the End*, Ibn Kathir repeats the same story under the same heading: 'A chapter on his fostering affinity between the Emigrants and the Ansar in the covenant he ordered to be written between them, and on the fraternization he ordered them to practice and his reconciliation with the Jews who were in Medina.' In both books, Ibn Kathir provides a historical introduction to the Charter, attempting to explain the reasons for such an affinity. 'In Yathrib,' he says, 'there were the quarters of the Jews of the Banu Qaynuqa', Banu al-Nadir and Banu Qurayza. They had come to Hijaz before the Ansar (Aws and Khazraj), during the reign of Bakhtunassar [Nebukhadhnassar], who, according to al-Tabari, had ravaged the land of Jerusalem. Then, at the time of the 'Arim Flood, when the tribes were scattered all over Arabia, the Aws and Khazraj came to Medina and stayed with the Jews, with whom they became allied, and they started to imitate them as they found them superior in their historical knowledge of the prophets. But God favoured the polytheists, guiding them to Islam, and cast down the others, who were jealous, unjust and too arrogant to follow the right path.' *Beginning and End*, Vol. 3–4, 262.

17. Walid Nuwayhid, *Islam and Politics: the Rise of the State at the beginning of the Mission* (Al-Islam wa 'l-siyasa: nushu' al-dawla fi sadr al-da'wa) Beirut, Markaz al-Dirasat al-Istratigiyya wa 'l-Buhuth wa 'l-Tawthiq, 1994.

9 The question of human rights in contemporary Islamic thought

Ridwan al-Sayyid

1. Khayr al-Din al-Tunusi, *The Best of Ways to Learn about Kingdoms* (Aqwam al-masalik li ma'rifat ahwal al-mamalik), edited by Munsif al-Shunoufi (Dar al-Tunisiyya, 1972), p. 50. For a critical reading of al-Tunusi's thought, see Mustafa al-Nifar, 'Khayr al-Din al-Tunusi; Good Management or a Modern State?' (Husn al-idara am dawlatun haditha?), *Al-Ijtihad*, 16–7, pp. 11–62.

2. Cf. Albert Hourani, *Arab Thought in the Age of Re-awakening, 1798–1939* (Al-Fikr al-'Arabi fi 'asr al-nahda, 1798–1939), Beirut: Dar al-Nahar, 3rd edition, 1977, p. 101 et seq. See also Fahmi Jad'an, *The Bases of Progress among Muslim Thinkers in the Modern Age* (Usus al-taqaddum 'inda mufakkiri 'l-Islam fi 'l-'asr al-hadith), Beirut, 1981, p. 112 et seq.

3. Rifa'a Rafi' al-Tahtawi, *The Ways of Egyptian Minds in the Pleasures of Modern Writings* (Manahij al-albab al-misriyya fi mabahij al-adab al-'asriyya), Egypt, 2nd edition, 1912, pp. 18–9.

4. Rifa'a Rafi' al-Tahtawi, *The True Guide for Girls and Boys* (Al-Murshid al-amin li 'l-banat wa 'l-banin), Cairo, 1872, p. 127.

5. *Ways of Egyptian Minds*, p. 46; and cf. Shaykh Hasan al-Marsafi, *Treatise of the Eight Sayings* (Risalat al-kalam al-thaman), edited Ahmad Zakariyya 'l-Shalaq, Cairo, 1984, p. 119 et seq.

6. Al-Tahtawi, *True Guide*, p. 127. Cf. 'Izzat Qarni, *Justice and Liberty in the Dawn of Modern Arab Awakening* (Al-'Adala wa 'l-hurriyya fi fajr al-nahda 'l-'Arabiyya 'l-haditha) (Kuwait: World of Knowledge Series, 1980).

7. Abu Hamid al-Ghazali, *The Gleaned in the Principles of Jurisprudence* (Al-Mustasfa fi usul al-fiqh) (Beirut: Dar al-Kutub al-'Ilmiyya, 1983), Vol. 2, pp. 242–4. Cf. Fahmi Muhammad 'Alwan, *The Necessary Values and the Objectives of Islamic Jurisprudence* (Al-Qiyam al-daruriyya wa maqasid al-tashri' al-Islami) (Cairo: Al-Hay'a al-Misriyya al-'Amma li 'l-Kitab, 1989), pp. 44–5.

8. Cf. Al-Shatibi (Abu Is-haq Ibrahim), *The Correspondences in Shariah Principles* (Al-Muwafaqat fi usul al-Shariah), commentary by Muhammad 'Abdallah Darraz (Egypt, n.d.), Vol. 1, p. 1. Cf. also the theory he derived from Imam al-Haramayn al-Juwayni (d. 478/1085), who was al-Ghazali's (d. 1111) *shaykh* who was the first to mention it in *Evidence and Synopsis* (Al-Burhan wa 'l-talkhis). See 'Abd al-Majid al-Saghir, *Fundamentalist Thought and the Problem of the Authority of Knowledge in Islam: A Study in the Rise of the Science of Usul and the Objectives of Shariah*, (Al-Fikr al-usuli wa ishkaliyyat al-sulta al-'ilmiyya fi 'l-Islam: qira'a fi nash'at 'il al-'usul wa maqasid al-Shariah), (Beirut: Dar al-Muntakhab al-'Arabi, 1994), p. 347 et seq. See also Ahmad al-Raysuni, *The Theory of Objectives in Imam al-Shatibi*, (Nazariyyat al-maqasid 'inda 'l-imam al-Shatibi) (Beirut: Al-Mu'assassa 'l-Jami'iyya li 'l-Dirasat wa 'l-Nashr, 1992), pp. 209–15. Also see my article, 'The Question of Man and his Rights in the Ashariyya School', (Mas'alat al-insan wa huquqihi fi 'l-madrasa 'l-Ash'ariyya), *Awraq Jami'iyya*, 2 (Winter, 1993), pp. 81–99.

9. Cf. 'Abd al-Majid Turki, 'Al-Shatibi and Contemporary Legislative *Ijtihad*' (Al-Shatibi wa 'l-ijtihad al-tashri'i 'l-mu'asir), *Al-Ijtihad*, 8, 1990, pp. 237–55. See also my article, 'Contemporary Islamic Thought and Human Rights' (Al-Fikr al-Islami 'l-mu'asir wa huquq al-insan), *Al-Insan al-Mu'asir*, Review No. 2, Summer 1995, pp. 26–43. See, further, my study, 'Modern Arabic Political Terminology: a Study in its Origins and Early Developments' in my book *The Politics of Contemporary Islam* (Siyasat al-Islam al-mu'asir) (Beirut, 1997), pp. 49–76.

10. Cf. Jad'an, op. cit., p. 259 et seq.

11. Al-Shatibi, op. cit., Vol. 1, pp. 11–12. Cf. Al-Tahir ibn 'Ashur, *The Objectives of Islamic Shariah* (Maqasid al-Shariah al-Islamiyya) (al-Dar al-Tunisiyya, n.d.), pp. 86–101. See also Salah al-Jorshi, 'The Objectives of Shariah between Muhammad al-Tahir ibn 'Ashur and 'Allal al-Fasi. The Issue is Still Open' (Maqasid al-Shariah bayn Muhammad al-Tahir ibn 'Ashur wa 'Allal al-Fasi. Al-muhimma ma tazal matruha), *Al-Ijtihad*, 9, 1991, pp. 195–210.

12. Cf. Wajih Kawtharani, *Selected Political Writings from* Al-Manar *Magazine* (Mukhtarat siyasiyya min majallat al-Manar) (Beirut: Dar al-Tali'a, 1980).

Cf. Raslan Sharaf al-Din, 'Religion and Religious Parties in the Arab Homeland' (Al-Din wa 'l-ahzab al-diniyya fi 'l-watan al-'Arabi), *Al-Wahda*, 96, 1992, p. 61.

13. Cf. Muhammad 'Abduh, *Islam and the Answer to its Critics* (Al-Islam wa 'l-radd 'ala muntaqidih) (Cairo, 1928); 'An Answer to a Recent Article by Hanotaux' (Radd 'ala *hadith* Hanutu al-akhir), *Al-Mu'ayyad*, 29 Rabi' al-Awwal, 1318 AH; *Islam and Christianity Support Science and Civilization* (Al-Islam wa 'l-nasraniyya ma'a 'l-'ilm wa 'l-madaniyya), *Al-Hilal*, 1960.

14. Charles Smith, 'The Crisis of Orientation; The Shift of Egyptian Intellectuals to Islamic Subjects in the 1930's', *IJMES*, pp. 382–410.

15. Cf. 'Abdallah al-'Alami, *Liberty and the Ottoman Parliament vis-à-vis the Teachings of the Quran*, (Al-Hurriyya wa majlis al-mab'uthan min ta'alim al-Qu'ran), (Ahliyya Press, 1913). Cf. Wajih Kawtharani, 'The Issues of Reform, Shariah and Constitution in Modern Islamic Thought' (Qadaya 'l-islah wa 'l-Shariah wa 'l-dustour fi 'l-fikr al-Islami 'l-hadith), *Al-Ijtihad*, 3, 1989, pp. 208–38.

16. Cf. Ridwan al-Sayyid, 'Beyond Missionary Work and Imperialism: a Study of Arabic Criticism of Orientalism' (Ma wara' al-tabshir wa 'l-isti'mar: qira'a fi 'l-naqd al-'Arabi li 'l-istishraq) in *Politics*, pp. 323–36. The first book to make this connection was published in Beirut, 1944, under the title *Missionary Work and Imperialism* (Al-Tabshir wa 'l-isti'mar) by Mustafa al-Khalidi and 'Umar Farroukh. Cf. Talal 'Atrisi, *Jesuit Missions* (Al-Bi'that al-Yasu'iyya) (Beirut: International Distribution Agency, 1987).

17. This is the logic inherent in works by 'Abd al-Qadir 'Oda, al-'Aqqad, Muhammad 'Abdallah Darraz, and others, published in the 1940s and early 1950s.

18. Abu 'l-A'la al-Mawdoudi, Sayyid Qutb, Muhammad Qutb and Muhammad Muhammad Husain, among others.

19. The Kingdom of Saudi Arabia had objected to three points mentioned in the International Declaration of Human Rights, namely: the marriage of a Muslim woman to a non-Muslim man; the right of a Muslim to change his religion; and the right of workers in Saudi Arabia to form labour unions. Cf. *Symposium on Islamic Shariah and Human Rights in Islam* (Nadwa 'ilmiyya hawla 'l-Shariah al-Islamiyya wa huquq al-insan fi 'l-Islam) (Beirut: Dar al-Kitab al-Lubnani, 1973), pp. 36–41. The text of the Islamic declarations appended to this essay conveys the impression that contemporary Muslim thinkers hold the same opinion concerning the first two points.

20. Cf. 'Ismat Sayf al-Dawla, 'Islam and Human Rights' (Al-Islam wa huquq al-insan), *Minbar al-Hiwar*, III, 9 (Spring 1988), pp. 33–9; Munir Shafiq, 'On the Intellectual Bases of the Concept of Human Rights in the West' (Hawla 'l-usus al-fikriyya li mafhoum huquq al-insan fi 'l-gharb), *Al-Insan al-Mu'asir*, 2, pp. 10–18; Muhammad 'Abid al-Jabiri, *Democracy and Human Rights* (Al-Dimuqratiyya wa huquq al-insan) (Beirut: Centre for Arab Unity Studies, 1994), p. 141; Cf. a leftist critique – similar to the Islamist critique – of the ideology of human rights, 'Isa Shaifji, 'A Critique of Human Rights Ideology: a Philosophic Idealism and a Political Nihilism,' in 'Isa

Shaifji and Hilmi Sha'rawi, *Human Rights in Africa and the Arab Homeland* (Huquq al-insan fi Ifriqiya wa 'l-watan al-'Arabi) (Cairo: Centre for Arab Studies, 1990), pp. 83–124; Mustafa al-Filali, 'Analysis of Human Rights: Documents and Declaration of Organizations' (Nazra tahliliyya fi huquq al-insan min khilal al-mawathiq wa i'lan al-munazzamat), *Al-Mustaqbal al-'Arabi*, 9, 1997, pp. 78–108.

21. Cf. Fat-hi 'Uthman, *Origins of Islamic Political Thought* (Usul al-fikr al-siyasi 'l-Islami: dirasa li huquq al-insan wa li wad' ri'asat al-dawla (al-Imama) fi daw' Shariaht al-Islam wa turathihi 'l-tarikhi wa 'l-fiqhi) (Beirut: Mu'assasat al-Risala, 1984), pp. 63–5; Muhammad Salim al-'Awwa, *On the Political System of the Islamic State* (Fi 'l-nizam al-siyasi li 'l-dawla al-Islamiyya) (Cairo: Dar al-Shurouq, 1989), p. 240 et seq.; Gordon Cramer, 'The Islamists and Talk of Democracy,' ("Al-Islamiyyun wa 'l-hadith 'an al-dimuqratiyya"), *Al-Ijtihad*, 5, Autumn, 1993, I, pp. 101–12. However, many liberal Arabs do not find this development sufficient. They insist on bypassing the entire Islamic tradition and accepting the International Declaration of Human Rights with no reservations, especially with regard to freedom of religion and to equality (between man and woman, the educated and the uneducated). Cf. *The Cultural Dimensions of Human Rights in the Arab Homeland*, (Al-Ab'ad al-thaqafiyya li huquq al-insan fi 'l-watan al-'Arabi), edited by 'Abdallah Ahmad al-Na'im (Cairo: Ibn Khaldoun Centre for Development Studies, 1993). See a sharp criticism of contemporary Islamic thought in its declarations of human rights in Ahmad al-Baghdadi, *Islamic Thought and the Universal Declaration of Human Rights* (Al-Fikr al-Islami wa 'l-i'lan al-'alami li huquq al-insan) (Kuwait, 1994).

22. 'Abd al-Qadir 'Oda, *Islam and our Political Situations* (Al-Islam wa awda'una 'l-siyasiyya) (Cairo, 1951); also, *Islam and our Legal Situations* (Al-Islam wa awda'una 'l-qanuniyya), 1950.

23. Muhammad 'Abdallah Darraz, *Morals in the* Quran (Dustour al-akhlaq fi 'l-Qur'an), translated by 'Abd al-Sabur Shahin (Beirut: Mu'assasat Al-Risala, 1982), pp. 238–41. There is a good review of 'vicegerency' in modern and contemporary Islamic thought in Rotraud Wieland, *Freiheit und Religion* (Mainz, 1993), pp. 179–209.

24. Cf., for instance, Mahmoud Shaltout, *Islam: Doctrine and Shariah* (Al-Islam: 'aqida wa Shariah) (Cairo, 17th edition, 1991), pp. 543–4; 'Ali 'Abd al-Wahid Wafi, *Human Rights in Islam* (Huquq al-insan fi 'l-Islam) (Cairo, 1957, pp. 171–98; Muhammad al-Ghazali, *Human Rights between Islam and the UN Declaration* (Huquq al-insan bayn ta'alim al-Islam wa i'lan al-umam al-muttahida), (n.p., 1993), pp. 245–61; 'Abd al-Salam al-Tirmanini, *Human Rights in Islamic Shariah*, (Huquq al-insan fi nazar al-Shariah al-Islamiyya) (Beirut: Dar al-Kitab al-Jadid, 1976).

25. This is the title of a book by Muhammad 'Amara: *Islam and Human Rights: Necessities, not Rights* (Al-Islam wa huquq al-insan: darurat, la huquq) (Kuwait: 'Alam al-Ma'rifa Series, 1985). 'Ali Jerisha calls such duties/rights 'inviolables'.

See his book, *Inviolables, not Rights: Human Rights in Islam*, (Hurumat, la huquq: huquq al-insan fi zill al-Islam) (Cairo: Dar al-I'tisam, [1987]), p. 35 et seq.

26. Al-Shatibi, op. cit., Vol. 1, p. 112.

27. Ann Elizabeth Mayer, *Islam and Human Rights: Tradition and Politics* (London: Westview Press, 1991). There are Arab and Islamic attempts in comparative studies, like that of Subhi al-Mahmasani, *The Principles of Human Rights: A Comparative Study in Islamic Shariah and Modern Laws* (Arkan huquq al-insan: bahth muqarin fi 'l-Shariah 'l-Islamiyya wa 'l-qawanin al-haditha) (Beirut: Dar al-'Ilm li 'l-Malayin, 1st edition, 1979); Muhammad Fat-hi 'Uthman, *Human Rights between Islamic Shariah and Western Legal Thought* (Huquq al-insan bayna 'l-Shariah 'l-Islamiyya wa 'l-fikr al-qanuni 'l-gharbi) (Cairo: Dar al-Shurouq, 1982); Muhammad al-Ghazali, op.cit.

28. For the text of this declaration, see: al-Ghazali, op.cit., pp. 262–328, and *Minbar al-Hiwar*, 9, (Spring, 1988).

29. *Human Rights in Islam* (Huquq al-insan fi 'l-Islam). This may be viewed as the first codification of the principles of Islamic Shariah vis-à-vis human rights. Introduction by Ibrahim Madkur, commentary by 'Adnan al-Khatib, published Damascus: Dar Tlas, 1st edition, 1992. For the Universal Declaration of Human Rights, the International Convention and the other international documents, I have referred to *Human Rights*, I, International and Regional Documents (Huquq al-insan: al-watha'iq al-'alamiyya wa 'l-iqlimiyya), edited by Mahmoud Sharif Basyouni, Muhammad Sa'id al-Daqqaq, and 'Abd al-'Azim Wazir (Beirut: Dar al-'Ilm li 'l-Malayin, 1st edition, 1988).

30. Ahmad al-Baghdadi, op. cit., p. 36.

31. Muhammad Mahmoud Rabi' and Isma'il Sabri 'Abdallah (eds), *Encyclopedia of Political Science* (Mawsu'at al-'ulum al-siyasiyya), Vol. 2, p. 1143.

32. Cf. George Maqdisi, 'Humanism in Classical Islam and in the Italian Renaissance', in Ihsan 'Abbas, Shereen Khairallah and Ali Z. Shakir, eds., *Studies in History and Literature* a Festschrift for Nicola Ziada on his 85th birthday, London: Hazar Publishing, 1992, pp. 15–22; also Maqdisi, *The Rise of Humanism in Classical Islam and the Christian West – With Special Reference to Scholasticism*, Edinburgh: Edinburgh University Press: 1990.

33. Cf. the discussion on 'the Universal and the Specific' in "Muqaddimat", *Moroccan Journal of Books*, 5, Winter 1996, p. 46 et seq.

34. Cf. for instance Christian Tomoshatt, Martin Grilet, Hans Küng, Peter Heine and Bassam al-Tibi, *Islam and the Internationality of Human Rights* (Al-Islam wa 'alamiyyat huquq al-insan), edited and translated by Mahmoud Munqidh al-Hashimi, Aleppo, 1995; and, 'Hamas Operations from the Human Rights Perspective,' ('Amaliyyat hamas min manzur huquq al-insan), in *Political Settlement: Democracy and Human Rights* (Al-Taswiyya al-siyasiyya: al-dimuqratiyya wa huquq al-insan), introduction by 'Abd al-Mun'im Sa'id, edited Jamal 'Abd al-Jawad, 1997. See also Muhammad 'Abid al-Jabiri, *Democracy and Human Rights (1994–1997)*.

(Al-Dimuqratiyya wa huquq al-insan, 1994–1997); 'Abdallah Ahmad al-Na'im, op. cit.

35. The Declaration was published in *Islamic Conference Documents, 1990* (Watha'iq al-'alam al-Islami, 1990), in 'Isa Shaifji and Hilmi Sha'rawi, op. cit., pp. 397–404; Su'ad al-Sabah, *Human Rights in the Contemporary World* (Huquq al-insan fi 'l-'alam al-mu'asir) (Kuwait: Dar Su'ad al-Sabah, 1997), pp. 170–2. The Declaration was subjected to analysis and critical commentary by Ahmad al-Baghdadi, op. cit.

10　The problematic of freedom and human rights in Arab-Islamic thought

Yousef Salama

1. Adib Ishaq, *Gems* (Al-Durar), Alexandria: Matba'at Jaridat al-Mahrousa, 1986, pp. 3–4.
2. Ibid., p. 4.
3. Ibid., p. 5.
4. Ibid.
5. Ibid., p. 6.
6. Ibid., p. 7.
7. Ibid.
8. Ahmad Lutfi al-Sayyid, *The Problem of Freedoms in the Arab World*, (Mushkilat al-hurriyyat fi 'l-'alam al-'Arabi) (Beirut: Dar al-Rawai', n.d., p. 15).
9. Ibid., p. 9.
10. Ibid., pp. 13–14.
11. Ibid., pp. 23–4.
12. Ibid., p. 12.
13. Ibid., p. 37.
14. Ibid., p. 39.
15. Ibid.
16. Ibid., p. 40.
17. Yousef al-Qardawi, *General Characteristics of Islam* (Al-Khasa'is al-'aamma li 'l-Islam) (Cairo: Dar Gharib li 'l-Tiba'a, 1st edition, 1977), p. 7.
18. Ibid., p. 37.
19. Yousef al-Qardawi, *How Imported Solutions have Slaughtered our Nation* (Al-Hulul al-mustawrada wa kaifa janat 'ala ummatina) (Cairo: Maktabat Wahba, 1st edition, 1977), p. 7.
20. Ibid., p. 52.
21. Ibid., pp. 80–1.
22. Ibid., pp. 81–2.
23. Ibid., p. 83.

24. Ibid., p. 121.

25. Ibid., p. 130.

26. Ibid., p. 122.

27. Muhammad Yousef Moussa, *Government System in Islam* (Nizam al-hukm fi 'l-Islam) (Cairo: Dar al-Fikr al-'Arabi, 1963), pp. 15–16.

28. Rashid al-Ghanoushi, *Public Freedoms in the Islamic State* (Al-Hurriyyat al-'aamma fi 'l-dawla al-Islamiyya) (Beirut: Centre for Arab Unity Studies, 1993), pp. 24–5.

29. Ibid., p. 97.

30. Ibid.

31. Ibid.

32. Ibid., p. 98.

33. Ibid., p. 101.

34. Ibid., p. 102.

35. Ibid., p. 103.

36. Muhammad Hussain Haykal, *Islamic Government* (Al-Hukuma 'l-Islamiyya) (Cairo: Al-Hay'a 'l-Misriyya al-'Aamma li 'l-Kitab, 1996), p. 37.

37. Al-Ghanoushi, op. cit., pp. 104–5.

38. Ibid., p. 105.

39. Muhammad al-Ghazali, *The Faith of the Muslim* ('Aqidat al-muslim) (Damascus: Dar al-Qalam, 7th edition), pp. 97–8.

40. Ibid., p. 99.

41. Ibid., p. 100.

42. Al-Qardawi, *Imported Solutions*, p. 7.

43. Ibid., p. 232.

44. Ibid.

45. Ibid., pp. 232–3.

46. Ibid., p. 133.

47. Yousef al-Qardawi, *The Islamic Solution: A Religious Obligation and Duty* (Al-Hall al-Islami: farida wa daroura) (Cairo: Maktabat Wahba, 3rd edition, 1977), p. 264.

48. Al-Ghanoushi, op. cit., p. 71.

49. Ibid.

50. Ibid.

51. Ibid., p. 37.

52. Ibid., p. 38.

53. Ibid.

54. Ibid.

55. Ibid., pp. 87–8.

56. Ibid., pp. 81–2.

57. Ibid., p. 88.

58. Ibid.

59. Ibid.

60. Ibid., p. 109.

61. Ibid.
62. Ibid.
63. Muhammad 'Abid al-Jabiri, *Democracy and Human Rights* (Al-Dimuqratiyya wa huquq al-insan) (Beirut: Centre for Arab Unity Studies, 1st edition, 1994), p. 42.
64. Al-Ghanoushi, op. cit., p. 109.

11 The issue of government in modern Islamic thought

Ahmad Barqawi

1. Muhammad 'Abdu, *Islam between Civilization and Science* (Al-Islam bayna al-madaniyya wa 'l-'ilm) (Cairo, n.d.), pp. 19–20.
2. Muhammad 'Abdu, *The Message of Monotheism* (Risalat al-tawhid) (Al-Thaqafa al-'Arabiyya Bookshop, n.d.), p. 23.
3. Muhammad 'Abdu, *Unknown Works* (Al-A'mal al-majhula) ed. 'Ali Shalash (London: Al-Rayyes Books, 1987), p. 73.
4. Ibid.
5. 'Abdu, *Message of Monotheism*, p. 194.
6. 'Abdu, *Islam between Civilization and Science*, pp. 140, 199.
7. 'Ali 'Abd al-Razzaq, *Islam and the Principles of Government* (Al-Islam wa usul al-hukm) (n.p., n.d.), p. 41.
8. Khalid Muhammad Khalid, *You do not Plough the Sea* (Likay la tahruthu fi 'l-bahr) (Cairo, 1955), p. 17.
9. Ibid., p. 18.
   [For the Christian teachings, see: *Ephesians*, 6, 5; *1 Timothy*, 6, 1. – EDITOR]
10. Ibid., p. 51.
11. Muhammad Shahrour, *Contemporary Islamic Studies on State and Society* (Dirasat Islamiyya mu'asira fi' l-dawla wa 'l-mujtama') (Damascus, 1994), p. 186.
12. Ibid., p. 196.
13. Ibid., p. 199.
14. Muhammad 'Awad, *Thoughts against Bullets* (Afkar didd al-rasas) (Cairo, 1972), p. 142.
15. *Adab wa Naqd*, 14, April 1984; details of the case against Nasr Hamid Abu Zayd, p. 80.
16. Sayyid Qutb, *Milestones along the Way* (Ma'alim 'ala al-tariq) (n.p., n.d.), pp. 8–25.
17. Muhammad Qutb, *Suspicions against Islam* (Shubuhat didd al-Islam) (n.p., n.d.), pp. 20–22.
18. 'Abbasi Madani, in ibid., p. 64.
19. Muhammad Sa'id Ramadan al-Buti, *Major Cosmic Certainties* (Kubra al-yaqiniyyat al-kawniyya) (Damascus, 1402 AH), 8th edition, pp. 272–3.
20. Ibid., p. 373.

21. Ibid., p. 374.
22. *Al-Musawwar*, No. 3720, 26 January 1996.
23. Sayyid Zahra, 'The Islam of the Rulers and the Ruled' (Islam al-hakimin wa islam al-mahkumin), *Adab wa Naqd*, 9, (July 1992), No. 83, p. 41.
24. Sa'd al-Hajj Hasan, 'Aspects of the Lebanese Entity' (Hawla simat al-kiyan al-lub-nani), *Al-Insan*, 1, Ramadan / April 1990.
25. Rashid al-Ghanoushi, *Public Freedoms in the Islamic State* (Al-Hurriyyat al-'aammah fi 'l-dawla al-Islamiyya) (Beirut, 1993), p. 510.
26. Ibid., p. 322.
27. Ahmad Barqawi, *Introduction to the Enlightenment* (Muqaddima fi 'l-tanwir) (Damascus, 1996), p. 101.

12 The Islamic intellectual Mahmoud Muhammad Taha on the impasse of human rights in Islamic legislation

Al-Nour Hamad

1. Arab Organization of Human Rights, *Annual Report*, Cairo, 1996.
2. Muhammad 'Abid al-Jabiri, *Formation of the Arab Mind* (Takwin al-'aql al-'Arabi) (Casablanca, 4th edition, 1991).
3. *Republican Brothers: Religion and Men of Religion across the Years* (Al-Din wa rijal al-din 'abra 'l-sinin) (Um Durman, 1975).
4. Mahmoud Muhammad Taha, *The Middle East Problem* (Mushkilat al-sharq al-awsat) (Sudan, 1967).
5. Op. cit.
6. This is the title given by his disciples to distinguish him from a traditional Sufi *shaykh*, or religious teacher.
7. 'Abdallah Boula, 'Mahmoud Muhammad Taha and Innovation in Islamic Thought' (Mahmoud Muhammad Taha wa 'l-tajdid fi 'l-fikr al-Islami), *Riwaq 'Arabi*, Cairo Centre for Studies on Human Rights (October, 1996).
8. Introduction to the special edition of *The Second Message of Islam* (Al-Risala al-thaniyya li 'l-Islam), Sudanese Organization for Human Rights (London, 1996). (On the eleventh anniversary of the author's execution.)
9. Op. cit.
10. Mansour Khalid, *The False Dawn: Numairy and the Distortion of Shariah* (Al-Fajr al-kadhib: Numairi wa tahrif al- Shariah) (Cairo: Dar al-Hilal, 1986).
11. Introduction to *The Second Message*.
12. Judith Miller, *God has Ninety-Nine Names*, New York, 1996.
13. 'Testimonies by the Staff of Cober Prison' (Shahadat al-'amilin fi sijn Kober) (Khartoum: *University Review*, 1985).
14. Introduction to *The Second Message*.

15. Boula, op. cit.

16. Ibid.

17. Introduction to *The Second Message*.

18. *The Second Message*.

19. M. M. Taha, *A Step towards Marriage in Islam* (Khutwa nahwa 'l-zawaj fi 'l-Islam) (Um Darman, 1971).

20. M. M. Taha, *Development of Personal Status Shariah* (Tatwir shari'at al-ahwal al-shakhsiyya) (Khartoum, 3rd edition, 1979).

21. Mohammed Arkoun, *Islamic Thought* (Al-Fikr al-Islami) (Algiers, 1993).

22. Introduction to *The Second Message*.

23. M. M. Taha, *La Ilaha illa Allah* (1969).

24. 'The Islamic Trinity' (Al-Thaluth al-Islami), in *The Second Message*.

25. Taha, *Personal Status Shariah*.

26. M. M. Taha, *Bases of the Sudanese Constitution* (Usus dustur al-Sudan) (1955).

27. M. M. Taha, *The Cultural Revolution* (Al-Thawra al-thaqafiyya) (Khartoum, 1972).

28. 'The Myth of Market Economy'; talk on National Public Radio (Washington, DC, July, 1997).

29. See his interpretation of 'We do not abrogate a verse . . .' above.

30. M. M. Taha, *The* Quran, *Mustafa Mahmoud and Modern Reading of Text* (Al-Qur'an, Mustafa Mahmoud wa 'l-fahm al-'asri) (Cairo, 1971.)

31. M. M. Taha, *Religion and Social Development* (Al-Din wa 'l-tanmiyya al-ijtima'iyya) (1974).

32. M. M. Taha, *Marxism in the Balance* (Al-Marxiyya fi 'l-mizan) (1973).

13 Human rights in contemporary Arabic thought

Burhan Ghalyoun

1. See Muhammad Sa'id al-Majdoub, *Public Freedoms and Human Rights* (Al-Hurriyyat al-'amma wa huquq al-insan) (Tripoli: Gross Press, 1991).

2. See Muhammad Khalid al-Az'ar, *Democratic Palestinian Political Culture and Human Rights* (Al-Thaqafa al-siyasiyya al-filastiniyya al-dimuqratiyya wa huquq al-insan) (Cairo: Centre for Human Rights Studies, 1995).

3. The need to use the instrument of 'human rights' in the United Nations to condemn Israeli violations of law in the Occupied Territories was undoubtedly the primary incentive of the Arab League in this field.

4. Nabih al-Asfahani, 'The Arab League's Position on Human Rights' (Mawqif al-jami'a al-'Arabiyya min huquq al-insan), *International Policy* (Al-Siyasa al-dawliyya), year 1, issue 39, January 1975, pp. 28–32.

5. Hasan al-Sayyid Nafi'a, 'The Arab League and Human Rights' (Al-Jami'a al-'Arabiyya wa huquq al-insan), *Arab Affairs*, 13, March 1982.

6. Muhammad 'Asfour, 'The Arab Human Rights Charter: a Pan-Arab imperative necessity' (Mithaq huquq al-insan al-'Arabi daroura qawmiyya wa masiriyya), *The Arab Future* (Al-Mustaqbal al-'Arabi), 9, 1983.

7. See the Charter's text in *Arab Affairs*, 80, December 1994.

8. 'The Arab League and the Human Rights Charter' (Al-Jami'a 'l-'Arabiyya wa mithaq huquq al-insan), *The Diplomat* (Al-Diblumasi) (London), June 1997.

9. Jalal 'Abdallah Mu'awwad, 'Legal Guaranties for Electoral Integrity in Arab Countries' (Al-Damanat al-qanuniyya li nazahat al-intikhabat fi 'l-duwal al-'Arabiyya), *File on Human Rights Issues* (Malaf qadaya huquq al-insan), Issue No. 1, (Cairo: Arab Organization for Human Rights, 1997).

10. Mugheizel argues, however, as follows: 'Despite the fact that many of the endorsed human rights charters remain as ink on paper, it is unfair to apply this statement to all Arab countries. There are different cases and these charters are treated with different measures of disregard.' (Joseph Mugheizel, *The Arab League: Reality and Aspiration* (Jami'at al-duwal al-'Arabiyya: al-waqi' wa 'l-tumuh), p. 381.)

11. Muhsin Awwad, 'The Future of Human Rights in the Arab World' (Mustaqbal huquq al-insan fi 'l-watan al-'Arabi), *The Arab Future*, 9, 1991.

12. Shibli Mallatt, 'Arab Constitutions and their Guardians' (Al-Dasatir al-'Arabiyya wa humatuha), *Second Intellectual Forum of the Arab Organization for Human Rights in Britain on 'Freedom of Expression and the Right to Political Participation'*, London, 21 August 1993.

13. Ahmad al-Rashidi, 'International Guarantees for Human Rights and their Application in some Arab Countries' (Al-Damanat al-dawliyya li huquq al-insan wa tatbiqatiha fi ba'd al-duwal al-'Arabiyya), Seminar at the Centre for Research and Studies.

14. Report of the Arab Organization for Human Rights, *Arab Human Rights* (Huquq al-insan al-'Arabi) (Cairo: Arab Organization, 1997), pp. 24–8.

15. Husain Jamil, 'Towards Establishing a Court for Arab Human Rights' (Fi sabil insha' mahkama li huquq al-insan al-'Arabi), in *Democracy and Human Rights in the Arab World.*

16. See, for example, Naji 'Alloush, 'American Imperialism and Human Rights' (Al-Impiryaliyya al-Amrikiyya wa huquq al-insan), *Arabic Thought* (Al-Fikr al-'Arabi), July–September 1991. Also Nadir Firjani, 'The West Employs Human Rights to Serve its Interests and Violates them to Achieve those Interests' (Al-Gharb yuwazzif huquq al-insan li khidmat masalihihi wa yantahikuha li tahqiq hadhihi 'l-masalih), *Al-Sha'b* newspaper, 1 December 1992, Cairo.

17. Arab public opinion constantly highlights the contrast between the positions taken by the United States and other major industrial countries in relation to Iraq's occupation of Kuwait, and Israel's occupation of Arab Palestinian, Lebanese and Syrian territories. It is not only the Arabs, however, who accentuate the issue. The double standards policies of the United States represent one of

the principal themes in the works of Noam Chomsky. See, for example, *Les dessous de la politique de l'Oncle Sam*, French translation, (Quebec: Edition Ecosociété, 1996).

18. Mundhir 'Anabtawi, 'The Role of the Arab Cultural Elite in Reinforcing Arab Human Rights' (Dawr al-nukhba al-'Arabiyya fi ta'ziz huquq al-insan al-'Arabi), *The Arab Future*, 55, September 1983.

19. 'Aliyyudin Hilal, 'Democracy and the Preoccupations of Contemporary Arabs' (Al-Dimuqratiyya wa humum al-insan al-'Arabi 'l-mu'asir), in *Democracy and Human Rights in the Arab World*, p. 7.

20. Munsif al-Marzouqi, *Human Rights: the New Vision* (Huquq al-insan, al-ru'ya 'l-jadida) (Cairo: Centre for Human Rights Studies, New Initiatives Series, 1996).

21. Burhan Ghalyoun, 'Democracy and Human Rights in the Arab World: The Problems of Transition and Difficulties of Participation' (Al-Dimuqratiyya wa huquq al-insan fi 'l-watan al-'Arabi, mashakil al-intiqal wa su'ubat al-musharaka), *The Arab Future*, 135, May 1990.

22. Established in early 1983, the Organization had no opportunity to hold its first General Assembly conference in an Arab country, and had therefore to meet in Limassol, Cyprus.

23. This project was also launched by expatriate Arab political and judicial activists. They gathered for a seminar organized in Syracuse, Italy, by the Higher International Institute for Criminology, 5–12 December 1986.

24. See *Arab Human Rights* (Huquq al-insan al-'Arabi), Cairo, 20 March 1987.

25. See the final statement of the conference held in Casablanca, 20–23 May, 1993.

26. Ibid.

27. Doha, 18–19 May, 1995.

28. The Final Report by the seminar *For a Better Arab Tomorrow: Current Arab Situations and Ways to Resolve the Crisis* (Nahwa ghad 'Arabi afdal: al-awda' al-'Arabiyya al-rahina wa subul tajawuz al-azma), held in Doha (see previous note).

29. 'Asfour, op. cit.

30. Ahmad Kamal Abu 'l-Majd, *A Contemporary Islamic Vision* (Ru'ya Islamiyya mu'asira) (Cairo: Dar al-Shurouq, 1991), p. 40.
This trend, which calls itself 'new', stems from the assumption that 'the application of the principles of Islam in contemporary society cannot be realized without a restoration of research and interpretation of the principles of jurisprudence and a continuation of the efforts of predecessors and Muslim scientists in this field. The renovation of jurisdiction must be preceded by the renovation of some of its principles.' (p. 25.)

31. Muhammad Ahmad Khalafallah, *The Quranic Origins of Progress* (Al-Usus al-qur'aniyya li 'l-taqaddum) (Cairo: Al-Ahali, 1984), pp. 124–7.

32. Malik ibn Nabi, 'Democracy in Islam' (Al-Dimuqratiyya fi 'l-Islam), in *Major Issues* (Al-Qadaya al-kubra) (Beirut: Dar al-Fikr al-'Arabi al-Mu'asir, 1991).

33. See 'Abdallah al-Na'im, *Towards Developing Islamic Legislation* (Nahwa tatwir al-tashri' al-Islami), translated Husain Ahmad Amin, (Cairo: Dar Sina, 1994).

34. Yusuf al-Qaradawi, talk on *Al-Shariah wa 'l-Hayat* programme, Al-Jazira Satellite Channel, Sunday, 16 February 1997, cited in 'Azzam al-Tamimi, 'Democracy in Islamic Thought' (Al-Dimuqratiyya fi 'l-fikr al-Islami), *Contemporary Affairs* (Shu'un al-'Asr), 1, 1997.

35. Muhammad 'Amara, *Islam and Human Rights, Necessities rather than Rights* (Al-Islam wa huquq al-insan, darurat . . . la huquq), Kuwait: *'Alam al-Ma'rifa* series, No. 89, 1985, pp. 15–6, 139–40. See also Ibrahim Madkour and 'Adnan al-Khatib, *Human Rights in Islam, the First Legistlation of the Principles of the Isamic Shariah about Human Rights* (Huquq al-insan fi 'l-Islam: awwal taqnin li mabadi' al-Shariah 'l-Islamiyya fima yata'allaq bi huquq al-insan), Damascus: Dar Tlas, 1992.

36. *Top Dignitaries Giving God's Ordinanaces* (A'lam al-muwaqqi'in 'an Rabb al-'alamin) Vol. 4, (Beirut: Dar al-Jil, 1973), p. 373.

37. Muhammad Salim al-'Awwa, *On the Political System of the Islamic State* (Fi 'l-nizam al-siyasi li 'l-dawla al-Islamiyya) (Cairo: Dar al-Shurouq, 1989).

38. Rashid al-Ghanoushi, 'Human Rights in Islam' (Huquq al-insan fi 'l-Islam), *Contemporary Affairs* (Shu'un al-'asr) 1, 1997.

39. Muhammad al-Ghazali, *The Teachings of Islam and the Declarations of the United Nations* (Al-Ta'alim al-Islamiyya wa i'lanat al-umam al-muttahida) (Alexandria: Dar al-Da'wa, 1993).

40. *The International Report on Human Rights in Islam* (Paris, London, The Islamic European Council, 1981).

41. Op.cit. See also Muhammad al-Sayyid Sa'id, 'Islam and Human Rights' (Al-Islam wa huquq al-insan), *Ruwaq 'Arabi*, January 1996.

42. Fat-hi Muhammad 'Uthman, *The Political Experience of the Contemporary Islamic Movement: Lessons of the Past and Horizons of the Future* (Al-Tajriba al-siyasiyya li 'l-haraka 'l-Islamiyya al-mu'asira, durus al-madi wa afaq al-mustaqbal) (Algiers: Dar al-Mustaqbal, 1991).

43. See Sayyid Qutb, *Milestones along the Way* (Ma'alim fi 'l-tariq) (Cairo: Dar al-Shurouq, 1979). Also, *In the Shade of the* Quran (Fi zilal al-qur'an), eight volumes, 7th ed., (Cairo: Ihya' al-Turath al-'Arabi, 1971).

44. Abu 'Abd al-Fattah 'Ali ibn Hajj, *The Final Say in Confronting the Injustice of Rulers* (Fasl al-kalam fi muwajahat zulm al-hukkam) Algiers: Islamic Salvation Front (Al-Jabha 'l-Islamiyya li 'l-inqaz), n.d.), p. 36.

45. Ibid., p. 119.

46. Ibid., p. 63.

47. In the Arab World today, there are 25 national organizations, three regional organizations, and scores of monthly, quarterly and annual periodicals. The Arab Human Rights Organization publishes an annual report covering all aspects of human resources and their violations in Arab countries.

48. Al-Marzouqi, op. cit.

49. Muhammad al-Sayyid Sa'id, 'Analysis of the Criticism against Human Rights Organizations' ('Tahlil al-naqd al-munahid li munazzamat huquq al-insan'), *Sawasiya* magazine, (Cairo: Centre for Human Rights Studies, December 1996).

50. Muhammad al-Sayyid Sa'id, 'Internal Problems in the Arab Human Rights Movement' (Al-Mashakil al-dakhiliyya li 'l-haraka al-'Arabiyya li huquq al-insan), *Ruwaq 'Arabi*, 3, 1996.

51. Bahiy al-Din al-Hasan, 'Towards a Coherent Strategy for the Human Rights Movement in Egypt' (Nahw istratijiyya munsajima li harakat huquq al-insan fi Misr), in ibid.

52. Hani Migalli, 'Identity Crisis: Has the Human Rights Movement Come of Age?' ('Azmat hawiyya: hal balaghat harakat huquq al-insan sinn al-rushd?'), in ibid.

53. Hani Shukrallah, 'Discussion Paper on the Current Strategic Conceptions and Options for the Egyptian Human Rights Organization' ('Waraqat niqash hawla 'l-tasawwurat wa 'l-khayarat al-istratijiyya amam al-munazzama al-misriyya li huquq al-insan fi 'l-lahza al-rahina'), in ibid.

54. *Human Rights: Ongoing Battles between the North and the South* (Huquq al-insan: ma'arik mustamirra bayna 'l-shamal wa 'l-janub), edited Amir Salim, (Cairo: Centre for Human Rights Studies and Judicial Information, 1994).

55. Burhan Ghalyoun, 'Politics and Morals: the Status of Human Rights in Arabic Thought' (Al-Siyasa wa 'l-akhlaq, makanat huquq al-insan fi 'l-fikr al-'Arabi), *Arabic Thought* (Beirut), 22, 1981.

56. 'Asfour, op. cit. Perhaps it is necessary, as many researchers argue, to improve the law curricula in Arab universities that concentrate on legal studies by setting up human rights sections within the departments of General Law and Political Science, covering such courses as: Public Liberties, International Human Rights Law, International Human Law, and Regional Human Rights Charters. This would enhance awareness and consciousness among those who apply these rights, such as judges, government functionaries and security officials. See 'Ali Kureimi, 'Arab Universities and Human Rights Teaching' (Al-Jami'at al-'Arabiyya wa tadris huquq al-insan), *Al-Mustaqbal al-Arabi*, 8, 1996. This theme is also underscored by Mustafa Kamil al-Sayyid, who believes that the scope for teaching these rights in Arab Universities is quite limited and its value either small or short-lived. Knowledge of human rights is therefore provided only for a small minority of students. See al-Sayyid, op. cit.

14 Human rights and social problematic in the Arab world

Fahmiyya Sharafuddin

1. Hisham Sharabi, *Cultural Critique of Arab Society at the End of the Twentieth Century* (Al-Naqd al-hadari li 'l-mujtama' al-'Arabi fi nihayat a-qarn al-'ishrin) (Beirut: Centre for Arab Unity Studies, 1990).

2. Since the issue of Burhan Ghalyoun's *Declaration for Democracy: the Political-Intellectual Structures behind Subordination, Backwardness and the Tragedy of the Arab People* (Bayan min ajl al-dimuqratiyya: al-buna 'l-asasiyya-al-fikriyya li 'l-taba'iyya wa 'l-takhalluf wa ma'sat al-umma 'l-'Arabiyya) (Beirut, Dar Ibn Rushd, 1978); many books and journals have highlighted this topic. For instance: *Democracy and Human Rights in the Arab World* (Al-Dimuratiyya wa huquq al-insan fi 'l-watan al-'Arabi) (Beirut: Centre for Arab Unity Studies, 1983); *Human Rights in the Arab World* (Huquq al-insan fi 'l-watan al-'Arabi) *Al-Fikr al-'Arabi* magazine, No. 65, July–September, 1991; and 'Isa Shaifji and Hilmi Sha'rawi, *Human Rights in Africa and the Arab World* (Huquq al-insan fi Ifriqiya wa 'l-watan al-'Arabi) (Cairo: Centre for Arabic Studies, 1994).

3. The Arab Development Institute has published many books on pan-national thought and pan-national development projects. For instance: Fahmiyya Sharaf al-Din et. al., *Studies in Pan-Arab National Thought* (Buhouth fi 'l-fikr al-qawmi 'l-'Arabi), Arab Development Institute, two vols, 1983–); Sadiq Jalal al-'Azm, *Self-Criticism after the Defeat* (Al-Naqd al-dhati ba'da 'l-hazima) (Beirut: Dar al-Tali'a, 1969).

4. On this point see Muhammad 'Izzat Hijazi et al, *Towards an Arab Sociology: Sociology and the Contemporary Arab Problems* (Nahwa 'ilm ijtima' 'Arabi: 'ilm al-ijtima' wa 'l-mishkila 'l-'Arabiyya 'l-rahina, in the *Arab Future Books* series, (Beirut: Centre for Arab Unity Studies, 1986); the seminar papers on *The Problematic of the Social Sciences in the Arab World* (Ishkaliyyat al-'ulum al-ijtima'iyya fi 'l-watan al-'Arabi), by a number of scholars, (Beirut: Dar al-Tanwir, 1984).

5. Salim Sari, 'Arab Social Scientists and the Study of Arab Social Issues: A Critical Approach' (Al-Ijtima'iyyum al-'Arab wa dirasat al-qadaya 'l-mujtama'iyya 'l-'Arabiyya, *Al-Mustaqbal al-'Arabi*, 75, Vol. 8, pp. 85–95.

6. Iyad al-Qazzaz, 'General Impressions of Sociology in Iraq, 1955–1970', in *Dirasat al-Khalij wa 'l-Jazira 'l-'Arabiyya* journal, Vol. 4, No. 16, 1987.

7. Muhammad Ahmad Khalifa, in *Problematic of the Social Sciences*, p. 7.

8. Muhammad 'Izzat Hijazi, 'The Current Crisis of Sociology in the Arab World' (Al-Azma 'l-rahina li 'ilm al-ijtima' fi 'l-watan al-'Arabi), in *Towards an Arab Sociology*, p. 17.

9. Sa'd al-Din Ibrahim, 'Abd al-Basit 'Abd al-Mu'ti and Fu'ad Ishaq al-Khoury, the seminar on 'Sociology and the Problems of the Arabs' (Nadwat 'ilm ijtima' wa qadaya 'l-insan al-'Arabi), in *Towards an Arab Sociology*, p. 207.

10. Al-Sayyid Yasin, 'Democracy and the Social Sciences: a Study on the Problems of Rationalization, Criticism and Commitment' (Al-Dimuqratiyya wa 'l-'ulum al-ijtima'iyya: dirasa hawl mushkilat al-tabrir wa 'l-naqd wa 'l-iltizam), a paper submitted at the seminar on *The Problematic of the Social Sciences*, op. cit.. See p. 289, where the writer stresses that the lack of serious social reform is a function of the absence of democracy in authoritarian states.

11. Hisham Sharabi, *The Patriarchal Society and the Problematic of the Underdevelopment of*

Arab Society (Al-Nizam al-abawi wa ishkaliyyat takhalluf al-mujtama' al-'Arabi), translated by Mahmoud Shuraih, (Beirut: Centre for Arab Unity Studies, 1992), p. 91.

12. In his *Cultural Critique of Arab Society*, Sharabi demonstrates how Arab identity is reflected in the image of the 'Other', and how the 'Other' depicts the image of the Arabs. See p. 33.

13. On this point see 'Isa Shaifji, 'The Concept of Human Rights in Africa', in *Human Rights in Africa and the Arab World*, op. cit.

14. Examples of this may be seen in developments in Algeria on the eve of the general elections and the statements made on democracy by the Islamic Salvation Front, and also in Rwanda and in daily happenings in Africa.

15. Isma'il Sabri 'Abdallah: 'Economic and Social Components for Democracy in the Arab World' (Al-Muqawwimat al-iqtisadiyya wa 'l-ijtima'iyya li 'l-dimuqratiyya fi 'l-watan al-'Arabi), *Al-Mustaqbal al-'Arabi* magazine, Year 2, No. 9, 1988, p. 77–89.

16. Ibid., p. 81.

17. Aliyyuddin Hilal, working paper for the seminar on 'Human Rights in the Arab World', in *Democracy and Human Rights in the Arab World*, p. 313.

18. Taher Labib, in ibid., p. 316.

19. See F. Sharaf al-Din et. al., *Studies in Pan-Arab National Thought* (Buhuth fi 'l-fikr al-qawmi 'l-'Arabi) Vol. 1.

20. Muhammad al-Majdoub, 'The Arab Individual and Human Rights' (Huquq al-insan al-'Arabi), *Al-Fikr al-'Arabi* magazine (Beirut: year 12, No. 65, July–September, 1991).

21. See the reports of the Arab Human Rights Organization and of the International Human Rights Organization and Amnesty International.

22. Fahmiyya Sharaf al-Din, *Culture and Ideology in the Arab World* (Al-Thaqafa wa 'l-idyulujiyya fi 'l-watan al-'Arabi) (Beirut: Dar al-Adab, 1994) (in Arabic); see also the French translation, *Culture et idiologie dans le monde arabe, 1960–1990* (Paris: Ed. L'Harmattan, 1994).

23. In his *Patriarchal Society*, p. 10, Sharabi argues that, in Naguib Mahfouz's novel *Bain al-Qasrain*, the father, whose power and influence are based on punishment, uses his authority as the essential instrument for repression.

24. Halim Barakat, *Contemporary Arab Society: A Social Exploration* (Al-Mujtama' al-'Arabi 'l-mu'asir: bahth istitla'i ijtima'i) (Beirut: Centre for Arab Unity Studies, 1984), p. 93.

25. 'Ali Zei'our, *Psychoanalysis of the Arab Self: Its Behavioural and Mythical Patterns* (Al-Tahlil al-nafsi li 'l-dhat al-'Arabiyya: anmatuha al-sulukiyya wa 'l-usturiyya) (Beirut: Dar al-Tali'a, 1977), p. 50.

26. Barakat, op. cit., p. 93.

27. 'Abd al-Qadir Zaghal, cited in Barakat, ibid., p. 181.

28. Barakat, ibid., p. 93.

29. Hisham Sharabi, *Embers and Ashes: Memoirs of an Arab Intellectual* (Al-Jamr wa 'l-ramad: mudhakkkarat muthaqqaf 'Arabi) (Beirut: Dar al-Tali'a, 1978).

30. Barakat, op. cit., p. 322.

31. Sharabi, *Patriarchal Society*, p. 28.

32. Barakat, op. cit., p. 327.

33. Ghassan Salama, 'Seminar on Human Rights in Arab Society' (Nadwat huquq al-insan fi 'l-mujtama' al-'Arabi), in *Human Rights in the Arab World*, p. 318. Salama highlights, among others, two causes for the absence of human rights in the Arab World: the anthropological environment of the exclusive, all-encompassing state, within which power is monopolized by one specific group; and 'the lack of any real democratic heritage, such as in the daily practice of democracy, at home and in the street . . . Under the circumstances, the lack of democracy is not a single inadequacy or drawback but rather an integral element of authoritarianism in the family, in the tribe and in society.' (p. 318)

34. Samir Amin, *Towards a Theory of Culture: A Critique of European Centrality and the Reverse European Centrality* (Nahwa nazariyya li 'l-thaqafa: naqd al-tamarkuz al-Aurobbi wa 'l-tamarkuz al-aurobbi 'l-ma'kus) (Beirut: Arab Development Institute, 1989).

35. Samir Amin, *On the Crisis in Arab Society* (Fi azmat al-mujtama' al-'Arabi), Cairo: Maktabat Madbouli (new revised edition), 1993.

36. Sharabi, *Patriarchal Society*.

37. Labib, op. cit., p. 316.

38. See Amin, *Towards a Theory of Culture,* op. cit., where the author draws a distinction between the idealistic metaphysical culture of the pre-capitalist revenue pattern and the positive culture of capitalism concomitant with capitalist expansion.

39. Amin, ibid.

40. Majdoub, op. cit.

41. Human Development reports, especially the Sustained Human Development reports issued by the United Nations Development Agencies since 1990.

42. Sharabi, *Patriarchal Society*.

43. Most Arab social scientists find a correlation between the status of women and the backwardness of Arab Society. See, for example, Barakat, op. cit.

15 The rights of Palestinians refugees

Salman Abu Sitta

1. 'Arif al-'Arif, *The Disaster: Disaster of Bayt al-Maqdis and of Paradise Lost, 1947–1952* (Al-Nakba, nakbat bayt al-maqdis wa 'l-firdaws al-mafqoud 1947–1952), 6 volumes, (Sidon: Al-Maktaba al-'Asriyya, 1956).

2. Muhammad Nimr al-Khatib, *The Events of the Disaster* (Ahdath al-nakba) or *The*

Palestine Disaster (Nakbat Filastin) (Beirut: Dar Maktabat al-Hayat, 2nd edition, 1967).

3. Kamil al-Sharif, *The Muslim Brothers in the Palestine War* (Al-Ikhwan al-muslimun fi harb Filastin) (Zarqa, Jordan: Maktabat al-Manar, 3rd edition, 1984).

4. Hasan Hat-hout, *Memoirs of an Egyptian Doctor – Palestine: the First Disaster* (Yawmiyyat tabib misri – Filastin, al-nakba al-ula), n.p., 1948. Another Egyptian doctor, working in Gaza in 1967, wrote of the execution of prisoners of war and the murder of doctors. See Ahmad Shawqi al-Fanjari, *Israel as I Knew It* (Isra'il kama 'araftuha) (Cairo: Dar al-Amin, 2nd edition, 1995).

5. 'Abdallah al-Tall, *The Palestine Disaster; Selections from 'Abdallah al-Tall, Commander in the Battle for Jerusalem* (Karithat Filastin – mudhakkarat 'Abdallah al-Tall, qa'id ma'rakat al-Quds) (Dar al-Huda, 2nd edition, 1990).

6. For further details on Ahmad al-Shuqayri's life and work, see Khayriyya Qasimiyya, *Ahmad al-Shuqayri: a Palestinian Arab Leader* (Ahmad al-Shuqayri, za'iman Filastiniyyan wa qa'idan 'Arabiyyan) (Kuwait, 1987).

7. Muhammad al-Farra, *Years without Anchor* (Sanawat bila qarar) (Cairo: Markaz al-Ahram li 'l-Tarjama wa 'l-Nashr, 1988).

8. The Institute for Palestine Studies publishes studies and periodicals on various aspects of the Arab-Israeli conflict, in Arabic (from Beirut), in English (from Washington) and in French (from Paris).

9. The Palestine Research Centre has issued a large number of pamphlets on the Palestine question, and also a journal, *Palestinian Affairs* (Shu'un Filastiniyya), from Beirut. After the exodus of Palestinians from Beirut, the journal was continued, on a reduced scale, in Cyprus.

10. Isma'il Shammout, *The Plastic Arts in Palestine* (Al-Fann al-tashkili fi Filastin), self-published, 1989.

11. See, for example, *The Palestine Question: Seminar of Arab Jurists on Palestine* (Al-Qadiyya al-Filastiniyya: nadwat al-qanuniyyin al-'Arab fi 'l-Jaza'ir), July 1967, Institute of Palestine Studies, Beirut, 1968. (22–27 July 1967, Published by the Institute for Palestine Studies, Beirut, 1968. See also: Bahjat Abu Gharbia's Memoirs: *In the Midst of the Palestinian Arab Struggle* (Fi khidumm al-nidal al-'Arabi 'l-Filastini) (Beirut: Institute for Palestine Studies, 1993); Salih al-Shar', *Palestine: Truth and History* (Filastin: al-haqiqa wa 'l-tarikh) (Amman: Majdalawi, 1996); also *Memoirs of a Soldier* (Mudhakkarat jundi) (Amman, 1989); Sadiq al-Shar' *Our Wars with Israel 1947–1973* (Hurubuna ma'a Isra'il, 1947–1973) (Amman: Dar al-Shurouq, 1997); Hasan Salih 'Uthman, *Palestine in the Life of the Hero 'Abd al-Halim al-Jilani* (Filastin fi sirat al-batal 'Abd al-Halim al-Jilani), (Amman: Dar al-Jalil, 1993); Yusuf Haykal, *Days of Youth, Images of Life and Pages of History* (Ayyam al-siba, suwar min al-hayat wa safahat min al-tarikh) (Amman: Dar al-Jalil, 1998); Hisham Sharabi, *Images of the Past: a Biography* (Suwar al-madi: sira dhatiyya) (Sweden: Dar Nelson, and Beirut: Bisan, 1993). Writers in English include Edward Said, Ghada al-Karmi, George Toubbeh, Serene

Husaini Shahid, Ibrahim al-Fawwal, Sa'id Abu 'l-Rish, Fawzi 'l-Asmar and Hala Sakakini.

12. See: 'Abd al-Latif Kanafani, *15, al-Burj Street, Haifa: Memories and Lessons* (15, Shari' al-Burj, Haifa, dhikrayat wa 'ibar) (Beirut: Bisan, 1996); Mustafa Mourad al-Dabbagh's voluminous encyclopaedic work *Our Homeland Palestine* (Biladuna Filastin) (Beirut: Dar al-Tali'a, 1974); Anis al-Sayigh, *The Geo-Demography of Occupied Palestine* (Buldaniyyat Filastin al-muhtalla) (Beirut: Palestine Research Centre, 1968). See also: Nabil Khalid al-Agha, *Major Cities of Palestine* (Mada'in Filastin) (Beirut: Arab Institute for Research and Publishing, 1993); Hatim Muhyiddin Abu 'l-Su'ud, *Cities of Palestine, a Stranger in his Homeland* (Mudun Filastin, gharib al-diyar fi 'l-diyar), (Arab Institute for Research and Publishing, 1993); and *Jaffa: the Fragrance of a City* (Yafa: 'itr madina), reviewed by Hisham Sharabi, Beirut: Dar al-fata 'l-'Arabi, and Nazareth: Yafa Research Centre, 1991; May Ibrahim Seikaly, *Transformation of an Arab Society 1918–1939*, (London-New York, 1995); (Haifa 'l-'Arabiyya 1918–1939), Beirut: Institute for Palestine Studies, 1997; Matta Sim'an Boury and Yusuf Ahmad Shibl, *Acre: Heritage and Memories* ('Akka: turath wa dhikrayat) (Beirut: Dar al-Hamra, 1992); Isber Munayyir, *Lydda in the Mandate and Occupation Periods* (Al-Lidd fi 'ahdai al-intidab wa 'l-ihtilal) (Beirut: Institute for Palestine Studies, 1997); Subhi Sa'd al-Din Ghosheh, *Our Sun Shall not Set* (Shamsuna lan taghib) (self-published, Kuwait, 1998).

13. A series on Palestinian cities was published by the Arab Organization for Education, Culture and Sciences, and the PLO Department of Culture. A number of books were written and published on Palestinian cities by their own inhabitants. The Centre for Study and Documentation at Birzeit University issued more than 20 books, exploring various aspects of geography, history, economics, society, education and health in every village. The most important element in these books is the testimony provided by inhabitants who lived through the disaster. Sharif Kana'na and Salih 'Abd al-Jawad played a significant role in completing these studies and field surveys, which now represent an important part of *Lest We Should Forget (All That Remains, in English): Palestinian Villages Destroyed by Israel in 1948 and the Names of their Martyrs*, edited by Walid al Khalidi, translated by Husni Zina, revised by Samir al-Dik, and published by the Institute for Palestine Studies in Beirut. This encyclopaedic work covers 418 of the 531 towns, villages and tribes where indigenous inhabitants were evicted and expelled during the Zionist invasion of Palestine in 1948.

14. This is my home village, 'Ma'in Abu Sitta'. I wrote its history on a poster showing rare pictures and the fruits of my visits to libraries and museums. It also shows aerial maps taken by the RAF in 1945. The poster is now kept at the Royal Geographical Society, the Public Record Office in London and other European libraries.

15. See, for instance: *Anecdotes* (Al-Khararif), compiled by Tawaddud 'Abd al-Hadi (Beirut: Dar Ibn Rushd, 1980); Victor Sahhab, *Traditions, Beliefs and Popular*

Handicrafts in Palestine, 1948 (Al-Taqalid wa 'l-mu'taqadat wa 'l-hiraf al-sha'biyya fi Filastin fi 1948), (Beirut: Dar al-Hamra, 1993); Salim 'Arafat al-Mubayyid, *The Folklore Geography of Popular Palestinian Proverbs* (Al-Jughrafiyya al-folkloriyya li 'l-amthal al-sha'biyya 'l-Filastiniyya) (Cairo: Al-Hay'a 'l-Misriyya li 'l-Kitab, 1986); Hasan al-Basha, *The Popular Palestinian Song, its Heritage, History and Art* (Al-Ughniyya al-sha'biyya al-Filastiniyya: torath, wa tarikh wa fann) (Damascus: Dar al-Jalil, 1979); Nimr Sirhan et al., *Archives of Palestinian Folklore* (Arshif al-folklor al-Filastini), 3 volumes (Amman: Department of Culture, Palestine Liberation Organization, 1985); 'Abd al-Karim 'Id al-Hashshash, *The Family in Palestinian and Arab Popular Proverbs* (Al-Usra fi 'l-mathal al-sha'bi 'l-Filastini wa 'l-'Arabi) (self-published, Damascus, 1988); *Arabic Folktales*, translated and edited by Inea Bushnaq (New York: Pantheon Books, 1986), a translation from *Al-Khararif.*

16. The writings of Tawfiq Kan'an have been kept in a library section named after him at Exeter University, England. See also *The Folklore Writings of Dr Tawfiq Kan'an* (Al-Kitabat al-folkloriyya li 'l-doktur Tawfiq Kan'an), translated and edited by Moussa 'Alloush, (Birzeit: Dar 'Alloush, 1998).

17. See, Jum'a Hammad, *Journey of Loss – Memoirs of a Refugee* (Rihlat al-daya' – dhikrayat laji'), 1986, and *A Bedouin in Europe* (Badawi fi Urobba), Matabi' al-Mu'assasa al-Sahafiyya 'l-Urduniyya, 1977. See also Ahmad Abu Khosa, *Be'er Sheva and Bedouin Life* (Bir al-Sab' wa 'l-hayat al-badawiyya), 3 volumes, (self-published, Amman, 1970, 1977, 1982). See also 'Abd al-Karim 'Id al-Hashshash, *Jurisdiction by Norm and Custom* (Qada' al-'urf wa 'l-'ada) (self-published, 1991); also *The Arts of Literature and Entertainment of the Naqab Tribes* (Funun al-adab wa 'l-tarab 'inda qaba'il al-naqab) (n.p., 1986). The most lucid and articulate book on Bedouin proverbs and customs is the book by Ishaq al-Diqs, *A Bedouin Childhood* (Tufulat badawi). See also Ghazi Falah's books on the Naqab Bedouins and their tragic conditions in the 80s of the twentieth century, in *The Forgotten Palestinians: The Negev Arabs 1906–1986* (Al-Filastiniyyun al-mansiyyun: 'Arab al-Naqab, 1906–1986) (al-Taybeh: Markiz Ihya' al-Turath al-'Arabi, 1989).

18. See Salma Khadra Jayyusi, *Anthology of Modern Palestinian Literature* (New York: Columbia University Press, 1992).

19. See, among his many writings, *Memoirs of Muhammad 'Izzat Darwaza* (Mudhakkarat Muhammad 'Izzat Darwaza), 6 volumes (Beirut: Dar al-Gharb al-Islami, 1993).

20. 'Ajaj Nuwayhid, *Memories of Sixty Years with the Arab March* (Mudhakkarat: sittoun 'aman ma' al-qafila 'l-'Arabiyya), edited by Bayan Nuwayhid al-Hout (Beirut: Dar al-Istiqlal, 1993).

21. 'Izzat Tannus, *The Palestinians: a Glorious Past and a Brilliant Future* (Al-Filastiniyyun: madin majid wa mustaqbal bahir) (Palestine Research Centre, PLO, 1982).

22. *Documents of the Palestinian National Movement 1918–1939* (Watha'iq al-haraka 'l-wataniyya 'l-Filastiniyya 1918–1939) – from the papers of Akram Zu'aytir,

1918–1939), edited by Bayan Nuwayhid al-Hout (Beirut: Institute for Palestine Studies, 2nd edition, 1984); and *The Palestine National Movement 1935–1939 – Diaries of Akram Zu'aytir, 1935–1939* (Al-Haraka al-wataniyya al-Filastiniyya – yawmiyyat Akram Zu'aytir, 1935–1939) (Beirut: Palestine Research Centre, 2nd edition, 1992).

23. See a review of Constantine Zurayq's work in Hisham Nashabeh (ed.), *Dirasat Filastiniyya: a Series of Studies in Tribute to Dr Constantine Zureik* (Beirut: Institute for Palestine Studies, 1988). See also Walid Qamhawi, *Disaster and Construction* (Al-Nakba wa 'l-bina'), 2 volumes, (Beirut: Dar al-'Ilm li 'l-Malayin, 2nd edition, 1962); and Hani 'l-Hindi and Muhsin Ibrahim, *Israel: The Idea, the Movement and the State* (Isra'il: fikra wa haraka wa dawla) (Beirut: Dar al-Fajr al-Jadid, 1958).

24. 'Abd al-Wahhab al-Kayyali, *Modern History of Palestine* (Tarikh Filastin al-hadith) (Beirut: Arab Institute for Studies and Publishing, 9th edition, 1985).

25. These scholarly studies deal with Palestinian rights according to international law, on the basis of new analytical research on the *nakba*. On the basis of studies in demography, water resources and agriculture, they demonstrate, contrary to Israeli contentions, that return to the land of Palestine is both feasible and possible. They also show that the US-adopted Israeli project for settlement is merely a new 'ethnic cleansing' project. See the following by Salman Abu Sitta: 'The Palestinian Right of Return: Sacred, Legal and Possible', *Al-Mustaqbal al-'Arabi*, No. 208, volume 19, (June 1996), pp. 4–38; *A Map of our Homeland Palestine: Palestinian Locations Depopulated in the Zionist Invasion of 1948* (London: Palestinian Return Centre, 1998). See also, 'The Essence of the Palestinian Conflict Was and Will Always be the Homeland and its People' (jawhar al-niza' al-Filastini kana wa sayabqa: al-watan wa ahluhu'), *Al-Hayat* newspaper, London, 9 September 1994, p. 7; 'The Forgotten Arabs: The Bedouins of Be'er Sheba" (Al-'Arab al-man-siyyun: badu Bi'r al-Sab'', *Al-Hayat* newspaper, London, two parts: 27 September 1995, p. 8, and 28 September 1995, p. 18; See also a series of four articles in *Al-Dustur* newspaper, Amman, on the Palestinian Right of Return emphasized as sacred, legal and possible: 'Transfer and Settlement in Zionist Thought' (Al-Tarhil wa 'l-tawtin fi 'l-fikr al-suhyuni), 3 September, 1997, p. 37; 'Return is Possible and Necessary for Peace' ('Al-'Awda mumkina wa daruriyya li 'l-salam'), 4 September, 1997, p. 16; 'The Right of Return and Compensation' (Haqq al-'awda wa 'l-ta'wid ma'an), 10 September, 1997 p. 35; and 'Practical Steps to Apply the Right of Return' ('Al-Khutuwat al-'amaliyya li tatbiq haqq al-'awda), 13 September, 1997, p. 36. See also 'Between Domestication and Settlement: the Battle for the Spurious Scholarship' (Baina 'l-tadjin wa 'l-tawtin: ma'rakat al-'ilm al-mashbuh), *Al-Hayat* newspaper, London, 6 August 1997, p. 7; 'Israel Sells the Lands of the Refugees and Registers their Property for Jews' (Isra'il tabi' aradi 'l-laji'in wa tusajjil mulkiyyataha li 'l-Yahud), *Al-Hayat* newspaper, London, 18 June, 1998, p. 8; 'A call for the establishment of an authority for Palestinian Land' (Da'wa ila insha' hay'at ard Filastin), *Al-Hayat* newspaper, London, 9 November

1998, p. 8; 'The Crimes of the Israeli War: Burning the People of al-Tireh Alive in 1948' ('Jara'im al-harb al-Isra'iliyya: harq ahali 'l-Tira ahya'an fi 'aam 1948), *Al-Hayat* newspaper, London, 5 April 1999, p. 8; 'Which Borders between Syria and Palestine and Israel?' (Ayy hudud baina Suriyya wa Filastin wa Isra'il?), *Al-Hayat* newspaper, London, 20 August 1999, p. 14; 'Israel Evades the Issue of Compensations in Order to Give Legal Legitimacy to Occupation' (Isra'il turawigh fi mawdu' al-ta'widat lintiza' shar'iyya qanuniyya lihtilaliha), *Al-Hayat* newspaper, London, 25 August 1999, p. 14; 'Toward a Unified Arab Position to Resist Settlement Projects' (Ila 'amal 'Arabi muwahhad li muqawamat mashari' al-tawtin), *Al-Safir* newspaper, Beirut, 24 August 1999, p. 17; 'Resolution 194 is Obligatory and Return is Possible in Practice' (Al-qarar 194 mulzim wa 'l-'awda mumkina 'amaliyyan), *Al-Safir* newspaper, Beirut, 25 August 1999, p. 19. And see Salman Abu Sitta, *The Register of Villages and Towns Depopulated during the Israeli Invasion in 1948* (Sijill al-nakba 1948: al-qura wa 'l-mudun allati ihtullat wa turida ahluha athna' al-ghazw al-Isra'ili 1948, fi 'l-dhikra al-khamsin lil-nakba) (London, Palestinian Return Centre, 1998).

26. See: *Samed al-Iqtisadi* magazine, the issue on Palestinian Refugees, Year 18, No. 105–106, 1996; *Shu'un al-Awsat* magazine, Year 7, No. 70, March 1998; see also Muhammad Khaled al-Az'ar, '1948 Arabs in Palestine, A Futuristic Outlook' ('Arab thamaniya wa arba'in fi Filastin, ru'ya mustaqbaliyya), *Shu'un 'Arabiyya* magazine, No. 72, December 1992; and 'Israel's Attempts to Settle the Issue of Palestinian Refugees' (Al-Madakhil al-Isra'iliyya li taswiyat qadiyyat al-laji'in al-Filastiniyyin"), *Shu'un 'Arabiyya* magazine, No. 79, September 1994; Hala Nawfal Rizqallah, *Palestinians in Lebanon and Syria: a Comparative Demographic Study 1948–1995* (Al-Filastiniyyun fi Lubnan wa Suriyya: dirasa dimugrafiyya muqarana 1948–1995) (Beirut: Dar al-Jadid, 1998); Majid Kayyali, *Settlement and the Issues of the Final Solution* (Al-Taswiyya wa qadaya al-hall al-niha'i), Beirut: Centre for Strategic Studies and Documentation, 1998. See also Suhayl al-Natour, *The Situation of the Palestinian People in Lebanon* (Awda' al-sha'b al-Filastini fi Lubnan) (Beirut: Dar al-Taqaddum al-'Arabi, 1993); Camile Mansour, ed., *The Palestinian People in the Interior: the Background of the Economic, Social and Political Intifada* (Al-Sha'b al-Filastini fi 'l-dakhil: khalfiyyat al-intifada 'l-siyasiyya wa 'l-iqtisadiyya wa 'l-ijtima'iyya) (Beirut: Institute for Palestine Studies, 1990). One of the earliest and most significant books on this subject is Sabri Jiryis, *The Arabs in Israel* (Al-'Arab fi Isra'il), 2 volumes (Beirut: Research Centre of the Palestine Liberation Organization, 1967); see also 'Aziz Haydar, *Palestinians in Israel under the Oslo Agreement* (Institute for Palestine Studies, 1997). Most of these studies are published in English except for Nouri al-'Uqabi who has edited the *Sawt al-'Arabi* periodical since 1974.

27. Among these studies are: Jean Yves Ollier, *The United Nations Conciliation Commission on Palestine, 1948–1951* (Beirut: Institute for Palestine Studies, 1991); Ramadane Babadji, Monique Chemilier, *The Palestinian Right to Return and its*

Applications (Beirut: Institute for Palestine Studies, 1996); Salim Tamari *The Future of the Palestinian Refugees* (Beirut: Institute for Palestine Studies, 1996). Elia Zureik, *The Palestinian Refugees and the Peace Process* (Beirut: Institute for Palestine Studies, 1996), 'The Palestinian Refugees and the Right to Return', *Journal of Palestine Studies*, No. 19, summer 1994 (in Arabic).

28. See George al-Qusayfi, 'Palestinian Refugees and the Right of Return' (Al-Laji'un al-Filastinyyun wa haqq al-'awda), *Shu'un al-Awsat*, Year 7, No. 70, March 1998, pp. 75–99.

29. Walid Salim, *The Right of Return: The Palestinian Alternatives* (Jerusalem: Panorama, 1997); Yusuf Muhammad Yusuf al-Qara'in, *The Right of the Arab Palestinian People to Self-Determination* (Haqq al-sha'b al-'Arabi 'l-Filastini fi taqrir al-masir) (Amman: Dar al-Jalil, 1983); Faleh al-Tawil, *Palestinian Refugees: an Issue Waiting for a Solution* (Al-Laji'un al-Filastiniyyun: qadiyya tantazer hallan) (self-published, Amman, 1996); Muhammad al-Majdoub, *The Palestinians and the Right of Return* (Al-Filastiniyyun wa haqq al-'awda) (Beirut: Dar al-Isra', 1998).

16 Human rights in the heritage of the Yemeni National Movement

Ahmad Qayid al-Sa'idi

1. Ahmad Qayid al-Sa'idi, *The Yemeni Opposition Movement under the Reign of Imam Yahya ibn Muhammad Hamid al-Din (1904–1948)* (Harakat al-mu'arada 'l-Yamaniyya fi 'ahd al-Imam Yahya ibn Muhammad Hamid al-Din [1904–1948]), Sanaa: Yemeni Centre for Studies and Research (*Markaz al-dirasat wa 'l-buhuth al-Yamani*), (Beirut: Dar al-Adab, 1983), p. 6 et seq.

2. Muhammad Mahmoud al-Zubayri, *This is How the Sons of Yemen are Slaughtered* (Hakadha yudhbahu abna' al-Yaman), publication of the Yemeni Union (Al-Ittihad al-Yamani), Matba'at Ahmad Mukhaymar, n.d., the introduction; and also Muhammad Ahmad Nu'man, *The Sinful History* (Al-Tarikh al-athim), publication of the Yemeni Union, n.d., p. 7 et seq.

3. Ahmad Qayid al-Sa'idi, *The Yemeni National Movement in the Twentieth Century* (Al-Haraka 'l-wataniyya 'l-Yamaniyya fi 'l-qarn al-'ishrin), the introduction. Manuscript.

4. For more, see al-Sa'idi, *Yemeni Opposition Movement*, p. 48 et seq.

5. Ibid., p. 8.

6. See Muhammad Mahmoud al-Zubayri and Muhammad Ahmad Nu'man, *The Objectives of the Liberals* (Ahdaf al-ahrar), publication of the Yemeni Union, n.d., p. 11 et seq.

7. Cf. Muhammad 'Umar al-Habashi, *South Yemen: Politics, Economy and Society* (Al-Yaman al-janoubi: siyasiyyan wa iqtisadiyyan wa ijtima'iyyan), translated by Elias Farah, (Beirut: Dar al-Tali'a, 1967), p. 15 et seq.

8. *The Yemeni Encyclopedia*, Sanaa: Mu'assasat al-'Afif al-Thaqafiyya, 1992, Vol. 1, 324. Also Vitali Naomkin, *The National Front in the Struggle for the Independence of Southern Yemen* (Al-Jabha 'l-qawmiyya fi 'l-kifah min ajl istiqlal al-Yaman al-janoubiyya), translated Salim Touma, (Moscow: Dar al-Taqaddum, 1984), pp. 38–9.

9. For more, see Muhammad 'Atiyya 'l-Masri, *The Red Star Over Yemen* (Al-Najm al-ahmar fawqa 'l-Yaman), third edition, (Beirut: Mu'assasat al-Abhath al-'Arabiyya, 1988), p. 770 et seq. Also Muhammad 'Ali Luqman, *Aden Demands Self-rule* ('Adan tatlub al-hukm al-dhati), Aden: Fatat al-Jazira, n.d., Introduction.

10. Al-Habashi, op. cit., p. 36 et seq. Also Muhammad 'Ali 'l-Jafri, *Facts on Southern Arabia* (Haqa'iq 'an janub al-jazira 'l-'Arabiyya), publication of the Aden Labour Conference, Aden, n.d., p. 43 et seq. Also *Constitution of the League of the Sons of the South* (Dustour rabitat abna' al-janub), (Aden: Dar al-Janoub, n.d.), pp. 7–9.

11. Muhammad Ahmad Nu'man, *The National Movement in Yemen* (Al-Haraka 'l-wataniyya fi 'l-Yaman), publication of the Yemeni Union, (Aden: Al-Jamahir, 1959), p. 33 et seq. Also Ahmad Salih al-Sayyad, *Authority and Opposition in Contemporary Yemen* (Al-Sulta wa 'l-mu'arada fi 'l-Yaman al-mu'asir), (Beirut: Dar al-Sadaqa, 1992), p. 222 et seq. Also 'Abdallah al-Asnaj, *Yemen's Labourers in the Battle* ('Ummal al-Yaman fi 'l-ma'raka), publication of the Aden Labour Conference, n.d., p. 9 et seq.

12. See *The National Covenant of the Popular Democratic Union* (Al-Mithaq al-watani li 'l-ittihad al-sha'bi 'l-dimuqrati), Aden: Dar al-Jihad, n.d., Introduction. Also *The Constitution of the Labour Conference* (Dustur al-mu'tamar al-'ummali) (Aden: Dar al-Ba'th, 1960), p. 4.

13. Anonymous, *Plundered and Stricken Yemen* (Al-Yaman al-manhouba 'l-mankouba), Cairo, 1947, p. 1.

14. Muhammad Mahmoud al-Zubayri, *The Great Deception in Arab Politics* (Al-Khadi'a 'l-kubra fi 'l-siyasa 'l-'Arabiyya), publication of the Yemeni Union, Beirut, n.d., pp. 52–5.

15. Anonymous, op. cit., pp. 7–8.

16. Qasim Ghalib Ahmad, *Message from Hell* (Risala min al-jahim) (Aden: Al-Salam, 1378 AH/1958 AD, pp. 16–19.

17. Ibid., Introduction, p. 28.

18. Ibid., p. 29.

19. Ibid., p. 24.

20. Ibid.

21. Ibid., pp. 25–6.

22. Anonymous, op. cit., pp 48–9.

23. [The Yemeni writer Zayd Mutee' Dammaj has written a brilliant novel on this theme, entitled *The Hostage*. The novel was translated and published through PROTA (Project of Translation from Arabic), translated by May Jayyusi and Christopher Tingley, (New York: Interlink Books, 1994). – EDITOR]

24. Yemeni Expatriates, *The First Moan: From their Retreat, the Sons of Yemen Explain the Reasons for Emigration* (Al-Anna 'l-ula: abna' al-Yaman fi mahajirihim yashrahun asbab al-hijra), n.d., pp. 4–6.

25. Anonymous, op. cit., p. 23.

26. Muhammad Ahmad Nu'man, *To Understand the Cause* (Likay nafham al-qadiyya), publication of the Yemeni Union, Aden: Al-Salam, n.d., p. 6.

27. That is, Sayf al-Islam Ibrahim, the eighth son of Imam Yahya. He fled to the Aden colony and joined the Yemeni Liberals, who gave him the leading role in the Greater Yemeni Association which they established in 1946 to replace the Party of Yemeni Liberals. They gave him the title 'Sayf al-Haq' (sword of justice) to distinguish him from his brothers, who were all named Sayf al-Islam (sword of Islam). He was appointed President of the Consultative Council after the 1948 coup. When the revolt failed, he was arrested with the leaders of the coup and died six months later in prison in obscure circumstances. It was subsequently reported that he had been poisoned on the orders of his brother Imam Ahmad.

28. Anonymous, op. cit., pp. 76–80.

29. 'Abdallah Ahmad al-Dhifani, *The Nationalistic Trend in the Yemeni Liberal Movement, 1944–1948* (Al-Ittijah al-qawmi fi harakat al-ahrar al-Yamaniyyin, 1944–1948), M.A. thesis, 1985, Baghdad, supplement No. 6.

30. Ibid., appendix No. 6.

31. Al-Sa'idi, *Yemeni Opposition Movement*, supplement No. 1, p. 245.

32. Ibid., Appendix No. 4, pp. 25–9.

33. 'Ali Muhammad 'Abduh, *The Course of the Yemeni National Movement* (Masar al-haraka 'l-wataniyya 'l-Yamaniyya) (Sanaa: Ministry of Information and Culture, 1979), pp. 60–1.

34. Muhammad Mahmoud al-Zubayri and Muhammad Ahmad Nu'man, *The Demands of the People* (Matalib al-sha'b), n.d., p. 9 et seq.

17 Human rights in the historical texts of the modern Arab world

Bayan Nuwayhid al-Hout

1. From an interview with Constantine Zurayq, conducted by the writer in Beirut on 12 November 1997.

2. From an interview with Nicola Ziyada, conducted by the writer in Beirut on 20 November 1997.

3. Nicola Ziyada, *Shamiyyat: Studies in Civilization and History* (London: Riad al-Rayyis, 1989), pp. 286–7.

4. Philip K. Hitti, *Lebanon in History* (London: Macmillan, 1957), p. 477.

5. 'Abd al-'Aziz al-Duri, *Introduction to Arab Economic History* (Muqaddima fi 'l-tarikh al-iqtisadi al-'Arabi) (Beirut: Dar al-Tali'a, 1st edition, 1969), pp. 13, 19.

6. Ibid., pp. 81–2.

7. Muhammad Kurd 'Ali, 'The Freedom of Nations' (Hurriyyat al-umam), *Al-Mu'ayyad*, 5 Ramadan 1325 AH (1907 AD), in M.K. 'Ali, *The Ancient and the Modern* (Al-Qadim wa 'l-hadith), Cairo, 1925, p. 307.

8. 'Abd al-'Aziz al-Duri, *The Historical Formation of the Arab Nation: a Study in Identity and Awareness* (Al-Takwin al-tarikhi li 'l-umma al-'Arabiyya: dirasa fi 'l-hawiyya wa 'l-wa'i) (Beirut: Centre for Arab Unity Studies, 1984), p. 219; in *Al-Mufid* journal, January 1912.

9. Ibid., p. 218, note.

10. Ibid., pp. 179–82.

11. See al-Duri, *Historical Formation*, p. 256; 'Various Freedom-Loving Writers', *The Conference of Martyrs: the Conference that Announced the National Goals and Led Its Members to the Gallows*, (Beirut: *Al-Yawm* Newspaper Press, 1955), pp. 78–89. (Yusuf Yezbek wrote the preface to this book and published documents and essays on Arab martyrs in his historic magazine *Lebanese Papers* (Al-Awraq al-lubnaniyya), Beirut, 1955–8. In his view al-'Uraisi held a place of honour.) See also Sati' al-Husari, *Lectures on the Evolution of the Nationalist Idea* (Muhadarat fi nushu' al-fikra al-qawmiyya), (Beirut: Dar al-'Ilm li 'l-Malayin, 3rd edition, 1956), p. 215.

12. 'Various Freedom-Loving Writers', op. cit., pp. 78–9.

13. Ibid., pp. 81–90.

14. *Fata al-'Arab*, No. 1435, 15 December 1913, in: *Mukhtarat al-Mufid*, introduction by Naji 'Alloush, Beirut: Dar al-Tali'a, 1981, p. 119. (*Al-Mufid* journal, published by 'Abd al-Ghani al-'Uraisi, in collaboration with Fu'ad Hantash in Beirut, was subject to closure on many occasions, during which times it appeared under other titles. *Fata al-'Arab* was one of these.)

15. Lothrop Stoddard, *The Islamic World Today*, translated by 'Ajaj Nuwayhid, containing additional chapters and comments by Prince Shakib Arsalan, (Cairo: 'Isa al-Babi al-Halabi, 2nd edition, 1352 AH [1933 AD]); from Arsalan's chapter on 'Tripoli and Italy', Vol. 2, p. 64.

16. The 'Arab Nationalist Bloc' harks back to the early 1930s, or maybe even to 1929, as an underground nationalist movement at the American University in Beirut. Its presidents were, in chronological order: Constantine Zurayq (of Syria); Darwish al-Miqdadi (of Palestine); and Yunis al-Sab'awi (of Iraq).

17. Constantine Zurayq, Introduction, in *General Philosophical Works of Dr Constantine Zurayq*, (Beirut: Centre for Arab Unity Studies *and* The 'Abd al-Hamid Shuman Foundation, 1994), Vol. 1, p. 12.

18. Ibid., Vol. 1, p. 18.

19. 'Abdallah al-'Alayli, *The Arabs' Nationalist Constitution* (Dustur al-'Arab al-qawmi) (Beirut: Dar al-Jadid, 1966, reprint of 1st edition, 1941), p. 187.

20. Ibid., p. 195.

21. Ibid., p. 212.

22. Ibid.

23. Ibid.

24. Anis Sayigh, Introduction, in Anis Sayigh (ed.), *The Arab Intellectual: His Concerns and Work* (Al-Muthaqqaf al-'Arabi: humumuhu wa 'ata'uh) (Beirut: Centre for Arab Unity Studies *and* The 'Abd al-Hamid Shuman Foundation, 1995), pp. 10–11.

25. 'Ali Mahafza, 'The Future of Democracy in Jordan'; lecture delivered at the University of Jordan Student Union, Amman, 4 December 1995 (typewritten text), pp. 3–4.

26. Turkish Ottoman tradition held that ministers and others of high office should be known by their first name and their title; Rashid Pasha, who held the position of Prime Minister, was one of these. His fame however, lies in having been the first Ottoman reformer, since he was the driving force behind the law making all citizens equal (known as the Kalkhana Law) of 1839.

27. Medhat Pasha had at one time been an Ottoman prime minister, but he was far better known as the 'Father of the Constitution' and the 'Father of the Free Men'. He ended his days imprisoned and exiled in Ta'if (in present-day Saudi Arabia), where he died in 1883. It is believed he was killed by strangling.

28. 'Constitutional' rule under Sultan Abdul-Hamid lasted for a total of three years, divided into two periods: one at the outset of his reign, and the other at its close. His reign lasted from 1876 to 1909.

29. Najib 'Azuri (founder of the League of Arab Nations in the early twentieth century), *Awakening of the Arab Nation* (Yaqzat al-umma al-'Arabiyya), translated from the French original of 1905 by Ahmad Abu Mulhim, (Beirut: Arab Institute for Studies and Publication, 1978), pp. 37–38, 219.

30. Shakib Arsalan, *Autobiography* (Sira dhatiyya) (Beirut: Dar al-Tali'a, 1969), p. 35.

31. Khalil Sakakini, *Such Am I, O World* (Kadha ana ya dunia) (Jerusalem: Commercial Press, 1955), p. 47.

32. Al-Husari, op. cit., p. 197.

33. Muhammad 'Izzat Darwaza, *On the Modern Arab Movement* (Hawl al-haraka al-'Arabiyya al-haditha) (Sidon: Modern Library, 1950), Vol. 1, p. 60.

34. Muhammad 'Izzat Darwaza, *Memoirs 1887–1984: Record of the Arab Movement and the Palestinian Cause*, (Beirut: Islamic West Press, 1993), p. 462.

35. 'Abd al-Razzaq al-Hasani, *Modern Political History of Iraq* (Tarikh al-'Iraq al-siyasi al-hadith) (Sidon: Al-'Irfan Press, 1948), Vol. 1, pp. 192–3.

36. See the text of 'Basic Iraqi Law', in ibid., pp. 203–20.

37. 'Abdallah al-Qusaymi, 'King Abdul-Aziz', in *Al-Katib* magazine, February 1946; quoted in 'Abd al-'Aziz ibn 'Abd al-Muhsin al-Tuwayjiri, *To the Night Travellers Morning Called: King Abdul-Aziz: a Documentary Study* (Li surat al-layl hatafa al-sabah) (Beirut: Riad al-Rayyis, 1st edition, 1997), pp. 774–5.

38. Ziyada, op. cit., pp. 282–3.

39. Al-Duri, *Historical Formation*, p. 39.

40. Ibid., p. 141.

41. Ibid., pp. 142–4.

42. See Muhammad 'Amara (ed.), *Jamal al-Din al-Afghani: Complete Works: Political Writings*, (Beirut: Arab Institute for Studies and Publication, 1981), Vol. 2, pp. 63–100.

43. The Explorer 'K' ['Abd al-Rahman al-Kawakibi], *Features of Oppression and the Ends of Slavery* (Taba'i' al-istibdad wa masari' al-isti'bad) (Cairo: Al-Azhar, 1900), p. 107.

44. Ibid., pp. 128–9.

45. 'Abd al-Ghani al-'Uraisi, 'The Ottoman Constitution', in *Al-Mufid*, No. 751, 22 July 1911; published in *Al-Mufid: Selections*, pp. 56–9.

46. 'Abd al-Ghani al-'Uraisi, 'The Birth of the Prophet (Muhammad)', in *Al-Mufid*, No. 919, 29 February 1912; published in ibid., p. 26.

47. Yusuf Ibrahim Yezbek, 'In This Month of 1915, the First Group of Martyrs Was Executed', in *Lebanese Papers* magazine, 8th volume, August 1955; published in *Lebanese Papers*, Beirut: The Lebanese Pioneer Press, 1983, Vol. 1, p. 351. (This is a reprint of Yezbek's original magazine published from 1955–8; Ahmad Nasser was the witness who recorded the last speech of the martyr 'Abd al-Karim al-Khalil, and Michel Zakkur was the first to publish it in *Al-Barq* newspaper, Beirut, February 1919.)

48. Text of the Zincograph leaflet, in *The Arabs* magazine, Jerusalem, No. 16, 10 December 1932, p. 13.

49. 'Communiqué by the Arab Independence Party of Palestine on the Anniversary of the British Army's Conquest of Jerusalem', in ibid., p. 12.

50. Al-Tuwayjiri, in ibid., p. 829. (From a speech delivered by King Abdul-Aziz at a celebration in his honour, organized by the municipality of the then capital Mecca on 30 April 1930.)

51. Ibid., p. 621.

52. Al-Hasani, op. cit., Vol. 1, p. 4.

53. King Faisal I, in ibid., Introduction, p. 6.

54. Anis Sayigh, 'Dr Constantine Zurayq the Man', in *Constantine Zurayq: 65 Years of Contribution* (Constantine Zurayq, 65 'aman min al-'ata') (Beirut: Bisan, 1996), p. 6.

55. Zurayq, op. cit., Vol. 1, I, pp. 182–6.

56. Ibid., Vol. 1, I, pp. 187–8.

57. Ibid., Vol. 1, I, p. 140.

58. Ibid. (from his work *On the Battle for Civilization* (Fi ma'rakat al-hadara), first published 1964), Vol. 2, VI, pp. 882–3.

59. Ibid. (from his work *The Meaning of Nakba Revisited* [Ma'na 'l-nakba mujaddadan], first published 1967), Vol. 2, VII, pp. 1013–4.

60. Nicola Ziyada, *Lubnaniyyat: History and Pictures* (London: Riad al-Rayyis, 1st edition, 1992), p. 139.

61. Loc. cit.

62. Mahafza, 'The Role of Research Institutions in Developing the Human and Social Sciences in Arab Countries', in *Acta*, First International Conference on the Role of Research Institutions in Developing the Human and Social Sciences in Arab Countries and Turkey, Zaghwan, Tunisia: Al-Tamimi *for* Research and the Konrad Adenauer Institute, 1995, pp. 263, 278.

63. 'Ali, op. cit., pp. 50–1. (Originally a lecture delivered by him in Damascus at a gathering of state school teachers, entitled 'The Rise and Decline of the Arabs'.)

64. Darwaza, *Memoirs*, Vol. 1, pp. 460–2.

65. Yezbek, *The Story of the First of May in the World and in Lebanon: Memories, History and Texts* (Hikayat awwal nuwwar fi 'l-'alam wa fi Lubnan: dhikrayat wa tarikh wa nusus) (Beirut: Al-Farabi Press, 1974), p. 82.

66. Ibid., p. 105; quoting *Humanity* (*Al-Insaniyya*) newspaper, No. 2, 24 May 1925, p. 2.

67. [Qasim Amin was a famous Egyptian writer who rose to fame at the end of the nineteenth and the beginning of the twentieth centuries. Most importantly, he wrote about the liberation of women, and became a symbol of male open-mindedness on the subject. – EDITOR]

68. 'The Eastern Question' embodies the West's designs on the Ottoman state, which it called the 'Sick Man', meaning that the Ottoman state was nearing its end and the Western powers were entitled to take over its territories and divide them up among themselves. The fact that the West kept the Ottoman state intact, in the aftermath of the Crimean War of 1856 for example, should not be miscon-strued as any desire on the part of the West to save the Ottoman territories from division. The Western powers were merely waiting for the appropriate moment to go ahead with a plan they had prepared all along. The First World War pro-vided the perfect opportunity for this.

69. Muhammad Jamil Bayham, *Eastern Women in Western Culture* (Fatat al-sharq fi hadarat al-gharb) (Beirut, 1952), p. 11.

70. Bayham published the following books on women: *Women in History and Codes* (Al-Mar'a fi 'l-tarikh wa 'l-shara'i'), 1921; *Women in Modern Civilization* (Al-Mar'a fi 'l-tamaddun al-hadith), 1927; *Eastern Women in Western Culture* (Fatat al-sharq fi hadarat al-gharb), 1952; *Women in Arab Civilization and Arabs in Women's History* (Al-Mar'a fi hadarat al-'Arab wa 'l-'Arab fi tarikh al-mar'a), 1962; *Women in Islam and Western Civilization* (Al-Mar'a fi 'l-Islam wa fi 'l-hadara al-gharbiyya), 1980.

71. Hasan Hallaq (ed.), *The Historian-Scholar Muhammad Jamil Bayham (1887–1978): Pioneer of the Political, Social and Philosophical Renaissance in Lebanon and the Arab World* (Al-Mu'arrikh al-'allama Muhammad Jamil Bayham (1887–1978): min ruwwad al-nahda al-siyasiyya wa 'l-ijtima'iyya wa 'l-fikriyya fi Lubnan wa 'l-'alam al-'Arabi), Beirut, 1980, p. 107.

72. Nicola Ziyada, *My Times: Autobiography* (Ayyami: sira dhatiyya) (London: Hazar, 1992), Vol. 2, p. 137.

73. Al-'Alayli, op. cit., p. 192.

74. 'Abdallah al-'Alayli, *Where is the Wrong in That? A Correction of Concepts and an Innovative View* . . . (Aina 'l-khata'? Tas-hih mafahim wa nazrat tajdid . . .), (Beirut: Dar al-Jadid, 2nd edition, 1992), pp. 113–4.

75. See al-Afghani, op. cit., Vol. 1, pp. 63–100.

76. Al-Kawakibi, op. cit., p. 107.

77. Yezbek, 'Preface', in *Martyrs' Conference*, pp. 17–8.

78. Al-Duri, *Historical Formation*, quoting Jawdat al-Rikabi and Jamil Sultan (eds.), *The Social Reformer ' Abd al-Hamid al-Zahrawi's Intellectual Legacy* (Al-Irth al-fikri li 'l-muslih al-ijtima'i 'Abd al-Hamid al-Zahrawi) (Damascus: Supreme Council for Arts, Literature and Social Sciences, 1962), pp. 224–30.

79. 'Prince Shakib Arsalan speaks out on the Berber Edict and Demands that it be Erased from Existence', *Al-'Arab* magazine, Jerusalem, No. 38, 27 May 1933, pp. 3–4.

80. Shakib Arsalan, *The Bond of Unity Among Jihad Activists* ('Urwat al-ittihad bayn ahl al-jihad), Buenos Aires: *Arab Banner* (Al-'Alam al-'Arabi) newspaper, 1st ed., 1941, Vol. 1, p. 154. (Originally an essay written by him in Geneva, 25 May 1940.)

81. Shakib Arsalan, 'Al-Sunusiyya', in *The Present of the Islamic World*, Vol. 1, II, p. 164.

82. 'Abd al-Razzaq al-Hasani, *The Babiists in History* (Al-Babiyyun fi 'l-tarikh), (Sidon: Al-'Irfan Press, 1930); 2nd edition, published as *The Babiists and Baha'is: Past and Present: A Detailed Study of Kashfism and Shaykhism and how Babiism and Baha'ism Came into Being* (Al-Babiyyun wa 'l-baha'iyyun fi hadirihum wa madihum: dirasa daqiqa fi 'l-kashfiyya wa 'l-shaykhiyya wa fi kayfiyyat zuhur al-babiyya wa 'l-baha'iyya), (Sidon: Al-'Irfan Press, 1962).

83. 'Abd al-Razzaq al-Hasani, *Satan Worshippers in Iraq* ('Abadatu 'l-Shaytan fi 'l-Iraq) (Sidon: Al-'Irfan Press, 2nd edition, 1931); expanded 6th edition, published as *Yazidis: Past and Present* (Al-Yazidiyyun fi hadirihim wa madihim) (Baghdad: New Book Press, 1974).

84. 'Abd al-Razzaq al-Hasani, *Sabaea: Past and Present* (Al-Sabiyya qadiman wa hadithan), corrected reprint of 1st edition of 1925, (Cairo: Al-Khanji, 1931); expanded 5th edition published as *The Sabaeans: Their Past and Present* (Al-Sabiyyun fi hadirihim wa madihim), n.p., 1978.

85. Hujjat al-Islam Shaykh Muhammad al-Husain Kashif al-Ghata wrote the introduction to al-Hasani's *Babiists in History*, and the scholar Ahmed Zaki Basha wrote the introduction to his *Sabaea*.

86. Al-Hasani, *Yazidis*, p. 7.

87. Al-'Alayli, *Arabs' Nationalist Constitution*, pp. 207–8.

88. Ahmad al-Shurbasi, *Shakib Arsalan, The Prince of Eloquence* (Amir al-bayan Shakib Arsalan) (Cairo: Arab Book Press, 1963), Vol. 2, pp. 741–2. (A letter from Arsalan in Geneva to al-Sayyid Rashid Rida in Cairo, 2 April 1931.)

89. Arsalan, *Bond of Unity*, Vol. 1, pp. 45–6.

90. Ibid., p. 47.

91. Darwaza, *Modern Arab Movement*, Vol. 3, pp. 196–7.

92. *'Arif al-'Arif Papers: Palestinian Homes Torn Down by the Israelis 1967–1972: Gaza, a Window onto Hell* (Awraq 'Arif al-'Arif: al-dur al-filastiniyya allati hadamaha al-Isra'iliyyun 1967–1972: Ghazza, nafidha 'ala 'l-jahim), (Beirut: Palestine Liberation Organization, Studies Centre, 1973), 3rd collection, p. 469.

93. Ibid., 2nd collection, pp. 375–7.

94. Ibid., *Register of Immortality: Martyrs' Names in the Palestine War of 1967: The Palestinians in Israeli Jails 1967–1972* (Sijill al-khulud: asma' shuhada' harb Filastin 1967: al-filastiniyyun fi sujun Isra'il 1967–1972), 1st collection, p. 21.

95. Ibid., 1st collection, p. 49.

96. Walid Khalidi (ed.), *All That Remains: The Palestinian Village Occupied and Depopulated by Israel in 1948* (Washington DC: Institute for Palestine Studies, 1992), preface, p. xix.

97. Mustafa Murad al-Dabbagh, *Our Country Palestine* (Biladuna filastin), (Beirut: Dar al-Tali'a and the Hebron Regional Academics League Press, Vol. 6, 1974), II, pp. 180–2.

98. Khalidi, op. cit., p. 450.

99. Hajj Amin al-Husaini and 'Arif al-'Arif both managed to escape to Jordan.

100. Sami al-Dahhan, *Lectures on Shakib Arsalan* (Muhadarat 'an Shakib Arsalan) (Cairo: League of Arab States – Arab Academy for Higher Studies, 1958), p. 155.

101. Israel did not stop attacking Palestinian writers and men of letters; it even attacked the Institute for Palestine Studies in Beirut, intending to paralyze it entirely. Israel bombed the Institute with three missiles in 1974, setting a large part of the library on fire; and during its occupation of Beirut in 1982, it committed the theft, over a number of days, of the Institute's contents, transferring them to Israel in huge containers.

102. Al-Dabbagh, op. cit., Vol. 1 (1965), I, pp. 7–8.

103. Constantine Zurayq, *What to Do? Speaking to the Youthful Arab Generations* (Ma 'l-'amal? Hadith ila 'l-ajyal al-'Arabiyya al-tali'a) (Beirut: Centre for Arab Unity Studies, 1998), p. 25.

104. Robert Maynard Hutchins (chief editor), *The Great Conversation: The Substance of a Liberal Education. Great Books of the Western World* (Chicago: Encyclopaedia Britannica, 1952), pp. xx–xxi.

18 Patriarchy and human rights

'Abd al-Razzaq 'Eid

1. 'Abd al-Rahman Munif, *Cities of Salt* (Mudun al-milh), Beirut: Al-Mu'assasa 'l-'Arabiyya li 'l-Dirasat wa 'l-Nashr, 5 volumes, 1984–1989. See Vol. 3, *Variations on Night and Day* (Taqasim al-lail wa 'l-nahar), p. 237.

2. Friedrich Engels, *Origins of Family, Private Property and the State* (Al-Usra wa 'l-mulkiyya al-khassa wa 'l-dawla), translated from French by Adib Yusef (Beirut: Dar al-Farabi and Dar al-Kitab al-'Arabi, 1958), p. 95.

3. Ibid., p. 96.

4. Ibid., p. 115.

5. Claude Lévi-Strauss, *La pensée sauvage*, Paris, 1962. Translated by Nazir Jahil, (Al-Fikr al-barri) (Beirut: Al-Mu'assasa 'l-Jami'iyya li 'l-Dirasat, 1984), p. 162.

6. From Michel Foucault, *L'usage des plaisirs*, 1984. Translated by George Abi Salih and titlted, (Isti'mal al-ladhat) (Beirut: Markaz al-Inma' al-Qawmi, 1991), p. 151.

7. The nature of the Arabic terms *rabb al-bayt, rabb al-'a'ila, rabb al-'amal* ('master of the household', 'head of the family', 'employer') suggests a connection in signification between the word 'father' and the word 'God'. The proverbial saying, 'A father's anger is akin to God's anger', indicates a degree of identification between signifier and signified.

8. Hisham Sharabi, *Patriarchy and the Problematic of Backwardness in Arab Society*. (Al-Nizam al-abawi wa ishkaliyyat takhalluf al-mujtama' al-'Arabi), translated by Mahmoud Shureih, (Beirut: Centre for Arab Unity Studies, 1992), p. 107. See also Halim Barakat, *Contemporary Arab Society: a Sociological Exploration* (Al-Mujtama' al-'Arabi 'l-mu'asir: bahth istitla'i ijtima'i) (Beirut: Centre for Arab Unity Studies, 1984), p. 246.

9. Ayyoub Thabit, *The Declaration of Human Rights* (I'lan huquq al-insan), cited in Ra'if Khoury, *Modern Arabic Thought* (Al-Fikr al-'Arabi 'l-hadith), introduced and edited by Muhammad Kamil al-Khatib, 3rd edition, (Damascus: Ministry of Culture, 1993), p. 15.

10. Sharabi, op. cit., p. 109.

11. Ibid., p. 108.

12. Terry Eagleton, *Literary Theory* (Nazariyyat al-adab), translated by Tha'ir Dib, (Damascus: Ministry of Culture, 1995), p. 242.

13. Ibid., pp. 279–80.

14. Michael Rosaldo and Louise Lamger, *Women, Culture and Society* (Al-Mar'a, al-thaqafa, al-mujtama'), translated by Haifa Hashim, (Damascus: Ministry of Culture, 1976), pp. 109–39. Quoted from Turki 'Ali 'l-Rabi'u, *Violence, the Sacred, Sexuality and Women in Islamic Mythology* (Al-'Unf wa 'l-maqaddas wa 'l-jins fi 'l-mithulujiyya al-Islamiyya) (Beirut: Arabic Cultural Centre, 1994), p. 146.

15. Ibid., pp. 20, 144.

16. Sigmund Freud, *The Interpretation of Dreams* (Al-Hulm wa ta'wiluh), translated by George Tarabishi (Beirut: Dar al-Tali'a, 1976), pp. 95–6.

17. 'Abd al-Razzaq 'Eid and Yassin al-Hafiz, *Criticism of the Modernity of Backwardness?* (naqd hadathat al-ta'khkhur?) (Aleppo: Dar al-Sadaqa, 1996). For an understanding of the Lebanese issue, see Part 2, Chapter 1, 'Secularism from an Epistemological Perspective', pp. 154–76.

18. Nawal al-Sa'dawi, *Women and Sexuality* (Al-Mar'a wa 'l-jins), (Cairo-Beirut: Al-Nashirun al-'Arab, 1971), p. 25.

19. Mustafa Hijazi, *Social Backwardness: the Psychology of the Oppressed*, (Al-Takhalluf al-ijtima'i: madkhal ila sikulujiyyat al-insan al-maqhur), (Beirut: Institute for National Development, 1980), p. 212.

20. 'Abbas Makki, 'The Body: its Taboos, Anatomy and Explosive Symbolic Expressions' (Al-Jism: muharramatuh wa tashrihatuh wa ta'biratuhu 'l-infijariyya 'l-ramziyya) (Beirut: *Dirasat Nafsiyya* journal, Faculty of Arts, Lebanese University, 1974), p. 17. *Ibid.*, pp. 215–25.

21. Sharabi, op. cit., pp. 69–71.

22. Fatima al-Mernisi, *La harem politique* (Al-Harim al-siyasi), translated by 'Abd al-Hadi 'Abbas, (Damascus: Dar al-Hasad, 1990), p. 78.

23. Ibid., pp. 32–67.

24. Hadi 'l-'Alawi, *Chapters on Women* (Fusul 'an al-mar'a) (Beirut: Dar al-Kunuz al-Adadiyya, 1996), p. 32.

25. Al-Qurashi ('Imad al-Din Abu 'l-Fida Isma'il), *Interpretation of the Glorious* Quran (Tafsir al-Qur'an al-'azim), Vol. 1, (Beirut: Dar al-Qalam), pp. 422–3.

26. Al-'Alawi, op. cit., pp. 32–7.

27. Sura 2, *Al-Baqara*, 223.

28. Al-Tabari (Abu Ja'far Muhammad ibn Jarir) *Interpretation of the* Quran (Tafsir al-Tabari), Vol. 4, pp. 400–12, cited by al-Mernisi, op. cit., pp. 175–78.

29. Al-'Alawi, op. cit., pp. 51–2.

30. For further information on the *ifk*/untruth episode, see al-Qurashi, op. cit., Vol. 3, 231.

31. Sharabi, op. cit., pp. 123–44.

32. This is the main theme in Muhammad 'Abid al-Jabiri's book *Critique of the Arab Mind* (Naqd al-'aql al-'Arabi), Beirut: Centre for Arab Unity Studies, 3 volumes.

33. 'Abdallah al-'Aroui, *The Concept of Freedom* (Mafhoum al-hurriyya), (Beirut: Arabic Cultural Centre, n.d.), pp. 5–8.

34. Ibid., p. 59.

35. Khoury, op. cit., p. 176.

36. Z. L. Levine, *Modern Social and Political Thought in Lebanon, Syria and Egypt* (Al-Fikr al-ijtima'i wa 'l-siyasi al-hadith fi Lubnan wa Suriyya wa Misr), translated by Bashir al-Siba'i, (Beirut: Dar Ibn Khaldoun, 1978), p. 262.

37. Ibid., pp. 143–4.

38. See 'Abd al-Razzaq 'Eid, *Introduction to the Thinking of Ra'if Khoury* (Madkhal ila fikr Ra'if Khoury) (Cyprus: Ebal Institute for Research and Publishing, [1990?]) pp. 111–35.

39. Levine, op. cit., p. 264.

40. 'Abd al-Rahman al-Kawakibi, *The Features of Oppression* (Taba'i' al-istibdad), Cairo, n.d., p. 13.

41. Ibid., p. 104. See also 'Eid, *The Crisis of the Enlightenmen: the Legitimisation of Cultural Disparity* (Azmat al-tanwir: shar'anat al-fawat al-hadari), (Damascus, Al-Ahali li 'l-Tiba'a wa l-Nashr wa 'l-Tawzi', 1997).

19 Civil and political rights in Arab constitutions

Fateh Samih 'Azzam

1. This study is an abbreviated and updated version of *Arab Constitutional Guarantees of Civil and Political Rights*, published by the Cairo Institute for Human Rights in 1995. For their research assistance, I would like to thank my colleague Ms Ruba al-Salim and Mr Nasser Amin, Director of the Arab Centre for the Independence of the Judiciary and the Legal Profession.

2. See for example *Human Rights in the Arab World for 2000* (Huquq al-insan fi 'l-watan al-'Arabi 2000) and other annual reports of the Arab Organization for Human Rights (Cairo). Review also the web sites of Arab and international human rights organizations, including Amnesty International (www.amnesty.org) and Human Rights Watch (www.hrw.org).

3. See Tariq al-Khudairy, 'The Influence of Arab-Islamic Civilization on the Development of Human Rights: A Historical Perspective' (Athar al-hadara al-Islamiyya fi tatawur mawdu' huquq al-insan: nazra tarikhiyya) in *The Universal Declaration of Human Rights and the Situation in the Arab World* (Al-I'lan al-'alami li-huquq al-insan wa ahwal al-'alam al-'Arabi) (Cairo: Dar al-Mustaqbal al-'Arabi, 1989), pp. 3–48.

4. For further discussion, see Subhi Mahmasani, *Legal Systems in the Arab States: Past and Present* (Al-Awda' al-tashri'iyya fi 'l-duwal al-'Arabiyya: madiha wa hadiriha), fourth edition (Beirut: Dar al-'Ilm li 'l-Malayin, 1981), pp. 180–95.

5. Gamal Mursi Badr, 'Islamic Law and the Challenges of Modern Times', in Piscatori *et al.* (eds), *Law, Personalities and Politics of the Middle East* (Boulder-Washington: Westview Press, 1989), p. 33.

6. Arab Organization for Human Rights (AOHR), 'Introduction to the 1988 Report', in *Journal of Arab Affairs*, 9, p. 8. See also the AOHR Annual Report for 1989, p. 11. A complete translation of the Libyan Declaration is found in Blaustein and Flanz (eds), *Constitutions of the Countries of the World*, Release 92–3, Oceania: Dobbs Ferry, New York, May 1992. The translations in Blaustein and Flanz are rather poor, and I have reworded most translations in this essay.

7. Article 26, *The Great Green Charter for Human Rights in the Era of the Masses*, promulgated in Beida, 12 June 1988. Translated from an official Libyan government publication, n.p., n.d.

8. Mundher 'Anabtawi, *The Human Being: Rights and a Cause* (Al-Insan qadiyya wa huquq) (Tunisia: Arab Organization for Human Rights, 1991).

9. Arab Organization for Human Rights, Annual Report, 1988, p. 9. See also, Human Rights Watch/Middle East, *Human Rights in Iraq* (New York: HRW, 1990), p. 57.

10. This is a more accurate translation than the one found in Blaustein and Flanz (see note 6 above), which reads: 'The State ensures the considerations necessary to exercise these liberties which comply with the revolutionary, national and progressive trend.'

11. See the discussion in Erica-Irene Daes, *Freedom of the Individual Under Law*, UN Human Rights Center Study Series No. 3, (New York: United Nations, 1990), p. 116, at paragraph 169.

12. This is as found in the original government translation of the Charter. Rather than 'mankind', a better translation of the Arabic *bashar* would be 'human kind', which has neutral gender connotations.

13. See Adama Dieng, 'The Rule of Law and the Independence of the Judiciary: An Overview of Principles', in Center for the Independence of Judges and Lawyers (CIJL), *Constitutional Guarantees for the Independence of the Judiciary*, CIJL Yearbook No. 1, (Geneva: International Commission of Jurists, 1992), p. 22.

14. The original Sudanese Constitution was suspended after the military coup of 1989, and a state of emergency was declared which remains in force. Moreover, the country remains divided by civil war and affected by international and US sanctions.

15. Hamid Fayyad, 'Constitutional Law in the Arab World' (Al-Qanun al-dusturi fi 'l-watan al-'Arabi), in Arab Organization for Human Rights, *Journal for Arab Affairs*, 9, p. 71.

16. 'Abd al-Ghani al-Mani', 'A Legal-Constitutional Intervention' (Mudakhala qanuniyya dusturiyya), in Arab Organization for Human Rights, *Decision-Making in the Arab World from the Viewpoint of Democratic Legitimacy* (Sina'at al-qarar fi 'l-watan al-'Arabi fi dau' al-shar'iyya al-dimuqratiyya), Thought Forum Series, No. 5, Cairo: Dar al-Mustaqbal al-'Arabi, 1992, p. 110.

17. As amended by Laws No. 60 (1968), 37 (1972), 164 (1981) and 50 (1982).

18. See Muhammad Hilmi Murad, 'Egyptian Legislation Contrary to Human Rights' (Al-Tashri'at al-misriyya al-mujafiya li huquq al-insan), in *Egyptian Organization for Human Rights* (Huquq al-insan fi Misr), Thought Forum Series, No. 2, (Cairo: Dar al-Mustaqbal al-'Arabi, 1990), pp. 26–7.

19. The Arab Lawyers' Union has been calling for the cancellation of exceptional courts since its Fifteenth Conference, held in Tunisia in 1984. See *Arab Human Rights* (Huquq al-insan al-'Arabi), No. 7, December/January 1984, pp. 33–4. We find this demand repeated consistently in the annual reports of Arab and international human rights organizations.

20. See Human Rights Watch, Middle East Division, *Human Rights in Iraq* (New York: HRW, 1990), pp. 50–1.

21. Presidential Decree No. 49 of 1999, published in the *Palestinian Gazette*, Issue

No. 4 (May 1999). The decree was justified on the grounds of the British Emergency Regulations, which are fundamentally no longer applicable in the Occupied Palestinian Territories.

20 Arab political parties and human rights

Muhammad al-Sayyid Saʿid

1. For a review of modern Arab pluralistic experiences, see ʿAzmi Bishara, Muhammad al-Sayyid Saʿid (eds.), *Problematics in the Decline of Democratic Transformation in the Arab World* (Ishkaliyyat taʿathur al-tahawwul al-dimuqrati fi ʾl-watan al-ʿArabi), (Ramallah: Muʾassasat Muwatin, 1997).

2. On the organic relationship between political parties and democracies, see: Nuʿman al-Khatib, *Political Parties and their Role in Contemporary Ruling Systems* (Al-Ahzab al-siyasiyya wa dawruha fi anzimat al-hukm al-muʿasira) (Cairo: Dar al-Thaqafa li ʾl-Nashr wa ʾl-Tawziʿ, 1983); Leon Epstein, *Political Parties in Western Democracies* (New York: Praeger, 1962).

3. Depreciation of the value of the political party in western democracies is the main driving force behind the search for alternative channels for the democratic process, especially in relation to articulating and negotiating interests and creating a genuine participative society. See, for example, Joshua Cohen and Joel Rogers, *Associations and Democracy* (London: Verso, 1995).

4. See: Muhammad Sayyid Ahmad, *The Future of the Party System in Egypt* (Mustaqbal al-nizam al-hizbi fi Misr) (Cairo: Dar al-Mustaqbal al-ʿArabi, 1984); Nizam Barakat, 'Elections, Political Parties and Democracy' (Al-Intikhabat wa ʾl-ahzab wa ʾl-dimuqratiyya), in *Contemporary Electoral Systems* (Al-Anzima al-intikhabiyya al-muʿasira) (Amman: Dar Sindibad li ʾl-Nashr, 1995), p. 45.

5. Muhammad al-Sayyid Saʿid, in Bishara and Saʿid, op. cit., pp. 35–86.

6. This becomes very evident when we compare the performance of the opposition parties in consecutive parliamentary elections held in Egypt, Jordan, Tunisia and Yemen. For the relevant comparison, see: Hala Mustafa (ed.), *Parliamentary Elections in Egypt, 1995* (Al-Intikhabat al-niyabiyya fi Misr, 1995) (Cairo: Al-Ahram Centre for Strategic Studies, 1996), pp. 2–35; *Contemporary Electoral Systems*, p. 45. See also pp. 107–16 for a comparison of elections in Yemen, Tunisia, Lebanon and Morocco; Centre for Political and Strategic Studies, *The Strategic Arab Report* (Al-Taqrir al-istratiji al-ʿArabi) (Cairo: Al-Ahram, 1993–7); Ibn Khaldoun Centre for Development Studies, *The Civil Society Bulletin* (Nashrat al-mujtamaʿ al-madani), various issues, 1995–8.

7. On the Sudanese National Alliance and the Nairobi Declaration, see 'Muhammad Khayr', *Al-Hayat* newspaper, 13 August 1997.

8. Hasan Qurunful concludes that even in Morocco, where political parties seem

more deeply rooted and enjoy greater popularity, the results of the 1997 elections represent the beginning of a phenomenon that cannot be ignored – showing, among other things, a decline in the numbers of voters having an attitudinal identification with the political parties and a deterioration in the role of membership within specific parties. This is symptomatic of the trends governing voters' choices and of a decline in voter enthusiasm toward political parties. See: Hasan Qurunful, *The Political Elite and Power* (Al-Nukhba al-siyasiyya wa 'l-sulta) (Casablanca: Dar Ifriqiya, 1997); Hasan Qurunful, 'The Islamic Movement and Political Participation in Morocco' (Al-Haraka al-Islamiyya wa 'l-musharaka al-siyasiyya fi 'l-Maghreb), *Social Science Journal* (Kuwait: Majallat al-'Ulum al-Siyasiyya).

9. See: G. Grunberg, *L'instabilité du comportement electoral, en explication du vote*, Paris: P.F.N.S.P., 1989; M, Pederson, 'The Dynamics of European Party Systems. Changing Patterns of Electoral Volatility', *European Journal of Political Research*, 7 March, 1979.

10. On Egyptian administration parties, see Ahmad Zakariyya al-Shal'a, 'Social Structures of Egyptian Parties', in Ra'ouf 'Abbas, *Egyptian Parties 1922–1953* (Cairo: Al-Ahram Centre for Strategic Studies, 1996), pp. 80–4.

11. This phenomenon resulted, initially, from the fact that certain coups or military takeovers had not, as in Syria or Iraq, stemmed from established party bases. The 1952 revolution, for instance, did not have party affiliation but tried later to create an inclusive political framework. The 'National Union' was the first experiment whose essential mottoes reflected this all-encompassing national character as well as the bureaucratic nature of political and ideological thought. One of these mottoes was 'Union, Order and Work', which reflected the nature of the National Union.

It would be interesting to review the concept of the 'single party', such as the Arab Socialist Union in Egypt, and ascertain whether it represents a political party in the conventional sense or an administration party. In fact, it is closer to the latter than the former, and we may, in this connection, make the following generalization: a political party cannot of itself develop in the political arena unless it is structured as a 'power bloc'. By ruling out pluralism and competition, the 'single party' eliminates itself and denies itself as a party. Indeed, it condemns itself to becoming a party subservient to the administrative state apparatus – with which it often identifies and merges. The generalization applies, to a lesser extent, to nominally 'ruling' parties when the circulation of power, and free competition for assuming positions of power in open elections, are ruled out and blocked.

For Egypt's experience in this respect, see Derek Hopwood, *Egypt: Politics and Society 1945–1990* (London-New York: Routledge, 1993), pp. 186–90.

12. On the various Egyptian parties, see: Wahid 'Abd al-Majid, *Egyptian Parties From Within* (Al-Ahzab al-misriyya min al-dakhil) (Cairo: Kitab al-Ahali, 1993). On the Moroccan parties, see: Fayiz Sara, *Parties and Political Forces in Morocco* (Al-Ahzab

wa 'l-quwa al-siyasiyya fi 'l-Maghreb) (London: Riad Al-Rayyes Books and Publishing, 1990). It is interesting to note that the two parties have attempted to combine a civil and a religious character, albeit within a liberal and tolerant framework.

13. The notion of being in the 'middle' or 'centre' has an enormous appeal for Arab ruling regimes, especially during periods of shift toward conservative positions. It was from this perspective that President Sadat insisted the 'Party of Egypt', then the 'National Democratic Party' that came to power, be given the status of a party of the 'centre'. Earlier, in 1976, Sadat had announced his famous decision to establish platforms or rostra in the Arab Socialist Union. One was for the right, one for the left, while the third, which articulated the position of the president – and the state – was given the status of platform of the centre. On this point, see: Ahmad, *Future of the Party System in Egypt*; Hassan Nafi'a, 'Political Administration and the Crisis of Transition to a Multi-Party System', in 'Aliyyuddin Hilal (ed.), *The Egyptian Political System: Between Change and Continuity* (Al-Nizam al-siyasi al-misri: bayn al-taghayyur wa 'l-istimrariyya) (Cairo: Centre for Political Studies, Cairo University, 1995).

14. Ahmad Jabir al-Ansari, 'Transformations of Thought and Politics in the Arab East: 1930–1970' (Tahawwulat al-fikr wa 'l-siyasa fi 'l-sharq al-'Arabi), *'Alam al-Ma'rifa*, 25 November 1980.

15. On the history of the pan-national parties and its bearing on the issue of democracy see: 'The Development of the Concepts of Democracy in Modern Arabic Thought' (Tatawwur al-dimuqratiyya fi 'l-fikr al-'Arabi al-hadith), in *The Crisis of Democracy in the Arab World* (Azmat al-dimuqratiyya fi 'l-watan al-'Arabi) (Beirut: Centre for Arab Unity Studies, 1984), pp. 115–38.

16. On the purge of indigenous Ba'athists from party and state under the Ba'th regimes in Syria and Iraq, see: Nicholas Van Dam, *Struggle for Power in Syria: Sectarianism and Tribalism in Politics 1961–1995*, Cairo: Maktabat Madbouli, 2nd edition, 1995 (Arabic translation), pp. 174–95; John Bullock and Harvey Morris, *Saddam's War* (London: Faber and Faber, 1991), pp. 26–49.

17. A number of courageous and honest pan-national Arab intellectuals have maintained their faith in the principles of democracy and written noteworthy works dealing with democracy, modernization of Arab political structures and critical assessment of the experience of nationalists in government. See, for example: Costantine Zurayq, *Complete General Scholarly Works* (Al-A'mal al-fikriyya al-'amma) (Beirut: Centre for Arab Unity Studies, 1994); Munif al-Razzaz, *Freedom and its Problem in Underdeveloped Countries* (Al-Hurriyya wa mushkilatuha fi 'l-buldan al-mutakhallifa) (Beirut: Dar al-'Ilm li 'l-Malayin, 1965); Joseph Mugheizel, 'Islam, Arab Christianity, Arab Nationalism and Secularism' (Al-Islam wa 'l-masihiyya al-'Arabiyya wa 'l-qawmiyya al-'Arabiyya wa 'l-'ilmaniyya), *Al-Mustaqbal al-'Arabi*, 26, April 1981.

18. The contribution of the Centre for Arab Unity Studies is not confined to the

leading role it has played in the establishment of the Arab Human Rights Organization. The Centre has also initiated and coordinated a wide range of intellectual activities with a view to conceptualizing democratic and legal issues in the Arab world from pluralistic perspectives. In addition to the contributions made by its *Al-Mustaqbal al-'Arabi* journal, the Centre has organized many conferences on the issue. For an example of this endeavour, see *The Crisis of Democracy in the Arab World*, along with a host of studies and frequent seminars on the plight of democracy and human rights in *Al-Mustaqbal al-'Arabi*.

19. These ideas are forcefully projected by extremist groups such as al-Jihad and al-Jama'a al-Islamiyya, but are also clearly presented by moderate sectors of the Islamist movement. In this respect, see: Sami 'Awad Abu Sahiliyya, 'The Human Rights Controversy between the West and Islam' (Huquq al-insan al-mutanaza' 'alayha bayn al-gharb wa 'l-Islam), *Al-Mustaqbal al-'Arabi*, 164, October 1992; Zaki Ahmad, 'Democracy in Modern and Contemporary Islamic Discourse' (Al-Dimuqratiyya fi 'l-khitab al-Islami al-hadith wa 'l-mu'asir), in ibid.

20. Ridwan al-Sayyid, 'Contemporary Islamic Thought and Human Rights' (Huquq al-insan wa 'l-fikr al-Islami al-mu'asir), *Al-Hayat* newspaper, 22 December 1994; Fahmi Huwaydi, 'Islam and Democracy' (Al-Islam wa 'l-dimuqratiyya), *Al-Ahram* newspaper, Cairo, 1993.

21. On this point see: Muhammad Salim al-'Awwa, *The Political System of the Islamic State* (Al-Nizam al-siyasi li 'l-dawla al-Islamiyya) (Cairo: Dar al-Shurouq, 1989); Muhammad 'Amara, *Islam and Human Rights: Necessities not Rights* (Al-Islam wa huquq al-insan: darura la huquq) (Kuwait: 'Alam al-Ma'rifa, 1985).

22. On these documents, see *Riwaq 'Arabi*, Cairo Centre for Human Rights, No. 1, Vol. 1, January 1996, pp. 122–6.

23. See, for example: *Shaykh* 'Abd al-Salam Yassin, *Dialogue with the Respectable Democrats* (Hiwar ma' al-fudala' al-dimuqratiyyin) (Casablanca: Matbu'at al-Ufq, 1994); Huda Mitkis, 'Legitimacy and Religious Opposition' (Al-Shar'iyya wa 'l-mu'arada al-diniyya), in Mustafa Kamil al-Sayyid, *Political Transformations in the Arab World* (Al-Tahawwulat al-siyasiyya al-haditha fi 'l-watan al-'Arabi), Studies of the First French-Egyptian Seminar 1988, (Cairo: Centre for Political Studies, Cairo University, 1989).

24. For a review of these issues from a Western angle, see Elizabeth Mayer, *Islam and Human Rights* (Boulder, Colorado: Westview Press, 1991), pp. 143–62. From an Arab legal perspective, see Muhammad al-Sayyid Sa'id, 'Islam and Human Rights' (Al-Islam wa huquq al-insan) in *Riwaq 'Arabi* (Cairo Centre for Human Rights), 1, Vol. 1, January 1996, pp. 13–34.

25. For an example of this conservative position, which denies equality on the basis of a particular understanding of Quranic texts and on biological interpretation, see Muhammad al-Ghazali, *Islamic Directives and United Nations Declarations* (Al-Ta'alim al-Islamiyya wa i'lanat al-umam al-muttahida) (Alexandria: Dar al-Da'wa, 1993), pp. 119–632.

26. See various declarations of this type in: Muhammad Kamil Mahmoud, *The General Declaration of Human Rights in Islam* (Al-Bayan al-'aam li huquq al-insan fi 'l-Islam) (Cairo: Maktabat al-Adab, 1991); Ibrahim Madkour and 'Adnan al-Khatib, *Human Rights in Islam* (Huquq al-insan fi 'l-Islam) (Damascus: Dar Tlas, 1992). See also drafts of the Arab Declaration of Human Rights issued by the Arab League.

27. Muhammad Fat-hi 'Uthman, *Human Rights between Islamic Shariah and Western Law* (Huquq al-insan bayn al-Shariah al-Islamiyya wa 'l-qanun al-gharbi) (Cairo: Dar al-Shurouq, 1982).

28. The apostasy issue has generated heated controversy in the wake of events concerning Dr Nasr Hamid Abu Zayd, who fell victim to the most reactionary trends within Islamic currents in Egypt. The dispute culminated in a juridical judgement passed by one of the Court of Cassation judges. The judgement was a perfect expression of the views of the most fanatical elements within the extremist camp.

   The Muslim Brothers distinguish themselves, within the Islamic Movement, from the 'Takfir' tendency, which involves accusing others of unbelief (although some of them have, in fact, themselves been involved in this practice of charging others with infidelity, atheism and apostasy). This particular issue represents, nevertheless, one of the Brothers' main reservations concerning human rights and democracy. A prominent Jordanian leader of the Brothers argues as follows: 'Though Islamists have rejected democracy in the past, they accept it now. But which democracy do they accept? It is the democracy that rejects atheism and concurs in matters upon which we agree . . .' This is quoted from a statement by 'Abdallah Kazim in 'The Historical Chronicle of the Muslim Brothers Movement and its Intellectual Framework' (Al-Sira al-tarikhiyya li jama'at al-ikhwan al-muslimin wa marji'yyatuha al-fikriyya), in *Islamic Movements and Organizations in Jordan* (Al-Harakat wa 'l-tanzimat al-Islamiyya fi 'l-Urdun), produced by Hani Hourani, ed., Husain Abu Rumman, (Amman: Markiz al-Urdun al-Jadid li 'l-Dirasat, 1997), p, 31.

29. For these countries, see reports of Amnesty International and other human rights organizations. In the case of Sudan, see: Muhammad Ibrahim Naqad, *Issues of Democracy in Sudan: Variables and Challenges* (Qadaya al-dimuqratiyya fi 'l-Sudan: al-mutaghayyirat wa 'l-tahaddiyat) (Cairo: Dar al-Thaqafa al-Jadida, 1992), pp. 152–3; Haydar Ibrahim 'Ali, *Civil Society and Democratic Transformation in Sudan* (Al-Mujtama' al-madani wa 'l-tahawwul al-dimuqrati fi 'l-Sudan), introduced by Sa'd al-Din Ibrahim, (Cairo: Ibn Khaldoun Centre, Dar al-Amin li 'l-Nashr, 1996).

30. See the debate on the 'democratization' of the Islamic trend in Nabil 'Abd al-Fattah, Hala Mustafa and Diya' Rashwan, 'Political Islam – Is it a Democratic movement?' (Al-Islam al-siyasi – hal huwa haraka dimuqratiyya?), *Riwaq 'Arabi*, April 1996, pp. 59–81. See also: *Islamic Movements and Organizations in Jordan*, Markiz al-Urdun al-Jadid li 'l-Dirasat; François Borja, 'Islamists and the Democratic Transformation: Suggestions for Research' (Al-Islamiyyun wa

'l-tahawwul al-dimuqrati: muqtarahat li 'l-bahth), in Nivene 'Abd al-Mun'im Mas'ad, *Democratic Transformations in the Arab World* (Al-Tahawwulat al-dimuqratiyya fi 'l-watan al-'Arabi) (Studies of the Third French-Egyptian Seminar 1990), (Cairo: Centre for Political Studies, Cairo University, 1995), pp. 427–37.

31. The basic positions and policies of the Arab Communist parties may be traced in Elias Murqus, *History of Communist Parties in the Arab World* (Tarikh al-ahzab al-shuyu'iyya fi 'l-watan al-'Arabi) (Beirut: Dar al-Tali'a, 1964). See also Richard Staar, *Yearbook of International Communist Affairs*, Stanford University Press, Hoover Institution Publications, various years, especially 1975–1980.

32. During the early stages of the development of 'progressive' Arab regimes, especially in the 1960s, and after the far-reaching social transformations achieved in these countries, communists disregarded the savage treatment they received and gave the regimes their full support. In the words of Rif'at al-Sa'id: 'Their conduct was a replica of the behaviour of the Japanese noblemen who wanted to demonstrate their chivalry through death. After all the killing and heartless torture, they all elevated themselves above their wounds and gave full support to Nasser. (Members of the Communist Party – Hadeto – declared such support even in the agony of their torture.)' See Rif'at al-Sa'id, *History of the Communist Movement in Egypt* (Tarikh al-haraka al-shuyu'iyya fi Misr) (Cairo: Dar al-Amal li 'l-Tiba'a wa 'l-Nashr, 1987).

33. For a more objective assessment of the political discourse and practice of the Iraqi communist party up to the last Ba'th coup, see: Hanna Batatu, *The Old Social Classes Revolutionary Movement in Iraq* (Princeton: Princeton University Press, 1978); Majid Khadduri, *Republican Iraq: A Study of Iraqi Politics since the Revolution of 1958* (Oxford: Oxford University Press, 1969), p. 115 *et seq.*; Rif'at al-Sa'id, *Writings on Marxism* (Kitabat an al-marxiyya), Cairo: Sharikat al-Amal li 'l-Tiba'a wa 'l-Nashr. More recently, following the US-led alliance war against Iraq, the party issued the *Democratic Tomorrow* (Al-Ghad al-Dimuqrati) magazine, which shows a profound interest in the issue of democracy. On the Sudanese communist party, see 'Ali, op. cit., pp. 117–8.

34. For the transformation in the political thought of the Iraqi communist party during the two stages of alliance and struggle against the ruling Ba'ath Party, see Pierre Jean Louisar, 'Iraq and Democracy Impossible: the Trap of the National State', in Mas'ad, op. cit.

35. This is often a dubious issue, since the views of Arab Marxists on the one hand and Soviet Marxists on the other tend to become confused. Western writings, in any interpretation of the attitudes of communists and communist parties in the Arab world of the 1960s and 1970s, normally refer to Soviet positions. In fact, only ideological considerations, specific beliefs and domestic conflicts within these parties can explain the communists' neglect, in countries ruled by 'progressive' regimes, of the question of democracy in its established constitutional sense.

The use of the term commonly became confused with other notions such as 'people's democracy'.

There are numerous references for these Western interpretations. See, for example, George Lenczowski, *Soviet Advances in the Middle East* (Washington DC: American Enterprise Institute, 1972).

36. See Muhammad Jamal Barout, 'The Syrian Communist Movement and Questions of Destiny' (Al-Haraka al-shuyu'iyya al-suriyya wa as'ilat al-maseer), *Al-Hayat* newspaper, 10, 11, 12 November 1998.

One political analyst from Sudan asks: 'To what extent was the undemocratic role of the left (in the 1950s and the 1960s) an optional alternative? And what therefore are the limits of actual responsibility for this role and the possibilities for amends?' His answer is that the responsibility rests with the nature of societies and with the Arab ruling regimes as much as with the communist parties' mechanical discourse grounded in historical determinism. See 'Abd al-'Aziz al-Sawi, 'Leftist Political Parties: the Role and the Limits of Responsibility' (Al-Ahzab al-yasariyya wa 'l-dimuqratiyya: al-dawr wa hudud al-mas'uliyya), *Al-Hayat* newspaper, 11 November 1997.

37. On liberalism and democracy, see Richard Bellamey, *Liberalism and the Modern State* (Oxford: Polity Press, 1992).

38. On the development of liberalism in modern political thought, see Albert Hourani, *Arabic Thought in the Liberal Age* (Oxford: University Press. Oxford, 1970).

39. After the re-emergence of the Wafd on the political scene, it was thought the party would represent the principal opposition. Considering the constraints imposed on the integrity of the voting process, the electoral performance of the party in 1983 was notable. In the 1995 elections, however, the party obtained only a handful of seats. This was a result not simply of rigging, but of deterioration in the party and its shrinking popular support. See Mustafa, op. cit.

40. See the party leader's address, 'The Nation's Holiday' ('Eid al-umma) in the Egyptian *Al-Wafd* newspaper, 10 November 1998. The party defines itself as 'the new Wafd: a political party that believes in democracy based on party plurality and political freedom'. See *Al-Hayat* newspaper, 24 September 1992.

41. See: Hasan Urid, *Al-Hayat* newspaper, 1 December 1997, and 11 November 1998. See also Sara, *Parties and Political Forces in Morocco*, pp. 18–23.

42. On the principles of the Nida' al-Jadid (New Appeal) Society, see Sa'id al-Najjar, *Modernizing the Political and Economic System in Egypt* (Tajdid al-nizam al-siyasi wa 'l-iqtisadi fi Misr) (Cairo: Dar al-Shurouq, 1997).

43. We are now witnessing a unique pattern in party positioning, with major parties bypassing domestic divisions in the interest of local, regional and international developments. There is more inter-party agreement than intra-party consent. This is, in fact, what occurred during the second Gulf crisis. See Muhammad al-Sayyid Sa'id, 'Future of the Arab System after the Gulf Crisis' (Mustaqbal

al-nizam al-'Arabi ba'd azmat al-khalij), '*Alam al-Ma'rifa*, February 1992, pp. 102–3.

44. The state's manipulation of parties – by drawing some of them closer for a while, or pushing them away for a while, and by playing on their contradictions the whole time – is a regular feature of current party politics. What applies to Yemen in this case applies also to Palestine, Tunisia and Egypt.

    An observer of the Yemeni scene reveals how the state uses some of the weapons in its arsenal for this purpose. These include: the promotion of dissent within parties; the creation of spurious entities which are then deployed to confront the real parties; and triggering conflict between the parties and employing the powers and resources of the state to attract or intimidate and enfeeble them. See Muhammad 'Abd al-Malik al-Mutawakkil, 'The Democratic Experience in Yemen' (Al-Tajriba al-dimuqratiyya fi 'l-Yaman), in Bishara and Sa'id, op. cit., p. 286.

45. See: Barout, op. cit.; Munsif al-Marzouqi, 'Wavering Democratic Transition in Tunisia' (Ta'athur al-tahawwul al-dimuqrati fi Tunis), in Bishara and Sa'id, op. cit. pp. 349–50.

46. See the resolutions of the first Conference of Arab Parties in *Al-Mustaqbal al-'Arabi*, 217, March 1997, p. 163.

47. In Algeria the ruling regime has rejected the first and second Rome Documents, which encapsulated the 'democratic consensus' and condemned political extermination. The regime was forced, nevertheless, to restructure the political system by taking guidance from the 'formalities' of the democratic set-up. On the other hand, the underlying fact of party conflicts in Algeria is that the major parties continue to support democracy and the democratic system.

48. See the *Public Opinion Poll on Issues of Democracy and Participation*, conducted by Al-Ahram Centre for Political and Strategic Studies, Cairo, 1998.

49. 'Azmi Bishara, 'Reality and Thought in Civil Society: a Middle Eastern Reading' (Waqi' wa fikr al-mujtama' al-madani: qira'a sharq awsatiyya), in Bishara and Sa'id, op. cit., p. 393.

50. An instance of such dialogues is the meeting held by human rights activists at the Arab and international levels, and representatives of moderate Islamic trends. (Committee of Advocates for Human Rights, *Islam and Justice: a Discussion on the Future of Human Rights in the Middle East and North Africa*, New York, May 1997.)

21 Labour laws and human rights

Asma Khader

1. Ibrahim 'Ali Badawi al-Shaykh, 'Human Rights Between the International Community and Regional Communities', (Huquq al-insan baina 'l-mujtama'

al-duwali wa 'l-mujtama'at al-qawmiyya), *Egyptian Magazine for International Law*, (Al-Majalla 'l-Misriyya li 'l-qanun al-duwali), article (34), (Cairo, 1978), p. 269 *et seq.*

2. Muhammad Salim Tarawneh, *Human Rights and their Guarantees*, (Huquq al-insan wa damanatuha) 1st edition, (Amman: Ja'far Printing Press, 1994), p. 179 *et seq.*

3. Muhammad Sa'id Majdoub, *Public Freedoms and Human Rights*, (Al-Hurriyyat al-'amma wa huquq al-insan) 1st edition, (Tripoli, Lebanon, 1986), p. 15 *et seq.*

4. See the International Covenant on Economic, Social and Cultural Rights (articles 6, 7, 8, 9, 10), ratified by Jordan, Algeria, Sudan, Syria, Somalia, Iraq, Kuwait, Lebanon, Libya, Egypt, Morocco and Yemen.

5. It is noteworthy that labour laws include most principles of the Universal Declaration of Human Rights regarding labour, with some differences springing from social and political factors. Jordanian Labour Law No. (8) for 1996 is regarded as one of the most recent labour laws to attempt to conform its provisions to those in the Universal Declaration of Human Rights and international conventions.

6. Article (7) stipulates that: 'The states parties to the present Covenant recognize the right of everyone to the employment of just and favourable conditions of work, which ensure in particular: remuneration which provides all workers, as a minimum, with: fair wages and equal remuneration for work of equal value without discrimination of any kind, in particular women being guaranteed conditions of work not inferior to those enjoyed by men, with equal pay for equal work.'

7. Paragraph (2) of article (10) stipulates that: 'Special protection should be accorded to mothers during a reasonable period before and after childbirth. During such periods, working mothers would be accorded paid leave or leave with adequate social security benefit.' For example, conventions and recommendations issued by the ILO regarding women may be divided into three categories. The first relates to the protection of the motherhood of working women. The second relates to the elimination of discrimination between men and women in the field of work. The third relates to conditions of work for working women and how these can be provided and safeguarded.

8. Other reasons, besides those noted above, have limited the development of labour legislation in Arab countries. One of these is the agricultural rather than industrial nature of Arab societies. Others include the existence of traditions, illiteracy and societal considerations vis-à-vis women's work.

9. The 13 states in question are Tunisia, Jordan, Sudan, Egypt, Kuwait, Lebanon, Algeria, Libya, Iraq, Saudi Arabia, Syria, Yemen and Morocco.

10. Article (4) of the Charter stipulates that: 'Arab countries agree to work towards achieving a similar level of labour legislations and social securities.'

11. The Arab Labour Organization has issued numerous conventions, namely:

Convention (1) for 1966 regarding working levels.

Convention (2) for 1967 regarding the transfer of labour forces.

Convention (3) for 1971 regarding minimum social securities.

Convention (4) for 1975 regarding the transfer of labour forces (amended).

Convention (5) for 1976 regarding working women.

Convention (6) for 1976 regarding working levels (amended).

Convention (7) for 1977 regarding occupational safety and health.

Convention (8) for 1977 regarding union freedom and rights.

Convention (9) for 1977 regarding vocational training.

Convention (10) for 1979 regarding paid study leaves.

Convention (11) for 1979 regarding group negotiation.

Convention (12) for 1980 regarding agricultural workers.

Convention (13) for 1981 regarding the working environment.

Convention (14) for 1981 regarding the Arab worker's right to social securities when moving to another Arab country for work.

Convention (15) for 1983 regarding the determination and protection of remuneration.

Convention (16) for 1983 regarding social services for workers.

12. Article (32) of the Tunisian Constitution stipulates that: 'Conventions are not enacted unless they are ratified. Ratified conventions override laws.'

13. Other countries include Egypt, Sudan and Kuwait.

14. Labour legislation appeared in Tunisia in 1904, in Sudan in 1908, in Egypt in 1909, in Algeria in 1910, in Lebanon in 1943, in Palestine in 1927, in Jordan in 1960, in Qatar in 1962, and in Abu Dhabi in 1966.

15. According to this definition, the criterion for determining whether or not the principles are constitutional is a formal one. See Ibrahim 'Abd al-'Aziz Shiha, *Public Constitutional Principles*, (Al-Mabadi' al-dusturiyya al-'amma) (Beirut: al-Dar al-Jami'yya li 'l-Tiba'a wa 'l-Nashr, 1982), p. 15 *et seq.*

16. Kamal Ghali, *Principles of Constitutional Law and Political Systems* (Mabadi' al-qanun al-dusturi wa 'l-nuzum al-siyasiyya) 3rd edition, (Damascus: New Press, 1971–2), p. 9 *et seq.*

17. There are similar provisions in most Arab constitutions. See, for example: article (59) of the Algerian Constitution; and article (56) of the Permanent Constitution of the Democratic Republic of Sudan for 1973; article (41) of the Kuwaiti Constitution for 1962; and article (13) of The Egyptian Constitution for 1971.

18. See paragraph (a) of article (27), and articles (67), (70) and (71) of the Jordanian Labour Law for 1996. Article (69) stipulates that: 'The Minister shall determine the following after consulting the competent official parties:

a Industries and types of work in which the work of women is prohibited;

b Periods of time during which the employment of women is prohibited and their exceptions'.

19. Absolute equality means that every human being, male or female, has the right to work, regardless of his/her age, culture, reputation, etc.

20. Article (24) of the Universal Declaration of Human Rights stipulates that: 'Everyone has the right to rest and leisure, including reasonable limitation of working hours and periodic holidays with pay.' Article (25) stipulates that: 'Everyone has the right to a standard of living adequate for the health and well-being of himself and his family, including food, clothing, housing and medical care, and necessary social services, and the right to security in the event of unemployment, sickness, disability, widowhood, old age or other lack of livelihood in circumstances beyond his control.'

21. In 1981, the International Labour Union issued the International Convention for workers with family responsibilities (No.156). Paragraphs (1) and (2) of article (3) stipulate that: 'With a view to creating effective equality of opportunity and treatment for men and women workers, each member shall make it an aim of national policy to enable persons with family responsibilities, who are engaged or wish to engage in employment, to exercise their right to do so without being subject to discrimination and to the extent possible, without conflict between their employment and family responsibilities.'

22. Jordanian Labour Law No. (8) for 1996 defines remuneration as: 'All that is due to a worker in return for his work, be it monetary or in kind, in addition to all other dues of all types stipulated in the law, work contract, internal system, or that have come to be paid, with the exception of remuneration due to overtime work.'

23. The Universal Declaration of Human Rights has been regarded as embodying the group of fundamental principles for human rights, which have come into existence as a result of numerous efforts, especially on the part of intellectuals and those struggling for women's issues in general.

24. See the text of this article in the introductory part of this section.

25. These conventions include: Convention No. (100) for 1951 regarding equality in pay for male and female workers when the labour is equal; the anti-Discrimination law in Employment and Occupation Convention No. (111) for 1958; the Social Policy (Basic Aims) and Standards Convention No. (117) for 1962; and equal opportunities for work among men and women No. (142) for 1975.

26. It should be noted that Jordan has ratified this convention.

27. It should be noted that neither Jordanian Labour Law No. (8) for 1996 nor the annulled Labour Law No. (21) for 1960 explicitly stated these principles.

28. Labour Law No. (137) for 1981.

29. Ahmad Zaki Badawi, *Individual Work Contracts in Arab and Foreign Legislation*, ('Iqd al-'amal al-fardi fi tashri'at al-'amal al-'Arabiyya wa 'l-ajnabiyya) (Labour Office: Studies and Research Series, 1982), p. 21.

30. For example, government employees are subject to Civil Service Law No. (1) for 1988.

31. These jobs include: private drivers, child minders and wet nurses.

32. Badawi, op. cit., p. 22.

33. Most harassment cases are swept under the carpet by paying the employee or sending her back to her country under threat of accusing her of theft.

34. Exceptions in Bahrain, the Arab Republic of Yemen and Libya include workers in agricultural institutions, while in Bahrain and Libya those working on operating and fixing machinery needed for agriculture are subject to the labour laws of those countries.

35. The countries in question are Morocco, Tunisia and Algeria.

36. Besides Jordan, there are other categories excluded from the labour laws of a number of Arab countries. These are, briefly, as follows:

   1 Workers in small stores which are not operated by machinery and employ fewer than five workers. This exception is present in the United Arab Emirates and Kuwait.

   2 Naval officers, engineers and navigators. This exception is present in Bahrain and Libya.

   3 Workers hired to do emergency and temporary work. This exception is present in the United Arab Emirates, Bahrain, Qatar, Kuwait and the Arab Republic of Yemen.

   4 Major jobs whose occupants are agents authorized by the job owners in practising their authority. This exception is present in Bahrain only.

   5 Members of the armed forces, police and security forces. This exception is present in the United Arab Emirates, Somalia and Qatar.

37. These means include:

   1 Protecting workers from health hazards and dangers from machinery.

   2 Providing necessary conditions for improving the working environment and working methods.

   3 Achieving compatibility between the nature and conditions of work and those assigned to do work, both healthwise and technically.

   4 Providing workers with awareness and training on safety methods and also providing them with personal prevention tools and the means of using them.

   5 Being aware of any health or social hazards which may face workers and working towards eliminating them.

   6 Protecting production equipment such as buildings and machinery.

38. See article (78) of Jordanian Labour Law No. (8) for 1996.

39. See article (79) of the same law.

40. See article (80) of the same law.

41. See article (81) of the same law.

42. See article (82) of the same law.
43. See article (83) of the same law.
44. See article (85) of the same law.
45. See article (84) of the same law.
46. See Ahmad Zaki Badawi, *Social Welfare of Workers in the Arab World*, (Al-Ri'aya 'l-ijtima'iyya li 'l-'ummal fi 'l-watan al-'Arabi), Workers' Literary Series No. 17, Baghdad: Arab Institute for Workers' Culture and Labour Research, n.d., p. 12 *et seq*.
47. Article (57) of Jordanian Labour Law No. (8) for 1996 specifies certain cases in which workers may be obliged to work overtime. These include preparation of annual inventories, budgets, final statements of accounts and clearance sales.
48. For example, Egypt issued Law No. (79) for 1975, amending Law No. (25) for 1977, regarding insurance against occupational accidents, health insurance against old age, and insurance against incapacity, death and unemployment. Syria issued Law No. (92) for 1959, regarding occupational accidents and insurance against old age, incapacity and death. Lebanon issued Decree No. (3955) for 1963, regarding insurance against occupational accidents, old age, incapacity, death and illness, and provision for maternity leaves and family allowances. Bahrain issued the Second Security Law by Decree No. (24) for 1976, regarding insurance against occupational accidents, old age, incapacity and death.
49. See Badawi: *Social Welfare*, p. 32 *et seq*.
50. See article (7) of the convention noted.
51. Article (32) of the UN Convention on the Rights of the Child (1989) stipulates that: 'States parties recognize the right of the child to be protected from economic exploitation and from performing any work that is likely to be hazardous or to interfere with the child's education, or to be harmful to the child's health or physical, mental, spiritual, moral or social development.'
52. Some of these conventions are:

    1 Convention No. (59) on the required minimum age of the child to work in the industrial sector.
    2 Convention No. (16) concerning medical examination for children and young people working at sea.
    3 Convention No. (6) concerning night work of children working in the indus trial sector.

53. See article (74) of Jordanian Labour Law No. (8) for 1996.
54. It is noteworthy that the Jordanian Labour Law's definition of the minimum age for juvenile employment is higher than that stipulated in international conventions and some Arab legislation, and without any distinction between the jobs juveniles may be employed to do. For example, international conventions, in respect of industrial activities, have prohibited the employment of juveniles

under the age of 15. With regard to farming activities, Convention No. (10) for 1921 prohibits the employment of juveniles under the age of 14. The Jordanian legislature has tended to give greater consideration to the conditions of juveniles in this regard.

55. See articles (57–64) of Arab Convention No. (6) for 1976 regarding working levels (amended).

56. See article (41) and article (2/4) of Qatari Labour Law No. (3) for 1962.

57. See article (1963) of Saudi Labour Law No. (21) for 1389 (AH).

58. It is noteworthy that articles and provisions of the Jordanian Labour Law have exceeded Arab and international levels with regard to defining the minimum age of juveniles for employment, as it prohibits the employment of juveniles under the age of 16.

59. See article (76) of Jordanian Labour Law No. (8) for 1996.

60. See article (76) of Jordanian Labour Law No. (8) for 1996, article (163) of Saudi Labour Law No. (21) for 1389 (AH), and article (21) of United Arab Emirates Law No. (8) for 1980.

61. See article (75) of Jordanian Labour Law No. (8) for 1996, article (161) of Saudi Labour Law No. (21) for 1389 (AH), article (23) of United Arab Emirates Law No. (8) for 1980, and article (43) of Qatari Labour Law No. (3) for 1962.

62. This has, for example, been stipulated in the labour legislation of Jordan, Iraq, Bahrain, Oman and the United Arab Emirates.

63. This has, for example, been stipulated in the labour legislation of Jordan, Bahrain, Saudi Arabia, Qatar and the United Arab Emirates.

64. This declaration became known as the Declaration on the Rights of Disabled Persons.

65. It is noteworthy that the UN Convention on the Rights of the Child (1989), in article (23), stresses the rights of disabled children and the duty of providing them with the necessary care and attention.

66. Some conventions and recommendations contain provisions regarding motherhood. These include:

International Labour Convention No. (110) for 1958, regarding agricultural workers.
International Labour Recommendation No. (110) for 1958, regarding the same issue.
International Labour Recommendation No. (12) for 1921, regarding the protection of motherhood for female agricultural workers.
Convention No. (149), Recommendation No. (157) for 1977, regarding workers in the nursing field.

67. Arab Recommendation No. (3) for 1979 prohibits denying workers their right to study leave due to differences in sex.

68. Jordanian Labour Law No. (8) for 1996 includes special provisions regarding leaves for men and women. These provisions include:

Not calculating weekends as part of the annual leaves unless they occur within them (article 61/A).

An agreement may be reached to accumulate weekend holidays and take them as days off within a period of time not exceeding one month if the employee was residing outside his workplace (article 61/B).

The worker has the right to pay instead of unused annual leaves, if his services were terminated before he used up all or part of his annual leaves (article 64).

Sick leave may be defined as 14 days (article 65).

Workers may be granted a paid leave of 14 days to undertake the pilgrimage, after the completion of five years' service and once only (article 66/A/2).

A worker may be granted an unpaid leave of four months if he enrols at a university, institute or college accredited by the official authorities (article 66/B).

69. See article (50) of Jordanian Labour Law No. (21) for 1950 (annulled).

70. Article (10) of Arab Convention No. (5) for 1976, regarding working women, stipulates that: 'A working woman has the right to a fully paid maternity leave before and after childbirth, for a period not less than ten weeks. Leave after childbirth should be not less than six weeks. During this period, the employment of the working woman is prohibited.'

71. Countries which determine the working woman's right to maternity leave in accordance with her years of service have aimed at distinguishing between fully paid and partially paid maternity leave. These countries include Egypt and Saudi Arabia.

72. It is noteworthy that Egyptian labour law has limited the number of maternity leaves to three. This may be part of the government's policy towards birth control in view of large family sizes in Egypt.

73. Algerian and Mauretanian labour laws grant working women the longest maternity leave, in accordance with the relevant Arab laws and Arab and international conventions.

74. There was no similar provision in Jordanian Labour Law No. (21) for 1960 (annulled).

75. Ahmad Zaki Badawi, *Provisions Organizing the Employment of Women in Arab Labour Laws* (Baghdad, 1983), p. 52 *et seq.*

76. See Convention No. (4) for 1919, Convention No. (41) for 1943, and Convention No. (89) for 1948.

77. See Convention No. (45) for 1930.

78. See Recommendation No. (4) for 1919, and Convention No. (13) for 1921.

79. See Convention No. (136) and Recommendation No. (144) for 1971.

80. See Convention No. (141) and Recommendation No. (1) for 1977.

81. See Convention No. (127) and Recommendation No. (128) for 1976.

82. See Convention No. (116) and Recommendation No. (95) for 1952.

83. See Arab Convention No. (1) for 1996, regarding Arab working levels, Convention No. (6) for 1976, regarding Arab working levels (amended), and Convention No. (5) for 1976, regarding working women.

84. Article (3) of International Convention No. (89), regarding Women's Night Work, issued by the International Labour Organization, stipulates that: 'Women, without distinction of age, shall not be employed during the night in any public or private industrial undertaking, or in any branch thereof, other than an undertaking in which only members of the same family are employed.'

22 Child rights in Arabic culture

Violette Dagher

1. See Munsif al-Marzouqi, 'Sa'sa'a', in the *Short World Encyclopedia* (Al-Mawsu'a al 'alamiyya al-musaghghara): *Devotion to Human Rights* (Al-Im'an fi huquq al-insan) (Beirut-Damascus: Al-Ahali, 2000).

2. Adapted from: Haytham Manna', 'Child Rights in Arab-Islamic Culture', *Riwaq 'Arabi*, 1 (English edition), January 1997.

3. Ibid.

4. These three *hadith*s are quoted in Jad al-Haqq 'Ali Jad al-Haqq, *Childhood in Islamic Shariah Law* (Al-Tufula fi zill al-shariah al-Islamiyya) (Cairo: Al-Azhar, September 1955), reprinted from *The Grand Conquest* (Al-Fath al-kabir) (Cairo: Mustafa al-Babi al-Halabi, 1350 AH).

5. Manna', op. cit.

6. Al-Hasan ibn 'Ali ibn al-Husain ibn Shu'ba al-Harrani, *Geniuses in the Prophet's Lineage* (Tuhaf al-'uqul 'inda al rasul), Treatise on Laws by 'Ali ibn al-Husayn, p. 263; to be published along with other Islamic legal documents, edited Ghanim Jawad.

7. Manna', op. cit.

8. Muhammad 'Atiyya al-Abrashi, *Islamic Education and its Philosophers: Stages of Child Rearing* (Al-Tarbiyya al-Islamiyya wa falsafatuha: marahil tarbiyat al-tifl), n.p., n.d., p. 52.

9. 'Urayb ibn Sa'd al-Katib al-Qurtubi, *The Embryo and the Management of Pregnant Women and Newborn Infants* (Khalq al-janin wa tadbir al-habala wa 'l-mawludin) (Algiers: Medicine and Pharmacology College Press, 1956); including a French translation by Noureddin 'Abd al-Qadir and Henri Jaillet.

10. Ibn Sina, *On Politics* (Kitab al-siyasa), in Mahmoud al-Hajj Qasim Muhammad, *History of Arab Pediatrics* (Tarikh tibb al-atfal 'inda 'l-'Arab) (Baghdad: Ministry of Culture and Arts, 1978), p. 134.

11. Ibn Miskawayh, *Cultivation of Good Manners* (Tahdhib al-akhlaq) (Beirut: Scientific Books, 1985), and Mohammed Arkoun, *The Humanist Tendency in Arab Thought* (Naz'at al-ansana fi 'l-fikr al-'Arabi) (Beirut-London: Al-Saqi, 1997), p. 143.

12. Manna', op. cit., 23.

13. Ibid.

14. Ibn Sina, *The Canon of Medicine* (Al-Qanun fi 'l-tibb), Baghdad: Al-Muthanna, n.d., Vol. 1, 157.

15. 'Abd al-Rahman al-Kawakibi, *Features of Oppression and the Ends of Slavery* (Taba'i' al-istibdad wa masari' al-isti'bad) (Al-Qur'an al-Karim Press, 1973), p. 103.

16. Ibid., p. 107.

17. Violette Dagher, 'Korsak', in *Short World Encyclopedia*.

18. Ibid.

Index

Names beginning with al- are filed under the letter following the dash, e.g. al-Ghanoushi is entered as al-Ghanoushi, Rashid but filed under G. References to notes are entered as, for example, 648n.

A

'Abbasi Madani 316
'Abd al-Jabbar 20–21, 134–135, 219, 582n
'Abd al-Jawad, Salih 621n
'Abd al-Qadir 'Oda 258
'Abd al-Razzaq, 'Ali 311–312, 314–315, 476
'Abdallah, Isma'il Sabri 379
'Abdu, Muhammad 304–311
Abdul-Aziz, King of Saudi Arabia 449, 452
Abdul-Hamid, Sultan 447, 629n
abortion, prohibition of 47
Absent canonical obligation, The 82
al-Abshihi, Shihab al-Din Muhammad ibn Ahmad 31
Abu 'Ali ibn Sina 566
Abu Bakr 48, 58, 126, 192
Abu Bakr al-Razi 173, 565–566
Abu Hanifa, Imam 34–36, 198, 199
Abu Hazim 27
Abu Hudhayl al-'Allaf 219
Abu 'l Fath al-Shahrastani 37, 194, 214, 218, 219, 220
Abu 'l-Majd, Ahmad Kamal 362, 614n
Abu Musa al-Ash'ari 198–199
Abu Sa'id 215–216
Abu Sihliyya, Sami al-Dib 259
Abu Sitta, Salman 397–398
Abu Zahra, Muhammad 199
Abu Zayd, Nasr Hamid 642n
academic freedom 455
Aden 410–414
Aden Association 413
Adib Ishaq 274–277
Adunis 588n
al-Afghani, Jamal al-Din 450, 458
African and Asian Writers' Conference (Beirut,

1967) 454–455
Agreements (al-Shatibi) 254
agricultural workers 550–551, 649n
Ahmad, Qasm Ghalib 417–419
Ahmad al-Turaqi, Mulla 207
Ahmad ibn Hanbal 198
Ahmad ibn Idris al-Shafi'i, imam 195
A'isha 113, 119–120
'Alawi, Hadi 'l- 482–483
al-'Alayli, Shaykh 'Abdallah 444–445, 457, 461, 469, 470
Algeria 319–320, 462–463, 497, 501, 504, 505, 506, 547, 559, 645n, 652n
'Ali, M.K. 455
'Ali ibn Abi Talib 194, 201–202, 203, 204–205
'Ali ibn al-Husayn 565
'Ali ibn Hajj, Abu 'Abd al-Fattah 367–368
'Ali ibn Muhammad al-Walid 211–212
All that remains (Khalidi) 399–400
allegorical works 142–148, 583n–584n
ALO. *see* Arab Labour Organization (ALO)
'Amara, Muhammad 188, 363–364
Amin, Samir 388, 481, 619n
Amnesty International 344, 371
'Amr bin Kulthoum 1
'Amr ibn al-As 86
'Anabtawi, Mundhir 354–355, 356, 492
Anas ibn Malik, Imam 198
angels, status 44–45, 136–137, 141–142
animal rights 128
apostasy 48–49, 92–96, 100, 154, 155, 293–294, 302, 315, 327–328, 331, 524, 581n–582n, 642n. *see also* religious freedom
Arab Court of Human Rights 351
Arab Human Rights Charter (1994) 346–349, 351, 360–361

Arab Labour Organization (ALO) 540–541,
546, 547, 551–552, 554, 557, 558, 560,
646n–647n, 648n, 652n
Arab Lawyers' Union. *see* Union of Arab
Lawyers
Arab League Charter (1945) 346
Arab Nationalist Bloc 628n
Arab Nationalist Conference 520–521
Arab Organization for Human Rights 356, 359,
368, 372, 614n
Arab Renaissance 485–488, 569
Arabic culture
attitudes to authority 7–9, 356, 386–387
criticism of West 255–257, 281–284, 318,
324–326, 338–339, 366–368, 378–379, 450
and democracy 510–535
and failure of reform movements 319–323,
382–383, 514, 528
images of the body 159–160
and individualism 40–43
influence of Arabic language 476–477
influence of Enlightenment 81, 275–276,
486–487
influence of French Revolution 129,
183–184, 486–487
influence of Western culture 253–254, 255,
274–277, 297–302, 305–306, 324–326,
377–379, 380–383, 467–468, 518,
526–527, 567
interdependence of politics and religion 85,
153–157, 282–290
and liberalism 280–302
and modernization 13–14, 255–257, 283,
290, 293–295, 515–518
value system 386–390
Arabs' national constitution (al-'Alayli) 444–445
Arafat, Yasser 393–394
al-'Arif, 'Arif 392, 464–465, 466
Aristotle 23
Arkoun, Mohammed 185, 186, 201, 219
Armstrong, Karen 190, 222
al-'Aroui, 'Abdallah 485–486
Arzt, Donna 406
Asad, Muhammad 189
asceticism 173, 179–180, 222
al-Asfahani, Abu 'l-Qasim al-Husayn ibn
Muhammad ibn al-Fadl al-Raghib 24–26
'Asfour, Muhammad 360–361
al-Ash'ari, Abu 'l-Hasan 35, 36, 90–91, 199
al-'Ashmawi, Muhammad Sa'id 189
Asma bint Abu Bakr 111

assembly, right of 348, 429
association, right to 494–495
atheism 92, 96, 217. *see also* apostasy
authority
collective attitudes to 7–9, 356, 386–387,
445
of courts 350, 351, 503, 508–509
definitions 384
and democracy 510–535, 638n–645n
family life 384–387
of human rights declarations 265, 343–344,
348–349, 613n
Imamate 202–204, 209–211, 414–417,
419–420, 426, 596n
of intellectuals 139, 583n
interdependence of politics and religion 85,
153–157, 282–290, 449
legitimacy 200, 221, 288, 449, 485, 490–491,
503–505
Medina Charter 240
obligatory obedience 26–32, 85–90, 99, 101,
125–126, 137, 149–150, 289, 439–440
patriarchy 384–387, 473–488
of *ra'i* 32–33
and reason 308, 309–310
and secularism 308, 309–311, 490–491
of Shariah 266, 286–287, 288–289, 300–302,
309–310
and *shura* 50–51, 126–127, 215–216,
367–368
and women rulers 58–59
Averroes (Ibn Rushd) 60–61, 139
Avicenna (Abu 'Ali ibn Sina) 566
Awakening of the Arab nation ('Azuri) 447
'Azuri, Najib 447

B

Ba'ath parties 519–521, 640n
Babiists 632n
al-Badri, Yusuf 317
al-Baghdadi, Abu Mansour 92
Bahrain 495, 497, 544
Balfour Declaration 7, 11–12
Barakat, Halim 384–385, 386, 387
Barthes, Roland 476
Barud. *see Filastiniyyat* (al-Dabbagh)
Bashshar ibn Burd 134
Bassam al-Tibi 183
Battle of culture (Zurayq) 454
Bayhum, Muhammad Jamil 456–457, 631n
Beacon, The (al-Manar) 255

Bedouin, folklore and customs 622n
belief
    definitions 33–36
    and religious tolerance 33–40, 47–49
Ben Ali, Zein El-Abedeen 505
Berber Decree 458–459
Bernard, Michel 158
Best of ways to learn about kingdoms (al-Tunusi)
    253
blood money 235
    for non-Muslims 92–93
    for women 199
body 158–182
    and authority 163
    body/garment metaphor 169–172
    'cosmic' body 175–181
    definitions 160–161, 587n
    ideals 174–175
    in modern Western culture 158–159
    and physical pleasure 162–172, 173–175,
        180–181, 483–484, 585n, 586n–587n
    pre-Islamic culture 164–168
    status in Islamic doctrine 46, 159–160,
        168–182
    in Sufism 172–182
Borja, François 524
breastfeeding 559, 564
Britain
    Aden protectorate 412–414
    Balfour Declaration 7, 11–12
    influence on Arabic culture 567
    violation of Palestinian rights 451–452,
        463–464, 630n
al-Buti, Muhammad Sa'id 316–317
buying and selling, regulation of 115–116

C
Cairo 438–439
Cairo Declaration (1990) 259–260, 266–273,
    608n
caliphs 32
Call to the fair physical pleasure (Rashid Rida) 257
capital punishment 348, 492–493
Catholic Church 185
censorship 429, 455
Centre for Arab Unity Studies 520–521,
    640n–641n
change. *see* reform, failure of
charity 53, 54–55, 114–115
Charter on Human and Peoples' Rights in the
    Arab World 356–358, 614n

Charter on the Rights of the Arab Child
    571–572
children
    corporal punishment 567
    duty to parents 110–112
    hostages 419–420, 626n
    parenting practices in Islam 564–568
    rights of 117, 263, 264, 444, 546, 553–555,
        562–572, 650n–651n
    and work 444, 546, 553–555, 571,
        650n–651n
Chomsky, Noam 614n
Christianity
    Copts 154–155, 156
    definitions of man 161
    forced conversions 458–459
    and human rights 185
    and modernity 64, 81
    tolerance of 49, 92–93, 154–155, 191, 458
circumcision 163, 327
Cities of salt (Munif) 474
citizens 33, 443–444. *see also* human rights
Citizens not subjects: you do not plough the sea
    (Khalid) 312–313
civil rights 3–5, 489–509
codification, human rights. *see* human rights
    documents
collective rights 7–9, 112–118, 573n
colonialism, struggle against 271, 442–444,
    462–464, 470–471
commoners and elite 139, 142, 150–151
communal ownership 215
communist parties 525–527, 643n, 644n
community of believers. *see* umma
compensation 401, 493, 501, 623n–624n
    and divine justice 21
Conduct of marriage (al-Ghazali) 483
consensus 439–440, 644n–645n
constitutionalism 207–208
constitutions 489–509, 636n–638n
    limitation of government powers 500–509
    Ottoman Empire 446–448, 629n
    and respect for human rights 336–337,
        344–345, 349–351, 542–543, 647n
consultation (*shura*). *see* shura
Contemporary Arab society (Barakat) 385
Convention for the Elimination of All Forms of
    Discrimination Against Women (1979)
    546, 557
Convention on the Rights of the Child (1989)
    570, 650n, 651n

Copts 154–155, 156
Corbin, Henri 177, 178, 181, 203, 223
Council of Senior Religious Scholars 425
Covenant of 'Umar 2
crime. *see* justice; punishment
critical discourse 345, 368–373, 477–478
criticism. *see also* dissent
    and Islamic tradition 79–80
    of rulers 4, 8
    of Western culture 255–257
Critique of the Arab mind 41
Crown in the character of kings, The (al-Jahiz) 30

D

al-Dabbagh, Mustafa 465–466, 467
Daftari, Farhad 208, 213
Dammaj, Zayd Mutee' 626n
Darraz, Muhammad 'Abdallah 258–259
Darwaza, Muhammad 'Izzat 399, 448, 456,
    463–464, 466
Day of Human Rights 327
de Goeji, M. 215, 216
dead, respect for 108
Declaration of Human Rights (1948) 129, 130,
    133, 184, 295, 400, 537–538, 545, 546, 556,
    605n–606n, 646n, 648n
Declaration of the Rights of Man and Citizen
    (1789) 183–184, 277
Declaration of the Rights of Women (1979). *see*
    Convention for the Elimination of All
    Forms of Discrimination Against Women
    (1979)
Declaration on the Rights of Disabled Persons
    (1975) 555
democracy 221, 312–315, 317–318, 321–323
    definition of majority 445
    and dissent 99
    and Islamist parties 524, 641n–643n
    political parties 510–535, 638n–645n
    and respect for human rights 83, 279–280,
        336–337, 338–339, 353–355, 361–368,
        378–379, 443–444, 445–446, 486–488,
        515–535, 606n, 617n
    and *shura* 298–302, 367–368
dependence 386–387
Derrida, J. 75
despotism 5, 7–9, 307, 312–314
determinism 136, 151–152, 290–292, 582n
determinists. *see* 'Umayyads
al-Din, Nazira Zain 457
disabled persons, right to work 555–556, 651n

discrimination 22, 273, 497–498, 545–546,
    547–551, 649n. *see also* equality
dissent 49, 84, 90–102, 153–157, 188–189,
    197–198, 205, 221, 271, 273, 350–351
    apostasy. *see* apostasy
    cultural difference 381
    intellectuals 151, 325–326, 355–356,
        445–446, 471–472, 629n
    political parties 510–515
Dissenters 98, 194
divine rights 19–21
divorce 57–58, 199, 331–332
Djibouti 491
doctrinal disagreement 48–49, 92–96, 100,
    101–102
'double standard' in human rights. *see* human
    rights, theory vs. practice
Dupuy, J. 81
al-Duri, 'Abd al-'Aziz 439–440, 440–441

E

Eastern Question 631n
Economic and Social Commission for West
    Asia. *see* United Nations Economic and
    Social Commission for West Asia
    (ESCWA)
economics
    and politics 378–379, 382–383, 389–390
    Yemen 409–414
education 109–110, 127, 261–262, 270, 430,
    444, 533
    legal studies curricula 616n
    parenting practices in Islam 564–568
    religious education 565–567
    women 9, 332, 486
Egypt
    constitution 490, 495, 496, 497–498, 501, 502
    history 213, 306–307, 436, 506, 507
    labour laws 543, 548, 558, 650n, 652n
    politics 310–311, 314–315, 319, 516, 517,
        525, 527–528, 531, 532, 638n, 639n–640n,
        643n, 644n
    religious freedom 154–156, 315, 642n
elections 221, 446, 504–505, 638n
elite and commoners 139, 142, 150–151
emanation discourse 345, 360–368
emergency laws 349, 429, 505–507, 508–509,
    637n–638n
emigration 5, 420–421
Emigration: an event that changed the course of history
    (Abu Khalil) 244

Emirates 499, 500, 501, 547

Emissaries' Council (Constantinople, 1908)
      447–448

Engels, Friedrich 474

Enlightenment 81, 274–277, 486–487

environment, protection of 403, 623n

equality 51, 55–59, 132, 185–186, 189–190,
      234, 268, 272, 277, 329–332, 426, 427, 428,
      449–450, 487–488, 497–498, 524, 538,
      561, 641n–642n
   definition 544–545, 648n
   and divine justice 39–40
   Qarmatians 214–215
   remuneration 538, 546–548, 648n
   She's (Shi'ites) 203–204
   Sunnis 199
   Syria 456

ESCWA. see United Nations Economic and
      Social Commission for West Asia
      (ESCWA)

European culture
   and equality 185–186
   individual vs. nation 40, 41, 43, 378–379
   influence on Arabic culture 253–254, 255,
      274–277, 305–306, 377–379, 380–383,
      467–468
   Islamic criticism of 255–257, 318, 324–326,
      338–339

evil, and divine justice 21

exceptional courts 506–507, 508–509,
      637n–638n

executive authority, government 503–505

expediency discourse 345–351

F

Faisal, King of Iraq 448–449, 452

faith. see belief

Fakhr al-Din al-Razi 173

family
   authority and identity 384–387, 474–475
   parenting practices in Islam 564–568
   protection of workers' rights 549–550
   rights and duties 110–112, 262–264, 269,
      270

Faraj, Muhammad 'Abd al-Salam 82

al-Farra, Muhammad 394

al-Fasi, Muhammad 'Allal 463

fathers. see patriarchy

Features of oppression (al-Kawakibi) 487–488, 569

Felix Arabia. see Yemen

female circumcision 163, 327

feminism 389

feudalism 481

Filastiniyyat (al-Dabbagh) 465–466

fiqh (jurisprudence) 148–150. see also Shariah

First moan, The 419–420

For a better Arab tomorrow: current Arab situations
      and ways to resolve the crisis (1995) 359–360

Formation of the Arab mind (al-Jabiri) 324

France 442, 462–463

free will 38–39, 134–135, 217, 220, 290–292,
      296–297, 320–321

Freedom of nations (Muhammad Kurd 'Ali)
      440–441

freedom of opinion 90–102, 125–127, 137,
      348, 426, 429, 447–448, 449–455,
      493–494. see also dissent; shura
   and patriarchy 477–478

French Revolution 129, 183–184, 486–487

From peasants to revolutionaries (Sayigh) 395

Fuda, Faraj 154, 155

Fudhoul Pact 1

fundamentalist groups 98
   Iran 206–207

funding, human rights organisations 369

funerals, respect for 108

G

Garaudi, Roger 191, 220

garment, body/garment metaphor 169–172

geography, Palestine 401–403

al-Ghanoushi, Rashid 95–96, 183, 285–286,
      287–289, 294–296, 297–300, 317–318, 365

Ghaylan al-Dimashqi 39, 40, 217

al-Ghazali, Abu Hamid Muhammad 107, 139,
      154, 169, 171–172, 174, 196, 290–292, 483,
      584n–585n, 641n

Gibb, Sir Hamilton 198

Gibran Khalil Gibran 572

gnosticism 178–179, 218, 223–224

God
   attributes 32, 37, 160, 219, 583n
   names 141
   rights 19–21

Goeji, M. de 215, 216

Goldstein, Eric 348–349

government 200, 273, 303–323. see also politics;
      rulers
   appointment to public office 430
   executive authority 503–505, 508–509
   hostage-taking 419–420, 626n
   Islamist political parties 514, 642n–643n

government (*cont.*):
  limitation of powers 282–285, 286–287,
    309–310, 311, 312–314, 349–351,
    425–431, 500–509
  opposition parties 4, 153–157, 513–514,
    529–535, 638n–645n
  and religion 33, 315–323
  secularism 304–311
  and *shura* 50–51, 126–127, 215–216
  states of emergency 349, 429, 505–507,
    508–509
Great Arab Revolt 451–452, 519
Great books of the Western World 469–470
Great religious leadership (Rashid Rida) 257
Great Sedition 31
Greater Islamic Association 413
Greater jurisprudence 35
Greater Yemeni Association 421
Greece, political system 26–27
Green Charter (1988) 492–493, 494, 498
guardianship 329–330, 336, 483

                          H

hadiths 45
  'abrogated' verses 332–337
  authenticity 30
  on buying and selling 115–116
  on communal relationships 112–118
  on education 109–110
  on equality 51, 190, 329–337
  on family 564–565, 566
  on human rights 47–48, 49, 51, 103–130,
    329–337
  on justice 22–23, 124–126
  on man 141
  on marriage 120
  on obedience 29–30, 85
  on relationship between right and duty 18
  on religious duties 59
  on responsibility 32–33
  on right to life 47, 106–107
  on right to privacy 116–117
  on right to work 108
  on rights of non-Muslims 93–96, 117–118
  on rights of specific groups 93–96, 116–124
  on sin 46, 110
  on slavery 121–124, 190
  on women rulers 58–59, 483
  on women's rights 55–59, 118–121, 199, 483
al-Hafiz, Yassin 480
Hallaq, Hasan 457

Hamdan ibn Ash'ath al-Qurmati 213, 215
al-Hamidi, Khalid ibn Salih 601n
Hanbal ibn Ishaq 87
harassment, protection from 550, 560–561,
    649n
Hasan, Bahiy al-Din 370
Hasan, Sa'd al-Hajj 317
al-Hasan al-Basri, Abu Sa'id 38–39, 87, 217,
    222
al-Hasan ibn 'Ali ibn Abu Talib 50
al-Hasani, 'Abd al-Razzaq 460–461
Hassan II, King of Morocco 517
Hathout, Hasan 393
hatred, incitement of 273
al-Hawwat, 'Ali 245
Hayy ibn Yaqzan (Ibn Tufayl) 142–148,
    583n–584n
heads of state 504–505, 508. *see also* rulers
health, right to 128
health and safety laws 551–552, 559–561,
    649n–650n
Higher Islamic Council (United Nations)
    184–185
Hijazi, 'Izzat 375
Hilal, 'Aliyyudin 355–356
history
  19th-20th century 253–255, 256–257,
    435–472, 481–482, 485–488
  Arab Renaissance 485–488, 569
  Berber Decree 458–459
  early Islamic period 1, 33–34, 97–98,
    121–124, 150–151, 186–192, 246,
    329–330, 482–483
  Egypt 213, 306–307
  Great Arab Revolt 451–452, 519
  Great Discord 192–194
  Great Sedition 31
  Greek city states 27
  human rights movements 344–345
  Iraq 448–449
  Isma'ilis 208–209
  Jordan 446
  Maghreb 458–459
  Medina Charter 239–249, 600n–603n
  Mu'tazilis 217
  Ottomans 200–201, 256, 306–307, 438–439,
    440, 446–448, 459–460, 490, 629n, 631n
  Palestine 392–396, 397–400, 451–452, 457,
    463–467, 630n
  Persian Empire 27
  post-independence 353–356, 377–380

pre-Islamic period 1, 164–168, 482–483
Qarmatians 213–216
She's (Shi'ites) 201–208
Sudan 326–328
Sunnis 195–201
Syria 448, 455–456, 519
'Umayyads 37, 38, 39, 151–152
Wahhabis 226–228
Yemen 407–431, 625n–627n
Hitti, Philip 198–199, 438–439
Hodgson, Marshall 202
homes, and right to privacy 116–117, 272, 428.
    see also khutat
Hostage, The (Dammaj) 626n
hostages 419–420, 626n
human rights. *see also* specific rights, e.g. civil
    rights, religious freedom
  children. *see* children
  codification. *see* human rights documents
  collective vs. individual rights 4–5, 7–9,
    103–130, 468–469, 573n
  constitutionally guaranteed rights 336–337,
    344–345, 349–351, 542–543, 647n
  critical discourse 345, 368–373, 477–478
  Day of Human Rights 327
  definitions 17–18, 183–186
  and democracy 83, 279–280, 336–337,
    338–339, 353–355, 361–368, 378–379,
    443–444, 445–446, 486–488, 531–535,
    606n, 617n
  early Islamic period 1–2
  emanation discourse 345, 360–368
  expediency discourse 345–351
  family life 110–112, 262–264
  funding of organisations 369
  history of 344–345, 435–472
  Islamic doctrine 47–61, 103–130, 183–228,
    258–259, 290–302, 361–368
  life 47, 106–107, 188, 191, 268–269, 348,
    492–493, 562–564
  natural rights 435, 437, 444–445, 470–472
  necessities/needs 196–197, 363–364
  non-government organisations (NGOs)
    344, 351, 353–354, 356–360, 368–373,
    396, 534–535, 615n, 645n
  ownership 264, 271–272
  and patriarchy 473–488, 634n
  persecution of activists 372–373
  political discourse 345, 352–360, 370–373,
    515–535
  pre-Islamic period 1

privacy 116–117, 269, 272
relationship between right and duty 18–21,
    84, 99, 106, 183–184, 265, 292–293,
    296–297, 363, 365–366, 493–494, 588n
and religious tolerance. *see* religious freedom
right to return 394, 397–398, 400–403,
    405–406, 621n, 623n–625n
rights of specific groups 198–199, 234,
    236–238, 239, 331, 358–359, 553–556
social care 272
and social problematic 374–390, 617n–619n
theoretical-philosophical aspects 467–470
theory vs. practice 3–6, 129–130, 131–157,
    258, 326, 349, 353–356, 370–373, 382,
    461–467, 613n, 613n–614n
women's rights. *see* women's rights
work 10, 108, 260–261, 271
human rights documents 183–186, 259–273,
    424–431
  Arab Human Rights Charter (1994)
    346–349, 351, 360–361
  Arab Labour Organization conventions
    540–541, 546, 547, 551–552, 554, 557, 558,
    560, 646n–647n, 648n, 652n
  authority of 265, 343–344, 348–349,
    360–361, 613n
  *For a better Arab tomorrow: current Arab situations
    and ways to resolve the crisis* (1995) 359–360
  Cairo Declaration (1990) 259–260, 266–273,
    608n
  Charter on Human and Peoples' Rights in the
    Arab World 356–358
  Charter on the Rights of the Arab Child
    571–572
  comparison of 259–265, 357, 492–509,
    537–541, 607n, 636n–638n, 645n–646n.
    see also labour laws
  Convention for the Elimination of All Forms
    of Discrimination Against Women (1979)
    546, 557
  Convention on the Rights of the Child (1989)
    570, 650n, 651n
  Declaration of Human Rights (1948) 129,
    130, 133, 184, 262, 264, 295, 400,
    537–538, 545, 546, 556, 605n–606n,
    646n, 648n
  Declaration of the Rights of Man and Citizen
    (1789) 183–184, 277, 486
  Declaration on the Rights of Disabled
    Persons (1975) 555
  Green Charter (1988) 492–493, 494, 498

human rights documents (*cont.*):
   Human rights in Islam (1992) 259, 260–261,
      262, 263–264, 607n
   International Covenant (1966) 260, 261,
      263, 492–509, 538–539, 545, 546,
      553–554, 556–557, 646n
   International Islamic Declaration of Human
      Rights (1981) 259, 260, 262, 263, 264
   International Labour Organization
      conventions 539–540, 545–546, 547, 554,
      555–556, 557, 560, 646n, 648n, 651n, 653n
   International report on human rights in Islam
      (1981) 365, 615n
   Islamic criticism of 295
   Medina Charter 229–249, 600n–603n
   National Charter (Yemen, 1956) 427–431
   Personal rights (al-'Alayli) 469, 470
   Sacred National Charter (Yemen, 1947)
      426–427
Human Rights Watch for the Middle East
   348–349
humanism 75
   images of the body 158–159
humans. *see* man
Husain ibn Mansour al-Hallaj 179–180, 225,
   226, 587n
Husain Muruwwa 204
al-Husari, Sati' 448
Hussein, Saddam 529
Hutchins, Robert 469–470
Huwaydi, Fahmi 581n–582n

I

Ibn al-Azraq, Abu 'Abd Allah 23–24
Ibn al-Khayyat 218
Ibn al-Muttahar al-Hilli 206
Ibn 'Arabi, Muhyi 'l-Din 139–140, 176,
   177–178, 225–226, 587n
Ibn 'Ayniyya 111
Ibn Hanbal 87
Ibn Hani' al-Andalusi 8
Ibn Hazm 54
Ibn Hisham, Abu Muhammad 'Abd al-Malik
   230, 240, 602n
Ibn Kaldoun 200, 203, 222, 601n
Ibn Kathir, Abu 'l Fida' Isma'il 241–242, 601n,
   602n, 603n
Ibn Manzur 40–41, 42–43
Ibn Marwan, 'Abd al-Malik 38
Ibn Miskawayh 566–567
Ibn Nabi, Malik 362

Ibn Qays, al-Ahnaf 563
Ibn Qayyim al-Jawziyya 364–365
Ibn Rushd, Abu 'l Walid Muhammad 60–61,
   139
Ibn Sina, Abu Ali 566
Ibn Taymiyya 98, 189, 227
Ibn Tufayl, Abu Bakr 142–148, 583n–584n
Ibn 'Umar 38, 86
Ibrahim, Sa'd al-Din 375
identity
   and family 384–387
   and Islamic tradition 71–83
Ikhbariyyoun (communicators) 206–207
ILO. *see* International Labour Organization
   (ILO)
Imamate 202–206, 209–211, 414–417, 426,
   596n. *see also* rulers
imperialism 605n
Imru'u al-Qays 164–166
incitement of hatred 273
individual. *see also* man
   definitions 40–43, 68–69
   and freedom 453–454
   in Islamic tradition 62–83, 185, 336
   and liberalism 278–280, 378–379
   rights of 4–5, 7–8, 103–112, 501, 573n
infanticide, prohibition of 47, 562–564
inheritance 474, 475
   women's rights 57, 330, 455
Institute for Palestinian Studies 395, 399–400,
   404, 466, 620n, 633n
intellectuals
   authority 139, 583n
   and dissent 151, 325–326, 355–356,
      445–446, 471–472, 629n
   freedom of expression 454–455
   persecution of 315, 450, 451, 462–463,
      466–467, 630n, 633n
International Conference on Human Rights
   (Vienna, 1993) 129, 372
International Covenant (1966) 260, 261, 263,
   492–509, 538–539, 545, 546, 553–554,
   556–557, 646n
International Islamic Declaration of Human
   Rights (1981) 259, 260, 262, 263, 264
International Labour Organization (ILO)
   539–540, 545–546, 547, 554, 555–556,
   557, 560, 646n, 648n, 651n, 653n
International report on human rights in Islam (1981)
   365, 615n
Iran 206–208

Iraq 448–449, 493, 494, 495, 497, 506–507, 519–521, 525, 526, 529, 543, 643n
Islam and our political situations ('Abd al-Qadir 'Oda) 258
Islam and the principles of government (al-Razzaq) 311, 314–315, 476
Islamic culture. *see* Arabic culture
Islamic directives and United Nations declarations (al-Ghazali) 641n
Islamic discourses 90–91
Islamic doctrines 183–228
  Isma'ilis 209–213, 214
  Mu'tazilis 20–21, 98, 133–137, 217–221
  Qarmatians 213–216
  She's (Shi'ites) 201–208
  Sufism 172–182, 221–226
  Sunnis 86–88, 195–201
  Wahhabis 226–228
Islamic state. *see umma*
Islamic texts
  authority of 77–79, 153, 240, 286–287, 300–302
  on buying and selling 115–116
  on communal relationships 112–118
  on dissent 92, 93–94, 97
  on education 109–110
  on equality 51, 189–190, 234, 329–337
  on family 110–112, 564–568
  on human rights 47–48, 49–51, 103–130, 186–192, 229–239, 329–337, 361–368, 522, 523–524
  on *jizya* 581n–582n
  on justice 22–33, 124–126
  on man 43–45, 67–71, 140–142
  on marriage 120
  on obedience 26–32
  on relationship between right and duty 18–21
  on religious duties 59, 107, 135, 227–228
  on religious tolerance 33–40, 47–49, 92–96, 191
  on right to life 47, 106–107, 188, 191, 563
  on right to privacy 116–117
  on right to work 108
  on rights of non-Muslims 93–96, 117–118
  on rights of specific groups 51–61, 93–96, 116–124
  on sin 45–46, 110, 220–221
  on slavery 121–124, 190
  on women's rights 55–59, 118–121, 190–191, 199, 483–484, 524
Islamic theology. *see* kalamology; theology

Islamic world today (Stoddard) 628n
Islamist political parties 514, 521–524, 641n–643n
Isma'ilis 208–213, 214
Israel 11, 353–356, 359, 391–406, 464–467, 619n–625n
Istiqlal party (Morocco) 528–529
Italy 442

J

al-Jabiri, Muhammad 'Abid 185, 204, 221, 245, 301, 324, 485
Jafar al-Sadiq 203
jahiliyya 316
al-Jahiz 30, 175
jails. *see* prisons
Jamal Pasha 450, 451
Jamil, Hussein 351
Jawhar al-Siqilli 213
Jawish, Abdul-Aziz 93–94
jihad 23, 82, 522
jizya 132, 151–152, 155, 581n–582n
Jordan 446, 495, 502, 507, 638n
  labour laws 541–542, 542–543, 544–545, 546, 548, 549–551, 552, 554, 556, 558, 559, 561, 646n, 647n, 648n, 650n–651n
Judaism
  definitions of man 161
  and modernity 64
  tolerance of 49, 92–93, 191, 234, 236–238, 239
  Western persecution of 11
Jumblat, Kamal 454–455
jurisprudence. *see fiqh* (jurisprudence)
justice 20–21, 124–126, 199, 203–204, 214–215, 235, 496–501
  definitions 25, 192, 439
  and equality 39–40, 272, 428, 497–498
  exceptional courts 506–507, 508–509, 637n–638n
  independence of judiciary 350, 351, 500–503, 506–507, 508–509, 637n–638n
  and obedience to rulers 22–33
  and reason 220–221
  and religious tolerance 33–40
  witnesses 56, 330

K

kalamologists
  on justice 20–21, 25
  on religious tolerance 33–40

kalamology 133–137
  definition 132
  justification for class divisions 139, 142
Kan'an, Tawfiq 398
Kana'na, Sharif 621n
Karamani, Hamid al-Din 210
al-Kawakibi, 'Abd al-Rahman 450, 458,
  487–488, 569
al-Kayyali, Abdul Wahhab 399
Khalafallah, Muhammad Ahmad 362
Khalid, Khalid Muhammad 312–313
Khalid ibn al-Walid 54–55, 123
al-Khalidi, Walid 399, 466
Khalifa, Ahmad Muhammad 375
al-Khalil, 'Abd al-Karim 451, 630n
al-Khatib, Shaykh Muhammad Nimr 393
Khoury, Ra'if 486–487
al-Khurasani 207
khutat 421. *see also* homes, and right to privacy
kibbutzim, failure of 402–403
al-Killini 203
kinship, rights and duties 112, 480
knowledge 583n
  and authority 139, 583n
  right to 49, 127, 262, 270. *see also* education
Korsak, Janusz 570
Küng, Hans 185
Kuwait 497, 502, 544, 547, 552–553, 558

L

Labib, Taher 387
Labour Federation, Yemen 413
labour laws 536–561, 645n–653n
  scope 548–551, 649n
land rights, Palestine 394, 397–398, 400–403,
  405–406, 621n, 623n–625n
language and thought 476–477
law. *see also* Shariah
  constitutionally guaranteed rights 496–501
  as guarantor of freedom 279–280, 349–351,
    373, 378, 616n
  history of 490–491
  labour laws 536–561, 645n–653n
  social welfare laws 551–553, 649n–650n
League of National Action 462–463
League of the Children of the South 413
Lebanon 456–457, 498, 505, 525, 553, 558, 561
leisure, right to 538, 551–552, 554, 560, 561
Letter to my daughter (Abu Sitta) 397
Lévi-Strauss, Claude 475
Lewis, Bernard 208

liberalism 274–302. *see also* secularism
  definitions of freedom 274–280
  and individual rights 278–280, 378–379
  Islamic criticism of 281–302
  political aspects 282, 283–284
  political parties 527–529, 532, 644n
  Yemeni Nationalist Movement 414–431
Liberation of woman (Qasim Amin) 487
Libya 442, 462, 491–492, 492–493, 494, 498,
  544, 558
life, right to 47, 106–107, 188, 191, 268–269,
  348, 492–493, 562–564
literature
  freedom of expression 454–455
  Hayy ibn Yaqzan (Ibn Tufayl) 142–148,
    583n–584n
  images of the body 164–168, 170–171,
    175–182
  Palestinians 396–400, 621n–623n, 633n
  Yemeni Nationalist Movement 414–431
love, physical. *see* physical pleasure

M

al-Maghout, Muhammad 5
Maghreb, history 458–459, 462–463
Mahafza, 'Ali 446, 455
Ma'in Abu Sitta 621n
Mallatt, Shibli 350
Ma'luf, Jamil 486
man. *see also* individual; women's rights
  mar' 42
  philosophical views of 138–139
  relationship with God 290–292
  status in Islamic doctrine 43–45, 46,
    103–105, 131–132, 136, 138–142, 161,
    185–186, 187–188, 210–213, 223–226,
    258–259, 285–286
  violent impulses 82–83
al-Manar (Rashid Rida) 255
al-Mani, 'Abd al-Ghani 504
Manna, Haytham 567
Maqdisi, George 267
al-Ma'rour ibn Suwayd 122
marriage 120, 169, 262, 263–264, 269, 483,
    585n, 586n–587n
  cross-religious marriage 199, 457
  pre-Islamic period 167
martial laws 349, 429. *see also* emergency laws
Marx, Karl 474–475
Marxism 525–527, 643n–644n
al-Marzouqi, Munsif 356, 369

Mashhur, Mustafa 155
Mashriq, history of 435–462, 463–472
Massignon, Louis 226
materialism, Islamic criticism of 257
Mauritania 491, 561, 652n
al-Mawardi, Abu 'l-Hasan 86
al-Mawdoudi, Abu 'l-A'la 95–96
Mayer, Ann Elizabeth 259
Meaning of catastrophe revisited (Zurayq) 454
Medhat Pasha 447, 629n
media, freedom of 273, 429, 447–448
Medina Charter 229–249, 600n–603n
    aims 242–244, 245, 248–249
al-Mernisi, Fatima 482
Message of monotheism ('Abdu) 307
Messenger's sayings. *see hadiths*
Migalli, Hani 370
military occupation of homes 421
Miller, Judith 328
minorities, protection of 497–498
al-Miqdad ibn 'Amr al-Kindi 122–123
missionaries, and imperialism 605n
Modern history of Palestine (al-Kayyali) 399
modernity 12
    and Arabic culture 13–14, 255–257, 382–383
    and Islamic tradition 64–65, 71–83, 219,
        283, 290, 293–295
    and politics 515–518
monotheistic religions
    definitions of man 161
    tolerance of 49, 92–93, 191
Morocco 491, 503, 517, 528–529, 638n–639n
mothers
    parenting practices in Islam 564–568, 572
    rights of 111, 119, 556–559, 646n, 651n,
        652n
    theological significance 175–181
Moussa, Muhammad Yousef 284–285
Mu'awiya ibn Abi Sufyan 582n
al-Mufid 440–441, 628n
Mugheizel, Joseph 613n
Muhammad Baqir al-Bahbaha'i 207
Muhammad ibn 'Abd al-Wahhab 227–228
Muhammad Kurd 'Ali 440
Muhammad's sayings. *see hadiths*
al-Mukhtar al-Thaqafi 204
Munif, 'Abd al-Rahman 474
murder, punishment for 92–93, 199, 235
Muslim Brotherhood 155, 393, 522–523, 529,
        530, 642n
Muslim state. *see umma*

Muslims and human rights: religion, law and politics
        (Abu Sihliyya) 259
Mu'tazilis 20–21, 98, 133–137, 217–221
mysticism 69, 139–148. *see also* Sufism

N

al-Nabigha al-Ja'di 171
Na'ini, al-Mirza Muhammad Husain 207–208
nakba 391–406, 454, 463–467, 619n–625n
al-Nasafi 54
al-Nashshar 596n
Nasir Khosraw 215, 216
Nasser, Gamal Abdul 436
National Charter (Yemen, 1956) 427–431
National Islamic Party (Sudan) 521
nationalism 356, 442–444, 470–471
    Arab Nationalist Bloc 628n
    League of National Action 462–463
    pan-national political parties 519–521
    Yemeni Nationalist Movement 407–431,
        625n–627n
Nationalist awareness (Zurayq) 453
natural freedom 274–276
natural rights 435, 437, 444–445, 470–472
al-Nazzam 218
necessities/needs, and human rights 19–20,
        196–197, 363–364
neighbours' rights 113
New woman (Qasim Amin) 487
night work, restrictions on 560, 561
non-government organisations (NGOs) 344,
        351, 353–354, 356, 368–373, 396,
        534–535, 615n, 645n
non-Muslims 150. *see also* apostasy
    jizya 132, 151–152, 155, 581n–582n
    rights of 93–96, 117–118, 154–155,
        198–199, 234, 236–238, 239, 247
Nu'man, Muhammad Ahmad 421
nursing leave, working mothers 559

O

obedience 26–32, 84–102, 289, 386–387
    definitions 84, 149–150
    to God 187–188
    and right to disagreement 90–102, 125–127,
        137
Oman 491
opinion, freedom of. *see* freedom of opinion
opposition parties 4, 153–157
Organization of the Islamic Conference
        266–267. *see also* Cairo Declaration (1990)

Oslo Agreement, failure of 404–405
Ottomans 200–201, 256, 306–307, 438–439, 440, 446–448, 459–460, 490, 629n, 631n
overtime 552, 650n
ownership 264, 271–272

P

Palestine, our country (al-Dabbagh) 465–466, 467
Palestine Research Centre 395, 620n
Palestinian Declaration of Independence (1988) 344
Palestinian Liberation Organization (PLO) 393–394
Palestinians 359, 391–406, 451–452, 457, 463–467, 507, 619n–625n, 630n
pan-national parties 519–521, 640n–641n
parents
    authority 384–387, 473–488
    rights and duties 110–112, 270, 564–568
Paris Academy of Political Ethics 185
Paris Conference (1913) 441, 628n
Party of Yemeni Liberals 425
patriarchy 384–387, 473–488, 572, 634n
    and freedom of opinion 477–478
pay. *see* remuneration
Peace of the intellect (al-Karamani) 210
pensions 553
Persian Empire, political system 26–27
person. *see* individual; man
Personal rights (al-'Alayli) 469
Petrochovski, S. 593n
philosophy 138–139
physical pleasure 162–172, 173–175, 180–181, 480–484, 585n, 586n–587n
Plato 60–61, 223
pluralism 226, 460–461
poetry, images of the body 164–168
political rights 3–5, 199, 273, 429–430, 446–449, 489–509
    and divinely appointed rulers 203, 205–208
    and freedom 276–277, 278, 354–356
    meetings and unions 348, 429, 430, 494–495, 538
    right to dissent 49, 84, 90–102, 153–157, 188–189, 197–198, 205, 221, 271, 273
    self-determination 271, 347, 394, 400
politics. *see also* government; rulers
    Arabic culture 41–42, 378, 379–380, 606n
    consensus 439–440, 644n–645n
    and duty of obedience 22–33, 85–90
    and economics 378–379, 382–383, 389–390

elections 221, 446, 504–505, 638n
    failure of reform movements 319–323, 382–383, 514, 528
    Greeks vs. Persian Empire 26–27
    Islamist political parties 514, 521–524, 641n–643n
    opposition parties 4, 153–157, 510–515, 529–535
    party systems 505, 510–535, 638n–645n
    persecution of human rights activists 372–373, 381
    political discourse 345, 352–360, 370–373, 515–535
    post-independence 5, 353–356
    and religion 153–157, 200–201, 234, 236–238, 239, 282–290, 304–311, 320–323
    and violence 88–89, 98, 100–101, 315, 322–323, 523
polygamy 57–58, 191
poor, support for 233, 551–553, 649n–650n
predestination 37, 38–39
presidents 504–505. *see also* rulers
princes 32
prisons 417–419
    prisoners of conscience 4, 381, 382
    use of torture 216, 350, 497
privacy, right to 116–117, 269, 272, 428, 429
progress, and Islam 253–255
promise, of Paradise 37, 221
property rights 264, 271–272
Prophet's sayings. *see* hadiths
Psychoanalysis of the Arabic self (Zei'our) 384
public health 128
punishment 19–20, 233–234, 235, 272, 428, 524. *see also* justice
    apostasy. *see* apostasy
    blood money 92–93
    capital punishment 348, 492–493
    corporal punishment of children 567, 569
    use of torture 216, 350, 497
purity, and body 162

Q

al-Qaradawi, Yusuf 363, 366
al-Qaradhawi, Yousef 280–284
al-Qardawi, Yusuf 155, 292–294
Qarmatians 213–216
Qasim Amin 487
Qatar 500
Qays and Layla 181
al-Qazazz, Iyad 375

quarantine 128

Quran
   'abrogated' verses 330–331, 332–337
   on apostasy 48
   authority of 77–79, 153, 219, 240, 329–337
   on dissent 92, 93–94, 97
   on equality 51, 189, 329–337
   on family 111, 564
   historical context 70–71
   on human rights 47–48, 49–51, 186–192,
      329–337
   on *jizya* 581n–582n
   on justice 22, 25, 37
   on man 44–45, 67–71, 140–142
   on obedience 27
   on relationship between right and duty
      18–21
   on religious tolerance 47–49, 191
   on right to life 188, 191, 563
   on rights of specific groups 51–61
   on *shura* 49–51
   on sin 45–46
   on slavery 190
   on women's rights 55–59, 190–191,
      483–484

Qurunful, Hasan 638n–639n
al-Qusaymi, 'Abdallah 449
al-Qushayri 179–180
Qutb, Muhammad 316, 366–367

R

radicalization 75–76, 79–80
Rafiq al-'Azm 441
ra'i 32–33
Rashid Pasha 446, 629n
Rashid Rida, Sayyid Muhammad 255, 256–257
Rashid Rida, Shaykh 198
al-Rashidi, Ahmad 350
reason 217–218, 219–221, 308, 309–310, 318
reform, failure of 319–323, 382–383, 514, 528
refugees 358–359, 391–406, 430, 619n–625n
   resettlement 406
Relief and Works Agency. *see* United Nations
   Relief and Works Agency (UNRWA)
religion
   allegories 142–148, 583n–584n
   and education 565–567
   images of the body 158, 159–160
   and politics 153–157, 200–201, 234,
      236–238, 239, 282–290, 304–311, 320–323
   pre-Islamic period 167–168

and reason 217–218, 220–221
religious duties 59, 107, 162
religious freedom 2, 47–49, 92–96, 131–132,
     155, 191–192, 197–199, 212–213, 247,
     270, 348, 449–455, 458–461, 524. *see also*
     apostasy
   cross-religious marriage 199, 457
   Egypt 154–156, 315
   Sufis 226
   and worship 296–297
   Yemen 429
remuneration 538, 546–548, 648n
repentance 37, 48
responsibility
   and free will 39
   of *ra'i* 32–33
   spiritual responsibility 74
rest, right to 538, 551–552, 554, 560, 561
return, right to 394, 397–398, 400–403,
     405–406, 621n, 623n–625n
Revival of the sciences of religion (al-Ghazali) 483
Revolutionary Court 506–507
Richard, Jan 202, 206
righteousness 52–53
rights. *see* human rights
roads, rights of way 116
Rousseau, Jean-Jacques 275–276
rulers 32–33, 199–201, 363, 503–505, 508–509.
   see also authority
   duties of 50–51
   Imam 202–206, 209–211, 414–417, 426,
     596n
   legitimacy 200, 221, 288, 449
   obedience to 26–32, 85–90, 205–208
   women rulers 58–59, 483

S

Sabaenism 49, 632n
Sacred National Charter (Yemen, 1947)
   426–427
Sadat, Anwar 506, 640n
al-Sa'dawi, Nawal 480
safety at work. *see* health and safety laws
Sa'id, Muhammad al-Sayyid 370
al-Sa'id, Rif'at 643n
al-Sakakini, Khalil 447–448
Salama, Ghassan 387, 388, 619n
salat, importance of 162
Sa'sa'a ibn Naji ibn 'Iqal 562–563
Saudi Arabia 449, 491, 498, 543, 605n
al-Sawi, 'Abd al-'Aziz 644n

Sayf al-Haq Ibrahim 421–424, 627n
Sayigh, Anis 399–400, 445, 452–453, 466–467,
    629n
Sayigh, Rosemary 395
al-Sayyid, Ahmad Lutfi 277–280
secret trials 500, 506–507, 508–509, 637n
secularism 155–156, 206, 284–290, 308,
    309–311, 317–318, 321, 490–491. *see also*
    liberalism
Selections from every fine art 31
self-determination, right to 271, 347, 394, 400
self-harm. *see* suicide
servants, rights of 550, 649n
al-Shafi'i, Muhammad ibn Idris 28–29
Shafiq al-Balkhi 158, 173
Shahrour, Muhammad 313–314
al-Shak'a 199–200
shakhs 42
Shakib Arsalan, Prince 442, 447, 458–460,
    461–463, 466, 628n
Shaltout, Shaykh Mahmoud 94–95
Shammout, Isma'il 620n
Sharabi, Hisham 385, 386, 387, 480, 481,
    618n
al-Sharastani. *see* Abu 'l Fath al-Shahrastani
Shariah 254–255, 604n. *see also fiqh*
    (jurisprudence); law
    authority of 266, 286–287, 288–289,
        300–302, 309–310, 329–331, 334–337,
        360–362, 439–440, 449
    definition of person 73–75
    on human rights 361–368, 522, 523–524
    and justice 25, 124
    on religious duties 135
    on right to life 106–107
    on women's rights 120–121, 524
al-Shariah wa 'l-hayat (television series) 77–79
al-Sharif, Kamil 393
al-Shatibi 95, 254
Shawqi, Ahmad 569
shepherds. *see ra'i*
She's (Shi'ites) 201–208
    fundamentalist groups 206–207
Shukrallah, Hani 371
al-Shuqayri, Ahmad 394
shura 49–51, 126–127, 188–189, 215–216, 286
    and democracy 298–302, 329–330, 336,
        367–368
sin 45–46, 110, 220–221
    and status of belief 34–35, 217
slavery 121–124, 190, 204–205, 216, 329

So that there will be no sedition (Huwaydi)
    581n–582n
social problematic
    and human rights 374–390, 617n–619n
    research priorities 374–376
socialism 337, 338–339, 525–527
society
    commoners and elite 139, 142, 150–151
    communal ownership 215
    definitions 40–43
    and human rights 372–373, 616n
    right to social justice 51–55, 114–115
    social welfare laws 551–553, 649n–650n
    Yemen 410–414
Somalia 558, 559
soul, definitions of 160–161, 223–224
Sources of the self: the making of modern identity 73
sovereignty, women's rights 58–59. *see also*
    guardianship; women's rights
special needs, and right to work 555–556, 651n
spirit, definitions of 160–161
spiritual responsibility 74
State Security Court (Palestinian Authority) 507
states of emergency 349, 429, 505–507,
    508–509, 637n–638n
Stoddard, Lothrop 628n
Sudan 326–328, 502, 504, 505, 521, 525, 526,
    544, 637n
Sufism 172–182, 221–226. *see also* mysticism
    gnosticism 178–179
Suhaym 170
al-Suhrawardi 178–179, 223–224
suicide 106–107
Sunnis 195–201
    and justice 86–88
al-Sunusi, Ahmad al-Sharif 460
Supreme Courts 502–503
Syria 448, 455–456, 494, 503, 506, 507,
    519–521, 531, 543, 644n

T

al-Tabari 136, 483–484, 602n
Taha, Mahmoud Muhammad 324–339, 362
al-Tahawi, Abu Ahmad 87
al-Tahtawi, Rifa'a Rafi' 253–255
al-Tall, 'Abdallah 393
taxation 53–54, 426, 430
    exemptions from 54–55
    jizya 132, 151–152, 155, 581n–582n
    zakat 53, 54–55, 425
Taylor, Charles 73

techno-bureaucratic parties 515–518
terrorism 75–76, 81, 523. *see also* violence
Thabit, Anton 486
theocracy 288–289, 449
    Imamate 202–206, 209–211, 596n
theology. *see also* kalamology
    and modernization 303–304
    rights of God vs. rights of men 19–21
tolerance 1–2, 131–132, 150–157, 191–192,
        212–213, 226, 234, 236–238, 239, 247, 270,
        429, 458–461
    cross-religious marriage 199, 457
    of unbelief 33–40, 92–96, 293–294
Tongue of the Arabs, The 40–41, 42–43
torture, use of 216, 350, 497
Towards a theory of culture (Amin) 388
trade, regulation of 115–116
traditionalization 79–80. *see also* radicalization
treason. *see also* apostasy
Treatise, The (al-Shafi'i) 28–29
Treatise on rights ('Ali ibn al-Husayn) 565
Tunisia 491, 504, 505, 507, 517, 531, 541, 544,
        559, 638n, 647n
al-Tunusi, Khayr al-Din 253, 254, 603n
al-Turabi, Hassan 296–297, 300–301
al-Tuwayjiri, 'Abd al-'Aziz ibn 'Abd al-Muhsin
        452
tyranny 5, 7–9, 307, 312–314, 519–521

U

'Ubada ibn al-Samit 86
'Umar al-Mukhtar 442–443
'Umar ibn al-Khattab 2, 56, 85–86, 126,
        192–193, 482
'Umayyads 37, 38, 39, 151–152
umma. see also Arabic culture; government;
        politics
    communal ownership 215
    consensus 439–440, 644n–645n
    definitions 40–43
    duties of non-Muslims 53, 54–55
    pan-national political parties 519–521,
        640n–641n
    and right to dissent 153–157, 286–287,
        298–302, 445
    rights of non-Muslims 93–96, 117–118,
        154–155, 198–199, 234, 236–238, 239,
        247, 331, 360, 524
    and secularism 155–156, 206, 284–290,
        298–302
    social justice 114–115

women's rights. *see* women's rights
UN Declaration of Human Rights (1948). *see*
        Declaration of Human Rights (1948)
Union of Arab Lawyers 358–360, 637n
unions 348, 429, 430, 494–495, 538
United Arab Emirates (UAE) 499, 500, 501,
        547
United Nations Economic and Social
        Commission for West Asia (ESCWA)
        404
United Nations Relief and Works Agency
        (UNRWA) 404–405
United Nations Security Council 394, 400
United States 11–13, 353–356, 613n–614n
unity 179–182, 224–225
Universal Declaration of Human Rights (1948).
        see Declaration of Human Rights (1948)
universal rights 442. *see also* human rights
        documents
UNRWA. *see* United Nations Relief and Works
        Agency (UNRWA)
al-'Uraisi, 'Abd al-Ghani 440–442, 450–451,
        628n
'Urayb ibn Sa'd al-Katib al-Qurtubi 566
'Urwa ibn Hakam ibn Hizam 115
'Uthman 193–194
'Uthman, Muhammad Fat-hi 366

V

Veiling and unveiling, The (al-Din) 457
veils 191
Vers une théologie chrétienne du pluralisme religieux 81
viceregency of man 44–45, 285–286. *see also*
        man, status in Islamic doctrine
violence 81–83. *see also* terrorism
    as political protest 88–89, 98, 100–101, 315,
        322–323, 523

W

Wafd party (Egypt) 528, 532, 644n
Wahhabis 226–228
war 82
warning, against sin 37, 221
Wasil ibn 'Ata' 37, 217
water resources 403, 623n
Way to the dignities of Shariah 24–26
weak and oppressed, rights of 51–55, 114–115
Wellhausen, Julius 201
West
    attitudes to human rights 10–13, 133, 184,
        353–356, 378–379, 382

West (*cont.*):
  attitudes to Islam 82, 184, 476
  role in Arab-Israeli conflict 11, 394,
    399–400, 403, 623n
Western culture
  Enlightenment 81
  and humanism 75
  images of the body 158–159
  individual vs. nation 40, 41, 43
  influence on Arabic culture 253–254,
    274–277, 297–302, 305–306, 377–379,
    380–383, 450, 467–468, 485–487, 518,
    526–527, 567
  Islamic criticism of 255–257, 281–284, 318,
    324–326, 338–339, 366–368, 378–379
Where is the wrong in that? (al-'Alayli) 457
witnesses 56, 330
women's rights 9–10, 55–61, 118–121, 129,
    190–191, 199, 262–264, 269, 330,
    331–332, 389, 455–457, 474–475, 487,
    524, 619n
  cross-religious marriage 199, 457
  dispensations from religious duties 59
  divorce 57–58, 331–332
  education 9, 332, 486
  and female circumcision 163, 327
  inheritance 57, 330, 455
  as mothers 111, 119, 264, 270, 556–559,
    646n, 651n, 652n
  and patriarchy 478–479, 480–484
  pre-Islamic period 482–483
  protection from harassment 550, 560–561,
    649n
  right to life 47, 191, 562–563
  in Shariah 74–75
  as wives 119–120, 163, 169–172, 483,
    586n–587n
  work 10, 456–457, 542, 544–548, 549–550,
    556–561, 646n, 647n–648n, 651n–653n
work 271
  agricultural workers 550–551, 649n
  children's rights 444, 546, 553–555, 571,
    650n–651n
  family businesses 549–550

health and safety laws 551–552, 560–561,
    649n–650n
labour laws 536–561, 645n–653n
overtime 552, 650n
pensions 553
protection from harassment 550, 649n
remuneration 538, 546–548, 648n
right to 108, 260–261, 348, 430, 431, 461,
    537–544, 645n–647n
right to leisure 538, 551–552, 554, 560,
    561
rights of persons with special needs
    555–556, 651n
women's rights 10, 456–457, 542, 544–548,
    549–550, 556–561, 646n, 647n–648n,
    651n–653n

Y

Yahya, Muhammad 317
Yahya ibn Muhammad Hamid al-Din, Imam
    410
Yathrib. *see* Medina Charter
Yazidis 460–461
Yemen 498, 501, 504, 505, 638n, 645n
  economics 409–411
  history 407–431, 625n–627n
  political rights 421–431, 496
Yezbek, Yusuf Ibrahim 451, 456, 630n
Young woman and the old men, (al-Din) 457

Z

al-Zahrawi, 'Abd al-Hamid 458
zakat 53, 54–55, 425
al-Zamakhshari, Abu 'l-Qasim al-Husayn ibn
    Muhammad ibn al-Fadl al-Raghib 19,
    27–28, 44, 50, 136–137
Zarzur, 'Adnan 77–79
Zaydis 98
Zei'our, Ali 384
Zionism 11, 353–356, 402–403, 447
Ziyada, Nicola 436, 449–450, 453–454, 457,
    471
Zurayq, Constantine 436, 443–444, 452–454,
    468–469, 471